6122
AF764145

Seeking Justice at the Court of the Khans of Khiva

Brill's Inner Asian Library

Edited by

Michael R. Drompp
Devin DeWeese
Mark C. Elliott

VOLUME 38

The titles published in this series are listed at *brill.com/bial*

Seeking Justice at the Court of the Khans of Khiva

(19th–Early 20th Centuries)

Paolo Sartori
Ulfat Abdurasulov

BRILL

LEIDEN | BOSTON

Cover illustration: Sayyid Islām Khwāja (d. 1913), grand-minister (*vazīr-i akbar*) of the Khanate of Khiva. Picture courtesy of the Ichan-Qal`a State Museum, Khiva.

Library of Congress Cataloging-in-Publication Data

Names: Sartori, Paolo, 1975- author | Abdurasulov, Ulfat, 1977- author.
Title: Seeking justice at the court of the khans of Khiva (19th–early 20th centuries) / Paolo Sartori, Ulfat Abdurasulov.
Description: Leiden ; Boston : Brill, 2020. | Series: Brill's inner Asian library, 1566-7162 ; volume 38 | Includes bibliographical references and index.
Identifiers: LCCN 2020007965 (print) | LCCN 2020007966 (ebook) | ISBN 9789004419391 (hardback) | ISBN 9789004427907 (ebook)
Subjects: LCSH: Justice, Administration of—Khivinskoe khanstvo—History—19th century—Sources. | Justice, Administration of—Khivinskoe khanstvo—History—20th century—Sources. | Justice, Administration of—Uzbekistan—History—19th century—Sources. | Justice, Administration of—Uzbekistan—History—20th century—Sources.
Classification: LCC KLW12.9 . S44 2020 (print) | LCC KLW12.9 (ebook) | DDC 347.587—dc23
LC record available at https://lccn.loc.gov/2020007965
LC ebook record available at https://lccn.loc.gov/2020007966

Typeface for the Latin, Greek, and Cyrillic scripts: "Brill". See and download: brill.com/brill-typeface.

ISSN 1566-7162
ISBN 978-90-04-41939-1 (hardback)
ISBN 978-90-04-42790-7 (e-book)

Copyright 2020 by Koninklijke Brill NV, The Netherlands.
Koninklijke Brill NV incorporates the imprints Brill, Brill Hes & De Graaf, Brill Nijhoff, Brill Rodopi, Brill Sense, Hotei Publishing, mentis Verlag, Verlag Ferdinand Schöningh and Wilhelm Fink Verlag.
All rights reserved. No part of this publication may be reproduced, translated, stored in a retrieval system, or transmitted in any form or by any means, electronic, mechanical, photocopying, recording or otherwise, without prior written permission from the publisher.
Authorization to photocopy items for internal or personal use is granted by Koninklijke Brill NV provided that the appropriate fees are paid directly to The Copyright Clearance Center, 222 Rosewood Drive, Suite 910, Danvers, MA 01923, USA. Fees are subject to change.

This book is printed on acid-free paper and produced in a sustainable manner.

Contents

Preface and Acknowledgments XI
Note on Transcription and Nomenclature XX
Glossary XXII

Introduction 1
1 Crime and Punishment in an Uzbek Khanate 1
2 The Historical Setting 12
3 Who Were the *Yasāvulbāshīs?* 21
4 *ʿArż* as a Form of Governance 35
5 On Protocol 45
6 Documents 50
7 What Was the Cost of the *ʿarż?* 72

Documents

1 **Rescripts (*Texts in Chaghatay*)** 81 (*231*)
1 28 Ẕī al-ḥijja 1328 / 30 December 1912. A Rescript by the *yasāvulbāshī* about a Dispute over Inheritance 81 (*231*)
2 9 Shavvāl 1328 /13 October 1913. A Rescript by the *yasāvulbāshī* about a Dispute over the Payment of Dowry 83 (*232*)
3 13 Shavvāl 1328 /17 October 1913. A Rescript by the *yasāvulbāshī* about a Dispute over Landownership 86 (*233*)
4 23 Ẕī al-ḥijja 1328 / December 25 1910. A Rescript by the *yasāvulbāshī* about A Marital Dispute 88 (*234*)
5 17 Ẕī al-ḥījja 1328 / 19 December 1910. A Rescript by the *yasāvulbāshī* about a Dispute over Debts 90 (*235*)
6 7 Shavvāl 1328 / 11 October 1910. A Rescript by the *yasāvulbāshī* about a Dispute over an Ancestral Undivided Property 92 (*236*)
7 17 Shavvāl 1328 / 21 October 1910. A Rescript by the *yasāvulbāshī* Instructing an Attendant to Investigate the Circumstances of a Dispute 94 (*237*)
8 13 Ẕī al-qaʿda 1336 / 20 August 1918. A Rescript by the *yasāvulbāshī* about a Dispute over a Contested Inheritance 96 (*238*)
9 7 Rabīʿ al-ṣānī 1336 / 19 January 1918. A Rescript by the *yasāvulbāshī* about a Dispute over Landownership 98 (*239*)

10 24 Rabīʿ al-avval 1335 / 7 January 1917. A Rescript by the *yasāvulbāshī* about a Dispute over Landownership 100 (*240*)
11 17 Shaʿbān 1328 / 26 May 1918. A Rescript by the *yasāvulbāshī* about a Case of Murder 102 (*241*)

2 **Reports (*Texts in Chaghatay*)** 104 (*242*)
12 8 Shavvāl [?]. A Report by *qāżīs* to the *yasāvulbāshī* about a Marital Dispute 104 (*242*)
13 4 Rabīʾ al-s̱ānī 1335 /27 January 1917. A Report by a Provincial Governor to the *yasāvulbāshī* about a Dispute over Custody 106 (*243*)
14 24 Ṣafar 1334 / 30 December 1915. A Report by a Provincial Governor to the *yasāvulbāshī* about a Dispute over a Dowry 108 (*244*)
15 Jumādī al-s̱ānī 1336 / March 1918. A Report by a Provincial Governor to the *yasāvulbāshī* about a Case of Robbery 109 (*245*)
16 Rabiʿ al-avval 1335 / December 1916. A Report by a Provincial Governor to the *yasāvulbāshī* about a Case of Domestic Violence 111 (*246*)
17 27 Rajab [1330] / 12 July [1912]. A Report by a Provincial Governor to the *yasāvulbāshī* about a Dispute over Water Rights 114 (*247*)
18 22 Jumādī al-avval 1335/ 15 March 1917. A Report by a Provincial Governor to the *yasāvulbāshī* about Maintenance Works of the Irrigation System 116 (*248*)
19 1328 / 1910. A Report by *qāżīs* to the *yasāvulbāshī* on Land Assessment Works 119 (*249*)
20 19 Ẕī al-ḥijja 1334 / 16 October 1916. A Report by a Provincial Governor to the *yasāvulbāshī* about a Marital Dispute 121 (*250*)
21 27 Ramażān 1336 / 6 July 1918. A Report by a Provincial Governor to the *yasāvulbāshī* about a Dispute over Debts 123 (*251*)
22 16 Rabīʿ al-s̱ānī 1335 / 8 February 1917. A Report by Provincial Governor and the *qāżīs* to the *yasāvulbāshī* about a Dispute over Landownership 125 (*253*)
23 27 Shaʿbān 1336 / 08 June 1918. A Report by a Provincial Governor to the *yasāvulbāshī* about the Death of a Man Involved in an Altercation 128 (*255*)
24 Jumadī al-s̱ānī 1336 / March–April 1918. A Report by a Provincial Governor to the *yasāvulbāshī* about Malfeasance 130 (*256*)
25 7 Muḥarram 1336 / 23 October 1917. A Report to the *yasāvulbāshī* about a Case of Murder 133 (*259*)

26 19 Jumādī al-s̱ānī 1332 / 14 May 1330. A Report by a Provincial Governor to the *yasāvulbāshī* about a Dispute over Landownership 136 (*261*)

27 1335 / 1916-1917. A Report by a Provincial Governor to the *yasāvulbāshī* about a Case of Robbery 138 (*263*)

28 8 Muḥarram 1335 / 3 November 1916. A Report by *qāżīs* to the *yasāvulbāshī* about a Case of Extortion 140 (*264*)

29 9 Shaʿbān 1334 / 10 June 1916. A Report by a Provincial Governor to the *yasāvulbāshī* about a Dispute over Losses Caused by Yomut Turkmens 141 (*265*)

30 28 Ramażān 1336 / 7 July 1918. A Report by a Provincial Governor to the *yasāvulbāshī* about Malfeasance 143 (*266*)

31 10 Rabīʿ al-s̱ānī 1332 / 7 March 1914. A Report to the *yasāvulbāshī* about the Extinguishment of a Debt 145 (*267*)

32 15 Shavvāl 1328 / 9 October 1910. A Report by a Provincial Governor to the *yasāvulbāshī* about the Extinguishment of a Debt 148 (*268*)

33 9 Rabīʿ al-avval 1335 / 2 November 1917. A Report by a Provincial Governor to the *yasāvulbāshī* about the Extinguishment of a Debt 150 (*269*)

34 n.d. A Report of *qāżīs* to the *yasāvulbāshī* about a Dispute over Landownership 152 (*271*)

35 8 Ramażān 1336 / 17 June 1918. A Report by a Provincial Governor to the *yasāvulbāshī* about Rights on a Thoroughfare 153 (*272*)

36 Jumādī al-avval 1336 / February–March 1918. A Report by a Group of Officials to the *yasāvulbāshī* about a Dispute over Taxes in Favor of Yomut Turkmens 154 (*273*)

3 **Notifications (*Texts in Chaghatay*)** 157 (*275*)

37 8 Ramażān 1334 / 8 July 1916. A Notification by a Provincial Governor to the *yasāvulbāshī* about a Case of Assault and Robbery 157 (*275*)

38 25 Ẕī al-qaʿda 1334 / 22 September 1916. A Notification by a Provincial Governor to the *yasāvulbāshī* about a Case of Robbery 159 (*276*)

39 25 Ẕī al-qaʿda 1334 / 22 September 1916. A Notification by a Provincial Governor to the *yasāvulbāshī* about a Case of Animal Theft 161 (*278*)

40 15 Jumādī al-s̱ānī 13[?] / [?]. A Notification by a Provincial Governor to the *yasāvulbāshī* about a Case of Armed Robbery 163 (*280*)

41 5 Rajab 1336 / 16 April 1918. A Notification by a Provincial Governor to the *yasāvulbāshī* about a Case of Robbery and Assault 167 (*284*)

42 n.d. A Notification by *qāżīs* to the *yasāvulbāshī* about a Case of Domestic Violence 170 (*287*)

43 Shaʿbān 1335 / May–June 1917. A Notification by a Provincial Governor and *qāżīs* to the *yasāvulbāshī* about a Man's Death 172 (*288*)
44 18 Shaʿbān 1334 / 19 June 1916. A Notification by a Provincial Governor to the *yasāvulbāshī* about a Case of Bride-Kidnapping 174 (*290*)
45 26 Jumādī al-avval 1336 / 09 March 1918. A Notification by a Provincial Governor to the *yasāvulbāshī* about a Case of Bride-Kidnapping 176 (*292*)
46 7 Jumādī al-s̱ānī 1336 /19 March 1918. A Notification by a Provincial Governor to the *yasāvulbāshī* about a Case of Robbery and Homicide 178 (*293*)
47 17 Rabīʿ al-s̱ānī 1335 / 9 February 1917. A Notification by a Provincial Governor to the *yasāvulbāshī* about a Case of Assault 181 (*295*)
48 22 Rabīʿ al-s̱ānī 1335 /14 February 1917. A Notification by a Provincial Governor to the *yasāvulbāshī* about a Case of Animal Theft 183 (*296*)
49 22 Rabīʿ al-avval 1335 / 15 January 1917. A Notification by a Provincial Governor to the *yasāvulbāshī* about a Double Homicide 184 (*297*)
50 18 Rajab 1336 / 29 April 1918. A Notification by a Provincial Governor to the *yasāvulbāshī* about Multiple Cases of Robbery and Homicide 185 (*298*)
51 Z̤ī al-s̱ānī 1335 / September–October 1917. A Notification by a Provincial Governor to the *yasāvulbāshī* about a Case of Robbery 187 (*299*)
52 5 Shaʿbān 1336 / 15 May 1918. A Notification by a Provincial Governor to the *yasāvulbāshī* about a Dispute over Rights of Inheritance 188 (*300*)
53 12 Z̤ī al-qaʿda 1336 / 19 August 1918. A Notification by a Provincial Governor to the *yasāvulbāshī* about a Case of Animal Theft 190 (*301*)
54 15 Jumādī al-avval 1335 / 8 March 1915. A Notification by a Provincial Governor to the *yasāvulbāshī* about a Case of Homicide 192 (*303*)
55 5 Jumādīʾ al-avval 1329 / 3 March 1911. A Notification to the *yasāvulbāshī* about a Case of Homicide 194 (*305*)
56 25 Ṣafar 1335 / 20 December 1916. A Notification by a Provincial Governor to the *yasāvulbāshī* about a Case of Robbery 197 (*308*)
57 2 Jumādī al-avval 1335 / 24 February 1917. A Notification by a Provincial Governor to the *yasāvulbāshī* about a Case of Robbery 200 (*311*)
58 27 Rajab 1339 / 5 April 1921. A Notification by a Provincial Governor to the *yasāvulbāshī* about a Case of Robbery 201 (*312*)
59 1334 / 1915–1916. A petition to the *yasāvulbāshī* regarding a Case of Robbery and Assault 203 (*313*)

60 1335 / 1916–1917. A Notification by a Provincial Governor to the *yasāvulbāshī* about a Dispute over an Unpaid Debt 205 (*314*)
61 14 Ẕī al-qaʿda 1337 / 10 August 1919. A Letter by the Turkmen Yomut Leader Junayd Khān to the *yasāvulbāshī* about the Appointment of a New *qāżī* to Solve Conflicts among the Ata Turkmens 207 (*315*)
62 8 Ramażān 1332 / 30 July 1914. A Notification by a Provincial Governor to the *yasāvulbāshī* about the Intention of the Disputing Parties to Solve the Dispute before the Khan 210 (*316*)
63 24 Rabīʿ al-ṣānī 1332 / 21 March 1914. A Notification by a Provincial Governor to the *yasāvulbāshī* about the Intention of the Disputing Parties to Solve the Dispute before the Khan 212 (*317*)

4 ***Qāżīs*' Reports (*Texts in Chaghatay*)** 213 (*318*)
64 *n.d.* A Report by a *qāżī-ra'is* about the Intention of the Disputing Parties to Solve the Dispute before the khan 213 (*318*)
65 7 Shaʿbān 1267 / 6 June 1851. A Report by a *qāżī-ra'is* to Authorities in Khiva about the Outcome of a Conflict at a Local Bazaar 215 (*320*)
66 *n.d.* A Report by a *qāżī* to the Royal Court about a Dispute over Land Ownership 216 (*321*)
67 *n.d.* A Report by a *qāżī* to the Royal Court about an Unspecified Dispute 218 (*322*)
68 *n.d.* A Report by a *qāżī* to the Royal Court about a Conflict over an Unpaid Fee and an Ensuing Case of Assault 219 (*323*)
69 *n.d.* A Report by a *qāżī* to the Royal Court about a Case of Homicide 221 (*324*)
70 *n.d.* A Report by *qāżīs* to the Royal Court about a Case of Homicide 222 (*325*)
71 *n.d.* A Report by a *qāżī* to the Royal Court about a Case of Homicide 224 (*326*)
72 *n.d.* A Report by a *qāżī* to the Royal Court about a Case of Homicide 226 (*327*)
73 *n.d.* A Report by a *qāżī* to the Royal Court about a Case of Homicide 227 (*328*)

Facsimiles 329
Bibliography 439
Index of Places 449
Index of Proper Names 452

Preface and Acknowledgments

This book originates from a casual conversation which took place in the historical citadel of Khiva nearly a decade ago. In August 2010, we were on a field-research mission to inspect collections of Islamic manuscripts located in remote collective farms in the region of Khorezm, in the territory of Uzbekistan and the subsidiary republic of Qaraqalpaqstan. Rumors had it that private libraries, which had been preserved throughout the Soviet period, were becoming the subject of public attention in those days. In several instances farmers had appeared before local authorities in the city of Urgench (Uzbekistan) and brandished legal deeds crafted in the 19th century to lay claim on the land, which once, so they said, had belonged to their ancestors. In other cases, heirs to families of scholars (*ʿulamāʾ*) from Khoja-eli (Qaraqalpaqstan) were deploying their 'genealogical charts' (*shajara*s) and 'initiatic affiliations' (*silsila*s) to boast of their privileged status before village communities, a move which soon gave a spur to conflicts over moral authority.

Excited to find out more about how in post-Soviet Central Asia people were deploying texts coming from a distant past, we hit the road towards Khiva to meet our informants. Taken by surprise by the sweltering heat of the summer in Khorezm, we found shelter in the cramped room of one of the cells of a madrasa dating back to the reign of Muḥammad Raḥīm Khān Fīrūz (1864–1910). The premises, once called upon to serve as a haven for students, had been recently repurposed as the office of Komiljon Khudaybergenov, an employee of the State Historical Museum. Proceeding from one topic in the history of the Khanate of Khiva to the other, Khudaybergenov unexpectedly laid out on the table what at first looked like a standard student notebook of the Soviet period. The only distinguishing feature of this otherwise uninspiring item was that it was elegantly written by hand in the Arabic script, not in Cyrillic as one would have expected. The notebook belonged to one ʿAbdullāh Bāltaev (1890–1966), a native of Khiva who during the 1950s and 1960s authored an impressive number of works (nearly ninety) covering a dazzling range of topics about the pre-Soviet history of Khorezm.[1] Most of his 'notebooks' (*daftar*, as he himself titled them) are in fact a bricolage of personal observations, stories recounted from memory, copies of records found in the archives, and excerpts of court chronicles written during the rule of the khans of Khiva. Several of them had been known for years because Bāltaev had written them upon commission

1 K. Abdullaev, *Naqshlarga bitilgan umr: Abdulla Boltaevning hayoti va ijodiy faoliyati* (Tashkent: Ghafur Ghulom nomidagi Adabiyot va sanʿat nashriyoti, 1995).

by Uzbek academics, who in turn bequeathed them to the al-Beruni Institute of Oriental Manuscripts in Tashkent in the 1960s. The majority of his *daftars*, however, have been jealously preserved by his descendants in Khiva and thus inaccessible to historians from abroad. Coming back to the one notebook laid out before us, we immediately noted something puzzling about it. The title read as follows: 'The first part of this *daftar* is devoted to the submission of *ʿarż* in the Khanate of Khiva.'[2] It took us some time and a good dose of head-scratching to find out that the a section of the notebook was in fact a detailed account about the court protocol to hear complaints (*ʿarż*) from the population at the court of the khans of Khiva.

At that time we knew from modern studies of Islamic law under the Mamluks of Egypt about the institution called *maẓālim*, which functioned as an appellate court. We were also familiar with scholarship devoted to Ottoman history, which has shown how subjects often appealed to the chancery (*dīwān*) of the Sultan with a grievance (*shikāyat*) to seek redress.[3] We were unclear, however, as to whether the same system applied in the Ottoman Empire – a system in which litigations were heard either by judges (*qāżīs*) out of their own volition or by the royal court[4] – was enforced in Khorezm and Central Asia in general. Therefore, nothing seemed more appropriate than to delve into Bāltaev's work. Reading the following extended quotation[5] will help, we hope, reproduce in purely dramatic terms how we proceeded into discovering what the *ʿarż* was:

> Having exited the private apartments (*īchkarī ḥarām*), every day, [approximately] two and a half hours before sunset, the khan spends time in the audience hall (*kūrūnīsh-khāna*) near the marble stone, sitting on the wooden podium called 'the throne' (*takht*), on the spot marked [in the drawing] with the number '1.' Said throne was usually covered with felt carpets. The khan sat facing the entrance door, which is marked with the number '7,' for it was through this door that the people (*khalq*) came close to him in order to submit a petition (*ʿarż*). After the khan entered [the audience room] and took his place, one of the heads of the [palace] guard (*shāṭirlār bāshlīghī*) went out to the gates of the palace, where usually the subjects (*fuqarā*), coming from every district (*rāyūn*), village and city,

2 1 – *ūshbū daftarda Khīva khānlīgīnī ʿarż surāsh tartībī yāzīlghān.*

3 See infra for a discussion of this scholarship.

4 J. Baldwin, "Petitioning the Sultan in Ottoman Egypt," *Bulletin of the School of Oriental and African Studies* 75.3 (2012), pp. 499–524; S. Ayoub, "'The Sulṭan Says': State Authority in Late Ḥanafī Tradition," *Islamic Law and Society* 23.3 (2016), pp. 239–278.

5 ʿAbdullāh Bāltaev, *Daftar* (*no. 22*), MS Khiva, Private collection of Odilbek Abdullaev, fols. 55–64 (Western pagination).

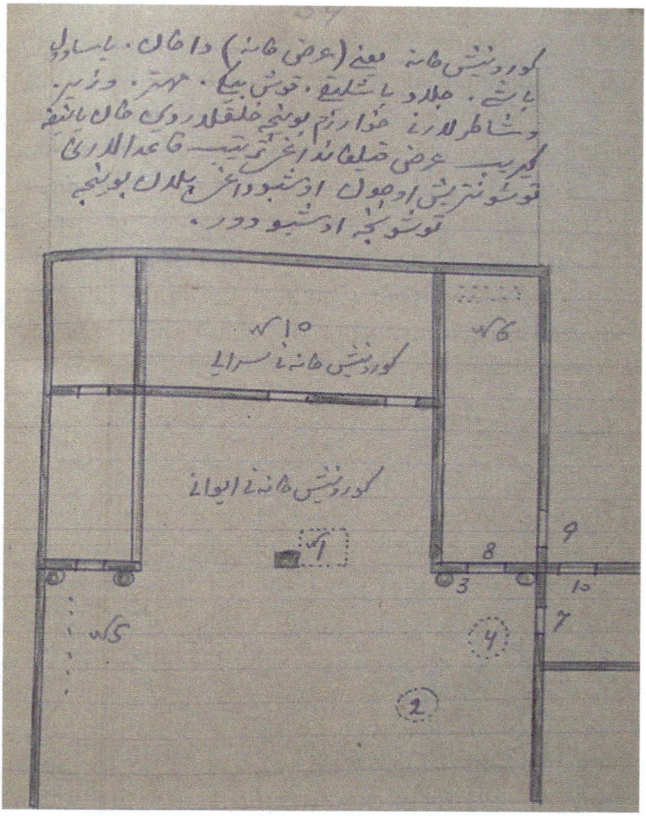

FIGURE 1 The audience hall (*kūrūnīsh-khāna*) for the *ʿarż* in the royal citadel, Khiva. Drawing by ʿAbdullāh Bāltaev. Particular of *Daftar* (*no.* 22), MS Khiva, Private collection of Odilbek Abdullaev, fol. 54 (Western pagination).

gathered at the appointed time to submit a petition (*ʿarż qilish ūchūn*). Turning to him, the chief of the guard exclaimed: 'If among you there are people who have come for the *ʿarż*, come in!' Upon hearing this call of the guard, the people in waiting passed through the gate to the courtyard of the palace, whence each petitioner, in order of priority, one by one, walking through the door [marked] with the number '7' was supposed to enter another room [marked] with the number '4.' No matter how many people arrived, each of them had to proceed to the room [marked] with no. '4,' where they would stand. From this point, the petitioner, standing and facing the khan, greeted the ruler, then with his arms folded, said: 'Sovereign, I have a request (*taqṣīr ʿarżīm bār*)!' To which the khan [usually] replied: 'Speak out!' Meanwhile, the *yasāvulbāshī*, who was in charge

> of the political affairs of the khanate (*siyāsī īshlarī*), and who attended the ceremony on the spot [marked] with the number '3', turned to the petitioner and in a threatening voice repeated: 'Speak out!' Upon hearing such a loud voice, and fearing possible punishments, [often] the petitioner became speechless and could not utter a single word. At that point the khan ordered: 'Take him!' Upon hearing this order, the *yasāvulbāshī* shouted out in the same threatening voice the [following] order to the executioners: 'Take him!' The head of the executioners, who too was standing on the spot [marked] with no. '3,' grabbed the afore-mentioned subject violently (*ghażab birlān*) and led him through the door [marked] with the number '8' into a long room [marked] with the number '6.' Here the petitioner is entrusted to special executioners (*makhṣūṣ jallād*). The petitioner will stay here until the khan passes an order to the *yasāvulbāshī* as to how to proceed. Meanwhile, the head of the executioners, returning [to the audience room], again takes his place [marked] with the number '3.' After some time, the next petitioners will come again to the khan through the door [marked] with the number '7.' Following the same procedure, they will appeal to the khan. If any of them, without fearing the menace [of the *yasāvulbāshī*] and remaining firm, can speak out, then the khan will order: 'Go outside and wait!' Upon hearing these words, the same *yasāvulbāshī*, in the [usual] threatening voice, will repeat the command to the petitioner. At which order, the petitioner will proceed to go out passing through the doors [marked] with the numbers '8, 9, 10.'

It was only when we reached the end of Bāltaev's memoirs that we could clarify conclusively that the legal system of *ʿarż*, which the Khivan savant referred, was in fact far removed from what we had learnt from studies devoted to the legal history of other regions of the Islamic world. In 19th- and early 20th-century Khorezm, justice was firmly in the hands of the Qonghrats, the dynasty ruling over the region, and therefore the subjects of the khans brought their affairs to whom was in power, either locally or at the center of the khanate. Here is how Bāltaev explained the matter:

> […] Each city and district in the region of Khorezm, that is in the Khanate of Khorezm, is [administered by] a separate governor (*ḥākim*). If the people living in this area had to file claims, they appealed to the governor of their own district (*khalqlārnī daʿvā īshlārī būlsa shūl rāyūnidāgī ūzīnī ḥākimīgha ʿarż qīlādī*). If the claims were particularly serious, the governors could not solve them, [and so] the people went to Khiva to appeal to

> the khan. This is why petitioners came before the khans in the manner we explained above to submit their serious claims for consideration. For this reason, every day [the khan] heard two or three major cases, [submitted by people coming from all over] Khorezm. If [there were a great number of such cases], he often heard four or five, but no more [than that]. For this reason, every day the khan went to the audience room, where he sat on the afore-mentioned throne for 15, but no more than 20 minutes. He did so both in winter and in summer, and even when it snowed. After hearing the petitions, the khan dismounted from the throne and entered a large edifice (*sarāy*), under a portico [marked] with the number '10.' As he sat there, 32 high officials entered to greet the khan (*salām birīb*). Some of them stayed in this edifice [with the ruler]. Others left as soon as they greeted him. Among the high-rank officials, the *qūshbīgī*, the *mihtar*, the *yasāvulbāshī*, as well as the *maḥrams*, and the *īshīk-āghās* were obliged to stand beside the khan starting from the submission of the petitions until he left for his private apartments. Because if the khan orders that someone be executed, imprisoned or beaten with a whip because for some reason he became angry, when such order is issued, [the abovementioned officials] should stand beside him. Even after the khan left for his private apartments, [the abovementioned officials] were supposed to stay at that place for about 10–15 minutes, and only if no order followed during this time, could they then go. These were the procedures and rules to submit petitions to the khans. I have seen with my own eyes how among the khans of Khorezm, Fīrūz Muḥammad Raḥīm Khān, his successor Isfandiyār Khān, and his successor Sayyid ʿAbdullāh Khān, from the late 19th to the early 20th century, followed such procedures [to hear] the petitions submitted [to them]. I wrote them down from my own memory for whomsoever among our offspring in the future may show an interest in history.

As soon as we closed Bāltaev's *daftar*, our search for more information on the *ʿarż* began. We had found out that there was a highly distinct way for subjects of the khans of Khiva to seek redress. But we did not know how to *document* it. No one prior to us had ever noticed the phenomenon and our informants in Khorezm tended to dismiss the historical significance of our *trouvaille*. 'Bāltaev noted down every kind of trivia!' – this is what we were told time and again. But there was a further layer of complexity. At that time we were granted access to a massive documentary corpus consisting of records issued by *qāżīs* in Khorezm in the 19th and early 20th century, which had been recently catalogued. Those legal deeds said nothing about the *ʿarż*. One could say that the legal system called *ʿarż* and the *sharīʿa* courts presided over by judges were far removed from each other, if not two worlds apart. In fact, they were not. Upon our return to Tashkent, we pursued our investigation further. And it was again by chance that, while looking in the al-Beruni Institute for works crafted in Khorezm which could shed more light on the *ʿarż*, we came across yet another *daftar* penned by Bāltaev. We had barely begun to leaf through it, when we found a description of a case of manslaughter occurring in the Khanate of Khiva at the turn of the 20th century.[6] The case involved two peasants in the province of Shavat: one went by the name of Īgām Birdī Raḥim Birdī ughlī, the other was known as Jumʿa Niyāz Ātash ughlī. The matter at stake was their respective water shares: each party blamed the other for having used more than their fair share of water for purposes of irrigation. It was an ordinary affair, to be sure, which originated from a trivial complaint: 'You took too much of it, while I had less' (*san suvnī kūb īchdīng man āz īchdīm dīb*). However, the conflict quickly morphed into a quarrel with the peasants insulting each other and coming to blows. Īgām Birdī hit Jumʿa Niyāz on the head with the handle of a shovel. As a result of the injuries caused by the strike, Jumʿa Niyāz died. As soon as the people informed the father and relatives of the victim about the incident, they got hold of the culprit, tied him up, loaded him on a cart, and hit the road to Khiva. Upon arrival in the city, the father of the deceased secured permission to appeal (*ʿarż*) to the royal court and sought a fair retribution. During the hearing in the presence of the sovereign, the accused Īgām Birdī acknowledged that his strike proved fatal for his opponent. This was enough for the ruler, Muḥammad Raḥīm Khān II, to sentence Īgām Birdī to death by hanging (*dārgha āsīb*). Dissatisfied with such a decision, however, Ātash, the father of the victim, appealed to the ruler once again: 'Your Majesty,' he said, 'let me kill this man with my own hands, for only in this way will I take [revenge for] the blood of my son' (*taqṣīr bu ādamnī uldīrīsh ikhtiyārīnī menga bersāngīz chūn-ki ūz qūlīm birlān uldurub ūghlīmnī qānīnī ālsām dīb*). Muḥammad Raḥīm Khān II allowed the aggrieved party to take revenge. Meanwhile, having learned about this decision, the parents and the relatives of Īgām Birdī too appealed to the khan and pleaded to entrust the capital punishment to the executioners. However, the ruler turned down the appeal. We shall now gloss over Īgām Birdī's public dismemberment, which Bāltaev describes in gruesome detail. The execution took place before the eyes of his relatives, we learn, who unable to tolerate all that horror, abandoned themselves to despair.

---

6 ʿAbdullāh Bāltaev, *Daftar*, MS Tashkent, Institut Vostokovedeniia im. Abu Reikhana Beruni Akademii Nauk Respubliki Uzbekistan [henceforth IVANRUz], inv. no. 11978, fols. 18a–19a.

Nothing could be done to avoid that revolting sight, Bāltaev reminds us, for all that affair represented the 'sovereign's wrath' (*pādishāh ghażabī*).

The episode described by Bāltaev may seem familiar to many. Indeed, almost no Khorezmian travel account by European authors went without reports of thieves hanging from gallows,[7] or escaped slaves impaled on stakes, dying agonizing deaths. The picture was usually further embellished with accounts of a special hole in the central square in front of the Khan's palace, where those suspected even of minor crimes would have their throat slit.[8] 19th-century travelogues thus offer a bleak picture of the dispensation of justice in Khiva, where judicial power was disposed of according to the mere whim of the despotic khan, ready to take his subjects' lives for the smallest fault.[9]

It is of course true that 19th-century Central Asian regimes were far from a model of humanity and tolerance by any contemporary standard. The rulers of the Uzbek khanates were merciless towards their political opponents, whom they often had killed either publicly, or in secret;[10] one notes, for example, records from the khan's chancery, which inform us about rewards given to participants of raids for delivering the ears and heads of enemies.[11] In addition, it appears that Persian or Russian slaves caught committing crimes, or trying

7 [Turpaev], "Dnevnik perevodchika armianina Turpaeva, poslannogo v 1834 g. iz Novo-Aleksandrovskogo ukrepleniia v Khivu (perevod s armianskogo)," in M.N. Galkin, *Etnograficheskie materialy po Srednei Azii i Orenburgskomu kraiu M.N. Galkina* (St. Petersburg: Izdanie Ia.A. Isakova, 1868), p. 284.

8 Anon., "Razboinich'e gnezdo," *Illiustrirovannaia nedelia* 50 (25 December) (St. Petersburg, 1873); E. Lobasevych, "Pokazaniia russkikh plennykh, byvshikh v Khive, dannoe 16-go iunia Orenburgskomu general-gubernatoru," *Turkestanskii Sbornik*, vol. 42 (St. Petersburg, 1871), p. 89.

9 It is remarkable that this narrative continued to develop in the later historiography of the Soviet and even post-Soviet periods, see M. Niiazmetov, *Poisk konsensusa. Rossiisko-khivinskie geopoliticheskie otnosheniia v XVI–nachale XX v.* (St. Petersburg: Peterburgskoe vostokovedenie, 2010), pp. 113–115.

10 On the details of brutal assassination of the political opponents by the Qonghrat dynasts see Muḥammad Yūsuf Bayānī, *Shajara-yi Khwārazmshāhī*, MS Tashkent, IVANRUz, inv. no. 9596, fols. 330a, 331a, 357a; Muḥammad Rižā Āgahī, *Gulshan-i dawlat*, IVANRUz, inv. no. 7572, fol. 15a; 'Abdullāh Bāltaev, *Khwārazm ta'rīkhīga matiryallār* (*Khīva 1950*), MS Tashkent, IVANRUz, inv. no. 9320, fols. 5a–6b.

11 TsGARUz, f. I-125, op. 2, d. 82. ll. 1–2; d. 83, l. 1. TsGARUz = Tsentral'nyi Gosudarstvennyi Arkhiv Respubliki Uzbekistan, Central State Archive of the Republic of Uzbekistan. Abbreviations used in references to Russian archives: f. (fond), holding; op. (opis'), inventory; d. (delo), file; l. (list), sheet; ob. (oborot), verso.

to escape on multiple occasions, were often condemned to exemplary executions, including impalement on stakes.[12]

However, it need not be that the investigation of any wrongdoing, either a misdemeanor or a felony, inevitably ended in the ruthless punishment of the accused. It is only when we go beyond the emphasis on capital punishment that we begin to appreciate the specific features of the *ʿarż* and recognize that there is something in Bāltaev's account which is less familiar to us: the implementation of the *ʿarż* did not require the involvement of any jurist or judge of any rank (*shaykh al-islām*, *qāżī kalān*, and *aʿlam*). Bāltaev is adamant about the fact that it is first to the governor and then to the sovereign that subjects turn for redress, not to legal scholars (see infra, 'Introduction').

In the light of this knowledge, however, it remained to be explained why the royal court did not produce any documentation of its various activities during the performance of the *ʿarż*. That was what we thought. In the year 2011 and again in 2014, and for the subsequent five years, we enjoyed privileged access to the Central State Archive of Uzbekistan, and more specifically, its collections of records from Khorezm. It was because of such an extended, indeed exceptional, opportunity to work with local materials that we were able to identify a significant paper trail left by the *ʿarż* in Khiva. This is an extensive collection of records (including several thousand folia) issued by various officials of the Khanate of Khiva, which illuminate how the royal court reviewed and processed petitions submitted by subjects. This collection, which Soviet archivists called the 'Yasaulbashi collection,' supplied the documentary corpus upon which to write this book.

Carrying out such a complex and long-term team-work would have been impossible without financial and institutional support in Uzbekistan. The seeds of this research were planted within the framework of the project 'The Archives Talk: Writing the Social History of Colonial Central Asia,' which was funded by the VolkswagenStiftung in the years 2010–2013. But it was thanks to a START prize awarded by the Austrian Science Fund (FWF) in 2013 for the project 'Seeing like an Archive: Documents and Forms of Governance in Islamic Central Asia' (Start Program Y-704), that we could carry out and complete our work in the years 2014–2019. We are indebted to these funding agencies for their generous support.

During the preparation of this book, we were assisted by a team of colleagues and research partners in Tashkent and Khiva. Initial transcription of a

12 Ḥasan-Murād Laffasī, *Āzādnāma*, MS Tashkent, IVANRUz, inv. no. 12581, fols. 4a–4b; Bābājān Safarov, *Khwārazmda būlūb ūtgān qūlchīlīq ahvāllārīnīng vāqiʿalārī*, MS Tashkent, IVANRUz, inv. no. 11254, fols. 85b–86b.

selection of records from the 'Yasaulbashi collection' was supplied by a group of Uzbek Ph.D. students. We are grateful to Khushnud Abdurasulov, Ikromjon Azizov, Akmal Bazarbaev, Nargiza Ismatova, Nasriddin Mirzaev, and Qahramon Yaqubov, for their help. During various stages in the evolution of this book, we took advantage of consultations and administrative assistance rendered by Dilorom Alimova, Bakhtiyar Babajanov, Nizomiddin Gulboev, Muhayyo Isakova, Komiljon Khudaybergenov, James Pickett, and Nuryogdi Toshov.

We would like to express our appreciation to the staff of academic institutions, in particular the Institute of History and the Institute of Oriental Studies of the Uzbek Academy of Sciences, the Central State Archive in Tashkent, the State Museum 'Ichan-Qal`a' in Khiva and the Institute of Iranian Studies at the Austrian Academy of Sciences. We are also grateful to the anonymous reviewer for Brill, whose comments and painstaking attention to the manuscript helped immensely to improve the volume, to Thomas Welsford for fabulous copyediting, and to Patricia Radder and Kathy van Vliet for their support of the project. Special thanks go also to Devin DeWeese, editor of the *Brill Inner Asian Library* series, for envisioning a place for the volume in this venue.

Note on Transcription and Nomenclature

For Islamic names and terms, we have adopted the transliteration system for Arabo-Persian used by the *International Journal of Middle East Studies*. In so doing, we have opted for a simple one-to-one correspondence between grapheme (in the original Arabic script) and phoneme (in the Latin). We have been agnostic with regard to the presumed pronunciation of words in Chaghatay[1] (Central Asian Turki or Eastern Turkic) and therefore avoided introducing any phonetic distinction between front and back vowels characteristic of the Turkic languages spoken in Central Asia. Our transcription of Russian follows the *Chicago Manual of Style* differing only in the rendering of *iu* and *ia* instead of *yu* and *ya*.

Writing practices in Khorezm clearly show that Chaghatay orthography was relatively unstable at the turn of the 20th century. Varying levels of literacy

---

1 In this work the term 'Chaghatay' is used conventionally in a broad sense as a synonym of Eastern Turkic (*Turkī*) as in E. Schluessel, *An Introduction to Chaghatay: A Graded Textbook for Reading Central Asian Sources* (Mountain View, CA: Michigan Publishing, 2018), pp. vi–x. In Western scholarship, 'Chaghatay' is often distinguished from 'Turki' in order to emphasize two distinct phases in the evolution of the Eastern Turkic literary language. The term 'Chaghatay' is deployed thus to refer to late Timurid literature ('Alī Shīr Navā'ī and Bābūr) and to emphasize its Persianate features, while 'Turki' is preferred when addressing works crafted in the Eastern Turkic language from the 17th to the 19th century. Some scholars have regarded the adoption of the term 'Chaghatay' as controversial on account of its Orientalist genealogy, for its occurrences in Central Asian Turkic literature are in fact sparse. See, for example, B. Péri, "Notes on the Literary-Linguistic Term 'Čaġatay': Evaluating the Evidence Supplied by Native Sources." In *Altaica Budapestinensia MMII: Proceedings of the 45th Permanent International Altaisitic Conference (PIAC) Budapest, Hungary, June 23–28, 2002*, ed. A. Sárközi and A. Rákos (Budapest: Research Group for Altaic Studies, Hungarian Academy of Sciences – Department of Inner Asian Studies, Eötvös Loránd University, 2003), pp. 248–55. While there is no doubt that Central Asian authors overwhelmingly preferred the term *Turkī* to *Chaghatāy* when referring to the Eastern Turkic language regardless of the period in which they wrote, in 19th-century Central Asia the term *Chaghatāy* enjoyed in fact some traction. The famous Khivan court historian Muḥammad Riżā Mīrāb Āgahī, for example, claimed to have written his chronicle titled *Shāhid-i Iqbāl* in the *Chaghatāy* language. Also, Şeyh Süleyman Efendi Buhârî employed the term *Chaghatāy* in his Eastern Turkic-Ottoman Turkish bilingual dictionary published in Istanbul in 1880/1, which included poems penned by another 19th-century Khivan savant, Shīr Muḥammad Mīrāb Munis. Equally, it seems to us that to distinguish between two different linguistic phases (an earlier one 'Chaghatay', and a later one 'Turki') is to put in place an artificial separation between texts produced in different epochs, a separation which local consumers of literature in the Eastern Turkic language hardly perceived. How else could we explain the fact that in the early 20th century in Khorezm the sophisticated oeuvre of 'Alī Shīr Navā'ī was assembled together with the more prosaic works of, say, Ṣufī Allāh Yār into literary miscellanies?

among the scribal apparatus of the Khanate of Khiva as well as exposure to different ethnic communities were evidently the main reasons behind spelling variations. One complicating factor for the transliteration system that we have employed is the variety of orthographic forms for certain proper names and toponyms. Rather than adopting a normatively prescriptive approach towards such variations, regarding one textual rendering as correct and another as wrong, we have instead reproduced all the terms in the form in which they appear in whatever text is under discussion. We have therefore noted all spelling variations and, where possible, also distinguished Oghuzisms (e.g., *ād* instead of *āt*). Another mark of orthographic instability is represented by the use of various patronymic terms: *ughlī, bin, valad-i,* and *qīzī, bint, dukhtar-i.* We have sought to render these terms as they appear in the texts. Finally, our documentary corpus includes variations in the ligature of prepositions and postpositions. For the sake of clarity and uniformity, we have rendered them as conjoined.

Place names have been rendered in two distinct ways. When translating texts or quoting directly therefrom, we have rendered all place names with diacritics with the exception of several terms (Hazarasp, Khiva, Khoja-eli, Manghit). In the rest of the book, place names have been rendered without diacritics.

Most of the unpublished material on which this volume is based comes from post-Soviet archives, and the citation of the archival material thus follows the standard system used in Russian studies. The archival collection, the inventory, the file, and the folio are indicated respectively with the following Russian abbreviations: f. (*fond*), op. (*opis'*), d. (*delo*), and l., ll. (*list, listy*), ob. (*oborot*).

Glossary

ābkhurī qāzū	canals' maintenance works
adrā yir	uncultivated land
aʿlam	senior jurist
ālghūdār	creditor
āltī ātār	lit., 'firing six shots'; a type of rifle
ʿamaldār	official
amānat	deposit, custody
amīn	trustee
amr-i ʿālī	royal order
amvāl va ashiyāʾ	possession
ānt	oath; a legal procedure adopted in *sharīʿa* courts
āqā/āghā	lord, honorific title attached to the names of senior officials
āqsaqāl	headman of a village or rural community
ʿarż / ʿarż-dād	formal procedure whereby a subject submits a grievance to the ruler and files a claim with the royal court
ʿarż / ʿarīża / ʿarīża-nāma / ʿarż-dāsht	petition
ʿārżgūy / ʿārżchī	petitioner, see also *dādkhwāh*
ʿarż-khāna / ʿarż-jāy	chamber of petitions in the royal residence
āryāq	'Russian' or 'right' side of the lower Amu Darya under the jurisdiction of the Russian Empire from 1873
āṭlīgh (āṭlīq) yirī	lands allotted predominantly to Turkmen tribes
āyghāq	informant
bātman	unit of weight; in the 19th and early 20th century it was *ca.* 20 kgs
bāy	a title usually attached to the names of provincial governors
bāyluv khaṭṭī	binding letter
birdānka	Berdan rifle
bīsh-ātār	lit.: 'firing five shots'; most probably 3-line Mosin rifle
biy	tribal elder
būyrūq / būyrūq-i ʿālī	royal warrant
dādkhwāh	petitioner
dafn	burial
daftar	register; cadastre
dargāh-i ʿālī	royal court

daʿvā	claim
daʿvāgar	claimant, plaintiff
davr	unit (community) of water-users
dīvān	scribe, see also *mīrzā*
farsang / parsakh	parasang; in 19th-century Central Asia between 9 and 10 km
fāsid daʿvā	void claim; unsound claim
fatak	royal rescript
fātiḥa / fātiḥa-khwānd	betrothal
fuqarā	subjects
dahabāshī	lit. 'commandant of ten'; head of the court guard
gumān / gumāndār	suspect
gunāh	misdemeanor; culprit
guvāh	witness, see also *shāhid*
ḥākim	provincial governor
hamrāh	accomplice to crime, see also *yūldāsh*
ḥaram	dynasts' private chambers
ḥavlī	house, household
ḥukm	legal ruling, decision, judgment
ibrāʾ	acquittal of a claim; waiver
īchkarī	inner quarter of the house
ʿidda	post-divorce waiting period
ijāra	rent
īl-ādamlārī	representatives of a local community
īl / īlāt	community
īl-qarāvullārī	communal militia
ahl-i īlāt	members of a community
inkār	denial of a claim
iqrār	acknowledgement, admission
īshān	title employed to denote Sufi *shaykh*s; also a honorific title added to *qāżī*s
īshīk-āqā	lit., 'doorkeeper'; a courtier who guarded the entrance to khan's audience-hall
īzchī	lit., 'one who follows tracks'; scout
īzchī fulī	the payment for the scout
jallād	executioner
janāza	burial prayer
janjāl	conflict
jarāhat	wound, injury; see also *majrūḥ*
jāy	house
jazā	punishment, see also *taʿzīr*

ūlūm jazāsī	capital punishment
kafīl	guarantor
kadkhudā	community elder
kadkhudā fulī	reward to the elders of a communities for the achievement of a settlement
kātībāna	payment or reward to scribe
kharājāt	expenses
kāranda	tenant
khaṭ	written document
khātūn	wife, see also *żaʿīfa*
khūn	compensation for murder
kiyāv	husband; son-in-law
kūrūnīsh-khāna	audience hall
maḥram	confidant; a chamberlain, an individual close to the Khivan khans, who was also endowed with the right to access the dynasts' private chambers (*ḥaram*)
mahr	dowry
majrūḥ	wound, injury; see also *jarāhat*
manāt	local designation for Russian rouble
maqtūl	slain man; murdered
mardum	people
masʾala	juristic case
masjid / masjid qavmī	mosque community
mawżiʿ	locality
mazār	cemetery, shrine
miḥtar	high-rank official in the Khanate of Khiva
mīrāṣ	inheritance
mīrshab	policeman
mīrzā	scribe, see also *dīvān*
muʾaẕẕin	the crier who calls the faithful to prayer
muddaʿī	plaintiff
muddaʿā ʿalayh	respondent, defendant
muftī	jurist
muhranā	payment or reward to an official for affixing his seal
mulk / milk	property
murāfaʿa	litigation
murīd	disciple
muʿtabar ādam	reliable person
mutavallī	administrator of a *vaqf*
nāchār	woman

nafaqa	post-divorce financial support
nawkar	liegeman; guard
āṭlī nawkar	mounted liegeman
nikāḥ	marriage
ʿaqd-i nikāḥ	marriage contract
pashshāb	chief of police in localities
pīshkash	gift
qalʿa	fortress, city
qalʿa kāsiblār	city dwellers
qālīng	customary bride-price
qāmchī	lit., 'whip'; lashing a culprit of the whip during or after interrogation
qamtū	cross-examination
qāndār	sworn enemy
qarīndāsh	relative
qariya / *qariya ādamlār*	elderly people, see also *yāsh-kattalār*
qasam	oath, see also *ānt*
qarż	debt
qavm	community
qāżī / *qāżī-īshān*	judge
qāżī ʿaskar	lit., 'military judge'; along with the *qāżī kalān*, the *qāżī ʿaskar* was the chief judge of the Khanate of Khiva
qāżī kalān	chief judge
qibla	southern side
qūshbīgī	high-rank official
rižālashūb	reaching an agreement
ṣadaqa	donations, alms
ṣāf (būlūb)	satisfaction
ṣaghīr	minor; underage child
sāqā	upper part of a canal
saqa qāzū	maintenance of the upper streams of a canal
salām	court ceremony of greeting the khan
shahādat	testimony
shāhid	witness, see also *guvāh*
sharīʿatgha qūshdūk/ *sharīʿatgha tāpshūrdūk*	transferring the case on to the *qāżī*s
shikāyat	grievance
sū	lit., 'water'; a measure to quantify a water share
sūdkhūr	money-lender

ṣulḥ	peaceful settlement; amicable settlement
siyāsat	violence during interrogation
surāq	procedure of inquiry
taʿāmul	established practice
tābiʿ	province
taftīsh	investigation
ṭanāb	square measure; in 19th-century Khorezm it consisted of 3600 *gaz*, or was equal 0,37–0,39 *ha*
ṭāʾifa	tribal clan
takht	throne
ṭillā	Khivan gold coin.
ṭanga/tanga	Khivan silver coin. In early 20th century, the average rate for reciprocal payments was set at 20 Russia *kopecks* per *tanga*.
tayāq	lit., 'stick'; a stick used during or after interrogation
taʿzīr	punishment, see also *jazā*
tuhmat	calumny
tūy	wedding ceremony
ūghrī	thief
ūlūk	corpse
ʿurf-ʿādat	custom; customary law, see also *ʿādat*
ūrūsiya	Russia
vaʿda	vow
vajh	reason
bī vajḥ-i sharʿī	unlawfully, illegally
vaqf	charitable endowment
vaqf-nāma	endowment deed
vāriṡ	heir
yālghān	deceit; false information
yarāshīb	reconcile; reconciliation
yūghūchi	corpse washer
yūldās	accomplice to crime, see also *hamrāh*
yūzbāshī	lit., 'commandant of one hundred', 'centurion'; a middle-rank official of the khanate
yasāvul	court attendant
yasāvul ḥaqqī	attendant's fee
yasāvulbāshī khiẕmatī	office or chancellery of *yasāvulbāshī*
yāsh-kattalār	elderly people, see also *qariya ādamlār*
yigīt	young man
żarar	loss
żaʿīfa	wife, see also *khātūn*

Introduction

> Wise men have said: dominion is like a young plant, and punishment is like water; it is surely necessary and essential to keep the roots of this plant fresh and irrigated with this water so that the flowers of safety and the fruits of security come forth.
>
> SHIR MUḤAMMAD MUNIS, *Firdaws al-iqbāl*[1]

1 Crime and Punishment in an Uzbek Khanate

This book sets out to shed light on the juridical field of the Khanate of Khiva at the end of the 19th and at the beginning of the 20th century. The 'Khanate of Khiva' is the term employed in Western historiography to denote the political formation[2] that was put in place by the Qonghrats. The latter were a dynasty of Uzbek origins, which ruled roughly between the last quarter of the 18th century and 1920 over the region known as Khorezm (Ar. *Khwārazm*), one of the biggest oases of Central Asia, traversed by the Amu Darya and nestled within the territory of what is today Uzbekistan, Kazakhstan, and Turkmenistan.

The main objective of this work is to show that prior to Sovietization the dispensation of justice in Khorezm depended mostly on a group of officials representing the dynasty in power, and lacking specialised legal training. It is important to pause to reflect on this aspect of the legal system developed by the Muslim principality that we refer to as 'the Khanate of Khiva,' for conventional wisdom says that the practice of law in pre-modern Muslim societies was usually the business of the *ʿulamāʾ*, i.e., the scholars of Islam. As we shall

1 Shir Muhammad Mirab Munis and Muhammad Riza Mirab Agahi, *Firdaws al-iqbāl: History of Khorezm*, translated from Chaghatay and annotated by Yu. Bregel (Leiden and Boston: Brill, 1999), p. 335. Here we slightly revised Bregel's translation.

2 The expressions 'Khivan Khanate' and 'Khanate of Khiva' are a calque from the Russian *Khivinskoe khanstvo*, applied by Tsarist bureaucrats at least from the second half of the 17th century The expression, of course, is not derived from the terminology deployed by local literati to address the rule of the Uzbek khanal dynasties in Central Asia from the 18th- to the early 20th-century. On this question, see B. Fragner, "Die „Khanate": Eine zentralasiatische Kulturlandschaft vom 15. bis zum 19. Jahrhundert," *Zeitschrift für Kulturgeschichte* 9.1 (2008), pp. 33–75.

© KONINKLIJKE BRILL NV, LEIDEN, 2020 | DOI:10.1163/9789004427907_002

see in detail, especially in the records that we provide here in translation, the situation in 19th and early 20th century Khorezm under the rule of the khans was entirely, and indeed remarkably different. The scholars of Islam were subject to a power system, which made them subservient to the royal court and the representatives of the dynasty. This specific aspect of post-Nadirid Central Asian legal culture has already been noted in Paolo Sartori's *Visions of Justice:* Sharīʿa *and Cultural Change in Russian Central Asia*[3] and the present book is designed to serve as a companion to that work to explore further how such legal culture survived, evolved, and changed during Russian domination. Also, to examine more closely practices of dispute settlement, which involved the royal court, in Khiva may open a window to comparisons with the Khanate of Khoqand and the Emirate of Bukhara and help us appreciate the degree of diversity within Central Asia, especially in the domain of law.

As a whole, the documents presented here mirror a world that was not structured and regimented into a rigid set of legal institutions. Indeed, the variety of cultural practices and the interplay of different sets of power relations produced a very dynamic set of legal relations. This left open a space for negotiation and consensus. Moreover, the space for negotiation was not confined to the localities and provinces, but was still available even after cases had been brought for hearing at the royal palace.

In order to illustrate our argument, let us turn our attention to one example. On the spring evening of 12 April 1913, near to a farmstead in the small Khorezmian settlement of Chavandur in the vicinity of Hazarasp, an alarming series of events were unfolding. The elders of the local community gathered in the house of one of the inhabitants. They had been cast into confusion by the sudden news that the farmstead had been surrounded by a group of distinctly suspicious-looking armed men on foot and on horseback. The general demeanor of these men left no doubt that they had serious plans to break into the farmstead by force. The owners of the house and members of the community knew very well why the attackers intended to break in. It was because a minor, an orphan boy called Rajab, had been detained there by the inhabitants of the village several hours earlier on suspicion of involvement in a homicide. The people around the perimeter of the farmstead were clearly associates of the boy and were determined to have him released, if necessary by means of an armed raid, so that the other participants in the crime should not be exposed. For this reason, when the elders received the news about the siege, they quickly arranged for the gates of the farmstead to be closed from the inside.

3 P. Sartori, *Visions of Justice*: Sharīʿa *and Cultural Change in Russian Central Asia* (Leiden: Brill, 2016), chapter 1.

By the time sun began to rise and the siege had been lifted, the community leaders were exhausted with fear and nervous anticipation. They then decided to make their way to the residence of the provincial governor (*ḥākim*), in the nearest urban center. The elders took Rajab with them.

The episode just described is taken from one of the many dispatches sent from the governors of the provinces of Khorezm to the royal court in Khiva in the early twentieth century. The letter is a routine report from the governor of Hazarasp, a small town in the southern part of the oasis which was subject to the Khanate of Khiva, and it informs the central agencies in the capital, specifically the office of the *yasāvulbāshī* (see infra), about the incident just described and about the details of the preceding and subsequent events.[4]

Further on, we learn from the same report that a few days earlier the elders of the community called Chavandur had reported to the *ḥākim* about a bloody raid carried out by a group of armed men on the farmstead of a local inhabitant called Khudāy Bīrgān b. Ismāʿīl. Besides the robbery of property, the raid had resulted in the murder of the head of the family, Khudāy Bīrgān himself, while members of his household had suffered severe knife wounds. Some days later, near another farmstead located within the territory belonging to the same community, a boy was arrested while begging for alms. One of the villagers was observant enough to recognize the youngster as an infamous thief who had previously worked in the bazaars of Petro-Aleksandrovsk. The latter was the administrative center of the 'Amu-Darya Department' (*Amudar'inskii otdel*), which had been organised out of the former lands of the khanate located on the right bank of the Amu Darya river,[5] and was now under the jurisdiction of the Russian Empire. The boy was swiftly handed over to members of the communal militia (*īl-qarāvullārī*) and to the elders (*īl-kadkhudālārī*), who gathered in the home of a respected resident, in preparation for their journey to the provincial governor the next morning.

The contents of the report also inform us about how events developed at the governor's residence on the morning after the night raid. Further inquiries by the *ḥākim*, and the confessions extracted from the boy under duress, led to the capture of the head of the criminal group, a man called Safā. On his arrest, several firearms were also confiscated: a Berdan rifle, a pistol and cartridges. The head of the group confessed that the weapons had been obtained on the Russian side of the Amu Darya, from soldiers quartered there. The *ḥākim* carried out some supplementary inquiries and drew up a detailed protocol of

4 See below, Doc. 40.

5 *Āryāq* (lit.: 'that side') was a term used in Khiva for the territory on the right bank of the Amu Darya, under the jurisdiction of the Russian Empire from 1873.

the circumstances surrounding the other raids, and then sent all the arrested members of the criminal group under convoy to the khan's palace in Khiva for further investigation.

The legal case described here is part of an extensive collection of records written in Chaghatay (otherwise known as Central Asian Turki) called 'the *yasāvulbāshī* documents,' held in the Central State Archive of the Republic of Uzbekistan in Tashkent. The name of the collection comes from Soviet archival taxonomy (*dokumenty iasaulbashi*) and reflects the fact that most of its constituent parts (c. 5000) are rescripts (*fatak*) issued by the chancery of the *yasāvulbāshī*, which was one of the highest posts in Khivan courtly hierarchy in the early 20th century.[6] In 1948 the records were transferred to the Central State Archive from Urgench, where they had been first gathered at the Khorezmian Provincial Archive together with other collections of documents crafted at the chancery of the Khanate of Khiva under the Russian protectorate (1873–1920).[7] Zoia Agafonova, one of the archivists involved in the process of rearranging the records for the Central State Archive, explained that, even if the collection in question came into being after the Russian subjugation of the khanate, 'the *yasāvulbāshī* documents' had to be included into a larger inventory of records, which reflect scribal practices in Khiva *prior* to the Russian conquest.[8] What led archivists to proceed in this fashion, says Agafonova, was the fact that 'all these records were written in the Arabic script, and that small notes were assembled in folders in a primitive way, without any order and without any attempt to determine their contents.'[9] In other words, Soviet archivists in Tashkent assumed that, by dint of their purported unrefined form, 'the *yasāvulbāshī* documents' were more reminiscent of local writing traditions than reflective of later chancery practices introduced by the Russians, which were thought to be more elaborate and modern-looking. As we shall see in detail, the records crafted by scribes serving the *yasāvulbāshī* represent in fact a documentary innovation, which manifested itself in full only during the period of the Russian protectorate and which left only occasional and indeed scanty records prior to 1873.

From a thematic point of view, 'the *yasāvulbāshī* documents' all concern either the hearing of grievances from the khan's subjects on a wide range of

6 We shall discuss the office in question in greater detail later in the book.

7 Akt ot 29 iiulia 1948 g, TsGARUz, f. I-124, courtesy of Muhayyo Ishakova.

8 The inventory of records in question is known as 'The chancery of the khan of Khiva' (*Kantselariia Khana Khivinskogo*) and consists mainly of records written prior to 1873, which were carted off to St. Petersburg in the wake of the Russian siege of Khiva. The archival signature of this collection is TsGARUz, f. I-125, op. 2.

9 Interview conducted by Muhayyo Ishakova in April 2014.

issues, or the proceedings of subsequent investigations. As noted earlier, the collection is substantial and most of the records preserved therein represent one compositional genre, i.e., rescripts. To better exemplify the complexity of the system of dispute settlement at work in Khorezm under the Qonghrats, however, we opted to bring generic diversity into sharp relief and thus decided to offer in translation a selection of 73 records, which, though small, can exemplify several compositional genres dating from 1910–1920. The reader will therefore find notifications, reports, and promissory notes (*bāyluv khaṭī*), together with rescripts.

Now that we have presented the documentary corpus used in this work, let us come back to the system of conflict resolution reflected in our sources and which was known in Khorezm as *ʿarż* (or *ʿarż-dād*). Here it is important to emphasize that its peculiarity lies in the central role played by the royal court (*dargāh-i ʿālī*) in Khiva in enforcing the settlement of disputes. Taken together, the documents we selected enable us to demonstrate that the khans and their officials were the primary judicial authorities to whom most petitioners addressed their claims. This book thus sets out to explore the Islamic juridical field of 19th- and early-20th-century Khorezm, a space in which there operated various institutions and officials, at the center of which stood the royal court of the local khans. The notion of 'juridical field' is derived from the work of the French sociologist Pierre Bourdieu and it is here employed to refer to a power field which 'is determined by two factors: on the one hand, by the specific power relations which give it its structure and which order the competitive struggles (or, more precisely, the conflicts over competence) that occur within it; and on the other hand, by the internal logic of juridical functioning which constantly constrains the range of possible actions and, thereby, limits the realm of specifically juridical solutions.'[10] As we will show, Muslims brought their affairs to state officials because the latter had the power to coerce parties to achieve a settlement and enforce a decision, either formally or informally. Significantly, it was a clear sense of hierarchy rather than an abstract notion of jurisdiction that informed Muslims' decisions to take legal action. Indeed, in contemporary Khorezm, the responsibility for the resolution of conflicts fell on the royal court and the governors, while *qāżīs* did not adjudicate of their own volition. The earliest attestation to this peculiar state of affairs comes from the Russian envoy to Khiva Nikolai Murav'ev who, in 1822, noted that *qāżīs* 'do not have any right to hear cases ... [with the exception only of] conflicts of little significance' and when they do so 'they have to report to

10 P. Bourdieu, "The Force of Law: Toward a Sociology of the Juridical Field," *Hastings Law Journal* 38 (1986–87): 816.

the khan about any given wrongdoing or crime.'[11] In fact, judges usually heard cases when the royal court or the governors instructed them to do so, mostly in cases in which defendants denied a claim (*inkār*) against them. As we shall see, a denial activated the transferal of a case to a *qāżī*. We shall return to this topic and discuss the subordination of *qāżīs* to Qonghrat court officials as we move to analyze legal proceedings.

Seeking Justice at the Court of the Khans of Khiva is based on a cachet of records mainly produced by the bureaucracy of a khanate and consequently adopts a state-centric approach. Neverthteless, the documents that we selected for this volume allow us to do more than just look at the juridical field in a Central Asian oasis from the narrow confines of a royal court. When and where possible, we equally considered the actions of people that moulded the everyday life of the khanate in the center and at the margins. Indeed, our records present us with a range of different individuals: a courtier in Khiva, a Qaraqalpaq fisherman on the shores of the Aral Sea, a Turkmen pastoralist in the riparian forests of the Amu Darya, a merchant from Urgench, a provincial governor in Khoja-eli, as they all moved around, took initiatives to defend their rights and pursued their own goals. The documents that we selected, open up a world in motion, where each individual case casts light on various microcosms of the Khanate of Khiva at the beginning of the twentieth century. It is our hope that the documents collected here will allow readers to feel that they are *witnessing* something of everyday life in Khorezm and thus appreciate their extraordinary cumulative effect. Furthermore, the records here assembled also allow us to uncover a complex world of social and legal relations in an Uzbek khanate over the course of the second decade of the twentieth century: a time of great political turbulence. The Khanate of Khiva had been a protectorate of the Russian Empire for around four decades by the time described in these documents. It was a protectorate with a very undefined and elusive status: it had no right to its own foreign policy or armed forces, but it had retained, albeit only partially, its right to preserve established forms of governance and 'traditional' institutions and practices.[12] At the same time, although formal interventions of imperial and colonial agencies in the internal life of the khanate were minimal, various Khivan agencies and khanal subjects regularly encountered Russian bureaucratic practices and could thus liaise with Russian institutions

11 N.N. Murav'ev, *Puteshestvie v Turkmeniiu i Khivu v 1819 i 1820 godakh gvardeiskogo general'nogo shtaba kapitana Nikolaia Murav'eva, poslannogo v sii strany dlia peregovorov, pt. 2* (Moscow: Tipografiia Avgusta Semena, 1822), p. 35.

12 For more information on this, see U. Abdurasulov and P. Sartori, "Neopredelennost' kak politika: razmyshliaia o prirode rossiiskogo protektorata v Srednei Azii." *Ab Imperio* 3 (2016), pp. 139–155.

at both informal and official levels. Read in this light, the records are a bricolage of small stories of right and wrong coming from Muslim communities in Khorezm. Unedifying as some of the stories are, however, they should be read against the backdrop of historically meaningful events such as the First World War, the overthrow of the Romanovs in February 1917, the October Revolution and the establishment of the Bolshevik dictatorship. Although the epicenters of these events were far from Khorezm, the shockwaves quickly rippled out to a region which, seen from St Petersburg and the offices of imperial ministries, seemed like a distant periphery. Each and every topic just mentioned is significant to make sense of the broader socio-cultural context in which our records were crafted, and they require extended and dedicated reflections, an exercise which falls out of the purview of this book.

Before we turn to a detailed description of the legal procedure in Khorezm known as *ʿarż-dād*, a term that denotes a formal ceremony in which a subject submits a grievance to the ruler and files a claim with the royal court, several notes of caution are in order. First, as elsewhere in the Islamic world, a petition (*ʿarż*) represents a default mode of communication between the chancery and a subject, whether an officeholder or a member of the general populace. Indeed, any form of communication with the royal court, whether a plea of allegiance or a news report (*vāqiʿa*),[13] was formulated as a petition and crafted in compliance with the requirements of this genre. However, under the Qonghrats, the terms *ʿarż-dād* and *ʿarż* were used specifically to denote a system of justice at the center of which were the khan and his court. It would be misleading to characterize this system as a 'petitioning system,' a term that connotes a larger body of textual practices that includes, but it is not co-exstensive with, the legal institutions under consideration. When it comes to examine 'petitions' as an instrument to seek redress when confronting official malfeasance, historians of Islam usually regard such records as the output of the so-called *maẓālim* system. This has to do with the fact that, under the rule of other Islamic dynasties elsewhere in the history of the Middle East, the term *maẓālim* has been deployed by scholars to refer to a situation in which the royal court operated as a court of second instance.[14] But this was not the case in Khorezm, where

13 On news reports (*vāqiʿa-navīsī*) and the ensuing compositional genre, see P. Sartori, "Seeing Like a Khanate: On Archives, Cultures of Documentation, and 19th Century Khorezm," *Journal of Persianate Studies* 9.1 (2016), pp. 241–250.

14 J. Nielsen, *Secular Justice in an Islamic State: Maẓālim under the Baḥrī Mamlūks, 662/1264–789/1387* (Leiden: Nederlands Historisch-Archaeologisch Instituut te Istanbul. 1985), p. 9. Several recent studies, however, have pointed out that, in different historical contexts, the *maẓālim* courts did not operate as a court of second instance for cases of judicial misconduct alone. See C. Müller, "*Maẓālim* Jurisdictions at the Umayyad Court of Córdoba

Qonghrat subjects brought their claims directly to the court of the khan, without filing their lawsuits with the judges. In this context, the Khivan royal court seldom served as a higher court with powers of judicial review. In addition, the term *maẓālim* is conspicuous by its absence from 19th- and early-20th-century Khivan bureaucratese.[15]

Second, Khivan subjects presented their complaints to the khan *orally*, not in writing.[16] This marks a substantive and decisive difference from other legal practices attested in the history of the Islamic world, which required that Muslims present their complaints to the ruler in form of a written petition.[17] Of course, it is possible that the Qonghrat polity also welcomed written petitions and that Qonghrat chancery practices may have been as elaborate as elsewhere in the region. Indeed, the Qonghrats promoted a culture of documentation that has left to us the richest repository of Arabic-script texts from Central Asia covering the period from the late eighteenth century to the year 1873, the so-called 'Archive of the Khans of Khiva'.[18] This archive contains numerous records that may well fall within the generic rubric of 'petitions.'[19]

(Eighth-Eleventh Centuries CE)," in A. Fuess and J.-P. Hartung (eds.), *Court Cultures in the Muslim World: Seventh to Nineteenth Centuries* (London and New York: Routledge, 2011), pp. 93–104; Y. Rapoport, "Royal Justice and Religious Law: *Siyāsah* and *Sharīʿah* under the Mamluks," *Mamluk Studies Review* 16 (2012), pp. 71–102; Baldwin, "Petitioning the Sultan in Ottoman Egypt."

15 To date we know only of one occurrence of the term *maẓālim* in a Khorezmian context. We observe it in an endowment deed dating to the eighteenth century. The record refers to an episode when a man applied to the Khivan ruler Abu'l-Ghāzī Khān (1603–1663) to review the status of lands, which had earlier been the hereditary properties of his ancestors. The place where the khan received the petitioner in question is named in the document the *divān-i maẓālim*. See *Vaqf-nāma-yi khanaqāh-i Shaykh Sulaymān Ḥaddādī*, MS Khiva, GMIQ, inv. no KP-1326.

16 *khalqlār kīlīb khāngha ʿarżīnī āghzākī sūzlāb*, ʿAbdullāh Bāltaev, *Khīvada Tāsh ḥawlī bināsīning tāpāgrafiyasī*, Khiva 1950, MS Tashkent, IVANRUz, inv. no. 9321, fol. 24a.

17 Y. Ben-Bassat, *Petitioning the Sultan: Protests and Justice in Late Ottoman Palestine* (London: I.B. Tauris, 2013), pp. 24–28; M. Alam and S. Subrahmanyam (eds.), *Writing the Mughal World: Studies on Culture and Politics* (New York: Columbia University Press, 2012), p. 160.

18 This is the term of art to refer to a collection of records, which Russians found in the royal citadel during the siege of Khiva in 1873. Together with a collection of codices, which most probably belong to the khanal library, the records were carted off to St. Petersburg. Nobody studied them until the Soviet Orientalist Pavel Petrovich Ivanov 'rediscovered' them in the vaults of the Public Library of the city (then Leningrad). For more on the history and the main features of this collections, see Sartori, "Seeing Like a Khanate: On Archives, Cultures of Documentation, and 19th Century Khorezm."

19 For a preliminary attempt to assess the scope of the Archive of Khiva in relation to the archives of other Central Asian polities, see P. Sartori, "On Khorezmian Connectivity: Two or Three Things I Know about It," *Journal of Persianate Studies* 9.1 (2016), pp. 133–157.

Third, besides matters concerning the study of law and society in Central Asia and court protocol typical of an Uzbek khanate, the documents which we offer here in translation also help us illuminate aspects of the culture of documentation which the Qonghrats developed throughout the 19th century as well as changes in such culture, which manifested themselves after the establishment of the Russian rule in the region, and more specifically the creation of the Amu-Darya Department. What we mean by 'culture of documentation' inheres in a mesh of chancery practices and record-keeping activities at the state-level. Accordingly, a culture of documentation primarily manifests itself in the output of texts, which were conceived of as items of bureaucratic consumption. Clearly, if one does not attempt to understand the purposes for which a bureaucracy kept archives, one simply risks misrepresenting the function of the records one finds therein. As noted earlier, the systematic record keeping of rescripts issued by the office of the *yasāvulbāshī* began only after the Russian takeover and therefore one could say that our source base is mainly the product, though indirect, of Russian bureaucratic influence. What we mean by this is that, following the establishment of the Amu-Darya Department, scribes employed in Khiva were exposed to practices of record-keeping and the documentary regime of the Governorship-General of Turkestan. They therefore had plenty of possibilities to acquaint themselves with the Russian bureaucratic *habitus*. In turn, this might activate new documentary sensibilities leading to the production of records of a nature that did not exist prior to the Russian takeover, merely for preemptive purposes.[20] However, occasionally one can find records, though scanty, which suggest that the system of conflict resolution called *ʿarż-dād* produced a documentary output. The latter must have been connected to other scribal and archival practices in Khiva, which we see reflected in 'The Archive of the Khans of Khiva.' In an effort to understand the documentary value of records produced and preserved by the Qonghrats, our previous studies of Arabic-script records produced in Khorezm, and especially of 'The Archive of the Khans of Khiva,' suggested that we should think of documents as constitutive elements within some larger archival project and thus advocated a holistic approach to the study of documentary collections. The latter assumes that *all* the texts contained in an archive may reflect a specific utilitarian purpose by dint of their preservation by khanal agencies; and this requires that one consider how each and every text within that repository is somehow representative of the forms of governance adopted by the Qonghrats. The overall objective of this method is, thus, to move away from the usual tendency to

20 P. Sartori, 'Murder in Manghishlaq: Notes on an Instance of Application of Qazaq Customary Law in Khiva (1895)," *Der Islam* 88.2 (2012), pp. 217–257.

approach to Islamic archives simply as repositories of data to be extracted at will. Our purpose in the present volume, however, is not to cast a holistic gaze at the available documentary corpus.[21] While we have analyzed, of course, 'the *yasāvulbāshī* documents' collection as a whole, we equally thought it would be more useful for students of the history of the Uzbek khanates to pause to reflect on individual documentary items that exemplify behavioral patterns and forms of governance rather than on aspects of scribal and archival culture. Again, to the latter we plan to devote separate studies.

Fourth, our sources shed light on a system of conflict resolution that functioned in the region at least from the beginning of the nineteenth century. Since similar practices existed in the Emirate of Bukhara and the Khanate of Khoqand, this system may be regarded as representative of post-Chinggisid Central Asia:[22] it is with the demise of the 'Arabshahid empire that we observe a shift from earlier political configurations that centered on notions of shared sovereignty – whereby a territory was divided in appanages and assigned to different dynasts in the fashion of a condominium[23] – to a highly centralised and bureaucratised state formation, which came into being in the wake of Nādir Shāh Afshār's military campaign in Central Asia (1740). It would be misleading, in our view, to explain the prominence of Qonghrat officials in the local system of conflict resolution in light of a Chinggisid tradition, which had otherwise informed patterns of governance in Central Asia prior to the rise of the Uzbek khanates. Indeed, there is little of Chinggisid pedigree in the ways in which Qonghrat officials articulated their legal authority over the resolution of conflicts in Khorezm, unless one wants to superimpose a Chinggisid tradition on all things Central Asian regardless of the very meaning that we accord to such tradition. We learn from a 18th-century Russian observer that prior to the rise to power of the Qonghrats 'adjudication belonged exclusively to the clergy, but with the establishment of dynastic rule in the khanate, the clergy lost almost all its judicial power.'[24] This statement suggests that the system that we see reflected in the available evidence, where the khans of Khiva and their officials enjoyed more legal authority than the *qāżīs*, was certainly an innovation of the Qonghrats, at least in the oasis of Khorezm.

---

21 Ibid.

22 Sartori, *Visions of Justice*: Sharīʿa *and Cultural Change in Russian Central Asia*, pp. 40–103.

23 M. Dickson, "Uzbek Dynastic Theory in the Sixteenth Century," in *Trudy XXV Mezhdunarodnogo Kongressa Vostokovedov* (Moscow: Izdatel'stvo Vostochnoi Literatury, 1960), pp. 208–217; E. Binbaş, "Condominial Sovereignty and Condominial Messianism in the Timurid Empire: Historiographical and Numismatic Evidence," *Journal of the Economic and Social History of the Orient* 61.1–2 (2018), pp. 172–202.

24 Anon., "Turkmeniia i Khiva," *Vsemirnyi puteshestvennik* 8 (1870), p. 120.

It must also be added that, more broadly speaking, the Qonghrats perceived their rule as disconnected from and, to a certain extent, in opposition to the political history of the Chinggisids. Indeed, in his magnum opus the court historian Muḥammad Rīżā Mīrāb Āgahī described the rise of the Qonghrat dynasty as the moment in which 'the light of majesty and the candle of power of the Chinggisid *sulṭāns* stopped to shine and be resplendent.'[25] Rather than just offering an apologetic eulogy for the dynasts in power, here Āgahī is looking back at the history of Central Asia, and Khorezm in particular, and emphasizing that, starting from the first Qonghrat ruler Īltūzār (r. 1804–1806), the Uzbek khanate brought about a major discontinuity with earlier practices of governance, which consisted of doing away with the Chinggisid dispensation of shared sovereignty. Indeed, under the rule of Allāh Qulī Khān (1826–1842) the Qonghrats began in fact openly to associate themselves with the imagery of the Khorezmshahs, the Muslim dynasty ruling over Khorezm between the 12th and the early 13th century, which had attempted to resist the Mongol conquest.[26] By the end of the 19th century, the Qonghrats' identification with the Khorezmshahs had become a powerful and evident attribute of their sovereignty. Indeed, in his *Tawārīkh al-khawānīn*, an unofficial chronicle of the Qonghrats written between the years 1885 and 1894, the Khivan literatus and the Qonghrat prince Sayyid Ḥāmid Tūra Kāmyāb claimed that, when in 1770 Īltūzār's grandfather Muḥammad Amīn 'Īnāq returned from Bukhara and subdued Khorezm, 'he sat firmly in power on the throne of the Khwarazmshahness' (*Khwārazmshāhlīq takhtīda bar qarār kāmgār īrdī*).[27] Also, when introducing Īltūzār Khān to his readers, Kāmyāb argued that the Qonghrat dynast 'sat on the throne of Khwarazmshahness' (*Khwārazmshāhlīq masnadīda ūltūrdī*).[28] What was the intended meaning of the latter abstract noun? What did it mean to be a Khwarazmshah in his view? We can attempt to find an answer to these questions by looking at Sayyid Ḥāmid Tūra Kāmyāb's further characterization of Īltūzār's rule: 'he provided the people with justice and put order to the military; and he sought to run *alone* [our emphasis] the government in the province of Khorezm.'[29] This

25 *Chingīzīya sulṭānlārīnīng chirāgh-i shavkatī wa sham'-i dawlatī āftāb tābish[ī]dīn bī-nūr va bī-furūgh būlūb*, Muḥammad Rīżā Āgahī, *Riyāż al-dawla*, MS St. Petersburg, IVRRAN, inv. no. D-123, fol. 12a.

26 This was first noted by Yuri Bregel, see Munis and Agahi, *Firdaws al-iqbāl: History of Khorezm*, pp. vii–viii.

27 Sayyid Ḥāmid Tūra Kāmyāb, *Tawarīkh al-khawānīn*, MS Tashkent, IVANRUz, inv. no. 7717, fol. 84a.

28 Ibid., fol. 84b.

29 *'adl-u-dād bīla īlgā saranjām birīb lashkar-u-'askar yighīb tartīb qīldī va Khwārazm diyārīda ḥukmīn 'alāḥida yūrūtmāk īstādī*, ibid.

passage offers conclusive evidence of the fact that in the historical perception of Khivan court literati, the Qonghrats introduced forms of governance (and possibly also a political ideology), which were far removed from that of the Mongols and their notion of shared sovereignty. If the 17th century was the age of Chinggisid restoration, as Robert McChesney has suggested, then the 19th was in Khorezm most certainly the century in which local constituencies came to regard Chinggisid traditions as a thing of the past.

Fifth, and finally, it should be noted that anyone reading this book hoping to get a sense of what were the philosophical premises underpinning the practice of law in early 20th-century Khorezm will likely be disappointed. There is little legal material coming from Khorezm, and especially among the records published here, that would be useful for the historian of law who would like to explain the world of moral philosophy, today identified as legalism.[30] To be sure, our records tell us something about power relations, practices of divination to apprehend suspects, and proceedings of dispute settlement. To call such records 'legal' requires that one thinks of law not just as a bundle of rules, however, but as a field in which discourses, moral sensibilities, and statuses, cross and influence each other. Clearly, the documentary materials that we put together in this work conjure up notions of rules, either followed or transgressed, which evoke modes of conduct as well as the legislative power of orders. Furthermore, they are entangled in a discursive field, which is above the law, or beyond it, for that matter. Read in this light, the legal records here assembled explain very little about rules, their intended meaning, and their popular reception. They do, however, point to the pervasive character of legalism in social interactions.

2 The Historical Setting

The texts presented here are documents produced by the chanceries of different agencies of the Khanate of Khiva, active in both the capital city of Khiva and surrounding regions. The documents were all produced in the period between 1910 and 1920 – the time of the reign of the last two members of the Qonghrat dynasty in Khorezm: Isfandiyār Khān (1910–1918) and Sayyid ʿAbdullāh Khān (1918–1920). The period covered by the documents thus corresponds to the final decade of the khanate: in February 1920, the Qonghrat dynasty came to an end following a pro-Bolshevik coup; the territory itself of the khanate was

30 Paul Dresch and Hanna Skoda (eds.), *Legalism: Anthropology and History* (Oxford: Oxford University Press, 2012).

formed first into the Khorezm People's Soviet Republic (KhNSR), and then in 1924 was integrated into the newly formed Uzbek, Turkmen and Kazakh SSRs.[31]

The Khanate of Khiva was a rather small state in the lower delta of the Amu Darya, in the Khorezmian oasis, and had been under the rule of members of the Qonghrat dynasty since the end of the eighteenth century. The Qonghrats came to power after an extended period of turmoil and interregna, and managed to consolidate control and establish a somewhat centralised administration within a short period of time.[32] Besides the direct use of force, the dynasty's success rested in large part on the support of different population groups. To seek the consensus of various demographics enabled them not only to regulate, albeit for a relatively short time, contradictions with representatives of different communities within the oasis, but also to establish more or less stable relations with tribal groups, in particular with the various Turkmen, Qaraqalpaq and Qazaq tribes. This facilitated the settlement of the Qaraqalpaq tribes, especially on the northern and north-western edges of the oasis, extending the borders of direct Qonghrat rule up to the coast of the Aral Sea and the lower reaches of the Syr Darya in the north.[33]

From the very first decades of its rule, the dynasty was forced to confront the rising ambition of the Russian Empire, which aimed to increase its colonial possessions at the expense of territories lying to its south. After some unsuccessful attempts to make the khanate submit by force,[34] Russian troops under the command of general-adjutant K.P. von Kaufman made their triumphal march

---

31 The lands on the right bank of the Amu Darya and along the coast of the Aral Sea belonged to the Karakalpak Autonomous Region (*Karakalpakskaia Avtonomnaia Oblast'*), which was constituted in 1924 as part of the Kazakh ASSR. In 1932, it was given the status of an Autonomous Republic, initially as part of the RSFSR. Later, in 1936, the Karakalpak ASSR was formally integrated into the Uzbek SSR. For more information on the political and economic processes underwriting the formation of the Karakalpak ASSR, see N. Pianciola, "The Benefits of Marginality: The Great Famine around the Aral Sea, 1930–34," *Nationalities Papers* 48.2 (2019) Accessed online on 30 October 2019).

32 On the analyses of these events, see further Yu. Bregel, "The New Uzbek States: Bukhara, Khiva and Khoqand: *c.* 1750–1886," in N. Di Cosmo, A.J. Frank, P.B. Golden (eds.), *The Cambridge History of Inner Asia. The Chinggisid Age* (Cambridge: Cambridge University Press, 2009), pp. 398–400; W. Wood, "Khorezm and the Khanate of Khiva," in *Oxford Research Encyclopedia of Asian History*, https://oxfordre.com/asianhistory/view/10.1093/acrefore/9780190277727.001.0001/acrefore-9780190277727-e-284?rskey=q3bEVy&result=1#acrefore-9780190277727-e-284-div2–3 (Accessed online on 2 June 2019).

33 See, also, A. Shioya, "Irrigation Policy of the Khanate of Khiva Regarding the Lawzan Canal, 1830–1873." *Area Studies Tsukuba* 32 (2011), pp. 115–136; U. Abdurasulov, "The Aral Region and Geopolitical Agenda of the Early Qongrats," *Eurasian Studies* 14 (2016), pp. 3–36.

34 A. Morrison, "Twin Imperial Disasters. The Invasions of Khiva and Afghanistan in the Russian and British Official Mind," *Modern Asian Studies* 48.1 (2014), pp. 253–300.

through the capital city of Khiva to the khan's palace on 29 May 1873.[35] The ruler of Khiva Muḥammad Raḥīm Khān II (1864–1910) was forced to sign the Gandumian (Gandūmqān) peace treaty (12 August 1873). This required him to acknowledge his own status as the 'humble servant of the Emperor of All Russia', and Khiva's status as a 'vassal' of St. Petersburg.[36] Among other stipulations, the Khanate of Khiva lost the right to recruit a regular army, and to carry out its own foreign policy 'without permission from the Russian authorities.' Another consequence of the treaty was the annexation of all the lands along the right bank of the Amu Darya, 'with all the settled and nomadic peoples there'. The Amu-Darya Department (*Amudar'inskii Otdel*) was formed on these territories, covering over half of the former area of the khanate,[37] under the Governorship General of Turkestan, with its center in the fort of Petro-Aleksandrovsk.[38] It is common among scholars of Central Asia to define the new status of Khiva as a protectorate, by analogy with some of the British and French holdings in South Asia and Northern Africa, although the term was never actually used either in the records defining the relations between Khiva and St. Petersburg, or in the official correspondence between governmental agencies.[39] The Gandumian Treaty was a freestanding and vague set of regulations that did more to complicate than clarify the status of the Khanate of Khiva and its subjects *vis-à-vis* the Russian Empire.[40] The indeterminacy of the Gandumian Treaty

35 M.A. Terent'ev, *Istoriia zavoevaniia Srednei Azii s kartami i planami*, vol. II (St. Petersburg: Tipo-litografiia V.V. Komarova, 1906), p. 260; On the circumstances of the Russian takeover of Khiva in 1873, see A. Morrison, *The Russian Conquest of Central Asia, 1814–1907. A Study in Imperial Expansion* (Cambridge: Cambridge University Press [2020]), [Chap. 7] (forthcoming).

36 See "Mirnyi dogovor s Khivoi, ustanovlennyi v Gandemiane 12 avgusta 1873 g", TsGARUz, f. I-1, op. 27, d. 7, ll. 6–8; The text of the treaty is also available as an appendix to S. V. Zhukovskii, *Snosheniia Rossii s Bukharoi i Khivoi za poslednee trekhsotletie* (Petrograd: Tipo-litografiia N.I. Evstigneeva, 1915), 179–183.

37 The area of the annexed lands covered almost 76,000 km², i.e. around 58% of the territory of the khanate, see A.S. Sadykov, *Ekonomicheskie posledstviia ustanovleniia protektorata tsarskoi Rossii nad Khivinskim khanstvom*, PhD dissertation (Moscow 1954), p. 38 (unpublished).

38 Until 1874 the *Amudar'inskii otdel* was called the *Amudar'inskii okrug* (district), see T.G. Tukhtametov, *Amudar'inskii otdel: Sotsial'no-ekonomicheskoe i politicheskoe znachenie dlia Khorezmskogo oazisa* (Nukus: Karakalpakstan, 1955), p. 54.

39 For a rare example of the use of this term, although in an unofficial context, see D. N. Logofet, *Bukharskoe khanstvo pod russkim protektoratom*, vol. 1–2 (St. Petersburg: V. Berezovski, 1911).

40 For example, A. Kalmykov, a high-ranking official of the Ministry of Foreign Affairs of Russia, wrote in 1910, that, 'the [Gandumian] peace treaty was re-interpreted several times, and was used by various rerpresentatives of the Russian and Khivan authorities in different ways at different times,' see his *Sostoianie Khivnskogo khanstva i zhelatel'nye*

may have reflected a conscious political choice. Such a form of governance was far from unique in the age of European colonialism. As Kristin Mann and Richard Roberts have noted about the history of African protectorates, 'significant ambiguities existed surrounding the legal authority that parties possessed to conclude these protection agreements and impose the new systems of colonial rule that developed.'[41] A similar indeterminacy of the status of the 'vassal state', a fluidity of the norms governing the Gandumian Treaty, and a vagueness about the authority invested in the Russian colonial officials who were responsible for relations with Khiva, produced an environment similar to other colonial situations.[42] The main feature of the Russian Empire's relationship with its distant protectorate was a fundamental ambivalence. On the one hand, preserving the semi-independent khanate with a rather uncertain status among the empire's other remote colonial possessions seemed to be a politically very risky and costly undertaking that conflicted with imperial interests in the region. On the other hand, however, the uncertainty of the khanate's position suited various interest groups, given that it provided broad access to Khiva's internal resources without the need to build a complex and costly system for managing and monitoring the khanate's domestic situation. Thus, the strategic uncertainty in the relationship between the Russian Empire and its Khivan protectorate also constituted a consistent policy.[43] Colonial agencies did not intervene except to assert control over the maintenance of stability in the Khivan protectorate, and to defend the interests and rights of Russian subjects in the khanate. However, they would avoid meddling directly with the internal life, administrative, fiscal, and judicial practices of the khanate.[44]

---

reformy, TsGARUz, f. I-2, op. 1, d. 291, l. 102. For an English translation of the Gandumian Peace Treaty, see S. Becker, *Russia's Protectorates in Central Asia: Bukhara and Khiva, 1865–1924* (Cambridge, Massachusetts: Harvard University Press, 1968), pp. 316–318.

41 K. Mann and R. Roberts, "Slave Voices in African Colonial Courts: Sources and Methods." In *African Voices of Slavery and the Slave Trade, vol. 2: Essays on Sources and Methods*, eds. A. Bellagamba, S.E. Green, M.A. Klein (Cambridge: Cambridge University Press, 2016), p. 134.

42 G. Balandier, "Kolonial'naia situatsiia: teoreticheskii podkhod (1951)," *Ab Imperio* 2 (2013), pp. 29–64.

43 See further, P. Sartori, U. Abdurasulov, "Imperial Strategic Uncertainty: The Promises and Perils of a Russian Protectorate in Central Asia." In Nader Purnaqcheband, and Florian Saafeld (eds.) "*Aus den Tiefenschichten der Texte. Beitrage zur tuko-iranischen Welt von der Islamisierung bis zur Gegenwart*" (Reichert Verlag Wiesbaden 2019), pp. 233–264.

44 In detail, see A. Erkinov, "How Muḥammad Raḥīm Khān II of Khiva (1864–1910) Cultivated His Court Library as a Means of Resistance against the Russian Empire," *Journal of Islamic Manuscripts* 2 (2011), p. 41.

At the same time, the khanate was located within the imperial possessions,[45] and its subjects had regular encounters with imperial institutions. Consequently, not only administrative and chancery practices, but aspects of internal politics, patterns of mobility, and monetary and legal relations in Khiva were all directly or indirectly affected.[46]

On 16 August 1910, the ruler of Khiva, Muḥammad Raḥīm Khān II, died at the age of 66, having held the Khivan throne since the time of the Russian conquest. According to Russian officials, he had always managed to govern the country 'in the old way,' i.e., by doing everything in his power for Khiva to remain as before.'[47] Imperial authorities in Tashkent and St. Petersburg used the death of the old monarch as an opportunity to initiate a so-called programme of reforms, designed to modernize the khanate, to be carried out under his successor, the hereditary prince Isfandiyār (r. 1910–1918). The programme of reforms was developed by both the imperial and Khivan authorities, and proposed, among other things, to reorganise and institutionalise the administrative apparatus and to impose order on the financial system and organs of justice.[48] However, while these transformations were widely trumpeted by both Khiva and St. Petersburg, it turned out to be an extremely difficult task to put them into practice, in the absence of any real strategies for monitoring and control. Soon after, the First World War would put an end to the majority of these hopeful beginnings. Preoccupied by events on the European stage, the Russian agencies in Tashkent and St. Petersburg largely limited themselves to attempts to maintain control over local elites, to preserve a certain degree of stability and to prevent potential disorders in this distant periphery.[49]

The absence of a consistent policy of Russia towards its protectorate, sharply growing asymmetries of power between the metropole and its colonial possessions, and internal conflicts within the khanate's elites, fed into major

45 In 1881, after the fall of Kök-Tepe, the submission of the Akhal-Tekin oasis and formation of the Transcaspian Region (*Oblast'*), the Khanate of Khiva was surrounded by Russian imperial possessions around the entire perimeter of its borders. On the details of Russian conquest of Transcaspia, see Morrison, *The Russian Conquest of Central Asia, 1814–1907*, [Chap. 8] (forthcoming).

46 For other examples of the formalization of chancery practices in Khiva after the establishment of the Russian Protectorate, see Sartori, "Murder in Manghishlaq: Notes on an Instance of Application of Qazaq Customary Law in Khiva (1895)".

47 [N.K. Glushanovksii], *Mnenie Nachal'nika Amu-Dar'inskogo otdela General-maiora Glushanoskogo*, TsGARUz, f. 1–2, op. 1, d. 291, l. 134.

48 For more information on this, see Abdurasulov, Sartori, "Neopredelennost' kak politika: razmyshliaia o prirode rossiiskogo protektorata v Srednei Azii," pp. 139–155.

49 U. Abdurasulov, "Konflikt kak resurs: anatomiia 'turkmenskikh besporiadkov' v Khorezme, 1914–1916," *Ab Imperio* 3 (2018), pp. 141–186.

popular upheavals in the khanate in 1915–16. Protests by inhabitants of individual towns, dissatisfied with the character of Isfandiyār's government, in 1915, quickly spilled over into open armed resistance. The events of early 1916 had even greater resonance, when Turkmen leaders who had broken off allegiance managed to capture the capital of the khanate, and seriously threatened to overturn the order in the country. Only the intervention of Russian colonial forces, under the command of Lieutenant General A.S. Galkin, and their use of violently repressive measures against the rebels, enabled the temporary suppression of the uprisings.[50]

The political landscape of Khorezm in the second decade of the twentieth century was decisively shaped by the echoes of the February revolution of 1917 in Petrograd, and the Bolshevik coup that followed in October of the same year. As a distant province of the former empire of the Romanovs, Khiva found itself in a difficult situation. The Khivan authorities no longer had the support of the Russian army,[51] and were now forced to establish a new balance between the different forces that had been lifted up on the wave of recent events in the capital. In particular, these included the armed units of the Yomut Turkmen leader Qurbān Muḥammad Sardār (1857–1938), otherwise known as Junayd Khān, who, incidentally, appears in our documents.[52] Junayd Khān was one of the leaders of the rebellion of 1916, and had been forced to flee with his supporters from the Russian authorities to Iran and Afghanistan.[53] In the spring of 1917, on the wave of revolutionary events in the former empire of the Romanovs, Junayd returned to Khorezm with considerable reinforcements, and began to challenge the power of authorities in Khiva and Petro-Aleksandrovsk.[54] Another active player on the Khorezmian political

50 O. Qo'shjonov and N. Polvonov, *Khorazmdagi ijtimoii-siyosiy jarayonlar va harakatlar* (Tashkent: Abu Matbuot Konslat, 2007), pp. 239–246; Niiazmetov, *Poisk konsensusa. Rossiisko-khivinskie geopoliticheskie otnosheniia v XVI-nachale XX v.*, pp. 424–433.

51 When, in January 1918, news of the Bolshevik coup reached Colonel Zaitsev's Russian units quartered in Petro-Aleksandrovsk and in Khiva itself, the troops, which had until that point followed orders from the Provisional Government, then abandoned the khanate. See T.G. Tukhtametov, *Rossiia i Khiva v kontse XIX–nachale XX veka* (Moscow: Nauka, 1969), p. 126.

52 See docs. 24; 36; 45; 61.

53 Abdurasulov, "Konflikt kak resurs: anatomiia 'turkmenskikh besporiadkov' v Khorezme", p. 177; on Junayd Khān's subsequent fate, see Q. Rajabov, "Xorazmda istiqlol harakat va Junayidxon", *Jamiyat va boshqaruv* 1 (2000), pp. 36–43.

54 The political allegiance of the Russians in Petro-Aleksandrovsk was far from univocal at this time. Initially, the administration was loyal to the Provisional Government, but after the Bolshevik coup of October 1917, and especially after colonel I.M. Zaitsev's withdrawal from Khiva on 5 January 1918, the influence of the SRs and Bolsheviks grew, Becker, *Russia's Protectorates in Central Asia*, pp. 254–257.

scene at this time was a group of local reformers known as the Young Khivans (*yāsh khīvalīklār*). Inspired by the revolutionary events in Russia, and actively supported by Soviet and Bolshevik agencies in Tashkent and Charjuy, these reformers also contended for power in Khorezm. The interests of the leaders of the soldiers' soviets[55] also deserves to be taken into account, while a significant political role was played by the actual commanders of the Russian garrisons quartered on the territory of the neighbouring Amu-Darya Department and in Khiva itself.[56] Isfandiyār Khān tried to balance between these centers of power, with a varying degree of success. Thus, on 5 April 1917, in a concession to the demands of the Young Khivans, the khan signed a manifesto on the proclamation of a constitutional monarchy; the monarch's power was now to be limited by a 'parliament' (*majlis*) and a council of ministers (*nāẓir*).[57] However, only a few months later, in the autumn of 1917, Isfandiyār Khān put an end to all of these initiatives, with the support of the Turkmen leader Junayd Khān and the silent approval of General H. Mirbadalov, the commissar for the Provisional Government in Khiva. The members of the Young Khivan party and their supporters were pursued, arrested, and in certain cases subjected to show-trials and executions.[58]

For a while, Isfandiyār Khān managed to hold on to power in this way, making alliances with representatives of one group after another, until he was finally executed on the orders of the same Junayd Khān in autumn 1918.[59]

---

55 To a large degree thanks to the support of the soldiers' soviets, in April 1917, the Khivan reformers managed to force Isfandiyār Khān to sign a manifesto on the proclamation in Khiva of a constitutional monarchy: Tukhtametov, *Rossiia i Khiva v kontse XIX–nachale XX veka*, p. 122; I.V. Pogorel'skii, *Ocherki ekonomicheskoi i politicheskoi istorii Khivinskogo khanstva kontsa XIX i nachala XX vv.* (1873–1917 gg.) (Leningrad: Izdatel'stvo Leningradskogo universiteta, 1968), pp. 122–124; Becker, *Russia's Protectorates in Central Asia*, pp. 253–257.

56 For example, General Mirbadalov at least initially supported the pretensions of the Young Khivans. His predecessor, Colonel Zaitsev, supported revanchist anti-Bolshevik uprisings and, on 5 January 1918, left the khanate and moved with his troops to Samarkand, see Becker, *Russia's Protectorates in Central Asia*, pp. 270; Qo'shjonov and Polvonov, *Khorazmdagi ijtimoii-siiosiy jarayonlar*, p. 307.

57 R.A. Nurulin, "Obostrenie politicheskoi obstanovki v khanstvakh." In D. Alimova, and R. Radzhapova (eds.), *Turkestan v nachale XX veka: k istorii natsional'noi nezavisimosti* (Tashkent: Shark, 2000), pp. 289–290.

58 Becker, *Russia's Protectorates in Central Asia*, pp. 269–270; R.A. Nurulin, "Obostrenie politicheskoi obstanovki v khanstvakh," pp. 290–291, 296.

59 Khivan authors give different accounts of the circumstances of Isfandiyār Khān's killing: in the view of the court historian Ḥasan-Murād Laffasī, the ruler of Khiva was shot on the order of the Yomut leader Junayd, see Ḥasan-Murād Laffasī, *Gulshān-i sa'ādat*, MS Tashkent, IVANRUz, inv. no. 7797, fol. 100b. Another author, Pahlavān Niyāz Ḥājjī Yusupov,

Immediately after the execution of the khan, his brother Sayyid ʿAbdullāh Khān was placed on the throne. The latter's rule was largely nominal, as real power was now held by Junayd and his supporters.[60]

The dynasty managed to hang on to the throne for another year and a half in these conditions, before a series of pro-Bolshevik coups reached this distant frontier as well. On 1 February 1920 the forces of the Young Khivans captured the capital with support from Bolshevik detachments.[61] A day later, Sayyid ʿAbdullāh Khān, the last ruler of the Qonghrat dynasty, which had reigned in Khiva for over a century, was overthrown and exiled to the city of Krivoy Rog (Ukr.: *Kriviy Rich*) in Ukraine, where he spent the final years of his life.[62] In April 1920, on the territory of the former khanate, the Khorezm People's Soviet Republic was proclaimed: a pro-Bolshevik quasi-state, which was destined to sink into oblivion within four years, when it was incorporated into the newly formed national Soviet republics.

Our aim here is not to provide a detailed account of all the political processes, which one should take into account if one pursues a political history of the khanate. For our purposes, the processes are important inasmuch as they provide some background knowledge to contextualize the social, documentary, and legal practices reflected in our sources. Needless to say that the political background outlined above did shape aspects of communal life, and particularly those aspects with which our documents are most concerned: instability, access to weapons, and the rise of violence within Khorezmian society. Indeed, from the very beginning of the protectorate period, we observe a constant flow of news reports from Khiva to Petro-Aleksandrovsk and Tashkent. While formally claiming to stay out of the internal affairs of its protectorate, the Russian administration had in fact vested interests in keeping key aspects of the khanate's internal life under control. The bureaucratic pressure which the Russian colonial administration exerted on the protectorate stimulated the

---

reports that on Junayd's order, one of his men 'slit the throat' of Isfandiyār during an audience, see Pahlavān Niyāz Ḥājjī, [*Khāṭiralar*], MS Khiva, Private Collection of Anvar Otaboev, fol. 231b.

60 ʿAbdullāh Bāltaev, *Khwārazm taʾrīkhīga matiryallār* (*Khīva 1950*), MS Tashkent, IVANRUz, inv. no. 9320, fol. 21; Pahlavān Niyāz Ḥājjī, [*Khāṭiralar*], MS Khiva, Private Collection of Anvar Otaboev, fols. 233b–234b.

61 Becker, *Russia's Protectorates in Central Asia*, pp. 286–289; R.A. Nurulin, "Likvidatsiia Khivinskogo khanstva i obrazovanie Khorezmskoi Narodnoi Sovetskoi Respubliki," in D. Alimova, and R. Radzhapova (eds.), *Turkestan v nachale XX veka: k istorii natsional'noi nezavisimosti*, pp. 297–305.

62 ʿAbdullāh Bāltaev, *Khwārazm taʾrīkhīga matiryallār* (*Khīva 1950*), MS Tashkent, IVANRUz, inv. no. 9320, fol. 22a.

development of new chancery practices in Khiva such as the cross-referencing of documents. The reforms begun by the Russian and Khivan authorities in Khiva in 1910 facilitated even greater bureaucratisation and standardisation of a range of administrative and legal practices. Indeed, the reforms brought about a *formalization* of certain chancery practices for which we would otherwise have no records. One could say that such reforms were themselves responsible for the generation of the documentation under discussion here, for one unintended consequence of bureaucratisation was the increased visibility of dispute settlement in the documentary output of the khanate.

Another characteristic feature of the Russian presence was the formation of separate judicial and administrative jurisdictions on the Russian and Khivan sides of the Amu Darya. This allowed various individuals and groups, accused of having broken the law, to cross from side to side, making it harder for them to be caught and tried, as is revealed both directly and indirectly in our documentary materials.[63]

As already been noted, Khorezm experienced exceptional political turbulence during the second decade of the twentieth century. The resulting uprisings against the central authorities, clashes between different groups of the population, and raids by Turkmen groups on the agricultural settlements in the oasis inevitably entailed a rise in the levels of violence in society. For example, in one of the documents presented here, dated to April 1918, the authorities in Khiva received a report from a group of 'elders' representing the province of Tashhawz about the sharp rise in the number of robberies and armed raids in the localities and, more generally, 'the extreme instability in the province' (*Tāshavuż tavābiʿlārī kūb nādīnchdūr*).[64] In another document, also dated to April 1918, the central authorities were informed that the inhabitants and elders of another Khivan town, Khanqah, demanded the harshest possible punishments, including executions, for robbers, in order to reduce the numbers of such crimes: 'Without such measures,' the dispatch noted, 'the local communities will be unable to maintain any peaceful existence.'[65]

The documents of the chancery of the *yasāvulbāshī* are also full of appeals and grievances from members of various communities about raids and attacks by Turkmen bands. The increased number of militant groups, and the flow of weapons from outside, meant an increased use of firearms,[66] which is also

63 See, e.g., Doc. 56.

64 See below, Doc. 50.

65 Doc. 41.

66 For example, after the suppression of the uprisings of 1916 in Khorezm, the Russian command requisitioned from the Turkmen clans in the western part of the oasis alone around

reflected in our documents. Local inhabitants were able to acquire weapons from Russian soldiers quartered in the khanate and on the right bank, and also, apparently, in significant quantities from across the Turkmen steppe.[67]

All these factors either directly or indirectly played an important role in the production of the records which we present here. However, it would be misleading to say that it was specifically these events that defined the practices and mechanisms of dispute settlement in the khanate. Indeed, it would be perhaps helpful here to remind our readers that materials produced locally as well as Russian travelogues make it clear that the system of dispute settlement called *ʿarż-dād* had taken shape in Khorezm long before the Russian conquest and therefore prior to many political realignments and socio-cultural changes reflected in our records.

3 Who were the *Yasāvulbāshī*s?

Narrative sources and chancery documentation from early-20th-century Khiva are clear about one thing: the *yasāvulbāshī* reviewed the content of the appeals addressed to the khans and instructed appellants to refer to other Qonghrat court officials who would investigate cases and oversee the settlement of disputes. But the competence of the *yasāvulbāshī* also extended beyond the juridical field. In fact, our sources attribute to the *yasāvulbāshī* a broad variety of administrative functions: they organize troops[68] and carry out military raids,[69] they ensure internal order, and administer the collection of taxes; at times, they represent khanal authority when dealing with Turkmen[70] and Qaraqalpaq clans.[71]

6,000 firearms, and 10,000s of cartridges for them, see "[A.S. Galkin] *Doklad, 12.06.1916, no 173*", TsGARUz, f. I-1, op. 31, d. 1104, ll. 157–160.

67 On such channels of weapon supply into Khiva, see Niiazmetov, *Poisk konsensusa. Rossiisko-khivinskie geopoliticheskie otnosheniia v XVI–nachale XX v.*, pp. 422–432.

68 Munis and Agahi, *Firdaws al-iqbāl: History of Khorezm*, pp. 446, 452, 512; Muḥammad Riżā Āgahī, *Riyāż al-dawla*, MS St Petersburg, IVRRAN, inv. no. D-123, fol. 266a.

69 Munis and Agahi, *Firdaws al-iqbāl: History of Khorezm*, 475, 480, 494, 501; Muḥammad Riżā Āgahī, *Gulshan-i dawlat*, MS Tashkent, IVANRUz, inv. no. 7572, fols. 56a, 68a; Muḥammad Yūsuf Bayānī, *Shajara-yi Khwārazmshāhī*, MS Tashkent, IVANRUz, inv. no. 9596, fols. 343b, 345a.

70 Munis and Agahi, *Firdaws al-iqbāl: History of Khorezm*, p. 528; Muḥammad Riżā Āgahī, *Riyāż al-dawla*, MS St Petersburg, IVRRAN, inv. no. D-123, fol. 83a; Muḥammad Yūsuf Bayānī, *Shajara-yi Khwārazmshāhī*, MS Tashkent, IVANRUz, inv. no. 9596, fols. 330a, 333b; 343b.

71 Muḥammad Riżā Āgahī, *Gulshan-i dawlat*, MS Tashkent, IVANRUz, inv. no. 7572, fols. 45a; 58b–66b; 74a–74b; 262b–263a; [Girshfel'd and Galkin], *Voenno-statisticheskoe opisanie Khivinskogo oazisa. Sostavleno General'nogo Shtaba Kapitanom Girshfel'dom,*

In the past, the sheer variety of functions ascribed to *yasāvulbāshīs* seems to have misled scholars. Seymour Becker, for instance, characterised the responsibilities of the *yasāvulbāshīs* as those of a 'minister of war;'[72] 'Abdullāh Bāltaev, for his part, called such officials the 'heads of the secret chancery,'[73] while Yuri Bregel attributed to them policing functions.[74] First of all, we should clarify that the office of *yasāvulbāshī* does not seem to have featured among the prominent Khorezmian positions of state prior to the rise of the Qonghrat dynasty. For instance, while depicting the court protocol during the reign of Abu'l-Ghāzī Khān (1644–1663), local historians do not mention the *yasāvulbāshī* among the 32 higher court dignitaries who possessed the privilege of 'seating beside the khan.'[75] If we move to the reign of the Qonghrats, i.e., the early 19th century, we notice that chronicles mention *yasāvulbāshīs* as individuals entrusted by dynasts with important tasks, such as military campaigns, irrigation works, and participation in embassies. However, it is only later, from the mid-19th century, that we begin to observe certain holders of the post identified among the senior officials of the khanate,[76] and clearly exercising significant influence on the khanate's internal and foreign policy. Further, at the turn of the 20th century several authors listed the *yasāvulbāshī* among the most influential officials with a fairly wide and varied range of functions.[77] These officeholders, for instance, were remembered by their contemporaries

pererabotano Nachal'nikom Amu-Dar'inskogo otdela General-Maiorom Galkinym. Part 2 (Tashkent: Tipografiia Tashkentskogo voennogo okruga, 1903), pp. 21–22.

72 Becker, *Russia's Protectorates in Central Asia*, p. 180.

73 'Abdullāh Bāltaev, *Daftar* (*no. 22*), MS Khiva, Private collection of Odilbek Abdullaev, fol. 56b; see also M. Yŭldoshev, *Khiva khonligida feodal yer egaligi va davlat tuzilishi* (Tashkent: Ŭzbekiston SSR Davlat nashriyoti, 1959), p. 283, fn. 6.

74 Munis and Agahi, *Firdaws al-iqbāl: History of Khorezm*, p. 612, n. 640.

75 Ibid., 44.

76 In his survey of the Khanate of Khiva compiled in 1873, Alexander Kuhn provided a list of senior officials at the Khivan court, which includes the office of *yasāvulbāshī*, see A. Kun, *Ocherk istorii zaseleniia Khivinskogo khanstva s drevnykh vremen, sostav ego sovremennogo naseleniia, administratsiia i goroda khanstva*, 1873, IVRRAN, St. Petersburg, Arkhiv Vostokovedov, f. 33, d. 8, ll. 36–36 ob.

77 The Soviet scholar T. Tukhtametov named the *yasāvulbāshī* among the most senior officials in the khanate, alongside the *qūshbīgī* (*or qūshbegī*), the *mihtar* and the *dīvānbīgī*, see his *Amudar'inskii otdel: Sotsial'no-ekonomicheskoe i politicheskoe znachenie dlia Khorezmskogo oazisa*, p. 26; M. Yŭldoshev suggests that in the military hierarchy the *yasāvulbāshī* occupied the place directly behind the khan and the *amīr al-umarā*, who was appointed from among the close relatives of the khan. Yŭldoshev, *Khiva khonligida feodal yer egaligi va davlat tuzilishi*, pp. 283–284.

as being among 'the most senior officials in the khanate',[78] who in some cases kept control over the whole of 'the state's external and internal affairs.'[79] Again, it is only in this period when chancery records refer to them with the epithet of 'ministers' (*vazīr*).

If the rise of the position of *yasāvulbāshī* to one of the leading offices in the Khivan court hierarchy in the early 20th century is a clearly established fact, however, the process whereby this rise occurred – a process embedded in the political dynamics of 19th- and early 20th-century Khorezm – is far from clear. In the pages that follow we shall illustrate, albeit in broad terms, the range of responsibilities of the *yasāvulbāshī*s in the Qonghrat court hierarchy and the administration of the khanate. Furthermore, we shall attempt to uncover biographical information pertaining to individuals who occupied that office throughout the Qonghrat era, with emphasis on those of them who appear among the documents published in this book.

A note of caution is here in order. The spheres of competence of officeholders operating in the Khanate of Khiva were loosely defined and imperfectly distinguished. This state of affairs reflected a variety of factors, not only the nature of an officeholder's personal relations with the ruler, or his personal charisma, but also his ability, or inability, to manage relations within a large network and a wide variety of power groups. Such a model left room for political maneuvering by individual actors. This may explain why the sources and the scholarly literature supply contradictory information about the status and functions of the *yasāvulbāshī* in the web of power relations within the Khanate of Khiva.

The *Firdaws al-iqbāl*, a monumental history of the early Qonghrat dynasts, provides the first references to the activities of *yasāvulbāshī*s at the Khivan court. Over the reign of Muḥammad Raḥīm Khān I (1806–1825) two individuals – Qurbān Niyāz and Muḥammad Niyāz – occupied the office at the same time. Munis and Agahi, the authors of the *Firdaws al-iqbāl*, distinguished these two officials as the closest confidants of the khan (*maḥram-i rāz*),[80] who were bestowed with the epithet 'the pillars of the attendants and the cream of the servants.'[81] Both dignitaries are repeatedly mentioned also as participants in the numerous military campaigns of Muḥammad Raḥīm Khān I. More

78 [Nil Lykoshin], *Raport Nachal'nika Amu-Dar'inskogo Otdela, polkovnika Lykoshina, 28.11.1912 g., № 52*, TsGARUz, f. I-2, op. 1, d. 289, l. 176.

79 [Ḥasan-Murād] Laffasī, *Tazkirai Shuaro*, ed. P. Bobojonov (Urgench: Khorazm, 1992), pp. 56–57.

80 Munis and Agahi, *Firdaws al-iqbāl: History of Khorezm*, p. 446.

81 Ibid. pp. 512; 654, n. 1113.

often than not they acted as special commissioners at various military units.[82] Both *yasāvulbāshī*s also accompanied the Turkmen units – the most capable detachments of the Khivan army[83] – in military forays initiated by Qonghrats. It is worth mentioning that Muḥammad Niyāz was in charge of the Turkmen units consisting of Yomut clan members,[84] whereas Qurbān Niyāz was primarily dealing with Chawdurs.[85]

These two individuals continued to enjoy similar competences during the reign of Allāh Qulī Khān (1825–1842), son and immediate successor to Muḥammad Raḥīm I.[86] In 1839, after the death of Muḥammad Niyāz Yasāvulbāshī, his son Raḥmatullah Bāy was appointed to the office.[87] The latter appears to have held the post, with occasional interruptions, right up until his death in 1890.[88] According to some reports, not a single serious military campaign was undertaken by the Qonghrats without the involvement of this officeholder.[89]

A son of the second *yasāvulbāshī* Qurbān Niyāz, a certain ʿAbdullāh, also inherited the post following his father's death. Amongst the multiple responsibilities conferred upon ʿAbdullāh Yasāvulbāshī, the most notable was commanding military units of Chawdur Turkmens.[90] His successor in the post, Maḥmūd Niyāz Yasāvulbāshī, also had responsibility over Chawdur

82 Munis and Agahi, *Firdaws al-iqbāl: History of Khorezm*, pp. 480, 494, 512, 534. As Yuri Bregel noted, these functions of the two *yasāvulbāshī* in the Khanate of Khiva, as military inspectors and military commanders, emerged over the reign of Muḥammad Raḥīm Khān I, see Munis and Agahi, *Firdaws al-iqbāl: History of Khorezm*, p. 647, n. 1026.

83 Iu. Bregel', *Khorezmskie turkmeny v XIX veke* (Moscow: Izdatel'stvo vostochnoi literatury, 1961), p. 180.

84 Munis and Agahi, *Firdaws al-iqbāl: History of Khorezm*, pp. 501, 533.

85 Ibid., 528. Such simultaneous presence of two *yasāvulbāshī*s in the Khivan court a few decades later was also noted by Alexander Kuhn, see his *Ocherk istorii zaseleniia Khivinskogo khanstva s drevnykh vremen, sostav ego sovremennogo naseleniia, administratsiia i goroda khanstva*, 1873, IVRRAN, St. Petersburg, Arkhiv Vostokovedov, f. 33, d. 8, ll. 41ob.-42.

86 Muḥammad Riżā Āgahī, *Riyāż al-dawla*, MS St Petersburg, IVRRAN, inv. no. D-123, fols. 139b, 145a, 192a, 197b.

87 Ibid., fols. 227b, 229b.

88 The interruptions occurred in 1854–1855, when Raḥmatullah Yasāvulbāshī was arrested by ʿAbdullah Khān following a court intrigue, and again in the wake of the conquest of Khiva by the Russian army in 1873, when he was exiled to Kaluga along with Muḥammad Murād Dīvānbīgī. In 1880, they returned to Khiva and resumed their former posts; see Muḥammad Yūsuf Bayānī, *Shajara-yi Khwārazmshāhī*, MS Tashkent, IVANRUz, inv. no. 9596, fols. 355b, 465a, 480b–481a.

89 Yŭldoshev, *Khiva khonligida feodal yer egaligi va davlat tuzilishi*, p. 284; Bobojon Tarroh-Khodim, *Khorazm shoir va navozandalari*, eds. A. Otamurodova and O. Abdurahimov (Tashkent: Tafakkur qanoti, 2011), p. 32, fn. 1.

90 Bregel', *Khorezmskie turkmeny v XIX veke*, p. 178.

detachments.[91] Yet for a while, from the late 1850s to 1866, this *yasāvulbāshī* was also responsible for governing over the Qaraqalpaq clans in the Amu Darya delta, in particular for collecting taxes from them.[92] The members of the Russian embassy to Khiva in 1858, for instance, reported about their contacts with Maḥmud Niyāz Yasāvulbāshī, whom they called the 'temporary governor of the city of Qonghrat'[93] – the northernmost settlement of the khanate. We know that the 1858 diplomatic mission advanced towards Khivan borders accompanied by a sizable military detachment.[94] This, of course, caused anxiety among the members of the Qonghrat royal court, who were concerned about the somewhat porous northern borders of their state. Their anxiety escalated when the Russian navy appeared in the Aral Sea.[95] One may plausibly infer that Maḥmūd Niyāz Yasāvulbāshī was appointed to the Aral Sea littoral in the capacity of plenipotentiary official to defend against the threat of Russian expansion. The secretary of the Russian embassy, a certain E. Kilevein, provides information about yet another *yasāvulbāshī* – Raḥmatullāh – whom he encountered at the khan's court. Kilevein describes this officeholder as 'the main military figure' in the khanate.[96]

Thus, one may observe that under Qonghrat rule two *yasāvulbāshīs*, who had been occupying simultaneously the post, were empowered with a range of competences, with particular emphasis on military activities. Despite the notable ambiguity and indeterminacy of the competences of the various officials of the Khanate of Khiva, one can nevertheless identify a tendency to task

---

91 According to Bayānī, Maḥmūd Yasāvulbāshī occupied this office until 1878, when on suspicion of abuse of power and treachery he was removed from office and put under house arrest by order of Muḥammad Raḥīm Khān II, see Muḥammad Yūsuf Bayānī, *Shajara-yi Khwārazmshāhī*, MS Tashkent, IVANRUz, inv. no. 9596, fols. 477a–477b.

92 Muḥammad Rizā Āgahī, *Gulshan-i dawlat*, MS Tashkent, IVANRUz, inv. no. 7572, fols. 45a; 58b–56b; see also Iu.E. Bregel', *Dokumenty arkhiva khivinskikh khanov po istorii i etnografii karakalpakov* (Moscow: Nauka, 1967), pp. 20–21.

93 N.G. Zalesov, "Posol'stvo v Khivu i Bukharu Polkovnika Ignat'eva v 1858 godu," *Russkii vestnik* 2 (1871), p. 446.

94 Ibid., p. 427.

95 Letter of Colonel Ignat'ev to General Kovalevskii on 20 August [1858], ibid., p. 472.

96 E.B. Kilevein, "Otryvok iz puteshestviia v Khivu i nekotorye podrobnosti o khanstve vo vremia pravleniia Seid-Mokhammed Khana, 1856–1860," in *Zapiski Imperatorskogo Russkogo Geograficheskogo Obshchestva*. Bk. 1. (St. Petersburg, 1861), p. 11. The same individuals – Raḥmatullah Yasāvulbāshī and Maḥmūd Yasāvulbāshī – would be mentioned by Bayānī, a Khivan court historian, with regard to later events: both would be named among the military leaders who led the Khivan military formations during the conquest of the khanate by Russian troops in May 1873, see Muḥammad Yūsuf Bayānī, *Shajara-yi Khwārazmshāhī*, MS Tashkent, IVANRUz, inv. no. 9596, fol. 448a.

the *yasāvulbāshī*s with crucial areas of Qonghrat policy. Such responsibilities, and the particular trust that the rulers invested in the *yasāvulbāshī*s, inevitably reinforced their status within the Khivan court and administrative hierarchy.

It is striking, however, that Qonghrat court chronicles, while describing the multiple activities played by *yasāvulbāshī*s, are often silent about their role in hearing subjects' petitions. Nor do we hear much from foreign observers. For instance, Gregor von Helmersen and Grigorii Gens, the authors of a detailed survey of the khanate in 1840, noticed that Khivan subjects who wished to submit a petition to the royal court had first to contact the *mihtar* – one of the most influential officials in the khanate. In case of the latter's absence the appellants were expected to apply to the *qūshbīgī*, another senior official, 'and if he [too] is not present, then to the [courtier named] *Khwādjesh-maḥram*.'[97] Thus, when describing the circle of Khivan courtiers who were presently in charge of the resolution of disputes, Helmersen and Gens said nothing about any involvement by *yasāvulbāshī*s. Nor did Gregor Danilevskii and Friedrich Basiner, members of a Russian diplomatic mission to Khiva in 1842, make any mention of the *yasāvulbāshī*s' role while describing the process whereby subjects appealed to the royal court.[98]

The earliest reference to the direct involvement of the *yasāvulbāshī* in the hearing of petitions and their subsequent investigation belongs to Alexander Kuhn, who was appointed to carry out a thorough inspection of the khanate in the summer of 1873, in the wake of the conquest of Khiva by Russian troops. Kuhn depicts the competences of the *yasāvulbāshī*, especially in the system of dispensation of justice as follows:

---

97 Georg von Gens, Gregor von Helmersen, "Izvestiia o Khive, Bukhare, Kokande i severo-zapadnoi chasti Kitaiskogo gosudarstva", in *Istoriia Kazakhstana v zapadnykh istochnikakh XII–XX vv. Tom 5: Nemetskie issledovateli v Kazakhstane. Chast' 1*, ed. I.V. Erofeeva. (Almaty: Sanat, 2006), p. 36. On Khwājash Maḥram, one of the most influential courtiers in Khiva over the first half of the 19th century, see Muḥammad Riżā Āgahī, *Riyāż al-dawla*, MS St Petersburg, IVRRAN, inv. no. D-123, fol., 55a; Murav'ev, *Puteshestvie v Turkmeniiu i Khivu v 1819 i 1820 godakh*, pt. 2, pp. 33–34; [Iskander Batyrshin] "Zapiska mladshego perevodchika Orenburgskoi pogranichnoi komissii Iskandera Batyrshina o Khivinskom khanstve i khane Prisyrdar'inskikh kazakhov Ermukhammede (Ilekee) Kasymove," in *Istoriia Kazakhstana v russkikh istochnikakh XVI–XX vekov. Tom VI: Putevye dnevniki i sluzhebnye poezdki po iuzhnym stepiam XVIII–XIX veka*, eds. I.V. Eroffeva and B.T. Janaev (Almaty: Daik-Press, 2007), p. 307.

98 [G.I. Danilevskii], "Opisanie Khivinskogo khanstva, sostavlennoe v 1842 g. podpolkovnikom G.I. Danilevskim," in *Zapiski Imperatorskogo gepgraficheskogo obshchestva*. Kn. 5 (St. Petersburg, 1851), p. 134; Theodor-Fridrich Basiner, "Estestvenno-nauchnoe puteshestvie po Kirgizskoi stepi v Khivu," in *Istoriia Kazakhstana v zapadnykh istochnikakh XII–XX vv. Tom 5: Nemetskie issledovateli v Kazakhstane. Chast' 1*, ed. I.V. Erofeeva (Almaty: Sanat, 2006), pp. 354–355.

> The Esaul-bashi (=Yasāvulbāshī) is a military commander. There are two of them in the khanate: one commands the Turkmen Yomuts, the other the Chawdurs. It is their responsibility to command their forces as instructed by the khan, and in peacetime each in turn is required to be present when the khan receives *arzs* (petitions). Each Esaul-bashi has several helpers, also called Esauls. When he receives an order from the khan to investigate a specific petition, he sends one of his helpers with the petitioner to the site of the conflict. When the Esaul has finished his investigation, he takes 3½ *ṭangas* – 70 *kopeks* – from the petitioner for each *tash* (18 versts) that he has travelled while following up this matter. In the past, the Esaul-bashi had as his insignia for this post a [special] wand – an *asa* – with a silver cane-head, but now he simply has a knife at his belt.[99]

Kuhn's narrative therefore leaves little doubt that by 1873, at the latest, not only did *yasāvulbāshīs* take part in military campaigns and command Turkmen formations, but they also played a central role in the dispensation of justice. Kuhn's description also provides unambiguous evidence that the *yasāvulbāshī* participated in both the procedure of receiving petitions, and the subsequent activities, delegating his attendants (*yasāvul*) to the site of the conflict. The specifics of the *yasāvulbāshīs*' involvement in the resolution of conflicts, as witnessed by Kuhn in 1873, correspond to what we have reconstructed in the previous sections of the book.

A further expansion of the *yasāvulbāshī*'s status and authority can be observed during the period after the establishment of the Russian protectorate over Khiva, and especially from the early 20th century.[100] It is natural that tasks such as ensuring internal stability and governing over Turkmen subjects thus acquired increased importance for the Qonghrats. It does not come as a surprise that the *yasāvulbāshīs*, who were actually in command of the police forces and who possessed a long-standing institutional experience of dealing with the Turkmen subjects, gained additional authority and stature. Being promoted predominantly from among the khan's close associates (*maḥram*),[101] the

99 A. Kun, *Ocherk istorii zaseleniia Khivinskogo khanstva s drevnykh vremen, sostav ego sovremennogo naseleniia, administratsiia i goroda khanstva*, 1873, IVRRAN, St. Petersburg, Arkhiv Vostokovedov, f. 33, d. 8, ll. 41ob.–42.

100 Becker, *Russia's Protectorates in Central Asia*, pp. 74–76.

101 For instance, Mamat Yasāvulbāshī and Dawlat Murad Yasāvulbāshī, the prominent officials who occupied this office, had started their career at the court as 'the closest associates' of the Qonghrat ruler Muḥammad Raḥīm Khān II; see Tarroh-Khodim, *Khorazm shoir va*

yasāvulbāshī furthermore tended to enjoy royal confidence and often was in charge over the execution of secret and delicate assignments of the Qonghrat dynasts.[102]

We now come to the early 20th century, where we frequently encounter *yasāvulbāshī*s among the high-ranking officials of the khanate with a broad range of responsibilities and much recognised authority. Nil Sergeevich Lykoshin (1860–1922),[103] who as the newly appointed Head of the Amu-Darya Department paid a visit to the Khivan ruler Isfandiyār Khān in May 1912, described Yasāvulbāshī Muḥammad Yūsuf as 'one who occupies a prominent post at the court'[104] and who is 'respected by all.'[105] A few months later, in his report to the Governor-General of Turkestan, Lykoshin named the same *yasāvulbāshī* as 'the most important senior official' alongside Sayyid Islām Khwāja, this latter at the time being the 'chief minister' of the khanate (*vazīr-i akbār*).[106]

As a vivid indicator of the growing significance of the *yasāvulbāshī* position in the court hierarchy, in the early 20th century the designation of *yasāvulbāshī* in chancery documents is often coupled with the epithet of 'minister' (*vazīr*). The documents published in this work eloquently illustrate such a shift in writing practices. We thus observe instances of addressing this officeholder as 'refuge of the vizierate' (*vizārat-panāh*), 'noble vizier' (*vazīr al-kirām*), 'most eminent vizier' (*vazīr-i aʿẓām*), 'illustrious councilor' (*dastūr al-mukarram*).

---

navozandalari, p. 81; Bābājān Safarov. *Khwārazmda būlūb ūtgān qūlchilīq aḥvāllarī nīng wāqiʿalārī*. MS Tashkent, IVANRUz, inv. no. 11254/II, fols. 87–90.

102 See for instance ʿAbdullāh Bāltaev, *Khwārazm ta'rīkhīga matiryallār* (*Khīva 1950*), MS Tashkent, IVANRUz, inv. no. 9320, fol. 5a; Tarroh-Khodim, *Khorazm shoir va navozandalari*, p. 16.

103 Nil Sergeevich Lykoshin was an official of the Russian colonial administration in Turkestan as well as an Orientalist. He began his career in Turkestan in 1889 as a non-commissioned officer, advanced through the hierarchy, and, between 1914 and 1917, served as military governor of the Samarkand District (*oblast'*) with the rank of major general. Between 1912 and 1914 he served as head of the Amu-Darya Department and was closely involved in relations with the Khivan administration on a wide range of issues. He is also known for his historical and ethnographic interests in Central Asia, see A. Morrison, "Sufism, Pan-Islamism and Information Panic: Nil Sergeevich Lykoshin and the Aftermath of the Andijan Uprising," *Past and Present* 214.1 (2012), pp. 255–314.

104 N.S. Lykoshin, *Zapiska Nachal'nika Amu-Dar'inskogo Otdela Polkovnika Lykoshina o sovremennom sostoianii Khivinskogo Khanstva, 1912 god*, TsGARUz, f. I-2, op. 1, d. 314, l. 20ob.

105 N.S. Lykoshin, *Sovremennoe raspredelenie vlasti v Khanstve Khivinskom, 1912 god*, TsGARUz, f. I-2, op. 1, d. 314, l. 63ob.

106 According to Lykoshin, Muḥammad Yūsuf Yasāvulbāshī and Sayyid Islām Khwāja were the only two individuals around the khan who were bestowed with 'a special sabre with a red cloth covering,' like the one which the Khivan ruler himself 'wore instead of a crown when on parade;' see: [Nil Lykoshin], *Raport Nachal'nika Amu-Dar'inskogo Otdela, polkovnika Lykoshina, 28.11.1912 g., № 52*, TsGARUz, f. I-2, op. 1, d. 289, l. 176

This comes in stark contract with earlier records from the 1860s, when the epithet of vizier is not employed in connection with *yasāvulbāshī*s.[107]

Yuri Bregel noted that for most of the 19th century the epithet 'vizier' tended to be applied predominantly (if not exclusively) to two of the higher ranks of the khanate, namely the *mihtar* and *qūshbīgī*. He also argued that the concept of the 'vizierate', at least until 1860, was exclusively connected with these particular offices.[108] This is borne out also by local chroniclers who tended to confer the epithet *vazīr* solely upon holders of the post of *mihtar* and *qūshbīgī*.[109] Echoing 19th-century European observers' reports,[110] Bregel also identified the official duties of the *mihtar* and *qūshbīgī* as those of the 'minister of internal affairs' and 'minister of war' respectively, wherein the *mihtar*'s responsibilities included the running the civil administration and standing in for the khan in the latter's absence, while the *qūshbīgī* was responsible for administering the armies.[111] Meanwhile, as illustrated in the preceding part of this section, by the late 19th and early 20th century, some part of those responsibilities formerly exercised by the *mihtar* and *qūshbīgī* was taken over by the *yasāvulbāshī*. Hence, we may safely conclude that the rise of the formal competence and position of the *yasāvulbāshī*, especially observable by the early 20th century, and the integration of this office into the highest echelons of the khanate's court hierarchy, found its manifestation also in the epithets conferred upon them.

The fact that by the beginning of the 20th century *yasāvulbāshī*s held similar status to *qūshbīgī*s and *mihtar*s in court hierarchy is indicated also by Pahlavān Niyāz Ḥājjī Yusupov (1861–1936), who was one of the leaders of the Young Khivans. Describing a meeting in 1917 between the soldier-delegates of Russian garrison in Khiva and Isfandiyār Khān, the author, who was an eyewitness to the event, reported:

> … on one side of the terrace sat the *qażī*s and [other] *ʿulamā'*, and on the other – the members of the parliament (*majlis*), and above them sat the soldier-delegates – on chairs. The [three] viziers – the *qūshbīgī*,

107 In these earlier dispatches, more general epithets appear, such as *ʿizzat-panāh, saʿādat-dastgāh, ʿizzat va saʿādat-hamrāh*, see TsGARUz, f. I-125, op. 2, d. 159.

108 Yu. Bregel, "The Sarts in the Khanate of Khiva," *Journal of Asian History* 12.2 (1978), pp. 131–132.

109 See for instance, Muḥammad Rižā Āgahī, *Riyāż al-dawla*, MS St Petersburg, IVRRAN, inv. no. D-123, fols. 52b., 63a.

110 Murav'ev, *Puteshestvie v Turkmeniiu i Khivu v 1819 i 1820 godakh*, pt. 2, pp. 32–33; Basiner, *Estestvenno-nauchnoe puteshestvie po Kirgizskoi stepi v Khivu*, p 354; Stetkevich, "Ocherki Khivinskogo oazisa," *Voennyi sbornik* 3 (1892), p. 14.

111 Bregel, "The Sarts in the Khanate of Khiva," pp. 132–133.

> the *mihtar* and the *yasāvulbāshī* – were standing.... All rose from their places and loudly greeted the khan according to the long-established tradition.[112]

Let us now go over some details of the biography and career history of certain individuals who occupyied the office of *yasāvulbāshī* over the timespan covered by our documents, i.e. 1910–1920.

A sizable number of royal rescripts (*fatak*) were sealed by Muḥammad Yūsuf Yasāvulbāshī (d. 1917), a son of ʿAważ Niyāz Maḥram. The seal can be found in records issued between September 1910 and the middle of November 1917. The Russian officer Nil Lykoshin provides some important information concerning this official, whom he met in Khiva in 1912:

> ... Esaul Bashi Mukhammad Yusuf Afazniiaz Makhramov, 65 years. Being a childhood friend of the late khan [Muḥammad Raḥīm II] has served at the court since his youth, and was earlier a consul in Petro-Aleksandrovsk. He has been universally respected [in Khiva]. He maintains the old-fashioned way of life (*po-starinnomu*), and has not had his house altered to imitate the Russian style. [He is i]nclined to oppose reforms and innovations ...[113]

We find a brief reference to this Khivan official also in the work of Pahlavān Niyāz Ḥājjī Yusupov. Describing the events of October 1917, the author mentions his conversation with the 'late' Yūsuf Yasāvulbāshī, evidently alluding here to the latter's death shortly thereafter. This is also confirmed by information from our documents: the seals of Muḥammad Yūsuf Yasāvulbāshī are found on the rescripts right up until the middle of November 1917.[114]

Yet another figure who also occupied this office during the initial years of Isfandiyār Khān's reign was Shaykh Naẓar Bāy Yasāvulbāshī (d. 1917), one of the sons of Muḥammad Murād Dīvānbīgī (d. 1901). According to Laffasī, immediately after Isfandiyār Khān's succession to the throne in 1910, a whole series of senior officials were reshuffled, and Shaykh Naẓar Bāy was promoted to the post of *yasāvulbāshī*.[115] Although his occupation of this post during the period

---

112 Pahlavān Niyāz Ḥājjī, [*Khāṭiralar*]. MS Khiva, Private Collection of Anvar Otaboev, fols. 103b–104b.

113 N.S. Lykoshin, *Sovremennoe raspredelenie vlasti v Khanstve Khivinskom, 1912 god*, TsGARUz, f. I-2, op. 1, d. 314, l. 63ob.

114 See, e.g.: TsGARUz, f. I-125, op.2, d. 633, ll. 178, 179, 180.

115 Ḥasan-Murād Laffasī, *Gulshan-i saʿādat*, MS Tashkent, IVANRUz, inv. no. 7797, fol. 5b. According to another Khivan author, Bābājān Tarrāh, Shaykh Naẓar Bāy's promotion to

1910–1915 was rather intermittent – during his tenure he was briefly arrested, and periodically fell out of royal favour[116] – it appears in general that Shaykh Naẓar Bāy enjoyed considerable influence at the court[117] and great authority among the wider population.[118] Shaykh Naẓar Bāy's career owed much to the fact that he was a part of Muḥammad Murād Dīvānbīgī's powerful clan, whose members occupied a number of key positions and concentrated considerable resources in their hands.[119] As a member of this family, Shaykh Naẓar Bāy had been in the khan's 'cohort' from the very beginning and could expect promotion to high office. In his capacity as *yasāvulbāshī*, besides overseeing the settlement of the disputes, Shaykh Naẓar Bāy's spheres of competence also included 'the government of all the Turkmen affairs on behalf of the khan of Khiva'[120] and, in particular, responsibility for collecting *zakāt* from the Turkmen population.[121] In August 1915, in the wake of a major Turkmen uprising, Shaykh Naẓar Bāy was held responsible for the disorder and, upon the insistence of the Russian administration, removed from his post and exiled to Russian Turkestan (Chimkent).[122] After his return from exile in December 1916, he was effectively detached from active political activities.[123]

---

the office of *yasāvulbāshī* had occurred slightly earlier, during the last years of Muḥammad Raḥīm Khān II's reign, when he 'was bestowed with the rank (*mansab*) of *yasāvulbāshī* and commander of the armies of Khorezm (*askarbashilik*),' Tarroh-Khodim, *Khorazm shoir va navozandalari*, pp. 76–77.

116 For details, see U. Abdurasulov, "Tainy khivinskogo dvora: politcheskaia bor'ba v Khive v period Rossiiskogo protektorata," *Vostok svyshe* 3 (2015), pp. 38–56.

117 Some authors characterize Shaykh Naẓar Bāy as the leader of an influential political grouping at the court, opposed to the powerful minister Sayyid Islām Khwāja.

118 According to Laffasī, a contemporary to these events, when Shaykh Naẓar Bāy returned from exile in December 1916, the whole population of Khiva, 'from the ages of 7 to 70,' went out to meet him: Ḥasan-Murād Laffasī, *Gulshan-i sa'ādat*, MS Tashkent, IVANRUz, inv. no. 7797, fol. 83b.

119 The brothers of Shaykh Naẓar Bāy occupied the leading positions in the khanate: Ḥusayn Muḥammad Bāy held the post of *dīvānbīgī*, Ṣāḥib Naẓar Bāy, that of *mihtar*, while Āmān Kīldī Bāy was one of the khan's confidants (*maḥram*): Ibid., fol. 10a.

120 Laffasī, *Tazkirai shuaro*, pp. 52–53; Tukhtametov, *Rossiia i Khiva v kontse XIX–nachale XX veka*, p. 68.

121 A. Shioya, "Povorot and the Khanate of Khiva: A New Canal and the Birth of Ethnic Conflict in Khorazm Oasis, 1870s–1890s," *Central Asian Survey*, 33.2 (2014), p. 239; N. Tashev, "Zanimal li Mukhammad Yusuf Baiani dolzhnost' divan-begi?," *O'zbekiston tarixi* (2009/2), p. 18.

122 Ḥasan-Murād Laffasī, *Gulshan-i sa'ādat*, MS Tashkent, IVANRUz, inv. no. 7797, fol. 33a; Becker, *Russia's Protectorates in Central Asia*, p. 183.

123 According to Laffasī, Shaykh Naẓar Bāy died in Khiva in August 1917, a few months after his return from exile, Ḥasan-Murād Laffasī, *Gulshan-i sa'ādat*, MS Tashkent, IVANRUz, inv. no. 7797, fol. 97a.

FIGURE 2 The Khivan ruler Isfandiyār Khān sits (at the center) among his courtiers (1911). Muḥammad Yūsuf Yasāvulbāshī is in the front row, i.e., the first from the right. Shaykh Naẓar Bāy Yasāvulbāshī is the second from the left
PHOTO COURTESY OF VLAD YAKOVLEV, MOSCOW, RUSSIA

Examining the seals attached on rescripts also allows us to shed light on other individuals who held the post of *yasāvulbāshī* during the reign of Isfandiyār Khān and his successor, Sayyid ʿAbdullāh Khān, the last Khivan monarch. They also enable us to reconstruct the rough lengths of their tenures. For instance, a significant number of rescripts issued between 1911 and 1915 were stamped with the seal of Muḥammad Maḥram Yasāvulbāshī (d. 1915), a son of Muḥammad Ḥusayn.[124] Lykoshin, who happened to meet Muḥammad (Mamat) Maḥram in 1912, writes that at that time he was around 50 years old, and that he had begun his court career 'from his early years', as a *maḥram* ('confidant') of Muḥammad Raḥīm Khān II, but had 'only recently' been promoted to the office of *yasāvulbāshī*.[125] Along with hearing subjects' petitions, Muḥammad

124 The earliest rescript with the signature of Muḥammad Maḥram Yasāvulbāshī is dated to 16 April 1911 (see: TsGARUz, f. I-125, op. 2, d. 655, l. 30), while the latest is dated to 15 March 1915: TsGARUz, f. I-125, op. 2, d. 656, l. 11.

125 N.S. Lykoshin, *Sovremennoe raspredelenie vlasti v Khanstve Khivinskom, 1912 god*, TsGARUz, f. I-2, op. 1, d. 314, l. 63 ob. See also Tarroh-Khodim, *Khorazm shoir va navozandalari*, p. 16, fn. 4.

Maḥram was in charge also of the collecting of *zakāt* 'from the goods [delivered from] Bukhara as well as the [charges] due to [provision of services of] the *ughlāns*[126] (*bachchas*).'[127] The Khivan author Bābājān Safar-ūghlī (Safarov, 1891–1983) provides some interesting details about the provenance of this official, giving thereby a certain insight into the career trajectories of upwardly mobile courtiers in Khiva:

> A boy named Mamat came from Iran [to Khorezm] from Iran, having been sold into slavery. He was handsome and comely. Muḥammad Raḥīm Khān [II] chose him as his *bachcha*; and when he grew up, he made him his *yasāvulbāshī*.[128]

Mamat Yasāvulbāshī's seals suggest that he occupied this post over the period of time 1911–1915. Local authors also indicated that Mamat Yasāvulbāshī died in a battle with Yomut Turkmens in late 1915, wherein he was one of two commander of Khivan troops,[129] during the mass revolt against the central authorities.[130]

Seals further indicate that the post of *yasāvulbāshī* was then occupied, though only for a short while, by Āmān Kīldī Bāy,[131] a brother of the

126 Pers.: *bachcha* or *bachchabāzī*; Turk.: *ūghlān* (lit.: 'boy'; 'boy play'), a term used to refer to a practice documented in various regions of Central Asia, whereby older men employed the services of boys for purposes of entertainment. Although *bachchabāzī* is closely associated with pederasty, sources in fact paint a more complex picture. Evidently, in the Khanate of Khiva *bachchas* constituted a discrete social group administered by individuals known as *sāzanda*. The latter operated upon permission of the royal court in Khiva. *Sāzandas* were expected to pay a tax to the treasury as well as a fee to the families of the *bachchas*, see Gleb Snesarev, *Polevye zapisi: Khorezm, 1961*, AIEARAN, f. G.P. Snesarev, d. 10. ll. 21, 29, 45. On *bachchas* in Central Asia, see I. Baldauf, "*Kraevedenie* and Uzbek National Consciousness," *Papers on Inner Asia*, no. 20 (Bloomington, 1992).

127 N.S. Lykoshin, *Sovremennoe raspredelenie vlasti v Khanstve Khivinskom, 1912 god*, TsGARUz, f. I-2, op. 1, d. 314, l. 63ob. Similar reports about this dignitary appear in Laffasī. Specifically, the latter reports that the appointment of Muḥammad Maḥram as *yasāvulbāshī* occurred at the end of 1911, after he had been relieved from his earlier post as royal treasurer (*khazīnachī*), Ḥasan-Murād Laffasī, *Gulshan-i sa'ādat*, MS Tashkent, IVANRUz, inv. no. 7797, fols. 18b, 76a–77a, 80a.

128 Bābājān Safarov, *Khwārazmda būlūb ūtgān qūlchīlīq ahvāllārīnīng vāqi'alārī*, MS Tashkent, IVANRUz, inv. no. 11254, fols. 87b–88a; this statement also finds support in the work by Bobojon Tarroh, see his, *Khorazm shoir va navozandalari*, p. 16.

129 Ḥasan-Murād Laffasī, *Gulshan-i sa'ādat*, MS Tashkent, IVANRUz, inv. no. 7797, fol. 28a.

130 Ibid., fol. 80a. According to Safarov, Junayd Khān ordered Mamat Yasāvulbāshī to be put to death 'by burning', Bābājān Safarov, *Khwārazmda būlūb ūtgān qūlchīlīq ahvāllārīnīng vāqi'alārī*, MS Tashkent, IVANRUz, inv. no. 11254, fol. 88.

131 Kosbergenov claims that, in light of their economic status, Qaraqalpaq *bāys* enjoyed the same authority as did *ātālīqs* and *bīs*, see R. Kosbergenov, "Polozhenie karakalpalskogo

afore-mentioned Shaykh Naẓar Yasāvulbāshī. Although this individual often appears in our sources as operating in different capacities,[132] there had been hitherto no information regarding his activity in the position of *yasāvulbāshī*. Our documents provide clear evidence about Āmān Kīldī Bāy's occupation of this office in the period between early 1916 to March 1917.[133]

Starting from around the autumn of 1917 the office was occupied by Muḥammad Yaʿqūb Yasāvulbāshī. The latter was a son of the afore-mentioned Muḥammad Yūsuf Yasāvulbāshī, who had held this post a few years earlier. Evidently, Muḥammad Yaʿqūb inherited the post from his father in 1917 and, as the seals on rescripts clearly indicate, he continued to occupy the office right until early 1920.[134]

Contemporary with Muḥammad Yaʿqūb Yasāvulbāshī was another *yasāvulbāshī* named Dawlat Murād Maḥram (d. 1920), a son of Īsh Muḥammad. We find evidence regarding the circumstances of his promotion to the post of *yasāvulbāshī* in the various accounts of local authors. In October 1918, after the murder of Isfandiyār Khān by order of the Turkmen leader Junayid

---

naseleniia v Khivinskom khanstve v kontse XIX–nachale XX v.," in *Trudy Khorezmskoi arkheologo-etnograficheskoi ekspeditsii. III. Materialy i issledovaniia po etnografii karakalpakov*, ed. T.A. Zhdanko (Moscow: Izdatel'stvo Akademii nauk SSSR, 1958), p. 261. Yŭldoshev and Bregel argued that *bāys* were representatives of the merchants and could be found among attendants of the royal court, see, respectively, *Khiva khonligida feodal yer egaligi*, p. 257 and "The Sarts in the Khanate of Khiva," pp. 126–127. Bregel also noted that 'persons to whose names was added the title *bāy* in Khivan chronicles, were often governors of towns in the southern part of the country,' (Ibid., 127). Diplomas of appointment (*yārlīq*) from Khiva indicate that under the rule of the Qonghrats, *bāy* was also a title conferred upon individuals appointed to a specific administrative office. Documents courtesy of Komiljon Khudaybergenov.

132 See, e.g., Ḥasan-Murād Laffasī, *Gulshan-i saʿādat*, MS Tashkent, IVANRUz, inv. no. 7797, fol.10b; Tukhtametov, *Rossiia i Khiva v kontse XIX–nachale XX veka*, pp. 68–69. Akifumi Shioya notes that Āmān Kīldī Bāy shared responsibility for governing the Turkmens with his brother Shaykh Naẓar Bāy, Shioya, "Povorot and the Khanate of Khiva: A New Canal and the Birth of Ethnic Conflict in Khorazm Oasis, 1870s–1890s," p. 239.

133 We have a series of rescripts sealed by Āmān Kīldī Bāy in the year 1913: see, e.g.: TsGARUz, f. I-125, op. 1, d. 633, l. 196. However, such documents were a one-off, and moreover on the official seal the name is shown as Āmān Kīldī Bāy, without any indication that he held the post of *yasāvulbāshī*. It could be that during this time he periodically stood in for his brother Shaykh Naẓar Bāy Yasāvulbāshī to take petitions from the population when the latter was away. However, on seals from the many rescripts of 1916 to 1917, his name now figures as Āmān Kīldī Bāy Yasāvulbāshī, which indicates that by the time in question he did occupy the post officially. See, e.g.: TsGARUz, f. I-125, op. 1, d. 656, ll. 14–17.

134 See, e.g.: TsGARUz, f. I-125, op. 2, d. 633, l. 157; d. 656, l. 44.

Khān,[135] the former's brother Sayyid ʿAbdullāh Khān (1918–1920) acceded to the Khivan throne.[136] His enthronement was followed by the appointment of Dawlat Murād, who was known as a *maḥram*[137] of the former Khivan ruler Muḥammad Raḥim Khān II, to the post of *yasāvulbāshī*.[138] Owing to his close relations with Junāyid Khān, Dawlat Murād Yasāvulbāshī 'kept in his hand the whole [range of] of the state's external and internal affairs,'[139] whereas Sayyid ʿAbdullāh Khān, the nominal Qonghrat ruler, 'was rather a marionette' in the hands of his *yasāvulbāshī*.[140] Amongst Dawlat Murād's broad range of administration responsibilities, he was placed in charge of settling disputes amongst the population. The rescripts concerning the settlement of grievances with the seal of Dawlat Murād Yasāvulbāshī were issued down to the beginning of 1920,[141] until the fall of the Qonghrat khans of Khiva. In February 1920, a pro-Bolshevik *coup d'état* in Khiva brought the ruling khanate to an end. With the fall of the Qonghrat *ancien régime*, the office of *yasāvulbāshī* also sank into oblivion.

4 *ʿArż* as a Form of Governance

Allāh Qulī Khān initiated a range of projects to reconstruct the city of Khiva, aiming to turn the capital into one of the key symbols of Qonghrats' sovereignty. Allāh Qulī Khān's predecessors had been forced to concentrate most of their energies on firming up the power of the new dynasty, putting down uprisings of oppositional groups, and reorganising practices of state administration.[142] In some respects, Allāh Qulī Khān inherited a rather more secure regime

135 By a cruel twist of fate, Isfandiyār Khān was assassinated in the audience hall (*arż-khāna*) of his residence immediately following the conclusion of the ceremony of hearing of the subjects' petitions (*fuqarālārnī ʿarżī tamām bulghānīdān sūng*), Pahlavān Niyāz Ḥājjī, [*Khāṭiralar*]. MS Khiva, Private Collection of Anvar Otaboev, fols. 230b–231b.

136 ʿAbdullāh Bāltaev, *Khwārazm taʾrīkhīga matiryallār* (*Khīva 1950*), MS Tashkent, IVANRUz, inv. no. 9320, fols. 20a–20b.

137 On details of his biography, see Laffasī, *Tazkirai shuaro*, pp. 56–57; Tarroh-Khodim, *Khorazm shoir va navozandalari*, pp. 80–84.

138 Ḥasan-Murād Laffasī, *Gulshan-i saʿādat*, MS Tashkent, IVANRUz, inv. no. 7797, fol. 102a; Pahlavān Niyāz Ḥājjī, [*Khāṭiralar*]. MS Khiva, Private Collection of Anvar Otaboev, fols. 230b–231b.

139 Laffasī, *Tazkirai shuaro*, pp. 56–57; Pahlavān Niyāz Ḥājjī, [*Khāṭiralar*]. MS Khiva, Private Collection of Anvar Otaboev, fols. 233b.

140 *maḥż-i ism būlūb tūrghān*, ibid., fol. 233b.

141 See, e.g.: TsGARUz, f. I-125, op. 1, d. 633, l. 75.

142 Abdurasulov, "The Aral Region and Geopolitical Agenda of the Early Qongrats".

than his predecessors had done, together with 'a rich treasury and a powerful state,' as one Khivan court historian put it.[143] He was therefore able to turn his attention to the redevelopment of Khiva's urban architecture and one of the most notable of his initial enterprises was the construction of a new royal palace in Khiva called *Tāsh Hawlī* ('Stone Courtyard'). As part of this monumental project, the ruler commissioned the construction of a 'chamber of petitions' (*ʿarż-khāna*) that was designed to allow the khan to receive claimants and hear their grievances directly. The chamber was built so that the hearing would be 'suitable to the royal status' of the rulers (*pādshāhlīqgha lāyiq*), whereas, previously, hearings had taken place at the old royal court (*kuhna arīkda* [sic]),[144] which is to say, in the apartments of the khan, without any officially designated protocol.[145]

The court historian Muḥammad Yūsuf Bayānī (1858–1923) reports that in this, and in other buildings constructed in the places of regular residence of the Khivan rulers, the khan would spend an hour every day, before sunset, 'dispensing justice' (*ʿadl-u-dād mashghūl idīlār*) by hearing petitions from the public.[146] It is here that we can appreciate the importance of hearing the grievances of the populace for the Qonghrats: the dispensation of justice was not only a form of governance deployed to exploit fissures and cleavages among the populations and thus bring the ruler closer to the many concerns of his subjects, but was also a physical and permanent attribute of sovereignty, embodied in the architecture of the royal court.

Another Khivan author, ʿAbdullāh Bāltaev (1890–1966), described how the Qonghrat ruler Muḥammad Raḥīm Khān II used to visit the estates of his numerous offspring, scattered across different parts of the khanate. Such visits were usually accompanied by the hearing of petitions from the population (*ʿarż surāghāndūr*), in a room specially set aside for this purpose in such

143 Muḥammad Yūsuf Bayānī, *Shajara-yi Khwārazmshāhī*, MS Tashkent, IVANRUz, inv. no. 9596, fol. 250b.

144 ʿAbdullāh Bāltaev, *Khīva-da Tāsh-ḥawlī binā-sīning tāpāgrafiyasī*, Khiva 1950, MS Tashkent, IVANRUz, inv. no. 9321, fols. 3b, 5b.

145 *Avval vaqtdā ʿarż sūrāsh ūchūn qīlinādūrghān ʿimāratnī bāshlādī. Khīvanī pāytakhtī būlghān kuhna arīk avvalghī khānlārdīn qālghān īdāra būlghānī ūchūn būl jāy bitgāncha shūl kuhna arīkda ʿarż-dād sūrāb ūltūrdī 1839-nchī mīlādīdīn kiyin shūl bināgha qūshūb ʿarż-khāna binālārnī ham bāshlāb āltī yil īchindā ānī ham bitkāzdī 1254-nchī hijrī yilindā khān ūyindā ūltūrghān vaqtdā khalqnīng ʿarżlārīnī shūl banā qīlgān ʿarż-khānadā sūrāshnī davām qīldīrdī*; ibid., fol. 10a.

146 Muḥammad Yūsuf Bayānī, *Shajara-yi Khwārazmshāhī*, MS Tashkent, IVANRUz, inv. no. 9596, fol. 298a.

estates.[147] The same Muḥammad Raḥīm Khān II preferred to spend most of the long scorching Khorezmian summer in his suburban residence of Qibla Tāza-Bāgh. Here too he ordered the construction of an *ʿarż-khāna*, worthy of its royal function (*pādshālīqgha lāyiq*), where the sovereign also occupied himself with the settling of the grievances and suits filed by his subjects (*khalqī ʿarż-dādīnī ham shūl ḥāvlīda tīnglār īdī*).[148]

Further eloquent attestation to the importance of the Khivan ruler's participation in the regular hearing of lawsuits is found in a description left by Bābājān Tarrāh (1878–1971), who served Muḥammad Raḥīm Khān II as court poet and scribe (*mīrzā*). Describing the last years of the khan's reign, the author reports that the deterioration of the ruler's health, especially his partial paralysis, made the regular holding of hearing grievances very difficult (*khalqnī ʿarż-dādīgha chīqīshgha yaramas buldī*).[149] The khan himself, according to Tarrāh, proposed that the hearing of grievances from the public be delegated to the hereditary prince, Isfandiyār Tūra. Clearly fearing rumors among the population and possible disturbances caused by the absence of the ruler,[150] the khan's retinue was able to ensure his continuous personal involvement in the procedure. Here, Tarrāh puts an interesting argument into the mouth of one of the courtiers addressing the khan: 'Your Majesty! You have read the history; it is not proper [for the ruler] to devolve his authority (*ikhtiyār*) to his heir during his lifetime.'[151]

---

147 Specifically, he did this during his visits to his sons ʿIbādullāh Tūra in Rāfanīk and ʿAṣqar Maḥmūd Tūra, see ʿAbdullāh Bāltaev, *Khīva īsdalīklārī*, MS Tashkent, IVANRUz, inv. no. 11645, fols. 39b–40a; 82a.

148 Ibid., fol. 35b.

149 Bobojon Tarroh-Khodim, *Khorazm shoir va navozandalari*, p. 30. According to the author, he was tasked by the sovereign with keeping a record of, among other things, the khanate's poets and writers (*shoir*) and their creative works. As a result, he was in close contact not only with court literary circles but also with many prominent officials who regarded the composition of poetry as an effective way to make a successful career at court. Between 1965 and 1967, Tarrāh compiled an anthology of thirty-one court poets, along with his personal recollections. The first abridged edition of the text was published in 1994 as Bobojon Tarroh Azizov-Khodim, *Khorazm shoir va navozandalari. XIX asr okhiri–XX asr boshlarida Sayid Muhammad Rahimkhoni soniy davrida yashagan shoirlar haqida esdaliklar*, ed. Davlatyor Rahim (Tashkent: G'afur G'ulom nomidagi Adabiyot va san'at nashriyoti, 1994).

150 There was a genuine threat of potential uprisings in Khiva in the last month of Muḥammad Raḥīm Khān II's life, due to the incapacity of the ruler, as the extensive correspondence of representatives of the Russian colonial administration in Petro-Aleksandrovsk, Tashkent and St. Petersburg makes clear. For details, see Abdurasulov and Sartori, *Neopredelennost' kak politika: razmyshliaia o prirode rossiiskogo protektorata v Srednei Azii*, pp. 129–133.

151 Tarroh-Khodim, *Khorazm shoir va navozandalari*, p. 30. Russian officials who were with the khan at this time report that right until the end of his life, Muḥammad Raḥīm Khān treated his personal involvement in the reception of citizens' appeals with utmost solemnity and punctiliousness, refusing to even countenance the idea of entrusting the

As a result, a special 'carriage' (*araba*) was constructed to bring the khan to the 'chamber of petitions' (*'arż-jāy*) immediately before the ceremony. During the reception of petitioners, one of the court attendants (*'arż-dād maḥramī*), a certain Dawlat Murād Maḥram, would prop up the khan's back as he sat on his throne. 'Thus,' concludes Bābājān Tarrāh, 'Muḥammad Raḥīm Khān II heard the grievances of his subjects even within one year [of his death].'[152]

The regular hearing of public grievances had to be ensured, even during periods when the supreme ruler found himself outside of the khanate. The Khivan historian Ḥasan Murād Laffasī (1880–1949) informs us, for example, that Isfandiyār Khān during his periodic visits to St. Petersburg for an audience with the Russian emperor, appointed proxies for receiving public grievances (*fuqarānīng 'arż-dādī ūchūn*).[153] The same practice was also used by the khan when he found himself outside of the capital in extraordinary circumstances.[154]

Thus, for the khan himself and for those around him, the *'arż-dād* was more than simply a ritualised ceremonial. It is clear that it was an important attribute of the sovereign's power, an indicator of his ability to rule over territories that were highly varied both in account of their ecological niches and their social geography. Another episode that is telling in this respect occurred at the end of the reign of Isfandiyār Khān (r. 1910–1918). It is described in detail in the memoirs of Pahlavān Niyāz Ḥājjī Yusupov. In April 1917, against the backdrop of the revolutionary events in Petrograd, and under pressure from local reformers, the Khivan ruler Isfandiyār Khān was forced to support a range of legislative initiatives, designed to place significant limits on the power of the sovereign and, effectively, to establish a constitutional monarchy. The Young Khivans, who initiated the reform process, wanted to transfer most of the monarch's powers to the new representative body of a 'parliament' (*majlis*). Nonetheless they felt unable to strip the khan of his prerogative of receiving petitions from the population. Yusupov relates how Isfandiyār Khān became 'beside himself with anger' during a debate with political opponents who accused him of

---

ceremony to any of his close associates, including the hereditary prince Isfandiyār. When Rachinskii suggested that the khan should cancel his daily reception of petitioners, the latter replied that, 'it was not within his power,' see *Donesenie vracha Rachinskogo*, 29.05.1910, TsGARUz, f. I-2, op. 1, d. 291, ll. 28–28ob.

152 Tarroh-Khodim, *Khorazm shoir va navozandalari*, p. 30.

153 Ḥasan-Murād Laffasī, *Gulshan-i sa'ādat*, MS Tashkent, IVANRUz, inv. no. 7797, fols. 8a–8b, 17b, 80b, 83b.

154 One such circumstance, for example, occurred in spring 1916, when Isfandiyār Khān travelled, with all of his officials, to Tashhawz for a meeting with Lieutenant General A.S. Galkin, governor general of the Syr-Darya Province, after the latter had suppressed a large Turkmen uprising. At that time, the Khivan *qāżī* Dāmullā Khudāy Birgān Ākhund remained in Khiva in order to hear the claims of the public; ibid., fol. 64a.

attempting to usurp power in contradiction of the agreed legislative initiatives. In his rage, the khan exclaimed: 'I have already given over all of my administrative powers and authority (*ḥukūmatning ikhtīyārī*) to the parliament. The only powers that I have retained is the daily examination of petitions from the population (*ʿarż*).'[155] Thus, the *ʿarż*, in this narrative of Pahlavān Niyāz Ḥājjī Yusupov, even in the perception of the political players in Khorezm, appears as an exceptional prerogative enjoyed by the khan, and the essential attribute of his authority, without which it was impossible for him to be presented or perceived as a sovereign.

There are plenty of examples in the Muslim tradition of the image of a just ruler, who was able and ready to take an interest in and resolve the problems of his subjects, and act as the source of justice. However, in Khiva this was far more than mere symbolism: it was an important mechanism of administration. This prerogative and duty of the khan to 'dispense justice', which was so important even in ordinary times, took on an exceptional importance in the context of the turbulence experienced by Khorezm during the second decade of the twentieth century.

Indeed, at the end of 1915, the elites of various Khivan provinces,[156] supported by authoritative religious leaders called *īshāns*,[157] initiated an uprising against the central power, leading to the overthrow of Isfandiyār Khān and his closest associates. While accusing the authorities of various abuses, the leaders of the revolt also articulated the idea that the khan was unable to ensure the normal functioning of the mechanism of conflict resolution between his subjects. As one of the leaders of the revolt, a certain Muḥammad Amīn Dargha, put it, 'the population of the region of Manghit … are especially unhappy that the Turkmen headmen: Junayd Khān, Khān Īshān and Khwājam Khān … even settle the [internal] affairs of the Uzbeks, when the latter appeal to them.' In this situation, according to Dargha, 'the population undoubtedly feels the burden of the overlapping systems of authority.'[158] The inability of the central agencies to respond promptly and authoritatively to such petitions from their

155 Pahlavān Niyāz Ḥājjī, [*Khāṭiralar*]. MS Khiva, Private Collection of Anvar Otaboev, fol. 108.

156 The inhabitants of the Khivan provinces of Khoja-eli, Qiyat, Gurlen and Manghit took part in the uprisings; see Niiazmetov, *Poisk konsensusa. Rossiisko-khivinskie geopoliticheskie otnosheniia v XVI–nachale XX v.*, pp. 424–426.

157 According to the Russian colonial authorities, 'all the most prominent *īshāns* of the khanate,' took part in the uprisings, 'wishing to make an 'admonition' to the Khan, about his failure to live and act according to the *sharīʿa*' [Kolosovskii] *Raport Turkestanskomu General-Gubernatoru. 21.01.1916*, TsGARUz, f. I-2, op. 2, d. 546, l. 45.

158 [Magomed Amin Dargha Irnazarov], *Pokazaniia. 20.01.1916*, TsGARUz, f. I-2, op. 2, d. 546, l. 63.

subjects was leading to constant breaches of social harmony. The citizens were therefore forced to seek new sources of power to whom they could turn for the settlement of their disputes.[159] For example, due to the weakened authority of Isfandiyār Khān and his successor Sayyid ʿAbdullāh Khān during the years 1918–1919, the inhabitants of the regions of Khorezm were often obliged to take their grievances to the Turkmen leader Junayd Khān. Even so, our documents show that Junayd still found it worthwhile to follow the existing protocol, sending over the petitioners themselves, as well as the decisions on specific petitions for review and/or confirmation by the khan's court in Khiva.[160]

To ensure the hearing of grievances even in times of political turbulence represented for Khivan rulers a powerful instrument of governance. Following the death of the Khivan khan Muḥammad Amīn in 1855, for example, Sayyid ʿAbdullāh Khān was raised to the throne. The proclamation of the new khan did not follow the established dynastic tradition, which caused discontent and even open resistance from among influential court circles. In these circumstances, the Khivan chronicler Bayānī narrates, one of the first actions of the newly appointed khan was to announce to the population that, 'whenever there are petitioners (*dādkhwāh*) [...] our gates will always be open' to them, 'so that they can inform [us] at any moment of their misfortunes.'[161] Sayyid ʿAbdullāh Khān evidently aimed by this initiative (a) to send a message to the different groups of the population about his ability to carry out the key functions of a sovereign, and (b) to use his accessibility and openness to the needs of his subjects as a resource, allowing him to enlist the support and recognition of the population. This resource could then act as a counter-weight to the influence of his political opponents.

The accessibility of the khan was perhaps significantly more obvious than in other Central Asian Muslim polities of that time. But was the proximity of the Qonghrat subjects to the authorities in Khiva simply an illusion? It does not appear so. The Russian Turkologist Alexander Samoilovich, on a mission to Central Asia in 1906 and 1907, noted that 'the Khivan khan administers his people directly: every day he holds trials and dispenses justice, and every Khivan [subject] can attend his audience, unlike the Bukharan emir, who keeps himself far removed from his subjects behind a wall of officials and

159 As the governor of the Khiva province of Khoja-eli noted, a situation emerged where, 'it was as if there are several khans and nobody knows which one to submit to,' [Avez Khodja Murtaza Khodjaev], *Pokazaniia. 20.01.1916*, TsGARUz, f. I-2, op. 2, d. 545, l. 62.

160 E.g., see Doc. 45.

161 *Shavqat yūzīdīn amr ītdī dādkhwāhlār har qāchān kīlsalār ishīkīmīz yūzlārīga āchūq būlsūn hamma vaqtda kilīb ʿarżlārīn aytābīrsūnlār*, Muḥammad Yūsuf Bayānī, *Shajara-yi Khwārazmshāhī*, MS Tashkent, IVANRUz, inv. no. 9596, fol. 356b.

paperwork.'[162] His contemporary A. Kalmykov, an official serving the Russian Ministry of Foreign Affairs, similarly stated in 1910, that 'the Khanate of Khiva has maintained its patriarchal way of life to a greater degree than Bukhara. Every day the khan receives any subjects who have requests or grievances to bring to him, and he holds a firmer control over the activity of his officials.'[163]

A similar image of the accessible khan eager to listen to small stories of private misfortunes, is colorful illustrated by the case of the Russian merchant Ambrosimov, who in the 1840s managed to submit a personal appeal to the Khivan ruler Muḥammad Amīn Khān (r. 1845–1855). The description is remarkable since it records one of the few instances where an ethnic Russian not only successfully visited Khiva on his own initiative,[164] but also managed to gain permission from the khan to carry out trade in the Khivan bazaar. His account provides some fascinating evidence about the internal life of the Khanate of Khiva and, particularly importantly for our purposes, some specific details concerning the process of the *ʿarż* at the court of the Qonghrat rulers.[165]

When Ambrosimov arrived in Khiva, he received permission to enter the bazaar. At the same time, on the personal orders of the khan, he had all of his Russian coins taken from him, in return for which the Khivan authorities were supposed to pay him in units of local currency to the corresponding amount.[166] When, after a certain time, however, Ambrosimov had still not received the

162 A.N. Samoilovich, *Opisanie rukopisei knig, khraniashchikhsia v Khivinskikh pridvornykh knigokhranilishchakh i knigo-pechatniakh*, MS St Petersburg, RNB, f. 671, op. 1, d. 145, l. 1.

163 [A.D. Kalmykov] *Sostoianie Khivinskogo khanstva i zhelatel'nye reformy*, TsGARUz, f. I-2, op. 1, d. 291, l. 101.

164 The Khivan authorities were exceptionally suspicious of any foreigners. Even official Russian delegations were treated by the Khivan authorities with a high level of suspicion, and were strictly limited in their movements and contacts. For private individuals, especially ethnic Russians, the opportunities for visiting the khanate were extremely limited due to the opposition of the Khivan authorities. The interests of the few Russian merchants who traded with Khiva, were represented largely by Tatar and/or Armenian commercial agents, see Murav'ev, *Puteshestvie v Turkmeniiu i Khivu v 1819 i 1820 godakh*, pt. 2, p. 52; Turpaev, *Dnevnik perevodchika armianina Turpaeva*, p. 276; N. Mikhailov, "Rasskaz torgovtsa Ambrosimova o poezdke ego v Khivu," in *Materialy dlia statistiki Turkestanskogo kraia. Vol.* 2 (St. Petersburg: Tipografiia K.V. Trubnikova, 1873), pp. 23–24.

165 In fairness, the Russian merchant does not use this terminology. However, his description, and the sequence of events regarding the response to his petition, indicate that his description is one of the first witnesses to the *ʿarż* at the court of the Qonghrat rulers of Khorezm.

166 The Khivan authorities took these steps due to the severe shortage of precious metals in the khanate. Indeed, foreign coins were taken from both local and foreign merchants and re-struck into Khivan coins, see Murav'ev, *Puteshestvie v Turkmeniiu i Khivu v 1819 i 1820 godakh*, pt. 2, pp. 42, 52; "Opisanie Khivinskogo khanstva, sostavlennoe v 1842 g. podpolkovnikom G.I. Danilevskim," p. 139. L. Meier, "Kirgizskaia step' Orenburgskogo

promised money, he decided to remind the khan of his debt. Let us now turn to the pretext that Ambrosimov used to gain access to the monarch of Khiva:

> Four days later [after my arrival in Khiva], I decided to go to the khan myself. When I entered a wing [of the palace], one of the courtiers asked me the reason why I had come. I said that I had a request for the khan, but did not specify ... When I entered the hall ... [the khan] asked me why I had come, and whether I had a request for him. I did not explain to him directly that I had come for the money, but first spoke of a claim I had against one of my Kyrgyz [=Qazaq] debtors, who did not want to pay me his debt of 36 sheep.[167]

From the description it is clear that Ambrosimov knew perfectly well that one of the few opportunities for ordinary residents, including himself, to address the khan directly was the submission of petitions at the time of the *ʿarż*. Therefore, as a pretext to meet with the Khivan ruler, Ambrosimov referred not to his most actually pressing purpose, but rather to his debt dispute with a certain Qazaq merchant. It was this that he told the gatekeeper at the palace, providing him with the basis for his admission to the khan's presence. Naturally, this raises the question of how a Russian merchant, who had only just arrived in Khiva, knew about such a practice. It seems very likely that Ambrosimov received this information at the Khivan bazaar where he traded, and where, as he himself said, 'he made a fairly large range of acquaintances' and 'was friendly to everyone.'[168] Thus, the image of the khan whom his subjects could approach with their petitions was widely known and, in a way, a routine affair, sufficiently well known to every Khivan subject that even a Russian merchant, who had only just arrived in the city, could quickly learn about it.

Meanwhile, the narrative is no less remarkable for the way it enables us to reconstruct some of the procedural aspects of the process by which the khan heard petitions from his subjects:

> In response [to my grievance], the khan said, 'If your debtor refuses to pay, how can you prove [that what you say is true] ...?' I replied that all my workers know that he [the debtor] took the merchandise, and the headman who arrived with me also knows that. The khan first ordered for

vedomostva," in *Materialy dlia geografii i statistiki Rossii, sobrannye ofitserami General'nogo shtaba* (St Petersburg: Tipografii E. Veimara i F. Persona, 1865), pp. 209, 214.

167 Mikhailov, *Rasskaz torgovtsa Ambrosimova o poezdke ego v Khivu*, p. 365.

168 Ibid., 19.

> the headman to be sent for and asked him, whether the Kyrgyz [=Qazaq] was really in debt to me. The sultan confirmed this ... [Only after this] the khan ordered for my debtor to be sent for. When the [accused] Kyrgyz was brought by one sultan, I did not recognize him, [as] he was so frightened by the look that the khan gave him and the fierceness of his question, 'Are you in his debt?' The Kyrgyz answered in the affirmative ... Perhaps he would have denied it, if he had not noticed the mullah there, and so probably thought that he would have to testify on oath ...[169]

Given that the version of Ambrosimov's narrative that has come down to us was set down in writing not by himself but by the traveler Mikhailov, one may be led to question the accuracy of such information. Nonetheless, the description of the hearing of a claim at the court of the Khivan khan, as presented by Ambrosimov, largely corresponds to the procedures and protocols of the system of *ʿarż-dād* that we find reported in later sources, as we shall see below. As is also clear from the narrative, the khan responded to the petition of Ambrosimov by clarifying the evidential basis of the latter's claim. Only once he had done so did he order for the defendant to be brought to him. The description of the interrogation of the Qazaq defendant explains the presence during this procedure of a certain mullah (presumably a *qāżī*), who was ready if necessary – which is to say, if the defendant denied the claim – to make the latter testify on oath. This is another important feature of the procedure, which appears on several occasions in our documents, and which we will describe in more detail below. Finally, a third aspect revealed by Ambrosimov's description is the idea of communal responsibility: if the defendant fails to pay, it is incumbent upon his relatives or other members of his community to fulfil his obligations to the creditor.

At the conclusion of this hearing at the khan's court, the creditor received what he had requested. Then, once the claim had already been resolved, Ambrosimov took the opportunity to raise with the khan the question of the return of his money, thereby finally contriving to address the real reason of his visit to the khan.

Hence, the involvement of the royal court in the hearing of grievances, and the khan's direct or delegated involvement in settling conflicts between his subjects, had both practical and symbolic significance. The latter manifested itself in the ritualization of the ceremony, which reflected the khan's willingness to delve into the concerns and needs of his subjects and to administer

---

169 Mikhailov, *Rasskaz torgovtsa Ambrosimova o poezdke ego v Khivu*, pp. 365–366.

justice. For subjects throughout the khanate, this procedure was a unique opportunity to meet their ruler, convey their grievances to him personally, and receive assistance in the resolution of their disputes.[170] It is no accident that Lykoshin characterizes the procedure as 'a ceremony of singular service to the people, which gave the khan the reputation of being available to each of his subjects, personally listening to their grievances and restoring justice through his orders and decisions.'[171]

The motivations that prompted the populace to file their claims with the royal court varied considerably. They usually reflected the widely shared perception that agencies in Khiva were more powerful than provincial officeholders, such as a *qāżī*, and that the royal court's sanctioning of a ruling would ensure its execution. This state of affairs manifested itself well beyond the borders of the khanate. Qonghrat officials, for example, solved conflicts among the Qazaqs living in the Ust Yurt plateau and on the banks of the Uil River, who were formally Russian imperial subjects.[172]

Qonghrat officials arguably devoted so much attention to the mundane affairs of their subjects because the *ʿarż-dād* offered the central government the opportunity to monitor local affairs in a regular fashion and thus to make timely adjustments in response to changing social circumstances. Justice mattered to Qonghrat officials because it provided the state with knowledge about the society over which it ruled. Equally, the Khivan legal system allowed subjects to speak and be heard. Justice was contingent on participation.

Therefore, we know that at least for the duration of the Qonghrat period there was a ritualised ceremony at the court of the rulers of Khiva called the *ʿarż* or *ʿarż-dād*. We also know that it had real significance both for the ruling elite and for the population at large. However, what do we know about its procedures, if we exclude passing references by local Khivan authors and accounts by occasional travelers? Which individuals were involved in the proceedings of dispute settlements? How did the process work, what was the protocol, and which agencies were involved? The following sections will allow us to answer these, and other questions.

---

170 'During the *ars* (<*ʿarż*) not only [big] cases are decided, but [also] small family and domestic quarrels are being settled: a neighbour [can] drag [his] neighbour to court because of a few pennies, the neighbour of the neighbour because of a stolen chicken. No one is denied [a hearing],' A. Vamberi, *Ocherki Srednei Azii* (*dopolnenie k "Puteshestviiu po Srednei Azii"*) (Moscow: Tipografiia A.I. Mamontova, 1868), p. 86.

171 N.S. Lykoshin, *Zapiska Nachal'nika Amu-Dar'inskogo Otdela Polkovnika Lykoshina o sovremennom sostoianii Khivinskogo Khanstva, 1912 god*, TsGARUz, f. I-2, op. 1, d. 314, ll. 15–15 ob.

172 Terent'ev, *Istoriia zavoevaniia Srednei Azii s kartami i planami*, I, p. 179.

5 On Protocol

One of the few descriptions of the procedure of the *ʿarż-dād*, and perhaps the most detailed, belongs to the pen of Lykoshin, an official serving the Russian colonial administration in Turkestan. In late May 1912, just after his appointment as Head of the Amu-Darya Department, Lykoshin made his first journey for purposes of intelligence gathering to the lands within the Khanate of Khiva on the left bank of the Amu Darya. On arrival in Khiva, Lykoshin was received by senior khanal officials and was lodged in one of the rooms of the diplomatic suite, within the residence of Isfandiyār Khān. By a fortunate coincidence, one of the windows from this suite looked into the inner court of the khan's palace, where he used to take petitions from the population at this time.[173] This auspicious circumstance allowed the Russian officer to observe the entire ceremony of the *ʿarż-dād*, which he then described in the following account:[174]

> About six o'clock in the evening, the usually deserted courtyard, decorated with tall columns in the Moorish style, suddenly perked up ... Sometime later, the harem door opened, whence Isfandiyār Khān Bahādir proceeded to the place where he sits to mete out judgment and punishment. Not far from the only entrance into the courtyard there is a small stone platform, covered with a large felt mat. The khan sits on the dais in Asian style (*po-aziatski*), and before him they lay out an ancient gun in its case and a small hatchet, also old: these are the insignia of power. The khan wears an expensive gold-trimmed sabre of the Asian type, and on his head, in place of the usual fur hat, he has an equally large hat of lamb fur, but with a red top; this hat is the equivalent of a crown. By the khan's hand they place a kettle of green tea and a cup. Even before the khan's entrance, a *maḥram* ['khan's close associates'] takes up a position not far from the khan's dais and stands perfectly still, with his head bare. From time to time, these *maḥrams* are silently replaced by others newly entered into the courtyard. The old man Yūsuf Yasāvulbāshī begins the ceremony ... The time for parsing the people's grievances has come ... The khan's subjects complain to him about each other and ask for the

173 According to ʿAbdullāh Bāltaev, the diplomatic suite was located to the east of the *ʿarż-khāna*, and was constructed in 1874, in the 'European style' for Russian officials visiting the khanate, ʿAbdullāh Bāltaev, *Khīva īsdalīklārī*, MS Tashkent, IVANRUz, inv. no. 11645, fols. 39a, 69b.

174 N.S. Lykoshin, *Zapiska Nachal'nika Amu-Dar'inskogo Otdela Polkovnika Lykoshina o sovremennom sostoianii Khivinskogo Khanstva, 1912 god*, TsGARUz, f. I-2, op. 1, d. 314, ll. 15–16 ob.

> restoration of rights violated by others of his subjects. The petitioner, having entered through the door, stops at the entrance, quite far from the khan, so his grievance is pronounced in a very loud patter, the supplicant almost yelling, as if he hopes to prove the severity of his grievances and to penetrate the soul of the khan with his cries. The khan, having allowed the supplicant to finish his brief grievance, says only one word, turning to the *yasāvulbāshī*. This is probably an order to sort out the case. The petitioner exits, another enters.[175]

For all its virtues, this description obviously comes with a heavy dose of orientalist colour. Lykoshin was not simply a colonial official but also a prolific author and he could not resist the temptation to exercise a little literary flair here. He did not simply want to give a dry account of the procedural aspects, but tried to convey the atmosphere and spirit of the ceremony, and even its emotional context. His attention was caught by the 'tall columns in the Moorish style,' that adorned the room of the *ʿarż-khāna*, the very way that the ruler moved, 'not walking, but rather following,' the details of the latter's dress, the variety of the 'insignia of his power,' and emotions of the petitioners.

Nevertheless, Lykoshin's narrative, especially on points of procedural detail, is largely confirmed by the account of Bābājān Safarov, who was a contemporary of Isfandiyār Khān, although writing in the Soviet period. The differences between the descriptions of the *ʿarż-dād* in the writings of Lykoshin and Safarov are largely generic. After all, they were catering to different audiences: Safarov cobbled together an historical survey about the khanate, commissioned by Muhammadjon Yŭldoshev, a famous Uzbek Soviet academic working on the Khanate of Khiva, which was full of clichés about the despotic nature of Qonghrat rule. Lykoshin, instead, wrote under Tsarist rule and gathered intelligence for colonial agencies in Tashkent. While Lykoshin's description creates an atmosphere of wonderment summoned by the otherness of Khivan courtly culture, Safarov's detailed descriptions about 'executioners (*jallād*) standing with bared sabers,' 'guardsmen (*īshīk-āghā*), armed with axes,' or the foreman (*dahabāshī*)[176] accompanying the petitioner with a sabre 'at the ready,' conjure

175 Ibid.

176 *Dahabāshī* ('commander of the tenth'). According to Safarov, there were ten *dahabāshīs* at the royal palace in Khiva, each of them with ten *yasāvuls* under his command. During the hearing of people's grievances at court, the *dahabāshī* was responsible for escorting the supplicant to the audience-hall before the khan, see Bābājān Safarov, *Khwārazm taʾrīkhī (1864–1934)*, MS Tashkent, IVANRUz, inv. no. 1023, fol. 15b.

up images of the purported brutality of Khivan rulers.[177] But let us look more closely at Safarov's description:

> To receive petitions from the public (*fuqarālārnīng ʿarżdādlārī*), the khan dispenses justice (*ʿarż-dād qīlādī*) on a daily basis, sitting on his throne for one hour. Beside him sit the *qushbigī*, the *mihtar*, the *naqīb*, the *ātālik*, and the *shaykh al-Islām*.[178] The *mīrshab*,[179] together with ten other people – the *yūzbāshī*[180] and the *jallāds* – stand beside the khan

177 It should be noted that this same feeling of fear and timidity experienced by a subject when taking a complaint to the Khivan sovereign was also mentioned by the merchant Ambrosimov, discussed above. According to him, 'I had never felt [such fear] before the Russian authorities.' The face of Ambrosimov's respondent, a Qazaq merchant, was so disfigured by fear, that the Russian merchant hardly recognised him, see Mikhailov, *Rasskaz torgovtsa Ambrosimova o poezdke ego v Khivu*, p. 365.

178 Yuri Bregel noted that under the rule of the Qonghrats the *shaykh al-Islām* was prominent in name only, while the nature of his functions remains absolutely unclear. See Munis and Agahi, *Firdaws al-iqbāl: History of Khorezm*, p. 560.

179 *Mīrshab* is a term widely employed in records from 19th-century Central Asia to denote individuals fulfilling policing duties in urban settlements under the rule of the three Muslim principalities. It is important to clarify that much of the literature available on the administration of the Khanate of Khiva suggests that the *mīrshab* was on duty exclusively at night, see Urunbaev, A. et al. (eds.), *Katalog khivinskikh kaziiskikh dokumentov XIX–nachala XX vv.* (Tashkent, Kyoto: Izdatel'stvo Mezhdunarodnogo instituta po izucheniiu iazykov i mira Kiotskogo universiteta po izucheniiu zarubezhnykh stran, 2001), p. 658. There is no clear evidence which could be used in support of this argument. It should be also noted that according to Yuri Bregel, the post of *mīrshab* did not exist in the Khanate of Khiva, see Munis and Agahi, *Firdaws al-iqbāl: History of Khorezm*, p. 624, note 736, while Yŭldoshev notes, instead, that *mīrshab* were on duties everywhere in Khrorezm in every city and village (*shahar va daha mirshablari bŭlgan*), see his *Khiva khonligida feodal yer egaligi va davlat tuzilishi*, p. 280. Bābājān Safarov adds that the *mīrshab* represented also an office at the royal court, i.e., a man who was at the head of the guards in the citadel of Khiva and who was also responsible for policing duties in other cities (*khān pāytakhtīnī va shaharnī sāqlāvchī pāshshāflārnīng hamda jallādlārnīng bāshlūghī*), see his *Khwārazm taʾrīkhī (1864–1934)*, MS Tashkent, IVANRUz, inv. no. 10231, fol. 15a.

180 *Yūzbāshī* (lit. 'commandant of one hundred'; 'centurion') was a term used to denote a middle-rank office-holder in the military hierarchy of the Khanate of Khiva. In local sources, the term is applied to commandants (*sarkār*) of units of the Khivan arm, see Munis and Agahi, *Firdaws al-iqbāl: History of Khorezm*, p. 209. Munis also refers to an episode when Muḥammad Raḥīm Khān I in 1809 conferred grants on a certain Badal for his heroism while at the head of a unit of 100 *nawkars*, see ibid., 295. According to diplomas, the *yasāvulbāshī* appointed 'attendants' (*yasāvul*) to settle disputes among a pool of liegemen (*nawkar*) who usually were at the service of *yuzbāshīs* in Khiva. It seems there were ten such *yuzbāshīs* operating at the royal court, see Bābājān Safarov, *Khwārazm taʾrīkhī (1864–1934)*, MS Tashkent, IVANRUz, inv. no. 10231, fol. 15. At the same time, Khivan authors more often than not failed to distinguish between civil and

> with sabres bared. Two *īshīk-āghās*, armed with axes and knives, stand on either side of the gate, guarding the entrance to the reception room (*ʿarż-khāna*). Summoning the [next] petitioner (*ʿarżchī*), the foremen (*dahabāshī*) with unsheathed sabres, lead him into the reception room, where the *yasāvulbāshī* stands between the khan and the petitioner, who stops thirty metres from the khan's throne. [The *yasāvulbāshī*] conveys the petitioner's greeting and his petition to the khan and transmits the khan's questions and decision to the petitioner. So it occurs and has become the custom (*ʿurf-ʿādat*), that the khan should not communicate directly (*ūz tūghrisīdān*) with his subjects (*fuqarālār*).[181]

These passages from Lykoshin and Safarov offer a glimpse of early twentieth-century practices and, specifically, recount the ceremony as it was during the reign of Isfandiyār Khān (r. 1910–18). Emphasizing the ancient origin of the ceremony that, in his words, 'reeks of the past,' Lykoshin evidently assumed that what he saw reflected a long-standing legal practice taking place at the royal court. Similarly, Safarov's characterization of the ceremony as 'custom' (*ʿurf-ʿādat*) attests indirectly to the perceived antiquity of this practice.

Lykoshin and Safarov illuminate two key elements of the *ʿarż-dād* that point to the peculiarity of the practice. The first element, which is procedural, concerns the manner in which petitioners appealed to the ruler. Claimants always petitioned the khan orally and directly. Similarly, the ruler's response to a particular petition was delivered orally, through the medium of the *yasāvulbāshī*. It is tempting to see in the oral dimension of such petitions a manifestation of

---

military offices and therefore the term *yūzbāshī* could be also used to denote administrative functions. For example, Lykoshin refers to a certain Mamat Yūzbāshī who served in the capacity of governor of Gazavat in 1912 (*Sovremennoe raspredelenie vlasti v Khanstve Khivinskom, 1912 god*, TsGARUz, f. I-2, op. 1, d. 314, l. 64 ob.) and to another *yūzbāshī* who was at the head of Aq-Tepe and operated in the function of adjunct of the governor of Hilali (N.S. Lykoshin, *Zapiska Nachal'nika Amu-Dar'inskogo Otdela Polkovnika Lykoshina o sovremennom sostoianii Khivinskogo Khanstva, 1912 god*, TsGARUz, f. I-2, op. 1, d. 314, l. 45 ob.). On the *yūzbāshī* being the second most important officeholder at the provincial level after the governor (*ḥākim*) and working at the latter's instructions, see also S. Navruzov, "Puteshestvenniki i uchenye ob administrativnom ustroistve Khivinskogo khanstva XIX – nachala XX veka," *Obshchestvennye nauki v Uzbekistane* (1991/10), p. 47. On account of the information available in this report we can safely assume that Bahādir Maḥram Yūzbāshī was the governor of Tashhawz.

181 Bābājān Safarov, *Khwārazm taʾrīkhī (1864–1934)*, MS Tashkent, IVANRUz, inv. no. 10231, fols. 18b–19b.

earlier juridical practices, when the khan heard public grievances; and such practices are attested during the rule of Muḥammad Raḥīm Khān I.[182]

The second key element of the *ʿarż-dād* is the centrality of the *yasāvulbāshī*. This element is clearly institutional, for his function was not limited to attending the ceremony or to serving as an intermediary between the khan and the petitioner. The *yasāvulbāshī* and the special office under him (*yasāvulbāshī khiẕmatī*) would be responsible for initiating and overseeing all subsequent investigations into petitions and their resolution, as well as for handling and archiving the resultant documentation.

Even so, for all the remarkable detail of the two descriptions, they are both quite static. They describe the procedure and the practice of the ceremony, and actions limited specifically to the room in which the reception of grievances occurred. These writings offer very limited space for the reconstruction of the legal and administrative practices, which preceded, and, especially importantly, followed the appeal of the petitioner to the khan. In this respect Lykoshin's description could well lead a potential reader astray. Let us take, for example, the following conclusion drawn by Lykoshin, regarding the procedural aspects of the *ʿarż-dād*:

> It is hard to say to what degree matters of grievance brought to the khan are investigated ... However, informed people have said that ... it is not rare for even the most basic pieces of evidence to be lost in this simplified oral dispensation of justice ... [It can happen that] a grievance is taken to the khan for a second time, [in that case] the khan wishes to know the current state of the matter. Then the first person, to whom the matter has been entrusted, the *yasāvulbāshī*, summons the petitioner himself, and asks him, 'What did I tell you, when you came last time with your grievance?' The petitioner ... says to whom he was sent the first time. They summon the official ... and then there is nothing to be done, but to ask the petitioner [about the preceding course of investigation of the petition].[183]

It is unclear who is meant by the 'informed people,' to whose 'authoritative' opinion Lykoshin so readily appeals for his characterization of the hearings. However, the excerpt makes it very clear that we must confront the following questions: to what degree was the procedure of hearing petitions from subjects 'a simplified oral dispensation of justice,' as Lykoshin characterizes

182 Munis and Agahi, *Firdaws al-iqbāl: History of Khorezm*, pp. 423, 457.

183 N.S. Lykoshin, *Zapiska Nachal'nika Amu-Dar'inskogo Otdela Polkovnika Lykoshina o sovremennom sostoianii Khivinskogo Khanstva, 1912 god*, TsGARUz, f. I-2, op. 1, d. 314, ll. 16–16ob.

it? Did it really have an exclusively *oral* character, and did it really leave no documentary traces outside the walls of the *ʿarż-khāna*? What, in general, do we know about the further procedure, in particular from the time when, as Safarov and Lykoshin tell us, the *yasāvulbāshī* was entrusted by the khan with investigation of the matter? How was the process of following up a given episode carried out? Which agencies, whether in the capital or in the regions – at the level of the provincial governor or in local communities – could be brought into the process of hearing an appeal from a subject? Which mechanisms and practices were used to bring different sides of a conflict to a compromise? We will now turn directly to the documents of our collection, which help us to answer these questions, and to reveal the truly dynamic and complex world of relations of power, social connections, and legal processes within the Khanate of Khiva.

6 Documents

6.1 *Fatak*s

The *yasāvulbāshī* had a chancery referred to in the documents as the *khiẕmat*. The latter was housed in its own premises at the ruler's palace, and included scribes (*dīvān*), as well as a staff of *yasāvul*s – officials, mostly guards, with specific commissions.[184] The Khivan author Bābājān Tarrāh, who had himself served at the khan's court, reported that the *yasāvulbāshī* would follow an established procedure (*tartīb*), by asking the appellant about the contents of the petition and, depending on its nature, would then define the further course of its investigation. If necessary, the petition could be sent for a further hearing to the rulers of the cities (*qalʿa ḥākimlārigha*), in accordance with a written order from the royal court (*būyrūq*).[185] Similarly to Tarrāh, Bābājān Safarov also reports that in response to an appeal from subjects to their khan, a rescript (*fatak*) was written, affixed with the seal of 'one of the [two] *yasāvulbāshī*s,

184 A whole range of authors refer to the existence of such chanceries operating under the direction of khanal representatives. For example, Nikolai Murav'ev, who visited the khanate in 1820–21, reported that Khivan high-rank officials, 'each have their own scribe or Mīrzā, each with several officials under them, called the *divanbigi* … whom they use for various tasks,' Murav'ev, *Puteshestvie v Turkmeniiu i Khivu v 1819 i 1820 godakh*, pt. 2, pp. 33–34; see also A. Vamberi, *Puteshchestvie po Srednei Azii* (Moscow: Vostochnaia literatura, 2003), pp. 97–98.

185 Tarroh-Khodim, *Khorazm shoir va navozandalari*, p. 30.

who were in the khan's presence on that day.'[186] It is now to this type of record that we will turn.

Conventionally addressed to the disputing parties, *fatak*s stipulated the appointment of a special attendant who, acting as a plenipotentiary court representative, escorted the plaintiff back to the locale where the wrong had occurred, initiated the investigation with the help of local Qonghrat officials (governors, jurists, and notables), and facilitated the resolution of the conflict. The results of the investigation, together with the stipulations of the settlement, were then brought to the *yasāvulbāshī* office and recorded, in brief, on the reverse of the *fatak*. All these records were deposited at the office of the *yasāvulbāshī*, for use as evidence in the event of some future reopening of the case. The outcome of dispute settlements was duly recorded also in special registries (*daftar*s), containing the names of claimants (*dādkhwāhchīlār*) and attendants, and some basic information about the claim, as well as a summary of the resolution of the conflict.[187] The following example illustrates how the *yasāvulbāshī* appointed a guard as attendant (*yasāvul*) and instructed him to settle the case by means of a *fatak*.

> [*Recto*]
> Muḥammad Murād, from the locality of Vazir [in the province of] Gurlen, had purchased a plot of land [sized] 1,75 *ṭanāb* together with its appurtenances (*va ḥaqqīsī bīla*) from a certain 'Allām Birgān Chakka, who is [also] from Vazir, for 700 *ṭillā*. [The transaction] was notarised (*khaṭlāshīb*). He also bought [from the same individual] millet [to harvest from that plot] for [an additional] 50 *ṭillā*. Now [the seller] neither passed the land [to the purchaser], nor gave him the millet. For this reason (*vajh*), [the latter] filed a claim (*da'vā*) [to the royal court] against 'Allām Birgān Chakka and his son, Īr Muḥammad. Let [the parties] come to royal court (*dargāh-i 'ālī*) together with Qurbān Niyāz Yasāvul, who is the liegeman (*nawkar*) of Shukur 'Alī Īshīk Āqā, and solve [the dispute] (*ṣāflāshsūnlār*). The attendant's fee (*yasāvul ḥaqqī*) should not exceed two *ṭanga* per parasang.[188]

186 Bābājān Safarov, *Khwārazm ta'rīkhī (1864–1934)*, MS Tashkent, IVANRUz, inv. no. 10231, fols. 21b–22b, fol. 21b.

187 See, e.g., TsGARUz, f. I-125, op.2, d. 100. The register's header reads, 'Register of *yasauls* assigned to petitioners' complaints in the month of Muharram 1333 AH [November 1914].'

188 *Farsakh* (or *farsang*) is a measure of length in Iran and Central Asia, which is usually considered equal to 6 km. However, its length could in fact vary according to regions and depending on road conditions (like the 'heavy' and 'light' *farsakh* in Iran). In Central Asia in the 19th century *farsakh* was usually between 9 and 10 km, see E.A. Davidovich, *Materialy po metrologii srednevekovoi Srednei Azii*, Appended to V. Khints [Walter Hinz],

> Conveying the royal order (*amr-i ʿālīlārī*) of our lord, may his rule last forever, the warrant (*khaṭ*) was written on 25 Rajab 1336.[189]

Let us try to reconstruct the actions presented in this rescript and the course of events. A certain Muḥammad Murād, an inhabitant of the small town of Vazir (around 50 km north-west of Khiva)[190] situated in the province of Gurlen, bought a plot of land from a fellow villager, as well as a part of the harvest of millet grown on the plot. Despite the fact that a *qāżī* had notarised the deal, the seller was nevertheless refusing, or most probably taking his time, to transfer property he had sold to its new owner. Muḥammad Murād had evidently not found other arguments or instruments to resolve the problem, and so had been forced to set off for Khiva to file his grievance at the khan's palace. In response to his claim, the royal court crafted a rescript (*fatak*), stamped with the seal of the *yasāvulbāshī*. This document was formulaic in its structure: it included a short description of the contents of the claim, and an identification of the parties to the dispute, and stipulated the figure responsible for its further resolution – the *yasāvul*, appointed from among the members of the palace guards.[191] The *yasāvulbāshī* also sanctioned the sending of this person to the place of the altercation, and stipulated the sum due to be payed to the *yasāvul* for his services. The size of the payment was defined by the distance that the latter had to travel to reach the place of the conflict.

We learn about the results of the hearing in the locality thanks to a somewhat terse note subsequently recorded on the back of the same rescript by a scribe in the *yasāvulbāshī*'s chancery:

> [*Verso*]
> The claim of the afore-mentioned Muḥammad Murād against Allām Birgān was solved (*yarāshtūrūb*) by community elders (*kadkhudālārī*). This was made known [to the royal court] in the letter by the governor (*ḥākim*) of the Gurlen province. It was recorded on 2 Shaʿbān 1336.[192]

Musul'manskie mery i vesa s perevodom v metricheskuiu sistemu (Moscow: Izdatel'stvo vostochnoi literatury, 1970), p. 120. See also Munis and Agahi, *Firdaws al-iqbāl: History of Khorezm*, p. 570, n. 293.

189 TsGARUz, f. I-125, op. 2, d. 633, l. 151.

190 New (Taza) Vazir was located 7 km north of the town of Gurlen, see Munis and Agahi, *Firdaws al-iqbāl: History of Khorezm*, p. 565.

191 In most case, these were the guardsmen of the *yasāvulbāshī* himself.

192 TsGARUz, f. I-125, op. 2, d. 633, l. 151ob.

This brief notice provides at least evidence that the sending of a *yasāvul* to the site of conflict had an effect. The contents of the instructions indicate that the different sides of the conflict were brought to some kind of agreement. This small fragment also allows us to see different provincial agencies at work while resolving the conflict alongside the representatives of the court. Indeed, this note tells us that reconciliation was made possible by the involvement of the local community leaders. The fact that the information about the resolution of the conflict was reported to the khan's palace by the governor of the province himself perhaps indicates his own involvement in the process. It should be said that similar references to the involvement of community leaders and provincial governors are found in most rescripts of this kind. It is much rarer that the back of the rescripts we find reference to the involvement of official jurists such as a *qāżī* or a *muftī*. Thus, *pace* Lykoshin,[193] there is evidence to say that the system of conflict resolution centered in the royal court generated its own writing and archival practices.

Another notable feature of such rescripts is the use of various standardised formulae. For example, although this *fatak* specifically instructed the various disputing parties to appear in the khan's palace for the resolution of the conflict,[194] in the vast majority of cases (judging by the contents of such records), once the *yasāvul* had been delegated, the conflicts were actually resolved *in situ*. The details of the agreement were then reported to the office of the *yasāvulbāshī* by one of the parties, the *yasāvul*, or representatives of the local authorities (*ḥākims*, *qāżīs*). Nonetheless, it would be wrong to suppose that everything we just described was a sequence of empty formulae without any practical consequence. In fact, as we shall see below, such procedure left a space for any side in a dispute (whether the plaintiff or the defendant), if they were unhappy with the course of the hearing in the locality, to bring their dispute once again to the khan's palace in Khiva.

Let us take another example. One Dāmullā Muḥammad Karim Ākhūnd, the administrator (*mutavallī*) of an endowment (*vaqf*) supporting a madrasa, was determined to obtain payment from tenants working on a property belonging to the madrasas, as stipulated in the endowment deed (*vaqf-nāma*). In his attempts to obtain the agreed payment, the *mutavallī* appealed (*sharīʿatlāshūb*) to the local *qażīs* and received a decision (*ḥukm*) in his favour. However, this turned out to be insufficient to force the other sides to carry out their obligations. In any case, two of the tenants stubbornly persisted in their refusal to

---

193 See Lykoshin's emphasis on the fact that cases did not produce any written records at p. 49 of this book.

194 *yasāvul bīla mūndā darbār-i ʿālīlārīgha kīlib ṣāflāshsūnlār.*

make the stipulated payments. Finally, in the last resort, the *mutavallī* set off for Khiva. In response to his appeal to the khan, following the procedure that is by now familiar to us, the *mutavallī* received an official rescript (*fatak*), and an official representing the court was dispatched to the locale in which the dispute first took place.[195] Once again, we can reconstruct the further course of events from a brief note on the back of the document:

> … it has been established that from now on, the tenants of the [*vaqf*] property will pay the rent (*ijāra*) in [full] accordance with the [endowment] deed. This acknowledgement was made in the presence of the *yasāvul*.[196]

It is notable that neither the endowment deed, nor even the subsequent decision of the *qażī*s were decisive in resolving the dispute between the *mutavallī* and the tenants. It was only the former's appeal to Khiva, and the consequent appointment of a *yasāvul* to the locality that forced the different sides to reach a compromise. Therefore, there can be no doubt that the delegation of a *yasāvul*, together with the writing of rescript, could be crucial to the whole procedure of the receipt and settlement of subjects' petitions.

This raises interesting questions about the *yasāvul*s themselves. Who were they? In the vast majority of cases, the text of court rescripts indicate that the role of *yasāvul* was taken by low-ranking palace guards, from the retinue of the *yasāvulbāshī* himself or other palace officials. It is highly unlikely that such *yasāvul*s had any specific juridical training, unlike, say a *qāżī*, or a *muftī*. Their authority in the provinces was scarcely comparable with that held by provincial governors, *ḥākim*s. Of course, it is also hard to imagine that they would have been as involved in the local fabric of society as the leaders and authority figures in the local communities. Nevertheless, it was specifically the presence of the *yasāvul* that forced the opposing sides to reach a settlement. Evidently, it sent a kind of signal, forcing the parties to the conflict to look for a path towards resolution. When the khan's court sent its own representatives to the site of the conflict, its direct or indirect involvement provided an additional impulse for the different local groups (not just the direct participants in the dispute) to reach a compromise. The kind of role played by the *yasāvul*s therefore did not really depend upon their personal qualities and skills: it was more

195 With the seal Muḥammad Yaʿqūb Yasāvulbāshī b. Muḥammad Yūsuf Yasāvulbāshī.

196 TsGARUz, f. I-125, op. 2, d. 656, ll. 36–36ob.

a question of the 'aura of power' which surrounded a figure delegated from the royal court to the locality. The *yasāvul* thus sent a signal to the whole community, including both the parties in the dispute and the local authorities: the royal court expected the conflict to be resolved, regardless of the conditions on which an agreement was reached.

Perhaps this also explains the character of the notes on the reverse of the rescripts. The main purpose of this slightly disjointed and sparse information was to demonstrate that the claims of the opposing sides had been satisfied (*ṣāf būlūb*), and that the different sides had reached agreement (*riżālashūb*) and reconciliation (*yarāshīb*). As a consequence, the relevant agencies in Khiva were less interested in the details of how the conflict was investigated, or even the conditions on which an agreement had been reached, than in the mere fact that an agreement had been reached and the conflict had been resolved.

Thus, the royal rescripts shed light on the proceedings of settling disputes between khanal subjects. Specifically, they also show the important role played by the *yasāvulbāshī* and the *yasāvul*s, and give us a general picture of the various provincial agencies that could be called upon in an investigation. At the same time, the standardised and formulaic character of such documents somewhat limits the scope for a more detailed study of the character of the involvement of specific actors, whether that of the *yasāvul* himself, or of the various officials in the locality. In an attempt to follow up these aspects, we will therefore turn to the next group of documents: namely, the reports of provincial authoritities (mainly, provincial governors) sent to the office of the *yasāvulbāshī* in Khiva in response to rescripts about subjects' petitions. This group of documents allows us to gain a more detailed picture of what happened in the provinces, after the arrival of the *yasāvul* and/or the receipt of a rescript: how the local agencies were involved and the part that the *ḥākim*s and *qażī*s could play in the process of investigating petitions from citizens. This corpus of documents also enables us to see how different social groups were involved in reaching an agreement.

6.2 *Reports*

The second group of documents presented in this work are the reports (*ʿarīża*, *ʿarīża-nāma*, *ʿarīża-i īkhlāṣ*, *khaṭ*) sent back to the office of the *yasāvulbāshī* in Khiva from various agencies in the provinces, mostly from the provincial governors to whom the khan's court had entrusted the investigation of claims filed with the royal court. In such reports, the officials informed the central authorities in detail about the proceedings (*ṣurat-i vāqiʿa*) of the investigations underway, and the achievement of a reconciliation, or the reasons for failing to reach one. In this work we have included translations and descriptions of 25 such reports. To illustrate their structure and contents, let us turn to the following record:[197]

> Let it be known to the office of the *yasāvulbāshī*, the noble vizier (*vazīr al-kirām*), our lord (*āqāmīz*), that when Muḥammad Yūsuf from Tashḥavuż[198] appealed [to the royal court], he stated that he left 1100 *manāt* in custody (*amānat*) to Muḥammad Yaʿqūb Bāy from Qonghrat. [When the former] asked [the latter to return the sum, Muḥammad Yaʿqūb Bāy] did not give [anything] and denied [the claim]. In the wake of the involvement of the governor (*ḥākim āqā*) and the community elders (*kadkhudās*), [the respondent] returned to the claimant only 550 *manāts*, but he refused to pay the rest. Therefore, you instructed me to clarify whether it is true that Muḥammad Yaʿqūb returned only half of the 1100 *manāt* which he was entrusted and, in such a case, to extort the money from him and let the parties reach a satisfactory settlement (*riżālashtūrsūn*). As I questioned the parties, Muḥammad Yūsuf [argued] that he had given 1100 *manats* to Muḥammad Yaʿqūb who refused to return [the money]. Muḥammad Yaʿqūb denied (*munkir*) the claim (*daʿvā*) stating that he was never entrusted the money. I thus involved the *qāżī-īshāns*. Meanwhile, the tribal elders (*biylār*) and the representatives of the town dwellers (*qalʿa kāsiblārī*)[199] [requested] not to place the parties under oath (*ānt*). [Instead] they made Muḥammad Yaʿqūb pay 550 *manāt* to Muḥammad Yūsuf and a certificate of relinquishment (*ibrāʾ*) was drafted before the *qāżī-īshāns*. This is what we had to report to you. Whatever is your decision, you know best. This report (*ʿarīża*) was compiled on 4 Rabīʾ al-s̱ānī 1335 [27.01.1917].

Structurally, the sequence of events presented in the contents of this report can be divided into three parts. The first part narrates the actions undertaken

---

197 Doc. 13.

198 Tashhawz was a fortress circa 65 km north-west of Khiva on the right bank of the Shahabad canal, see Munis and Agahi, *Firdaws al-iqbāl: History of Khorezm*, p. 642, n. 972; Danilevskii, *Opisanie Khivinskogo khanstva*, p. 110; Basiner, *Estestvenno-nauchnoe puteshestvie po Kirgizskoi stepi v Khivu*, p. 348; *Ocherk istorii zaseleniia Khivinskogo khanstva s drevnykh vremen, sostav ego sovremennogo naseleniia, administratsiia i goroda khanstva*, 1873, IVRRAN, St. Petersburg, Arkhiv Vostokovedov, f. 33, d. 8, ll. 50–50 ob.

199 In vernacular sources from Khorezm the term *kāsiblār* is used to denote 'city dwellers.' In referring to events taking place in Tashhawz in 1915 Laffasī uses the term *kāsiblār* as a synonym of *qalʿa khalqī* ('the people of the city'). See Ḥasan-Murād Laffasī *Gulshan-i saʿādat*, MS Tashkent, IVANRUz, inv. no. 7797, fol. 32a.

by the parties to the conflict, before their petition had been sent to the khan's court in Khiva. Then, the author of the dispatch briefly recounts the contents of the rescript he had received from the khan's court, concerning the settlement of the petition. Finally, in the concluding section, the governor informs the chancery of the *yasāvulbāshī* about the results obtained by following the instructions in the rescript. If we try to reconstruct the course of events as they appear in the report cited here from the governor, then we are presented with the following picture. A certain Muḥammad Yūsuf, an inhabitant of Tashhawz insisted that he had earlier given an inhabitant of Qonghrat, another urban center in the north of the khanate, money for safe-keeping to the value of 1,100 roubles, which the latter had refused to return. In order to resolve the dispute that had arisen, Muḥammad Yūsuf, the creditor, appealed to the local governor, and brought representatives of the communities into the matter. The examination of the dispute by these agencies led the debtor to return half of the sum demanded. The plaintiff, however, did not consider this to be a satisfactory resolution, and decided to file a suit with the royal court in Khiva for the outstanding sum owed by the defendant. In response to Muḥammad Yūsuf's petition, the chancery of the *yasāvulbāshī* gave the following instruction to the same governor: to investigate the matter and, if possible, bring the two sides to a compromise. The governor's report picks up its narrative from here, concerning the course of the investigation he had initiated on the basis of the rescript from the royal palace. Thus the *ḥākim* reports that when the parties were questioned, the defendant, Muḥammad Yaʿqūb, refused outright to acknowledge the existence of an outstanding debt. The governor was forced to involve the local jurists, *qāżīs*, in the investigation, to carry out legal procedures, in this case, to make the parties swear an oath. As the author of the report tells us that at this moment, however, tribal leaders and the representatives of the urban population managed to persuade the defendant to avoid to take a cleansing oath, and instead to pay Muḥammad Yūsuf the money owed. When the latter received the whole sum owed to him, there in the court of the *qāżīs*, he notarised his acquittal of any further claims against the defendant. The governor of Tashhawz informed the central agencies of this settlement.

This particular case is instructive for a number of reasons. First of all, it clearly shows that provincial governors had the power to hear claims and resolve conflicts among the local population directly, which is to say, before the khan's court became involved. The authors of a detailed military-statistic survey of the Khanate of Khiva, prepared in the early 1900s, also mention that provincial governors held such powers. According to this source, the *ḥākim*s had the right to examine a 'claim,' to resolve all minor disputes 'decisively,' and also to 'arrest criminals.'[200] For these purposes, according to Alexander Kuhn, the governor had under him his own staff of *yasāvul*s, on the model of the royal court.[201] Various sources indicate that the great majority of conflicts between subjects were settled at the level of the community and provincial authorities, without involving the royal court. In the case we are considering here, Muḥammad Yūsuf also appealed first to the governor of Tashhawz. It was only when the plaintiff did not receive full satisfaction of his grievance (or perhaps, because he believed that the *ḥākim* had not played a sufficiently impartial role in the examination of his case), that he decided to send his petition to Khiva, in order to involve the khan's court in the investigation of his case.

Secondly, judging by this and other similar records presented in Section Two titled 'Reports' of the present work, even once the subject had submitted a petition to Khiva and a written rescript (*fatak*) and/or a *yasāvul* from the khan's court had been sent in response, it was still the provincial governors who were responsible for the resolving of the conflict *in situ* in the majority of cases. The documents show that the hearing could take place either in the residence of the *ḥākim* with him actually present, or without his direct involvement – for example, at the place where the parties to the dispute lived – through the medium of the *yasāvul* or the local elders. Either way, the governors were kept informed about the course and content of any investigation initiated by the Khivan authorities. It is noteworthy that in the document which we have just analyzed, the case was sent to Khiva for resolution by the same *ḥākim* to whom the plaintiff had appealed initially, and with whose resolution he had been dissatisfied. Evidently, as we have said before, the instruction from the court (and equally the sending of a *yasāvul*) gave an additional impulse to the resolution of the dispute, and brought the different sides to a peaceful agreement.

Another notable feature reflected in the document is the nature of the involvement in the case of *qāżī*s, which is to say jurists. As can be seen from this and from a number of other documents presented in the Sections Two and Three of the present work, *qāżī*s were brought in to examine conflicts between citizens at the stage where concrete expert knowledge were required. This happened, for example, when the different sides in a conflict, despite admonishments from representatives of the community and the local authorities, were unable to reach a compromise and continued to stand their ground. In such cases, expert testimonies were required, and these were the prerogatives of the

---

200 [Girshfel'd and Galkin], *Voenno-statisticheskoe opisanie Khivinskogo oazisa*. Part 2, p. 23.

201 A. Kun, *Ocherk istorii zaseleniia Khivinskogo khanstva s drevnykh vremen, sostav ego sovremennogo naseleniia, administratsiia i goroda khanstva*, 1873, IVRRAN, St. Petersburg, Arkhiv Vostokovedov, f. 33, d. 8, l. 44 ob.

qāżīs. Such procedures could include the witnessing of the notarial documents held by the different parties, the summoning and interrogation of witnesses, or, as we have seen above, making the parties swear an oath. The *qāżīs* and their trustees (*amīn*) also had to be brought in to clarify questions concerning property rights, fixation of precise boundaries of plots of land.

Document No. 16, section Two, is equally revealing for procedural aspects of the examination of citizens' petitions in the provinces. The governor of the town of Gurlen reports to Khiva that some time earlier an elderly woman had appealed to him with a grievance against her son-in-law. She claimed that the son-in-law had assaulted her daughter, Saʿādat Bīka, and then fled without trace. Having received this information, the governor had found two trustees (*amīnlār*), one for him, and for the *qāżī* of Gurlen. He wrote to them with instructions to inspect the bruises on the victim's body, with the assistance of the community elders (*īl-kadkhudā*). Meanwhile, the defendant, Yakshī Murāt, had learnt about the actions initiated against him by his wife's relatives, and responded by appealing directly to Khiva. He submitted a counter-claim to the khan's court, accusing his wife's relatives of holding her by force. The khan's palace had responded to this appeal by sending a rescript (*būyrūq-i ʿālī*) to the *ḥākim*, instructing him to examine the case and to resolve the conflict if possible. During the subsequent hearing of the case in the governor's residence, Yakshī Murāt's representatives demanded that the rest of the case be heard in the khan's palace. The governor was unable to refuse such a demand from one of the parties to the conflict, and so arranged for the girl to be escorted to Khiva (having first entrusted her to the community headman), along with the details about the *amīns*' inspection of the girl's bruises.

The report outlining this case is particularly noteworthy for the way it formulates the instructions from the officials at the khan's court to the governor on how to proceed with the case:

> … should [the plaintiff's] appeal be sound, the wife and husband should be reunited, otherwise (*bāshqa sūzī būlsa*) [the conflict] should be heard before the *qāżīs*. [If they refuse to comply], they should be sent [to the royal court for further examination].[202]

Thus the palace offers the governor the following possible options for resolution: (i) to reconcile the sides before taking the matter to a court of law; (ii) if the parties refuse to compromise, to use legal expertise, through the involvement of *qāżīs*; and (iii) if one of the parties refuses to be put on oath as witness,

202 Doc. 16.

then in the last resort to send the litigants to Khiva, for hearing by representatives of the khan's court.

As can be seen from the instructions from the court, cited by the *ḥākim* in his dispatch, the involvement of *qāżīs* in the process was quite precisely circumscribed. They would be called upon only if both sides in the conflict agreed to subject themselves to legal procedures in the *qāżī*'s court. This is demonstrated not only by the document cited here, but by a whole series of other testimonies. One anonymous contemporary Russian author, when describing the legal system of the khanate, noted that 'examination according to the Qur'ān (i.e. by the *qāżīs*) occurs in relatively few cases, and only when both sets of litigants agree …'[203] Moreover, as our documents show, even once the case had been passed over for the inspection of the *qāżīs*, the parties to the conflict were in fact still able to refuse to give testimony at any stage, and to insist that the case be transferred to the khan's court in Khiva.

It is also intriguing that even an elderly female petitioner, at the very beginning of the examination of the case of her daughter's beating, preferred to appeal to the local governor, rather than to the *qāżīs*, or the *muftīs*. It was the governor who initiated the investigation of the case, and it was on his instructions that the local *qāżīs* sent their trustee to witness the victim's body. At the same time, it would be wrong to imagine the *ḥākims* were the only figures in the provinces who were able to dispense justice, or that their powers were unlimited. The case in question provides an illustration. As we can see, as soon as he learnt about the investigative activities undertaken against him, the defendant Yakshī Mūrat decided to appeal to Khiva, with a counter-petition to the khan's palace. This was answered with written instructions from the central authorities. Although the instructions were addressed to the same *ḥākim* who had been hearing the case initially, it can reasonably be assumed that the receipt of instructions from the Khivan court somewhat strengthened Yakshī Mūrat's position in the following settlement. This in no way guaranteed him unequivocal success in the settling of his case. But it evidently reduced the likelihood of unfair (biased) actions on the part of the local authorities, or, specifically, of the governor. It is notable that Yakshī Mūrat's side would take advantage of the opportunity to refer the investigation to Khiva again, during the second examination of the case. We can only guess what might have motivated the second request for the examination of the case in Khiva. It is possible that Yakshī Mūrat's side once again felt the *ḥākim* was biased in this case. It is also possible that when he saw that the investigation of his case with the local governor was not going in his favour, Yakshī Mūrat was forced to refer

203 Anon., "Turkmeniia i Khiva," *Vsemirnyi puteshestvennik* 8 (1870), p. 123.

his case to Khiva, calculating that the different mechanisms of investigation at the court, and, perhaps, his personal contacts in the capital, would ensure a more favourable outcome for him. Whatever their motives, Yakshī Mūrat's side found it preferable to use this option, while the *ḥākim* had no choice but to agree to the demand of the defendant.

Another example of the readiness of the parties to a conflict to refer the investigation of their case to Khiva when necessary is found in the contents of Document No 18. In this text, the governor of the province of Ambar-Manaq reports the results of his investigation into a conflict between members of two communities of water-users (*davr*) in the province. The conflict flared up because the members of one of the communities had not fulfilled their obligations to clean out the irrigation channels. As a result, representatives of the neighbouring community decided to send a grievance to Khiva. In response, a rescript was sent to the local authorities on how to settle the matter. There was then an attempt to reconcile the two sides in the presence of the governor, but this was unsuccessful, so the latter had to call in *qāżīs* to carry out expert procedures. The governor's report gives an interesting description of the events that followed:

> The *qāżī-īshāns* from Manaq who are skilled in *sharīʿa* ordered the appellants to produce their witness (*guvāh*). When the appellants were about to bring their witness, [the defendant] Allāh Birgān Mīrshab stated that he intended to go to Khiva (*Khīvāgha bārūrman dīb*) [and address the dispute to the royal court].[204]

It is evident that procedures undertaken by the *qāżīs*, such as making the witnesses take an oath, and listening to their statements, could be a sufficient basis for making a decision (*ḥukm*) in favour of one of the parties. In such a case, the decision would, as a rule, be final and irrevocable, with practically no room for later appeals against it (or, at least, it was very unlikely any such appeals would be successful). In the present case, it appears that when the defendant's side saw the willingness of their opponents to present the requested witnesses to the court, and, consequently, foresaw that the decision of the *qāżīs* might not be in their favour, they broke off the procedure, by announcing their demand that the investigation of the case be transferred to Khiva. So, once again, we come across a case where such a demand from one of the parties is a sufficient basis both for the governor and for the *qāżīs* to end the investigation and refer the case to the khan's court.

204 TsGARUz, f. I-125, op. 1, d. 498, l. 44.

However, if we turn to the questions which Khivan subjects referred to their khan (both in the rescripts from the palace, and in the reports in reply from the officials in the provinces), then we may conclude that the option of appealing to Khiva was defined not by the level of 'importance' of the question, the legal character of the dispute or the monetary value of the claim, but above all by the readiness and motivation of subjects to set off to the court. This is also supported by ethnographic materials related to the Qaraqalpaq tribes around the Aral Sea coast. Kosbergenov gives the following information from his respondents on the nature of legal relations among the local Qaraqalpaqs:

> ... by custom the Qaraqalpaqs always referred first to the local *biy* when a dispute arose. If both sides were not satisfied with the decision of the *biy* and continued their dispute ... the litigation could be heard at courts of higher instances – the *ḥākim* and even the khan ... [In this case] the transfer of matters of dispute to courts of higher instances was not determined by the character of the claim, but depended *exclusively* on the economic position of the disputants.[205]

The Qaraqalpaqs on the coast of the Aral Sea, who were located at some distance from the center of the khanate, used the same option of petitioning the khan in Khiva that was available to other Khivan subjects, since this enabled them to bypass both clan leaders and governors. At the same time, Kosbergenov suggests, such an appeal to Khiva not only created a possibility for conflict with local power-holders, but also required significant expenditure, which subjects were by no means always ready to make.

6.3 *Notifications*

A certain 'Abdullāh, with the revealing nickname of *khāmbāsh* ('puzzled'), lived in a village on the outskirts of the town of Khanqah. On an ordinary spring morning in 1918, he set off to his plot of land, located at some distance from his farmstead. As was his habit, when he arrived, he walked towards a small barn, where, among his various agricultural tools, he came across a whole series of unfamiliar objects that, it appears, did not belong to him. Surprised by such an unexpected find, 'Abdullāh hurried to the home of Muḥammad Ya'qūb Khwāja, the administrator (*mutavallī*) of an Islamic endowment and who most probably enjoyed a certain degree of respect within the local community. When

205 R. Kosbergenov, "Polozhenie karakalpalskogo naseleniia v Khivinskom khanstve v kontse XIX–nachale XX v.," pp. 260–261.

Muḥammad Yaʿqūb Khwāja heard about the suspicious discovery by his fellow villager, he made the only proper decision he could make: to report what had happened to the governor (*bāy āqā*) of Khanqah, within whose administrative jurisdiction the community fell. The *mutavallī* and ʿAbdullāh loaded up the items they had found onto a camel, and set off to the governor's court in Khanqah. A group of dangerous robbers who had been plundering the area around Khanqah for several years were arrested as a consequence of this unexpected find. The details and sequel to this intriguing story are presented below, in the Section Three titled 'Notifications.'[206] The episode described here is noteworthy since it provides an excellent illustration of the possible patterns of behavior of inhabitants of Khorezm who found themselves in a situation of emergency. What should Khivan subjects do if they were victim to a robbery or a raid, a participant in a dubious situation, or, as in this case, if they made a suspicious discovery? Inhabitants of Khorezm at the beginning of the twentieth century had a more or less clear idea: they should hurry to the home of the community elders, and later, if the case was serious enough, to the governor's residence.

The corpus of documents presented in the third section of the book contains notifications to the office of the *yasāvulbāshī* from various agencies in the provinces, in particular from provincial governors, providing information (*ṣūrat-i vāqiʿa*) about various crimes committed on the territories within their jurisdiction and about the results of their investigations. They differ from the reports from the provincial governors, presented in Section Two, where the records were crafted as responses to undertakings to examine petitions initiated by the royal court. Section Three instead presents records issued by various provincial agencies to inform the royal court about the investigation of a range of wrongdoings, as well as descriptions of the measures undertaken to investigate and settle such matters. The records here termed 'notifications' shed light on cases that officials in the provinces of the Khanate of Khiva adjudicated of their own volition.

In the majority of cases of assaults, robberies, or murders, which are described in this section, the aggrieved parties appealed specifically to the provincial governors. As for the types of misdemeanors committed in the khanate, one European author reported that 'the most commonly occurring crimes are the following: theft, fraud, fights and often also murders …'[207] The notifications from provincial governors included in this work present a similar impression of the crimes committed in the khanate. Notably, the documents we have stud-

206 See Doc. 41.

207 M.I. Ivanin, *Khiva i reka Amu-Daria* (St. Petersburg: Obshchestvennaia pol'za, 1873), p. 62.

ied describe such misdemeanors specifically as crimes, which are designated as *jīnāyat* ('crime') or *gunāh* ('misdemeanor') in Khivan bureaucratese.

Like rescripts and reports, the genre of notifications is of little help to disclose the rules informing decision-making, patterns of behavior and conflict resolution. Let us illustrate what we mean by turning to one such text.[208] We learn from a missive from the governor of the province of Besh-Ariq that a thoroughbred horse was stolen from the courtyard of the property of an inhabitant of the settlement of Susalaq. When the victim learned what had happened, he quickly hired a scout, who managed to follow hot on the robber's trail, tracing them to the house of a certain Rūz Muḥammad. Having identified where the possible robber was staying, the victim took his case to the provincial governor, accompanied by the heads of his community (*īlātīnī āqsaqāl kadkhudālārī*). In response to this notification (*maʿlūm*) and the testimonies received, the governor tasked an official with bringing the suspect to him at his court. During the subsequent hearing the accused admitted under duress that he had stolen the horse, and also supplied further details of how he had committed the crime. This information led to the arrest of a further four of his accomplices (*yūldāshlārī*). These four were subjected to further interrogation under torture (*siyāsat ītūb sūrāldī*) in order to establish the extent of their guilt, and to reveal that they had then sold the stolen horse. The governor decided to place all five thieves (*ūghrī*) under arrest in special premises at their own expense.[209] Besides the 1,200 *ṭillā* owed to the victim as compensation, the communities' heamen took on the responsibility of covering the remaining expenses for the investigation, including the pay for the scout (*īzchī fulī*), reward for the heads of the communities (*kadkhudā fulī*) who had taken part in the investigation, and any remaining costs (*ghayri chiqghūn*). Then, since the details of the crime had been fully established, and the expenses had been fully compensated, the community elders asked to be the prisoners' guarantors (*kafīl*). On the basis of this appeal, the governor had sent the dispatch in question to Khiva, to the office of the *yasāvulbāshī*, asking whether the guilty parties could be entrusted to their guarantors. A short note on the margin of the document, obviously made by a scribe of the *yasāvulbāshī*, states that in response to this request from the provincial governor, the Khivan authorities approved the handing over of all the prisoners to the elders who would act in the capacity of guarantors.[210]

---

208 Doc. 39.

209 We should note that the assessment of the value of the stolen horse is given on the basis of the victim's own words.

210 Similar scenarios for the investigation of crimes are also mentioned in other documents; see Docs. 38, 53, 55, 57. For further reflections on the institution of *kafālat* and on the notion of communal responsibility, see S. Winter, "Le rôle du *kafīl* (garant) dans la

This example, which we have chosen almost at random from the general collection of such notifications, goes some way to convey the complex process involved in the investigation of a robbery. In the description just given, we can distinguish the individual initiative of the victim, who paid an expert scout, the active involvement of the community leaders, the role of the provincial governor and his guards, and finally, the presence of the central agencies of the capital, whose approval was needed for the final resolution of the case.

Together, the collection of documents at our disposal allows us to reconstruct (albeit in very general terms) the sequence and content of the procedural arrangements undertaken by various agencies when examining crimes and legal infringements. At the same time, it obviously must be acknowledged that the organization and conduct of investigations could vary from case to case, and did not necessarily always follow the exact details of the sequence described below.

The first formal step after a crime had been committed was the notification (*maʿlūm, khabar, ʿarż*) of the provincial authorities. The information was reported to the governor either by the victims themselves or by some other representatives of their community. If the incident had involved physical injury or death, the governor would have his assistant (*khiẕmatkār, ādam*) sent to the site of the crime, and would simultaneously instruct the local *qāżī*s to send their own trustee (*amīn*). Both trustees would then inspect the site of the crime and examine the body of the victim(s), always in the presence of representatives of the local community (*īl-ādamlārī*). It is evident that the results of such examinations were recorded in written form, since the governors' notifications refer to such materials. In the case of incidents that led to death, the relatives were only permitted to bury the body once the corresponding examinations had been carried out by the authorities.

The next stage can be called the investigation (*taftīsh*), and was divided into the search operations and the inquiry. The documents presented allow us to reconstruct some procedural details and practices of investigation used by the local agencies. For example, one of the first tasks of the investigation was to define the possible range of suspects. For this the governor asked the victim for possible suspects (*gumāndār*). If names were given, then the governor instructed his mounted guards (*āṭlī nawkar*) to bring such individuals to his residence for interrogation. In such cases, representatives of the local community, or elders',would take part in the arrest of the suspects in their place of

governance locale selon les contrats d'affermage fiscal à Tripoli au XVIIe–XVIIIe siècle," *Islamic Law and Society* 23.4 (2016), pp. 392–409.

residence. They were usually also present for the subsequent hearing in the residence of the governor.

Another method for carrying out investigations, often mentioned in our documents, was the use of expert scouts called *īzchī*, who could follow the tracks of the criminals if the conditions were right.[211] The use of such specialists appears to have been relatively widely practiced, especially in the case of thefts of livestock, and could often produce successful outcomes. This is indicated by a whole series of cases where the employment of a scout led to the identification of the place where the suspects lived and, in rarer cases, to the discovery of the stolen property itself. This was usually where the services of the scouts ended, since once the possible location of the criminals had been identified, the victim would then appeal to the provincial authorities to ask for someone to come and arrest the suspects and interrogate them. In this case too, the arrest of the suspects, especially if it happened in another locality, would happen in the presence of representatives of local society.

Another method of investigation mentioned in the documents is the use of informants (*āyghāq*). In this capacity, habitués of busy places such as the bazaars were often ready to share information with the victim's side for a defined reward.[212]

The documents also point to a whole range of other more elaborate practices for hunting criminals, involving the use of rituals of fortune telling and divination. For example, one of the documents tells how a certain mullah, who offered his services to deal with a case of theft, had two boys look into the water to identify the culprit.[213] In another case suspects for the theft of money were

211 In the late 19th century, the colonial official A. Lomakin collected interesting reports about how the Turkmens in the Transcaspian Region used trackers in the case of thefts. Although these materials concerned Turkmens, they still correspond to the practices mentioned in our documents: '… a group of people known as *īzchī* has formed: *īz* – following, hence *īzchī* – one who follows tracks, a searcher; their profession consisted of the search, for reward, in the tracks of lost property … One is amazed by the knowledge and skill with which an *īzchī* follows a track … This art, of course, takes many years of practice to perfect, and provides those Turkmens who have mastered it with a substantial income,' see A. Lomakin, *Obychnoe pravo u Turkmen* (*Adat*) (Ashkhabad: Parovaia Russkaia tipografiia K.M. Fedorova, 1897), p. 99.

212 In many of the documents the sums which could be paid to trackers and informants for their services are recorded. So, in the example mentioned above, concerning the investigation of the theft of a horse, the services of the *īzchī* were valued at 300 *ṭillā*, which were to be paid by the criminals. In another document (see below), individuals who had initiated a search for thieves managed to gain important information as to the whereabouts of the latter from an informant for the sum of 100 *manāt*.

213 *har kimnī māllārī ūghūrlānsa īkkī yāsh bālanī suvgha qārātīb ūghrīni tāpib birūr īrdīm*, see below Doc. 25.

found by 'scattering sand' (*tūfrāq tūktūrūb*).[214] The documents do not give any information as to the meaning of such practices, either legalistic or divinatory. Also they do not indicate how reliable any information gathered by such means was believed to be or whether it could be used in the subsequent process of investigating wrongdoings. However, it is clear that these practices and rituals were widespread in Khorezmian society in the early twentieth century.[215]

It is noteworthy that in the great majority of cases, searches were initiated and carried out by the victims or representatives of their communities. Only once the range of suspects had been established did the initiators of the search turn to the provincial authorities. The latter were needed for help in the subsequent arrest and escort of the suspects to the governor's residence for interrogation. It is clear that the arrest of the criminal had to be sanctioned by the provincial authorities, which helped to reduce the chance of open conflict between different groups and communities to whom the victims and suspects of a crime belonged.

Once the range of suspects had been established and they had been escorted to the governor's residence, there followed the next stage, the *surāq* or inquiry. The texts studied here are relatively sparing in their descriptions of the procedures involved in an inquiry, and the tactics of interrogation used. They simply indicate that the interrogation was carried out by the governor himself in the presence of representatives of both the side being questioned, and the victim's side. The governors often admitted in their notifications that during interrogations they had used force (*jazā, siyāsat*), in the form of lashes of the whip (*qāmchī*) or beating with a stick (*tayāq*). However, our texts do not allow us to define precisely how much force was considered acceptable in interrogations. Clearly, governors had the formal right to use force against suspects, but their ability to use this right could be limited by the authority of both the suspects themselves and their representatives.

If the accused did not acknowledge his or her guilt during the interrogation then they would be sent to Khiva, escorted by an armed convoy and the victim's party, for further hearing and the settlement of the case. If the details of the crime were established, and the accused was proved guilty, then they would be placed under temporary arrest at the governor's residence (*ūyga ṣālib*), until further instructions arrived from the center. If, as often happened,

214 Doc. 57. On geomancy and other occult sciences practiced in Central Asia in the period under consideration in this book, see M. Melvin-Koushki and J. Pickett, "Mobilizing Magic: Occultism in Central Asia and the Continuity of High Persianate Culture under Russian Rule," *Studia Islamica* 111 (2016), pp. 231–284. See, also, N. Lykoshin, "O gadanii u sredneaziatskikh tuzemtsev." In *Spravochnaia knizhka Samarkandskoi oblasti 1907 g. Vypusk IX*, ed. M. Virskii (Samarkand: Tipo-Litografiia G.I. Demurova, 1907), pp. 163–197.

215 AIEARAN, fond G.P. Snesarev, *Polevye zapisi*, no. 8 (1966), ll. 16, 23; no. 15 (1955), ll. 24, 70.

representatives of the community and relatives of those arrested were present, these would pay the damages and try to have those arrested handed over to them as guarantors (*kafīl*). In such cases, the governor would also ask for instructions from the court and the *yasāvulbāshī*, as to whether the criminals could be handed over to their guarantors.

To follow these procedural practices, let us turn to yet another investigation, in this case of a robbery carried out in one of the villages around Manghit in late 1916.[216] A certain elderly woman appealed to the provincial governor with a grievance against a group of people who had broken into her house and stolen some items that belonged to her, including some livestock, valuables and money. The woman identified (*gumānīm shūndīn tūrūr*) one of the robbers as a certain Sāriq Bāy. During the interrogation by the governor, the suspect denied having taken any part in the crime. Meanwhile, the leaders of the community (*āqsaqāl kadkhudālārī*) to which Sāriq Bāy belonged insisted on his innocence (*ūghrī īmās*), and petitioned the governor to give them six days to apprehend those responsible for the crime. In the course of their search, the community leaders came to the opposite 'Russian' side of the Amu Darya (*āryāq*), where they managed to find an informer (*āyghāq*). For a fee, the latter gave them two names of people who had sold part of the stolen property at the bazaar a few days earlier. However, since these individuals were currently located on territory under Russian jurisdiction, the *āqsaqāl* could not initiate a formal search for them, and so patiently waited for their return to the left, 'Khivan' side (*bū ṭarafghacha ūtgūncha*). As soon as the latter turned up in the bazaar of the town of Khitay under the Khivan jurisdiction, they were immediately arrested by representatives of Sāriq Bāy's community, accompanied by an assistant (*yūzbāshī*) of the governor. During the interrogation before the provincial governor, both of those arrested admitted to having committed the robbery, and also gave the names of their remaining accomplices (*yūldāsh*), three of whom were also arrested. Although the newly arrested individuals refused acknowledgment of guilt (*tuhmat*) for having taken part in the robbery, they nonetheless expressed their willingness to pay the cost of what had been stolen. The governor had no means to prove the guilt of the latter three, and so had his trustee escort all five under convoy to Khiva for their fates to be decided there.[217] In his report on this, the governor adds that, according to the local inhabitants, one of those arrested was a certain Tangrī Birdī, who was a known thief (*yamān ūghrī*), who had managed to escape capture for

216 Doc. 56.

217 Sāriq Bāy, who had been arrested earlier, is not mentioned among those taken under convoy to Khiva, which suggests that the earlier accusations against him had been withdrawn.

many years, having successfully hidden on the Russian side of the Amu Darya (*hīch tāpdūrmāy āryāqda qāchīb yūrgān īrdī*).

It is also striking that the true criminals were apprehended on the initiative of members of the community of Sāriq Bāy, who had earlier been arrested on the basis of the victim's statement. The gathering of information, the use of informants, and the pursuit of the suspects had all been carried out by these people, and at their own expense, as they tried to demonstrate the innocence of the suspects. The actions of the three other individuals arrested under suspicion of involvement in this crime are also worth noting: they insisted on their innocence but nonetheless expressed willingness to compensate the victim for the loss she had sustained during the robbery. In a modern context, such willingness might be taken as an informal admission of guilt on the part of the suspects. However, it is clear that according to notions of morality which had currency in early twentieth-century Khorezm, such willingness in no way indicated indirect admission of involvement. Both examples are telling: while a concept of 'presumed innocence' is one of the basic concepts of legal relations in the contemporary world, in Khorezm in the period in question, a suspect would instead have to demonstrate innocence. In the case of Sāriq Bāy, his non-involvement was proved by the efforts of members of his community, who sought out the real perpetrators of the crime. In the second case, individuals who were unable to present similar proofs of their innocence were forced to express their willingness to take upon themselves the compensation payment.

It is also important to note that in such notifications we very rarely find mentions of cases in which to deny a claim would precipitate a hearing by *qāżīs*. In light of the records and the proceedings we described above, it would be natural to expect that jurists would be called upon to bring suspects to produce testimony or witnesses to take oaths. However, the documents indicate that the *qāżīs* were only fleetingly involved in criminal investigations; their intervention was very often limited to a formal examination of injuries on the victims. Records show that subjects seem to have no particular interest in turning to *qāżīs* for help, preferring instead other mechanisms of conflict resolution.

There is no doubt that the provincial governors had a wide range of powers to initiate investigations, arrest suspects and to impose initial bail conditions. For example, the authors of a late 19th-century military-statistical survey of Khiva noted that:

> … the *ḥākim* has a fairly large degree of power over the population. He can imprison people suspected of crime and can place shackles upon them, he can inflict corporal punishment on the simple people, and he can decisively resolve all minor disputes. In order to ensure his orders are

> carried out ... the *ḥākim* usually has around 10 guards and a fairly large number of retainers, most of whom are his relatives.[218]

Given these powers, why in the cases discussed here did the governors have to refer matters to Khiva for resolution? And why, more generally, did the *ḥākim*s craft such detailed notifications, informing the central agencies about the circumstances of the cases under investigation?

Evidently, the actions of the governors need to be seen within the dynamics of the power relations within the khanate. We find officials of various walks of life and career backgrounds among the governors whose names appear in our records. For example, among them we find individuals who inherited the post, such as ʿAvaż Khwāja, the ruler of Khoja-eli, on account of his belonging to the local elite. Other *ḥākim*s, by contrast, could be just temporary appointees, selected among the relatives of senior court dignitaries.[219] The legal authority and judicial power of such dignitaries would often depend on the status and influence of their patrons at court.[220] We also meet a group of governors who were appointed by the khan from among his confidants (*maḥram*),[221] for whom a governorship was just a jumping-off point in their career, as in the case of Shaykh Naẓar Yasāvulbāshī. The picture becomes even more complex if we take into account the members of different ethnic groups that lived on territories administered by such governors – Qazaqs, Turkmens, Qaraqalpaqs – whose leaders certainly did not always accept the authority of the *ḥākim* who intervened in their affairs. In such circumstances, the legal authority of the *ḥākim* was not determined by his official tasks and administrative prerogatives. On the contrary, the legal authority of the governors in many respects was contingent upon their ability to situate themselves in this complex social context, to manage relations with local power groups and elites while still taking into account the balance of power at the royal court. This was especially the case when the parties to a conflict were members of different social, especially ethnic, groups often backed up by powerful figures. It does not come as a surprise that parties to a conflict could call on their influential patrons at the court in Khiva. In such cases, as can be seen in the records, the governors were forced

218 [Girshfel'd and Galkin], *Voenno-statisticheskoe opisanie Khivinskogo oazisa*, II, pp. 23–24.

219 Allāh Birgān Bāy b. ʿAvaż Niyāz Maḥram, the *ḥākim* of Urgench, was the brother of Muḥammad Yūsuf Yasāvulbāshī; Sayyid Ismāʿīl Khwāja, the ruler of Hazarasp, was the older brother of the *vazīr-i akbar* Sayyid Islām Khwāja (d. 1913).

220 For example, soon after the death of Sayyid Islām Khwāja, his brothers Sayyid Ismāʿīl Khwāja and Isḥāq Khwāja, respectively the governors of Hazarasp and Kunya-Urgench, were removed from their posts.

221 For example, Jumʿa Niyāz Maḥram b. Maḥmūd Dīvān, the ruler of Tashhawz.

to weigh up their actions against the possible consequences. It often happened that the governors in the provinces were not ready to intervene in a conflict between local groups, in case they themselves became drawn into the conflict.

This was the story, for example, with the investigation into the kidnap of a Qaraqalpaq girl, later recorded by the Soviet ethnographer Rzambet Kosbergenov. According to his account, a girl from a Qaraqalpaq tribe, having already been betrothed to another member of her tribe, was kidnapped by an Uzbek boy. Hoping to escape their pursuers, the young couple was forced to seek shelter in Turkmen nomadic encampments. The girl's relatives appealed to the governor of Shumanay, under whose jurisdiction they fell, with a demand that the girl be returned to her family and the boy be punished. The petitioners called upon an authoritative fellow-tribesman called Qāżī Bekbauli, who had close contacts with Khiva, to exert additional pressure. The governor, however, 'did not want to decide this matter independently,' since any decision could bring him into confrontation with different groups, and preferred to send the matter on to Khiva, for the agencies in the capital to settle.[222]

We should also not forget that the khan's accessibility, which we have already discussed, allowed individuals to appeal against the actions of the governor. One of our documents provides an example.[223] A person had been caught stealing and had been arrested by the victim's side. When interrogated by the local governor he not only confessed the crime, but also named an accomplice (*hamrāh*). At the same time, the leaders of his community managed to obtain his release under their guarantee (*kafīl*), on the pretext that they would carry out further investigations into his activities in the locality. As soon as he was released, however, the suspect set out to the khan's court, to petition for a more objective examination of his case. This led to the *ḥākim* sending his dispatch, in which he was forced to give a detailed account to Khiva to demonstrate that he had acted justly during the earlier investigation.

6.4 *Qāżīs' Reports*

Qāżīs are conspicuous by their infrequency of their appearance in the '*yasāvulbāshī* documents'. The fourth section of this book includes only a handful of reports, which *qāżīs* addressed to the royal court in Khiva. Most of these reports reflect how *qāżīs* attended to and fulfilled tasks which the royal court assigned to them and which ranged from hearing lawsuits to inspecting corpses for traces of lethal injuries. As we noted earlier, the infrequency with

222 Kosbergenov, "Polozhenie karakalpalskogo naseleniia v Khivinskom khanstve v kontse XIX–nachale XX v.", p. 262.

223 Doc. 51.

which *qāżīs* appear reflects their lower status in the hierarchy of power within the Islamic juridical field of Khorezm. That is, Qonghrats' subjects brought their grievances to representatives of khanal authority because the latter were more powerful and effective than *qāżīs* in enforcing judgments. Our observation does not amount to say that *qāżīs* did not hear cases. They usually did not hear cases of their own volition, but mostly when instructed to do so by the royal court and, especially, by the office of the *yasāvulbāshī*. It could also be that *qāżīs* did hear cases of their volition after those parties to a dispute agreed to bring their cases to judges instead of turning to the royal court officials (see Docs. nos 66 and 68). While they played a somewhat marginal role in hearing cases, *qāżīs* were central in the process of notarizing the resolution of conflicts. The records here assembled show that more often than not representatives of the Qonghrat royal court pursued reconciliation. When the latter was achieved, parties were obviously interested to secure proof of a peaceful settlement (*ṣulḥ*). *Qāżīs* therefore produced records solemnizing the stipulations of such settlements, which could include acknowledgments of acquittal (*ibrā'*) of a claim and all sorts of transactions.[224] Although such records rarely include references to disputes, they should nevertheless be read as *outcomes* of disputes.

7 What was the Cost of the *'arż*?

The account by Nyl Lykoshin, Head of the Amu-Darya Department, of his tour of inspection of the Khanate of Khiva in 1912 includes an intriguing story told to him by a certain Allāh Naẓar, an inhabitant of Tashhawz. The latter told the Russian official about his dispute with the local town's chief of police (*pashshāb*), which had left Allāh Naẓar with knife wounds. Allāh Naẓar submitted a petition to Khiva and, as a result of the investigation, the chief of police was found guilty and sentenced to pay 200 *ṭillā* (360 roubles, by Lykoshin's calculations). However, the victim only saw a quarter of that sum, since 100 *ṭillā* went to Muḥammad Yūsuf Yasāvulbāshī, who had investigated the case,' and an additional 50 *ṭillā* 'was the share that went to the attendant (*yasāvul* – P.S., U.A.) for their efforts.'[225] The episode is noteworthy, above all, because it

224 The phenomenon whereby 19th-century Central Asia *qāżīs* mostly operated as notaries has been the subject of a discussion in Sartori, *Visions of Justice: Sharī'a and Cultural Change in Russian Central Asia*, pp. 54–57.

225 N.S. Lykoshin, *Zapiska Nachal'nika Amu-Dar'inskogo Otdela Polkovnika Lykoshina o sovremennom sostoianii Khivinskogo Khanstva, 1912 god*, TsGARUz, f. I-2, op. 1, d. 314, ll. 46–46ob.

gives at least a vague idea of how the sums taken from the parties to a dispute were then distributed after the hearing of the case in Khiva.

Meanwhile, one of the reports from governors to the office of the *yasāvulbāshī* presented in Section Two also illustrates the substantial financial investment that a petitioner had to make when taking one's appeal to Khiva.[226] The governor informs the central agencies about the course of the examination of a petition which had earlier been submitted by a subject to the khan's palace, and reports how, during the subsequent hearing in the province, one of the defendants had insisted that the examination of the case be transferred back to Khiva. The *ḥākim* admits that he had tried to talk the defendant out of such a rash decision, since such an appeal to Khiva 'would end up costing the petitioner (*kharj*) 200 roubles (*manāt*).'[227] Unfortunately, the author of the report does not say anything about what he had in mind precisely by 'costs during the trip to Khiva.' Indeed, one is only left to wonder what may have been the items of expenditure that a petitioner had to take into account, when preparing to set off for Khiva.

It is notable that a similar amount of expenditure for the handing over of a petition and its examination in Khiva is also indicated by the authors of a grievance submitted to members of the 'Senate Review' (Rus. *Senatskaia Reviziia*) that had been initiated by the Russian imperial authorities in 1908–9 for the survey of their colonial possesions in Turkestan. The authors of the letter, inhabitants of Khiva who wished to remain anonymous, describe the wrongs of the local justice system to the director of the commission, Count Konstantin Konstantinovich Pahlen. In particular, they write that the procedure for the reception and examination of petitions from subjects had become a source of income for the officials involved, such that an examination of an ordinary petition to Khiva usually cost the petitioner around 100–200 *ṭillā*. A slightly smaller sum – 50 *ṭillā*, according to the authors of the missive addressed to Pahlen – would be taken during the hearing of a petition by provincial authorities such as the *ḥākims*.[228]

---

226 Doc. 21.

227 *Manāt* was the local designation for the Russian rouble. After the Russian takeover of Khiva in 1873 the two currencies, i.e., *manāt* and *ṭillā*, were used in the khanate. Though the exchange rate was not stable, the average rate during this period had been fluctuating between 1,6 and 1,8 Russian roubles (*manāt*) for one Khivan *ṭillā*, see ʿAbdullah Bāltaev, *Rivālūtsiyadīn avval qīshlāq khwājalīqīdā būlghān Khwārazm dīhqanlārīnī aḥvālī va kūrgan ʿazāblārī*, MS Tashkent, IVANRUz inv. no. 11978, fol. 23a; Iu.O.Ia., "Khivinskaia ten'ga v sviazi s nedavnim proshlym ten'govogo voprosa," *Turkestanskii sbornik*, vol. 464 (Tashkent, 1908), p. 122–8; [Girshfel'd and Galkin], *Voenno-statisticheskoe opisanie Khivinskogo oazisa*, II, p. 199.

228 RGIA, f. 1396, op. 1, d. 33, l. 101.

It would be tempting to treat the information coming from Lykoshin and the anonymous petitioners as part and parcel of the narrative, which was dominant in Central Asia under Russian rule, about the corrupt nature of power and, by extension, of the justice system in the Khanate of Khiva. Equally, the similarity between the figures provided by three different authors may suggest that indeed we are dealing here with established practices of corruption. At any rate, it seems obvious that, in a system without fixed payments, various official figures at both the central and provincial levels saw their involvement in the hearing of petitions as an important source of revenue.

The Khivan author Safarov emphasised that appellants would be meeting expenses as soon as they filed their grievance. One had to make a payment (*kātībāna*) to the court scribe (*divān*) for a rescript (*fatak*) to be drawn up and stamped by the Qonghrat chancery.[229] Mirzā ʿAbd al-Raḥmān, the translator and assistant of Alexander Kuhn, in his records composed in 1873, wrote that the court *divān*s would take for themselves 9 *ṭanga*s from everyone who came to the *ʿarż*.[230] The *yasāvulbāshī* also expected a separate payment (*muhrāna*) for affixing his seal to the instruction. The head of the court guard (*dahabāshī*) received his share of the payment for sending a mounted guard (*āṭlī yasāvul*) to the site of the conflict.[231] The latter would often have to travel tens of kilometres from the capital. Although in the rescripts the sum to be paid for the services of the escorts was strictly stipulated in the region of 2 to 4 *ṭanga* per parasang travelled, Safarov asserts that besides this formal pay, the petitioner would also have to cover his expenses (*kharj fulī*), including the fodder for his horse (*āṭ āvqātī*) for the whole course of the investigation of the case.[232]

The hearing of the conflict in the locality also meant involving community elders (*āqsaqāl*) and authoritative members of the community from both sides (*īl-ādamlārī*), who would expect to be hosted and given presents. Ethnographic data collected by Soviet scholars among the Qaraqalpaqs living on the northern edges of the khanate provides specific confirmation of this:

229 Bābājān Safarov, *Khwārazm taʾrīkhī (1864–1934)*, MS Tashkent, IVANRUz, inv. no. 10231, fol. 21.

230 Mirza Abdurakhman, [*Zapiski Mirza Abdurakhmana*], St. Petersburg, IVRRAN, Arkhiv Vostokovedov, f. 33, d. 134, l. 99 ob. On Alexander Kuhn and Mirzā ʿAbd al-Raḥmām, see O. Yastrebova and A. Azad, "Reflections on an Orientalist: Alexander Kuhn (1840–88), the Man and His Legacy," *Iranian Studies* 48.5 (2015), pp. 675–694.

231 Bābājān Safarov, *Khwārazm taʾrīkhī (1864–1934)*, MS Tashkent, IVANRUz, inv. no. 10231, fol. 22.

232 Chancery expenses are not specific to Khiva and its *ʿarż-dād* procedure, to be sure. One is put in mind that in other regions of Central Asia too to secure a fatwa, or a deed for that matter, required paying similar fees. See Sartori, *Visions of Justice: Sharīʿa and Cultural Change in Russian Central Asia*, pp. 63, 136, 264.

> Usually a court decision about a litigation would be settled in the province. The authorities would arrive in the village and stay at the house of whoever had initiated proceedings. The plaintiff would have to slaughter his livestock and host ... his entire retinue. The examination of a case could sometimes last a week. The costs for the plaintiff would rise constantly; he would be forced to make concessions ... The higher the level of jurisdiction, the greater the scale of hospitality required ...[233]

We should also not forget the cost of involving a provincial governor, and paying for the services of *qāżīs*, regardless of whether they brought their legal expertise in the form of an interrogation of the witnesses, an oath-taking, or simply by notarising either an amicable settlement (*ṣulḥ*) or a withdrawal of the claim (*ibrā*ʾ), following an out-of-court settlement of the conflict.

The question of the many malfeasances by senior officials, particularly in connection with the examination of petitions, was often raised by members of the colonial administration in the region. In late 1910, under pressure from colonial officials, the Khivan authorities initiated administrative reforms, designed to root out a system based on Qonghrat officials' discretion, and instead to introduce fixed payment from the treasury. For example, the first point of the so-called Programme of Reform, undertaken in January 1911, declared:

> The khan of Khiva, considering the [present system of] remuneration of official persons to be old-fashioned, and incommensurate with [the demands of] the present time ... has ordered for the introduction of an arrangement of daily payments to all the officials of the khanate, commensurate with the character of the official duties they carry out.... For this reason, all payment [formerly] taken from the population [for the benefit of] the Khivan treasury and as payment for court officials is now cancelled. In particular, the following payments are cancelled: payments taken [from the population] for the Khivan treasury for fixing compensation for murder (*khūn*) to [the value of] 1/10 [of the value of the compensation], also the payment of 10 *ṭillā* [taken by] *yasāvul*s and *maḥram*s, on their appointment to investigate murders; the payment of 5 *tillā* during the investigation of cases of injuries; also the payment taken by *ḥākim*s for investigating matters of theft and robbery [to the cost of] 1/10 [of the value of the compensation]. Besides this, for the drawing up and delivery of documents (*ḥujjat khaṭ*), and for the making of decisions (*ḥukm*) about

233 Kosbergenov, "Polozhenie karakalpalskogo naseleniia v Khivinskom khanstve v kontse XIX–nachale XX v.", pp. 260–261.

> claims (*da'vā īshlār*), [it is not permitted for] *qāżīs* to take more than 5 *ṭanga* from every 1,000 *ṭanga* [of the sum demanded in the claim] ... All of these payments are cancelled in their entirety and without exception.[234]

As a consequence of these initiatives, there were also attempts to fix the cost of the services of the *qāżīs* and *hākims*. We also have a written instruction from the Khivan central authorities, addressed to the *qāżīs* of one of the towns of the khanate (sealed by Sayyid Islām Khwāja – the grand *vazīr* of the khanate), regulating the sphere of powers and the pricing for drawing up documents:

> [It is permitted for *qāżīs*] to take a payment in the form of *muhrāna* and *kātībāna* for the notarisation of any kind of document (*khaṭ*) in their chamber (*maḥkama*); and also *kātībāna* for registration (*daftar ītūlgāndā*) of such documents, calculated at half a *ṭanga* for every 100 *ṭanga* [of the value of the transaction] and at 5 *ṭanga* from every 1,000 *ṭanga* [of the value of the transaction], but not to demand anything above the [sum] stipulated. When the documents are notarised, and no [precise value of the claim] is to be stipulated, as for example in the case of [the notarisation] of a document concerning the withdrawal by one person of a claim (*da'vā*) against another person, or equally [the drawing up of] other such documents, then the payment for such types of services is fixed at [the value of] no more than 2 *ṭanga* [per document drawn up].[235]

However, these initiatives were largely declarative, and they evidently did little to change things much at an institutional level. The practice of *kormlenie* ('feeding'), i.e., distributing stipends to officials, which was the central component of the system of power relations in the Khanate of Khiva, could not be replaced by fixed payments for senior officials. Attempts to regulate such a sophisticated and flexible system, even simply by introducing fixed rates, resulted in ineffective half-measures. What is more, even this formal initiative was not fully realised.[236] Without realistic mechanisms for its enforcement, informal agreements continued to dominate, and so the examination of petitions, claims and conflicts between citizens continued to be seen as an important source of income for the individuals involved.

---

234 GMIQ, Khiva, KP-3687, fols. 2a–2b.

235 TsGARUz, f. I-125, op. 1, d. 579, l. 2.

236 Abdurasulov and Sartori, "Neopredelennost' kak politika: razmyshliaia o prirode rossiiskogo protektorata v Srednei Azii," p. 144.

Safarov notes that during the hearing of a case at the court, besides the fixed fees, it was expected that the petitioner and the defendants would make various payments to the *yasāvulbāshī*, and that they would also bring 'gifts as a mark of gratitude' (*pīshkashlar bilān qūllūq qīlandī*) to various courtiers who could have a positive influence on the resolution of the case. Even after the decision had been made, the claimant or the defendant, depending on who had been successful, would have to bring yet another present to the *yasāvulbāshī*, 'commensurate with the value of the claim.'[237]

Moreover, the Khivan author writes that examination of a case in Khiva could drag on 'for two to three months.' Given that it was usual for 'ten to fifteen' authoritative fellow villagers and elders of the community to escort the litigants to Khiva, the living costs for the latter during their stay in the capital could add an additional burden for the litigants. As a good illustration, Safarov writes how during the days of the *ʿarż*, there were always money-lenders (*sūdkhūrlār*) plying their trade 'at the entrance to the khan's palace,' ready to provide litigants with the necessary sums at interest. Of course, Safarov's information cannot be taken at face value; it must be remembered that the work was composed in 1957, i.e., four years after the death of Stalin, in a state where entirely different ideological and epistemological paradigms dominated. It therefore reflects a number of preconceptions, especially in the section concerning the justice system. Nonetheless, it is clear that a journey to Khiva for examination of a case at the khan's palace was no cheap undertaking by any means.

Therefore, a somewhat ambivalent picture has emerged, wherein on the one hand the khan of Khiva was in fact reasonably accessible for subjects who wished to appeal to him, but where the practical realization of such access could end up being distinctly expensive for them.

So, once again, the question arises: why did subjects decide to go to Khiva? The answer is both complicated, and simple. Litigants usually had to pay a considerable amount of money to have their cases heard. Obviously, sometimes the larger part of the expenses would fall on the shoulders of the losing side.[238] Thus, petitioners might be able to recoup their costs. Therefore, on the one hand, a claimant planning to take a petition to Khiva would have to weigh up the possible expenses that further examination of the case could incur, against

237 Bābājān Safarov, *Khwārazm taʾrīkhī (1864–1934)*, MS Tashkent, IVANRUz, inv. no. 10231, fols. 21b–22b. For comparative purposes, see A. Wilde, *What is beyond the River? Power, Authority and Social Order in Transoxania (18th–19th Centuries)*, 3 vols. (Vienna: Austrian Academy of Sciences Press, 2016).

238 Some of the royal rescripts stipulate that the *yasāvulbāshī*'s expenses should be paid by the side found guilty.

what could be won if the case was decided in their favour. Meanwhile, the defendant would also have to calculate the risks of such an undertaking. So if they felt their position was not sufficiently secure, they would be much better off trying to resolve the case in the locality, without a hearing in Khiva. They might therefore accept the claimant's conditions partially or in full in order to reach a compromise.

Still, it would be misleading to explain the motives of the people who decided to set off to the royal court solely on the basis of financial or material factors. An excellent illustration is provided by the following story, found in the writings of the mid-nineteenth-century Russian author Galkin, who carried out ethnographic research among the Turkmen tribes on the eastern shore of the Caspian Sea. Galkin presents the story of a Turkmen woman from the Caspian gulf of Qara-Bogaz, who wanted to divorce her husband. According to Galkin, this woman was well aware that such a divorce was hardly possible within the legal and ethical norms of the Turkmen locality, so she decided to petition the khan in Khiva, where she was able to secure a public divorce.[239] Of course, there are good reasons to suspect this story, recorded by a Russian author, may be apocryphal. However, it is still quite telling, in the sense that it can explain why the protagonists in our documents, during an interrogation by the *ḥākim*, or before the *qāżī*, so often opted to leave the room and set off for Khiva. With an appeal to the khan's court in Khiva, the resolution of a conflict would receive new publicity. Hence it could allow simple people the chance to receive satisfaction (which was otherwise hard to attain) for injuries to their self-worth, and to restore their sense of dignity before the community to which they belonged.

239 M.N. Galkin, *Etnograficheskie i istoricheskie materialy po Srednei Azii i Orenburgskomu kraiu* (St. Petersburg: Izdanie Ia.A. Isakova, 1868), p. 33.

Documents

SECTION 1

Rescripts

Document 1: A Rescript by the *yasāvulbāshī* about a Dispute over Inheritance[1]

Introduction

A certain Muḥammad Jān passed away. His wife Āyimsūn Bīka and Qūchqār, underaged son of Muḥammad Jān and stepson of Āyimsūn Bīka, inherited from him some money and a horse. Bīk Jān, Āyimsūn Bīka's brother, kept all this wealth in custody (*amānat*). He did so most probably by acting in the capacity of guardian for the underage. At some point in time Āyimsūn Bīka asked Bīk Jān to entrust to her the inheritance left to her and her son, but Bīk Jān refused to do so. Āyimsūn Bīka thus took legal action against her brother. She went to Khiva and filed there a claim with the royal court. The *yasāvulbāshī* issued a warrant ordering an attendant (*yasāvul*) to go to the place and deal with the conflict. Negotiations evidently proved insufficient to achieve an extra-judicial reconciliation, and the case was then transferred to a judge (*qāżī-īshān*), who summoned the parties. At the hearing Bīk Jān counterclaimed that his sister had already relinquished the claim. According to a legal procedure often adopted in *sharīʿa* courts, the judge put Āyimsūn Bīka under oath (*ānt*).[2] She swore an oath and the judge consequently ruled for the restitution of the inheritance and compensation for the horse that had in the meantime been sold.

Translation

A certain Āyimsīn Bīka[3] together with Qūchqār, who is Jumʿa Niyāz's minor (*ṣaghīr*) stepson (*ūgāy ūghlī*), gave 50 *ṭillā* in cash, 50 *ṭillā* in promissory note (*khaṭ*), and one horse in deposit (*amānat*). Since [the afore-mentioned goods] were not returned [to their proprietors], they filed a claim (*daʿvā*) against a certain Bīk Jān. Let [the parties] together with Muḥammad Raḥīm Bāy Yasāvul, who is the liegeman (*nawkar*) of Muḥammad Yūsuf Yasāvulbāshī, come to the royal court (*dargāh-i ʿālī*) of our lord, may his rule last forever, and solve [the dispute] (*ṣāf būlsūnlār*). The attendant's fee (*yasāvul ḥaqqī*) is 4 *tanga* per parasang. This warrant (*khaṭ*) was registered on 28 Ẕī al-ḥijja 1328 [30.12.1910].

1 TsGARUz, I-125, op. 2, d. 633, ll. 7–7ob.

2 Sartori, *Visions of Justice:* Sharīʿa *and Cultural Change in Russian Central Asia*, chap. 5.

3 This is a spelling variation of Āyimsūn Bīka, see below *verso* side of the document.

© KONINKLIJKE BRILL NV, LEIDEN, 2020 | DOI:10.1163/9789004427907_003

Seal: Muḥammad Yūsuf Yasāvulbāshī b. Avaż Niyāz Maḥram

[Verso:] Khudāy Qulī from Manāq[4] and Āyimsūn Bīka bint Shīr Niyāz, from the Būrlāq community (*qavm*), acting on behalf of themselves and as a guardian (*aṣālatan ūz ṭarafīdīn viṣāyatan*) of her minor son (*ṣaghīr ūghlī*) Qūchqār b. Muḥammad Jān, had lodged a claim (*daʿvā qīldī*) against Bīk Jān valad-i Shīr Nīyāz, from Māylī Jengel.[5] [The claim] regarded a horse valued at 50 *ṭillā* and 50 *ṭillā* in cash. Since [the respondent] answered that he had [already] returned the goods and discharged [himself from any obligation], the onus of the oath (*ant*)[6] fell on Āyimsūn Bīka and her husband Jumʿa Nīyāz b. Raḥmān Birdī. According to the subsequent ruling (*ḥukm*), 50 *ṭillā* in bonds and 100 *ṭillā* in cash were given [to the claimants] in the presence of the *qāżī-īshān*. [This occurred] on 8 Muḥarram 1328 [19.02.1910].[7]

4 Manaq, otherwise known as Ambar or Ambar-Manaq, was a settlement located 45 km north-west of Khiva, see "Opisanie Khivinskogo khanstva, sostavlennoe v 1842 g. podpolkovnikom G.I. Danilevskim," p. 103; A. Kun, *Ocherk istorii zaseleniia Khivinskogo khanstva s drevnykh vremen, sostav ego sovremennogo naseleniia, administratsiia i goroda khanstva*, 1873, IVRRAN, St. Petersburg, Arkhiv Vostokovedov, f. 33, d. 8, l. 45 ob. ʿAbdullāh Bāltaev mentioned Manāq among the 24 administrative units at the head of which at the end of the 19th century there was a governor (*ḥākim*), see his *Khīva īsdalīklārī*, MS Tashkent, IVANRUz, inv. no. 11645, fol. 108a. Bāltaev employs a Soviet term to denote such administrative unit, *rāyūn* < Rus. *raion*.

5 Māylī Jengel or Māylī Chungul is indicated between Gurlen and Ambar and corresponds to the modern village of Mayli Jengel which is located circa 11 km south-west of Gurlen, see Munis and Agahi, *Firdaws al-iqbāl: History of Khorezm*, p. 610, n. 615; Georg von Gens, and Gregor von Helmersen, "Izvestiia o Khive, Bukhare, Kokande i severo-zapadnoi chasti Kitaiskogo gosudarstva," p. 24.

6 Spelling variation of *ānt*.

7 The date is incorrect, otherwise it would seem that the judge issued the ruling a year prior to the claim being filed with the royal court. It is thus more likely that the date was 8 Muḥarram 1329, that corresponds 8 January 1911.

Document 2: A Rescript by the *yasāvulbāshī* about a Dispute over the Payment of Dowry[8]

Introduction

In 19th-century Central Asia a wedding consisted of three main rituals. One was the 'betrothal' consisting of the reading of the opening *sura* of the Qur'ān (*fātiḥa*) with which the bride and the groom commit to the wedding. The other was the solemnization of the marriage (*nikāḥ*) usually before a mullah in the form of a contract (*ʿaqd-i nikāḥ*).[9] The third ritual was the celebration (*tūy*).[10] The first two took place at the house of the bride, but expenses for the organization of the celebration fell exclusively on the groom's family.[11] The latter expenses were called *tūyāna* and consisted mainly of gifts to the bride's family. The family of the groom paid also a bride-price called *qālīng*, which might include a sum of money as well as other goods such clothes and jewelry. While *mahr* is the default normative Islamic term for bride-price, our sources do not distinguish between Islamic and customary bride-price. We are therefore inclined to infer that, in Khivan bureaucratese, *qālīng* was perceived and used as a synonym for *mahr*.[12] However, while one would expect the dower to be paid directly to the bride and thus become her property,[13] our sources show that *qālīng* was usually paid to her parents. Khorezmian *muftī*s opined that such payment should be regarded as temporary. In this way, the bride-price was given in deposit (*amānat*) to parents, but the wedded brides would

8 TsGARUz, I-125, op. 2, d. 633, ll. 1–10b.

9 *Mullās* and *imāms* usually needed the permission from an office-holder (more often than not a *qāżī*) to perform the marriage. See, for instance, *Katalog khivinskikh kaziiskikh dokumentov XIX–nachala XX vv*, docs. 791, 842, 993, 1081, 1091, 1283.

10 N.P. Lobacheva, "K istorii slozheniia instituta svadebnoi obriadnosti (na primere kompleksov svadebnykh obychaev i obriadov narodov Srednei Azii i Kazakhstana)," in *Sem'ia i semeinye obriady u narodov Srednei Azii i Kazakhstana*, ed. G.P. Snesarev (Moscow: Nauka, 1978), p. 144. Lobacheva also suggests that among settled Uzbeks (including the population of Khorezm) it was common to deliver the customary bride-price prior to the engagement, ibid., p. 173.

11 S.N. Abashin, "Kalym i makhr v Srednei Azii: o "granitsakh" v sotsial'nykh otnosheniyakh," in *Chelovek i pravo. Kniga o letnei schkole po iuridicheskoi antropologii*, eds. N.I. Novikova and V.A. Tishkova (Moscow: Institut etnologii i antropologii RAN, 1999), pp. 155–161.

12 This supports the view expressed in Abashin, *Kalym i makhr v Srednei Azii*, p. 159. *Sharīʿa* courts' documents from Khorezm, instead, use only the term *mahr* to refer to bride-price. See *Katalog khivinskikh kaziiskikh dokumentov XIX–nachala XX vv.*, docs. 849, 871, 907, 933.

13 O. Spies, "Mahr", *The Encyclopaedia of Islam, second edition*, eds. P. Bearman et al. (Leiden: Brill, 1991), Vol. VI, pp. 78–80.

recover their property after the solemnization of the marriage.[14] The following document recounts a conflict that sparked in the wake of an engagement: the groom's father failed to deliver the entire bride-price to the bride's family, who subsequently filed a claim with the royal court in Khiva. There the *yasāvulbāshī* issued a warrant and entrusted it to an attendant. The brief report drawn by the attendant on the verso side of the document indicates that the latter convened the parties and persuaded the groom's father to pay the remaining bride-price and commit to the defrayment of other wedding gifts. The note also suggests that the agreement was solemnised before a *qāżī* in the form a certificate of acknowledgment (*iqrār*) in the presence of two witnesses. One may infer that the certificate in question was, in fact, a marriage contract.[15]

Translation

Saʿādat Bīka Muḥammad Ṣafānīng qīzī, and Khāl Murād Khudāy Bīrgān ūghlī are engaged (*fātiḥa-khwānd ītib*). While the [bride's parents] received 30 *ṭillā* as [part of] the customary bride-price (*qalīng pūlī*), the [groom] failed to pay the remaining sum as well as other liabilities concerning the wedding (*qālgan tūyāna lavāzim*). He avoided providing explanations and four years have passed without his giving any notice. For this reason (*vajh*), [Muḥammad Ṣafā] filed a claim (*daʿvā*) against [the groom's side]. Accordingly, let the parties come to the royal court (*dargāh-i ʿālī*) of our lord, may his rule last forever, together with Sulṭān Yūzbāshī Yasāvul and solve [the dispute] (*ṣāf būlsūnlār*). The attendant's fee (*yasāvul ḥaqqī*) should not exceed more than 2 *tanga* for each parasang. This warrant (*khaṭ*) was drawn up on Tuesday, 9 Shavvāl 1328 [13.10.1913].

Seal: Shaykh Naẓar Yasāvulbāshī b. Muḥammad Murād Dīvānbīgī

[Verso:] Saʿādat Bīka Muḥammad Ṣafā b. Yaʿqub Bāy qīzī, who belongs to the community (*qavm*) of Īsh Niyāz Bājbān in Manāq, went to Khāl Murād Khudāy Bīrgān b. ʿAvaz Muḥammad ūghlī, who is a member of the same community.

---

14 *Katalog khivinskikh kaziiskikh dokumentov XIX–nachala XX vv*, doc. 1075. It should be noted that in the description of the legal opinion (*rivāyat*) the dower is referred to as *kalym* (Rus. for '*qālīng*'), while the term does not occur In the original text of the record. For another such legal opinion, see TsGARUz, f. I-125, op. 1, d. 495, l. 9.

15 See, for instance, *Katalog khivinskikh kaziiskikh dokumentov XIX–nachala XX vv.*, doc. 205. There are several misinterpretations in the description of the document in question, where, for example, the term *ṣaghīr* is rendered as 'orphan' instead of 'minor,' see the original source in IVANRUz, Ashapberova Akliia, papka 3, unnumbered folio [5].

[The bride's party] received [the remaining part] of the customary bride-price (*qālīng mālī*) for organising the wedding ceremony (*tūy*). Khudāy Bīrgān said that he will deliver to Muḥammad Ṣafā new clothes together with other wedding gifts (*tūyānalār*). This [promissory note] was notarised (*iqrār yāzīldī*) in the presence (*shāhidlarī*) of the *yasāvul* and Gadāy Niyāz Bābā b. Ḥamīt Niyāz.

Document 3: A Rescript by the *yasāvulbāshī* about a Dispute over Landownership[16]

Introduction

A conflict over circa 2,8 ha of land sparked in Qosh-Kupruk, a locality on the left bank of the Ghaziabad canal.[17] The *yasāvulbāshī* thus issued a warrant with which he appointed an attendant (*yasāvul*) and instructed him to escort the claimant to the disputed place. The warrant served also to instruct a *qāżī* to appoint a trustee (*amīn*) to examine the deeds available to the parties and divide the land accordingly. This and other documents show that, when parties to a dispute agreed on the procedures of conflict-resolution adopted by the royal court, the *qāżī*'s role in the settlement of disputes was confined to extrajudicial functions such as the appointment of trustees, the examination of corpses, etc. The record indicates that the achievement of an agreement between the parties took place also before a *qāżī* who joined the trustee. It could be that the presence of the jurist conferred additional legal force and authority upon the reconciliation. It could also be that, once reconciliation was achieved, the *qāżī* notarised a document solemnizing an amicable settlement (*ṣulḥ*) whereby the parties agreed to a number of stipulations determining the access to the property in question.

Translation

Let it be known to our *qāżī ʿaskar-īshān*,[18] the transmitter of the prophetic law

---

16 TsGARUz, I-125, op. 2, d. 633, ll. 24–24 ob.

17 Ghaziabad (Gazavat) is the name of a fortified settlement in the lower reaches of the canal bearing the same name. Guliamov suggests that this fortification was erected in the mid-17th century, Guliamov, *Istoriia orosheniia Khorezma s drevneishikh vremen do nashikh dnei*, p. 202. According to Kuhn, in the second half of the 19th century the settlement included circa 50 shops and 3 mosques, *Ocherk istorii zaseleniia Khivinskogo khanstva s drevnykh vremen, sostav ego sovremennogo naseleniia, administratsiia i goroda khanstva*, 1873, IVRRAN, St. Petersburg, Arkhiv Vostokovedov, f. 33, d. 8, l. 46 ob. See also Munis and Agahi, *Firdaws al-iqbāl: History of Khorezm*, p. 613, note 648.

18 *qāżī ʿaskar* – (lit., 'military judge'). In the Khanate of Khiva *qāżī ʿaskars* were tasked with responsibilities expanding beyond disputes among the military. Records indicate clearly that they also heard misdemeanors among the wider populace, see *Katalog khivinskikh kaziiskikh dokumentov XIX – nachala XX vv.*, docs. 225, 311, 581, 718. Some authors also suggested that the office of *qāżī ʿaskar* coincided with that of the *qāżī ūrda* – a judge of the royal residence. Together with the *qāżī kalān* ('chief judge') the *qāżī ʿaskar* was regarded as the 'supreme judges over all judges of the khanate,' see A. Kun, *Ocherk istorii zaseleniia Khivinskogo khanstva s drevnykh vremen, sostav ego sovremennogo naseleniia, administratsiia i goroda khanstva*, 1873, IVRRAN, St. Petersburg, Arkhiv Vostokovedov, f. 33, d. 8, l. ll. 39–39 ob.; N.S. Lykoshin, *Sovremennoe raspredelenie vlasti v Khanstve Khivinskom, 1912 god*, TsGARUz, f. I-2, op. 1, d. 314, l. 64 ob.; Bābājān Safarov, *Khwārazm taʾrīkhī (1864–1934)*,

(*muravvij-i sharīʿat-i nabavī*), that Sulṭān Murād from Qūshkūfrūk[19] had a claim (*daʿvālī bulūb*) against ʿAbd al-Raḥīm Maḥram concerning [a plot of] land measured (*bar-kashīda*) 7½ *ṭanāb*.[20] Since [Sulṭān Murād] has submitted a petition (*ʿarż*) [to the royal court], let a reliable trustee (*muʿtabar amīn*) join Ḥasan Yasāvul, who is the liegeman (*nawkar*) of Muḥammad Yūsuf Yasāvulbāshī. Let the trustee reach [the place], examine their documents, determine the boundaries of this disputed land according to *sharīʿa*, and delimit [their possessions]. Conveying the royal order (*amr-i ʿālīlārī*) of our lord, may his rule last forever, [this warrant] was registered (*marqūm*) on 13 Shavvāl 1328 [17.10.1910].

Seal: Shaykh Naẓar Yasāvulbāshī b. Muḥammad Murād Dīvānbīgī

[Verso:] [The parties to the dispute agreed] to stay within the boundaries[21] [of their own possessions]. This was notified [to the office of the *yasāvulbāshī*] by their trustee (*amīn*) Mullā Tājī, who was adjoined by the *qāżī*, on 17 Shavvāl 1328 [21.10.1910].

MS Tashkent, IVANRUz, inv. no. 10231, fol. 13b. According to Bāltaev, the *qāżī ʿaskar*'s office (*qāżī-khāna*) was located within the madrasa of Muḥammad Amīn Khān in Khiva, ʿAbdullah Bāltaev, *Khīva īsdalīklārī*, MS Tashkent, IVANRUz, inv. no. 11645, fol. 28b.

19 Qosh-Kupruk – a locality on the bank of the Ghaziabad canal, 15 km north of Khiva, Munis and Agahi, *Firdaws al-iqbāl: History of Khorezm*, p. 594, n. 419; Gens, and Helmersen, *Izvestiia o Khive, Bukhare, Kokande*, p. 24; Basiner, "Estestvenno-nauchnoe puteshestvie po Kirgizskoi stepi v Khivu," p. 348; Danilevskii, *Opisanie Khivinskogo khanstva*, p. 106.

20 The *ṭanāb* was a square measure in Central Asia. In 19th-century Khorezm, a *ṭanāb* consisted of 3600 *gaz*, or was equal to 0,37–0,39 *ha*, see P.P. Ivanov, *Arkhiv khivinskikh khanov XIX v.: Issledovanie i opisanie dokumentov s istoricheskim vvedeniem* (Leningrad: Izdanie gosudarstvennoi publichnoi biblioteki, 1940), p. 20, fn. 3; Bregel', *Khorezmskie turkmeny v XIX veke*, p. 354, fn. 106.

21 The expression *tūrdūq* ('we stayed') conveys here the parties' undertaking not to trespass beyond the boundaries of their respective properties.

Document 4: A Rescript by the *yasāvulbāshī* about A Marital Dispute[22]

Introduction

A girl was promised in marriage to a man. The latter paid the customary bride-price to her family. The bride and the groom were then engaged. The marriage, however, did not take place. The groom filed a claim against the bride's father and another man with the royal court. The *yasāvulbāshī* subsequently instructed an attendant to solve the conflict. The parties reached an amicable agreement according to which the bride's father would pay back the bride-price to the groom, who, in exchange, relinquished his claim. This legal case is an insight into what we may term 'marriage-play.' A father agrees to wed his daughter and, for the engagement, he receives the customary bride-price. Should another would-be groom appear and offer a higher sum of money for the bride-price, the father will agree to wed his daughter to this second man instead. In such situations, parents usually take into consideration that they will have to face a lawsuit, pay back the entire bride-price to the first aspiring groom and perhaps even cover some other expenses. They will therefore agree to wed their daughters to a second man only if the latter offers a sum of money sufficient to cover possible losses and still represent a true economic advantage. It appears that in this case the first aspiring groom sued the bride's father together with the second would-be groom. As the respondents lost the case, the bride's father agreed to pay also for the second would-be groom and to act as his guarantor (*zar-kafīl*).[23] The stipulations of such agreements were notarised before a *qāżī* in a legal deed. The document clearly explains how the participation of the royal court's appointees in the dispute ensured and sanctioned the latter's settlement. Nothing in this records suggests that such negotiations were more in accordance with customary than Islamic law.

Translation

[A certain] Ibrāhīm paid the bride-price (*qālīng fūlī*), clothes and new [?]. While a betrothal was performed (*fātiḥa khwāndī*), Khadīcha Bīka was not handed over in marriage (*nikāḥ ītīb birmāgānlūr*). For this reason (*vajh*), he filed a claim (*daʿvā*) against [a certain] Ūrāż Muḥammad and Ramażān. Let [the parties] come to the royal court (*dargāh-i ʿālī*) of our lord, may his rule last forever, together with Muḥammad Jān Yasāvul, who is the liegeman (*nawkar*) of Shaykh Naẓar Yasāvulbāshī, and solve [the dispute] (*ṣāf būlsūnlār*). The

22 TsGARUz, I-125, op. 2, d. 633, ll. 30–30 ob.

23 On *zar-kafīl* (*kafīl-i zar*) see also, *Katalog khivinskikh kaziiskikh dokumentov XIX – nachala XX vv.*, p. 656.

attendant's fee (*yasāvul ḥaqqī*) is 4 *tanga* per parasang. The warrant (*khaṭ*) was completed on 23 Ẕī al-ḥijja 1328 [25.12.1910].

Seal: Muḥammad Yūsuf Yasāvulbāshī b. Avaż Niyāz Maḥram

[Verso:] On 7 Muḥarram Ibrāhīm b. Qāsīm received a promissory note (*almāqgha khaṭ*) for the return of 70 *ṭillā*, which relates to his claim (*daʿvā*) against Khadīcha Bīka b. Ūrāż from Tāza Bāzār[24] for the money he had given to her according to *sharīʿa*. [In exchange], he gave a certificate of relinquishment (*ibrāʾ khaṭ*) and [the dispute] was solved (*ṣāf būlūb*). [The contract] stipulates that [Khadīcha Bīka's] father, Ūrāż Muḥammad b. Ṭālib, who acts as guarantor (*zar-kafīl*), should pay the sum of money within one month. This notification (*khaṭ*) was registered in 1328.

24 We have been unable to identify this locale.

Document 5: A Rescript by the *yasāvulbāshī* about a Dispute over Debts[25]

Introduction

A certain Ūrāż Bāy owed 200 *ṭillā* to one Īsh Murād. They reached a preliminary agreement whereby Ūrāż Bāy had to pay Īsh Murād 30 *ṭillā* and entrust a horse to another man named Muḥammad Yūsuf. The animal was valued at 50 *ṭillā* and was to cover part of Ūrāż Bāy's debt. The creditor, however, did not count this payment as part of the debt. Consequently, Ūrāż Bāy decided to take legal action against both Īsh Murād and Muḥammad Yūsuf. He went to Khiva and filed a claim. An attendant escorted the claimant to meet the respondents. Muḥammad Yūsuf most probably denied that the payment of the horse was related to Ūrāż Bāy's debt with Īsh Murād. This lawsuit was therefore transferred to a *sharīʿa* court. There, as Ūrāż Bāy was unable to produce evidence, Muḥammad Yusūf, the respondent, took an oath and won the case. By contrast, the other claim concerning 30 *ṭillā* ended with a reconciliation sanctioned by the attendant. The document shows that, when the parties did not agree on a resolution of the conflict according to the stipulations proposed by the attendant, the latter could decide that the dispute would be adjudicated by a *qāżī*.

Translation

Ūrāż Bāy from Māylī Jengel[26] owes 200 *ṭillā* [to a certain] Īsh Murād from the citadel (*qalʿa*) of Khiva. [The debt has been] recorded (*khaṭlī*). [Ūrāż Bāy] enstrusted to [a certain] Muḥammad Yūsuf from Māylī Jengel a horse that was valued at 50 *ṭillā*, as part of his debt (*qarżgha birmākchī būlūb*). He also paid back 30 *ṭillā* [in cash] to the afore-mentioned Īsh Murād. [Nevertheless], the payments have not been counted [to cover the debt] and consequently [Ūrāż Bāy] is still liable for the [previously] recorded [*khaṭlī*] payment of 200 *ṭillā*. For this reason (*vajh*), [the latter] has filed a claim (*daʿvā*) against these individuals. Accordingly, let them come to the royal court (*dargāh-i ʿālī*) together with Raḥman-Qulī Yasāvul, the liegeman (*nawkar*) of Bahādir Bāy Īshīk-Āqāsī,[27]

---

25 TsGARUz, I-125, op. 2, d. 633, ll. 53–53 ob.

26 For the location of this place, see Doc. 1.

27 The *īshīk-āqā* or *īshīk-āqḥā* (lit. 'doorkeeper') was a courtier who guarded the entrance to the khan's audience-hall. According to different accounts, there were two of them in the Khivan royal palace. Their duties amounted mostly to staying at the entrance of the audience-hall (*ʿarż-khāna*) during the ceremonies when the khan heard grevances, see Bābājān Safarov, *Khwārazm taʾrīkhī (1864–1934)*, MS Tashkent, IVANRUz, inv. no. 10231, fol. 15b; A. Kun, *Ocherk istorii zaseleniia Khivinskogo khanstva s drevnykh vremen, sostav ego sovremennogo naseleniia, administratsiia i goroda khanstva*, 1873, IVRRAN, St. Petersburg, Arkhiv Vostokovedov, f. 33, d. 8, l. 42ob.

and solve [the dispute] (*ṣāflāshsūnlār*). The attendant's fee (*yasāvul ḥaqqī*) is 4 *tanga* per parasang. Conveying the royal order (*amr-i ʿālīlārī*) of our lord, may his rule last forever, this warrant (*khaṭ*) was written on 17 Ẕī al-ḥījja 1328 [19.12.1910].

Seal: Shaykh Naẓar Yasāvulbāshi b. Muḥammad Murād Dīvānbīgī

[Verso:] This claim (*daʿvā*) was transferred to a *qāżī* (*sharīʿatgha qūshūlūb*). With regard to the horse valued at 50 *ṭillā*, Muḥammad Yūsuf took an oath (*ānt*). The claim against the afore-mentioned Īsh Murād concerning 30 *ṭillā* was solved (*ṣaf būlūb*) without a hearing according to Islamic law (*sharīʿatda īshitilmāy*). [The resolution] was notarised (*khaṭlāshūb*). [The royal court] was informed on 22 Ẕī al-ḥījja 1328 [24.12.1910].

Document 6: A Rescript by the *yasāvulbāshī* about a Dispute over an Ancestral Undivided Property[28]

Introduction

Four brothers purchased a plot of land as an ancestral undivided property. Later three of them sought to divide the land amongst themselves thereby excluding their brother named Khudāyār. Accordingly, the latter filed a claim with the royal court, which appointed an attendant and issued a warrant. A certain mullah acted in the capacity of mediator and achieved an extra-judicial reconciliation. The parties agreed that Khudāyār would receive his share. The attendant sanctioned the outcome of the dispute. It is worth nothing that the attendant assisting the plaintiff was not the person who was appointed by the royal court. It is unclear what might have prompted this change. No more clear is the reason behind the mullah's participation in the resolution of the conflict. Was he someone known to the parties? At any rate, it seems that, without the sanction of the state, the mediation of the mullah alone would not have been enough to negotiate the case. Instead, it was only by filing a lawsuit with the royal court and subsequently involving an attendant that the claimant could compel the respondents to reach an agreement on the land.

Translation

Khudāyār acquired in partnership (*sharīk būlūb*) [with his brothers] 5 *ṭanāb* land. [Now the brothers] intend to divide this plot of land among each other without reimbursing what was due to him. For this reason (*vajh*), [Khudāyār] filed a claim (*daʿvā*) against his brothers, Iskandar, ʿAbdullāh, and Mavlām Birdī. Let them come to the royal court (*dargāh-i ʿālī*) of our lord, may his rule last forever, together with the *dahlīz maḥramī*[29] Muḥammad Raḥīm Yasāvul, and solve [the dispute] (*ṣāf būlsūnlār*). The attendant's fee (*yasāvul ḥaqqī*) is 2 *tanga* per parasang. This warrant (*khaṭ*) was registered on 7 Shavvāl 1328 [11.10.1910].

---

28 TsGARUz, I-125, op. 2, d. 633, l. 61–61 ob.

29 The *maḥram* (lit. 'confidant') was a chamberlain, an individual close to the Khivan khans, who was also endowed with the right to access dynasts' private chambers (*ḥaram*). *Dahlīz maḥramī* (lit. 'threshold's confidant') was evidently a chamberlain who served at the royal court, but who could not access the khan's private apartments. On *maḥrams*, see A. Kun, *Ocherk istorii zaseleniia Khivinskogo khanstva s drevnykh vremen, sostav ego sovremennogo naseleniia, administratsiia i goroda khanstva*, 1873, IVRRAN, St. Petersburg, Arkhiv Vostokovedov, f. 33, d. 8, l. 42 ob.

Seal: Muḥammad Yūsuf Yasāvulbāshī b. Avaż Niyāz Maḥram

[Verso:] [A certain] Mullā Khudāyār from Shīrshālī[30] solved the claim (*daʿvā*) of Khudāyār from Ḥāfiq[31] on the spot (*daʿvāsī īlātīdā yarāshīb*). So the conflict was solved and the plot of land [that was due to Khudāyār] will remain at his disposal. [The plaintiff] together with his attendant ʿAbdullāh Īshīk-Āqāsī came [to the royal court] and informed [us about this].

30 There were different places in the Khanate of Khiva known under the name of Shīrshālī (Sirshālī, Sirchali). The best known among them was a settlement at the outskirts of Khiva located on the bank of the channel of the same name, see ʿAbdullāh Bāltaev, *Khīva īsdalīklārī*, MS Tashkent, IVANRUz, inv. no. 11645, fol. 78a; Gens, and Helmersen, *Izvestiia o Khive, Bukhare, Kokande*, p. 25. Also, the 19th-century accounts often mentioned the settlement with a similar name in the vicinity of Hazarasp, see Īsh Murād ʿAlavī, *Taʾrīkhcha-yi Muḥammad Yaʿqūb Khwāja*, MS Tashkent, IVANRUz, inv. no. 845, fol. 3a; Gens, and Helmersen, *Izvestiia o Khive, Bukhare, Kokande*, p. 25.

31 We have been unable to identify this locale.

Document 7: A Rescript by the *yasāvulbāshī* Instructing an Attendant to Investigate the Circumstances of a Dispute[32]

Introduction

The following document shows the system of conflict resolution in Khorezm in all its bureaucratic complexity. A dispute involved parties living between the different administrative jurisdictions[33] of Qonghrat and Urgench. Qonghrat was a town situated on the lower delta of the Amu Darya, while Urgench was at the center of the oasis and thus relatively closer to Khiva. The claim must have been filed first with the governor of Urgench, who subsequently wrote to his opposite number in Qonghrat with the request to investigate the circumstances of the dispute. The governor in Qonghrat then wrote back to the official in Urgench. The latter was expected to summon the parties and hear the case. At that point, either the governor himself or the plaintiffs must have decided to resort directly to the royal court in Khiva to make sure that the central power would activate its chain of justice and solve the conflict. The royal court thus issued the following warrant where it informs a group of notables about the appointment of an attendant. The latter would gather all the information relevant to the dispute and get hold of the letter that the governor of Qonghrat had written to the one in Urgench. The royal court evidently expected the local level of the administration to entrust the plaintiffs to the attendant who would then escort them to Khiva where they will be heard.

Translation

Let it be known to Ātājān Āqsaqāl, Ūrāż, and another Ātājān that we sent *dahlīz maḥramī* ʿĀlim[34] Bāy Yūzbāshī to investigate the circumstances (*aṣl vāqiʿalārī taḥqīqlāb sūrāshīlmāq*) of the claim (*daʿvā*) of Muḥammad Ṣafā, Khudāy Birgān, and Īrsgul Bīka. [The attendant should] also collect a letter (*khaṭ*) regarding this claim, which the governor (*ḥākim*) of Qūngrāt[35] sent to the governor of

---

32 TsGARUz, I-125, op. 2, d. 633, l. 83.

33 For similar case, see below Doc. 46.

34 ʿĀlīm in the original version of the text.

35 In the early 20th century Qonghrat was relatively a small town consisting of 68 households, see [Girshfel'd and Galkin], *Voenno-statisticheskoe opisanie Khivinskogo oazisa, pt. II*, pp. 132–133; Munis and Agahi, *Firdaws al-iqbāl: History of Khorezm*, p. 602, n. 504. Lykoshin visited Qonghrat in the 1912 and noted the presence of a large bazaar where the residents of the khanate exchanged goods with 'the nomads inhabiting the neighbouring Russian territories and with the Khivan Turkmens and the Qazaqs who travelled westwards,' N.S. Lykoshin, *Zapiska Nachal'nika Amu-Dar'inskogo Otdela Polkovnika Lykoshina o sovremennom sostoianii Khivinskogo Khanstva, 1912 god*, TsGARUz, f. I-2, op. 1, d. 314, l. 35.

Urgench.[36] Now that we have examined this letter, let the above-mentioned individuals come together with the above-mentioned attendant (*yasāvul*) to the royal court (*dargāh-i ʿālī*) and explain the circumstances of the case (*bayān-i vāqiʿa*). Conveying the royal order (*amr-i ʿālīlārī*) of our lord, may his rule last forever, this warrant (*khaṭ*) was written on 17 Shavvāl 1328 [21.10. 1910].

Seal: Shaykh Naẓar Yasāvulbāshī b. Muḥammad Murād Dīvānbīgī, 1328.

[Verso:] 22 Shavvāl [1328]. The circumstances [of the case outlined in this] warrant were also recorded in the rescript [entrusted to the] attendant (*yasāvullī patak*).

36 Urgench (New Urgench) at the beginning of the 20 century was a major urban center and a commercial hub of the Khanate of Khiva. In the year 1873 Kuhn wrote that the city was the major market of the khanate. See his *Ocherk istorii zaseleniia Khivinskogo khanstva s drevnykh vremen, sostav ego sovremennogo naseleniia, administratsiia i goroda khanstva*, 1873, IVRRAN, St. Petersburg, Arkhiv Vostokovedov, f. 33, d. 8, l. 49. According to the data gathered by the Russian colonial administration in 1909, the city was a commercial and industrial center of the polity, with several major markets, storages of Khivan and Russian merchants, 4 cotton industries and various offices for transportations. See [Glushanovskii], *Diplomaticheskomu Chinovniku pri Turkestanskom General-Gubernatore, 20.02.1909*, TsGARUz, I-2, op. 1, d. 253, l. 7–7ob.

Document 8: A Rescript by the *yasāvulbāshī* about a Dispute over a Contested Inheritance[37]

Introduction

This case involves the right to pre-emptive purchase of property. A man passed away leaving a courtyard and some land to his heirs. When these possessions were put on sale in order to settle a debt, a son-in-law offered a sum of money to the heirs to acquire the entire property. It was at this moment when a third party defending the interests of the family advised the heirs to refuse the offer. The son-in-law filed the claim with the royal court, which subsequently issued a warrant appointing an attendant to oversee the case. The latter brought the parties to Khiva where they were reconciled in the presence of high officials, such as the *mihtar* and the chief judge (*qāżī kalān*) and others. We know from a source dating to the beginning of the early 20th century that the high-ranking officials[38] of the khanate who operated in Khiva always heard the appeals to the royal court every time that the ruler was absent.[39] In this case it was agreed that the plaintiff would purchase the possessions of the departed for a larger sum of money than he had earlier proposed. He thus entrusted the money to the heirs before the high-rank officials. In addition, the chief judge wrote a rescript (*fatak*) asking the judge in Hazarasp to notarize the contract of sale. This would suggest that the parties lived under the Hazarasp judge's jurisdiction. We observe here again how parties did not bring their cases to the closer legal authority, but instead resorted to central power to activate the khanal chain of justice.

Translation

Let it be known that Īsh Niyāz who was the father-in-law of Muḥammad Yaʿqūb from Sirshālī[40] died and left approximately three and half *ṭanāb* of land and a house (*ḥavlī*). When [these possessions] were put on sale to cover the debts (*qarż*) of the deceased, [Muḥammad Yaʿqūb] offered more than 200 *ṭillā* to purchase [the property]. [A certain Muḥammad Raḥīm] refused [the offer] and thereby made the heirs of the deceased (*mutavaffā vārislārī*) unhappy (*nā-rižā*

37 TsGARUz, I-125, op. 2, d. 633, l. 114.

38 See N.S. Lykoshin, *Zapiska Nachal'nika Amu-Dar'inskogo Otdela Polkovnika Lykoshina o sovremennom sostoianii Khivinskogo Khanstva, 1912 god*, TsGARUz, f. I-2, op. 1, d. 314, ll. 15–160b.; Bābājān Safarov, *Khwārazm taʾrīkhī (1864–1934)*, MS Tashkent, IVANRUz, inv. no. 10231; Bobojon Tarroh-Khodim, *Khorazm shoir va navozandalari*, eds. Anbara Otamurodova, and Ollanazar Abdurahimov (Tashkent: Tafakkur qanoti, 2011), p. 30.

39 See Ḥasan-Murād Laffasī, *Gulshan-i saʿādat*, MS Tashkent, IVANRUz, inv. no. 7797, fols. 8b, 17b, 64a, 84a.

40 On this locality see the footnote to Doc. 6.

ītgān). For this reason (*vajh*), [Muḥammad Yaʿqūb] has a claim (*daʿvā*) against Muḥammad Raḥīm. Let them come to the royal court (*dargāh-i ʿālī*) of our lord, may his rule last forever, together with Khwāja Niyāz Dahabāshī Yasāvul, who is the liegeman (*nawkar*) of [Muḥammad Yaʿqūb] Yasāvulbāshī and solve [the dispute] (*ṣāf būlsūn*). The attendant's fee (*yasāvul ḥaqqī*)[41] should not exceed 2 *tanga* per parasang. This warrant (*khaṭ*) was written on 13 Ẕī al-qaʿda 1336 [20.08.1918].

Seal: Muḥammad Yaʿqūb Yasāvulbāshī b. Muḥammad Yūsuf Yasāvulbāshī

[Verso:] [The afore-mentioned] Muḥammad Yaʿqūb bought the land and the house for 1500 *ṭilla* at the presence of the *mihtar*[42]*-āqā*[43] and other notables (*kattalār*). The chief judge (*qāżī kalān-īshān*) issued a warrant (*fatak*) [prescribing] the *qāżī*[44] of Hazārāsb to notarize [the settlement]. [This occurred on] 19 Ẕī al-qaʿda[45] 1336 [26.08.1918].

---

41 In the original text of the record the expression *yasāvul ḥaqq* is most probably a scribal error.

42 The *mihtar* (Pers. 'the highest') represented one of the highest ranks in the Khivan administration under the Qonghrats, see Bābājān Safarov, *Khwārazm taʾrīkhī (1864–1934)*, MS Tashkent, IVANRUz, inv. no. 1023, fol. 14b; Yu. Bregel, "The Sarts in the Khanate of Khiva," *Journal of Asian History* 12.2 (1978), pp. 129–135; Munis and Agahi, *Firdaws al-iqbāl: History of Khorezm*, pp. 560–561, note 251.

43 According to Kuhn, the *āqā*/*āghā* was one of the highest ranks at the court of the Qonghrats. This title was usually given to the members of the Sart elite of the khanate. *Āqā*s attended the khan's receptions during official events; see *Ocherk istorii zaseleniia Khivinskogo khanstva s drevnykh vremen, sostav ego sovremennogo naseleniia, administratsiia i goroda khanstva*, 1873, IVRRAN, St. Petersburg, Arkhiv Vostokovedov, f. 33, d. 8, ll. 36a–36b, 39. See also Bregel, "The Sarts in the Khanate of Khiva," p. 129; Munis and Agahi, *Firdaws al-iqbāl: History of Khorezm*, p. 560, note 252. Documents originating from the second decade of the 20th century show that *āqā* could also be used as an honorific title, like in the following cases: *mīrzābāshī-āqā* (TsGARUz, I-125, op. 2, d. 39, l. 13); *dīvānbīgī-āqā* (ibid., d. 41, ll. 2, 4); *maḥkamabāshī-āqā* (ibid., f. 6); *ḥākim-āqā* [see below, Doc. 13].

44 In the original the term *qāżī* is given in the plural form just as an honorific.

45 In the original text of the record, *Ẕī al-qaʿdā*.

Document 9: A Rescript by the *yasāvulbāshī* about a Dispute over Landownership[46]

Introduction

Two people sold a plot of land to a third man. Some time later, the sellers took legal action against the purchaser in order to recover their property. A *sharīʿa* court found that their claim was unsound. The plaintiffs disregarded the legal force of the latter ruling and thus continued to lodge lawsuits on the same case. As the plaintiffs did not allow the respondent to enjoy his rights on the plot of land now in his possession, the latter filed a claim against the former with the royal court in Khiva. The *yasāvulbāshī* issued a warrant instructing an attendant to deal with the case and settle the conflict. Most probably on account of his inability to reconcile the parties on the spot, the attendant transferred the case to a court presided over by a *qāżī*. We do not know whether the parties could produce testimony or written probative evidence. The document only tells us that the *qāżī* must have thought that the case was somewhat complex and thus required that each party produce a legal opinion (*masʾala*) issued by a jurist. Only the plaintiff did so, and he therefore won the case. We can safely assume that with the sanction of the attendant, this ruling would be enforced.

Translation

[A certain Iskandar and Āykhānīm Bīka] sold to Qilich Niyāz from Bīsh-Arīq[47] 7 *ṭanāb* of land for 1000 *ṭillā*. After that [Iskandar and Āykhānīm Bīka] regretted their action and claimed [the property back] (*daʿvālāshīb*). According to *sharīʿa* [their] claim (*daʿvā*) was found wrong (*nā-durust*). [However,] they repeated the claim. For this reason, [Qilich Niyāz] has a claim against Iskandar and Āykhānīm Bīka. Let them come to the royal court (*dargāh-i ʿālī*) of our lord, may his rule last forever, together with Jān Bik Sarhang Yasāvul, who is the liegeman (*nawkar*) of [Muḥammad Yaʿqūb] Yasāvulbāshī, and solve [the dispute] (*ṣāf būlsūnlār*). The attendant's fee (*yasāvul ḥaqqī*)[48] is 2 *tanga* per parasang. This rescript (*khaṭ*) was written on 7 Rabīʿ al-s̱ānī 1336 [19.01.1918].

46 TsGARUz, I-125, op. 2, d. 633, ll. 130–130ob.

47 Besh-Ariq (Bīsh-Ārīq) is a locality in the western environs of Hazarasp, see Munis and Agahi, *Firdaws al-iqbāl: History of Khorezm*, p. 573, note 322.

48 In the original text of the record the expression *yasāvul ḥaqq* is most probably a scribal error.

Seal: Muḥammad Yaʿqūb Yasāvulbāshī b. Muḥammad Yūsuf Yasāvulbāshī.

[Verso:] The claim (*daʿvā*) of the afore-mentioned Qilich Niyāz was transferred to a *qāżī* (*sharīʿatgha*[49] *qūshūlūb*). [The plaintiff] brought a legal opinion (*masʾala ālīb*) and [the court] issued a judgment (*ḥukm khaṭ*) according to which the land belongs to the plaintiff, while the defendants' claim is wrong (*muddaʿā alayhlārnī daʿvāsī nā-durust*). [This was recorded] on 8 Rabīʿ al-s̱ānī 1336 [20.01.1918].

49 *Sharāyitgha* in the original text of the record.

Document 10: A Rescript by the *yasāvulbāshī* about a Dispute over Landownership[50]

Introduction

In the hope of seizing another person's property, two individuals forged a legal deed. The aggrieved property-owner appealed to the royal court in Khiva. An attendant received instructions to deal with the conflict. Accordingly, he summoned the parties to a mosque community,[51] but he was unable to find a compromise that would suit them. He therefore proceeded to transfer the case to a *qāżī* who found that the initial claim was void. The jurist, however, opted not to issue a judgment in favour of the defendant and instead persuaded the parties to reach an amicable settlement, which he notarised in the form of a certificate of relinquishment. This case illustrates that judges could, in principle, initiate the settlement of a conflict at court by notarizing a certificate of relinquishment (*ibrāʾ*). Amicable settlements did not always require the intervention of a third party,[52] nor were they achieved outside of court alone. Judges would encourage the parties to reconcile, not only to avoid litigation, but also to mitigate the latter's outcome. From this perspective, the *qāżī*'s course of action was in agreement with the culture of reconciliation that manifests itself in the activity of the royal court.

Translation

Qurbān Niyāz and Khudāy Birgān produced a deed (*khaṭ chīqārīb*) and filed a groundless claim (*bī vajh daʿvā ītib*) against Jumʿa Niyāz from Rūzīm Būy for 5 *ṭanāb* of land. [The respondent's rights on the plot of land are attested by] a legal deed (*khaṭlī*). On these grounds (*vajh*), [Jumʿa Niyāz] has now a claim (*daʿvā*) against [them]. Let them come to the royal court (*dargāh-i ʿālī*) of our lord, may his rule last forever, together with Maḥramkhānachī Muḥammad

50 TsGARUz, I-125, op. 2, d. 633, ll. 190–190ob.

51 Under the rule of the Qonghrats the expression *masjid qavmī* ('mosque community') or simply *masjid* referred to the lowest administrative subdivision of the khanate. This could be a group of households (from five to dozens) or a parish of a particular mosque under the fiscal authority of an *imām* or *āqsaqāl*. One village or settlement could consist of one or several mosque communities. The expression *masjid qavmī* was of course used in the sense of an administrative unit among the sedentary population, while nomadic groups were subjected to different principles of tribal subdivision. See further on *masjid qavmī*, Bregel', *Khorezmskie turkmeny v XIX veke*, pp. 343–4; on the terminology regarding the tribal subdivision of Turkmens, see below fn. 427.

52 On the involvement of third parties in the resolution of conflicts in Central Asian *sharīʿa* courts, see P. Sartori, "The Evolution of Third-Party Mediation in *Sharīʿa* Courts in 19th- and Early 20th-Century Central Asia," *Journal of the Economic and Social History of the Orient* 54.3 (2011), pp. 311–352.

Riżā Yasāvul, [and] resolve [the dispute] (*ṣāf būlsūnlār*). The attendant's fee (*yasāvul ḥaqqī*) is 2 *tanga* per parasang. This warrant (*khaṭ*) was written on 24 Rabīʿ al-avval 1335 [07.01.1917].

Seal: Muḥammad Yūsuf Yasāvulbāshī b. ʿAvaż Niyāz Maḥram

[Verso:] [The attendant summoned the parties in] the Bāltāq Mīrāb mosque (*masjid*). [There] the plaintiff (*muddaʿī*) Jumʿa Niyāz from Rūzīm Būy, together with his fellow community (*qavm*) members, Khudāy Birgān, Qurbān Niyāz b. Īsh-Murād, were ordered [to bring their case] before a *qāżī* (*sharīʿatgha būyūrūlūb*). Their litigation (*murāfaʿa*) then took place before the *qāżī ʿaskar-īshān*. [The latter ruled that] the 5 *ṭanāb* of land belong to Jumʿa Niyāz, while the defendants' claim (*muddaʿi ʿalayhlārnī daʿvālārī*) was found void (*fāsid*). [The judge] notarised a certificate of relinquishment and reconciled [the parties] (*ibrāʾlāshīb ṣāflāshdīlār*). [This was recorded] on 29 Rabīʿ al-avval 1335 [22.01.1917].

Document 11: A Rescript by the *yasāvulbāshī* about a Case of Murder[53]

Introduction

A corpse was found lying on the shores of the Charkas lake. The leaders of a local community reported to the royal court about this apparent case of homicide. The office of the *yasāvulbāshī* issued a warrant instructing a *qāżī* to appoint a bailiff and request him to join an attendant dispatched by the royal court to examine the corpse and establish the circumstances of the death. The bailiff and the attendant reached the locality where the body was found and, in the presence of the representatives of the local community, examined the corpse and collected the available circumstantial evidence about the dead person. They then allowed the performance of the burial. Upon their return to Khiva, they informed the royal court that a local informant confirmed that the departed died a natural death and that his family did not intend to file any claims.

Translation

Let it be known to [our] *qāżī-īshān*, the symbol of *sharīʿa*, token of devotion, that Rūz Muḥammad Āqsaqāl and Jumʿa Niyāz from Gandūmkān[54] reported (*ʿarż*) [to the royal court] that [someone] killed an unidentified young mullah and his corpse lies on the shore of Charkas lake,[55] which belongs to a charitable endowment (*vaqf*) [established for the benefit] of a mosque. For this reason, let a trustworthy person (*muʿtabar ādam*) join Qalandar Dahabāshī,[56] who is the liegeman (*nawkar*) of [Muḥammad Yaʿqūb] Yasāvulbāshī, and let them together reach [the locality], examine the body of the abovementioned deceased with the afore-mentioned *āqsaqāl-kadkhudā*s and with particular care establish the causes of [his] death. [After that,] let them allow the burial (*dafn*) [of the corpse] and draft a report (*khaṭ ītib*). Let them then come to the royal court (*darbār-i ʿālī*) and report about the event. Conveying the royal order (*amr-i ʿālīlārī*) of our lord, may his rule last forever, this warrant (*khaṭ*) was written on 17 Shaʿbān 1328 [26.05.1918].

---

53 TsGARUz, I-125, op. 2, d. 656, l. 35–35ob.

54 Gandumkan is a settlement located 2 km. east of Khiva, see Munis and Agahi, *Firdaws al-iqbāl: History of Khorezm*, p. 559, note 247; Danilevskii, *Opisanie Khivinskogo khanstva*, p. 115. It is famous for the treaty between the Qonghrats and the Russians signed in August 1873.

55 We have been unable to identify this locale.

56 On *dahabāshī* see above, fn. 176.

Seal: Muḥammad Yaʿqūb Yasāvulbāshī b. Muḥammad Yūsuf Yasāvulbāshī.

[Verso:] Muḥammad Sharīf Khwāja, the bailiff (*ādam*) of the *qażī-īshān* and Qalandar Dahabāshī examined the afore-mentioned corpse (*ūlūk*). [They found] that he was [a certain] Bābā Jān, the grandson of Ṭāhir Qazāq. [A certain] Ṣābir Bāy, who is a kinsman [of the deceased], stated that the afore-mentioned Bābā Jān was somewhat absent-minded (*khayālatlīrāq*) and must have died of natural death. Wounds were not visible (*jarāhat*[57] *yūq īrkān*). [Ṣābir Bāy] said that [the family] has not any claim (*daʿvāmīz yūq*). [This was recorded] on 18 Shaʿbān 1336 [28.05.1918].

57 See *jarḥ* in A. Layish, *Sharīʿa and Custom in Libyan Tribal Society*, p. 292.

SECTION 2

Reports

Document 12: A Report by *qāżīs* to the *yasāvulbāshī* about a Marital Dispute[58]

Introduction

A man appealed to the *yasāvulbāshī* on account of his wife having left the conjugal dwelling. In filing his claim with the royal court, the man took legal action against his father-in-law as the latter did not allow him to recover his wife. The appellant therefore asked for someone to be appointed as attendant (*yasāvul*) who would oversee the case. We do not know whether the *yasāvulbāshī* appointed an attendant. However, hearsay about this claim filed with the royal court must have reached the respondent, as he decided to take legal action against the claimant. Indeed, the respondent appealed to the royal court and he too requested a *yasāvul*. It is important to note that the report emphasizes that the parties requested a specific individual to be appointed to act in the capacity of attendant. They must have done so in hope that their ties to the royal court would prove instrumental to reach an advantageous solution of the case. Be that as it may, the royal court appointed the attendant requested by the respondent. Given that the latter filed what we may term a 'counterclaim,' the attendant was joined also by two *qāżīs*. He then notified the *yasāvulbāshī* about the settlement of the dispute. The royal court was less interested in the procedures according to which the settlement was achieved before the *qāżīs* than in the fact that the parties reached a satisfaction of some sort. An additional indicator of the fact that the royal court was not concerned with the trivia of dispute settlement is the absence in the text of any information that could shed light on the stipulations of the settlement. In speaking of which, it should be noted also that the *qāżīs* did not mention the notarization of any contract of relinquishment nor any deed of settlement. This would suggest that, at least in this case, the parties did not regard written attestation as particularly important for their purposes. It is also worth dwelling on the intentions of the respondent who too appealed to the royal court. One wonders why he felt pressed to secure the involvement of an attendant from Khiva. One possible explanation is that he wanted to publicize his and his daughter's dissatisfaction with the claimant's behavior and therefore to confer on his arguments the attributes of a sound accusation. Involving a *yasāvul* would thus

58 TsGARUz, f. I-125, op. 1, d. 498, l. 14

© KONINKLIJKE BRILL NV, LEIDEN, 2020 | DOI:10.1163/9789004427907_004

be an instrument to affirm his own entitlements and let the larger community know that his daughter was right in leaving the conjugal dwelling.

Translation

Let the *yasāvulbāshī*, the refuge of happiness (*sa'ādat-panāh*) and repository of power (*ḥukūmat-dastgāh*), his serene highness (*janāb-i 'ālīlārī*), our lord (*āqāmīz*), know our sincere supplication. [A certain] Qurbān Bāy from Būmīrī[59] appealed (*'arż ītib*) [to the royal court]. He requested the appointment of Muḥammad Yūsuf Kākil Bī, the liegeman (*nawkar*) of Muḥammad Yūsuf Yasāvulbāshī, our lord, to the office of attendant (*yasāvul*) because [he claimed that] his father-in-law Khudāy Birgān is forcibly detaining (*zūrlīq qīlib*) his wife (*nikāḥlī khātūnim*) Arżīgul Bīka and does not allow her to come back. Khudāy Birgān too appealed (*'arż*) [to the royal court] and requested Muḥammad 'Ālīm Bāy Yūzbāshī [to act in capacity of an attendant. The latter] was appointed to act in the capacity of attendant (*yasāvul*) [to deal with the case of] Muḥammad Jān, Birdī Murād, Qurbān Bāy, and Khāl Jān Bīka who were all satisfied (*rāżīlīqgha kīlishdīlār*) [with the settlement]. Since the aforementioned individuals are all poor people and thus unable [to travel to Khiva] (*'ājiz va bīchāra*) in order [to notify the outcome of the dispute], we sent [this rescript] to your office. This letter (*khaṭ*) was written on 8 Shavvāl.[60] It is you who decides (*ṣāḥib ikhtiyār ūzlārī turūr*).

Seals: Qāżi va ra'is Dāmullā 'Abd al-Allāh
Qāżi va ra'is Dāmullā Allāh Birgān

59 We have been unable to identify this locale.
60 Year is missing.

Document 13: A Report by a Provincial Governor to the *yasāvulbāshī* about a Dispute over Custody[61]

Introduction

This document reflects the resolution of a conflict over custody (*amānat*). One Muḥammad Yūsuf gave some money to a certain Muḥammad Ya'qūb Bāy. When the latter refused to return the money, Muḥammad Yūsuf appealed to the governor (*ḥākim*) of Tashhawz. The governor and the leaders of the local communities attempted to settle the dispute. However, their attempt proved helpful only in part, for the respondent returned half of the sum. Consequently, the plaintiff decided to bring his grievance to the royal court. The *yasāvulbāshī* instructed Bahādir Maḥram Yūzbāshī, the governor of Tashhawz to hold an inquest and pursue a reconciliation. He also stipulated that, had the plaintiff indeed entrusted the said amount of money to the respondent, the governor should return the possessions to the plaintiff. When the governor summoned the parties and questioned them, the respondent denied the claim. The governor, therefore, transferred the case to the *qāżīs*. The latter would usually follow the procedure of adjudication which requires the counterclaimant to produce testimony. If the counterclaimant failed to do so, the claimant would be put under oath (*ānt*). If the latter refused to swear an oath, the *qāżīs* would put the counterclaimant under oath. The report explains that local tribal chiefs (*biylār*) and the representatives of the urban population acted in the capacity of mediators and persuaded the defendant to return the rest of the money in order to avoid the onus of the oath. They did so to prevent a direct confrontation and ensure that the parties would still be in a position to negotiate their entitlements. When the sum of money was delivered, the *qāżīs* notarised a certificate of relinquishment (*ibrā'*).

Translation

Let it be known to the office of the *yasāvulbāshī*, the noble vizier (*vazīr al-karām*), our lord, that when Muḥammad Yūsuf from Tashḥavuż appealed [to the royal court], he stated that he left his 1100 *manāt*[62] in custody (*amānat*)[63] to Muḥammad Ya'qūb Bāy from Qūngrāt. [When the former] asked [the latter to return the sum, Muḥammad Ya'qūb Bāy] did not give [anything] and denied [the request]. In the wake of the involvement of the governor (*ḥākim-āqā*) and the community elders (*kadkhudās*), [the respondent]

---

61 TsGARUz, f. I-125, op. 1, d. 498, ll. 16–16ob.

62 On *manāt*, see fn. 226 of the Introduction to this book.

63 On 'custody' (*amānat*), see *Katalog khivinskikh kaziiskikh dokumentov XIX–nachala XX vv.*, p. 649.

returned to the claimant only 550 *manats*, but he refused to pay the rest. Therefore, you instructed (*mihribān būlghān*) me to clarify whether it is true that Muḥammad Yaʿqūb returned only half of the 1100 *manāt* which he was entrusted to and, in such a case, to secure the remainder of the money from him and let the parties reach a satisfactory settlement (*riżālashtūrsūn*). As I investigated the case, Muḥammad Yūsuf [argued] that he had given 1100 *manāts* to Muḥammad Yaʿqūb, who refused to return [the money]. Muḥammad Yaʿqūb denied (*munkir*) the claim (*daʿvā*) stating that he was never entrusted the money. I thus involved the *qāżī-īshāns*. Meanwhile, the tribal elders (*biylār*) and the representatives of the urban population (*qalʿa kāsiblārī*) agreed not to place the parties under oath (*ānt*). [Instead] they made Muḥammad Yaʿqūb pay 550 *manāt* to Muḥammad Yūsuf and a certificate of relinquishment (*ībrāʾ*) was drafted before the *qāżī-īshāns*. This is what we had to report to you. Whatever is your decision, you know best. This report (*ʿarīża*) was compiled on 4 Rabīʿ al-ṣānī 1335 [27.01.1917].

Seal: Bahādir Maḥram Yūzbāshī

Document 14: A Report by a Provincial Governor to the *yasāvulbāshī* about a Dispute over a Dowry[64]

Introduction

This record refers to a case of a failed payment of bride price. In the wake of a betrothal consisting of the reading of the *fātiḥa*, the groom had to pay the bride price (*qālīng māl/pulī*) to the bride's father and fulfill the liabilities (*lavāzim*) to celebrate the wedding (*tūy*). As the groom failed to do so, the bride's father appealed to othe royal court. An attendant (*yasāvul*) was instructed to solve the case. The resolution of the conflict involved an element of publicity, which is referred to in the text by mentioning the presence of the representatives of the local community (*īl āqsaqāl va katkhudālārī*). The involvement of the judiciary is not mentioned.

Translation

Let it be known to the *yasāvulbāshī*, banner of glory (*'izzat-nishān*), our lord, that a certain Atā Bāy from Qirq-Yaf[65] appealed (*'arż*) to your office [and complained against] a certain Bik-Jān to whom he betrothed [his daughter] (*fātiḥa ītūb*). [Bik-Jān] paid Atā Bāy [only] 130 *manāt*s thereby failing to deliver the rest of his wedding dues (*lavāzim*); [nonetheless] Bik-Jān intended to marry (*nikāḥ*) Atā Bāy's daughter. Accordingly, an attendant (*yasāvul*) was sent [to make an investigation]. As a result, in agreement (*ittifāq*) with the *āqsaqāls-kadkhudās* of the community (*īl*) [Bik-Jān] paid in full the remaining part of the bride price and the wedding liabilities (*qālghān qālīngīnī va tūy lavāzīmlārīn*), while [Atā Bāy] agreed of his own will to celebrate the wedding (*tūy ītūb*). [The parties] were satisfied (*riżālashtūrūldī*) [with the settlement] before me (*mūndā*). This report (*khaṭ*) was compiled to inform you about this [event] on 24 Ṣafar 1334 [30.12.1915].

Seal: Muḥammad Ya'qūb b. [Jabbār Qulī Maḥram]

64 TsGARUz, f. I-125, op. 1, d. 498, l. 21.

65 Qirq-Yaf (or Qirq-Yab) was a settlement in the province of Hazarasp. By the mid 19th century Qirq-Yaf consisted of 150 households, see Gens, and Helmersen, *Izvestiia o Khive, Bukhare, Kokande*, p. 25. Bāltaev, named this settlement in his list of the early 20th century Khivan locales, 'Abdullah Bāltaev, *Khīva īsdalīklārī*, MS Tashkent, IVANRUz, inv. no. 11645, fol. 79a.

Document 15: A Report by a Provincial Governor to the *yasāvulbāshī* about a Case of Robbery[66]

Introduction

A certain ʿAbd al-Ṣamad Khwāja, from Tama,[67] filed a complaint with the royal court against three men for a case of robbery. The *yasāvulbāshī* instructed the local governor, Muḥammad Yūsuf Bāy b. Pahlavān Maḥram, to make an inquest. The latter summoned a public hearing with the help of local notables. On that occasion, an *āqsaqāl* from Naymān provided some useful information: the defendants had committed another crime in a neighbouring locale. This hearsay prompted the elders of Tama to take the defendants before the community of the locale where the previous crime had been perpetrated. While attending the hearing, the governor also found out about the presence of a man implicated with another conflict, which had been reported to the royal court and who was now with guarantors. This report is instructive as it shows that governors could decide not to interfere with the course of actions taken by the *kadkhudā*s and *āqsaqāl*s. By so doing, the governor effectively gave the *kadkhudā*s and *āqsaqāl*s free hand to collect facts relevant to the case and information on the *fama* of the defendants.

Translation

Let it be known to the *yasāvulbāshī*, banner of glory, our lord, that, in accordance with your instruction (*mihribān būlghān*) to report about the circumstances of the claim lodged by ʿAbd al-Ṣamad Khwāja from Tama against his respondents (*daʿvāgarlār*) named Ṭamʿa Pahlavān, Muḥammad Sharīf, and Īgām Birdī, four men were recognised (*dānūb*)[68] and brought to me (*mūnda*) for questioning. During the hearing which occurred in the presence of the *kadkhudā*s, a certain ʿAbd al-Raḥman Āqsaqāl from Naymān[69] joined and reported that these [respondents] had been recognised as those who broke also into a house of another community (*īlāt*) and committed robbery. At that point, the *kadkhudā-āqsaqāl*s of the abovementioned [individuals] mentioned that there are other rumours around them. [The elders thus decided] to take the respondents to the community [in which the robbery was perpetrated],

---

66 TsGARUz, f. I-125, op. 1, d. 498, ll. 25–50b.

67 Tama is 6 km southeast of Khanqah, see Munis and Agahi, *Firdaws al-iqbāl: History of Khorezm*, p. 574, note 330; Tama is also mentioned in fiscal registers as a locality belonging to a jurisdiction comprising about twenty mosqeu communities. See TsGARUz, f. I-125, op. 2, d. 385, ll. 12–14.

68 Most probably this is an oghuzism for *tānūb*.

69 Nayman was a settlement located ab. 20 km west-northwest of Khiva, see Munis and Agahi, *Firdaws al-iqbāl: History of Khorezm*, p. 605, note 553.

summon everybody [to clarify the circumstance of the crime], drive them back with great caution. They left [for that locale]. Amongst those [who attended the hearing] there was a certain Nafas who had previously appealed (*ʿarż ītib*) [to the royal court] with a false complaint (*yālghān*). Nafas' guarantors (*kafīl*) also were in this place. This is what happened and you know best. The report (*khaṭ*) was written in the month of Jumādī al-s̱ānī in the year 1336 [March 1918].

Seal: Muḥammad Yūsuf Bāy b. Pahlavān Maḥram

Document 16: A Report by a Provincial Governor to the *yasāvulbāshī* about a Case of Domestic Violence[70]

Introduction

This report to the *yasāvulbāshī* is written by the governor of Gurlen.[71] A woman named Niyāz Bīka filed a claim of assault against her son-in-law, Yakhshī Murāt, who had beaten Saʿādat Bīka and caused her injury. Consequently, Saʿādat Bīka had left the conjugal dwelling. The governor instructed the *qāżī*s of Gurlen to appoint a trustee (*amīn*) in order to examine the body of the injured party. He also ordered local notables – most probably elders from Saʿādat Bīka's community – to assist the trustee. Clearly in the attempt to defend himself from the accusation of assault and acquire a different standing before the royal court, Yakhshī Murāt filed a complaint claiming that the wife had broken the marriage bond (*nikāḥ*) by abandoning their conjugal dwelling and seeking refuge in her paternal home. The royal court issued a warrant instructing the governor to verify the veracity of Yakhshī Murāt's claim. Should the man's claim be found sound, Saʿādat Bīka would be returned to him. Otherwise, the dispute should be heard by *qażī*s. This mode of proceeding in the royal court is not unusual: other texts from Khiva and other regions of Central Asia show that a counterclaim usually pushed the royal court to transfer the dispute to a *sharīʿa* court. Unusual, however, is the fact that the royal court contemplated the possibility that the *qażī*s would not enjoy enough authority to either issue a judgment or settle the dispute. Indeed, the *yasāvulbāshī* ordered the governor that, should the aggrieved party refuse to submit to the *qāżī*s, she should be escorted back to the royal court. This is precisely what happened, for a man representing Saʿādat Bīka, most probably a guarantor, requested before the governor the implementation of this latter procedure. Saʿādat Bīka was consequently escorted to Khiva.

This document is interesting in many respects. First, it illustrates an instance in which a woman decided to bring her grievance to the office of the governor, not to the local *sharīʿa* court. In her eyes the judicial authority of the *qāżī*s evidently counted less than the power of the governor. Second, it illustrates

---

70 TsGARUz, f. I-125, op. 1, d. 498, l. 28

71 Gurlen is a town is about 50 km northeast of Khiva on the left bank of the Amu Darya, see also Munis and Agahi, *Firdaws al-iqbāl: History of Khorezm*, pp. 564–565, note 280; Basiner, *Estestvenno-nauchnoe puteshestvie po Kirgizskoi stepi v Khivu*, p. 347; Kun, *Ocherk istorii zaseleniia Khivinskogo khanstva s drevnykh vremen, sostav ego sovremennogo naseleniia, administratsiia i goroda khanstva*, 1873, IVRRAN, St. Petersburg, Arkhiv Vostokovedov, f. 33, d. 8, ll. 45ob.–46.

the royal court following an uncommon procedure, specific to cases involving alleged bodily harm: the governor would instruct the *qāżīs* to appoint a trustee to examine the body of the aggrieved party and ascertain the presence of injuries. The *qāżīs* and the trustee would not operate alone, however, since the governor also requested the presence of local notables during the inquest. All these courses of action seem to be constraining the legal authority of the *qāżīs* and relegating them to a marginal role. It should not come as a surprise of it was the trustee, not the *qāżīs*, to report directly to the governor. Third, this case shows how the populace in general perceived the royal court (as represented by the *yasāvulbāshī*) as the highest judicial instance to which the governor and most certainly the *qāżīs* were subordinated.

Translation

Let it be known to the office of the *yasāvulbāshī*, refuge of the vizierate (*vizārat-panāh*) and repository of power, our lord, that in this month of Rabīʿ al-avval an aged woman (*kanfir*) called Niyāz Bīka came and informed [me] that her daughter Saʿādat Bīka was the victim of assault, having been injured (*majrūḥ*)[72] by her husband Yakhshī Murāt, who later ran away. Proceeding from [this complaint], [I requested] the *qāżī-īshāns* of Gūrlān, who are the banner of Islamic law (*sharīʿat-shiʿār*), to appoint a trustee (*amīn*). I [also] have instructions to gather the *īl-kadkhudās* who, together with the trustee, reached the locality, examined the injured party and reported to [me] about their examination. Meanwhile Yakhshī Murāt appealed (*ʿarż*) [to the royal court and claimed] that the woman he had legally wedded (*nikāḥlī khātūnūm*) had repaired to her father's home and that her elder brother did not let her come back to him. [Accordingly it was then ordered by Your Excellency] to proceed in the following way: should [Yakhshī Murāt's] appeal be sound, the wife and husband should be reunited, otherwise (*bāshqa sūzī būlsa*) [the conflict] should be heard before the *qāżīs*. [If they refuse to comply], they should be sent [to the royal court]. When I was about to reconcile them according to the royal warrant (*būyrūq-i ʿālīlārīgha muvāfīq ālārnī yarāshtūrmāqchī*), a certain Muḥammad Ṣafā from Qūsh-Kūfrūk, who had apprehended the afore-mentioned Yakhshī Murāt, requested that the woman be sent to Khiva. [She] was entrusted to Khāl Murāt Āqsaqāl who escorted her to Your Excellency (*janābingīz*). The elderly

72 In the text *machrū*.

Niyāz Bīka requested me to let you know about the investigation. I thus inform your excellency what was reported (*bayān ītgānlār*) by the trustees (*amīnlār*) who inspected the woman [and found that she] had been beaten with a stick. This sincere petition (*ʿarīża-yi ikhlās*) was written in Rabiʿ al-avval 1335 [December 1916].

Seal:[73]

73 We have been unable to decipher the seal.

Document 17: A Report by a Provincial Governor to the *yasāvulbāshī* about a Dispute over Water Rights[74]

Introduction

The governor of Urgench reports to the *yasāvulbāshī* about the settlement of a dispute concerning the disposal of his allocated share of water. The text is instructive for it illuminates how the resolution of conflicts saw the participation of a constellation of actors representing different social forces. After a claimant submitted a petition to Khiva, a liegeman was appointed to act in the capacity of attendant (*yasāvul*). The latter summoned a hearing, most probably in Urgench, in the presence of both the governor and the representatives of the community to which the parties belonged. One may well imagine that local notables were invited to the hearing because they were endowed with local knowledge. Indeed, representing as they were the locale, they must have known the details of the dispute. The attendant and the governor pushed the parties to a settlement and sanctioned it.

Translation

Let it be known to the office of Muḥammad Maḥram Yasāvulbāshī,[75] refuge of the vizierat[76] and repository of nobleness (*najābat-dastgāh*), our lord, that a certain Muḥammad Yaʿqūb from Chātkūfrūk went to the royal court (*dargāh-i ʿālī*) and submitted a petition (*ʿarīża*) [claiming] that Bābā Jān, Ṣābir, Dūndī Bīka, Karīm Birgān, Qalandar and Saʿādat Bīka do not let water flow into his ditch (*suv yūlī*). He also mentioned that the afore-mentioned individuals had assaulted him and his brother. [The royal court thus] appointed Muḥammad Sharīf, the liegeman (*nawkar*) of ʿAbd al-Sattār Says,[77] [to the office of] attendant (*yasāvul*); [Muḥammad Yaʿqūb] drove [the attendant to the locale]. The

74 TsGARUz, f. I-125, op. 1, d. 498, l. 42.

75 On Muḥammad Maḥram Yasāvulbāshī, see the Introduction, p. 32.

76 In the original text of the record, *vizārat-fanāh*.

77 Yŭldoshev writes that in the Khanate of Khiva the term *says* means 'stable boy,' see his *Khiva khonligida feodal yer egaligi va davlat tuzilishi*, p. 234. Safarov claims, instead, that in Khiva *says* denoted an ascription of office at the royal court. He further notes that there were two of them who commanded 45 subordinates who were in charge of taking care of the Khan's stables, see Bābājān Safarov, *Khwārazm taʾrīkhī (1864–1934)*, MS Tashkent, IVANRUz, inv. no. 10231, fol. 15.

latter let the above-mentioned individuals reach a settlement (*yarāshdīlār*) in our presence (*ḥużūrīmizda*) together with the representatives of the local community (*ahl-i īlāt būlūb*). I wrote this notification (*khaṭ*) to inform your office on 27 Rajab (1330) [July 12, 1912].

Seal: Allāh Birgān Bāy b. ʿAvaż Niyāz Maḥram[78]

78 Prior to his appointment to the governorship of Urgench, Allāh Birgān Bāy b. ʿAvaż Niyāz Maḥram acted as Khivan consul in the Amu-Darya Department, see N.S. Lykoshin, *Sovremennoe raspredelenie vlasti v Khanstve Khivinskom, 1912 god*, TsGARUz, f. I-2, op. 1, d. 314, l. 64.

Document 18: A Report by a Provincial Governor to the *yasāvulbāshī* about Maintenance Works of the Irrigation System[79]

Introduction

The document reflects a conflict between two communities (*davr*) of water-users living along the lower bank of the canal Qūshbigī Yāf,[80] a stream of water which flows northwest from Lavzan, the latter being a distributor of the Amu Darya.[81] On behalf of one community, two individuals filed a lawsuit at the royal court claiming that the other water-users had not been fulfilling their duties of maintenance for the last two years. In Khorezm, upkeep of the irrigation system consisted of two main activities termed respectively *saqa qāzū* and *ābkhurī qāzū*. The first activity inhered in the cleaning of the upper streams (*saqa*) of a canal, and was under the direct competence of the principality, whereas the second referred to the cleaning of the distributaries (*ābkhurī*), an operation that fell on the local communities.[82] As we see in the document translated below, the communities of water shares were required to organize such maintenance works in accordance with established practices (*taʿāmul*). In this case the claimants lamented that, in neglecting the fulfillment of its duties, the neighbouring community impeded the correct flowing of the water to the lower part of the canal, thereby complicating the process of irrigation. In order to solve the conflict, the *yasāvulbāshī* enacted the procedure that we have already seen at work: he ordered a governor to make further inquiries into the case. The governor, in turn, was endowed with powers to assess the veracity of the claim and he was expected to enforce the fulfillment of the duties of maintenance, should he find that the claim was sound. Otherwise, if the respondents should counterclaim, the *yasāvulbāshī* expected the governor to

---

79 TsGARUz, f. I-125, op. 1, d. 498, l. 44.

80 This canal was built in 1857 by Ḥasan Murād Qūshbigī, see Ya.G. Guliamov, *Istoriia orosheniia Khorezma s drevneishikh vremen do nashikh dnei* (Tashkent: Izdatel'stvo Akademii nauk Uzbekskoi SSR, 1957), p. 231; Mirza Abdurakhman, *Dnevnik Mirzy Abdurakhmana, vedennyi vo vremia khivinskogo pokhoda*, IVRRAN, St. Petersburg, Arkhiv Vostokovedov, f. 33, op. 1, d. 221, ll. 24–29.

81 Y. Bregel, *An Historical Atlas of Central Asia* (Leiden-Boston: Brill, 2003), p. 67, map 33; Guliamov, *Istoriia orosheniia Khorezma s drevneishikh vremen do nashikh dnei*, pp. 218, 292; A. Shioya, "Irrigation Policy of the Khanate of Khiva regarding the Lawzan Canal, 1830–1873," *Area Studies Tsukuba* 32 (2011), p. 116.

82 See L. Kostenko, "Khivinskoe khanstvo v sel'skokhoziastvennom otnoshenii (s chertezhami)," *Voennyi sbornik* 4 (St. Petersburg, 1874), pp. 373–374; Guliamov, *Istoriia orosheniia Khorezma s drevneishikh vremen do nashikh dnei*, p. 261; I.M. Dzhabbarov, "Iz istorii tekhniki i kul'tury zemledeliia v iuzhnom Khorezme," in *Istoriia material'noi kul'tury Uzbekistana*, 2 (Tashkent: Fan, 1961), p. 277; Munis and Agahi, *Firdaws al-iqbāl: History of Khorezm*, p. 609, note 607.

transfer the case to the *qāżīs*. It is here important to observe that the formulaic expression to denote this last procedure – 'we entrusted it to the *sharīʿa*' (*sharīʿatgha qūshdūk/sharīʿatgha tāpshūrdūk*) – means simply that the case was transferred to the *qāżīs* who would hear the dispute according to the probative procedures of Islamic adjudication. This does not mean, however, that, the governor (or the attendant) did not hear cases according to *sharīʿa*. It means, instead, that the governor, for example, did not have the legal authority to request that the plaintiffs produce testimony, or that the respondents swear an oath, or to ask the parties to bring legal opinions in support of their position. Nothing in our texts suggests that governors (or attendants) implemented customary rules. By contrast, it is worth reminding that the involvement of *qāżīs* usually resulted in the production of written statements, whose stipulations were determined by local notables (*āqsaqāls/kadkhudās*), thereby giving ample room for considering the specifics of local circumstances, established practices, and customary notions of justice. The present document is also useful to illuminate the degree to which legal actors operating in the Khorezmian Islamic juridical field were aware of the legal instruments at their disposal. As soon as the respondents realised that the plaintiffs would produce testimony and win the case, the former informed the governor that they would bring the case to the royal court.

Translation

Let it be known to the office of the *yasāvulbāshī*, the refuge of the vizierate,[83] our lord, that Bābā Jān and ʿAbdu Karīm from Manāq [claimed that] above their community (*davr*), on the upper bank of the canal Qūshbigī Yāf, [there is a group of people] disposing of 20 water shares (*sū*)[84] under the supervision of Allāh Bīrgān Mīrshab and Nāvāẕā Mīrāb. During the last two years said latter group has not carried out the maintenance works (*qāzūshmāydūr*) in the lower part of the canal (*āyāq*). Since ancient times (*qadīmdīn*) it is established practice (*taʿāmul*) that all water users (*hamma ābjūrī*) should clean

83 In the original text of the record, *vizārat-fanāh*.

84 In Khorezm the term *sū* (lit. 'water') denotes a measure to quantify a water share. According to Yahya Guliamov the Qonghrats introduced standard irrigation units. As a result, they established that one *sū* was the quantity of water necessary to irrigate ten *ṭanāb* of land and they thus allocated ten *sū* to a community of landholders, which they termed *jabdī*, see Guliamov, *Istoriia orosheniia Khorezma s drevneishikh vremen do nashikh dnei*, p. 295. The Qonghrat bureaucracy recorded and updated the allocation of water shares to communities. They did so by making reference either to the communities, as in e.g. TsGARUz, f. I-125, op. 2, d. 508, or to the canals (*ābkhūr yāflār*), as in e.g. TsGARUz, f. I-125, op. 2, d. 510, l. 4.

the local ditches proceeding from the lower reaches towards the main stream (*saqa*). [As a result,] you ordered (*būyrūq*) to question the afore-mentioned people and [if the appeal is found to be sound], make them clean the canal according to the ancient practices. [You also instructed that,] should the [respondents] counterclaim (*bāshqa daʿvālār*), the dispute must be heard at *sharīʿa* [court]. We thus arranged for a hearing according to *sharīʿa*. The *qāżī-īshāns* from Manāq who are skilled in *sharīʿa* ordered the appellants[85] to produce their witness (*guvāh*). When the appellants were about to bring their witness, [the defendant] Allāh Bīrgān Mīrshab stated that he intended to go to Khiva (*Khīvāgha bārūrman dīb*) [and address the dispute to the royal court]. In wishing you well, we wrote this report (*khaṭ*) to inform you about this [event] on 22 Jumādī al-avval 1335 [15.03.1917].

Seal: Muḥammad Yaʿqub Bāy b. Jabbār Qulī Maḥram, 1334

85 In the original text of the record, *ariża-gūy*.

Document 19: A Report by *qāżīs* to the *yasāvulbāshī* on Land Assessment Works[86]

Introduction

This text is a *qāżīs*' report to the *yasāvulbāshī*. It recounts the case of a certain Jumʿa Niyāz who appealed to the royal court to complain that log bundles hampered the flow of water. The royal court reacted to his complaint by sending an attendant with a royal warrant (*nishāna-yi ʿālī*) that instructed the *qāżīs* in Yarmish[87] to collect information on the conflict. This required the *qāżīs* to go to the locality, inspect it and ask local elders, that is people endowed with privileged knowledge, to provide further clarifications. This otherwise brief report is instructive because it shows that *qāżīs*' activity was constrained by the instructions which they received from the royal court. Indeed, they limited themselves to execute orders and, consequently, their remit consisted of providing for the expertise of land assessors. They did not take any initiatives regarding the claim, though they established that it was not sound. They no doubt refrained from doing so because responsibility for solving the dispute lay with the royal court, not them. It is also important to note that, despite the somewhat trivial nature of the case, the arrival of an envoy who represented the royal court and brought instructions from the central power required the involvement of not just one *qāżī*, but three. This would suggest that *qāżīs* regarded accountability to the royal court as a key aspect of their activity.

Translation

He [God Almighty]! Let it be submitted for consideration (*maʿrūż bū ki*) to the *yasāvulbāshī*, His Excellency (*janāb-i ʿālī*), the most eminent minister (*vazīr-i aʿẓam*) and illustrious councilor (*dastūr al-mukarram*), our lord, that, in accordance with the content of the royal warrant (*nishāna-yi ʿālīlārī*) entrusted to Iskandar Maḥram, we went to the [place of the dispute] and saw that indeed on the western (*kūn-bātar*) border of the land of Muḥammad Niyāz b. Bīk Murād and Jumʿa Niyāz ʿAbd al-Karīm Murād ūghlī there is a thoroughfare.

---

86 TsGARUz, f. I-125, op. 1, d. 498, l. 54.

87 On the canal Yarmish, see Munis and Agahi, *Firdaws al-iqbāl: History of Khorezm*, p. 564, note 276; M.I. Ivanin, *Khiva i reka Amu-Daria* (St. Petersburg: Obshchestvennaia pol'za, 1873), p. 9; Guliamov, *Istoriia orosheniia Khorezma s drevneishikh vremen do nashikh dnei*, p. 200. We have not found in our sources any mention that would suggest that Yarmish was the name of a settlement. It may well be that it was the name of a large area, consisting of different communities of water-users, which were subject to the authorities of *qāżīs* indeed appointed to such area. It is interesting to note that in fiscal registers one can find the expression 'water-users of Yarmish' (*ābkhūr-i Yārmīsh*) as fiscal unit, while there is no mention of the locality in itself, see TsGARUz, f. I-125, op. 2, d. 387, l. 68–68ob.

[However,] there is no road leading to the water dumps (*chiqar suv yūlūsī yūq*).[88] We summoned the elders of this mosque community (*masjid qavmīnīng qariya ādamlārī*) and questioned them. They too confirmed that the thoroughfare belongs to the afore-mentioned Muḥammad Niyāz but that there is no road leading to the water dumps. [They also drew our attention to the fact that] along the sides of the afore-mentioned road there are log bundles belonging to ʿAbd al-Karīm which do not hamper passers. The document (*ḥujjat-nāma*) was registered (*marqūm*) in the year 1328 [1910].

Seals: Qāżī va ra'is-i Yārmīsh Dāmullā Muḥammad Yūsuf
Qāżī va ra'is-i Yārmīsh Dāmullā ʿAbd al-Ghafūr
Qāżī va ra'is-i Yārmīsh Dāmullā Bābājān Makhẕūm

88 The meaning of the term is unclear.

Document 20: A Report by a Provincial Governor to the *yasāvulbāshī* about a Marital Dispute[89]

Introduction

In the wake of a failure to consummate marriage due to her husband's sexual impotence, a woman announced her intention to divorce, a decision that led to a violent altercation between the families of the spouses. Consequently, the father of the woman submitted a petition to the royal court and filed a claim for battery and injury. The office of the *yasāvulbāshī* instructed the governor to solve the conflict. He did so, as this rescript emphasizes, by hearing the case 'according to Islamic law.' In the absence of additional empirical information, it is unclear what the governor actually meant by this. Most probably he advised the parties to reach a settlement, as we have seen governors following this procedure in similar cases. During the hearing, however, the respondent must have manifested dissatisfaction with the settlement's stipulations proposed by the governor and consequently expressed his willingness to file a counterclaim. The established procedure in such cases required that the governor transfer the case to the *qāżīs*. Things seem not to have changed substantively with the involvement of the *qāżīs*, however. Unhappy with the outcome of the adjudication offered by the judges, the husband manifested his intention to file a counterclaim with the royal court in Khiva. This course of action left the governor with no other choices than to send the parties to Khiva. Illuminating the authorial intentions leading to the production of this document seems here particularly important. On the one hand, one can infer that this text is merely a report of a local official, the governor, to the agency from which he had received instructions to proceed with the resolution of a conflict. On the other, the text also reflects the governor's attempt to elucidate the course of events that had occurred before the *qāżīs* in order to qualify his own position. Not only he had attempted, albeit unsuccessfully, to settle the dispute, but he also most probably participated in the attempted adjudication of the case before the *qāżīs*. By drafting this rescript, therefore, he must have sought to show the royal court that he and his subordinates, which is to say the *qāżīs*, had done everything in their power to settle the dispute. It is also important to note how the term *sharīʿa* could be used in two different meanings: one denoting 'Islamic law', the other as a metonym for '*qāżīs*' court.'

89 TsGARUz, f. I-125, op. 1, d. 498, ll. 56–56ob.

Translation

Let it be known to the office of the *yasāvulbāshī*, refuge of the vizierate and repository of power, our lord that a certain Qurbān Dūrdī Qarādāshlī[90] had appealed to the royal court (*darbār-i ʿālīlārīgha ʿarż ītib*) and was entrusted with a warrant (*nishāna*). [The content of his plea was the following:] when he decided to divorce (*āyirmāqchī*) his daughter from Bāyrām Sulṭān her husband (*kuyuv*)[91] due to the latter's failure to consummate marriage (*martnīng sharīʿat īshīgā yārāmāghān sabablī*),[92] Ārtūq Nīyāz, Ūrāż Nīyāz, Mullā Jūmʿa, ʿĀshīr, and Khwājam Birdī battered (*ūrūb*) his daughter, pulled her hair, caused bodily harm (*aʿżālārīn jarāhatdār ītib*) and also insulted [Qurbān Dūrdī]. On this account, the claim (*daʿvā*) of the afore-mentioned individuals was heard according to Islamic law (*sharīʿat bīrla*). Since [the parties] did not find an agreement (*yutūshmagāndīn kiyin*), I transferred [the case] to the *qāżīs* (*sharīʿatgha qūshūb*). However, when the groom's party came before the *qāżīs* (*sharīʿatgha bārgānda*), they announced that they will go to the royal court (*dargah-i ʿālīgha bārūrman*).[93] For this reason, I summoned the afore-mentioned [individuals] and dispatched them to your office. This petition (*ʿariża*) was registered on 19 Ẕī al-ḥijja 1334 [16.10.1916].

Seal: Muḥammad Karīm Yūzbāshī b. Ismāʿil

---

90 Qaradashli is an ethnic term designating a Turkmen tribe that came to the oasis of Khorezm in the first half of the 19th century. According to Bregel, groups belong to this tribe settled in the lower reaches of the Yarmish canal as well as in the northeastern district of Hilali (Yilanli), see his *Khorezmskie turkmeny v XIX veke*, pp. 31–32. In Khivan chronicles they are referred to as *Qarādāshlī* or *Qarādāshlī khalqī*, see Mūnis and Āgahī, *Firdaws al-iqbāl. History of Khorezm*, p. 962.

91 In Uzbek the term *kuyov* carries both the meaning of 'groom' and 'son-in-law.' This word-choice makes perfect sense if we think that, in this part of the narrative, it is the woman's father who accounts the events.

92 'Due to his inability to fulfill what is due to him as a man according to *sharīʿa*.' This is clearly a circumlocution to express a case of sexual impotence. The term *mart* may well be a phonetic rendering of the word *mard*, ('male', 'masculine'). For revealing comparisons, see A. Layish, *Sharīʿa and Custom in Libyan Tribal Society: An Annotated Translation of Decisions from the Sharīʿa Courts of Adjābiya and Kufra* (Leiden: Brill, 2005), doc. 37.

93 In the original text of the record, *dargah*.

Document 21: A Report by a Provincial Governor to the *yasāvulbāshī* about a Dispute over Debts[94]

Introduction

A man filed a claim for debt against three individuals with the royal court in Khiva. He received a royal rescritpt (*fatak*) instructing the governor with jurisdiction over the claimant to settle the dispute. By involving the local elders, the governor was able to settle things between the claimant and two respondents. The latter acknowledged their debts and honored them. In exchange, the plaintiff relinquished his claims. The third respondent, however, did not admit his debt. The denial of the claim activated the transfer of the case to a *qāżī*. The judge, however, refused to hear the case. The claimant reported about the unsuccessful hearing to the governor, who summoned the *qāżī* in an attempt to clarify the issue. The *qāżī*, in turn, blamed the governor for having instigated the plaintiff against him and manifested his willingness to transfer the case to the royal court. The governor tried to persuade the judge that going to Khiva would be an unfortunate move: to file a claim with the *yasāvulbāshī*'s office would cost him a considerable amount of money and it would also go counter to the royal court's previous instructions, i.e., to solve the case according to *sharīʿa*. The judge did not follow the advice of the governor who was thus obliged to write a report informing the royal court that he sent the *qāżī* and the third respondent to Khiva to file a counterclaim against the plaintiff. On the basis of this document, we observe that the governor transfers to *qāżī*s a case every time a respondent denies a claim. The transfer of the case from the governor to the *qāżī*s signals the changing nature of the dispute: while the governor usually attempts to achieve the resolution of the conflict through mediation, and while the involvement of a third party endowed with recognised authority (such as the governor) is instrumental in securing the parties' satisfaction, *qāżī*s, instead, are expected to follow Islamic probative procedures thereby enhancing the confrontational aspect of the dispute. The document is instructive also because it shows that at any stage of the dispute settlement, the parties could always resort to the royal court to express their dissatisfaction and achieve redress.

Translation

Let it be known[95] to the *yasāvulbāshī*,[96] refuge of the vizierate and repository of power, our lord, that a certain Ṣālīḥ, a man (*ādamī*) of Muḥammad

94 TsGARUz, f. I-125, op. 1, d. 498, ll. 65–64–64ob.

95 *Maʿlūm wa huvaydā* in the original text of the record.

96 *Yasāvīlbāshī* in the original text of the record.

Karīm Yūzbāshī['s entourage], appealed to the royal court claiming (*darbār-i ʿālīlarīgha ʿarż qīlīb*) that Mullā Ghāyib Qāżī owes him 600 *manāt* and 1½ *bātman*[97] of rice, Mullā Bikjān owes him 8 *būt*[98] and 15 *qadaq*[99] of sugar, Ūstā Qurbān Niyāz owes him 80 *manāt* [and] a robe, ʿIbādullāh owes him 400 *manāt* [and] a cart. [Ṣālīḥ] received a *fatak* [from the royal court]. As soon as we became acquainted with the content of this order, we summoned these people and interrogated them. The afore-mentioned Ūstā Qurbān Niyāz admitted (*iqrār*) [his debt] and returned [it]. ʿIbādullah too acknowledged [that] his debt amounted to 240 *manāt* and nothing else. These 240 *manāt* were paid back [to Ṣālīḥ]. The notables of the community (*īl kadkhudā-āqsaqāls*) had [Ṣālīḥ] relinquish his other claims (*bāshqa daʿvāsīn*) [against Ūstā Qurbān Niyāz and ʿIbādullāh]. Since Mullā Bikjān did not acknowledge [his debt], we passed [the case] over to the *sharīʿa*. According to *sharīʿa,* it was incumbent on Ṣālīḥ to produce testimony (*guvāhgha tūshīb*). [Since he failed to do so], Mullā Bikjān took an oath (*ānt*).[100] [But] after that the *qāżī-īshān* stated: 'I shall not hear your dispute; go away!' (*murāfaʿa*[101]*-ngiznī sūrāmāyman tūr kīt*). Mullā Bikjān together with Ṣālīḥ came [to me] and informed me about what the *qāżī-īshān* had said. Consequently, I summoned the *qāżī-īshān* and asked him to explain to me his words. He answered that as Ṣālih had also filed a claim against him, he intended to go to Khiva together with Mullā Bikjān. I have attempted to persuade [the *qāżī-īshān*] not to involve the royal court (*ūzī Khivanī ṭalab qīlmāsa*) [since] travel would cost (*kharj*) him 200 *manāt*. I even said that the [royal] order (*mihribānchiliqlārī*) prescribes that the case be solved according to *sharīʿa*. [But the *qāżī-īshān*] accused me of having advised Ṣālih to [sue him] and acquire [from the royal court] a rescript [with allegations] against him. [The *qāżī-īshān*] then left. Because of this incident, we sent the afore-mentioned Mullā Bikjān and the *qāżī-īshān* to your noble office. The state of the case (*ṣurat-i vāqiʿa*) was recorded on 27 Ramażān 1336 [06.07.1918].

Seal: Khwāja Niyāz Bāy b. ʿAbdullāh Maḥram, 1335

---

97 The *bātman* was a unit of weight. In the 19th- and early 20th-century Khanate of Khiva it was *ca.* 20 kgs, see Ivanin, *Khiva i reka Amudaria*, 46 (footnote); *Katalog khivinskikh kaziiskikh dokumentov XIX–nachala XX vv.*, p. 651.

98 Local rendering for the Russian *pud*, a measure for weight equivalent to 16,380 kgs.

99 The *qadāq* or *qadāgh* was a unit of weight, equivalent to 409.5 gms, see A. Abdurasulov, *Khiva* (*Tarikhiy-etnografik ocherklar*) (Tashkent: Ŭzbekiston: 1997), p. 89.

100 It is unclear what was the procedure followed by the *qāżī* here.

101 *Murāfīʿa* in the original text of the record.

Document 22: A Report by Provincial Governor and the *qāżīs* to the *yasāvulbāshī* about a Dispute over Landownership[102]

Introduction

This is a rescript that five *qāżīs* of Gurlen and the local governor addressed to the *yasāvulbashī* in the wake of a claim over a plot of land filed with the royal court. The dispute revolved around an area amounting to 5 *tanāb* which was the object of a transaction between individuals. The representative of the local mosque community, however, held that that the plot of land belonged, instead, to a larger area that was endowed to the benefit of the mosque as part of a charitable endowment (*vaqf*). The *qāżīs* and the governor went to the place in question, summoned the elders, and asked them to provide information about the legal status of the land. In absence of documentary evidence that could attest to the rights on this land, the elders testified that the area did not belong to the endowment and that who sold it had disposed of it in the capacity of proprietor. There is ample documentary evidence from 19th-century Central Asia showing that *qāżīs* usually operated in the capacity of land assessors on behalf of the chanceries of the khanates.[103] It was also common in Central Asia that, in the absence of written attestations, elders provided testimony (*shahādat*) either to renew the stipulations of endowments or to update the legal status of estates belonging to them.[104] Most importantly, however, we should appreciate the public dimension of a dispute over landed property rights. Besides the presence of the elders, the authors of this rescript emphasize the involvement of the mosque community.

Translation

Let it be known to the *yasāvulbāshī*, refuge of the vizierate[105] and repository of power,[106] our lord, that [we proceeded] according to your instruction (*būyrūq*) to notify to your office whether a plot of land measuring 5 *ṭanāb*, which a certain Bāshlūgh Jumʿa Murād and one Ādina Murād, from the Qara-Tāylī clans[107]

---

102 TsGARUz, f. I-125, op. 1, d. 498, l. 75.

103 P. Sartori, "Colonial Legislation Meets *Sharīʿa*: Muslims' Land Rights in Russian Turkestan," *Central Asian Survey* 29.1 (March 2010), pp. 43–60.

104 P. Reichmuth, "'Lost in the Revolution': Bukharan waqf and Testimony Documents from the Early Soviet Period," *Die Welt Des Islams* 50.3–4 (2010), pp. 362–396.

105 *Vizārat-panā* in the original text of the record.

106 *Ḥukūmat dastgā* in the original text of the record.

107 Qara-Tāylī referred to a sub-group of the Imreli Turkmens. Bregel considered them as the third major group of Turkmens in Khorezm after the Yomuts and the Chawdur see Bregel', *Khorezmskie Turkmeny v XIX veke*, pp. 31, 42. In the text of this record the expression Qara Tāl should be read as a toponym, rather than an ethnic designation.

(*jamāʿa*)[108] sold to a certain Muḥammad Ūraż, belongs to the 20 *ṭanāb* of land endowed (*vaqf*[109] *ītgān*) to the benefit of Qūl Muḥammad Īshān's mosque. [For that purpose you ordered us] to go to that place, gather the elders (*qariyalār*), and question them. We reached that locality, gathered the elderly people, and examined in the presence of all the dwellers (*jamʿ-i kaṣīrlār*) that all the four boundaries of the 20 *ṭanāb* of *vaqf* land correspond to the endowment deed (*vaqf-nāma*).[110] However, [we discovered that] there was a canal called Ūlūgh Tāza Yārghān crossing the afore-mentioned *vaqf* land which was not mentioned in the endowment deed. Secondly, when we questioned the individuals who sold 5 *ṭanab* of that land as their property as well as the elders – namely Khudāy Birgān valad-i Ṣafar Niyāz, Muḥammad Panāh Dārugha valad-i Aḥmad, Sayyid Niyāz valad-i Ṣafar Niyāz (another man), Jumʿa Niyāz valad-i Ṭaghāy Murād, Allah Birgān Dārugha valad-i Qūtlūq Murād, Khāl Murād valad-i Sīytak, Pahlavān Niyāz valad-i Atā Niyāz, Khāl Murād valad-i Qūshmān, Khudāy Birgān (another man) valad-i Khāl Muḥammad, Khāl Murād valad-i Muḥammad Ghālī – whether the 5 *ṭanāb* indeed belonged to the *vaqf* of the mosque or they were outside, they stated that these 5 *ṭanāb* of land were the property (*ḥaqqī va mulkī*) of the sellers and should not be considered as [part of the] endowment. When we questioned them as to whether they could produce written evidence (*ḥujjat khaṭī*) or a royal warrant (*pādshāhlīq-dīn ālghān yārlīq-i ʿālī*) showing that they owned the land, they stated that in the wake of two floods, the locality was destroyed and therefore all the written evidence attesting to the properties of the Qara Tāl clans got lost and that, beside the endowment deed, there is no written evidence left for [said] *vaqf* land. [The elders further stated] that from the outset [the sellers] owned the land which they made use of (*mutaṣarrif būlūb ūltūrghān mulklārī dūr*). Equally, they stated and testified (*akhbār va shahādat*) that they would bear the responsibility in this life and hereafter should they hide that the afore-mentioned 5 *ṭanāb* were included in the endowment and were considered *vaqf* land. We informed you about the state of the case (*ṣurat-i vāqiʿa*); now you know best [what to do]. This report (*khaṭ*) was written on 16 Rabīʿ al-ṣānī 1335 [08.02.1917].

---

108 *Jamʿa* in the original text of the record.

109 *Vāqf* in the original text of the record.

110 *Vāqf-nāma* in the original text of the record.

Seals: ʿAbd al-Raḥīm Bāy[111]
Qāżī va raʾis Muḥammad Qurbān[112]
Qāżī-yi Gūrlān Dāmullā Bābājān
Qāżī-yi Gūrlān Dāmullā Muḥammad Yaʿqūb
Qāżī-yi Gūrlān Muḥammad Karīm Khwāja
Qāżī-yi Gūrlān Dāmullā Ūrāż Muḥammad

111 We have been unable to decipher the seal.
112 We have been unable to decipher the seal.

Document 23: A Report by a Provincial Governor to the *yasāvulbāshī* about the Death of a Man Involved in an Altercation[113]

Introduction

This record recounts the settlement of a dispute initiated by a dead man's relative filing a claim with the royal court and suggesting that the cause of death was an altercation that had occurred between the departed and another man. According to the order (*būyrūgh*) of the court to make an inquest and settle the dispute, the governor summoned the relatives of the departed who stated that the man was seriously ill prior to the altercation and, for this reason, they do not have any claims against the respondent. One may well imagine that prior to the summons, mediators assisted the parties to achieve an amicable settlement. In view of a monetary compensation, the claimant relinquished his claim while the respondents received a deed of relinquishment. The document shows the logics of filing a claim with the royal court: it triggers a procedure of inquest that obliges the parties to find a compromise over a conflict in order to achieve a settlement.

Translation

Let it be known to the office of *yasāvulbāshī*, refuge of the vizierate[114] and repository of power, our lord, that Ḥaqq Muḥammad and Sharīf from the community (*qavm*) of Mullā Yūsuf Āqsaqāl in Shāhābād[115] got into an altercation with each other . Given the death of Sharīf, we [proceeded] in accordance with your instruction (*būyrūgh*) to investigate the claim [filed by his relatives] (*daʿvā*), to resolve the conflict according to Islamic law on the spot (*shūl ṭarafda sharīʿat farmāyishī bīla sāflāshtūrūb*) and to report the results [of the proceedings] to your office. We thus summoned and questioned the heirs (*varaṣalārī*) of the deceased Sharīf, [namely] his son Jumʿa Niyāz and wife Qurbān Bīka of Sharīf, together with his brothers Rajab Bāy and Mullā Īsh Bāy. His heirs stated that Sharīf had fought [with Ḥaqq Muḥammad] three days before his death and that he was also sick (*kasal*). They thus acknowledged the relinquishment of the claim against Ḥaqq Muḥammad. Later [Jumʿa Niyāz Sharīfnī ūghlī], acting on his own behalf (*ūz ṭarafīdīn*) and as representative (*vakīl*) of his mother Qurbān Bīka with the testimony (*shahādat*) of his witnesses (*guvāhlār*), Yūsuf Āqsaqāl and Rajab Bāy, certified (*khaṭlāshtūrūb*) before the *qāżī-īshāns* of

113 TsGARUz, f. I-125, op. 1, d. 498, l. 86.

114 In the original text of the record, *vizārat-fanāh*.

115 Shahabad (Shavat) is a town located 35 km north-west from Khiva along the middle section of the canal bearing the same name, see Danilevskii, *Opisanie Khivinskogo khanstva*, p. 114; Ivanin, *Khiva i reka Amu-Daria*, p. 9; Munis and Agahi, *Firdaws al-iqbāl: History of Khorezm*, p. 564, note 278.

Shahabad the death (*mawt*) of his father and the relinquishment of his claim. This is the state of the case (*ṣūrat-i vāqiʿa*) which was recorded on 27 Shaʿbān 1336 [08.06.1918] and was sent to your office.

Seal: Muḥammad Ṣafā Ātālīq[116] b. ʿAbdullāh Ātālīq

---

116 Muḥammad Ṣafā Ātālīq was governor of Shahabad. The term *ātālīq* was an ascription of status that we usually find attached to the names of the leaders of the major Uzbek tribal groups in Khorezm. This title was in use at court already under the rule of Abū ʾl-Ghāzī Khān, see Munis and Agahi, *Firdaws al-iqbāl: History of Khorezm*, p. 45. The majority of the tribal leaders who played a central role in the political events of the region at the end of the 17th and in the 18th century used the title *ātālīq*, see N.I. Veselovskii, *Ocherki istoriko-geograficheskikh svedenii o Khivinskom khanstve s drevneishikh vremen do nastoiashchego* (St. Petersburg: Tipografiia brat. Panteleevykh, 1877), p. 213; Munis and Agahi, *Firdaws al-iqbāl: History of Khorezm*, p. 560, note 251. Under the Qonghrats who pursued policies to undermine the local tribal aristocracy, one can observe a meaningful devaluation of the titles representing earlier, local tribal traditions (as was the case with the titles *ātālīq* and *īnāq*). The Russian embassador to Khiva (1819–20) N. Murav'ev pointed out that Muḥammad Raḥīm Khān 'deprived [the notables] of all their privileges and left only their titles;' and, 'these tribal leaders barely have a say …; and they do not participate in the [political] affairs,' see his *Puteshestvie v Turkmeniiu i Khivu v 1819 i 1820 godakh gvardeiskogo general'nogo shtaba kapitana Nikolaia Murav'eva, poslannogo v sii strany dlia peregovorov, pt. 2* (Moscow: Tipografiia Avgusta Semena, 1822), pp. 34–35. According to Kuhn, in 1873 *ātālīq* was a 'honorific title' (*pochetnoe zvanie*) which was granted to the leaders of four Uzbek tribes: Qonghrat, Manghit, Uyghur and Qipchaq, see his *Ocherk istorii zaseleniia Khivinskogo khanstva s drevnykh vremen, sostav ego sovremennogo naseleniia, administratsiia i goroda khanstva*, 1873, IVRRAN, St. Petersburg, Arkhiv Vostokovedov, f. 33, d. 8, l. 39. It is noteworthy that in his notes on the political hierarchy in Khiva, which related to the beginning of the 20th century, Nil Lykoshin does not mention the title *ātālīq* among the officials serving the royal court and who played a meaningful role in the life of the Khanate, see N.S. Lykoshin, *Sovremennoe raspredelenie vlasti v Khanstve Khivinskom, 1912 god*, TsGARUz, f. I-2, op. 1, d. 314, ll. 63–64. One can therefore infer that under the rule of the Qonghrats the granting of the title *ātālīq* did not carry with itself the same privileges which were once given to the Uzbek tribal aristocracy. As an honorific title, it had also little to do with specific administrative duties. For this reason, one observes that at the end of the 19th century and at the beginning of the 20th century individuals with the title of *ātālīq* served in very different capacities such as governors (*ḥakīm*), ibid., l. 64ob.

Document 24: A Report by a Provincial Governor to the *yasāvulbāshī* about Malfeasance[117]

Introduction

A group of liegemen from Hazarasp appealed to the royal court in Khiva and complained about an instance of fiscal malpractice, which involved the governor of the city and other local power holders who had levied a special 'ammunition tax' (*yarāgh fūlī*). In the work *Gulshan-i sa'ādat*, the Khivan chronicler Laffasī writes that at the beginning of 1918, after the withdraw of the Russian army from the territory of the khanate, the Khivan ruler Isfandiyār Khān (r. 1910–1918) was obliged to seek the protection from Junayd Khān, one of the leaders of the Yomut Turkmens.[118] The latter took advantage of his newly acquired position of political authority and obliged the khan to provide for the resources necessary to quash the revolts of other Turkmen groups. In complying with the request of Junayd Khān, Isfandiyār Khān thus levied from the population a supplementary tax, which Laffasī termed the 'bullets tax' (*ūq pūlī*).[119] From a chronological point of view, the events referred to in this document (March–April 1918) perfectly match the accounts provided by Laffasī. The claim of the liegemen relates to the fact that their status traditionally exempted them from the payment of taxes, while their possessions became subject to taxation. As the document suggests, the royal court sent to the local governor a series of instructions meant to regulate this conflict, which, however, remained a dead letter. The local governor explained that, because of the inaccuracy of the appellants, he could not follow the orders coming from Khiva. He also explained in detail the reason for acting as he did with regard to the taxation of the local residents and the imposition of a new tax. He takes great care to illustrate the fact that his actions did not represent his own initiatives, but that he merely executed orders coming from the center of power. The governor also confirms that, since he was appointed relatively recently, the forms of taxation applied by his predecessors were still in place. He then goes on to explain that he ordered his subjects to establish the rate of taxation and return money in those cases when subjects paid more than what was due. This document shows that the instructions coming from Khiva were sometimes entrusted not directly to their addresses, but to the claimants who could operate also without attendant (*yasāvul*). The text is noteworthy also because it offers evidence, albeit indirectly, on the compilation of fiscal registers. In this case, we observe that

117 TsGARUz, f. I-125, op. 1, d. 498, ll. 87–87ob.

118 On this personality, see the Introduction, pp. 17–18.

119 Ḥasan-Murād Laffasī, *Gulshan-i sa'ādat*, MS Tashkent, IVANRUz, inv. no. 7797, fols. 99a–100a.

*āqsaqāl*s first compiled the list of taxpayers for every mosque, which they subsequently passed on to the governor and the royal court in Khiva.

Translation

Let it be known to the *yasāvulbāshī*, the refuge of the vizierate, our lord, that two liegemen (*nawkar*), Mullā Dawlat and Tājī Bāy from Hazārāsp, filed a petition (*ʿarż*) [to the royal court] stating that the governor had imposed on them the payment of a weapon tax (*yarāgh fūlī*), gave them inappropriate orders (*bī yumish* [?] *khiẕmat*) and levied from them more than [the previously stipulated] 10 *manāṭ* for the Yomuts' expenses. From your order (*būyrūq*) dating 13 Jumādī al-ṡānī prior to this 3 or 4 times I was given instructions (*fatak*) not to interfere with the petitioners (*ʿārżgūy*), which I did not follow, and that, should I endure with such behavior, I would be dismissed from the office of governor. My reply (*ʿarż*) is that, when I summoned the *bāy* and *āqsaqāl*s and announced to them the [content of the] incoming instructions regarding the collection of the tax on the weapons, they discussed and agreed (*ittifāq*) to fulfill their duties, and we had thus informed His Excellency and Muḥammad Raḥīm Bāy about that. After that there came another instruction [to impose the tax] on wealthy men (*qadāratlī ādamlārdīn*). After we announced [the content of that order] to the *bāy* and *āqsaqāl*s, the *āqsaqāl*s of each mosque community (*masjid qavmī*) compiled a register of names (*ād ba ād daftar*) belonging to the wealthy men, handed it over [to me] on 22 Jumadī al-ṡānī. I forwarded the registers in our possession to his excellency. As your order [came] to levy the tax [from the people listed] in the register, I ordered the *āqsaqāl*s to collect the weapon tax (*yarāgh fūlī*). But until now neither the liegemen (*nawkar*) nor the other residents (*ghayrī fuqarā*)[120] have been taxed; nor was I aware of the instructions (*fatak*) which the petitioners obtained. I had heard of them [only] from Muḥammad Amīn Dīvān Bābā. [As a result], I had these claimants be brought before me. I questioned them and examined their rescript (*fatakni kūrūb*). I asked them who required that they pay the tax on weapons. Since they answered that it had been the *āqsaqāl*s, I summoned and questioned the latter; but they did not confirm [the liegemen's statement] (*bīkār*). I then asked [the claimants] why they did not bring the rescript immediately in the wake of their receipt, [and they answered that] they were willing to produce them upon request [to pay] the weapon tax. Secondly, whatever was the amount of *manāṭ* collected for the Yomuts' expenses, we acknowledge that it had been

120 The term *fuqarā* was mostly used to designate 'subjects' and referred to ordinary taxpayers as distinct from other individuals enjoying fiscal privileges, see Munis and Agahi, *Firdaws al-iqbāl: History of Khorezm*, pp. 570–571, note 297.

collected when Īsma'īl Khwāja[121] was [on duty as] governor. And since I was appointed to the [office of] governor [of Hazarasp] neither the liegemen nor the other residents were taxed over again [to meet] such expenses. As soon as the *yūzbāshīs*[122] informed me about the amount of money which the liegemen paid under the rule of Īsma'īl Khwāja, I have instructed the *yūzbāshīs*, who were about to go along with [a certain] Muḥammad Raḥīm Bāy, to calculate for me within three-four days the amount of revenues collected from the *bāys* and the community (*īl*) to the benefit of the Yomuts. [I equally ordered that], should have the taxes exceeded [a fair amount,] the exceeding part must be paid back to the liegemen, otherwise we will inform your office [and request new instructions regarding] the petitioners. Whatever your decision, I shall let you know accordingly. Other than that, I know nothing else regarding what the petitioners said. If you ask the *yūzbāshīs* [to clarify] whether the petitioners provided false information (*yālghāndīn dalīl kūrgāzīb*) when they stated that the governor imposes [the fulfillment of] inadequate duties and levies from them the tax on weapons to the benefit of the Yomuts; and [if you also] ask Muḥammād Āmīn Dīvān Bābā [to ascertain] whether I had [the liegemen] bring me their notifications [precisely] because they had avoided to do so, [then] you would certainly see whether the word of the petitioners is trustful or deceitful. [At any rate,] I have informed Your Excellency (*janāb-i humāyūnlār*) that [these claimants] are used to submit ill-founded petitions (*yālghāndīn dalīl kūrgāzīb 'arż itīb yūrgānlīgī*). It is you who decides and knows best. Our sincere petition (*'ārīża-i īkhlāṣ*) was recorded at the end of the month of Jumadī al-ṣānī 1336 [March/April 1918].

Seal: 'Abd al-Raḥīm Bāy b. Muḥammad Karīm Bāy

121 The author clearly refers to Sayyid Ismā'il Khwāja, the elder brother of the grand-minister (*vazīr-i akbar*) Sayyid Islām Khwāja (d. 1913). In 1912 Lykoshin refers to Sayyid Ismā'il Khwāja as the governor of Hazarasp at the age of 45 years. See N.S. Lykoshin, *Sovremennoe raspredelenie vlasti v Khanstve Khivinskom, 1912 god*, TsGARUz, f. I-2, op. 1, d. 314, l. 64.

122 On the *yuzbāshī* being the second most important official at the provincial level after the governor (*ḥākim*) and working at the latter's instructions, see Introduction p. 47 fn. 180.

Document 25: A Report to the *yasāvulbāshī* about a Case of Murder[123]

Introduction

A woman was shot. Her son, a certain ʿAbdullāh Khwāja, reported the homicide to an official, most probably the local governor. He claimed that the perpetrator of the homicide had first attempted to shoot him with a pistol, but that he missed him and hit instead his mother. The murderer, claimed ʿAbdullāh Khwāja, was a certain Mullā Qurbān Niyāz Bāy who after firing fled away, but lost his sheepskin hat in the vicinity of the house. By following an established procedure usually applied in cases of homicide, the official requested the *qāżīs* to examine the crime scene and inspect the corpse. The jurists sent two individuals, including a man acting in the capacity of bailiff. The latter reported back and confirmed that the woman was murdered by a bullet, which perforated her breast. At the same time, the respondent, Mullā Qurbān Niyāz Bāy appealed to the royal court in Khiva and denied the claim. His account of the incident was substantially different. From our document it transpires that the story behind the murder of the woman was more complex: ʿAbdullāh Khwāja, claimed Mullā Qurbān Niyāz Bāy, had conconcted a stratagem with two men, who were suspected of highway robbery, to lure Mullā Qurbān Niyāz Bāy to the house of ʿAbdullāh Khwāja and to kill him. We do not know the reasons why they did so: most probably the three men wanted to settle previous scores with Mullā Qurbān Niyāz Bāy or perhpas they simply wanted to get rid of him because he could be instrumental in identifying them as the culprits in a case of robbery. In any case, when Mullā Qurbān Niyāz Bāy approached the house of ʿAbdullāh Khwāja, the two men fired at him. They missed him, however, and he was able to flee. The royal court sent a royal warrant to the local official, which instructed him to hear the dispute according to *sharīʿa*. The official did not transfer the case to the *qāżīs*, though. He questioned the parties and the robbery suspects himself, but he was unable to reconstruct the dynamics of the murder: the sheepskin hat did not belong to Mullā Qurbān Niyāz Bāy and the suspects denied their participation in the robbery. Moreover, he heard local notables who confirmed evidence of the murder, but who excluded the involvement of Mullā Qurbān Niyāz Bāy. This document also provides insights into the investigation procedures of robbery cases. It appears that in Khorezm people followed a procedure of divination consisting of having two young boys look into the water to identify the suspect. Most probably this procedure was to be followed when testimony was not enough to establish the identity of the thieves.

123 TsGARUz, f. I-125, op. 1, d. 498, ll. 92–92ob.

Translation

Let it be known to the office of Muḥammad Yūsuf Yāsavulbāshī,[124] the refuge of the vizierate,[125] our lord, that a certain ʿAbdullāh Khwāja from the mosque community (*masjid qavmī*) of Yādgār Khwāja came here and informed me that during the evening prayer (*khūftān vaqtī*), when he was sitting at his place [and talking] to Mullā Khāl Bāy, the *imām* of the [local] mosque, [somebody] knocked at his door. [ʿAbdullāh Khwāja] went out and a certain Mullā Qurbān Niyāz shot at him with a pistol (*ṭubbāncha*). The bullet, however, did not reach him and he ran away. [At that moment] his mother, Ūlūgh Jān Bīka, [who was in the house,] came [to the door]. Mullā Qurbān Bāy fired another shot that hit her in the breast and exited from her back. He then ran away too [but] left his sheepskin hat there. [ʿAbdullāh Khwāja] brought the bullet and the sheepskin hat [to me]. As a result both Mullā Bābā Jān Mullā Bājbān ūghlī, who was dispatched by the *qażī-īshān*, and Ātā Jān Makhẕūm, who was dispatched by myself, went in their [joint] capacity as trustee (*amīn*) to examine [the crime scene]. [When] they returned, they reported that [the story of] the woman being shot was true (*rāst īrkān*): and they stated that [the bullet] hit her in the breast and exited from her back. Later the afore-mentioned Mullā Qurbān Bāy went to [royal court] and on 2 Ẕī al-ḥijja[126] he brought to me a royal warrant (*nishāna*) whereby [Mullā Qurbān Bāy] stated the following: 'in cases of theft [the aggrieved party usually come to me as] I could determine the identity of the thief by having two children look into the water.[127] Two thieves Khallī and Muḥammad Żiyā, who had stolen the possessions (*māl*) of a certain Mūsā Khwāja, summoned me to the house of a certain ʿAbdullāh [Khwāja]. [When I reached that place, the thieves] fired twice with a rifle (*āltī ātār*)[128] intending to kill me. However, the bullets did not hit me and I

---

124 The text here refers to Muḥammad Yūsuf b. ʿAvaż Niyāz Maḥram who acted in the capacity of *yasāvulbāshī* between 1910 and 1917, see the Introduction, p. 30.

125 In the original text of the record, *vizārat-panā*.

126 In the original text of the record, *Ẕā al-ḥijja*.

127 *man har kimnī māllārī ūghūrlānsa īkkī yāsh bālanī suvgha qārātīb ūghrīni tāpib birūr īrdīm.*

128 At the beginning of the 20th century two types of rifles were mostly employed in the khanate: the Berdan rifle, which was referred to in local sources as *birdānka* (see the footnote to Doc. 40), as well as the 3-line Mosin rifle with an internal magazine of five shots, which explains why our material refers to it as *bīsh ātār* (Turki for 'firing five shots'), see N.S. Lykoshin, *Zapiska Nachal'nika Amu-Dar'inskogo Otdela Polkovnika Lykoshina o sovremennom sostoianii Khivinskogo Khanstva, 1912 god*, TsGARUz, f. I-2, op. 1, d. 314, l. 250b. The expression *āltī ātār* (Turki for 'firing six shots') may be intended to refer to the G-98 Mauser rifle, which fired cartridges from a five-shot magazine. If desired, the rifle could also be equipped with a sixth cartridge, by placing one in the trunk.

managed to run away.' [Since the royal warrant further instructed that] this case be reviewed according to *sharīʿa*, I [proceeded to] question Mullā Qurbān Bāy and asked him whom the sheepskin hat belongs to. He answered that it does not belong to him. Then they brought Khallī and Muḥammad Żiyā [before me]. When I questioned them, they stated that it has been a year since they last went to ʿAbdullāh [Khwāja]'s house. They never fired at Mullā Qurbān Bāy, nor did they steal Musā Khwāja's possessions. Regarding the royal warrant which your office [entrusted to] Khudāy Naẓar Yūzbāshī and sent to me, I had the *āqsaqāl-kadkhudā*s of ʿAbdullāh Khwāja summoned [before me]. When I questioned them, they informed me that as soon as they heard about the case, they immediately went [to ʿAbdullāh Khwāja's place] and they stated it was true that the woman had been shot, [but] they do not know who fired. The *āqsaqāl-kadkhudā*s of Mullā Qurbān Bāy gave testimony to (*shāhidlīq*)[129] that they have never seen him wandering about aimlessly (*bihūda yūrgānīnī*). This is the state of the case (*ṣūrat-i vāqiʿa*) as I heard it; but it is you who knows best (*ṣāḥib-i rāʾy üzlārī bīlūrlār*). This notification was written on 7 Muḥarram 1336 [23.10.1917].

Seal:[130]

129 *Shāydlīq* in the original text of the record.
130 We have been unable to decipher the seal.

Document 26: A Report by a Provincial Governor to the *yasāvulbāshī* about a Dispute over Landownership[131]

Introduction

The document recounts the investigation of a claim which was led by a local governor. The plaintiff claimed he was the owner of a plot of newly irrigated state land, which during a cadastration campaign initiated by the Khivan authorities in 1910[132] was assigned to someone else. This occurred in his absence. The office of the *yasāvulbāshī* issued a royal warrant (*nishāna*) which instructed the governor of Khanqah to deal with this case. The latter requested the local *qāżīs* to collect information on the process of cadastration. The judges proceeded to question the residents of the locality and clarify the conditions in which the entitlements on the contested land had been conferred. In contrast to the statement provided by the claimant, local residents testified that the claimant had in fact abandoned the land showing little interest in the process of cadastration. The governor deferred any decision to the office of the *yasāvulbāshī*. It is noteworthy that when requesting from the *yasāvulbāshī* a final decision on the case, the governor warned the royal court that in his region similar lawsuits of recovery of property abounded. Presumably, a ruling on this specific lawsuit might have well served to establish a precedent to deal with other such cases. This case shows how *qāżīs*' role in dispute settlements was confined to one of legal advisors.

Translation

Let it be known to the office of the respected and honorable (*ʿizzatlū ḥurmatlū*) Shaykh Naẓar Yasāvulbāshī,[133] our lord, that [a certain] Qalandar from Hāzārāsp filed a petition to the royal court (*dargāh-i ʿālīlārīgha ʿarīża ītib*). He stated that a certain Jumʿa Niyāz, together with Bikjān and Nār Muḥammad, have profited from his absence and thus [changed] the registration [of his possession amounting to] approximately 3 *ṭanāb* of land in the cadastre (*ṭanāb daftarī*). [Accordingly,] a royal warrant (*nishāna*) was entrusted to the afore-mentioned [Qalandar]. As soon as I became acquainted with [the content of said] order (*būyrūq*), I examined the register and found out that the afore-mentioned land had been recorded under the name of Jumʿa Niyāz; and Qalandar also confirmed that he had been absent [when this incident occurred]. Thereafter I wrote (*khaṭ birdūm*) to the *qāżīs* of Hāzārāsp [and instructed them] to question all those individuals who appear in the cadastral [register] and who belong to the [local]

131 TsGARUz, f. I-125, op. 1, d. 498, l. 93–93ob.

132 For more information, see p. 16.

133 On Shaykh Naẓar Bāy Yasāvulbāshī , see pp. 30–31.

community (*īlātni tamāmī ādamlārī*) and to send a report. The *qażī-īshāns* questioned the people who were present and sent to me a report, [which says] that [the local community] testified (*shahādat*) that said Qalandar was present [during the cadastration]; that they had asked him whether he would keep the notarised property (*khaṭlī mulkīngīnī tūtārdūrmūsan*), and that, on account of his [repliying] that he would not keep [the property], and his abandoning it, Jum'a Niyāz [and his associates] kept it [for themselves]. The [judges] reported to me [these] events (*vāqi'alār*). Now Qalandar testifies (*shahādat*) that he was absent [during the process of cadastration], while the community (*īlāt*) was present and stated that he had left [the land]; a scribe (*dīvān*) too was there. As a result, this was recorded into the cadastre and registered under the name of a certain Jum'a Niyāz. So if [you] order to allot the land again to Qalandar [in accordance with] his [original] documentation (*khaṭī bīla*), then such receipt should be taken from Jum'a Niyāz and handed over [to Qalandar]. If [you] bestow your mercy (*mihribān*) [and thus consider] that in the wake of the abandonment of a property and the latter's transfer to a cadastre (*falānd*),[134] [such land] should not be allotted again, then Qalandar's claim should be made null (*da'vānī qūymāqī kirāk*). In the province of Hāzārāsp there are many people who first abandon the untilled land (*fartāpta*[135] *yirlār*), which they are allotted (*ṭanāb būlūjāqdā*), but then they regret [having done so] and file a claim (*da'vā*) [to recover their property]. There must be approximately 3–4000 such cases. I dispatched to your office the *qażī-īshāns*' report (*yāzghān khaṭī*), the claimant (*da'vāgar*), and the two parties. Whatever will be the mercy you bestow [upon us], I shall proceed accordingly. This is the state of the affairs and it was submitted to your office on 19 Jumādī al-s̱ānī 1332 [14.05.1914].

Seal: Ḥājjī Muḥammad Bāy b. Amīn al-Dīn Bāy 1330[136]

---

134 Phonetic rendering of the Russian word *plan* ('plan,' 'outline').

135 This was the corrupted form of the Persian *partāfta* ('left'). In the Khanate of Khiva the term was used to designate abandoned land. The term entered the bureaucratese of the Russian colonial administration in the form *partau*, see [Girshfel'd and Galkin], *Voenno-statisticheskoe opisanie Khivinskogo oazisa*, 2, p. 16; K. Sarybaev, *Agrarnii vopros v Karakalpakii (konets XIX–nachalo XX vekov)* (Nukus: Karakalpakstan, 1972), p. 38.

136 Lykoshin notes that in 1912 this man was the 39 year-old governor of Khanqah, who lived in a luxurious edifice adorned with European furniture. See his *Sovremennoe raspredelenie vlasti v Khanstve Khivinskom, 1912 god*, TsGARUz, f. I-2, op. 1, d. 314, ll. 64–64ob; Idem, *Zapiska Nachal'nika Amu-Dar'inskogo Otdela Polkovnika Lykoshina o sovremennom sostoianii Khivinskogo Khanstva, 1912 god*, TsGARUz, f. I-2, op. 1, d. 314, l. 13.

Document 27: A Report by a Provincial Governor to the *yasāvulbāshī* about a Case of Robbery[137]

Introduction

A Turkmen appealed to the royal court in Khiva to report a case of robbery. The royal court reacted by appointing an attendant who proceeded to mediate the case. In the presence of the governor of Tashhawz, the attendant organised a public hearing with the headmen representing the communities of the two parties and achieved a settlement. The notification of the settlement addressed to the office of the *yasāvulbāshī* acquires the status of a pledge indicating that the parties recognised the obligation to avoid new conflicts. From this we should infer that in this specific case the parties to the dispute must have regarded the involvement of a *sharīʿa* court as less effective than representatives of the royal court to achieve the instrumental purposes of avoiding further conflicts. It also suggests that, in cases of disputes, communities in Khorezm regarded legal deeds as less legally forceful than the knowledge, which such communities preserved and could thus transmit orally, about the achieved stipulations of the settlement. We here encounter yet another case which reminds us that, in spite of the ubiquity of written records and especially legal deeds in Central Asia, among certain communities oral testimony carried more probative weight than did documentary evidence. Most probably this phenomenon originates from the fact that the embodiment of and the participation in a shared knowledge were crucial for the process of forging a cohesive a community. If seen from this point of view, the practice of prefering oral testimony to written evidence may not reflect the enduring legacy of Islamic juristic principles,[138] rather be born out of specific social circumstances.

Translation

Let it be known to the *yasāvulbāshī*, the banner of glory and happiness (*ʿizzat-va saʿādat-nishān*), our lord, that a certain Kildī Muḥammad, a Chawdur[139] [Turkmen] claimed that in his absence, during the night, [two people called]

137 TsGARUz, f. I-125, op. 1, d. 498, l. 94.

138 For a discussion on the tension between written evidence and oral testimony in Islamic law, see J. Marglin, "Written and Orality in Islamic Law: Documentary Evidence and non-Muslims in Moroccan *Sharīʿa* Courts," *Comparative Studies in Society and History* 59.4 (2017), pp. 884–911.

139 Chawdur was the name of one of the major Turkmen tribes in Khorezm. During the 19th and early 20th century some groups of Chawdur inhabited the westword and north-westword fringes of the Khorezmian oasis, see N.S. Lykoshin, *Zapiska Nachal'nika Amu-Dar'inskogo Otdela Polkovnika Lykoshina o sovremennom sostoianii Khivinskogo Khanstva, 1912 god*, TsGARUz, f. I-2, op. 1, d. 314, l. 24ob.; Bregel', *Khorezmskie Turkmeny v XIX veke*, pp. 30, 42.

Qūshān and ʿAnna Muḥammad broke into his house and robbed him of 300 *manāt*. Accordingly, ʿAyd Bāy, the liegeman (*nawkar*) of Ghāyib Yūzbāshi, was appointed [by the royal court] in the capacity of attendant (*yasāvul*). [The latter together with] the *kadkhudā*s of Kildī Muḥammad and his opponents (*sūzīnīng daʿvāgarlārī*) – Qūshān and ʿAnna Muḥammad – came [before me] and reconciled the two parties. And now in order to avoid further disturbances among the population (*fuqarālārnī halāk būlmāslīqī vajhīdīn*), this notification was entrusted to the liegeman. We inform your office about this event. This report (*khaṭ*) was written in the year 1335 [1916–17].

Seal: Jumʿa Niyāz Maḥram b. Maḥmūd Dīvān[140]

140 A governor of Tashhawz, see N.S. Lykoshin, *Sovremennoe raspredelenie vlasti v Khanstve Khivinskom, 1912 god*, TsGARUz, f. I-2, op. 1, d. 314, l. 64ob.; Ḥasan-Murād Laffasī, *Gulshan-i saʿādat*, MS Tashkent, IVANRUz, inv. no. 7797, fols. 29b., 63b.

Document 28: A Report by *qāżīs* to the *yasāvulbāshī* about a Case of Extortion[141]

Introduction

Two *qāżīs* notified the *yasāvulbāshī*'s office about their hearing of a case of extortion. Little information is provided on the procedure applied at court; emphasis, instead, is put on the fact that a third party representing the khan reconciled the disputing parties on account of their kinship ties (*qarindāsh*). The judges also indicate that they issued a certificate of acquittal bearing the unusual name of 'cleansing document' (*khaṭ-i pāk*). Apparently, whoever crafted this text knew that his addressee was not interested in the details of court proceedings; instead, it was important for purposes of an important principle at the Khivan royal court – to record that the conflict had been peacefully solved.

Translation

Let it be known to the office of the *yasāvulbāshī*, refuge of the vizierate and repository of power, our lord, that Allāh-Yār Makhẕūm from Nāymān[142] appealed (*ʿarīża*) [to the royal court] stating that when he attempted to recover his 3 *ṭillā* from a certain Khāl-Murād Vafāh and Ṣafar, the latter extorted from him 24 *ṭillā*. You bestowed your mercy (*mihribān*) [upon us] and appointed Qalandar, [your] servant (*khiẕmatkār*), [to the office] of attendant (*yasāvul*). When they [all] came here to Khidir-ilī-Qalʿa,[143] since the two parties had kinship ties,[144] they both took a certificate of acquittal (*khaṭ-i pāk*)[145] and achieved satisfaction (*riżālīq*). As the residents [of this town] suffer from indigence (*ʿājizlīq*), they prayed [their lord] to be benevolent. This notification was compiled on 8 Muḥarram 1335 [03.11. 1916].

Seals:[146]

---

141 TsGARUz, f. I-125, op. 1, d. 498, l. 95.

142 On Nayman, see above, p. 109n69.

143 Clearly Khidir-ili, a settlement located along the canal bearing the same name between Gurlen and Vazir, see Munis and Agahi, *Firdaws al-iqbāl: History of Khorezm*, p. 613, note 652.

144 On the notion of *qarindāsh* in the Islamic juridical field of Khorezm, see further Sartori, "Murder in Manghishlaq: Notes on an Instance of Application of Qazaq Customary Law in Khiva (1895)".

145 In the original text of the record, the Persian genitive is rendered as *khaṭī-yi pāk*.

146 We have been unable to decipher the seals.

Document 29: A Report by a Provincial Governor to the *yasāvulbāshī* about a Dispute over Losses Caused by Yomut Turkmens[147]

Introduction

The years 1915–1916 were marked by major rebellions by the Yomut Turkmens against the central authorities in Khiva.[148] Sources tell us that these rebellions were followed by episodes of highway robbery perpetrated against the local population, which brought about a wave of lawsuits filed with the royal court against the Yomuts.[149] A contemporary of those events, the court historian Ḥasan-Murād Laffasī explained that authorities in Khiva gave orders to record all these lawsuits in separate registers (*ūlūgh daftar*) in order to require that the tribal headmen of the Yomut Turkmens compensate the victims of these offences.[150] Chronologically, the events recorded in the present document match with the Turkmen rebellion of 1916, which was quashed by a punitive expedition led by the Russian general A.S. Galkin. The quashing of this rebellion was instrumental to ensure that representatives of the Yomut Turkmens would compensate the population in cases of robbery and destruction.[151] The document is a governor's report requested by the agencies in Khiva and addresses a complaint of a resident of a settlement in the district of Hilali (otherwise known as Yilanli). In this case, the Yomut Turkmens were accused of ravaging agricultural works and a canal. Following the order of the royal court, the official summoned the disputing parties. In the presence of the governor, the parties determined the value of the damages and the amount of compensation due. While the text tells us that the aggrieved party expressed satisfaction at the compensation, there is no evidence of the notarization of a certificate of amicable settlement or any other legal deed. It is interesting to note that part of the sum determined for the compensation was levied by the governor to pay fees for the agencies in Khiva, i.e., the attendant as well as the trustee.

147 TsGARUz, f. I-125, op. 1, d. 498, ll. 98–98ob.

148 Becker, *Russia's Protectorates in Central Asia: Bukhara and Khiva, 1865–1924*, pp. 182–185, Abdurasulov, "Konflikt kak resurs: anatomiia 'turkmenskikh besporiadkov' v Khorezme, 1914–1916," pp. 141–186.

149 Pahlavān Niyāz Ḥājjī, [*Khāṭiralar*]. MS Khiva, Private Collection of Anvar Otaboev, fols. 31b–32b.

150 Ḥasan-Murād Laffasī, *Gulshan-i saʿādat*, MS Tashkent, IVANRUz, inv. no. 7797, fols. 26b, 51a.

151 Ibid., fol. 81a; Pahlavān Niyāz Ḥājjī, [*Khāṭiralar*]. MS Khiva, Private Collection of Anvar Otaboev, fol. 37b.

Translation

Let it be known to Āmān Kīldī Yasāvulbāshī,[152] refuge of the vizierate and repository of power, our lord, that last year the Yomuts, against our will (*zūrlāb*), [trampled through] the fields belonging to the Dūrman mosque in Hilālī[153] causing great damage to said fields and the crops of several dwellers (*fuqarālār*) and passing through a canal. As a result, a certain Bābājān Sayyid appealed (*ʿarż ītīb*) [to the royal court] and received a warrant (*nishāna*) which he brought [to me]. Accordingly, I summoned the appellant (*ʿarżgūylār*) and the Yomuts who had passed through the canal. I sent a trustee (*amīn*) to the landowners (*yir īgālārī*) whose crops had been ruined, and instructed him together with the *āqsaqāl-kadkhudās* to examine [the damages]. I had [the Yomuts] pay 150 [*ṭillā*] to [compensate] the loss (*żararlārī*)[154] that the aforementioned [landowners] had suffered and thus settled amicably (*rizālīqgha yitdīlār*) [the dispute]. Besides, I have additionally levied 50 *ṭillā* from those who had damaged the canal as a payment for the trustee and the attendant (*amīn fūlī va yasāvul ḥaqqī*). From this [sum of money], I have sent 25 *ṭillā* to your office. This letter (*maktūb*) was recorded on 9 Shaʿbān 1334 [10.06.1916].

Seal: Muḥammad Yūsuf Bāy b. Muḥammad Yaʿqūb Divān

---

152 See on Āmān Kīldī Yasāvūlbāshī the Introduction to this volume, pp. 33–34.

153 Hilali (Yilanli) was a town on a lower stream of Shahabad channel, located circa 85 km north of Khiva, see Kun, *Ocherk istorii zaseleniia Khivinskogo khanstva s drevnykh vremen, sostav ego sovremennogo naseleniia, administratsiia i goroda khanstva*, 1873, IVRRAN, St. Petersburg, Arkhiv Vostokovedov, f. 33, d. 8, ll. 46ob.-47; Munis and Agahi, *Firdaws al-iqbāl: History of Khorezm*, p. 650, note 1072.

154 In the original text of the record, *zarārlārī*.

Document 30: A Report by a Provincial Governor to the *yasāvulbāshī* about Malfeasance[155]

Introduction

A man appealed to the royal court in Khiva and he filed a claim of extortion against the governor of Kat. Said extortion allegedly occurred when the governor heard a case in which the appellant was found guilty of assault and bodily harm. On that occasion, the appellant dispensed a substantial sum of 305 roubles. He gave 100 roubles to the injured party for medical treatment, while he paid the rest to award the attendant and a middle-man who presumably had strong ties to the governor. When the claim of extortion reached the governor, the latter had leeway to deal with the case as he saw fit, regardless of the fact that he himself was one of the disputing parties. He organised a hearing in a court presided over by *qāżīs* and had the appellant confess that the direct payment to the governor never occurred. Though the *qāżīs* seem not to have issued any specific documentation to support the governor's position, in the mind of the governor the appellant's confession before the local notables would ensure some kind of absolution. The governor of Kat then wrote to the *yasāvulbāshī* explaining that the aggrieved party might indeed have been extorted of that sum of money, but he was unaware that a number of officials involved in the previous hearing had harassed the appellant. In reporting to Khiva, the governor did not address the question of extortion, but accused the claimant of slander.

Translation

Let it be known to the *yasavūlbāshī*, refuge of the vizierate and repository of power, our lord, that a certain Muḥammad Yaʿqūb from Kāt[156] had appealed (*ʿarż ītīb*) [to the royal court] stating that the governor (*ḥākīm*) had taken from him 290 *manāt* and that a certain Āllah-Birgān, who was an attendant (*ādlī*),[157] had taken 15 *manāt*. Regarding the warrant (*nishāna*) [which the

155 TsGARUz, f. I-125, op. 1, d. 498, l. 103.

156 Kat (New Kat) is a town situated circa 35 km north of Khiva, see Danilevskii, *Opisanie Khivinskogo khanstva*, l. 108; Kun, *Ocherk istorii zaseleniia Khivinskogo khanstva s drevnykh vremen, sostav ego sovremennogo naseleniia, administratsiia i goroda khanstva*, 1873, IVRRAN, St. Petersburg, Arkhiv Vostokovedov, f. 33, d. 8, ll. 46ob.-47; Munis and Agahi, *Firdaws al-iqbāl: History of Khorezm*, p. 563, note 275.

157 *Ādlī* is a spelling variation (probably an Oghuzism) of *ātlī* ('horsemen'). In 19th- and early 20th-century Khiva this term was employed to denote the cavalry as opposed to 'infantry' (*piyāda*), as well as an armed horseman, see Iu.E. Bregel', *Dokumenty arkhiva khivinskikh khanov po istorii i etnografii Karakalpakov* (Moscow: Nauka, 1967), p. 31; Munis and Agahi, *Firdaws al-iqbāl: History of Khorezm*, p. 586, note 384.

appellant received from the royal court], I inform you (*ʿarż-i ikhlāṣimīz*) that the afore-mentioned Muḥammad Yaʿqūb together with his two younger brothers (*īnī*) had assaulted a certain Ātā-Murād and his two women (*nāchār*), wounded his head and caused injuries (*majrūḥ*) all over their bodies without any reason (*tamāmī aʿżālārīnī bī-vajḥ*). In this regard, I took 100 *manāt* [from Muḥammad Yaʿqūb's side] and handed over to the injured [parties] (*majrūḥlār*) [to cover] the expenses for the [medical] treatment (*malḥam fulī*); afterwards I settled the dispute (*daʿvāsīnī ṣāflāshtūrūb īrdūk*). [Now] together with the trustee (*āmīn*) sent [by the royal court], I went to the *sharīʿa* court (*dār al-qażā*) in Kāt. Before the *qāżī-īshān*s and in the presence of the afore-mentioned [Muḥammad Yaʿqūb's] *katkhudā-āqsaqāl*s gathered there, I asked [the claimant] when he had given to me 290 *manāt*. He replied that he personally had given 290 *manāt* not to me, but that he had given said sum to Muḥammad Yūsuf Bāy; and that the latter had returned therefrom [only] 63 *manāt*. He acknowledged (*iqrār*) that before the *qāżī-īshān*s. When Muḥammad Yūsuf was asked where the rest of the money was, he said that the attendant (*yasāvul*) and *kadkhudā*s had taken 27 *manāt* and that a guard (*qaravul*), a certain Yomut called Sardār, had taken 100 *manāt*. I was not aware tha these sums had been taken [from him]; but the reason for Āllāh-Birgān's taking 15 *manāt* is that during a period of four months [the latter had acted in the capacity of attendant] since Muḥammad Yaʿqūb had assaulted somebody and wounded his head; hence [Āllāh-Birgān] was paid the attendant's fee (*yasāvul ḥaqqī*). Now [the victim of the assault] too is ill. However, Muḥammad Ya'qūb has used slanderous and inappropriate words against me (*ḥaqqārat-namā va nāshāyista sūzlār*). You decide as you wish. The petition (*ʿarīża-nāma*) was written on 28 Ramażān 1336 [07.07.1918] and sent to your office.

Seal: Ātā Bīk b. Raḥīm Birdī Bīk, 1335

Document 31: A Report to the *yasāvulbāshī* about the Extinguishment of a Debt[158]

Introduction

Two residents of Hilali appealed to the royal court in Khiva with the aim of securing permission to extinguish a part of their debts before their creditors by selling plots of land in their possession. In answering this appeal, the royal court entrusted them with a warrant that instructed the provincial governor to collect the necessary circumstantial evidence on the case and report to Khiva. In the wake of a consultation with the debtors and their creditors, the governor assessed the potential value of the plots of land and determined also a way to extinguish the debt. The latter required that the sum of money resulting from the sale of the debtors' possessions would be distributed proportionally among the creditors according to the amount of their credit. As for the remaining part of the debt, the governor proposed the issuance of promissory notes to each creditor, which determined the sum of money that the debtors still owed to their creditors. From the document it transpires that the office of the *yasāvulbāshī* agreed on the proposed procedure, but it also stipulated that creditors who were subjects of the Russian Empire should be paid first, while the subjects of the khanate would be compensated only later. In addition, the office of the *yasāvulbāshī* asked the governor to report on the implementation of the extinguishment of the debt. It is of significance that both here and in other cases of debts preference is accorded to Russian subjects. Such preference reflects one of the stipulations included in the peace treaty between the Russian Empire and the Khanate of Khiva signed in Gandemian in 1873.[159]

The document is interesting also for another reason. It shows the degree to which the royal court in general and the office of the *yasāvulbāshī* in particular was involved in cases of debts involving private individuals. Such involvement was no mere formality. The document illustrates that the *yasāvulbāshī* required the governor to collect the information that would be useful for the agencies in Khiva to assess the case. In this regard, the documentation produced by the chancery of the Commandant of the Amu-Darya Department allows us to shed light on the procedural aspects of the resolution of conflicts originating from debts. In 1912 Colonel Nil S. Lykoshin crafted a report to the Governor-General of Turkestan that explaind that, until recently, issues concerning debts fell within the competence of governors of the khanal provinces.

---

158 TsGARUz, f. I-125, op. 1, d. 498, ll. 63–63ob.

159 Art. 14 of said treaty stipulated that: 'In case of claims regarding debts from either Russian or Khivan subjects, the former enjoy precedence to receive the payment of debts,' Zhukovskii, *Snosheniia Rossii s Bukharoi and Khivoi za poslednee trekhsotletie*, p. 181.

Creditors who had claims for unextinguished debts directly appealed to the governors. The latter would instruct their attendants to deal with such cases. However, in the summer of year 1912, as Lykoshin notes, agencies in Khiva forbade governors to appoint attendants to collect debts from the population. In particular, from that moment on creditors who were Russian subjects were required to appeal directly to the royal court, while the governors were instructed to inform the office of the *yasāvulbāshī* about the wealth in possession of debtors.[160] In his missive addressed to Lykoshin, the Qonghrat ruler Isfandiyār Khān informed him that such a procedural change was prompted by a very bad harvest that impoverished the population and which obliged the Khivan chancery to take the financial situation of his country under direct control. The chancery therefore took measures that would facilitate the reconfiguration of debts with Russians and help the Khivan subjects avoid having to sell all their possessions.[161]

Translation

He [is the Almighty]! Let it be submitted for consideration (*maʿrūż ūl-kīm*) to the office of the *yasāvulbāshī*, refuge of the vizierate, our lord, that a certain ʿAvaż Niyāz and Khudāy Bīrgān, residents (*fuqarālār*) of Hilālī, brought [me] a royal warrant (*nishāna-yi ʿālī*) [endorsing their intention] to sell their land (*yir jāylār*) in order to pay their debts (*qarż*). I discussed the matter together with the creditors (*ālghūdārlār*) and they explained to me that someone intends to purchase ʿAvaż Niyāz's land for the sum of 125 *ṭillā*. Should [this sum of money] be distributed [among creditors, the latter would receive] 12 *tanga* for each five *ṭillā* [of debt]. [Someone else] is willing to offer 200 *ṭillā* for Khudāy Bīrgān's real estate; if the creditors divide [among themselves] this sum of money, it looks like (*ūkhshāydūr*) they would receive more than 3 *tanga* for each *ṭillā* [of debt]. This is how they answered [my question]. I shall proceed to order them whatever you decide [regarding this matter]. They also applied for a document (*khaṭ*) attesting to the sum of money which will not be covered [by such an arrangement]. Should you agree also on this, I kindly ask you to clarify with a notification whether [the creditors] should receive a document which does not include a rate of interest (*bī-ijāra*) given that [the debtors] do not own their houses anymore, or the creditors should not receive any such document for what is still due to them and take [only] in accordance to the form of payment [they agreed upon] regardless of the amount of their debt. Praise be

160 [N.S. Lykoshin] G. Turkestanskomu General-Gubernatoru, 28.08.1912, no 43. TsGARUz, f. I-2, op. 1, d. 289, l. 137ob.

161 Ibid., l. 140.

to Allah, Lord of the Worlds! The nobleness of this government is [a sign of] tranquility; and we are wholly dedicated to praise in your favour. This sincere petition (*ʿarīża al-ikhlāṣ*) was written on 10 Rabīʿ al-s̱ānī 1332 [07.03.1914].

Seal[162]

[Verso:] If creditors agree, let [the debtors] sell their properties (*yir va jāy māllārī*) according to the rule of Islamic law (*sharīʿat farmānī bila*). First of all [the debt] must be paid to the creditors from the subjects of Russia (*ūrūsiya fuqarāsī*) and the remainder [of the money] must be given to the [local] creditors of this [left] side [of the Amu Darya]. As for the remainder of the debt the creditors must be provided with a document of guarantee (*khaṭ itīb*). And finally, let us know [on the performance] by [official] letter. 10 Rabīʿ al-s̱ānī 1332 [07.03.1914].

162 We have been unable to decipher the seal.

Document 32: A Report by a Provincial Governor to the *yasāvulbāshī* about the Extinguishment of a Debt[163]

Introduction

An individual appealed to the royal court with the aim of recovering a debt of 90 *ṭillās* from a certain Rūzī Bāy Tājīk. In response to this appeal, the *yasāvulbāshī* issued a warrant to the governor of Khanqah and sent an attendant to deal with the dispute according to the established practice. The attendant proceeded to make an inventory of the debtor's possessions to estimate their value. Then the governor of Khanqah decided to sell the possessions in order to expiate the various debts of Rūzī Bāy Tājīk according to the order of the royal court. In the meantime, three creditors who were subjects of the Russian empire[164] claimed to enjoy right of precedence in debt cases and therefore insisted that their debts be covered by the entire sum of money that resulted from the sale of Rūzī Bāy Tājīk's possessions. In this way, the other creditors who were subjects of the Khivan protectorate would not receive anything. Unable to resolve the dispute on the spot, the governor of Khanqah decided to send the debtor together with a guarantor directly to Khiva, and let the royal court decide on the case.

Translation

Let it be submitted for consideration to the *yasāvulbāshī*, the recipient of the ruler's trust (*muʿtamad al-sulṭān*) and the confidant of the king (*muqarrab al-khāqān*), his excellency (*janāblārī*), our lord, that a certain Rūzī Bāy Tājīk owes (*ḥaqqī bār*) ʿIbādullāh Bīk from Khivā 90 *ṭillā* and this [debt] has been notarised (*khaṭlī*). [As ʿIbādullāh Bīk appealed to the royal court,] he was entrusted with a rescript (*fatak*) and an attendant (*yasāvul*) was instructed to recover [his property] according to Islamic law (*muvāfiq-i sharīʿa*).[165] [As a result,] the provisions of the shop of the afore-mentioned Rūzī (*dūkān asbāblārī*) were sold for 163 *manāṭ* and 89 *tiyn*.[166] Then I intended to cover the debt of one creditor (*ālghīdār*) whom [Rūzī Bāy] owed 45 *manāṭ* and proceed to divide (*taqsīm*) [the remaining sum] among other creditors according to the order of

163 TsGARUz, f. I-125, op. 1, d. 498, l. 71–71ob.
164 See Doc. 31 for a discussion on this topic.
165 In the original text of the record, *muvāfiq*.
166 Chagahtay rendering of the Russian 'kopek.'

the chancery (*dīvān-khāna*).[167] [But at that point,] Maksīm Ūralskī,[168] Astafī,[169] and Muḥammad Jān Nūghāy told me that they will take all the money and will not share them with any other. They also required that I hand over the money to them and inform the chancery about their contentions (*ʿarżlārīmīz*). I did so on 16 Jumādī al-s̱ānī but since I have not yet received any reply I wrote once more with regard to the contentions of those Russians (*ūrūsīlār*). Since Rūzī Bāy Tājīk stated that he himself intends to appear before your office on Saturday, I entrusted him to a guarantor (*kafīl*), a certain Yūldāsh from Khanqah. This is the state of the case which was written to you (*ṣurat-i vāqiʿa ūshbū-dūr*). I compiled this letter (*khaṭ*) on 15 Shavvāl 1328 [09.10.1910].

Seal: Ḥājjī Muḥamad Bāy b. Amīn al-Dīn Bāy[170] 1327[?]

167 In the chronicles written at the court of the Qonghrat khans, the term *dīvān-khānā* is seldom employed, and in the rare instances of its appearance it serves as a synonym for 'meeting-hall' (*kūrūnīsh-khāna*). See, for example, Munis and Agahi, *Firdaws al-iqbāl: History of Khorezm*, p. 614, fn. 662. Furthermore, in the documentary collection known as 'The Archive of the Khans of Khiva' we do not find occurrences of this term. We are therefore prone to think that the idea of a centralised chancery originated from bureaucratic exchanges between the Russian colonial administration and the Khanate of Khiva after 1873.

168 This *nisba* refers to the city of Ural'sk (until 1775 Yaitsk), a trade settlement on the right bank of the river Ural.

169 Most probably, this is a corrupted form of the Russian personal name Astafii.

170 Governor of Khanqah, see Doc. 26, fn. 136.

Document 33: A Report by a Provincial Governor to the *yasāvulbāshī* about the Extinguishment of a Debt[171]

Introduction

A local official, Bābā Jān Yuzbāshī b. Pahlavān, addressed a report to the *yasāvulbāshī* in compliance with previous instructions. A certain Ūrāż Bāy had appealed to the royal court and attempted to secure the support of the latter in the payment of his debts. In reply to this appeal, the royal court ordered the official in the locality of Qīlich Niyaz Bāy to gather circumstantial evidence and, in particular, to provide for an estimation of Ūrāż Bāy's possessions and clarify the citizenship of the creditors thereby excluding the presence of Russian subjects among the latter. The involvement of Russians would have implied a specific procedure of pay-back to follow.[172] The inquiry showed that Ūrāż Bāy was not in the position to extinguish his debts. The official thus proceeded to have the creditors postpone the payment for two more years without imposing any interest rate. This document shows that the involvement of Khiva in the resolution of debt cases was important for the appellants unable to pay their debts, to postpone payment and thus avoid insolvency.

Translation

He [is the Almighty]! Let it be known (*bū nav' ma'lūm*) to the office of *yasāvulbāshī*, the refuge of the vizierate, and the repository of power, our lord, [the following:] a certain Ūrāż Bāy from Qīlich Bay had appealed (*'arż*) to your office. He [stated that] he was indebted to a few people, that [such a debt] had been notarised (*khaṭlī qarż*), and that he intended to sell his 12,5 *ṭanāb*s of land to return the loan (*adā ītmākchī dūrmān*). [As a result, you instructed me to determine] the amount of the debt he had, the value of his land, whether he had other possessions, whether he was indebted with Russian subjects (*ūrūsiya fuqarāsī*), and whether his possessions (*amvāl va ashiyā'lārī va yirī*) could compensate for his debts, and his creditors (*ālghūdārlār*) would agree to such a pay-back. Since [you instructed me] to answer such queries with a written notification (*khaṭī bīla*), I proceeded to calculate the amount of money that should be paid to the creditor[s.] [It was determined that] his debt amounts to 555 *ṭillā*. His 12,5 *ṭanāb*s of land are not worth 100 *ṭillā* since they were left uncultivated (*adrā*). He also owns an old cart, two calves (*ūchāk*) and a donkey. He seems not to have debts with Russian subjects. Since the land and other possessions were not worth enough to extinguish his debts, all the creditors of the same locality jointly agreed (*ittifāq bīla*) to give the afore-mentioned Ūrāż

171 TsGARUz, f. I-125, op. 1, d. 498, ll. 45–45 ob.

172 See Doc. 31 and 32 of this section.

Bāy two more years without any interest (*bī fīdā*).[173] This is the state of the case (*ṣurat-i vāqiʿa*). I submitted this report (*ʿarīża*) to your office to inform you and you know best. [The report] was registered on 9 Rabīʿ al-avval 1335 [02.01.1917].

Seal: Bābājān Yūzbāshī b. Pahlavān

On 11 of Rabīʿ al-avval the report was handed over to [the office of] the *yasāvulbāshī*, our lord, by a certain Qurbān. It was then registered and kept [in the office].

173 *Fīdā* is clearly a spelling variation of the word *fāʾida* ('advantage').

Document 34: A Report of *qāżīs* to the *yasāvulbāshī* about a Dispute over Landownership[174]

Introduction

A party to a dispute concerning the delimitation of two properties appealed to the royal court. It appears from the tersely-worded document that the legal status of a road delimiting two properties constituted the main subject of the dispute. The *yasāvulbāshī* appointed an attendant and dispatched him together with the *qāżīs* of Yarmish[175] to that place with instructions to solve the conflict. Once they reached the locality, the judges and the court attendant proceeded to involve the elders (*qariyalār*) of the local community who provided expert knowledge on the road. The elders also intervened directly into the conflict in the attempt to mediate between the parties. But it was only with the direct involvement of the *kadkhudās* and *āqsaqāls* that the parties came to a reconciliation. It is important here to note that, though brief, this notification bearing the seals of the Islamic judges draw a sharp distinction between the 'elders' and the 'notables' of the community who acted in the capacity of *kadkhudās* and *āqsaqāls*. This would suggest that it may be misleading to equate the latter with the notion of 'elders.' In addition, it could be that the individuals bearing the title of *kadkhudās* and *āqsaqāls* indeed were seen by the locals as state appointees, i.e., members of the community with a specific ascription of status.

Translation

Let it be known to the *yasāvulbāshī*, the most eminent minister and illustrious councilor (*dastūr al-mukarram*), his excellency , our lord, that, according to the royal warrant (*nishāna-yi ʿālī*) sent to us together with [an attendant] Iskandar Yasāvul, we went [to the disputed place] and saw the road which ʿAbd al-Karīm mentioned [in his petition]. We have then summoned the elders of this community (*qavmīng qariya ādamlārī*) and questioned them concerning this road. The elders came and suggested that both parties discharge their claims (*san-ham qūy san-ham qūy daʿvāngnī*). The *kadkhudā-āqsaqāls* of the community settled the dispute with the volition of the two parties. This notification (*ruqʿa*) was addressed to your office by Vāṣiḥ Bāy.

Sels: Qāżī va ra'is-i Yārmīsh Dāmullā Muḥammad Yūsuf
Qāżī va ra'is-i Yārmīsh Dāmullā Bābājān Makhẕūm

---

174 TsGARUz, f. I-125, op. 1, d. 498, l. 50.
175 On Yarmish see Doc. 19, fn. 87.

Document 35: A Report by a Provincial Governor to the *yasāvulbāshī* about Rights on a Thoroughfare[176]

Introduction

This document is another report of the governor of Besh-Ariq, in reply to a royal warrant which he had previously received from agencies in Khiva. A certain Qurbān Niyāz had appealed to the royal court and complained that a group of people were illegally using a thoroughfare (*arāba yūlī*)[177] that was situated within his possessions. They did so by force and disregarding the fact that a local *qāżī* had already ruled in favour of the appellant. When the *yasāvulbāshī* instructed the governor to take the measures needed to achieve a settlement, the latter summoned the parties together with the representatives of their communities and had them negotiate a settlement. Noteworthy is the fact that, in reporting to the royal court about the outcome of the dispute, the governor explains that the appellant's rights on the thoroughfare were recognised in accordance with an established practice (*avvalghī taʿāmulī būyūncha*). This would suggest that the appellant could not provide written evidence that could serve as an attestation to his rights; hence, the conflict with his opponents. In addition, the report emphasizes that the representative of the local communities agreed on the stipulations of the settlement. We can safely assume that their assent conferred on the settlement additional legal force, which in all probability the first *qāżī*'s ruling did not have.

Translation

Let it be known to the office of *yasāvulbāshī*, refuge of the vizierate, our lord, that Qūsh Niyāz, Qurbān Niyāz, Rūz Muḥammad, Bābā, Ātā Niyāz, Jumʿa Naẓar, Sayyid, Ṣafā, and Iskandar forcefully (*zūrlīq ītib*) have been using the thoroughfare (*ʿarāba yūlī*) belonging to Qurbān Niyāz, thereby disregarding a legal ruling (*sharīʿat amrīgha ham rizā būlmāy*). As a result, I [summoned the parties], made them subject to cross-examination (*qamtū*), and had them speak. According to the claim (*muddaʿāsīgha muvāfiq*) and in compliance with earlier practice (*avvalghī taʿāmulī būyūncha*), the road was returned to the appellant (*ʿariża-gūy*) Qurbān Niyāz in agreement (*ittifāq*)[178] with the *nāib*s and *āqsaqāl-kadkhudā*s of the community (*īlāt*). [The dispute thus] was solved (*rizālāshtūruldī*). I compiled this letter (*khaṭ*) to inform your office about this on 8 Noble Ramażān 1336 [17.06.1918].

Seal: Muḥammad Yūsuf Bāy b. Pahlavān Maḥram 1334

---

176 TsGARUz, f. I-125, op. 1, d. 498, l. 53.

177 *Arāba* in the original text of the record.

178 *Ittīfāq* ('agreement') in the original text of the record.

Document 36: A Report by a Group of Officials to the *yasāvulbāshī* about a Dispute over Taxes in Favor of Yomut Turkmens[179]

Introduction

This document is a report by the governor of Besh-Ariq to the royal court. He replies to the office of the *yasāvulbāshī*, after the local residents appealed to the royal court and complained that the Yomut Turkmens of the Ushak clan, which were quartered in the vicinity, attempted to levy a tax thereby causing unrest. The governor explained that it was the Russian army stationed within the Khanate of Khiva which was responsible for this instance of attempted confiscation: lacking as they were the resources to supply the Russian garrisons that protected the regime of Isfandiyār Khān from internal and external challenges,[180] agencies in Khiva decided that the local population would need to meet such expenses (*chiqqūn fūlī*). When in January 1918 Russian soldiers left the khanate, Isfandiyār Khān was obliged to find an agreement with Junayd Khān, one of the most powerful leaders of the Yomuts of Khorezm. The latter took responsibility to defend Isfandiyār Khān's regime from the challenges to power posed by other Turkmen leaders.[181] In exchange, Isfandiyār Khān delegated to him several powers. Furthermore, this allowed impose a number of exceptional taxes for the upkeep of his troops.[182] Another reason for collecting such taxes was that, as shown by this document, the royal court issued a royal warrant that allowed the leaders of the Turkmen clans of Ushak to collect taxes from the population in order to meet expenses for their presence in the territory and their ammunition. The governor's report indicates that payment was the result of negotiations with the leaders of local communities, while the amount paid reflected the size of the local population and the latter's solvency. In this regard, the appellants objected to the payment of this tax thereby breaking the consensus of the local residents (*īl ittifāqlārīgha ītmāy*) and jeopardizing the fulfillment of the instructions coming from Khiva. Together with the local headmen, the governor of Besh-Ariq invited the royal court to take

179 TsGARUz, f. I-125, op. 1, d. 498, ll. 89–89ob.

180 Russian soldiers were stationed within the territory of the Khanate of Khiva on a permanent basis in 1915 after the suppression of another major uprising of the Turkmen against the central authorities. See Becker, *Russia's Protectorates in Central Asia*, pp. 183, 185. In January 1918 all the Russian units headed by Colonel I.M. Zaitsev left the territory of the khanate on account of the intensification of the struggle for power between the Bolsheviks and their politcal opponents in Tashkent, as well as in other parts of the former Russian Empire. Ibid., p. 211.

181 Ibid.

182 How authorities in Khiva collected money and food from the population to the benefit of Junayd Khān and his army is described in details by Ḥasan-Murād Laffasī, *Gulshan-i saʿādat*, MS Tashkent, IVANRUz, inv. no. 7797, fols. 98b–99a.

punitive measures (*jazā'*) against those who disobeyed warning that such a behavior might lead to deferral in the payment of such taxes or even to the residents attempting to recover what they had already paid.

Translation

Let it be known to the *yasāvulbāshī*, the refuge of the vizierate (*vizārat-panāh*), our lord, that representatives of one mosque community (*masjid qavmī*), namely ʿAbd al-Rahmān, Allāh Birgān, Muḥammad Nīyāz Khwāja, Īsh Nīyāz, Qūsha Khwāja, and Muḥammad Yaʿqūb Khwāja, had appealed (*ʿarż*) to the royal court (*darbār-i ʿālīlārī*). They had stated that when the Yomut clans (*ṭā'ifalār*) were passing on the way to Bīsh-Ārīq, they requested that [the locals] should take over their expenses (*kharājāt*) and thus pay daily allowances (*chiqqūn-fulī*). The afore-mentioned Yomut clans (*jamāʿalār*)[183] [claimed that] they can levy [such payments] from the localities in which they stop (*mihmān tūshgān yirdīn sūrāshsalār dīb*). Now I inform you about the situation. Since the treasury (*ghazina*)[184] did not possess enough resources to cover the *chiqqūn-fulī* for the Russian soldiers (*ūrusīya ʿaskarlārī*), the royal court instructed (*nishāna*) the *āqā-nāībs*, and *āqsaqāl-kadkhudās* of Bīsh-Ārīq to collect the provisions (*kharjīlār*) from the [local] communities (*īlāt*) according to their size (*andāzasī miqdārīda*). Moreover, the Bīk of Ūshāq [Turkmens][185] together with Amān Nīyaz Bīk, who act on behalf of the Yomut clans (*jamāʿalār*), reached Bīsh-Ārīq and, in accordance with the rescript (*fatak*) of the royal court, the *āqā-nāībs* should find a mutual agreement (*ittifāq īlān*) in order to cover the expenses [of the Yomuts] wherever they stay. In addition, the *bāys* and other residents (*fuqarālār*) were ordered [to pay] for their their ammunition (*bīsh-ātār*).[186] [That means] that all the expenses should be allocated

183 As noted by Bregel, Khivan sources lack a more or less systematic terminology to address the tribal segmentation of the Turkmens. This means that one term could refer to different units of the tribal structure. See, Bregel', *Khorezmskie turkmeny v XIX veke*, p. 18. For this reason, we render the terms *ṭā'ifa* and *jamāʿa* in their conventional meaning of 'clan.'

184 This is a spelling variation of Ar. *khazīna* ('treasury'), which is also in use in modern colloquial Uzbek.

185 One of the main groups of the Yomut-Turkmens was the Bayram-Shali, a sub-group of which was called Ushak, see, Bregel', *Khorezmskie turkmeny v XIX veke*, p. 27. Contemporary sources point to this tribal group being headed by a *bik*. See N.S. Lykoshin, *Zapiska Nachal'nika Amu-Dar'inskogo Otdela Polkovnika Lykoshina o sovremennom sostoianii Khivinskogo Khanstva, 1912 god*, TsGARUz, f. I-2, op. 1, d. 314, l. 26 ('Ushak-begi'); Ḥasan-Murād Laffasī, *Gulshan-i saʿādat*, MS Tashkent, IVANRUz, inv. no. 7797, fol. 84a (*ūshāq tīrasining muhrdār bigī*) and etc.

186 On the *bīsh-ātār* rifles as well as the ammunition taxes see above the footnote to Doc. 25.

upon a mutual agreement (*ittifāq itīb*) among each [administrative] unit (*vāḥid*). All the residents, with the exception just of the afore-mentioned appellants, paid the state taxes (*manūt-i pādshāhī*) and the *chiqqūn-fulī*. And since the afore-mentioned petitioners rejected the communal consensus and behaved disobediently (*sarkashlīk*), all the *āqā-nāībs* agreed to append their seals [on this notification]. If the afore-mentioned appellants are not be punished (*jazā'*) adequately, the payment of the taxes due to the tribes will be delayed (*ta'khīr tāpib*) and the residents too will take back what they have already paid. This sincere petition (*'arīża-yi ikhlāṣ*) was written on Jumādī al-avval 1336 [February–March 1918].

Seals: Muḥammad Yūsuf Bāy b. Pahlavān Maḥram
Ḥasan Āqā b. Khudāy Birgān Āqā 1336
Muḥammad Ya'qūb Bāy b. Ismā'il Jān Bāy
Atā Niyāz Bāy b. Muḥammad Niyāz Bāy 1317

SECTION 3

Notifications

Document 37: A Notification by a Provincial Governor to the *yasāvulbāshī* about a Case of Assault and Robbery[187]

Introduction

This is a notification by the provincial governor of Besh-Ariq about the settlement of a dispute prompted by a case of assault and robbery. The document shows that the governor summoned the parties and their representatives and obliged them to reconcile. The governor achieved the settlement of the dispute. He himself led the investigation, meted out punishment against the culprits, and collected compensation for the aggrieved party. This all happened without the involvement of jurists. The document is unclear about who initiated the investigation. Did the governor follow the instructions of the *yasāvulbāshī* or did he respond to an appeal directed to him? The document offers little evidence to solve these questions. As other documents in this section show, however, it is likely that provincial governors enjoyed powers to hear claims filed directly with them. It is important to note that, like in many other cases, this report emphasizes the participation of local constituencies in the settlement of the dispute (*īlātīnī nā'ib āqsaqāl kadkhudālārīnī ittīfāqlārī bīla*). One can argue that, by dint of their involvement in the resolution process, the representatives of social groups conferred on the settlement supplementary legal force. The stipulations of the settlement are unclear, though. The meager contents of the document and the terse nature of its prose suggest again that agencies in Khiva had little interest in the details of the process by which the dispute was settled.

Translation

Let it be known to the *yasāvulbāshī*, refuge of the vizierate, our lord (*āqā*), that I summoned the appellant (*ʿarżgūy*) – Qūsh Naẓar from Khwājalīq[188] – and the respondents (*daʿvāgarlār*)[189] – Qurbān Niyāz, Rūz Muḥammad, Ātā Murād, Tīngr[ī] Birdī, Allāh Birdī, Mavlām Birdī, Ṣābir, Qurbān Niyāz, Qūtlūq Murād, and Khwāja Dūrdī. According to the appeal (*ʿarż*), [the

187 TsGARUz, f. I-125, op. 1, d. 498, l. 18.
188 We have been unable to identify this locale.
189 *Daʿvāgar*, evidently wrong here.

© KONINKLIJKE BRILL NV, LEIDEN, 2020 | DOI:10.1163/9789004427907_005

afore-mentioned ten individuals] had unlawfully (*bī vajh-i sharʿī*)[190] assaulted the appellant, injured (*jarāḥat*)[191] [different] parts of his body, impaired (*maʿyūb*) one hand, and [also] robbed him of 2000 *manāts*. In agreement (*ittifāq*)[192] with the *nāʾib* and the *āqsaqāl-kadkhudā*s of the community (*īlāt*), I punished (*jabrlāndīm*) them and extracted from them 2000 *manāts*. The conflict (*daʿvā*) was solved (*khālīṣ ūtūb*) and the two parties were reconciled (*riżālashtūrūldī*). This report (*khaṭ*) was compiled on the 8 of Noble Ramażān 1334 [08.07.1916].

Seal: Muḥammad Yūsuf Bāy b. Pahlavān Maḥram

190 In the original text of the record, *bī vajh-i sharʿ*.
191 See on *jarḥ* the footnote to Doc. 11, fn. 57.
192 *Ittīfāq* in the original text of the record.

Document 38: A Notification by a Provincial Governor to the *yasāvulbāshī* about a Case of Robbery[193]

Introduction

In this notification the Besh-Ariq provincial governor (*ḥākim*) Muḥammad Yūsuf Bāy informs the royal court about the outcome of an investigation of a case of robbery perpetrated against an individual from the locality of Sārt Ālācha. The aggrieved party himself followed the traces of the thieves, caught one of them and took him before a local official. The latter threatened to resort to corporal punishment. It is noteworthy that the term *siyāsat* is here employed to refer only to violence exerted by a state representative. Under threat, the first suspect confessed his crime and provided the names of his associates. As the latter too were found and it was ascertained that the three men indeed perpetrated the act of robbery, the case was settled by the official representatives of a local community who arranged for a monetary compensation to the victim. The governor thus notified the office of the *yasāvulbāshī* and asked for further instructions. In so doing, he asked whether the thieves should be put under detention, sent to Khiva, or handed over to a guarantor. Presumably, the author inquired as the community's representatives must have suggested that a guarantor be involved so that the thieves would avoid further sanctions. The personnel of the *yasāvulbāshī* who filed this notification noted in the margin of the text that the thieves were first detained by the local governor and were later freed. It is noteworthy that this and other cases of robbery fell within the purview of the local governor, though Islamic legal theory (*furūʿ al-fiqh*) is adamant about ascribing such felonies to *qāżīs*.

Translation

Let it be known to the office of the *yasāvulbāshī*, refuge of the vizierate, our lord, that several thieves broke into the household (*havlī*) of a certain Muḥammad Raḥīm, from Sārt Ālācha,[194] belonging to Sayyid Āqsaqāl's community (*qavm*), and stole 4 *bātman* of wheat, 4 dresses (*ishtūf*) and 4 silk robes. The owner of the house followed their traces and caught a certain Khwāja Nīyāz whom he brought [to me; the thief's] associates (*yūldāshlārī*) [however] escaped. When I questioned Khwāja Nīyāz about his associates and the stuff (*vajh*) they stole, I threatened to punish him with a stick (*tayāqlamāqchī būlūb sīyāsat ītūb*). He confessed (*iqrār*) that his companions Tūra and Minglī took the afore-mentioned items and run away, while he [alone] was caught. Later I was able to catch his two associates and they too confessed.

---

193 TsGARUz, f. I-125, op. 1, d. 498, ll. 57–57ob.

194 We have been unable to identify this locale.

With the disclosure of their offence (*ūghīrlīqī ẓāhir būlghānī ūchūn*), the *nā'ibs* and *āqsaqāl-kadkhudās* [of the community] arranged compensation to the afore-mentioned Muḥammad Raḥīm, which amounted to 400 *ṭillā* for the goods that had been stolen. In reporting about the crime (*jināyat*) committed by these thieves, I kindly ask you to clarify with a letter (*khaṭ bīla*) whether I should dispatch them to your office, or detain them here (*mūndā ūyga sālīb*), or hand them over to a guarantor (*kafīl*). This notification (*khaṭ*) was compiled on 25 Ẕī al-qa'da[195] 1334 [22.09.1916].

Seal: Muḥammad Yūsuf Bāy b. Pahlavān Maḥram 1334

[Verso:] The thieves were detained at the residence of the provincial governor (*hākimnī ūzī sāqlāb*). It was [then] ordered [by the royal court] to free them.

195 In the original text of the record, *Ẕā al-qa'da*.

Document 39: A Notification by a Provincial Governor to the *yasāvulbāshī* about a Case of Animal Theft[196]

Introduction

The author of this notification is, again, the governor of Besh-Ariq, Muḥammad Yūsuf Bāy. The document reflects the solution of a case of animal theft in a rural environment. It shows how the investigation began with the victim hiring a scout to pursue the suspects. It was the self-same victim who then informed the community representatives (*āqsaqāl-kadkhudās*) and a local governor that by following the traces of his stolen horse, he could identify one of the suspects. The governor instructed a liegeman to bring the suspect before him. Once at the residence of the official a confession was extracted by violent means. The confession proved instrumental in identifying the associates of the first suspect, who gave a similar confession under duress. The governor proceeded to detain the thieves. In the attempt to recover the property of the victim, the official questioned them about the location of the horse. As the animal was no longer available to them – presumably, they had already sold it –, the governor arranged for a monetary compensation to the victim. As a result, the notables of the community to which the thieves belonged entrusted to the governor a sum that was sufficient to cover the horse's value and the expenses for the other individuals, i.e., the scout and the other *āqsaqāl*s, who had been involved in the investigation. At this point, the governor notified the office of the *yasāvulbāshī* about the investigation and requested instructions regarding the payment and the measures of restraint to adopt for the thieves. The *yasāvulbāshī* instructed the governor to compensate the aggrieved party with 1200 *tillā*s, to pay 300 *tillā*s to the scout and to entrust the culprits to a guarantor (*kafīl*). The value of the text lies in the fact that it clearly reflects how in the Khanate of Khiva the dispensation of justice was contingent on the involvement of governors and community representatives rather than the judiciary who, as in this case, are not even formally involved in the case. The text also shows that the victim of a theft was more than just a claimant who could only rely on officials who will investigate the case. By contrast, he himself played a decisive role as he initiated the investigation by hiring a scout for himself who would aid him to identify the thieves.

Translation

Let it be known to the office of the *yasāvulbāshī*, refuge of the vizierate, our lord, that a horse was stolen from the household (*ḥavlī*) of a certain

196 TsGARUz, f. I-125, op. 1, d. 498, ll. 59–60ob.

Khwāja Murād from Sūsalāq,[197] belonging to the community (*qavm*) of ʿĀvaz Muḥammad Āqsaqāl. [The owner] together with a scout (*īzchī*) followed the traces of the horse which led to the house of Rūz Muḥammad Chūchī. Khwāja Murād, the horse's owner, together with *āqsaqāl-kadkhudā*s of that community (*īlātī*) came and reported to us about the event (*ḥādiṣa*). I sent someone who brought Chūchī [before me] and I told him that the horse's traces led to his house. [I have ordered] that he be lashed twenty-thirty times (*qāmchī ūrūb*) to force him to tell the truth (*rāstnī āytghan dīb*). [After that] Rūz Muḥammad confessed (*iqrār*) that, together with ʿAbd āl-Raḥīm, Yūsuf Khwāja, Abdāl Khwāja, and Allāk Tāynav [?], he opened one side of Khwāja Murād's gate and drove the horse away. On the basis of his confession, [I have given instructions] to bring the afore-mentioned associates (*yūldāshlār*) who were already corporally punished (*siyāsat ītūb*) and questioned. They too provided a confession which corresponded to the statement of Rūz Muḥammad Chūchī. In this respect, the afore-mentioned five thieves were detained (*ūyga sālīb*) and were instructed to find the horse and to be of some help. The thieves stated that there was no horse and there was no way to find it. Then I asked Khwāja Murād what price the horse was valued at. Khwāja Murād answered that once he had been asked to sell his horse for 1200 *ṭillā*, but he had refused to do so. As a result, the *āqsaqāl-kadkhudā*s of the Ḥasan Aqā Bābā community (*īlāt*) took from the five thieves the sum of 1200 *ṭillā*, as a payment for the horse, and 300 *ṭillā* for the scout as well as other expenses met by the *kadkhudās*. I took the total sum of 1500 *ṭillā* and kept it here with me. Now in informing you, I kindly ask you to clarify with a letter (*khaṭ bīla*) whether I should pay to the owner of the horse, the scout, and the *kadkhudā*s what is due to them and take over also the other expenses; whether I shall detain (*ūyda sāqlānīb*) the thieves or let them out on a guarantor (*kafīl*); and whether I should send all of them together with the total sum of money to your office. This notification (*khaṭ*) was written on 25 Ẕī al-qaʿda[198] 1334 [22.09.1916].

Seal: Muḥammad Yūsuf Bāy b. Pahlavān Maḥram 1334

[Verso:] An order was issued that 1200 *ṭillā* be given to the owner of horse and 300 *ṭillā* whom it was due; the thieves should be let out on a guarantor.

197 We have been unable to identify this locale.
198 In the original text of the record, *Ẕā al-qaʿda*.

Document 40: A Notification by a Provincial Governor to the *yasāvulbāshī* about a Case of Armed Robbery[199]

Introduction

Ismāʿīl Khwāja b. Ibrāhim Khwāja, a governor of Hazarasp, was informed about a case of armed robbery, which led to the murder of one person and the injury of several individuals. Without receiving instructions from the royal court, he initiated an investigation. Following a procedure that was typical of murder cases, the governor acted in cooperation with local *qāżīs* and appointed two trustees who went to the locale and gathered information. The following day the resident of another nearby locale was recognised as one of the culprits. The boy was detained, a fact that prompted his associates to attempt to free him at gunpoint. Local notables, however, were able to hand the boy over to the governor. After questioning him, Ismāʿīl Khwāja established the involvement of the boy and his associates in the murder under investigation. One such associate, a certain Ṣafā was found in possession of weapons. A further series of hearings that involved the representatives of local constituencies helped the governor establish that Ṣafā was at the head of a group of outlaws consisting of 15–20 people who had committed other crimes. Ismāʿīl Khwāja thus handed over the offender over to a policeman (*mīrshab*) for temporary detention and dispatched the other associates to the royal court for further inquiries. The notification does not mention any hearing held at the court of the *qāżīs* and it seems, instead, that it was the provincial official who independently from other institutions initiated and led the preliminary investigation.

Translation

Let it be known to the *yasāvulbāshī*, refuge of the vizierate, our lord, that this year[200] on 3 Jumādī al-ṣānī I was informed (*khabar*) that the night before unknown people killed one Khudāy Bīrgān b. Ismāʿīl in the locality (*mawżiʿ*) of Chavāndūr. Thereafter I and the *qāżī-īshāns*, the banner of Islamic law, [appointed] two trustees (*amīnlār*) and dispatched them to that locale. The trustees together with the *kadkhudā-āqsaqāls* and other representatives of the local community (*īl-ādamlārī*) reached the place [of the crime] and inspected it. They found out that somebody had broken open the door on the southern side [of the house], knocked down the door in the vestibule (*dahlīz*) and killed the afore-mentioned [Khudāy Bīrgān b. Ismāʿīl]. When they examined the body of the slain man (*maqtūl*) they noticed that the top and left parts of his

---

199 TsGARUz, f. I-125, op. 1, d. 498, ll. 33–33ob.

200 Due to damage at the end of the document we have been unable to identify the exact date of the events described.

head had been injured (*jarāḥatdār*). [The trustees and the others proceeded to question the relatives of the deceased:] the son of the slain man, Birdī Shukūr, his wives, Dar Jān Bīka and Jumʿa Bīka, and his daughter, Rāżiya Bīka. [All these individuals] explained that 15 unknown people had broken into the house and committed the offence. Birdī Shukūr's two temples and his forehead were injured. The head of his wife, Zulaykhā Bīka, was also injured. And Rāżiya Bīka's left hand was injured as well. They were all questioned whether they knew someone among the [15 individuals] whom they mentioned, but they answered that they were unable to recognize anyone. [The relatives of the slain man] also stated that [a number of items] were stolen: Birdī Shukūr's 10 *bātman* of grain, 20 *ṭillā* in *manāt* paper money; Rāżiya Bīka's one Turkish veil (*amīrgānī rūymāl*),[201] 1 *tirmā* [?], 6 pairs of veils, 7 pairs of striped veils, 3 *yalāk* [?] made of silk, 2 dresses (*kūynāk*); 2 *ṭillā* in coins and 40 *ṭillā* in *manāt* paper money which belonged to their father, and 2 quilts. Khudā Shukur, [another] son of the slain man, informed [the trustees] that they stole from him approximately 30 *bātman* of grain. This is the state of the case (*ṣurat-i vāqiʿa*). Then, on the fourth day of this month, on Tuesday evening before the bedtime prayer (*khuftan*), one boy (*bala*) came to the house of a certain Muḥammad Jān Qara Qurbān Kharrāt ūghlī, in the locality of Ātāliq. He cried that he was an orphan from Bīk Ābād[202] and that nobody ever gave him a place to stay. It was then that Muḥammad Yaʿqūb the *mu'azzin* [recognised this boy] as a very dangerous thief from the land on the right bank of the Amu Darya (*Āryāqlī*). Muḥammad Yaʿqūb explained that the boy is known to him because of dealings he had at the market on the right bank of the Amu Darya. As a result, the boy was brought to the local sheriffs (*īl-qarāvullārī*). The latter drove him to the local elders (*īl-kadkhudālārī*). While [the elders] were holding a reception at the house of a certain Bābā Jān Shaykh, a woman (*nāchāra*) came from the inner quarter (*īchkarīdīn*)[203] and warned that the house was surrounded by horsemen and two of them had already climbed on the roof. When the elders

---

201 *Amīrgān* was a neighbourhood in Istanbul, see F. Steingass, *A Comprehensive Persian-English Dictionary* (London: Routledge&Kegan Paul Limited, 1963 [first ed. 1892]), p. 102. It may also be that *amīrgān* refers to the American type of cotton, which was introduced in Central Asia in the wake of the Russian conquest.

202 The term refers to the locale of Bekabad (in the local Khorezmian dialect, pronounced as Begovat), that Bregel located 7 km west-southwest of Urgench, see Munis and Agahi, *Firdaws al-iqbāl: History of Khorezm*, p. 587, note 387.

203 In early 20th-century Central Asia houses were divided by a wall which prevented men who were not agnatic members of the family (*nā-maḥram*) from entering into contact with the female members of the family (*maḥram*). This space of seclusion was called *īchkarī* (inner quarter), see D. Northrop, *The Veiled Empire: Gender and Power in Stalinist Central Asia* (Ithaca ad London: Cornell University Press, 2004), p. 365.

went out they saw that two horsemen and several footmen were ready to storm (*hujūm*) the house and free the boy. Thereupon [the elders] got frightened, locked the gates and sat out in wait. On the next morning the elders brought [the boy] to me. When I asked him what his name was, he answered that he was Rajab Qurbān Niyāz ūghlī, from the lineage (*tīra*) of ʿAvaẓ Bakhshī[204] and that he came from the county (*būlūshī*) of Tūrtkul[205] [damage in the text]. One month earlier he had crossed [the Amu Darya river] over to this bank and ever since he has been committing robbery here together with Qūybāq Qazāq, Bāy Naẓar, Jumʿa Niyāz from Shirshālī, Khwāja Niyāz, Muḥammad Ṣafā, Sayyid Murād and a certain Ṣafā from Chavāndūr. He also explained that this latter Ṣafā from Chavāndūr carries a gun and cartridge cases. We thus sent [our] men after Ṣafā and found him alongside with a black rifle, a pistol (*tufāncha*) and 23 bullets for Berdan [rifles] (*birdānka ūqī*).[206] As they took him before us, we asked Ṣafā where he had acquired all this. He answered that the year before, while he was aiding Russian soldiers (*rusiyya ʿaskarlārī*) [to reach the locality of] Tāsh-Saqā[207] with his cart, he could purchase [the weapons] from one soldier for 1 *manāt*. Then 2 months ago he took this gun and the pistol which had been left in the custody (*amānat*) of his relatives, namely Ḥājjī ʿAbd Allāh, Ḥājjī, and Nīyāz Muḥammad in the settlement (*manzīl*) of Āq Qamīsh[208] in *āryāq*, with the consent of the representatives and the elders of the community

---

204 The term *bakhshī* occurs often in Khorezmian sources written in the 19th and the early 20th century and it usually couples with the names of the headmen of several Turkmen tribes. According to Bregel, this term was in use especially among the Yomut Turkmens of Khorezm, see his *Khorezmskie turkmeny v XIX veke*, pp. 124–125; 128–129. One could therefore infer that the boy belonged to a group of Yomuts.

205 Turtkul, or Petro-Aleksandrovsk, was the administrative center of the Amu-Darya Department (*otdel*), i.e., the part of the Khivan Khanate, which was conquered by the Russians and included into the Governorship-General of Turkestan in 1873. The Amu-Darya Department was established as an administrative unit on August the 21st 1873 and it was located circa 40 miles from Khiva. For more on this subject, see the introduction to this volume.

206 *Berdanka* is the colloquial form for the Russian rifle invented by the American colonel Hiram Berdan in 1868. See also above, the footnote to Doc. 25.

207 In 1828 Allāh Qulī Khān found on the locale of Tūyūklī on the west bank of the Amu Darya a stony base where to erect a new and more resistant sluice gate of the Palvan-Yab canal. The place was renamed Tāsh Saqā, lit. 'canal's stony sluice gate.' People began to use this term with reference also to the surrounding areas, including the elevations situated on the south-eastern fringes of the Khoresmian oasis, see Guliamov, *Istoriia orosheniia Khorezma s drevneishikh vremen do nashikh dnei*, pp. 142, 220, 265. Tāsh Saqā is situated close to Hazarasp.

208 The Āq Qamīsh tract is located on the right bank of the Amu Darya, south-east of Petro-Aleksandrovsk, in one of the crossing points of the river on the route from Bukhara to Khiva. It is therefore situated on the opposite side of Tāsh Saqā.

(*īl-ādamlārī īlān kadkhudālārīnī sūzī īlān*) [of that locality]. When I asked him about the patronymics [of the people who kept the weapons] he was unable to answer. He then stated that he carried the weapons through Hazarasp and no one knew about it. We verified his statements with the representatives and the elders of the community; the latter answered that they never told him to keep the weapon (*miltūq*) and knew nothing about this weapon. Thereafter, we summoned Jum'a Niyāz, Khwāja Niyāz, Muḥammad Ṣafā, Sayyid Murād and Ṣafā, a knife grinder from the locality of Shirshālī in Chavāndūr and showed them to the boy, who could not recognize anybody except for Ṣafā from Chavāndūr. We then questioned the afore-mentioned [Ṣafā], but he denied (*munkir*) [everything]. The afore-mentioned boy, whose name was Rajab, said to [Ṣafā]: 'every day early in the morning (*har āqshām*) you took me to the shore of the lake in Āq Maydān and brought me back on horse every evening at the bedtime prayer (*namāz-i shām*). And we also went together to the house of the afore-mentioned slain man, and while I was looking after the horses, my accomplices tumbled down the door and entered into the house. Then there was a scream, but I didn't know [precisely] how things went.' We thus asked him how many people [were involved] and he answered that he was in a group of twenty. He also told us that Qūybāq Qazāq gave him 3 *manāt* and sent him to steal the horse of the afore-mentioned Muḥammad Jān Qara and it was Ṣafā who showed us the house [to raid]. Let it be known [to the *yasāvulbāshī*], that we also questioned the boy about various horses and houses which were recently robbed in Hazarasp, and he answered that they stole them and provided evidence (*'alāmat*) [for the robbery]. This is the state of the case (*ṣurat-i vāqi'a*). On the basis of the evidence which Rajab the boy produced, we handed over Ṣafā to the policeman (*mīrshab*). The rifle, the pistol and the 23 cartridge cases, which we found together with Rajab the boy, were put on a horseman and sent to your office. This missive (*maktūb*) was written on 15 Jumādī al-ṣānī 13 (?).[209]

Seal: Ismā'īl Khwāja b. Ibrāhim Khwāja[210]

209 A damage in the text.

210 Sayyid Ismā'il Khwāja was governor of Hazarasp and the elder brother of the grand-minister (*vazīr-i akbar*) Sayyid Islām Khwāja (d. 1913), see also the footnote to Doc. 24.

Document 41: A Notification by a Provincial Governor to the *yasāvulbāshī* about a Case of Robbery and Assault[211]

Introduction

An *āqsaqāl* informed the governor of Khanqah about a case of robbery and assault, the victims of which suffered heavy bodily injuries. The governor initiated the investigation by instructing the *qāżīs* to collect circumstantial evidence about the case and report to him. Around the time when the governor received said report, one of the victims died of his injuries. An unexpected development of the investigation occurred when someone who was not involved in the case found that the robbers had hidden the loot in his shed. He decided to bring the loot to Khanqah where one of the victims of the robbery recognised the goods as his possessions. The governor hired a scout[212] who tracked the three thieves. The culprits were detained and brought to Khanqah where the governor questioned them. However, the suspects denied any responsibility. In the meantime, the officials representing the communities to which the three thieves belonged appealed officially to the governor. They asked him to intercede to the royal court in order to impose capital punishment upon them. Interestingly, they did so by claiming that they would not be able to enjoy a peaceful life (*farāghat*), should these three men be left free. The latter were known to be repeat criminal offenders, who had already shown themselves to be particularly skillful in avoiding sanctions. The governor took a pragmatic course of action: he requested that the *yasāvulbāshī* explain to the head of the Qonghrat principality that, if released, the culprits would certainly commit the same crimes again and cause great disturbance to the local populace. Proceeding from this, he requested that they be executed.

This document clearly exemplifies the limitations of governors' powers in the process of conflict resolution. They could initiate investigations, which consisted of collecting information from the victims and testimony, as well as detain the suspects and question them. Governors could also request, if they deemed it necessary, the help of the representatives of the local communities, the *āqsaqāl*s and the *qāżīs*. However, when they had to take a final decision on the case and mete out punishments to offenders, they inevitably had to consult agencies in Khiva and ask further instructions.

---

211 TsGARUz, f. I-125, op. 1, d. 498, l. 97.

212 The investigation here clearly consists of the activity of path-finding. See, in particular, TsGARUz, f. I-125, op. 1, d. 498, ll. 100–100b: a case of horse theft which was investigated only by way of path-finding.

Translation

Let it be known to the office of *yasāvulbāshī*, the recipient of the state's trust (*muʿtamad al-dawlat*) and the confidant of the ruler (*muqarrab al-ḥażrat*), our lord, that at the end of Jumādī al-s̱ānī, on Thursday early in the morning (*āẕānda*) Jabbār Birgān Āqsaqāl, from the mosque [community] (*masjid*) of Mullā Muḥammad Raḥīm in Jingān,[213] came and informed [me] that during the night [several] thieves broke into the house of a certain Īsh-Jān. They broke Īsh-Jān's hand and beat his brother Qul Muḥammad on the head with a cane and cut his flesh with a knife. [Also,] they took away all his possessions from the house. Immediately after [that], I instructed the *qāżī-īshāns* to go [there]. Two hours after the *qāżī-īshāns* came back with a written report on the case (*ṣūrat-i vāqiʿalārīnī khaṭ*), the afore-mentioned Qul Muḥammad died. Informed [about this], I ordered the *qāżī-īshāns* to send someone (*kīshī*) to deal with the burial of the deceased man. Later I had someone appointed as a scout (*īzchī*) and sent him [after the thieves]. At mid-day Muḥammad Yaʿqūb Khwāja, the administrator of an endowment (*mutavallī*), together with ʿAbdullāh brought some goods on a camel. In the presence of the Khanqah elders (*yāsh-kattalār*) I examined them. I [thus] instructed a man to go and bring the afore-mentioned Īsh-Jān with his people over [to me]. When they were shown those goods, they recognised them as their own possessions. For this reason, before the Khanqah elders and at the presence of the communities' (*īlāt*) *kadkhudās*, the goods were entrusted to Jabbār Birgān, the *āqsaqāl* of his [Īsh-Jān's] the community. Then, I questioned Muḥammad Yaʿqūb Khwāja where he had found such things. ʿAbdullāh Khāmbāsh answered that on his land which abuts on the southern side (*qibla*) of his household, there was a shed (*dūlā*). When he went there to collect some tools for agriculture, he noticed that inside there were laid a few [other] things. He then went to Muḥammad Yaʿqūb Khwāja and informed him about this. Later he came back there and examined [those items] together with [Muḥammad Yaʿqūb] Khwāja who decided to load them on a cart in order to bring them to the governor's residence (*bāy āqānī ḥavlīsīgha*). At once he took his camel, loaded the goods, and brought them here. The scout came back. At first he began to follow the traces leading to the shed where the goods were found, and then he moved on and reached the house of a certain Qurbān Bāy from Qiyāt[214] and Hamrāh. [They] took [2 men] out from their place. [The scout then followed the traces leading] to

213 We have been unable to identify this locale.

214 Qiyat is located 30 km north of Khiva, see Bregel, *An Historical Atlas of Central Asia*, p. 67 (map 33).

the house of [another] thief, a certain Muḥammad Sharīf from Nawkhāṣ.[215] [At this point], the scout established that these three men were the thieves. He handed them over to my assistant (*khiẕmatkār*), who was accompanying him and brought them all [before me]. When I questioned the three men, they all denied (*inkār*) [the felony]. I inform your office that the thief Muḥammad Sharīf had previously gone to Khiva [as defendant] a number of times and remained unpunished. The *kadkhudā-āqsaqāls* of [Muḥammad Sharīf] together with the *kadkhudā-āqsaqāls* and the community [representing] the thieves Qurbān Bāy and Hamrāh have come [here] and requested (*ʿarż*) that I intercede to the noble office of our sovereign (*khiẕmat-i humāyūnlārīgha āytib*) [and explain] that if these three men will not be put to death (*ūltūrtūrūb birmāsangīz*), the [appellants] would not be able to leave in peace as ordinary subjects (*fuqarā būlūb*). For this reason, I inform you that I hope that you intercede to the noble office of our sovereign and proceed to execute them (*ūltūrmākgha taraddud*[216] *qīlsalār*). If you let [these thieves] free to return [home], their people (*ūlāt*) and the other residents (*fuqarālār*) will not be living in peace. I thus sent these three men, the written report of the *qāżī-īshāns* about the state of the case and this notification via the Qarāvul Qahqa Bīk from Khānqāh. This is the state of the case, which was compiled and handed over to your office on 5 Rajab 1336 [16.04.1918].

Bīkjān Bāy Ḥājjī Muḥammad Yār Qāżī ūghlī, Allāh Birgān Kavādan ūghlī, Ḥājjī Karīm Qūlī Tūrsūm Bāy ūghlī, Najm al-Dīn Allāh Birgān Ḥājjī ūghlī, Yūsuf Bāy Ḥājjī Iskandar ūghlī.

Seal: Āqmuhr Ḥajjī Muḥammad Bāy[217]

215 Nawkhast was located 7,5 km southwest of Khanqah, see *Khiva khonligida feodal yer egaligi va davlat tuzilishi*, p. 593, note 408; Danilevskii, *Opisanie Khivinskogo khanstva*, p. 249.

216 In the original text of the record, *taraddūd*.

217 On Ḥājjī Muḥammad Bāy b. Amīn al-Dīn Bāy, the governor of Khanqah, see above, Doc. 26, fn. 136.

Document 42: A Notification by *qāżīs* to the *yasāvulbāshī* about a Case of Domestic Violence[218]

Introduction

This is a judicial notification, which the *qāżīs* of Khoja-eli addressed to the *yasāvulbāshī*. It recounts the unsuccessful outcome of a hearing and the attempt to mete out a punishment. In the wake of an assault and bodily harm, a woman appealed to the provincial governor of Khoja-eli. The latter instructed an attendant to bring the two parties before the *qāżīs*. As the defendant admitted the assault, the judges proceeded to appoint a woman trustee to examine the body of the claimant and assess the presence of injury. The examination disclosed various instances of bodily harm and the *qāżīs* consulted with a *muftī* who opined that the defendant should be punished. When the *qāżīs* intended to put in practice the opinion of the jurist, the defendant questioned the authority of the jurors and left the hearing. With regard to the intentions behind the production of this document, it is unclear whether it was the *qāżīs* who felt obliged to inform agencies in Khiva about the unorthodox behavior of the defendant. One should not exclude, however, that the claimant might have an interest in the acquisition of such a document from the *qāżīs*, especially if the claimant attempted to pursue redress with the office of the *yasāvulbāshī*. Be that as it may, this certificate clearly shows that the defendant had acknowledged his unlawful behavior and evidently the woman could use this document as a supplementary evidence to produce during a new hearing. Regardless of the fact that the document reflects the outcome of a hearing held by *qāżīs*, it was the governor of Khoja-eli who initiated the process of conflict resolution and instructed the jurists to hear the case.

Translation

Let it be known to the office of *yasāvulbāshī*, banner of glory, our lord, may his power increase, that a certain woman (*musammāt*) called Ḥanīfa Bīka, from the Shīrīn mosque community (*masjid qavmī*) in [the district of] Khoja-eli,[219]

---

218 TsGARUz, f. I-125, op. 1, d. 498, l. 29.

219 Khoja-eli is a city located on the left bank of the Amu Darya. The northern part of the city is close to the lower delta of the Amu Darya where the river divides into a number of emissaries. In the 17th century the city changed its appearance several times due to changes in the course of the Amu Darya and the subsequent resettlement of various tribal groups in the lower delta of the river and the formation of the so-called Aral province. See Guliamov, *Istoriia orosheniia Khorezma s drevneishikh vremen do nashikh dnei*, p. 211; B.V. Andrianov, "Etnicheskaia territoriia karakalpakov v severnom Khorezme, (XVIII–XIX vv.)," in *Materialy i issledovania po etnografii karkakalpakov. Trudy Khorezmskoi arkheologo-etnograficheskoi ekspeditsii*, III, ed. T.A. Zhdanko (Moscow: Izdatel'stvo Akademii nauk SSSR, 1958), p. 45. According to Kuhn, in the second half of the 19th century, Khoja-eli

appealed (*ʿarż*) to the governor (*ḥākim*) and claimed that her husband, a certain Ṣādiq, unlawfully (*bī vajḥ-i sharʿī*) assulted her, causing injury (*jarāḥat*). [The governor] dispatched an attendant (*yasāvul*) [to the locality], [instructing him] to find the husband and deliver the two parties to us [the *qāżīs* of Khoja-eli]. Later, when we questioned the man, he admitted (*muqirr*)[220] the assault. Then we appointed a faithful and pious woman (*mūʾmina va mutadayyina bir khātūn*) as trustee (*amīn*) [and instructed her] to examine [the body of] the afore-mentioned [claimant]. The trustee informed us that indeed in various parts [Ḥanīfa Bīka] showed signs of bodily harm. We [therefore] decided that the [case] of this woman represents a juristic case (*masʾala*). As we were putting in practice (*ʿamal*) the opinion of the *muftī* and thus intended to inflict a punishment (*taʿzīr*) according to Islamic law (*sharīʿat parmāyish*[221] *bīla*), the defendant stood up and said: 'No!' Then he left [the hearing]. This alone is what occurred before us. No financial issues (*fūl-tanga ḥāditha*) [were discussed]. The event was recorded.[222]

Seals: Qāżī[223]
Qāżī-yi Khwāja Īlī[224]
Qāżī-yi Khwāja Īlī Dāmullā Muḥammad Ṣāliḥ Khwāja
Qāżī-yi Khwāja Īlī Dāmullā Bābā Jān Khwāja

---

was a relatively important settlement surrounded by a fortified wall with more than 200 shops and 16 mosques, *Ocherk istorii zaseleniia Khivinskogo khanstva s drevnykh vremen, sostav ego sovremennogo naseleniia, administratsiia i goroda khanstva*, 1873, IVRRAN, St. Petersburg, Arkhiv Vostokovedov, f. 33, d. 8, l. 52.

220 *Muqīrr* in the original text of the record.

221 This is a spelling variation of *farmāyish*.

222 The document lacks information on the date of its compilation.

223 We have been unable to decipher the seal.

224 We have been unable to decipher the seal.

Document 43: A Notification by a Provincial Governor and *qāżīs* to the yasāvulbāshī about a Man's Death[225]

Introduction

This document is a notification, which the governor of Urgench and 2 *qāżīs* addressed to the *yasāvulbāshī*. It offers an account in succinct fashion about the death of a man from Gurlen who had come to Urgench to seek redress. While the man was traveling, he fell mortally ill and sought shelter at the place of an acquaintance. When the latter felt that the man's death was imminent, he sought the advice of the governor and the judges in order to avoid possible claims directed against him. The governor together with two jurists proceeded to instruct two trustees who, in the presence of the elders of the local community, listed the possessions of the man. At that point, the man left Urgench and headed back home. But *en route* he died. The agencies in Urgench took care of the funeral ceremonies and the burial. The possessions of the departed were entrusted to a corpse-washer. The production of this notification followed a course of action undertaken by the relative of the departed. It is, however, possible that, as all the officials were held accountable to the administrative center of the khanate, the governor and the *qāżīs* felt pressed to inform authorities in Khiva.

Translation

Let it be known to the office of the *yasāvulbāshī*, refuge of the vizierate and repository of nobility, our lord, that Muḥammad Ya'qūb Īsh Muḥammad ūghlī from Gurlen, who is a member of Bābā Jān Yūzbāshī's community (*qavm*), came to Urgench to claim redress (*ṭalabkārlīghī qīlib*), but he fell sick. He thus repaired to the house of his acquaintance, a certain Vays Bāy from Urgench, a member of the Khwāja Fārsā community (*qavm*). In this respect Vays Bāy informed me and the *qāżī-īshāns* that Muḥammad Ya'qūb was ill and he was laying at his place. As a result, together with the *qāżī-īshāns*, I dispatched two individuals (*ādam*) to Vays Bāy's place to question Muḥammad Ya'qūb and clarify whether he had unpaid credits and other possessions. Muḥammad Ya'qūb answered before the community's elders (*qavm āqsaqāl-kadkhudālārī*) that he possessed nothing except 8 *manāt*, 1 sickle and 1 donkey. He then rode out on his donkey, but *en route* to his home he died. That happened at the time of the midday prayer (*fīshīn*).[226] As the information came, the *qāżī-īshāns* appointed a trustee (*amīn*) and I appointed another, [and the two of them] brought the corpse washers (*yūghūchilār*). The latter prepared a funeral ceremony, read

225 TsGARUz, f. I-125, op. 1, d. 498, ll. 38–37.
226 Spelling variation of *peshin*.

the *jānaza*-prayer, and buried him (*dafn*) [under] the protection (*amānat*) of Qarā Āʿlam Bābā, peace be upon him. I entrusted the donkey and the sickle of the departed as well as his 8 *manāt*, 3 old robes, an old caftan, and a hat (*jūkirma*) to the corpse-washer Khudāy Bīrgān. We wrote this report (*khaṭ*) to inform your office about the state of the case on Shaʿbān 1335 [May 1917].

Seals: Allāh Birgān (?) b. ʿAbd al-Raḥīm Bāy
Qāżī-yi Ūrganch Dāmullā ʿAṭaullāh b.[227]
Qāżī-yi Ūrganch Dāmullā Ātājān b. Bābā Ṣūfī-yi marḥūmī 133[?]

227 We have been unable to decipher the seal.

Document 44: A Notification by a Provincial Governor to the *yasāvulbāshī* about a Case of Bride-Kidnapping[228]

Introduction

Three representatives of a community (*īlāt*) in the locality of Qara-Mazi informed the governor of Khanqah about the detainment of a boy and a girl. According to their report, the two had come to the locality, but the status of their relationship aroused the suspicion of the local population. The governor questioned the couple and was able to establish that it was a case of bride-kidnapping: the young man had kidnapped the girl in Tashhawz and was heading to a relative of his in the province of Khanqah. On account of such circumstances the governor first summoned the father of the girl and then decided to dispatch the parties to the royal court in Khiva. This document evidently reflects the outcome of a preliminary investigation which the official led autonomously in the province.

Translation

Let it be known to Amān Kīldī Bāy Yasāvulbāshī, refuge of the vizierate and repository of nobleness, our lord, that on 16 Shaʿbān Jabbār Bīrgān Āqsaqāl, Tangrī Bīrgān Bāy, and Ūstā Yaʿqūb from Qara-Mażū[229] have captured and brought [to me] a [young] woman (*nāchār*) and a young man (*yigīt*). They informed me that these two [individuals] had visited their community (*īlāt*) and were treated as guests. But, regarding their behavior as inappropriate (*yūrūshlārīnī nāqūlāy kūrūb*), the [elders] detained them. For this reason, I questioned these two runaways (*qāchqūnchīlār*) [and I found out that] the young man kidnapper comes from Tāshḥavuż, whereas the girl (*qīz*) is from Manāq. When the afore-mentioned girl came to Tāshḥavuż to visit her grandfather Khudāy Bīrgān Chūychī, the afore-mentioned young man from Tāshḥavuż, whose name is Iskandar, kidnapped (*ālīb qāchīb chiqīb*) the girl and kept her at his household (*jāy*) for two months. Afterwards he took her to the boat (*kīma*) of a certain Āta Murād from Chātkūfrūk,[230] proceeded to a place close to Qara-Mażū, and when he was heading to the place of his relative (*qarīndāsh*), a certain ʿAbdullāh, in the province (*tābiʿ*) of Khanqah, he had already arranged that all his possessions be sent to the same place. [Then] we asked the young woman whether she was married or [simply] engaged to this

---

228 TsGARUz, f. I-125, op. 1, d. 498, ll. 46.-46ob.

229 Qara-Mazi is a settlement located circa 7 km east of Urgench and circa 7 km northwest of Khanqah. In the middle of the 19th century it consisted of 200 households, see Munis and Agahi, *Firdaws al-iqbāl: History of Khorezm*, p. 601, note 503.

230 We have been unable to identify this settlement.

man (*san kīshīgha nikālī*[231] *yā-ki fātiḥalī īrdīngmū*). She answered that she was neither married nor engaged to anyone. For this reason, we summoned the girl's father from Manāq and we sent them and the young man Iskandar, who had kidnapped the girl, all together, to your office. Now we rely on your mercy (*miḥrabān*) as you know best. This letter (*khaṭ*) was written on 18 Shaʿbān 1334 [19.06.1916].

Seal: ʿAbd al-Raḥīm Bay b. Muḥammad Yūsuf Baqqāl

231 Spelling variation of *nikāḥlī*.

Document 45: A Notification by a Provincial Governor to the *yasāvulbāshī* about a Case of Bride-Kidnapping[232]

Introduction

In this document the governor of Ghaziabad informs the *yasāvulbāshī* about the settlement of a dispute achieved by a certain Qurbān Muḥammad Sardār.[233] This mediator was, in fact, no one other than Junayd Khān, the famous leader of the Turkmen Yomuts. Junayd Khān played an important role in the political events of the second decade of the 20th century, when after January 1918, he became the *de facto* ruler of the khanate and left only formal powers of government to Isfandiyār Khān in Khiva.[234] Junayd's stronghold was situated in the lower reaches of the Ghaziabad canal, in the locality of Bedrikent close to the settlement of Takhta. The latter functioned at that time as the alternative capital of the Khanate of Khiva.[235] Takhta was close to Ghaziabad where the appellants mentioned in this document attempted to seek redress from Junayd Khān. The dispute that he was called to solve was the following. A woman initiated a divorce with the consent of her husband. After that, her relatives and the members of her community determined the amount of her liability (*nafaqa*) to be paid by her former husband during the waiting period (*ʿidda*), that is until the moment when she would be wedded to another man. However, during this waiting period, she was kidnapped by another man. The representatives of her community as well as her relatives appealed to Junayd Khān and requested the woman's return. It is important, of course, to note that the appellants referred in this case not to the agencies in Khiva, nor to the local governor who would usually deal with such cases. Instead they sought help from Junayd Khān, apparently regarding him as a source of greater authority and a man who had all the resources to solve this case of bride kidnapping.

Translation

Let it be known to the *yasāvulbāshī*, banner of glory, our lord, that when I was at the place (*jāyīdā*) of Qurbān Muḥammad Sardār-Āqā, the inhabitants (*fuqarālārī*) of Ghāzī-ābād appealed (*ʿarż ītīb*) to Sardār-Āqā [stating that] the husband of Ūstā Muḥammad Niyāz's daughter divorced (*āyirīb*) his wife by his own will (*ūz riżālīqī bīla*). Her community (*īlātī*) and her relatives determined her [waiting-period] maintenance (*nafaqa*) for Mullā ʿUthmān. [But]

232 TsGARUz, f. I-125, op. 1, d. 498, l. 48.

233 According to Bregel', the term *sardār* was employed to denote the leader of tribal units as well as the elders of Turkmen tribes. It also had the wider connotation of military leader. See Bregel', *Khorezmskie Turkmeny v XIX veke*, pp. 132–133.

234 See the Introduction to this volume (pp. 17–19) as well as Docs. 24, 36, 61.

235 Becker, *Russia's Protectorates in Central Asia*, p. 221.

a certain Jumʿa Niyāz from Nawkhāṣ kidnapped the woman. Now the people request that the woman be found and returned to the people responsible for her (*igāsīgha qūshūb*) as well as that the royal court be informed. This letter (*khaṭ*) was compiled on 26 Jumādī al-avval 1336 [09.03.1918].

Seal: ʿAbd al-Karīm Maḥram b. ʿAbd al-Raḥīm Maḥram 1331

Document 46: A Notification by a Provincial Governor to the *yasāvulbāshī* about a Case of Robbery and Homicide[236]

Introduction

This document sheds light on a case of robbery in a private household, which ended with a death. As soon as he was informed about the case, the governor of Khanqah sent his representative together with a trustee of the *qāżīs* in order to inspect the corpse and the murder scene. It is important to note that after this procedure, the relatives were allowed to perform the funerary rituals. If we consider that according to local practices, the corpse of the departed had to be buried in the shortest possible time, we can infer that the procedures of investigations initiated by the governor had to work efficiently. Once the corpse was inspected and the murder scene examined, it was decided to use a scout who could determine the place where to apprehend the robbers – in this case the house of a certain ʿAbdullāh from Būyqazāq. Since the suspects were found within the jurisdiction of the neighbouring province of Besh-Ariq, the governor of Khanqah sent a notification (*fatak*) to the Besh-Ariq governor as well as two liegemen to apprehend the suspects. The latter were then escorted to Khiva by the *āqsaqāl*s of their community and a local *qāżī*. The same document also illuminates another case of robbery. It provides detailed information about the preliminary investigation, the apprehension of the suspects and their escort to Khiva. It is important to note that even a cursory comparison between this and other documents shows the complex set of procedures that officials on the spot were expected to follow, a fact suggesting the existence of clear instructions issued by agencies in Khiva to the individuals representing the authority of the royal court in the territory of the khanate. Despite the established procedures regarding the investigation of robbery and murder cases, we observe an important difference among the courses of action taken by the various officials. It seems that in certain cases provincial governors were free to lead the investigation, question the suspects, resort to violence (*siyāsat*) against them and take a final decision on the case. In other cases, governors felt obliged to send the suspects directly to the royal court in Khiva for further investigations. The documents do not provide enough information to establish the specific circumstances that prompted the application of such procedures. However, it is important to appreciate the fact that the report of the governor makes it clear that it was the appellants from Khanqah who requested the direct involvement of the royal court and explained the necessity of severely punishing the offenders to prevent the reiteration of such felonies.

236 TsGARUz, f. I-125, op. 1, d. 498, l. 78.

Translation

Let it be submitted (*ma'rūż*) for consideration to the office of the *yasāvulbāshī*, the recipient of the state's trust and the confidant of the ruler (*muqarrab al-ḥażrat*), our lord, that on 3 Jumādī al-ṣānī a certain Sātim and Atā Jān from Qūlān Qara Bāghlī,[237] who belong to the mosque (*masjid*) [community] of Ḥażrat-i Pahlavān informed me that [a band of] thieves broke into the house of Muḥammad Ya'qūb Āqsaqāl during the night and one of them climbed on the roof. [At that time], Muḥammad Ya'qūb Āqsaqāl's son was on the roof watching over (*qarāvullīq*) [the house]. [The thieves] strangled him, and came down into the house, and stole the household goods. In another room a woman (*nāchār*) and the youngest son of Muḥammad Ya'qūb Āqsaqāl were sleeping. As [the thieves] came closer to them, the child (*bala*) recognised one of the thieves as his uncle 'Abdullāh. [Then] 'Abdullāh gagged the child. After this, [the thieves] stole all the household goods and went away. The next morning when [I was] informed about [the incident], I had the *qażī-īshāns* provide for a trustee (*amīn*), whom I sent with one of my assistants [to the place of the murder]. As soon as they reached [the locality] and examined the dead man, they gave instructions [to proceed] to bury (*dafn*) [him]. Then a scout (*īzchī*) was brought. Among [the footsteps left by] the thieves, he recognised those of a man (*piyāda*) and a camel [which] led to the house of a certain 'Abdullāh from Būyqazāq.[238] After that Muḥammad Ya'qūb Āqsaqāl came in person and informed [me] that he too considered that 'Abdullāh was a suspect (*gumāndār*). As a result, I sent two Yomut liegemen (*nawkar*) with a written notification (*fatak*) to the house of the governor (*ḥākim*) of Besh-Ariq. The latter added an assistant (*kīshī*). These people went to 'Abdullāh's place, and brought him here together with a certain Jumāsh. I thus inform you that I sent the thieves 'Abdullāh and Jumāsh, together with the afore-mentioned Muḥammad Ya'qūb Āqsaqāl, Īsh Jān Āqsaqāl, and Sātim to your office accompanied by Khāl Bāy Qāżī. Let it be known that a thief broke into the summer house of a certain Muḥammad Raḥim Bāy from Dūrghāvīk and stole the agricultural tools, a mosquito net, one teapot with a cup, one pitcher, one share of the wooden plaugh and some straw. The next morning [the owner hired] a scout [who followed the traces of the thieves] leading to the house of a certain Jum'a Niyāz from Buvāy. When they got there, they did not enter Jum'a Niyāz's house'; [instead,] they came to me and as soon as they informed [me about what they had found], I sent two Yomut liegemen with the notables of the communities of the parties [to the dispute] to [Jum'a Niyāz's house]. They

237 We have been unable to identify this locale.

238 We have been unable to identify this locale.

identified one pitcher, one mosquito net, one teapot with a cup [as the stolen goods]. Afterwards the afore-mentioned thieves Jum'a Niyāz and Bābā, were brought here; as [I proceeded] to question them, at first they denied (*inkār*) the accusation; however, later they confessed (*būyūn būldīlār*). Let it be known to you that the things which they found were returned to Muḥammad Raḥim Bāy and these two individuals were also sent to your office together with Khal Bāy Qāżī. This is the state of the case. [This notification] was addressed to your office on 7 Jumādī al-s̱ānī 1336 [19.03.1918].

Let it be [also] known that the elders (*yāsh kattalār*) of Khanqah requested that the capital punishment (*ūlūm jazāsī*) be meted out to 3 or 4 among these notorious thieves; otherwise the number of thieves would increase day by day. [So] it was written.

Seal: Āqmuhr Ḥājjī Muḥammad Bāy[239]

239 On this individual, see Doc. 26, fn. 136.

Document 47: A Notification by a Provincial Governor to the *yasāvulbāshī* about a Case of Assault[240]

Introduction

A certain ʿAbdullāh from a locality called Uyghur appealed to the provincial governor and informed him that one ʿIbādullāh assaulted his wife and fled. The official initiated the procedure of investigation and instructed the *āqsaqāl* of the locality to find the suspect. After his arrest, ʿIbādullāh agreed to compensate the aggrieved party and the dispute was settled. It is important to note that, while informing the royal court about the outcome of the investigation procedures that he undertook, the local official attempted to distance himself from the settlement and its stipulations. Indeed, he emphasised in the report addressed to the agencies in Khiva that it was the parties themselves together with the representatives of their communities who reached a peaceful settlement. However, the report clarifies that the official played a crucial role in the distribution of the money paid by the defendant among the individuals who were involved in the process of mediation. The necessity to craft this document came when the claimant decided to appeal to the royal court. Most probably, ʿIbādullāh, who was not satisfied by the stipulations of the peaceful settlement, appealed to the agencies in Khiva and complained that during the process of reconciliation, the mediators demanded from him a substantial sum of money and resorted to violence. Once he received instructions to explain the circumstances of ʿIbādullāh's appeal, the officials attempted to persuade the royal court that such an appeal was unsound.

Translation

Let it be known to Amān Kīldī Bāy Yasāvulbāshī, refuge of the vizierate and banner of glory, our lord, that a certain ʿIbādullāh has assaulted the wife of a certain ʿAbdullāh from Ūyghūr[241] without any reason (*bī-vajh*) and caused her injury (*jarāḥat*) at one eye. For this reason, when I was about to detain ʿIbādullāh with the intention of questioning him, he ran away. After that I ordered his *āqsaqāl* to find him. Because of this, the next day he was found at the place of a certain Qūshāq and brought before me. All the *āqsaqāl-kadkhudās* reconciled the parties themselves outside [away from my sight] (*ūzlārī tashqārīda yarāshtūrūb*): [they] had [ʿIbādullāh] pay 10 *ṭillā* for the expenses for the [medical] treatment

240 TsGARUz, f. I-125, op. 1, d. 498, l. 84.

241 Bregel identified two localities under the name Uyghur or Yaman-Uyghur in the 19th and the beginning of the 20th century. The first one was situated east of Khanqah on the bank of the Amu Darya, see Munis and Agahi, *Firdaws al-iqbāl: History of Khorezm*, p. 621, note 710. The second locality bearing the same name was found on the right bank of the Amu Darya within the administrative unit of the Uyghur lake, see ibid., p. 627, note 770.

(*malḥam fulī*), as well as, some money to the *kadkhudās* (*kadkhudā fulī*) and to my attendant (*yasāvul ḥaqqī*), thus altogether 36 or 37 *ṭillā*. From this sum I was entrusted 17 *ṭillā* as payment for my assistance (*saʿī say*[242] *fulūngīz*) and the rest was spent for the *kadkhudās* and my attendant and for the medication. [But] now the afore-mentioned ʿIbādullāh has come before me escorted by a [court] attendant (*yasāvul*) and argued that the *āqsaqāls*, Mullā Qurbān Bāy and Yūldāsh, had beaten him and extorted from him 75 *ṭillā*. His allegations are groundless (*sūzī bīkāra dūr*). This is the state of the case. This notification (*khaṭ*) was compiled on 17 Rabīʿ al-s̱ānī 1335 [09.02.1917].

Seal: ʿAbd al-Raḥīm Bāy b. Muḥammad Yūsuf Baqqāl

242 *Say* in the original text of the record.

Document 48: A Notification by a Provincial Governor to the *yasāvulbāshī* about a Case of Animal Theft[243]

Introduction

In this report, a local official, most probably the governor of Manaq, writes to the agencies in Khiva with regard to a claim of horse theft. The suspect of the latter offense was a man from Manaq who had temporarily resided in the house of the aggrieved party. The suspect was sent to the governor and questioned. As the respondent denied responsibility, the governor decided to send the parties to the royal court, which would hear the case. Records from the Governorship-General of Turkestan and Bukhara indicate that in these two latter regions cases of horse-theft usually fell within the purview of *qāżīs*. The fact that in Khorezm such cases were instead heard by the royal court reinforces, once again, the idea that under the Qonghrat system of administration *qāżīs* occupied a somewhat low position in the Islamic judicial hierarchy.

Translation

Let it be known to the office of the *yasāvulbāshī*, refuge of the vizierate,[244] our lord, that a certain Qūtlūq Murād Ṣūfī from Tāshḥavuż came and informed me that six months ago a certain Qūrbān Bāy from Manāq who had resided at his place, stole [his] horse and a sheep-skin. [Qūtlūq Murād Ṣūfī also told me that] he has now found [Qūrbān Bāy] at the Manāq bazaar. As a result, I questioned the afore-mentioned Qūrbān Bāy who denied (*munkir*) [the theft]. [Accordingly,] I sent to your office the afore-mentioned Qūrbān Bāy accompanied by a liegeman on a horse (*nawkar-i āṭlī*) together with Qūtlūq Murād Ṣūfī, the owner of the [stolen] horse. I wrote this letter (*khaṭ*) to inform you about this [event] on 22 Rabīʿ al-s̱ānī 1335 [14.02.1917]. I wish you good health.

Seal: Muḥammad Yaʿqūb Bāy b. Jabbār Qulī Maḥram[245] 1334

243 TsGARUz, f. I-125, op. 1, d. 498, l. 62.

244 In the original text of the record, *vizārat-fanāh*.

245 Given the context of this and another document (Doc. 20) with the same seal, Muḥammad Yaʿqūb Bāy b. Jabbār Qulī Maḥram was evidently the governor of Manaq in the years 1916–1917.

Document 49: A Notification by a Provincial Governor to the *yasāvulbāshī* about a Double Homicide[246]

Introduction

A resident of an unidentified settlement who was a member of the Qaradashli Turkmens informed an official of the Khanate of Khiva about a double homicide. His niece and a young man were murdered by an unidentified individual. The claimant requested the appointment of a trustee to make an inquest, a fact suggesting that most probably the person filing the lawsuit with the royal court was cognizant of the legal instruments which were at his disposal. The Qonghrat official sent his trustee (*amīn*) together with the *qāżī* to investigate the place where the homicide occurred and collect the circumstantial evidence. In the wake of this procedure, the two corpses were handed over to their families to perform the funerary rituals and the burial. The main intention behind the production of this report is to inform agencies in Khiva that the families of the two murdered do not have any claims against each other on account of the two being killed together.

Translation

Let it be be submitted for consideration to the *yasāvulbāshī*,[247] refuge of the vizierate and repository of power,[248] our lord, that on 8 Rabīʿ al-avval a certain Āghā Qaradāshlī[249] came [before me] and submitted an appeal (*ʿarż ītdī*). [He stated] that somebody had killed the daughter of his elder brother Fakhr, and a young man (*bir yigit*), and thus asked that a trustee (*amīn*) be appointed [to investigate the case]. I sent a trustee together with the *qazī*[250]*-īshān* so that they would examine together [the corpses]. They have examined the corpses (*mayitlār*) and handed them over to their relatives. I asked the *qażī-īshān* whether there were any injuries visible [on the bodies] (*jarāḥatī*[251] *bār-mū*). He answered that in a few places [the bodies showed] knife and stick wounds. I asked the relatives of both the deceased whether they had any claims (*daʿvā*)[252] [against each other]. They answered that, on account of the fact that [they] were killed together, they do not have any [mutual] claims. I wrote this letter (*khaṭ*) on 22 Rabīʿ al-avval 1335 [15.01.1917].

Seal: Muḥammad Karīm Yūzbāshī b. Ismāʿil 1334

---

246 TsGARUz, f. I-125, op. 1, d. 498, ll. 70–70ob.
247 *Yāsavulbāshī* in the original text of the record.
248 *Ḥukūmat dasgā* in the original text of the record.
249 On the Qaradashli Turkmens, see the reference in Doc. 20, fn. 122.
250 *Qāzī* in the original text of the record.
251 *Jārājatī* in the original text of the record.
252 In the original text of the record, *davā*.

Document 50: A Notification by a Provincial Governor to the *yasāvulbāshī* about Multiple Cases of Robbery and Homicide[253]

Introduction

This report illuminates instances of robbery at gunpoint and homicide that were perpetrated in the district of Tashhawz in the spring of 1918.[254] The local official initiated an investigation and a series of hearings, which allowed him to establish that the perpetrators of these offences were Turkmen Yomuts who were loyal to a certain Sayyid Niyāz.[255] The report clearly suggests that the governor was requesting the agencies in Khiva to intervene with some concrete measures against such Turkmen outlaws.

Translation

He [is the Almighty]! Let it be known to the *yasāvulbāshī*, the banner of glory, our lord, that in the mosque (*masjid*) [community] of Chaʿsh [?] Mīrāb in Kāt, on the bank of the Yarmīsh [canal], four thieves on horse (*āṭlī*) and other six men on foot (*fīyadā*) broke into the houses of Raḥīm Bāy and Ātā Murād. They took a pair of bulls and a cow belonging to Raḥīm Bāy, shot and killed the wife of the afore-mentioned Ātā Murād, and stabbed one of his peasants thereby causing bodily harm (*yārādār*). In the locality of Chalang, five or six men broke into the house of a certain Ḥaytan. They took his cow, [then] they shot and killed him. In the course of three days similar events occurred again all around the locality of Tashḥavuż. It has been reported that those Yomuts on horses and on foot who robbed the houses, drove away the livestock, and murdered several people belong to Sayyid Niyāz's [group of] mounted and foot-men. Moreover, these men frightened the residents (*fuqarā*) of Tashḥavuż by blackmailing and robbing them (*sindā fulān nimarsa va fulān vajʿalārīm bār dīb*) and taking other appropriate and improper courses of action (*bī tigīsh bī ūrūn va bīr qāra īshlārnī ītīb*) against the law (*bī sharīʿat bī vajh-i sharʿī*)[256] and this is the reason behind disturbances in the district of Tashhawz (*kūb nādīnch*[257] *dūr*). [These thieves] robbed the residents of the locality of several thousand *manāt*

---

253 TsGARUz, f. I-125, op. 1, d. 498, ll. 88–88ob.

254 On the events that occurred in the spring of 1918 see Introduction, pp. 17–19.

255 Sayyid Niyāz was most probably the head of one of the various groups of Yomut Turkmens. We have been unable to dig out more information on this individual as his name does not figure in the list of Turkmen (Yomut) leaders drawn by Lykoshin in 1912. Nor do local historians such as Ḥasan-Murād Laffasī and Pahlavān Niyāz Ḥājjī Yusupov mention his name in their works focusing on the political events of the second decade of the 20th century.

256 In the original text of the record, *bī vaj-i shar*.

257 This is an Oghuzism for *nātīnch*.

as well as horses and sheep. To inform your office about all this, the [present] notification (*khaṭ*) was written on 18 Rajab 1336 [29.04.1918].

Seal: Jumʿa Niyāz Muḥammad Maḥram b. Māḥmūd Divān[258]

258 On this individual, the governor of Tashhawz, see Doc. 29.

Document 51: A Notification by a Provincial Governor to the *yasāvulbāshī* about a Case of Robbery[259]

Introduction

The victim of a robbery, a certain Ish-Jān Bāy, identified the perpetrator as one Khudāy Birgān Qūl, whom he took before a local official. The latter questioned the suspect who admitted his responsibility and provided the name of his accomplice. The leaders of the community of the aggrieved party successfully requested that the plaintiff be handed over to them under guarantee. Then they left for an unidentified destination. It is unclear whether the guarantors requested the release of the defendant so that the latter could assist them to collect supplementary circumstantial evidence on the crime scene. At any rate, it seems that the culprit's release did not leave the official particularly satisfied. Indeed, in reporting to the agencies in Khiva, he clearly refers to the need to take more serious measures against the culprit and he therefore provides information attesting to his bad fame. One could safely assume that the release of the culprit occurred against the will of the local official.

Translation

Let it be known to the *yasāvbāshī*,[260] the banner of glory and happiness, our lord, that in the wake of robbery in his house, Ish-Jān Bāy recognised his water jug in the hands of a certain Khudāy Birgān Qūl and he thus took the latter before me. When I questioned him [Khudāy Birgān Qūl] acknowledged (*iqrār*)[261] that, together with an accomplice, he stole the jug along with one sheep and [some] wheat. After that the *āqsaqāl*s and *kadkhudā*s told [us] that they would go to the community (*īlāt*), inquire about the case, and bring [the suspect] back to me; thus, in acting in the capacity of guarantor (*kafīl*), they took [the thief] with themselves and went away. That night a horseman (*āṭlī*) left for Khiva [with information] regarding Ish-Jān Bāy's case. Now, [it seems that] Khudāy Birgān Qūl is indeed a depraved unruly man (*kūp bīhūda yamān ādam*). The letter (*khaṭ*) was compiled in Jumādī al-ṣānī 1335 [September–October 1917] to inform your office about such [events].

Seal: Jumʿā Niyāz Maḥram b. Maḥmūd Dīvān

---

259 TsGARUz, f. I-125, op. 1, d. 498, ll. 72–72ob.

260 This is a spelling variation of *yasāvulbāshī*.

261 *Īqrār* in the original text of the record.

Document 52: A Notification by a Provincial Governor to the *yasāvulbāshī* about a Dispute over Rights of Inheritance[262]

Introduction

An *āqsaqāl* died living no direct heirs. The officials representing the constituency to which the deceased belonged took the initiative to consult with the local governor. In compliance with established bureaucratic practices, the latter sent one of his men together with a *qāżī-īshān* to collect circumstantial evidence regarding the man who had just passed away. They could establish that he had only a younger sister. There was, however, another *āqsaqāl* claiming kinship ties to the deceased and therefore rights on the inheritance. The governor's trustee and the judge thus questioned the local elders who dismissed the relevance of such a claim. The emissaries of the governor proceeded to list the possessions as well as the pending debts of the deceased. In his missive to the *yasāvulbāshī* the governor puts emphasis on the fact that the list was drawn in public at the presence of the local officials as to solemnize the involvement of state authorities in this matter. It seems, however, that the emissaries of the governor could not dissuade the *āqsaqāl* from pursuing his goal: the officials representing his constituency provided additional information thereby sustaining his claim to be a natural heir of the deceased. At this point, the governor must have felt obliged to defer to the *yasāvulbāshī*'s judgment. A palpable sense of impatience transpires from this notification as we find the governor urging the authorities in Khiva to act swiftly in order to counteract the rapacity of the locals.

Translation

Let it be submitted for consideration to the office of the *yasāvulbāshī*, refuge of the vizierate, and repository of power, our lord, that Bābājān Āqsaqāl [who belongs to the group of] Qonghrat Āchī Qūylī[263] died. In the light of this

262 TsGARUz, f. I-125, op. 1, d. 498, ll. 96–96ob.

263 Apparently, Achamayli – one of main subdivisions of the Qonghrat tribe in Khorezm along with Kok-Uzak, Balghali, and Qanjighali, see Alexander Kun, *Ocherk istorii zaseleniia Khivinskogo khanstva s drevnykh vremen, sostav ego sovremennogo naseleniia, administratsiia i goroda khanstva*, 1873, IVRRAN, St. Petersburg, Arkhiv Vostokovedov, f. 33, d. 8, ll. 9ob.-10; K.L. Zadykhina, "Uzbeki del'ty Amu-Dar'i," in *Trudy Khorezmskoi arkheologo-etnograficheskoi ekspeditsii*, I. *Arkheologicheskie i etnograficheskie raboty Khorezmskoi ekspeditsii. 1945–1948*, eds. S.P. Tolstov, and T.A. Zhdanko (Moscow: Izdatel'stvo Akademii nauk SSSR, 1952), p. 338; Munis and Agahi, *Firdaws al-iqbāl: History of Khorezm*, p. 575, note 350. The text clearly refers to a group of Qonghrat Uzbeks who lived in the Besh-Ariq district. They were resettled in this locality at the beginning of the 19th century after the Qonghrat rulers of Khiva conquered the Aral province in 1811. See Guliamov, *Istoriia orosheniia Khorezma s drevneishikh vremen do nashikh dnei*, p. 216.

information, we sent [there] a man (*ādam*) in our service together with the *qāżī-īshān*; when the latter questioned whether the deceased left any heirs (*vāriṡlār*), it seemed that he had only one younger sister. [But] a certain Qūchqār Āqsaqāl apparently alleged that he was a close relative [of the deceased] and that he was heir to his possessions. The *āqsaqāl*s and the other *kadkhudā*s of the community (*īl*) [of the deceased] did not consider [Qūchqār Āqsaqāl] as a true heir. Since he [=the deceased] has no other sons, nor daughters, [it was decided] to draw up a list (*rūykhaṭ*) in the presence of the *āqsaqāl-kadkhudā*s of all the debts (*qarżlār*), the landed properties (*yir-mulk*), and the other possessions of the afore-mentioned [deceased man], and the list was then sent to your office. Some *kadkhudā*s of Qūchqār Āqsaqāl's community (*īlāt*) state that he is a true heir and relative of the deceased; I thus [ask you] to notify [to me] with the letter (*khaṭ bīla*) whatever be your mercy before the possessions recorded on the list are lost. This letter (*khaṭ*) was compiled on 5 Shaʿbān, 1336 [15.05.1918].

Seal: Muḥammad Yūsuf [b. Pahlavān Maḥram][264]

264 Cf. the seal of Doc. 38.

Document 53: A Notification by a Provincial Governor to the *yasāvulbāshī* about a Case of Animal Theft[265]

Introduction

One Jumʿa Naẓar informed a local governor that he recognised on the horse of a certain Qūsh Naẓar the gear which had been stolen from him a year earlier together with his horse at the bazaar of Khanqah. Consequently, the local governor questioned the suspect. The governor obliged the suspect, under threat of punishment, to admit the theft of the horse. The two parties' representatives agreed that the horse would be returned to his owner, while the defendant should be temporarily detained by the governor. Following an established procedure, the governor wrote to the *yasāvulbāshī* and asked for further instructions with regard to the defendant. What the governor wanted to know from the Khivan authorities was whether he had to free the defendant under guarantee and thus satisfy the plea of his representatives, or to escort him to the royal court, most probably for a subsequent hearing. The *yasāvulbāshī* instructed the governor to release the defendant under guarantee. This document is noteworthy because it reflects how a dispute originating from a case of horse theft could be solved through preliminary investigations and negotiations led by the representatives of the two parties. This procedure of conflict resolution differs substantially from the procedure of adjudication of horse theft which *qāżīs* followed in other urban centers in Central Asia.[266]

Translation

Let it be known to the office of the *yasāvulbāshī*, the refuge of the vizierate, our lord, that last autumn the horse of a certain Jumʿa Naẓar, [a member of] the community (*qavm*) of Allāh Bīrgān Āqsaqāl, who belongs to the mosque community (*masjid īl*) of Āmān Yūzbāshī in Qonghrat, was stolen at the market of Khanqah. So far he has not found the thief. This year on 8 Ẕī al-qaʿda[267] he brought before me a certain Qūsh Naẓar valad-i Dawlat Murād as he had recognised on the latter's horse the harness (*yūna*) [belonging] to his own animal which had been stolen. I asked [Qūsh Naẓar] where he got this harness from since it appears that it [previously] belonged to [Jumʿa Naẓar's] stolen horse. He stated that he bought it at the market in Khanqah. I proceeded to a precautionary inquiry (*iḥtiyāṭ bīla taftīsh itīb*) and asked him again how the

265 TsGARUz, f. I-125, op. 1, d. 498, ll. 90–91.

266 On the procedure of adjudication followed by Central Asian *qāżīs* when they heard cases of horse theft, see P. Sartori, "Birth of a Custom: Nomads, *Sharīʿa* Courts and Established Practices in the Tashkent Province, ca. 1868–1919," *Islamic Law and Society* 18.3–4 (2011), pp. 293–326.

267 In the original text of the record, *Ẕā al-qaʿda*.

harness of a stolen horse could appear [from him]. [I also encouraged him] to tell the truth (*tūghrīsīn*) otherwise he would be punished (*sangā jazā' bīrīlūr*). In this regard Qūsh Naẓar said (*dīb*) that last autumn at the market of Khanqah he had stolen [Jum'a Naẓar's] horse and then sold it to a Qazaq for 30 *ṭillā*. After that the *kadkhudā-āqsaqāls* of both parties (*īkkī ṭaraf*) arranged for the delivery of Qūsh Naẓar's stolen horse to Jum'a Naẓar and thus reconciled them (*rižālāshdūrdīlār*). The *āqsaqāl-kadkhudās* of Qūsh Naẓar, the thief, also pleaded (*iltimās*)[268] for [the release of] the culprit (*gunāh*) and for that reason the latter was kept [in custody] (*sāqlāndī*). Should this reflect your intention, I could let him free and thus satisfy the plea of his *kadkhudās*. Otherwise, if you order (*parmāyish*) to send him [to Khiva] I shall have him dispatched to your office. This notification (*khaṭ*) was written on 12 Ẕī al-qa'da[269] 1336 [19.08.1918].

Let the fact not be hidden that, satisfying the plea of the *āqsaqāl-kadkhudās*, Qūsh Naẓar was handed over to Qahqa Vakīl and Qurbān Āqsaqāl, who will act in the capacity of guarantors (*kafīl*).

Seal: Muḥammad Yūsuf Bāy b. Pahlavān Maḥram

268 In the original text of the record, *īltimās*.

269 In the original text of the record, *Ẕā al-qa'da*.

Document 54: A Notification by a Provincial Governor to the *yasāvulbāshī* about a Case of Homicide[270]

Introduction

This document provides an account of a case of blood feud. A man was found hanging from a tree. Once rumors about this event reached the local governor, the latter sent two trustees to the place where the murder had been committed. The trustees were joined by local notables and together they carried out the preliminary investigation. As they proceeded to question the relatives of the murdered man, the trustees unfolded a story of adultery: the victim had entertained an extra-conjugal relation with another woman. According to the statements of the relatives, the husband of the adulteress together with other three men broke into the house of the victim, abducted him, and tied up his wife. The family of the murdered man was clearly waiting for a retaliation to take place, since the father had already alerted local notables that the suspects were their 'sworn enemies' (*qāndār*) and about the latter's intention to murder his son. The suspects were heard, but they denied the claim. The governor decided to entrust them to the policeman, while the widow was handed over to a guarantor. With this notification the governor of Hazarasp asked the *yasavūlbāshī* to provide further instructions.

Translation

Let it be known to the *yasavūlbāshī*, the banner of glory, our lord, that on 13 Jumādī al-avval on Monday evening, i.e., yesterday, in the locality (*mavżiʿ*) of Chavāndūr there occurred the [following] event: a certain Khudāy Birgān [b.] Ish Niyāz was hung to death on a tree in front of the door [of his house]. This is the case (*vāqiʿa*), about which they informed [me]. I sent my own trustee (*amīn*) and one from the *qāżī-īshān*s, the banner of Islamic law. When the trustees, together with the *āqsaqāl-kadkhudā*s and the local people (*mardum*) examined [the crime scene], permission was given to bury the corpse (*dafn*). [Then they proceeded to] question [the relatives of the departed] before the *kadkhudā*s. [Somebody explained that] that night in the house of the murdered man (*maqtūl*) slept his father Ish Niyāz, his mother Jumʿa Bīka, his sister Shakar Bīka, together with her husband Pahlavān, and his uncles Ḥusayn and ʿAbdullāh. The murdered man slept with his wife (*khātūnī*) Raḥmiya Bīka in another room. For this reason the others were unaware of the case. The next morning, the afore-mentioned ʿAbdullāh went outside for the ritual ablutions (*ṭahārat*) and saw [Khudāy Birgān hanging]. Without knowing the circumstances of the case, he [immediately] informed the afore-mentioned Ḥusayn.

270 TsGARUz, f. I-125, op. 1, d. 498, ll. 109–109ob.

[At that point, they all] went outside and saw [him]. This is the state [of the case]. After that they [the trustees] questioned Raḥmiya Bīka, the wife of the murdered. She said that the day before a certain Vays Niyāz, ʿAbd al-Raḥman, Ādam Bāy Tuqalāq, and another man had come [to her house], took her husband, while one of them confined her [in the room]. She [explained that] she was unaware of what was going on (*bī-khavar*)[271] and that she does not know anything else [since] the door had been locked from the outside. When they asked her who had confined her, she said that she would recognize him if she saw him and she recounted his features (*nishānalārīn*). They showed her a certain Qurbān Niyāz and she recognised him [as the offender]. Then they asked why those men had undertaken such a course of action against her husband. She answered that her husband had had an affair (*īshī bār*) with the wife of the afore-mentioned Vays Niyāz. Afterwards they proceeded to question the relatives of the murdered: Ish Niyāz, Jumʿa Bīka, and Shakar Bīka. [Ish Niyāz] explained that Vays Niyāz and ʿAbd al-Raḥman were their sworn enemies (*qāndārmīz*) and they wanted to kill his son [Ish Niyāz] and the latter's wife, Raḥmiya Bīka, and that he had informed everybody about [their intention] well in advance. They thus questioned Qalandar Āqsaqāl and Ghāyib Naẓar Arbāb, who confirmed that they had been informed. Then they questioned Vays Niyāz, ʿAbd al-Raḥman, Adam Bāy Taqalāq, and Qurbān Niyāz, who denied (*munkir*)[272] [the claim]. Afterwards the four men were handed over to the policeman (*mīrshab*). The abovementioned Raḥmiya Bīka was entrusted to a guarantor (*kafīl*). This is the state of the case (*ṣūrat-i vāqiʿa*) which I [sent to your] office in wait for your mercy. The notification (*maktūb*) was compiled on the 15th of the current month [Jumādī al-avval] in 1335 [08.03.1915].

Seal: Ismāʿil Khwāja b. Ibrāhim Khwāja[273]

271 Phonetic rendering for *khabar* ('information').

272 In the original text of the record, *munkīr*.

273 The governor of Hazarasp. See on this individual Doc. 40, fn. 208.

Document 55: A Notification to the *yasāvulbāshī* about a Case of Homicide[274]

Introduction

A mailman[275] living in the territory of the Urgench province headed off to the post office in Petroaleksandrovsk (Turtkul) in the Amu-Darya Department. When he returned to his place he found the dead body of his wife lying nearby his house. He then appealed to the local governor and sued his neighbour whom he suspected of homicide. The local governor held an inquiry. He appointed a trustee (*amīn*) to inspect the body for evidence of bodily harm. He also heard the leaders of the local communities. As the respondent categorically denied the claim, the local governor informed the office of the *yasāvulbāshī* and requested further instructions. The verso of the document indicates that the plaintiff agreed to settle the murder case amicably (*ṣulḥ*) in consideration of a sum of money.

Translation

He [is the Almighty]! Let it be known to the office of the *yasāvulbāshī*, the refuge of vizierate and repository of nobleness, our lord, that a certain Sayyid Ḥājjī Bāy ūghlī living in Urgench, in the locality (*mavżiʿ*) of Ghāybū on *āṭlīgh* lands,[276] appealed (*ʿarż itīb*) by stating (*dīb*) that on Monday 26 Rabīʿ al-s̱ānī

274 TsGARUz, f. I-125, op. 1, d. 498, ll. 110–110ob.

275 During the period of Russian rule, the Khanate of Khiva had two stations that offered postal services. Though both stations were administered by Russians, Khivan authorities paid for their upkeep. One of them, the telegraph station named 'Khiva' was opened in the city of Khiva on 1 November 1912, later than the period to which this document refers, see TsGARUz, f. I-125, op. 1, d. 289, ll. 174–174ob. The other station was called 'New Urgench' (*Novo-Urgenchskoe Pochtovo-telegrafnoe otdelenie*) and was much more significant than 'Khiva' on account of the scope of its communications and activities. Nil Lykoshin indicates that the 'New Urgench' station was manned by 'servants' (*dzhigity*) taken from the local population, who delivered the mail into and from the khanate through Petro-Aleksandrovsk and Charjuy, see his *Zapiska Nachal'nika Amu-Dar'inskogo Otdela Polkovnika Lykoshina o sovremennom sostoianii Khivinskogo Khanstva, 1912 god*, TsGARUz, f. I-2, op. 1, d. 314, ll. 29ob-30. In the remote settlements of the khanate the local population hired *dzhigits* who offered the service of postmen. If we consider that the events described in this document occurred in Urgench, we can infer that the mailman mentioned in the text was serving the 'New Urgench' station and therefore communicated with Petro-Aleksandrovsk.

276 *āṭlīgh* or *āṭlīgh* (*āṭlīq*) *yirī* is usually referred to land allotted predominantly to Turkmen tribes that settled in Khorezm under the rule of the Qonghrats with rights of possession in return for military service. The term *āṭlīgh* (from *āṭlī* – 'cavalryman') would suggest that Turkmens were expected to fill the ranks of the cavalry of the Khivan army. See Bregel, *Khorezmskie Turkmeny v XIX veke*, pp. 100–105. After the establishment of the Russian protectorate in Khiva in 1873, the fiscal status of *āṭlīgh*s was made subject to change. While

he had left for Turtkul[277] for the post office (*fūchta khizmatī*)[278] and left his wife (*ʿayāl*) Ūghūl Bīka Pahlavān-qīzī alone at his place (*ūyūmda*). When he made home on 27 Rabīʿ al-ṣānī after the delivery of the mail, he noticed that the entrance door was locked. For this reason, he gave a cry but he did not hear anything. After that he decided to get information from his close neighbour (*yaqīn qūnkūshīm*), a certain Ḥājjī Pahlavān ūghlī. On his way there, about a half *ṭanāb*[279] away from his house he found the dead body (*ūlūkīn*) of his wife. She had been killed with a knife and [Sayyid Ḥājjī Bāy ūghlī claims] it was [his neighbour] Ḥājjī Pahlavān ūghlī who killed her: the latter knew that his wife possessed 150 *manāt*. Accordingly, he said he would take care of the corpse: he took a trustee (*amīn*) there, buried the dead (*ūlūknī jāylāb*) and came back. With regard to the murdered woman and Ḥājjī Pahlavān ūghlī, I gathered their *āqsaqāl*s, namely Īsh Muḥammad Āqsaqāl Bābā Niyāz ūghlī, [who is appointed] by royal warrant (*ʿ'ināyatnāmalī*) [as well as] Jumʿa Niyāz Āqsaqāl Ibrāhīm ūghlī, Bābājān Āqsaqāl ʿAbdullāh ūghlī, Qurbān Bāy Āqsaqāl Raḥmān Bīrgān ūghlī, Ḥājjī Niyāz Bālṭa Niyāz ūghlī, Sulṭan Bāy Shīrīm ūghlī, Vays Niyāz ʿAbdullāh ūghlī, Īr Niyāz Tūra ūghlī, Bābājān Bālṭa Niyāz ūghlī, and Sattār-Qulī Muḥammad Saʿīd ūghlī. I initiated an inquiry into this case (*taftīsh*) and questioned them. They said that Sayyid Ḥājjī Bāy ūghlī and Ḥājjī Pahlavān ūghlī were indeed close neighbours and that there was no one else besides these two neighbours who lived in the [immediate] vicinity. They said that the two houses are located ¼ *farsaq*[280] away from their [= the *āqsaqāls*] places. They had no idea about how [these neighbours] behaved to each other. They also stated that they had never heard of the afore-mentioned Ḥājjī Pahlavān ūghlī being involved in similar circumstances in earlier periods. [The *āqsaqāl*s also stated that] whatever they may speculate (*taraddud*) on this case, they are unable to understand [what happened]. Sayyid Ḥājjī Bāy ūghlī stated that

---

during earlier periods they had to provide for military service, now Turkmens possessing *āṭlīgh* would pay for a tax at a fixed rate called *salghut-kesme*. The average size of *āṭlīgh yir* was circa 30 *ṭanāb* which would yield a payment of 12 *ṭillās*, that is 21 *roubles* and 60 *kopeks* or 72 *kopeks* for every *ṭanāb*. See N.S. Lykoshin, *Zapiska Nachal'nika Amu-Dar'inskogo Otdela Polkovnika Lykoshina o sovremennom sostoianii Khivinskogo Khanstva, 1912 god*, TsGARUz, f. I-2, op. 1, d. 314, ll. 25ob-28; Bregel', *Khorezmskie turkmeny v XIX veke*, p. 101; T.G. Tukhtametov, *Rossiia i Khiva v kontse XIX–nachale XX v. Pobeda Khorezmskoi narodnoi revoliutsii* (Moscow: Nauka, 1969), p. 97.

277 Local term employed to denote the citadel of Petro-Aleksandrovsk, the center of the Amu-Darya Department. See also Doc. 42.

278 Phonetic rendering of the Russian word *pochta* ('post office').

279 As a unit of length in 19th-century Khorezm a *ṭanāb* was equal to 60 *gaz*, whereas 1 *gaz* = 102–104 cm. Hence, half a *ṭanāb* is approx. 30–31 m.

280 This is a spelling variation of *farsakh*.

it was Ḥājjī Pahlavān ūghlī who killed his wife and no one else. As a result, I questioned the afore-mentioned Ḥājjī Pahlavān ūghlī and he said that he is absolutely unaware of what had happened. Now, I inform your office about the answers the *āqsaqāl*, the plaintiff (*mudda'ī*), and the defendant (*mudda'ā 'alayhi*) gave when I questioned them. This is the state of the case (*ṣurat-i vāqi'a*). The notification (*maktūb*) was registered on 5 Jumādī' al-avval 1329 [03.05.1911].

On 6 Jumādī al-ṣānī 1329 [04.06.1911], Sayyid the mailman acknowledged (*iqrār*) that he agreed (*rāżī būldūm*) on a peaceful settlement (*ṣulḥ*) for the murder of his wife Ūghūl Bīka bint-i Pahlavān [in consideration of] 250 *ṭillā* from Ḥājjī b. Pahlavān, in the presence of his *kadkhudā*s namely Bābā Jān Āqsaqāl, Jum'a Niyāz Āqsaqāl, Īsh Muḥammad Āqsaqāl, and Qurbān Bāy Āqsaqāl.

[No seal]

Document 56: A Notification by a Provincial Governor to the *yasāvulbāshī* about a Case of Robbery[281]

Introduction

This is a report about an an inquiry held by the governor of Manghit into a case of robbery. The victim explained that seven men had broken into her house and taken away animals and other possessions. The *āqsaqāl-kadkhudās* of the community to which the victim belonged asked the governor for permission to investigate the case further. As they suspected that the thieves had already found refuge somewhere under Russian jurisdiction, the *āqsaqāl-kadkhudās* crossed the Amu Darya. They addressed themselves to an informant who told them that part of the booty had been already sold. At this point, however, they could identify the culprit. They waited for him on his way back to the territory of the Khanate of Khiva and apprehended him with one accomplice in the market of Khitay (Khtay), a town between Gurlen and Manghit. He was brought before the governor and questioned. The thief admitted his responsibility and he was escorted with his accomplices to the office of the *yasavulbāshī*. It is important to note that the people who initiated an autonomous investigation and apprehended the thief were the leaders of the community to which the initial suspect himself belonged. It was their initiative that led to the exculpation of the first suspect. It is also noteworthy that, though the suspect admitted his guilt, the governor of Manghit argued for the importance of taking measures against him and his accomplices on account of his bad notoriety as outlaw.

Translation

Let it be submitted for consideration to the office of the *yasāvulbāshī*, refuge of the vizierate and repository of power, our lord, that on 12 Ṣafar a certain Ūghūl Kamfir[282] from Qum-Sangar[283] came [here] and informed me that 7 people had broken into her house and stolen one black-coloured mare, a new bullock cart, and three fat rams, and one dower chest (*ārja*) with money to the value of 16 *bātmāns* of cotton (*fakhta*),[284] 15 *qadāqs* of silk, 4 silk *mīsk* [?], 4 *pādshahī* [?], 2 shirts, 4 silk dressing gowns (*tūn*), 4 shawls, 2 hairpins (*tūrma*) [?], 2 pieces of strong silk (*qatīgh shāhī*) [?], 300 *manāt* in paper money, and one silver bracelet.

---

281 TsGARUz, f. I-125, op. 1, d. 498, ll. 114–114ob.

282 This is a spelling variation of *kampīr* ('old woman').

283 The text most probably refers to the locality of Qum-Senger mentioned in Khivan chronicles without any other indication as to its precise location. See Munis and Agahi, *Firdaws al-iqbāl: History of Khorezm*, p. 649, note 1051.

284 This is a spelling variation of *pakhta* ('cotton').

When I asked her whether she suspected anyone (*gumāndārīng bār mū*), she replied that she recognised among the seven men who had broken into her house only a certain Sāriq Bāy and that he is her suspect (*gumānīm*). After that I [ordered that] Sāriq Bāy be brought [to me]. When I questioned him, he denied (*munkir*) [the claim]. Accordingly, the *āqsaqāl-kadkhudā*s stated that it is unlikely that Sāriq Bāy is the thief and it is necessary to hold an inquiry within [the next] five or six days. Perhaps, they will be able to find some other people. His *āqsaqāl*s, Īsh Niyāz and Bālta Bāy went to the other side of the Amu Darya (*āryāq*). There [they found] an informer (*āyghāq*), a certain Ṣafar Qazāq who for 100 *manāt* told them that the thieves were Tangrī Birdī and Dūstān Īshjān Qazāq ūghlī from Qum-Sangar who had come [there] and sold the horse and the bullock cart. When [the *āqsaqāl*s] were staying in the house of a certain Bāl Muḥammad, Tangrī Birdī reached [the territory of the khanate]. While Tangrī Birdī was on the other side [of the Amu Darya], they did not say a word to him until he crossed over to this side with his companion Qazāq Dastān he was apprehended by Ibrāhīm Yūzbāshī and Īsh Niyāz Āqsaqāl in the market of Khitay.[285] When our man, Ibrāhīm Yūzbāshī, questioned him, Tangrī Birdī answered that he had sold the horse and the cart in the Amu-Darya Department in a county (*būlūsh*) under [the jurisdiction of a certain] ʿInāyat Būlūsh and that 3 rams had been slaughtered in the house of Ūrāż Muḥammad Āqsaqāl Yūsuf Makhẕūm ūghlī from Qum-Sangar. When he asked them who were their accomplices (*yūldāshlār*), they named Dawlat, Qul Muḥammad, Allash Āränlī, Ūrāż Muḥammad Makhẕūm and Khufar Bāy the Qazāq from Qum-Sangar. Ibrāhīm Yūzbāshī and the *āqsaqāl* brought the thieves to us. I questioned the thieves. Tangrī Birdī and Qazāq Dastān answered that they took only the horse, the cart, and 3 rams, and nothing else. After I questioned the accomplices of Tangrī Birdī and Qazāq Dastān, i.e., Dawlat, Qul Muḥammad, and Allash Āränlī. They answered that for them [such an allegation] is a calumny (*tuhmat*), but they will pay for the stolen things (*māl*), should I ask them to do so. Their accomplices Ūrāż Muḥammad Makhẕūm and Khufar Bāy the Qazāq have run away and they have not been found yet. Therefore, I sent to your office those who confessed (*būyūn*) Tangrī Birdī, Qazāq Dastān, and their accomplices, Dawlat, Qul Muḥammad, and Allash Āränlī together with Ībrāhīm Yūzbāshī. Let it be known that among the afore-mentioned thieves Tangrī Birdī over the course of three or four years has been a notorious thief (*yamān ūghrī*). Nobody

285 Khitay (Khtay) – a fortress approx. 21 km northwest of Gurlen, halfway between Gurlen and Manghit, see Munis and Agahi, *Firdaws al-iqbāl: History of Khorezm*, p. 631, note 828

could apprehend him as he had escaped to the other side of the Amu Darya. Tangrī Birdī's father too is tired (*bīzār*) of him. You know best. This is the state of the case (*ṣūrat-i vāqiʿa*). This petition (*ʿarīża-nāma*) was written on 25 Ṣafar 1335 [20.12.1916].

Seal: Muḥammad Niyāz Bāy b. Qāsim Dīvān[286]

286 The author of this report was a certain Matniaz Kasymov, who according to Lykoshin was the governor of Manghit in 1912, see his *Sovremennoe raspredelenie vlasti v Khanstve Khivinskom, 1912 god*, TsGARUz, f. I-2, op. 1, d. 314, l. 64ob. From the beginning of the 19th century, the town of Manghit was located on the right bank of the Atalyk Arna (Manghit-arna) canal, c. 85 km from Khiva. See Danilevskii, *Opisanie Khivinskogo khanstva*, p. 108; Alexander Kun, *Ocherk istorii zaseleniia Khivinskogo khanstva s drevnykh vremen, sostav ego sovremennogo naseleniia, administratsiia i goroda khanstva*, 1873, IVRRAN, St. Petersburg, Arkhiv Vostokovedov, f. 33, d. 8, l. 48 ob.; Guliamov, *Istoriia orosheniia Khorezma s drevneishikh vremen do nashikh dnei*, p. 202. This place should not be conflated with Manghit-Qalʿa, which is located on the west bank of the Karabaili emissary on the lower delta of the Amu Darya.

Document 57: A Notification by a Provincial Governor to the *yasāvulbāshī* about a Case of Robbery[287]

Introduction

In the wake of a robbery, a man sought redress before a local governor. The defendants denied the claim and the governor was clearly unable to reconcile the parties. At that point, the claimant decided to bring the issue before the royal court in Khiva. There are two interesting aspects to this text. Firstly, we observe again how the leaders of the community take upon themselves the responsibility of identifying and apprehending the culprit. It is, however, at this point that the text becomes less clear. It seems that the *āqsaqāl-kadkhudās* resorted to geomancy. Indeed, we learn that the local notables were expected to establish the amount of the theft by a ritual which is called 'sand scattering' (*tūfrāq tūktūrūb*), which consisted of scattering some sand on the traces left by the thieves. Secondly, the defendant expressed his intention to refer to the royal court in Khiva and requested from the local governor a 'binding letter' (*bāyluv khaṭī*), ensuring that the case was under review by local officials.

Translation

Let it be known to the office of *yasāvulbāshī*, banner of excellence, our lord, that 'Avaż-Murād came [to me] and informed [me] that when he left for the market in Manghit [several] thieves broke into his house and stole 994 *ṭillā* in *manāt* banknotes. The *āqsaqāl-kadkhudās* [of the appellant] came [to me] and requested to be given a period of 1–2 days so that they can scatter some soil and look into it (*tūfrāq tūktūrūb kūrāy*). Later they came back and, by scattering some soil, they predicted that 930 *manāt* [were stolen]. After that the afore-mentioned 'Avaż-Murād came and stated that he suspected (*gumāndār*) [three] *bāys*, i.e., Vays, Khāl-Murād and Īrkīn. I held an inquiry about these three men and questioned them, but they denied (*munkir*) [the claim]. [At that point], 'Avaż-Murād said that he would go to the royal court (*dawlat-i ā'lāgha bārūrman*) and requested a binding letter (*bāyluv khaṭī*). They [agreed] to gather at your office (*khiẕmatīngizdā tāpīlmāqchī būldīlār*) in five days, that is next Tuesday. Yūsuf Ṣafāsh ūghlī will be the guarantor (*kafīl*) for these three men. [But] you know best (*ṣāḥib-i ikhtiyār*). This letter (*khaṭ*) was written on Thursday 2 Jumādī al-avval 1335 [24.02.1917].

Seal: [?] Yūzbāshī b. Raḥmatullāh Yasāvulbāshī

---

287 TsGARUz, f. I-125, op. 1, d. 498, l. 113.

Document 58: A Notification by a Provincial Governor to the *yasāvulbāshī* about a Case of Robbery[288]

Introduction

In the wake of a case of robbery, the leader of a local community (*āqsaqāl*) appealed to the provincial governor. The latter operated according to an established procedure and appointed a trustee (*amīn*) to initiate a preliminary investigation and collect circumstantial evidence. He also resorted to the local *qāżīs* and instructed them to provide their own fiduciary, a mullah who would join the investigation. The governor then decided to notify the *yasāvulbāshī* about the course of actions he undertook. In so doing, he listed all the items which had been stolen. This document is clearly the notification which the local governor sent to the agency in Khiva most probably waiting for further instructions.

Translation

Let it be known to the office of the *yasāvulbāshī*, refuge of the vizierate and repository of power, our lord, that on Monday evening in the middle of the night several thieves broke into the home of Tājī Niyāz, who is a member of the community (*qavm*) of Muḥammad Murād Bāy, and stole a pair of oxen, a colt, and a ram among his livestock (*māl ashiyā' lār*). Among his possessions they took [a pair] of new boots and [a pair] of old ones, two robes, 2 felt rugs and six face-veils and a woman's dress [?],[289] a [piece of] striped fabric (*ālācha yalāk*)[290] and a small jug, three sheepskins, a tea pot and two [tea] cups, one *bātman* of sorghum and one *bātman* of millet and paper money worth 100 *manāts*. While they were taking the afore-mentioned items, they locked up in the house [Tājī Niyāz's] son and his wife. They then tied Tājī Niyāz's hands behind his back, fastened [a rope around] his shoulders, and left. As soon as an *āqsaqāl* of the community (*īlātnī āqsaqālī*) informed me, I dispatched one person together with one *mullā* given by the *qāżī-īshāns* [to reach the place and investigate the incident]. Now I address to your office this notification (*khaṭ*) which [lists] the stolen items and [recounts] the event [of the robbery]. Whatever

288 TsGARUz, f. I-125, op. 1, d. 498, ll. 31–31ob.

289 *Nāchar kūylāk* in the original text of the record.

290 In the text, the striped material is also referred to as *yalāk*. We have been unable to establish the meaning of this word.

your mercy, you know better. The notification was compiled on 27 Rajab 1339 [05.04.1921].[291]

Seal: Muḥammad Ṣafā Ātālīq b. ʿAbdullāh Ātālīq 1335[292]

291 The date is clearly wrong as, after the Young Khivans seized power in February 1920 with the help of the Bolsheviks, they liquidated the office of provincial governor and replaced them with revolutionary committees (*revkomytety*) and soviets. See Becker, *Russia's Protectorates in Central Asia*, p. 225; I.V. Pogorel'skii, *Ocherki ekonomicheskoi i politicheskoi istorii Khivinskogo khanstva*, p. 215. Therefore, it is very unlikely that the office of governor and *yasāvulbāshī* could exist in April 1921. In addition, the seal bears the year 1335, i.e. 1916/17.

292 On this individual and on the term *ātālīq*, see Doc. 23, fn. 116.

Document 59: A petition to the *yasāvulbāshī* regarding a Case of Robbery and Assault[293]

Introduction

In this appeal (*ʿarż*), a certain ʿAbd al-Aḥad Sālim addressed the *yasāvulbāshī* to file a claim of assault and abuse. The appellant was most probably a *shaykh* who had come with his disciples to Khiva in order to perform a pilgrimage and offer donations. When he and his associates reached their inn, they noticed that somebody was attempting to break in. Though this person managed to escape, they could nevertheless establish his identity since in running away he had left his knife behind him. The appellant also informed the local community elder, thereby evidently publicizing the event. As a result, the relatives of the individual who was identified as the burglar retaliated by assaulting and cursing the *shaykh* and his disciples. It is important to note that in filing this complaint, the appellant did not limit himself to offering an account about the brutality and the slanderous behaviour of his assailants. He also noted that one of the offenders had wounded his forehead, a fact which would have prompted an appeal to a local authority against the *shaykh*. ʿAbd al-Aḥad Sālim thus appealed to the *yasāvulbāshī* to secure the involvement of the royal court which could have protected him from the abuses of the local community. This notification substantially differs from other texts presented in this section as it was not issued by an official.

Translation

He is the Almighty! We appeal (*ʿarżimīz*) to the *yasāvulbāshī*, refuge of the vizierate and repository of power, our lord, [to report about the following incident]. I, your humble servant (*duʿāgūy*), together with my disciples (*murīdlār*) came to the [royal court] of the Khwārazmshāh,[294] peace be upon him, and prayed for the sake of [his Majesty], may his rule last forever. We came here to offer donations (*ṣadaqa*) and, having done so, after the evening prayer (*khuftan*)[295] we made return to the inn (*musāfir-khāna*) where we stayed. It was at that point that one [of my disciples] went outside and saw that someone was breaking the lock of the southern door [of our lodge]. [Our associate] asked him: 'Who are you?', but he ran away. [However] we found that his name was Niẓām [because] he had left his knife [there]. We then addressed the

293 TsGARUz, f. I-125, op. 1, d. 498, l. 32.

294 For a discussion of the significance of this epithet, see p. 11.

295 This is a spelling variation of *khuftān*.

āqsaqāl-bābā[296] and informed him [about what had occurred]. [Later] when we were resting outside of our place, the brothers [of Niẓam] together with his father came to us. The father ordered them to hit us (*ūrūng dīb*) and so they beat the three or four of us; and they also cursed us a lot (*kūb ḥaqārat*) while beating us. [In the brawl] one of the younger brothers[297] hit the door lock and wounded his forehead. Then they left to file a complaint (*ʿarż*) against us. This is the event that occurred.[298]

Seal: ʿAbd al-Aḥad Sālim, 1334

296 *Bābā* was most probably intended as a honorific expression to refer to the *āqsaqāl* in question.

297 In the text *bālasī*, 'his child'. It clearly refers to one of the children of Niżām's father, i.e., one of Niżām's brothers.

298 On the basis of the seal we can conclude that the text was not produced earlier than 1915.

Document 60: A Notification by a Provincial Governor to the *yasāvulbāshī* about a Dispute over an Unpaid Debt[299]

Introduction

The governor of Besh-Ariq notifies the office of the *yasāvulbāshī* that a dispute regarding an unpaid debt was brought before the judges. The latter considered the circumstantial information (*akhbār*) coming from individuals representing the community to which the claimant belonged together with others who acted on behalf of the community of the defendant. The judges examined the evidence, had a few individuals swear an oath as a form of rebuttal to the claim, and refused to hear the dispute. It appears that the judges resorted to the examination of written evidence produced by the defendants and the taking of oaths as preparatory procedures to weigh the soundness of the claim. Indeed, as they did not proceed with the trial, the judges did not rule that the claim was null. Instead, they simply dismissed it as irrelevant. The document clearly shows that in this specific case the judges acted in the capacity of legal advisors for the Qonghrat royal court.

Translation

Let it be known to our *yasāvulbāshī*, the undefeatable seat of glory (*ʿizzat-maʾāb mā-lā-iktisāb*), our lord, that a certain Ādīna Murād from Ṭama last year [filed a lawsuit] against Jumʿa Niyāz and Muḥammad Yaʿqūb Bāy by stating that they owed him [the equivalent of] 1200 *kalta qāmīsh*.[300] He waived his claim (*daʿvā*) after he received 29 *ṭillā* and handed [to them] over a certificate (*khaṭ*) [of relinquishment]. Also, he [had filed a claim] against his brothers Khudāy Birdī and Muḥammad Sharīf, [saying] that they owed him 6 bundles of alfalfa. Accepting 15 *ṭillā*, he gave a certificate [of relinquishment] to them (*khaṭ bərīb īrkān*). This year too he claimed (*daʿvā qīldī*) 11½ *batmān* of undusked rice (*shālī*) against his brother, a certain Bābā Jān, whom he brought before the *qażī-īshāns*. [In the course of the hearing] before the [*qażī-*] *īshāns*, the notables of the claimant's community gathered (*īlātī-nīng nāʾib āqsaqāl kadkhudālārī jamʿ būlūb*) and informed and [legally] acknowledged (*iqrār būlūb akhbār qildīlār*) that Ādīna Murād's claim, itself unsound, is null (*ūzī nāḥaq tūtghūchī daʿvāy-i qāq tūrūr*). Qalandar Nāyib, Bābā Jān Bāy, Durbīk, Bābā Niyāz, Sayyid, Bābā Jān Bāy, and the community of the defendants (*muddaʿā ʿalayhi*) Jumʿa Niyāz and Bābā Jān, stated (*akhbār*) that the claim was unsound. A certain

299 TsGARUz, f. I-125, op. 1, d. 498, l. 77.

300 *Kalta qāmīsh* ('short cane'), a grass of the Poaceae family growing in riverine areas, which was used as fodder and construction material.

Sayyid Muḥammad Aqā from Baghat,[301] Raḥmān Birdī Āqsaqāl, Tāza Bāy, and Ya'qūb Bāy stood [there too]. The [*qażī-*] *īshān*s informed us that, since they examined the documents and let the afore-mentioned individuals take several oaths rebutting [the claim] (*bir nicha daf'a qasam aytdī*), they will not further proceed with the hearing (*murāfa'a*). Now you know best. The petition (*'arīża-nāma*) was compiled in 1335 [1916–17].

Seal: Shāh Murād Bāy b. Dawlat Murād Bāy[302]

301 Baghat is a locality ca. 40 km northeast from Khiva and 16 km east of Yangi-Ariq, see Munis and Agahi, *Firdaws al-iqbāl: History of Khorezm*, p. 594, note 421; Bregel, *An Historical Atlas of Central Asia*, p. 67.

302 The governor of Besh-Ariq, the grandson of Muḥammad Murād Divānbīgī, see N.S. Lykoshin, *Sovremennoe raspredelenie vlasti v Khanstve Khivinskom, 1912 god*, TsGARUz, f. I-2, op. 1, d. 314, l. 64 об.

Document 61: A Letter by the Turkmen Yomut Leader Junayd Khān to the *yasāvulbāshī* about the Appointment of a New *qāżī* to Solve Conflicts among the Ata Turkmens[303]

Introduction

The author of this text was Muḥammad Qurbān Sardār, better known as Junayd Khān. He was *de-facto* ruler of the Khanate of Khiva in the period 1918–1919.[304] In the case illutrated by this document, the author wrote to the *yasāvulbāshī* and conveyed to him the request of a certain Īshān Āgha Jān. The latter was the leader of the Ata Turkmens[305] living on the right bank of the Amu Darya. He had asked Junayd Khān to intercede with the khan and the chief judge in Khiva with regard to the appointment of a new *qāżī* to solve conflicts among the Ata Turkmens living in the area between Fitnak and Darghan Ata, on the one hand, and their fellow tribesmen living on the other bank of the river under the jurisdiction of Russia, on the other. It is noteworthy that the appellant bore the title of *īshān* which, on its own, is usually employed to denote Ṣufi *shaykhs*.[306] It is worth emphasizing that not always were *īshāns* fellow tribesmen of the Turkmens among which they lived.[307] It is also noteworthy that

---

303 TsGARUz, f. I-125, op. 1, d. 498, l. 22

304 See the Introduction to this volume as well as Docs. 24, 36, 45, and 61.

305 'Ata' was the name of a Turkmen tribe that the Qonghrat rulers allowed in the 1820s and the 1830s to settle in Khorazm on the fringes of the Balkhan bay and close to the Balkhan mountain range, see Bregel', *Khorezmskie turkmeny v XIX veke*, p. 35. Later, in the wake of a series of conflicts with the Yomut Turkmens, the Atas were allowed to move to the south-eastern regions of the khanate. According to Alexander Kuhn, this resettlement occurred under the ruler of Sayyd Muḥammad Khān (1856–1864), see his *Ocherk istorii zaseleniia Khivinskogo khanstva s drevnykh vremen, sostav ego sovremennogo naseleniia, administratsiia i goroda khanstva*, 1873, IVRRAN, St. Petersburg, Arkhiv Vostokovedov, f. 33, d. 8, ll.14a–14b. The main area in which the Atas resided was the territory on the south-eastern borders of the khanate, see Bregel, *An Historical Atlas of Central Asia*, p. 75. In addition, a branch of the Ata Turkmens lived also on the right bank of the Amu Darya in the Aq-Qamysh district, see Bregel', *Khorezmskie turkmeny v XIX veke*, pp. 35–36. Kuhn suggests in 1873 the Ata Turkmens amounted to 1000 households, the pastures of which were situated in the south-eastern border of the khanate on both sides of the Amu Darya, see his *Ocherk istorii zaseleniia Khivinskogo khanstva s drevnykh vremen, sostav ego sovremennogo naseleniia, administratsiia i goroda khanstva*, 1873, IVRRAN, St. Petersburg, Arkhiv Vostokovedov, f. 33, d. 8, ll.14a–14b. See further N.S. Lykoshin, *Zapiska Nachal'nika Amu-Dar'inskogo Otdela Polkovnika Lykoshina o sovremennom sostoianii Khivinskogo Khanstva, 1912 god*, TsGARUz, f. I-2, op. 1, d. 314, l. 24 ob.

306 Of course, this is not the case with formulations such as e.g. *qāżī-īshān*.

307 Bregel', *Khorezmskie turkmeny v XIX veke*, p 76, fn. 28; S.M. Demidov, *Turkmenskie ovliady* (Ashkhabad: Ylym, 1976), p. 20. William Wood argues that in the 18th and the 19th century Turkmen tribes usually conferred 'special land and water right' upon such individuals who claimed saintly descent in order to persuade them to join the tribe, see his "The Sariq Turkmens of Merv and the Khanate of Khiva in the early Nineteenth Century" (Unpublished Ph.D. Dissertation. Indiana University, 1999), p. 16.

both the intercessor, Īshān Āgha Jān, and the invidivual recommended to the post of *qāżī* Mullā Najm were residents of the Amu-Darya Department. As a consequence, regardless of the formal subdivision among Ata Turkmens between two different jurisdictions, they retained strong social and cultural ties and recognised the spiritual authority of the same leaders. Presumably, the request coming from the leader of the Ata Turkmens was possible on account of the fact that at that time (August 1919) Junayd Khān enjoyed authority not only over a substantial part of the territory of the Khanate of Khiva, but also on the right bank of the Amu Darya, when he was preparing an attack against the pro-Bolshevik garrison in Petro-Aleksandrovsk in the hope of establishing his power on both sides of the river.[308] Agencies in Petro-Aleksandrovsk had little resources to prevent the residents on the right bank of the Amu Darya from aligning themselves with him, especially given that the ruler of Khiva Sayyid ʿAbdullāh (1918–1920) was in fact Junayd Khān's puppet khan. The use of the title of *qāżī* among the Turkmens of Khorezm was mostly honorific and therefore signalled a tribal affiliation rather than a specific madrasa background. The document in question also shows that the appointment to the position of *qāżī* might satisfy the necessity of a specific community rather than representing a policy of the center. No less important is to note that the *yasāvulbāshī*'s authority to appoint a *qāżī* suggests that the judicial authority of the latter was less than the former's. Hence, the local population perceived him as the most natural addressee of appeals.

Translation

Let it be known (*iʿlām ūl-kīm*) to the *yasāvulbāshī*, refuge of the vizierate, repository of nobleness, and banner of glory, our lord, that our Āgha Jān Īshān from the Amu-Darya Department requested that one judge (*qāżī*) be appointed to solve the conflicts (*daʿvā janjāllār*) among the members of the Ātā [tribe] in the other side of the Amu Darya and [their tribesmen living] between Pitnak[309] and [the shrine of] Darghan-Ata,[310] mercy be upon him.

308 See Becker, *Russia's Protectorates in Central Asia*, p. 223; Qoʻshjonov, and Polvonov, *Khorazmdagi ijtimoiy-siyosiy jarayonlar*, pp. 306–307.

309 Pitnak (Fitnak) is a locality approx. 80 km southeast of Khiva, see Munis and Agahi, *Firdaws al-iqbāl: History of Khorezm*, p. 577, note 359; Danilevskii, *Opisanie Khivinskogo khanstva*, p. 109; N.S. Lykoshin, *Zapiska Nachal'nika Amu-Dar'inskogo Otdela Polkovnika Lykoshina o sovremennom sostoianii Khivinskogo Khanstva, 1912 god*, TsGARUz, f. I-2, op. 1, d. 314, l. 31.

310 On the locality of Darghan Ata (or Darghan), see Kun, *Ocherk istorii zaseleniia Khivinskogo khanstva s drevnykh vremen, sostav ego sovremennogo naseleniia, administratsiia i goroda khanstva*, 1873, IVRRAN, St. Petersburg, Arkhiv Vostokovedov, f. 33, d. 8, l. 32; Guliamov, *Istoriia orosheniia Khorezma s drevneishikh vremen do nashikh dnei*, pp. 117, 141.

For this reason, we appeal to you so that you can convey our request to our Majesty (*ḥaẓratīmīz*) and the *qāżī kalān-īshān*, to entrust Mullā Najm from the Amu-Darya Department, with a seal together with a diploma of appointment (*yārlīq bila muhr ālīb birsūnlār*). That was the request of our Īshān [Āgha Jān]. This request (*khaṭ*) was written on Sunday 14 Ẕī al-qaʿda 1337 [10.08.1919].

Seal: Muḥammad Qurbān Sardār b. Ḥājjī Bāy, 1337

Document 62: A Notification by a Provincial Governor to the *yasāvulbāshī* about the Intention of the Disputing Parties to Solve the Dispute before the Khan[311]

Introduction

Two liegemen sued a Qazaq. They most probably did so before a local governor. When negotiations proved insufficient to determine a resolution, the parties made a vow (*vaʿda*)[312] to solve their conflict before the khan. They did so in the presence of an official who recorded their vow and entrusted this document to one of the plaintiffs. The vow consisted of several stipulations. Firstly, they agreed to meet in Khiva within three days. Secondly, they determined that, if one party failed to appear before the royal court in time, the latter would appoint an attendant (*yasāvul*) to assist the other party. The *yasāvul* should escort the attendee to meet with the absentee and act in the capacity of mediator. The absentee party should be also made liable to pay the attendant's fee. The document was then entrusted to one of the plaintiffs and it is likely that he would produce it to the royal court in Khiva upon his arrival.

Translation

Two liegemen (*nawkar*) from Qīlīch Bay,[313] Khāl Nīyāz Yūzbāshī and Ṣafar Muḥammad filed a claim (*daʿvā*) against Ḥamza the Qazāq. As [the parties] were willing to pursue the resolution of the conflict before the royal court of our excellence, let his rule last forever (*dargāh-i ʿālīlarīda ṣāf būlmāqchī būlūb*), they made a vow (*vaʿda*) to [attend to this task] within 3 days. They also promised that, if within the afore-mentioned period one [party] does not turn up at the court of the sovereign (*dargāh-i ʿālam-panāh*) and does not find [the

---

311 TsGARUz, f. I-125, op. 1, d. 498, l. 41.

312 This is a procedure also applied in dispute settlements according to Qazaq customary law, see Sartori, "Murder in Manghishlaq: Notes on an Instance of Application of Qazaq Cutomary Law in Khiva (1895)," p. 243.

313 Qlich Bay (Qīlich Niyāz Bāy) was a settlement located circa 70 km west of Khiva on the bank of the canal bearing the same name, see Basiner, *Estestvenno-nauchnoe puteshestvie po Kirgizskoi stepi v Khivu*, pp. 347–348; Danilevskii, *Opisanie Khivinskogo khanstva*, p. 106. Kuhn reported in 1873 that unlike many other Khorezmian cities of the time Qlich Niyaz Bay was not surrounded by city walls and residents' houses were scattered among various gardens, see his *Ocherk istorii zaseleniia Khivinskogo khanstva s drevnykh vremen. sostav ego sovremennogo naseleniia, administratsiia i goroda khanstva*, 1873, IVRRAN, St. Petersburg, Arkhiv Vostokovedov, f. 33, d. 8, l. 47.

other party], the party who does go should inform [the royal court] and receive an attendant (*yasāvul*), while the absentee should pay the latter's fee (*yasāvul ḥaqqī*). I entrusted this notification (*khaṭ*) to the afore-mentioned Khāl Nīyāz Yūzbāshī on Friday 8 Ramażān 1332 [30.07.1914].

Seal: Muḥammad Laṭīf Khwāja b. ʿAbd al-Karīm Khwāja, 1331

Document 63: A Notification by a Provincial Governor to the *yasāvulbāshī* about the Intention of the Disputing Parties to Solve the Dispute before the Khan [314]

Introduction

This document is very similar to the preceding one. A chieftain of a group of Qaradashli Turkmens sued a Qazaq for the theft of a camel. He most probably did so before a local governor. When negotiations proved insufficient to determine a resolution, the parties made a vow (*va'da*) to solve their conflict before the khan. The vow consisted of several stipulations. Firstly, the two parties agreed to meet in Khiva within five days. Secondly, they determined that, if one party failed to appear before the royal court in time, the latter would appoint an attendant (*yasāvul*) to assist the other party. The attendant would escort the attendee to meet with the absentee and act in the capacity of mediator. The absentee party would be also made liable to pay the attendant's fee. The document was then entrusted to the proxy and it likely that he would produce it to the royal court in Khiva upon his arrival.

Translation

A certain Qīlich Vakīl[315] Qarādāshlī[316] filed a claim against Chupān Bāy, a Qazāq, for the death of a camel. As [the parties] were willing to go to the royal court (*dargāh-i 'ālīlarīda*) to pursue the resolution of the conflict (*ṣāflāshmāqchī būlūb*), they have made a vow (*va'da*) to [attend to this task] within 5 days. They [thus expressed] the intention to meet before the court of the sovereign (*dargāh-i 'ālam-panāh*) within the afore-mentioned [period of] 5 days. They also promised in our presence (*ḥużūrimīzda*) that, if within the afore-mentioned period one [party] does not turn up at the court of the sovereign and does not find [the other party], the party who does go should receive an attendant (*yasāvul*), while the absentee should pay for the latter's fee. I entrusted this binding promissory note (*bāyluv khaṭī*) to Qīlich Vakīl on Monday 24 Rabī' al-s̱ānī 1332 [21.03.1914].

Seal: Muḥammad Laṭīf Khwāja b. 'Abd al-Karīm Khwāja

---

314 TsGARUz, f. I-125, op. 1, d. 498, l. 43.

315 *Vakīl* (or *vekil*) – one of the common designations in 19th-century Khorezm used for the Turkmen tribal aristocracy, see Bregel', *Khorezmskie turkmeny v XIX veke*, p. 129.

316 On Turkmen clan Qaradashli, see above the footnote 90 to Doc. 20.

SECTION 4

Qāżīs' Reports

Document 64: A Report by a *qāżī-ra'is* about the Intention of the Disputing Parties to Solve the Dispute before the khan[317]

Introduction

This a report that a *qāżī-ra'īs*[318] addressed to the ruler after that the royal court requested that he examines the status of a woman after the death of her husband. Somebody must have appealed to the agencies in Khiva claiming that the widow had in fact married another man before the expiration of the mandated waiting period (*'idda*). In an earlier report, the jurist explained that a number of people had already acknowledged that the husband had passed away six months earlier. Such an acknowledgement was most probably notarised in a *sharī'a* court and attested to the expiration of the widow's waiting period. The judge, however, wanted to show himself to be particularly diligent in fulfilling the request of the royal court and claimed that the afore-mentioned acknowledgment had been made in bad faith. He thus heard another man, presumably somebody influential within the local community, who provided a testimony corroborating the information about the expiration of the waiting period. The judge went on to question the woman and put her under oath. As the woman did not refrain from swearing, the *qāżī* solemnised the new marriage. This document illuminates at least three aspects of Islamic legal culture in 19th-century Khorezm. Firstly, Khivan subjects must have assumed that, amid the variety of legal services supplied by the Qonghrats, the royal court could solve issues pertaining to Islamic family law. Secondly, to solemnize the marriage of a contract for a widow who was suspected to be still in her waiting period required the *qażī* to gather all the available circumstantial evidence on her status. Thirdly, before writing this report, the jurist had taken for granted that he would have to go to the royal court and report orally about the state of the case. This would suggest that the *qāżī* had already accounted for his own activity directly to the chancery in Khiva.

317 TsGARUz, f. I-125, op. 2, d. 606, ll.1–10b.

318 It was quite common among jurists in 19th-century Khorezm to be appointed to both the office of 'judge' (*qāżī*) and 'moral enforcer' (*ra'īs*), see Sartori, *Visions of Justice:* Sharī'a *and Cultural Change in Russian Central Asia*, appendix I.

© KONINKLIJKE BRILL NV, LEIDEN, 2020 | DOI:10.1163/9789004427907_006

Translation

He is the Almighty! Let us address one hundred thousand praises and encomia to his majesty (*ḥaẓrat*), the trustee of the sultanate (*amīn al-salṭana*) and the pillar of the state (*rukn al-dawla*), the beloved of the learned ones (*muḥibb-i ʿulamā*), the friend of the poor ones (*mushfiq-i fuqarā*), and fortune-bearing refuge for the outcasts (*ghurabā-nīng darbār-i falak-madār*); and let the rays of the sun illuminate the recesses of the mind (*maʿlūm żamīr*). You have been informed (*maʿrūża būlghān*) that Māmā Jān Bīka's husband died six months ago. Mullā Īr-Niyāz, Jukān Ṣūfī, Muḥammad Niyāz Mīrāb, Razzāq Bīrdī Makhẓūm, ʿIbādullāh Maḥram, Bābā Jān Jarchī, Muḥammad Niyāz Bāy and other such people (*mūndāgh ādamlār*) confirmed it (*iqrār būldīlār*).[319] [However,] we do not believe (*bāvar qilmāyin*) what they said and we did not solemnize the marriage (*nikāḥ*). [A certain] Sayyid Riżā Khwāja Īshān also said that he testifies (*shāhidmīz*) that the waiting period (*ʿidda*) of this woman (*khātūn*) has [already] elapsed. After that, we held an inquiry (*mubāshir būlūb*). We questioned her whether she was pregnant and whether her waiting period [has already passed] (*ḥamlīn va ʿiddasīn sūrāshīb*). We put her under oath (*ānt bīrīb*). [In the end] we contracted (*ʿaqd qilīb*) [a marriage between] her and Pahlavān Niyāz. Four months passed when he went to Urgench and [there] the *raʾīs*es, as soon as they knew that he got married, gave him a certificate [of marriage] and extorted (*zūrdīn*) from him a fee for contracting a marriage (*nikāḥāna*). All the afore-mentioned people were present at the marriage which your supplicant solemnised on the basis of their testimony (*sūz*). When we asked your confidant (*maḥram*) whether we too were summoned [to Khiva], he answered: 'No!' For this reason, we did not come, but we illustrated instead the case by writing (*qalam tīlī bīla*). Otherwise, your supplicant (*duʿāgūylārī*) would not have the smallest reason to write [and indulge in] such disrespect (*mūndāgh bī-adablīk*). Peace be upon you! The paper given by Muḥammad Riżā has finished. Your supplicant cannot not find appropriate paper to write in the desert. Would you give us 20 reams (*dasta*) of paper? You know best. Or do you want [us] to write on any kind of paper which is to be found [here]? If you give us some paper, [please consider that] ʿIbādullāh Maḥram lives close to your supplicant. Lord! Lord! Lord!

Seal: Qāżī va raʾīs Maḥmūd b. Dāmullā Muḥammad Karīm

---

319 This is most probably a scribal mistake, for the intended meaning should have been formulated either as *muqirr buldīlār* or *iqrār qildīlār*.

Document 65: A Report by a *qāżī-ra'is* to Authorities in Khiva about the Outcome of a Conflict at a Local Bazaar[320]

Introduction

A local *qāżī-ra'is* informed *qāżīs* in Khiva about the outcome of a conflict over a place at a bazaar, which ended with an assault and bodily harm. At first, the defendants denied responsibility. However, after the deposition (*akhbār*) of other people, they proposed to the aggrieved party an amicable settlement (*ṣulḥ*). The latter consisted of a withdrawal of the claim in consideration of a sum of money. In his report to the agencies in Khiva, the *qāżī* emphasised that it was the defendants who took the initiative to end the conflict amicably without, that is, his direct involvement. While this document is addressed to other *qāżīs*, it is equally possible that the claimant first appealed to the royal court and that the latter instructed jurists in Khiva to deal with the case. The procedure at this point trickled down to the hearing of the *qāżī*. Most probably, judges in Khiva fulfilled the same duties of the *yasāvulbāshī* at an earlier stage in the history of Qonghrat rule over Khorezm.

Translation

Let it be known to the *qāżīs* of Islam and the respected governors that [a certain] Tājī Niyāz, a draper (*bazzāz*), filed the claim (*'arż*) that he had placed his personal possessions (*māl*) in someone's unused workshop (*dūkān*) located at the entrance of the market. A certain Khudāy Birgān and Shafī' Bābā told him to leave [the premises of] the shop. [Then] they unlawfully (*bī vajh-i shar'ī*) assaulted him and broke one tooth. Furthermore, they dislodged one other tooth and shifted two. [As a result], he came with one tooth in his hand and three wobbly teeth in his mouth. Khudāy Birgān and Shafī' Bābā denied (*inkār*) [the claim]. Three or four men came and confirmed (*akhbār qīldīlār*) that they [= the accused] assaulted [Tājī Niyāz]. [At that point,] the afore-mentioned Khudāy Birgān and Shafī' Bāy went outside. [When they came in] they expressed their willingness to reach an amicable settlement (*ṣulḥ qīlmāqchī*) by offering 5 *ṭillā* [to Tājī Niyāz] and telling him to withdraw the claim (*da'vāngnī qūy dīb*). [This is] the state of the case [and it] was submitted [to you]. You know best. The document (*khaṭ*) was written on 7 Sha'bān 1267 [06.06.1851].

Seal: Qāżī va ra'is 'Abd al-Ya'qūb[321]

320 TsGARUz, f. I-125, op. 2, d. 606, ll. 7–70b.

321 We have been unable to decipher the seal.

Document 66: A Report by a *qāżī* to the Royal Court about a Dispute over Land Ownership[322]

Introduction

This is a report about the adjudication of a conflict over landownership in Astana, which originated from a division of inheritance. During the hearing both parties produced written evidence, a situation that led the *qāżī* to require testimony from the claimant. The latter complied with the request, while the defendant did not appear before the *qāżī*. He let the jurist know, instead, that he would bring the case to the royal court in Khiva. It is interesting to note that the hearing first occurred in a *sharīʿa* court after the two parties mutually agreed to solve their case before a *qāżī*. We may infer that such an agreement was reached in order to avoid filing a lawsuit in Khiva and paying the fees entailed by the implementation of royal justice. This case also clearly shows that in the eyes of the conflicting parties, the courts presided over by *qāżī*s and the royal court in Khiva represented two alternative legal forums among which locals could choose to pursue their own interests. Equally, we should be alerted to the fact that this report attests to the existence of a judicial hierarchy according to which *qāżī*s were expected to report to the royal court, even when parties first resorted to the former.

Translation

After the fulfillment of one hundred thousand praises to our Prince, the refuge of the vicariate (*nāyibat-panāh*), the master of alchemy (*tūra-mīznīng janāb kīmyā taʾṣīrlārī*), the repository of government, the knower of subtleties (*daqīqa-shunās*) who grasps the basis of Greek philosophy (*Falāṭūn asāsī*), let it be known (*ʿarż būkīm*) that Mūʾmin Khwāja and his brothers' sons came to our office in Āstāna[323] and filed a lawsuit (*murāfaʿagha ūltūrdīlār*). Each party produced a written document (*khaṭ*). Mūʾmin Khwāja's mother entrusted to her son a document illustrating that [the land] is her property (*mulkīm dīb*). The other party possesses a document showing that [the land] is their grandfather's property. They also said that the land [in question] belongs to their grandfather who entrusted the deed to them. For this reason, I required them to provide witnesses (*guvāhgha sālīb*). And when they brought their witnesses, I was informed that Mūʾmin Khwāja had gone to the city [of Khiva] (*shahargha kītīb tūr*). This is the state of the case as it occurred before us. [But] you know best. Everything is temporary. Peace be upon you and those who follow the

322 TsGARUz, f. I-125, op. 2, d. 606, l. 8.

323 Astana is located 16 km east of Khiva, see Munis and Agahi, *Firdaws al-iqbāl: History of Khorezm*, p. 594, note 416.

right path! I am sorry; I am sorry. Furthermore, many people say that the land is Amīn Khwāja's property.

Seal: Qāżī-yi shar'-i sharīf Muḥammad Murād ustād-i karīm-i 'aṣr va khasām az ḥadd-i ziyād

Document 67: A Report by a *qāżī* to the Royal Court about an Unspecified Dispute[324]

Introduction

This document is a report that a *qāżī* sent to the royal court in Khiva. In compliance with the instructions (*nishāna*) that he had received, the jurist summoned the parties to a dispute.

Translation

Let it be known from this appellant, a man of long-standing service and of one hundred thousand weaknesses, to the office of our prince (*tūra-bīk*), his excellency, the pillar of the state, [a man] of noble dignity and exalted quality (*rafīʿ manzilat sutūda khiṣlat*), [a man] of angel-like trait (*firīshta-ṭayyinat*), the confidant of the *amīr*s and the best of lords, the defender of the poor, the supporter of the weak, a man who applies the religion of Muḥammad, the patron of the law of the Prophet, who is the cause of security and tranquillity, that a certain Burīnjuq Dūrdī was given your order whereby the conflict between the abovementioned Durdī with Muḥammad Nafas and Muḥammad Qīlich be solved by collecting the *kadkhudā*s of both parties in accordance with their customs (*ūz dastūrlārī birla*). Having accepted [your order] wholeheartedly, we sent a message from Durdī to the aforementioned Muḥammad Nafas and Muḥammad Qīlich. Muḥammad Nafas appeared, but Muḥammad Qīlich failed to do so. Perhaps, as we heard, Durdī has insulted him [Muḥammad Qīlich]. Now you know best. Lord! Lord! Lord!

Seal: Qāżī Jān Muḥammad b. Mullā Muḥammad Dūrdī

324 TsGARUz, f. I-125, op. 2, d. 606, ll. 10–10ob.

Document 68: A Report by a *qāżī* to the Royal Court about a Conflict over an Unpaid Fee and an Ensuing Case of Assault[325]

Introduction

The administrator of a charitable endowment (*vaqf*) attempted to collect rent from a tenant. The latter assaulted the administrator, who was also cursed at by the tenant's younger brother. The aggrieved party filed a claim against the two people before a judge. The *qāżī* sent someone who apprehended the tenant's younger brother and brought him before the *qāżī*. At this point, the trustee sued the young man. The local community gave testimony in favour of the claimant and the judge had the defendant punished by lashing. Later that day the tenant came before the judge and filed a claim against the administrator. The *qāżī* postponed the hearing. When the tenant appeared again before him, the former stated that the administrator's relatives had attempted to kill him and that he wanted to bring the case to the royal court in Khiva. Though the *qāżī* recommended the claimant to wait for the arrival of the administrator, the former nonetheless left for Khiva. There are two possible readings of this notification. It could be a sort of cover letter that the peasant asked the *qāżī* to write in order to provide the royal court with the necessary information to process his appeal. It may equally be that the judge took the initiative to compile this letter in order to explain to the royal court the reason why the conflict had not been solved at his court. This text clearly illustrates how the populace perceived the royal court as an alternative venue to the *sharīʿa* court.

Translation

After countless praises to the caliph of the greatest sultan, the deputy of estimable khans, beloved among the scholars and compassionate towards his subjects (*khalīfa al-sulṭān al-aʿẓam wa nāvib al-khāqān al-muḥtaram muḥibb al-ʿulamā mushfiq al-fuqarā*), our petition (*ʿarżimīz*) is [as follows]: Dāmullā Raḥmatullāh came on Friday before the prayer time and stated that a certain ʿAbd al-Raḥman had beaten him when [the former] had come to him in order [to collect a share] in wheat of the *vaqf* ['s produce]. [He also stated that ʿAbd al-Raḥman's] younger brother had cursed (*sūkdī*) [him]. After that, I dispatched a man (*kīshī*), who brought [ʿAbd al-Raḥman's] young brother [before me]. [At this point, Dāmullā Raḥmatullāh] filed a lawsuit (*murāfaʿa qīldilār*). [ʿAbd al-Raḥman's] young brother denied [the claim] (*munkir*). Subsequently, a community (*bir būlak jamāʿa*) witnessed that the cursing had indeed taken place. After that, I punished him (*taʿzīr*). As they beat [him] six times, [Dā]mullā [Raḥmatullāh] expressed satisfaction. Then, at the night prayer

---

325 TsGARUz, f. I-125, op. 2, d. 606, l .17.

(*khuftan*), the afore-mentioned ʿAbd al-Raḥman appeared [before me] and [expressed his intention] to file a lawsuit (*murāfaʿ qīlajaq būlūb*) against the afore-mentioned [Dā]mullā [Raḥmatullāh]. I told him to come the next day. He came on Saturday morning at the prayer time and stated that in the evening, on his way back, three relatives (*qarīndāsh*) of [Dā]mullā [Raḥmatullāh] attempted to kill him. [He also claimed] that the traders got him out of [his assailants] and escorted him away. ʿAbd al-Raḥman said that he wants to appeal to the Prince, His Majesty (*tūra ḥażratimīzgha ʿarżimīz bār*). I recommended first to relinquish the claim of cursing and then to go [to Khiva]. [I also suggested] ʿAbd al-Raḥman to wait for [Dā]mullā [Raḥmatullāh] to come. But prior to his arrival, ʿAbd al-Raḥman left [for Khiva] in order to appeal to you. The notification (*ʿarīża-nāma*) has been written.

Seal: Qāżī[326]

326 We have been unable to decipher the seal.

Document 69: A Report by a *qāżī* to the Royal Court about a Case of Homicide[327]

Introduction

In the vicinity of Pitnak, a judge received instructions from the royal court in Khiva to make an inquest into a case of homicide. This document is a rescript to such instructions. It does not provide any detail which may be helpful to shed light on the contours of the case. Instead, the judge informs his addressee about his having proceeded precisely according to the instructions which he had received from agencies in Khiva. He thus asked the local *kadkhudās* to verify whether a certain man witnessed the homicide. The judge's rescript explains that *kadkhudās* have established that the testimony provided by the alleged witness is unreliable by dint of his interests in the properties belonging to the departed. The document shows that the *qāżī* acted exclusively within the purview of the instructions coming from the royal court. He had no authority to initiate an inquest of his own volition.

Translation

After uttering one hundred thousand words of praise and worship, my supplication (*ʿarż būkīm*) to the highest threshold of our Majesty – may his rule prosper! – [he who is] his majesty, the caliph of the merciful, the shade of the Almighty, the personification of Alexander [the Great], the guardian of Caesar, the source of peace and well-being (*ḥażrat khalīfa al-raḥmān ẓill al-subḥān iskandar-nishān qaysar-pāsbān bāʿiṣ al-amn wa al-īmān*), is that we summoned the *kadkhudās* of Pitnak and interrogated (*sūrāshdūq*) them. Afterwards they said that the testimony of [a certain man] [who claimed] that he and his wife (*żaʿīfa*) saw [the culprit] is deceitful (*yālghān*). But he himself was deprived of his share of inheritance (*mīrāṣ*), and [thus] intended to murder [the deceased one] and take possession of his property (*mulkīgā īgā būlmāqchī*). He seems also to have forcibly seized (*bāsīb ālīb*) the deeds (*khaṭ*) belonging to the underage children (*ṣaghirlār*) of the deceased. I held an inquiry into the matter and sent [a report] to His Excellency. The *kadkhudās* would know more about the departed. But you know best, [my Lord: you are] the follower of [He who is] the eternal divine one, may your rule last forever.

Seal:[328]

327 TsGARUz, f. I-125, op. 2, d. 37, l. 1.
328 We have been unable to decipher the seal.

Document 70: A Report by *qāżīs* to the Royal Court about a Case of Homicide[329]

Introduction

The leaders of the 'Arab community sought for redress against the residents of Qara-tupe and appealed to the royal court. The agencies in Khiva instructed an attendant to deal with the case. The latter reached the locality and during the negotiations beat one of the respondents (i.e., a resident of Qara-tupe) thereby causing severe injuries. The injured man later died. The homicide triggered a new appeal to the royal court that instructed the local *qāżīs* to inspect the corpse in the presence of other liegemen and the leaders of the local community and report back. This document is the succinct report that the *qāżīs* addressed to the royal court. The examination of the corpse consisted only of verifying the presence of bodily injury. It is clear that the *qāżīs* acted in the capacity of legal advisors alone and complied with the instructions that they had received from the royal court.

Translation

Our petition (*'arż*) to our excellent lord (*janāb-i 'ālīlārī*), our Prince (*tūra-bīk*), is [as follows:] the residents (*fuqarālār*) of Qara-Tūfa[330] appealed (*'arż*) to your office (*khiẕmatīnkiz*) [and complained] that the 'Arab clan (*ṭā'ifa*)[331] escorted a man, a certain Qūtlī Murād, to our place [in the capacity of] attendant (*yasāvul*). [The latter] assaulted a certain 'Abd al-Raḥīm Ṣūfī causing bodily injury (*majrūḥ*). As a result of these blows (*żarb*), the afore-mentioned Ṣūfī has died. You had showed your mercy and instructed your supplicants (*du'āgūylār*) to send our men (*ādamimīz*) together with several *kadkhudā*s to inspect the deceased. Thus we together with the *kadkhudā*s of this locality (*mavżi'*) examined the corpse (*ūlūk*). The back showed bruises (*kūk bār īrkān*). This is all

329 TsGARUz, f. I-125, op. 2, d. 37, ll. 5–5ob.

330 Most probably this refers to Qara-tupe, a place located 2–3 km southeast Khiva, see Ivanov, *Arkhiv khivinskikh khanov XIX v.*, p. 36 and Munis and Agahi, *Firdaws al-iqbāl: History of Khorezm*, p. 591, note 405.

331 In 1873 Kuhn noted the presence of communities of 'Arab that amounted to 348 households and resided in the province of Khiva. Regardless of the fact that the majority of them took the custom and the language of the local population, they identified themselves as 'Arabs and avoided to mix with other local groups. See A. Kun, *Ocherk istorii zaseleniia Khivinskogo khanstva s drevnykh vremen, sostav ego sovremennogo naseleniia, administratsiia i goroda khanstva*, 1873, IVRRAN, St. Petersburg, Arkhiv Vostokovedov, f. 33, d. 8, ll. 17–17ob.

what your supplicants found out (*maʿlūm*). Now you know best (*ūzlārī ṣāḥib-i ikhtiyār*). Be resplendent! Peace be upon you!

Seals: Qāżī va raʾīs ʿUmar Khwāja[332]
Qāżī Raḥman Birdī[333]

332 We have been unable to decipher the seal.
333 We have been unable to decipher the seal.

Document 71: A Report by a *qāżī* to the Royal Court about a Case of Homicide[334]

Introduction

A judge sent a report to the ruler in Khiva after he had examined a homicide scene. The *qāżī* provides a cursory description of the two corpses and their clothes. He puts emphasis on the fact that the two bodies were found on the private estates of the khan on a public thoroughfare. This place was situated relatively far away from where the two individuals, who belonged to the Uzbek tribal group called Manghit, usually resided. The judge took this initiative most probably on account of the established practice that the community residing where a corpse is found should be held liable for the homicide and thus compensate the family of the deceased. The absence of blood is also noted as if the *qāżī* wanted to suggest that the two bodies had been carried there after the homicide.[335] The author gives account of the fact that the corpses were buried in the presence of official representatives of the settled and tribal communities living in the district. Apparently, the *qāżī* had seized the occasion of the burial to collect other information on the two departed, but besides the tenants inhabiting the lands belonging to the ruler, nobody had heard of the assassination. In writing to the royal court, the *qāżī* fulfils most probably the instruction to inspect the corpses and describe their belongings. He evidently complies with such a request alone thereby avoiding having to take other initiatives.

Translation

[After] innumerable and endless praises for the well-being of our Prince, let his life and throne thrive, let it be no secret that we executed Your order (*amrlārī*) to the best of our ability. One of the dead (*mayit*) was a white-bearded (*āqsaqāl-līq*) *qulchamāq* [?] [man]. The old man had two old robes (*tūn*), a Qazaq kaftan (*chakmān*), an old knife, and [a pair of] old boots. The second [dead man] was a young man with no beard (*bī-saqāl yigīt*). He had three robes: one of them was red, another was white *bālqī* [?], and [the third] was an old one. He had one white skull cap (*taqiya*), one [dark] blue hat (*shifirma*). These two corpses lie on the land of his majesty [the Khan] (*ḥaẕratimīznīng yirlārī*), on a public thoroughfare (*rāh-i ʿāmma*). No blood was found around them. Between [the place where] the corpses [lie] and Manghit people (*ahl*) there are circa 20 *ṭanāb* of land. The *kadkhudā*s of the tenants

334 TsGARUz, f. I-125, op. 2, d. 37, l. 6.

335 For another homicide case in which a similar juristic thinking is applied, see Sartori, *Visions of Justice:* Sharīʿa *and Cultural Change in Russian Central Asia*, p. 83.

(*kāranda*), those of the Qipchaq [people], those of the Arabachī,[336] and those of the Manghit came and buried [the corpses]. It seems that the Qipchaq officials (*ʿamaldārlār*) were not informed [about these homicides]. [Only] the tenants informed their own *qāżī*, while the *kadkhudā*s of Manghit did not hear anything [about the homicides].

Seal: Qāżī[337]

---

336 Bregel' writes that the Turkmen tribe Arabachi in the first half of the 19th century settled mostly on the right bank of the Amu Darya. He also suggests, however, that in the 1860s a group of Arabachi was granted some land around Uyghur. See his *Khorezmskie Turkmeny v XIX veke*, p. 36.

337 We have been unable to decipher the seal.

Document 72: A Report by a *qāżī* to the Royal Court about a Case of Homicide[338]

Introduction

A *qāżī* informs the royal court in Khiva about the case of a woman who was found dead on the bank of a canal. The leaders of the local community suspected her husband of murder. The *qāżī* thus resorted to torture and the respondent admitted responsibility for the murder. The community leaders conferred additional probative value on this confession by confirming that the culprit had a bad reputation. In reporting to the royal court the jurist asked for further instructions with regard to the culprit's detainment and his punishment. The *qāżī* referred to a pronouncement of the local community leaders who warned him that, if the culprit were left unpunished, his behavior would oblige them to leave the country for another place.

Translation

After sending myriads of praises, our plea (*ʿarż*) to the threshold of the heavens' seat, our Majesty – may his rule prosper! –, the caliph of the merciful, the shade of the Almighty, is [as follows]: someone assaulted and killed his wife (*żaʿīfa*) on the bank of the Khāṣṣa [canal].[339] He brought and left [her body] on one side of Shah-Bābā's cemetery (*mazārāt*). I gathered the *kadkhudā*s and questioned them. They said that it was her husband (*kuyāvī*)[340] who killed her. Consequently, I put the husband under torture (*qiynādūq*). He confessed (*iqrār*) that he was the one who murdered and abandoned her. Even the *kadkhudā*s avowed that this damned [murderer] is an extremely bad (*ziyāda yamān*) [type of man]. [They also warned me that,] should he avoid [the consequences] of this event (*ḥāditha-dīn qūtūlūb chīqsa*), he would force them all to move. But you know best (*ṣāḥib-i ikhtiyār*). The petition (*ʿarż-dāsht*) was written. [My Lord: you are] the follower of [He who is] the eternal divine one, may your rule last forever. Amen and [thanks be to God who is] the Lord of the universe. And another supplication is that the deceased woman had neither relatives nor anyone else.

Seal:[341]

---

338 TsGARUz, f. I-125, op. 2, d. 37, l. 7.

339 Judging from the accounts of Munis and Agahi, the Khāṣṣa canal was located in the vicinity of Hazarasp, see Munis and Agahi, *Firdaws al-iqbāl: History of Khorezm*, pp. 417, 487.

340 In contemporary usage, *kiyāv* means son-in-law.

341 We have been unable to decipher the seal.

Document 73: A Report by a *qāżī* to the Royal Court about a Case of Homicide[342]

Introduction

Agencies in Khiva received notification about the murder of a certain ʿAẓīm Bāy. Consequently, they instructed a local *qāżī* to examine the corpse and collect circumstantial evidence about the case. Together with a *yasāvul* from Khiva, the *qāżī* reached the scene of the homicide and examined the corpse in the presence of the local community. He determined the presence of bruises, but he was unable to ascertain what caused the death. In reporting to the royal court in Khiva, the *qāżī* added hearsay information, which he had collected from the locals. He referred to an earlier conflict between the family of ʿAẓīm Bāy and certain people who had caught him in the night, most probably as he was trying to break in. On that occasion, ʿAẓīm Bāy was in possession of a knife. The people disarmed him, but he escaped. It is likely that the *qāżī* thought that this information could be relevant to establish a list of suspects for the homicide case.

Translation

After fulfilling [the duty] of exalting (*ʿariża-dāsht adāsīdīn sūngra*) [our Lord], our petition to the sublime office of our prince and our plea (*ʿarż*) is that, in order to comply with your noble order (*amr-i ʿālī*) to examine the corpse (*ūlūk*) of a certain ʿAẓīm Bāy, the son of Shahrī Bīka, ascertain the presence of wounds, injuries, and [any other] signs on all parts of his body, arrange for the *janāza* prayer to be performed, oversee his burial (*dafn*), and entrust to an attendant (*yasāvul*) a report (*khaṭ qīlīb*) [to your office, we proceeded as follows:] the attendant and I reached [the place where] the corpse [was to be found], gathered all the [local] people (*ūlūgh va kichīklārīn*), and took off his clothes, and examined him. We noticed the presence of blood coming from his mouth and nose; and from his chest to the lower part of his navel as well as under his armpits there were bruises (*kūk*). The body was not broken or deformed, nor was it severely injured. We could not ascertain what had produced (*vajh*) those bruises. Besides this, a month prior to this occurrence, people who were denouncing Shahri Bika (*daʿvāgarlār*) brought an old robe, a knife, and a

342 TsGARUz, f. I-125, op. 2, d. 37, l. 9

tūzūk [?]. [They said that] they had caught ʿAẓīm Bāy in the night on the roof but he ran away leaving his knife, and a *tūzūk* [?]. This is the state of the case (*ṣūrat-i vāqiʿa*) [that] was submitted [to your consideration]. You know best. Lord! Lord! Lord!

Seal:[343]

343 We have been unable to decipher the seal.

Texts in Chaghatay

Document 1

حضرتمیز دام دولته [*][1]
جمعه نیازنینک اوکای اوغلی قوچقار صغیرنینک و آیم سین[2] بیکه
امانت تابشورولغان ایلیک طلالیق تنکه
برلان ایلیک طلالیق خط و بر آتین برماکان
وجه دین بیک جان غه دعواسی بار ایرکان محمد یوسف
یساول باشی نی نوکری محمد رحیم بای یساول برلان یکلیب [*]
نینک درکاه عالی لاریدا صاف بولسون لار یساول حقی
هر فرسخیغه تورت تنکه دیب ماه ذو الحجه نی
۲۸ نجی سیدا خط بیتلدی
۱۳۲۸ نجی یلدا
مهر: محمد یوسف یساولباشی ابن عوض نیاز محرم

[verso]

مناقلی خدای قلی
بورلاق لی قومیدین آیم سون بیکه
بنت شیر نیاز اصالتًا اوز طرفیدین وصایتًا
صغیر اوغلی قوچقار ولد محمد جان طرفیدین دعوی قیلدی بیک جان
ولد شیر نیاز مای لی جنکل لی بر آط بهاسی ایلیک طلا و ایلیک طلا نقد تنکه
اول جوابی بریب صاف قلدیم دیکانی اوچون
ایری جمعه نیاز بن رحمن بردی برلان آیم سون بیکه غه انت
بریلیب حکم ایتکان و ایلیک طلانی خطی برلان یوز طلا تنکه نی
قاضی ایشان حضوری دا برکان ماه محرم ۸ نجی
۱۳۲۸

1 The sign * refers to expressions which in the original version of the document are written outside the body of the text and are cross-referenced. Conventionally, such expressions appear at the top of the document; thus we have placed them at the beginning of the text.

2 This is a textual variation of آیم‌سون, see below *verso* side.

© KONINKLIJKE BRILL NV, LEIDEN, 2020 | DOI:10.1163/9789004427907_007

Document 2

حضرتمیز دام دولته[*]
محمد صفانینک قیزی سعادت بیکه نی خدای بیرکان اوغلی
خالمرادغه فاتحه خواند ایتب قلینک پولیدین اوتوز طلا بیریب
قالغان تویانه لوازم و قلینک پولین تولدوروب بیریب آلمای
و یا جوابین بیرمای تورت ییل بویان خبرلاشمای یورکانی
وجهیدین آلارغه دعواسی بار ایرکان سلطان یوزباشی
یساول بیله یکلیب[*] نینک درکاه عالی لاریدا صاف
بولسونلار داغی هر فرسخیغه ایکی تنکه دین زیاده یساول حقی
برماسون لار دیب ماه شوال نینک
توقوزلانجی‌سی سه شنبه کونی خط
بیتلدی ۱۲۳۸
مهر: شیخ نضر یساولباشی ابن محمد مراد دیوان بیکی

[verso]

مناق دا ایش نیاز باجبان قومیدین
محمد صفا بن یعقوب بای نی قیزی سعادت بیکه نی
مذکور قوم دین خدای بیرکان بن عوز محمدنی اوغلی خالمرادغه بارغان سونکرا
طوی ایتب برماک بولغان قالینک مالی نی الیب بولغان ایمدی توزوک لباس لاری بیله
طویانه لارین برور دیب مذکور محمد صفا بیله خدای بیرکان نی
اقراری یازیلدی شاهدی یساولی و هم کدای نیاز بابا بن حمیت نیاز

Document 3

حضرتمیز دام دولته [*]
مروّج شریعت نبوی قاضی عسکر ایشانمیزنینک معلوم لاری بولغایکیم
قوشکوفروک سلطانمرادنینک برکشیده یتی یاریم طناب یری
عبد الرحیم محرم نینک یری برلان دعوالی بولوب عرض ایتکان اوچون
محمد یوسف یساولباشی نینک نوکری حسن یساول نینک
یانیغه بیر معتبر امین بیرسونلارکیم مذکور امین باریب آلارنینک
قولیداغی خط لارین کوروب دعوالی یرلارین شریعت بیرلان
حدود اربعه لارین معلوم قیلیب چاک ارالارین آیریب
بیرماک کا دیب [*] نینک امر عالی لاری برلان ماه شوال نینک
۱۳ لانجی سیدا ۱۳۲۸ لانجی یلدا مرقوم بولدی
مهر: شیخ نصر یساولباشی ابن محمد مراد دیوان بیکی

[verso]

اوز حدیمیزدا توردوق دیب معلوم قیلدی لار امین
لاری برلان دیب ماه شوال ۱۷ نجی سیدا ۱۳۲۸
قاضی دین قوشولغان امین ملا تاجی

Document 4

حضرتمیز دام دولته [*] ابراهیم نینک قالینک فولی و لباس و توزوک لارین بریب بولغان فاتحه خواندی خدیجه بیکه نی نکاح ایتب برماکان لاری وجهیدین اوراض محمد برلان رمضان لارغه دعواسی بار ایرکان شیخ نظر یساولباشی نینک نوکری محمد جان یساول برلان کلیب [*] نینک درکاه عالی لاریدا صاف بولسون لار یساول حقی هر فرسخ غه تورت تنکه دیب ماه ذو الحجه نی ۲۳ نجی سیدا خط بتلدی ۱۳۲۸ نجی یلدا

مهر: محمد یوسف یساولباشی ابن عوض نیاز محرم

[verso]

ماه محرم نینک یتی سیدا ابراهیم بن قاسم خدیجه بیکه تازه بازارلی بن[3] اوراض غه مذکور بولغان دعواسین شریعت دا برکان فولیکه یتمش طلا قای تیب آلماقغه خط الیب صاف بولوب ابراء خط آلوشغان مذکور فول نی مدتی بر آی زرکفیلی اتاسی اوراض محمد بن طالب تورور دیب بو خط مرقوم بولدی ۱۳۲۸

3 sic; clearly should be بنت.

Document 5

حضرتمیز دام دولته [*]
مایلی جنکل لی اوراضبای نینک خیوه قلعه لی ایشمراد دیکان دین
خطلی ایکی یوز طلا قرضی بار بولوب شول دراک دین مایلی جنکل لی
محمد یوسف غه ایلیک طلاغه بهالاب بر آط برکان مذکور
قرضی غه برماک چی بولوب ینه اوتوز طلا مذکور ایشمرادغه بریب
مذکور برکان لاری نی حساب ایتمای خطلی ایکی یوز طلانی آلغانی
وجهیدین مذکور آدم لارغه دعوی سی بار سبب لی بهادر بای
ایشیک آقاسی نی نوکری رحمنقلی یساول بیله موندا درکاه
عالی لاریغه کیلیب صاف لاشسون لار داغی یساول غه
فرسخی غه تورت تنکه یساول حقی برسون دیب [*] نینک
امر عالی لاری بیله ۱۷ نجی ماه ذی الحجه دا
خط بیتلدی ۱۳۲۸ نجی یلدا
مهر: شیخ نضر یساولباشی ابن محمد مراد دیوان بیکی

[verso]

اوشبو دعوی نی شریعت غه قوشولوب
ایلیک طلا بهالیق آت درکیدن محمد یوسف غه
آنت برکان و مذکور ایشمرادغه اوتوز طلا
دعوی سین شریعت دا اشیتلمای صاف بولوب
خط لاشیب درکاه عالی لاریغه معلوم قیلیب
چیقدی ذو الحجه ۲۲ نجی
۱۳۲۸

Document 6

حضرتمیز دام دولته [*] خدایار برلان بیشطناب یرنی شریک بولوب آلیب آنینک قرضیغه بیریشمای یرنی بولوب آلماقچی بولغان لاری وجهیدین برادرلاری اسکندر و عبد الله و ملا مبردی دیکانلارغه دعواسی بار ایرکان دهلیز محرمی محمد رحیم یساول بیرلان یکلیب [*] نینک درکاه عالی لاری دا صاف بولسونلار داغی یساول حقی هر فرسخ غه ایکی تنکه دیب ماه شوال نینک ۷ لانچی سیدا اوشبو خط مرقوم بولدی ۱۳۲۸ لانچی یلدا

مهر: محمد یوسف یساولباشی ابن عوض نیاز محرم

[verso]

شیرشالی لی ملا خدایار حافق داغی خدایارنینک
مذکور ایتکان دعواسی ایلاتیدا یراشیب همراه یکلیب یری اوزیدا
توراتورغان بولوب صافلاشیب کیتدیلار عبدالله اشیک آقاسی یساولی بیرلان
یکلیب معلوم ایتدی

Document 7

حضرتمیز دام دولته [*]
آتا جان آقسقال اوراض ینه دیکر آتا جان لارغه سوز اولکیم
محمد سفا بیله خدای برکان و ایریس کل بیکه لارنینک
دعوی لارین اصل واقعه لارین تحقیقلاب سوراشیلماق
وجهیدین و ینه مذکورلارنینک قونکرات حاکمی دین اورکنج
حاکمی غه اوشبو دعوی حقیدا آلیب کیلکان خط نی آلیب
کیلماک اوچون دهلیز محرمی عالیم[4] بای یوزباشی نینک یباریلدی
ایمدی خط کورکاچ مذکور آدم لار مذکور یساول بیله موندا
درکاه عالی لاریغه کیلیب بیان واقعه لارین
آیتسون لار دیب [*] نینک امر عالی لاری بیله
۱۷ نجی ماه شوال دا خط بیتلدی
۱۳۲۸ نجی یلدا
مهر: شیخ نضر یساولباشی ابن محمد مراد دیوان بیکی

[verso]
شوال ۲۲
بو خط هم یساول لی پتک غه داخل واقعه سینی آنکه یازیلدی

4 Textual variation of عالم.

Document 8

حضرتمیز دام دولته [*]
سرشالی لی محمد یعقوب نی قاین آتاسی ایش نیاز اولوب آندین تخمیناً اوچ یاریم طناب
یر
و بیر حولی قالیب آنی قرض لاری اوچون ساتیلیب شول یرنی اوزی ایکی یوز طلا
زیاد بیریب آلماقچی بولغانیدا بیرمای مذکور متوفانی ورثه لاری نی نارضا ایتکانی
وجه دین محمد رحیم دیکان غه دعواسی بار ایرکان یساول باشی نی نوکری
خواجه نیاز ده باشی یساول بیرلان کیلیب [*] نینک درکاه عالی لاری دا
صاف بولسون داغی یساول حق[5] اوچون هر فرسخی غه
ایکی تنکه دین زیاد بیرماسون دیب ماه ذی القعده نی ۱۳ نجی سیدا
خط بتیلدی
۱۳۳۶ نجی ییلدا
مهر: محمد یعقوب یساولباشی ابن محمد یوسف یساولباشی

[verso]

مذکور محمد یعقوب یر برلان حولی نی
مهتر آقالارنی حضوری و باشقه
کنه لارنی یانی دا بیر مینک بیشیوز طلاغه
ساتغون آلیب قاضی کلان ایشان
هزاراسب قاضی لاری غه فتک بریب صافلاسون
دیب ۱۹ لانجی ماه ذی القعدا[6] دا بتلدی ۱۳۳۶

5 sic.
6 Textual variation of ذی القعده.

Document 9

حضرتمیز دام دولته [*] بیش آریقلی قیلچ نیازغه یتی یاریم طناب یرنی مینک طلاغه ساتیب سونکرا پشیمان ایتب دعوالاشیب شریعت بیرلان دعواسی نادرست بولوب ینه آنکا دعوا قیلاتورغان لاری وجه دن اسکندر و آیخانیم بیکه دیکان لارغه دعواسی بار ایرکان یساولباشی نی نوکری جان بک سرهنک یساول بیرلان کیلیب [*] نینک درکاه عالی لاری دا صاف بولسون لار داغی یساول حق[7] هر فرسخغه ایکی تنکه دیب ۷ نجی ماه ربیع الثانی دا خط بیتلدی ۱۳۳۶

مهر: محمد یعقوب یساولباشی ابن محمد یوسف یساولباشی

[verso]

مذکور قیلچ نیازنی دعواسی شرایت[8] غه قوشولوب مسئله آلیب
و هم حکم خط بریلیب یر اوزی نکی بولوب مدعا علیه لارنی
دعواسی نادرست بولغان دیب ۸ لانجی ماه ربیع الثانی دا
۱۳۳۶

7 sic.

8 Textual variation of شریعت.

Document 10

حضرتميز دام دولته [*]
روزيم بوى لى جمعه نيازنى خطلى بيش طناب يريغه
خط چيقاريب بى وجه دعوا ايتيب يوركانلارى
وجه دين قربان نياز بيله خداى بيركانلارغه دعواسى
بار ايركان محرم خانه چى محمد رضا يساول بيله
كيلب [*] نينك دركاه عالى لاريدا صاف
بولسون لار داغى يساول حقى هر فرسخيغه
ايكى تنكه برسون ديب ٢٤ نجى
ربع الاولدا خط بيتلدى ١٣٣٥
مهر: محمد يوسف يساولباشى ابن عوض نياز محرم

[verso]

مذكور مدعى روزيم بويلي مسجد بالتاق ميراب دا
جمعه نياز بن عوض نياز بيله مذكور قوملى خداى بركان و قربان نياز
بنون ايشمرادلارنى شريعت غه بويورولوب قاضى عسكر ايشان دا مرافعه لاشيب
مذكور بيشطناب ير جمعه نيازنيكى بولوب مدعى عليه لارنى دعوى لارى فاسد
بولوب
خط ابراءلاشيب صاف لاشديلار ديب ٢٩ نجى ماه ربيع الاولدا ١٣٣٥

Document 11

حضرتمیز دام دولته [*]
شریعت شعار دیانت آثار قاضی ایشانیمیزغه اعلام اولکیم
کندومکانلی روز محمد آقسقال و جمعه نیازلار عرض قیلدیلارکیم
چرکس کولی نی لبیدا مسجدنی وقفی دا نامعلوم بر یاش یکیت ملانی اولتوروب
دورلار اولوکی یاتیب دور دیب شول سبب لی بر معتبر آدم لارینی
یساولباشی نوکری قلندر دهباشینی یانیغه قوشسونلارکیم آلار
همراه باریب مذکور آقسقال کدخدالاری بیله مذکور
اولوک نی جسدلارین احتیاط لاب کوروب نی طریقه دا
اولتوروب دورلار شولارنی دقت لاب بیلیب خط
ایتب دفن ایتلماکی غه جواب بریب واقعه سینی
موندا دربار عالی لاریغه کیلب آیتسون لار دیب [*] نینک
امر عالی لاری بیله ۱۷ نجی ماه شعبان دا
خط بیتلدی ۱۳۳۶ نجی ییلدا
مهر: محمد یعقوب ابن محمد یوسف یساولباشی

[verso]

مذکور اولوک نی قاضی ایشان نی آدمی محمد شریف خواجه
برلان قلندر ده باشی کوروب دورلار طاهر قزاق نی
آختوقی بابا جان ایرکان خوستاری صابر بای نی اوزی آیدیکیم مذکور بابا جان
اوزی خیالات لی راق ایردی اوز اجلی غه اولوب دور جراحت
یوق ایرکان هیچ کیم غه دعوالاریمیز یوق دیب معلوم ایتدی لار ۱۸ لا نجی
ماه شعبان دا ۱۳۳۶

Document 12

سعادت پناه و حکومت دستگاه یساول باشی آقامیزنینک جناب عالی لاریغه عرض و اخلاصمیز بوکیم بومیر بلی قربان بای دیکان عرض ایتب محمد یوسف یساول باشی آقامیزنینک نوکری محمد یوسف کاکل بی نی یساول قیلب نکاحلی خاتونیم مسماة ارض کل بیکه نی آتاسی خدای برکان دیکان زورلیق قیلب برمایدور دیکان عرضی بیله و خدای برکان مذکورهم عرض ایتب محمد عالیم[9] بای یوز باشی نی عرض ایتب محمد جان و بردیمراد و قربان بای و خالجان بیکه لارغه عالیم[10] بای یوزباشی مذکورنی یساول قیلب مذکور آدملار همه لاری راضی لیق غه کیلش دیلار و مذکور آدملار نینک عاجز و بیچاره بولغانلیقی وجهیدین خذمتلاریغه ارسال قیلندی ماه شوال نینک سکزیده خط بتلدی صاحب اختیار اوزلاری توررلار

مهر: قاضی و رئیس داملا عبدالله[※]

قاضی و رئیس داملا الله برکان[※]

9 sic.

10 sic.

Document 13

وزير الكرام يساولباشى آقامزنينك خدمتلاريغه معروض اولكم تاشحوضلى محمد يوسف عرض قيلدى قونكراتلى محمد يعقوب باى ديكان غه آمانت تافشوروب قويغان بر مينك بر يوز مناتم بار بولوب سوراغانمده بيرماى منكر بولوب سونكره حاكم آقابيله كدخدالارغه معلوم قيلب ايرديم بيشيوز ايليک مناتم نى بيريب قالغان حقيم نى بيرمايدور ديب ايمدى شونى سوراشيب محمد يعقوب غه بر مينک بر يوز منات تافشوروب بيشيوز ايليک مناتين بيريب قالغان حقين بيرما كانى راست بولسه قالغان حقين آليب بيريب رضالاشتورسون ديب محربان[11] بولغان ايركان لار شونى سوراشيب كوردوک بر مينک بر يوز منات محمد يعقوب غه تافشوريب قويب ايرديم سوراسام بيرمايدور ديب محمد يوسوف نى ايتكان دعواسيغه محمد يعقوب منكا تنكه تافشورغانينک يوق ديب منكر بولغان

[verso]

بولغانيدين سونكره قاضى ايشان لارغه قوشولغان ايركان سونكره بى لار و قلعه كاسب لارى همه اتفاق بيله ايكى لارين آنت لاشتورماى بيشيوز ايليک منات غه اصلا ايتب محمد يعقوب دين محمد يوسف باى غه بيش يوز ايليک منات آليب بيريب قاضى ايشان لار حضورلاريده ابراء خط لاشتورغان ايركان لار خدمت لاريغه معلوم قيلورمز نه محربان[12] بولسه لار صاحب اختياردور لار ديب اوشبو عريضه ١٣٣٥ ماه ربيع الثانى نينک ترتلانجى سيده يبتلدى

١٣٣٥ لانجى سيده ٤ لانجى ماه ربيع الثانيده

مهر: بهادر محرم يوزباشى

---

11 Textual variation of مهربان.

12 sic.

Document 14

عزت نشان یساول باشی آقانینک معلوم لاری بولسونکیم قرق یافلی
آتابای دیکان خذمت لاریغه عرض ایتوب بیکجان دیکان قزیم نی فاتحه
ایتوب بیر یوز اوتوز منات بریب باشقه لوازیم لارین ایتمای نکاح
ایتماکچی تورور دیب یساول کیلتورکان ایرکان شول سببلی موندا
ایل آقسقال کتخدالارنی[13] اتفاقی بیله باقی قالغان قالینکینی و
توی لوازیم لارین بتمام آلیب بریب اوز رضالیقی ببله
توی ایتوب برماکچی بولوب رضالاشدوریلدی اوشبونی
معلوم قیلورمیز دیب ۲٤ ماه صفرده
خط بتلدی ۱۳۳٤ نجی یلده
مهر: محمد یعقوب بای ابن [جبار قلی محرم]

13 Textual variation of کدخدا.

Document 15

عزت نشان یساول باشی آقانی معلوم لاری بولغایکیم تمه لی
عبد الصمد خواجه ننک دعواکرلاری طمعه پهلوان و محمد شریف
و ایکام برکان دیکان لارنی مونده حضوریده بولغان
واقعه لاری بیله یازوب یبارسون دیب مهربان بولغان ایرکانسز
مذکور تورت آدم نی دانوب قالدیم دیب کیلتورب ایردی
مذکورلارنی واقعه لارنی سورالماقمز اوچون کدخدالارنی
حضوریده سوراتیب اولتورغانمزده نایمانلی عبد رحمان
آقسقال دیکان کیلب آیدی اقشام بزلارنی ایلات
مزده هم بر اویی غه توشیب نمرسه لارنی الغان شول
لار ایرکان بول لارنی دانوب قالغان ایرکان لار

[verso]

دیب آیغان حالی ده مذکورلارنی کدخدا آقسقال لاری
ی[14] بول لارنی باشقه سوزلاری هم کوب تورور دیب
ایلات غه باروب همه نی جمعلاب یخشی احتیاط
ایتب بارلاشیب کیلتورورمیز دیب آلیب
کتیب ایردی لار شول لارنی ایچنده نفس دیکان
باروب عرض ایتیب یورکان یالغان سوزلاب
مذکور نفس دیکان ننک کفیل بولغان آدم لاری هم
مونده اویده ایردی مذکورلارنی واقعه سی
شول ایردی صاحب اختیار اوزلاری دیب
ماه جمادی الثانی ده بو خط بیتلدی
۱۳۳۴ لانچی یلده
مهر: محمد یوسف بای ابن پهلوان محرم

14 sic.

Document 16

وزارات پناه حکومت دستکاه یساولباشی آقامیزنینک خذمتلاریغه معروض اولکم اوشبو ماه
ماه[15] ربیع الاولده نیاز بیکه دیکان کنفر کیلیب معلوم قیلدی قیزیم سعادت بیکه نی ایری
یخشمرات دیکان اوروب مجرو[16] ایتب قاچیب کتدی دیب شول توغریده شریعت شعار
کورلان قاضی ایشان لاریدین بیر امین آلیب ایل کدخدالاری نی یغناب آلارهم
امین بیله مذکور ناچارنی کوروب کدخدالاری بیله کیلیب صورات[17] واقعه نی معلوم
قیلیب ایردی لار ایمدی لیکدا مذکور یخشمرات دیکان نکاحلی خاتونوم آتاسینی اویغه
کتیب ایردی اکاسی منکا قوشوب یبارمایدور دیب عرض ایتکان سببلی شول عرضی
راست بولسه خاتونین ایریغه قوشسون باشقه سوزی بولسه شریعت بیله بیتکارسون بولماسه
موندا قوشوب یبارسون دیکان بویروق عالی لاریغه موافیق[18] آلارنی موندا یرا
شتورولماقچی بولغاندا مذکور یخشمرات نی تلیدان یانیغه آلیب بارغان قوشکوفریکلی
محمد صفا دیکانلار مذکور ناچارنی خیواغه قوشوب یبارماک نی طلب ایتکان لاری
سببلی آقسقالی خالمرات غه قوشوب جنابنکیزغه یباریلدی اوشبو بیان بولغان لارنی
معلوم ایتسانکز ایرکان دیکان نیاز بیکه کنفرنی التماسیغه کورا تیاق یکان ناچارنی
کورکان امین لارنی بیان ایتکان لارینی ازبرای جنابنکیزغه معلوم قیلیب
ماه ربیع الاولده عریضه اخلاص مرقوم بولدی ۱۳۳۵ نچی یلي

مهر: [※]

15 Repeated word.
16 Textual variation of مجروح.
17 Textual variation of صورت.
18 Textual variation of موافق.

Document 17

وزارت فناه[19] نجابت دستکا محمد محرم یسولباشی اقانینک معلوملاری بولغایکیم چاتکوفروکلی محمد یعقوب دیکان درکاهی عالی لاریغه باریب مینینک سو یولومدین سو برمای باباجان و صابر و دوندی بیکه وکریم برکان و قلندر دیکان و سعادت بیکه دیکان لار آقام بیله ایکیمیزنی اوردیلار دیب عرضه ایتیب عبد الستار سیس نینک نوکری محمد شریف نی یساول ایتیب آلیب کیلکان ایرکان یمدی مذکور لارنی اهل ایلات بولوب بیزنینک حضوریمیزده یراشدیلار اوشبونی خدمتلاریغه معلوم ایتامیز دیب

٢٧نچی ماه رجبده خط بیتلدی

١٣٣۵

مهر: الله برکان بای ابن عوض نیاز محرم

---

19 Textual variation of پناه.

Document 18

وزارت فناه[20] یساولباشی آغامیزنینک خذمت لاریغه معلوم لاری بولسونکم مناقلی باباجان و عبدکریم لار قوشبیکی یاف نینک آیاقچی آبخوری دورمیز یوقاری سیده الله بیرکان میرشب و نواذا میراب باشلغی دا یکیرمه سو اکی یلدین بری ایاقدین توشوب قازوشمایدور قدیم دین تعامل آیاقیدین توشوب همه آبخوری سقه سیغه چه قازوشماق ایردی دیب مذکورلارنی سوراشب قدیمدین تعامل برلان تینکلاشتوروب قازدوروب برسون و اکر باشقه دعوالاری بولسه شریعت برلان تنکلاشتورسونلار دیکان بویروق لاریغه موافق مذکورلارنی شریعت لاشتوروب ایردوک شریعت شعار مناق قاضی ایشانلاری ارضه کویغه کواه بویروب تورورلار ارضه کوی کواه اوتکارماکچی بولغانده خیواغه بارورمن دیب الله برکان میرشب لار جواب آیتیب تورورلار اوشبونی معلوم قیلورمیز دیب

۲۲نچی ماه جمادی الاولده ساغ سلامت لیک لارین تیلاب خط بتلدی ۱۳۳۵

مهر: محمد یعقوب بای ابن جبار قلی محرم ۱۳۳۴

20 sic.

Document 19

وزیر اعظم دستور المکرم اَعنی یساول باشی آقه میزنینک جناب عالی لاریغه معروض بوکه اسکندر محرم برلان یباریلکان نشانهٔ عالی لاری مضمونی برله باریب کوردوک محمد نیاز بن بیکمرادنینک و عبد الکریم اوغلی جمعه نیازنینک یری نینک کونباتر طرفیده مذکور محمد نیازنینک ارابه[21] یولوسی بار و چقر سو یولوسی یوق ایرکان و ینه مسجد قومی نینک قریه آدملارینی چاقورتوب تحقیق لاب سورادوق آلار هم آیدیلار محمد نیاز مذکورنینک ارابه[22] یولوسی بار تورور چقر سو یولوسی یوق تورور دیب مذکور یول نینک ایکی طرفیده هم عبد الکریم مذکور نینک قایمه بولوب تورغان یغاچلاری بار تورور اوتکوچی لارنینک یغاچ مذکورغه ضرری یوق تورور دیب حجت نامه مرقوم بولدی ۱۳۲۸

مهر: قاضی و رئیس یارمیش داملا محمد یوسف [※]

قاضی و رئیس یارمیش داملا عبد الغفور [※]

قاضی و رئیس یارمیش داملا بابا جان مخذوم [※]

21 Textual variation of عرابه.

22 sic.

Document 20

وزارة پناه حکومت دستگاه یساول باشی آقانیتک
خدمت لاری غه معروض اولکیم قراداشلی قربان دوردی دیکان
دربار عالی لاری غه عرض ایتب نیشانه یکلتوردی قیزیم
بایرام سلطان نینک کیوی مرت نینک شریعت
ایشی کا یاراماغان سببلی مذکور قیزیم نی آیرماقچی بولغانیم دا
مذکور قیزیم نی آرتوق نیاز و اوراض نیاز و ملاه جمعه
و عاشیر و خواجمبیردی لار اوروب ساچی نی یولوب اعضالارین
جراحت دار ایتب منکا خوارلیق بیردی لار دیب

[verso]

شولوجهیدین مذکورلارنی دعواسینی شریعت بیرله سوراشیلدی
اخیری یتوشماکان دین کین شریعت غه قوشوب یبارکانمیزده
کیو طرفی شریعت غه بارغانده درکاه عالی غه بارورمن
دیکان سببلی مذکورلارنی خدمتلاریغه قتو قوشوب
یباریلدی دیب ۱۹ نجی ماه ذی الحیجه دا اوشبو عریضه
مرقوم بولدی ۱۳۳٤ نجی یلده
مهر: محمد کریم یوزباشی ابن اسماعیل

Document 21

وزارت پناه حکومت دستکاه یساویل[23] باشی آقامیزغه معلوم و هویدا بولغایکم محمد کریم یوزباشینی آدمی صالح دیکان دربار عالیلاریغه عرض قیلب ملا غایب قاضیدا آلتی یوز منات بر یاریم باتمن بورونج حقیم بار و ینه ملا بکجاندا سکز بوت اون بش قدق شکریم بار و ینه اوستا قربانیاز ده سکسان منات بر چفانیم بار و ینه عبادالله دیکاندا تورت یوز منات بر عربه م[24] بار دیب فتک آلیب کیلب اوشبو فتک مضمو نیدین آگاه بولیب مذکور آدملارنی چاقریب سوراغانمیزده مذکور اوستا قربانیاز اقرار بولیب بردی و ینه عبادالله دیکان هم منده ایکی یوز قرق منات حقی بار باشقه حقی یوقدیب اقرار بولدی اوشبو اکی یوز قرق منات نی آلیب بریب باشقه دعوی سین ایل کدخدا آقسقاللاری قویدو ردیلار ملا بکجان دیکان اقرار بولماغان سببلی شریعت غه قوشدوق شریعت بیله صالح دیکان کواهغه توشیب ملا بکجان آنت غه کیلب دور آندین سونک قاضی ایشان آیتب تورورلار من سیزلارنی مرافیعه[25] نکزنی سورامایمن تورکیت دیبدور مذکور ملا بکجان بیله صالح کیلب قاضی ایشان بزلارغه شونداغ دیدیلار دیکان سببلی قاضی ایشان نی چاقریب نه اوچون مونداغ دیرسیز دیکاندا جوابیدا آیته دور اوشبو صالح دیکان نی منینک بیلان هم دعوی سی بار من خیوه[26] بارورمن ملا بکجان هم بارسون دیر بز هرچند تولّا قیلدوق فقرا اوزی خیوه نی

---

23 Textual variation of یساول.

24 Textual variation of عرابه with the first-person singular possessive suffixe م.

25 Textual variation of مرافعة.

26 Suffix غه is clearly missed here.

طلب قیلماسه ایکی یوز منات باریب کیلکونچه خرج بولور و ینه شریعت فرمایشی بیله صاف بولسون دیکان مهربانچلق لاری هم بار دیسک اوشبو صالح غه اوزینک آیتب منی اوستمکا فتک آلیب کیلب دور دیب توریب کیتی

[verso]

اوشبو واقعه سببلی مذکور ملا بکجان بیله قاضی ایشان نی خذمت با شرافت لاریغه قوشدوق دیب یکرمه یتی لانچی ماه رمضاندا صورت واقعه مرقوم بولدی ۱۳۳۶

مهر: خواجه نیاز بای ابن عبدالله محرم۱۳۳۵

Document 22

وزارت پنا[27] حکومت دستکا[28] یساولباشی آقانینک معلوم لاری بولغایکیم قره تالیلی جماغه لاریدین باشلوغ جمعه مراد و آدینه مرادلارنینک

محمد اورض غه ساتغان بیش طناب یری قل محمد ایشان نینک مسجدیغه واقف[29] ایتکان یکرمه طناب موقوفه غه داخل مو و یا

موقوفه دین تشقاری مو شولارنی مذکور یرلارنی اوستیغه باریب قاریه لارینی جمع ایتب سوراشیب بیان واقعه لارینی

مونده معلوم ایتسونلار دیکان بویروق لاریغه موافیق[30] مذکور یرنینک اوستیغه باریب تابعی مذکورنی قاریه لارینی جمع ایتب

واقف[31] ایتکان یکرمه طناب یرلاری نینک جمه کثیرلار بیله کورکانمیزده حدودی آربعه لاری واقف نامه[32] غه موافق کیلدی

لیکین واقف[33] مذکورنینک ایچیندین بر اولوغ تازه یارغان دیکان یاف اوتار ایرکان اول یاف نی ذکری واقف نامه[34] ده

بیان ایتولمایدور ۲ نچی بیش طناب یرنی ملکیم دیب ساتغان آدم لاردین باشقه قاریه بولغان خدای برکان دارغه ولد

صفر نیاز و محمد پناه دارغه ولد احمد و سید نیاز ولد صفر نیاز دیکر و جمعه نیاز ولد ظایمراد و الله برکان دارغه ولد قوتلوقمراد

و خالمراد ولد سیتک و پهلوان نیاز ولد اتانیاز و خالمراد ولد قوشمان و خدای برکان دیکر ولد خال محمد و خالمراد ولد محمد علی

دیکانلاردین مذکور بیش طناب یر مسجید مذکورنینک موقوفه سیغه داخل مو و یا تاشقاری مو دیب سوراغانیمیزده مذکور بیش طناب یر

---

27 Textual variation of پناه.

28 Textual variation of دستگاه.

29 Textual variation of وقف.

30 Textual variation of موافق.

31 sic.

32 Textual variation of وقف‌نامه.

33 sic.

34 sic.

ساتغان آدملارنی حقی و ملکی دور واقف[35] غه داخل ایرماسدور دیکانلاری توغرینده آلارنینک اوز حقی ملکی ایرکان لیکی غه

قول لاریده حجت خطی یاکه پادشاهلیق دین آلغان یارلیق عالی لاری بارمو دیکانیمیز ده تابه مذکورنینک بر یکی مرتبه سوآلیب

خراب بولغان سببلی قره تال جماعه لارینی ملکی داغی آنینک دیک حجت جط لاری شول آندا یوق بولوب کیتکاندور مذکور واقف[36]

یرلاریده هم واقف نامه[37] دین باشقه حجت خطی یوقدور اوّلدین متصرف بولوب اولتورغان ملک لاری دور واکر ساتیلغان

بیش طناب یر واقف[38] بولغان یرنینک ایچینده داخل بولوب واقف[39] ایرکان لیکی نینک آیتماساق بو دنیا و اخرتده ضمانی

بزلارنینک ذمه لاریمیزغه بولسون دیب و جمع کثیرلارنی حضوریده اخبار و شهادت برکانلاری سببلی صورات واقعه نی

جناب لاریغه معلوم قلدوق ایمدی صاحب اختیار اوزلاری بیلورلار دیب ۱۳۳۵ نچی یلي ۱۶ نچی ماه ربع الثانی آیده خط بتلدی

مهر: عبد الرحیم بای [※]

قاضی و رئیس [※] محمد قربان [※]

قاضی کورلان داملا بابا جان [※]

قاضی کورلان داملا محمد یعقوب [※]

قاضی کورلان محمد کریم خواخه [※]

قاضی کورلان داملا اوراض محمد [※]

---

35 sic.
36 sic.
37 sic.
38 sic.
39 sic.

Document 23

وزارت فناه[40] حکومت دستگاه یساول باشی اقامیزنی خذمتلاریغه معلوم بولغایکم شاه اباد

موضعیداغی ملا یوسف اقسقال نینک قومیداغی حق محمد بیله شریف دیکانلار اوروشوب مذکور

شریف اولکان سبب لی الارنینک دعوالارینی سوراشیب شول طرفده شریعت فرمایشی بیله

سافلاشتوروب آخیرین مونده بیلدورسون دیکان بویروغلاری نینک توغروسیده مذکور اولکان

شریف نینک ورثه لارینی چاقریب سورالدی مذکور شریف نی اوغلی جمعه نیاز و خاتونی مسماة قربان بیکه

و برادرلاری رجب بای و ملا ایشبای دیکانلاردین مذکور ورثه لاری آیدیلار شریف مذکور وقت

موتیدین اوچ کون اوّل اوروشوب ایردی اندین هم اوّل کسل ایردی بزلارنینک حق محمد

دیکانغه دعوامیزنی اوتدوک دیب اقرار قلیب کیتدیلار اندین سونکره مذکور شریف نی

اوغلی جمعه نیاز دیکان نی اوز طرفیدین اصل ایتب اناسی قربان بیکه مذکوره نی طرفیدین وکیل بولوب

کواهلاری مذکور یوسف اقسقال و رجب بای لارنینک شهادتی بیله الارنی موت اوتکانین شاه اباد

قاضی ایشانلارین خط لاشتوروب مذکورلارنینک دعوالارین اوتوب خط لاشغانین خذمتلاریغه

۱۳۳۶نجی یلده ماه شعبان نینک یکرمه یتی سیده صورة واقعه نی بیتب یباریلدی

مهر: محمد صفا آتالیق ابن عبدالله آتالیق

40 sic.

Document 24

وزارت پناه یساولباشی آقانینک معلوم لاری بولسونکیم هزاراسب لی ملا دوست وتاجی بای دیکان نوکرلار باریب

حاکم بزلاردین یراغ فولی سوراب و هم بی یمش خدمت بویوروب یموت لارنی خراجاتی اوچون اون مناط

فول لاریمیزدین کوفراق آلدی دیب عرض ایتکان سببلی عرضکوی لارغه دخل ایتماسون موندین مقدام[41] سنکا

اوج تورت مرتبه فتک یباریلدی عمل ایتمای سن ایمدی موندین سونکره بو طریقه ایتسانک سنی حاکم لیکدین

چقاریلادور دیب ۱۳ نچی جمادی الثانی دا یازغان بویروق لاری برابریدا عرضیمز بوکم یراغ توغریسیده

کیلکان بویروق لارنی بای لار و آقسقال لارنی یغناب اعلام ایکانیمزدا آلار سوزغه[42] سالیب یراغ

خذمتلارینی اورون غه کیلتورماک نی اتفاق ایکان لارینی محمد رحیم بای بیله جناب همایون لاریغه

معلوم ایتوب ایردوک انینک بعدیندا ینه قدارتلی آدام لاردین ایتماقغه بویرق بولیب آنی هم بای آقسقال

آقسقال[43] لارغه اعلام ایتکانیمیزدین سونک هر مسجد قومی نینک آقسقالی قدارتلی دیکان آدام لارینی آد به آد دفتر

ایتب ۲۲ نچی جمادی الثانی دا تافشوردی لار بیزداغی شول دفترلارینی جناب لاریغه یباریب شول دفترداغی فولنی

اوندوروب آلسون دیب بویروق بولغاندین سونک یراغ فولی نی اوندوبوب برینک دیب آقسقال لارغه

41 Textual variation of مقدم.

42 In text: سوغه.

43 Reapeted word.

بویوردوق شول آنغه چه نوکرلاردین و غریب فقرادین یراغ فولی سورالغانی یوق عرضکوی لارنی آلغان

فتک لاریدین هم خبریمیز یوقدور آلارنی فتک آلغان لیغی نی محمد امین دیوان بابادین ایشوتوب عرضکوی لارنی

آلدوروب سوراشوب فتک نی کوروب سیزلاردین کیم یراغ فولی سورادی دیکانیمیزدا بیزلاردین آقسقال لار

سورادی دیکان سببلی آقسقال لارنی آلدوروب سورالغانیدا آلارنی سوراغانی هم بیکار بولدی فتک نی نچون

آلغان واقتیده کیل توروب بیرمای سیزلار دیکانیمیزدا یراغ فولی سورالسه بیرماکچی ایرکان لار ۲ نچی

[verso]

یموت لارنی خراجاتی اوچون نچه مناط دین بیرکان بولسه لار ایسماعل خواجه حاکم وقتیده آلغان

دور بیز کیل کانیمیزدین بیان یموت خراجاتی دیب نوکرلارغه و غریب فقراغه تازه دین چقون سالغانی یوق

ایسماعیل خواجه نی حاکم واقتیده نوکرلارنی بیرکان فول لارینی یوزباشی لار بیزغه معلوم ایتکان لاری دا

محمد رحیم بای بیله بامرقاچی[44] یوزباشی لارغه اوچ تورت کون خبر ایتونک یموت لارغه بای لارنی ایکان

خراجاتی بیله ایلدین یغناب آلغان فول لارینی حیسابی کورولسون اگر ده آرتغان فولی بولسه نوکرلارغه

بیریلسون و اگر آرتماسه خذمتلاریغه سیزلارنی عرضینکیزنی معلوم ایتوب نی مهربانچیلیق لاری بولسه سزلارغه

ینه معلوم ایتارمیز دیب ایردوک آندین باشقه سوزلاری دین خبریمیز یوقدور عرضکوی لارنی حاکم

44 Obviously a distorted rendering of بارماقچی.

بیزلاردین یراغ فولی سوراب بی یمش خذمت بویوبوب یموت خراجاتی اوچون فول آلدی دیب یالغان دین

دلیل کورکازیب ایتکان عرضلارینی یوزباشی لاریدین و هم فتک نی کیل توروب بیرمای اوزیمیز

سوراتوب آلغانیمیزنی محمد امین دیوان بابادین سوراشوب کورسانکز البته عرض کویلارنی

سوزی نینک راست یلغان لیغی معلوم بولسه کیراک آلارنی عرض بیله یالغاندین دلیل کورکازیب

عرض ایتب یورکان لیکی نی ازبرای جناب همایون لاریغه معلوم قیلدوق ینه صاحیب اختیار

اوزلاری یخشی بیلورلار دیب ماه جمادی الثانی نینک اخیریدا عریضه احلاص مرقوم

بولدی ۱۳۳۶ نچی یلی

مهر: عبد الرحیم بای ابن محمد کریم بای

Document 25

وزارت پنا[45] محمد یوسف یاسول باشی آقا میزنینک خدمت لاریغه معروز[46] بوکیم یادکار
خواجه نی مسجد قومیدین عبدالله خواجه دیکان کلیب مونده معلوم قیلدی اویومکا خوفتان
وقتی مسجدیمیزنینک امامی ملا خالبای بیلان اولتوریب ایردیک قافوم نی قاقتی لار
تاشقاری چیقسام ملا قربان نیاز دیکان منی طبانچه بیلان آتدی منکا تیکمادی من قاچدیم
آنام اولوغ جان بیکه کلیب ایردی ایکنجی مرتبه آتدی اوق آنام نی کوکراکیدین کریب
آرقاسیدین چیقدی ملا قربان بای هم قاچیب کتیب چوکورمه سی اوشبو جایده قالدی
اوق بیله چوکورمه نی کلتوروب کورساتکانی سببلی قاضی ایشان طرفیدین ملا باباجان
ملا باجان اوغلی بیله بزنی طرفیزدین آتاجان مخذوم دیکان امین بولوب باریب کوریب کلیب
معلوم قیلدیلار مذکور ناچارنی آتقانی راست ایرکان کوکراکیدین کیریب آرقاسیدین
چیقیب دور دیب معلوم قیلدیلار سونکره مذکور ملا قربان بای خدمت لاریغه باروب
و ۲نجی ذالحجه[47] ده نشانه آلیب کلدی مضمونی نی کورساک من هر کم نی مال لاری اوغور
لانسه ایکی یاش باله نی سوغه قاراتیب اوغری نی تاپب برور ایردیم موسی جواجه
دیکان نی مالی نی اوغری آلغان سببلی اوغری لاری خاللی و محمد ضیا دیکانلار منی عبدالله

45 Textual variation of پناه.
46 Textual variation of معروض.
47 Textual variation of ذوالحجه.

دیکان نی اویغه چاقورتوروب اولتورماکچی بولوب منکا ایکی مرتبه آلتی آتار آتدیلار اوقی

تیکادی من قاچدوم دیب ایمدی شونی سوراشیب کوروب شریعت غه موافق بتکارسونلار مو دیب

[verso]

و ینه مذکور ملا قربان بای دین چوکرمه کیم نیکی دیب سورالغانده جواب بردی چوکرمه منکی ایرماس دیب

خاللی و محمد ضیا دیکانلارنی آلدوریب سورانمیزدا[48] بزلار بر یل دین بویانه عبدالله نینک

اویغه بارغانمیز یوق ملا قربان بای نی هم آتغانمیز یوق و موسی خواجه نی مال لارینی هم اوغری

لاب آلغانمیز یوق دیب ایردی سونکره خذمت لاریدین خدای نظر یوزباشی برلان یبارکان

نشانه لاری نی برابرینده هم چاقورتوروب سوراغانمیزده عبدالله خواجه نینک اقسقال کدخدالاری

موندا معلوم ایتادور بزلار مذکورلارنی حادثه سی وقتینده اشیتب باردوق ناچارغه اوق تیککانی راست ایرکان کیم اوق آتغانی نی بزلار بیلمایمیز دیرلار ینه ملا قربان بای دیکان

نینک اقسقال کدخدالاری آیتادور بزلار مذکور ملا قربان بای نی بهوده یورکانی نی کورکانمیز

یوق دیب شایدلیق[49] برورلار بزلارنینک ایشیتکان صورت واقعه لاریمیز اوشبو تورور و ینه صاحب رای اوزلاری بیلورلار دیب ۷ لانچی ماه محرم دا خط بتلدی ۱۳۳۶ یلدا

مهر: [※]

48 Textual variation of سوراغانمیزدا.

49 Textual variation of شاهدلیک.

Document 26

عزتلو حرمتلو شیخ نظر یساول باشی آقامیز خدمت لاریغه معروض اولکیم هزاراسب لی

قلندر درگاه عالی لاریغه عریضه ایتب تخمینًا اوچ طناب یریم نی اوزوم نی یوق وقتم دا جمعه نیاز

و بکجان و نار محمد دیکانلار طناب دفتری غه یازدوروب دور دیب مذکورغه نشانه مهربان بولوب ایرکانلار

بویروقلاری یکلکاچ طناب دفتری نی کورولدی یر جمعه نیازلار اسمی غه ایرکان قلندر مذکور من یوق ایردیم

دیدی آندین سونکره هزاراسب قاضی لاریغه خط بردوم ایلات نی تمامی آدم لاری نی طناب دا حاضر کیشی

لاردین سوراب خط ایتب یبارسون لار دیب قاضی ایشان لار بار آدم لاردین سوراب خط ایتب

یباریب دورلار قلندر مذکور بار ایرکان خطلی ملکی نکینی توتادورمو سن دیکاندا توتماس میز دیب

تاشلاغان سببلی جمعه نیازلار توتدی دیب شهادت برکان لارنی واقعه لاری نی یازیب یباریب دورلار

ایمدی قلندر یوق ایردوم دیر ایلات بار بولوب تاشلادی دیر یازغان دیوان هم بار ایردی دیب شهادت

برادور شول طریقه بولوب طناب دفتریغه یازیلیب ایرکان فلاند جمعه نیازلار اسمی غه بولوب کیتکان

ایمدی قلندرنی خطی بیله یرنی آنکا یانکغی دین برماکنی فرمایش قیلسه لار جمعه نیازلاردین خط آلیب

برماک کراک بولادور اکر تاشلاب فلاندغه اورناغاندین سونکرا یانکغی دین بریلماسون دیب

مهربان بولسه لار اولصورتدا قلندر دعوی نی قویماقی کراک هزاراسب تابعی دا فرتابته یرلاری نی

اوّل طناب بولوجاق دا تاشلاب سونکره پشیمان بولوب دعوی ایتب یورکان خلق کوب تورور

[verso]

تخمینًا اوچ تورت مینک نمرغه بارسه کراک هزاراسب قاضی ایشان لاری نی یازغان خطی نی

دعوی کرنی ایکی طرفی نی قوشوب خدمت لاریغه یباریلدی نه مهربان بولسه لار آنینک بیله بویورمیز

دیب صورت واقعه خدمت لاریغه عریضه قیلندی

۱۹ نجی جمادی الثانی آیی دا ۱۳۳۲ نجی یلدا

مهر: حاجی محمد بای ابن امین الدین بای ۱۳۳۰

Document 27

عزت و سعادت نشان یساول باشی آقانینک معلوم لاری بولغایکم چودر کلدی محمد اوزیم اویوم دا یوق ایردیم آقشام ایچیدا قوشان و عنّه محمد دیکان لار اوغورلاب اوچ یوز مناتیم نی آلدیلار دیب غایب یوزباشی نی نوکری عید بای یساول بولوب کیلیب ایمدی مذکور کلدی محمدنی سوزی نینک دعوی کرلاری قوشان و عنّه محمدلار برلان کدخدالاری ایکی طرف نی رضالیق غه یتکوردیلار و ایمدی فقرالارنی هلاک بولماسلیقی وجهی دین یساول نی قولیغه خط یازیب بیریلدی اوشبونینک خدمت لاریغه معلوم قیلامیز دیب بو خط بتیلدی ۱۳۳۵ لانجی یلدا

مهر: جمعه نیاز محرم ابن محمود دیوان

Document 28

وزارت پناه حکومت دستکاه یساول باشی اقالاریمزنی خذمتلاریغه معلوم لاری بولغای لارکم نایمان لی الله یار مخذوم دیکان اوچ طلامنی سوراغانده خالمراد وفاه و صفر دیکان لار یکرمه ایکی طلامنی الدیلار دیب عریضه اتکان توغروسنده خذمت کار قلندرنی یساول ایتب مهربان بولغان ایرکانلار مونده خدریلي قلعه سیکه کلکانلارینده ایکی طرافلاری قرنداش بولغان وجهیدن خطی پاک الوشوب رضالیق تاپلار فقرالاری عاجزلیق سببلی دعاء خیرلارین قلیب قالدیلار دیب اون سکزلانجی محرم ایده عریضه خطی بتلدی ١٣٣٥

مهر: [※]

[※]

Document 29

وزارت پناه حکومت دستکا[50] آمان کیلدی یساولباشی آقامیز خذمتلاریغه معروض اولغا یلارکیم هلالی لی مسجد دورمن دین یموتلار زورلاب اوتکان یل بیر نیچه فقرالارنی یر لاری نی و ایکین لاری نی بوزب یاف باریب اوتکان سبب لی باباجان سید دیکا عرض ایتیب نشانه آلیب کیلکانی غه موافق مذکور یاف باریب اوتکان یموتلار بیله مذکور عرض کوی لار بیله سوزلاشتورب مذکور یر ایکالاری نی بوزولغان ایکین لاری نی امین یباریب و اقسقال کدخدالاری بیله کورکازب مذکورلارنینک زرارلاری[51] اوچون بر یوز ایلیک آلیب بریب بیر بیرلاری بیله رضالیق غه یتدیلار و داغی مذکور یاف یارغانلاردین ایلیک طلا امین فولی

[verso]

و یساول حقّی آلندی شوندین خذمتلاریغه یکرمه بش طلا بریب یباردم دیب ۹نجی ماه شعباندا اوشبو مکتوب مرقوم بولدی ۱۳۳۴نجی یلي

مهر: محمد یوسف بای ابن محمد یعقوب دیوان

---

50 Textual variation of دستکاه.

51 Textual variation of ضرر.

Document 30

وزارت پناه حکومت دستگاه یساول باشی آقاغه کاتلی محمد یعقوب دیکان حاکم مندین
اون کم اوچیوز مناة آلدی الله برکان دیکان اون بیش مناة آلدی دیب عرض
ایتیب یرکان نشانه لاری نینک توغریسیده عرض اخلاصیمز بوکیم مذکور محمد یعقوب
ایکی اینیسی بیله آتامراد دیکاننی ایکی ناچاری بیله اوزینی اوروب کله لارینی یاریب
تمامی اعضالارینی بی وجه مجروح ایتکان بز شول توغریده یوز مناة آلیب مذکور
مجروح لارغه ملحم فلی‌سی اوچون بردوک اندن سونک دعواسینی صافلاشتوروب
ایردوک یبارکان امین لاری بیله کات دارالقضاسیغه قاضی ایشانلارنینک خضور
لاریغه باریب مذکورننک کدخدا آقسقال لاری نینک جعلاب بزکا سن قاچان
اونکم
اوچیوز مناة بردینک دیب سورالدی اول جوابیده دیدیکم من سیزکا اوز قولوم
برله اونکم اوچیوز مناة برکانیم یوق امّا من مذکور اونکم اوچیوز مناة نی محمد یوسف
بایغه
بریب ایردیم اندین التمیش اوچ مناة نی محمد یوسف مذکور منکا قایتیب بریب
ایردی دیب قاضی ایشانلارنینک حضوریده اقرار بولدی آندن سونک باقی مناة قایده
دیب محمد یوسف مذکوردین سورالغانده دیدیکم یکرمه یتی مناة نی یساولی وکدخدا
لاری آلدیلار و یوز مناة نی قره ول بولوب یاتغان سردار دیکان یموت آلدی دیدی
امّا بزنینک بولارنینک آلغان لاریدین خبریمز یوق امّا الله برکان مذکورنینک
آلغان اون بیش مناتینی سببی موت تورت لیقده مذکور محمد یعقوب بر آدم نی
اوروب کله سینی یاریب ایردی شول توغریده یساول حقی اوچون برکان ایرکان
آلان شول آدم هم یاتیب تورور امّا محمد یعقوب مذکور بزکا کوب حقارت نما و
ناشایسته سوزلارنی آیدی ایمدی صاحب اختیار اوزلاری تورور دیب
۲۸ نجی ماه رمضنده اوشبو عریضه نامه نی مکتوب ایتیب خذمتلاریغه ارسال
ایتیلدی
۱۳۳۶

مهر: آتا بیک ابن رحیم بردی بیک ۱۳۳۵

Document 31

هو
وزرات پناه یساولباشی آقامیزنینک خذمتلاریغه معروض اولکیم
هلالی فقرالاریدین عوضنیاز و خدا یبرکان دیکان یر جای لارین
صاتیب قرض لاریغه بیرماکچی بولوب نشانهٔ عالی آلیب کلیب
شولارنی آلغودارلاری سوزلاشیب عوض نیازنی یری نی
بر یوز یکرمه بیشطلاغه بر آدم آلماقچی بولوب تقسیم بولغان دا هر بیشطلاغه
اون ایکی تنکه دین یتوشوردیرلار خدا یبرکان دیکان نی یری نی
ایکی یوز طلا آلماقچی بولوب شونی آلغودارلاری هم تقسیم ایتماکچی
بولوب طلاغه اوچ تنکه دین زیاد یتوشور اوخشایدور شولارنی
جواب آلیب بویروق ایتسه لار فرمایش لاری بله بویورمیز و ینه
عرض یتوشماکان قول لاریغه خط آلماقچی دورلار آنی هم بیلدورسه لار
خط الغان دا بی اجاره بولور دیب اویلارمیز مُلکی بولماغان سبب لی

[verso]

یا الغودارلاری هر نه باری بولسه یتوشکانیغه لایق آلیب
قالغان حق لاری اوچون خط آلماسون دیرلارمو شولارنی بیان
واقعه لارین خط بله مهربان بولسه لار الحمد الله رب العالمین الآن
بو ظرف لاری نینک دولت لاری شرافتیدین فراغت لیک دور
دعاء خیرلاریغه مشغولدور دیب ربع الثانی دا ۱۰نجی ایدا
عریضه الاخلاص رقم تافدی ۱۳۳۲نجی یلی

مهر: [※]

آلغودارلار رضا بولسه شریعت فرمانی بله
یر و جای مال لارین ساتیب اول اوروسیه فقراسی بولسه
بریب قالغانین بو طرف فقرا آلغوداریغه بریب
قالغانیقه برسون خط ایتب بریب رضاسی غه
تنکه بریب اخری خط بله موندا معلوم قلسون دیب
۱۰لانجی ماه ربع الثانی دا ۱۳۳۲

Document 32

معتمد السلطان مقرب الخاقان یساول باشی آقامیز جناب لاریغه معروض
اولکیم خیوالی عباد الله بیک نی روزی بای تاجیک دا خطلی توقسان طلاّ
حقی بار موافیق[52] شریعت الیب بریلسون یساول بله فتک مهربان
بولوب ایرکان لار مذکور روزی نی دوکان اسباب لاری نی
بر یوز التمیش اوچ مناط ۸۹تین غه ساتیب قرق بیش مناط لیق
بر آدم دین آلغی دار خطی نی تمام آلغی دارلاری دیوان خانه دین
بولغان بویروق بله تقسیم اتیب بریلماکچی بولغانده اورالسکی مکسیم بله
استفی محمد جان نوغای لار بزلار اوزلاریمیز آلادورمیز لار
باشقه آدم لارغه برمای میز دیب تنکه نی بزغه تاپشوروب بزلارنی عرض
لاریمیزنی دیوان خانه غه معلوم اتینک دیب ۱۶نچی جمادی الثانی
آینده یازیب معلوم اتیلب ایردی هیچ بر جواب بولماین

[verso]

توروب ایردی ینه اوروس لارنی تازه دین جواب لاری نی
دوباره یازیب دیوان خانه غه معلوم ایتلدی داغی
روزی بای تاجیک نی حانقا لی یولداش دیکانغه کفیل غه بریلدی
شنبه کونی خدمت لاریغه اوزیم باریب معلوم بولادور
من دیکانی سبب لی صورت واقعه اوشبو دورکه
خدمت لاریغه تحریر ایتلدی
۱۵نچی شوال آینده خط بتلدی ۱۳۲۸
مهر: حاجی محمد بای ابن امین الدین بای ۱۳۲۷ (؟)

52 Textual variation of موافق.

Document 33

هو
وزارت پناه حکومت دستگاه یساول باشی آقانینک خذمتلاریغه بو نوع معلوم قیلورمزکیم
قیلچ بالی اوراض بای دیکان خذمتلاریغه عرض قیلغان ایرکان بیر نچه نفر آدم
لاردین خطلی قرضیم بارو اون یکی یاریم طناب یریم بار ساتیب قرضیم نی
ادا ایتماکچی دورمان دیب ایمدی شونی نچاقلی قرضی بار و یری نی بهاسی نه دور و باشقه
نمرسه سی بارمو اورسیه فقراسی دین قرضی بارمو اموال و اشیاءلاری
و یری قرضیغه یتوشورمو آلغودارلاری آلماقغه رضامو شولارنی خطی بیله موندا
معلوم قیلسون دیب شول سببلی مذکورنی آلغودارنی یغناب قرضی نی حساب
ایتولدی بیش یوز داغی ایلیک بیش طلا قرضی بار ایرکان و اون ایکی یاریم طناب یری
نینک بهاسی ادرا بولغانی اوچون یوز طلاغه آلمایدورلار و بر کهنه ارابه[53] و یکی اوچاک
و بر ایشاک بار ایرکان اوروسیه فقرسینیدین قرضی یوق ایرکان مذکورنینک یری و نرسه قرا
لاری قرضیغه یتوشماکانی وخهی دین بر یرداغی الغودارالاری اتفاق بیله مذکور اوراض بایغه ایکی یل
مدّتینچه لی بی فیدا[54] توردی لار مذکورنینک صورت واقعه سی بو طریقه ایردی

[verso]

خذمتلاریغه معلوم قیلماق اوچون بو عریضه یباریلدی صاحب اختیار اوزلاری
بیلورلار دیب ماه ربیع الاوّل نینک ۹ نجی کونی مرقوم بولدی

53 sic.
54 Textual variation of فائده.

۱۳۳۵ یلدا

مهر: بابا جان یوزباشی ابن پهلوان

۱۱نجی ماه ربیع الاولدا اوشبو خط یکلب یساولباشی آقا

دوردی کربان بیله بریب یازب دورلار

آلیب قویولدی

Document 34

وزیر اعظم دستور المکرم اعنی یساول باشی اقامیز نینک جناب عالی لاریغه معلوم لاری اولغایکم اسکندر یساول بیله یاریلکان نشانهٔ عالی لاری مضمونی بیله باریب عبد الکریم نی آیتغان یولنی کوردوک و شول قوم نینک قریه آدم لارینی یولنی سوراشماق اوچون چاقردق و قریه آدم لار کیلیب سنهم قوی سنهم قوی دعوانکنی دیب ایکی طرف نینک رضالیقی بیله کدخدا آقسقال لار یراشتوردیلار دیب خدمت لاریغه رقعه بتلدی دیب واصح بای

مهر: قاضی و رئیس یارمیش داملا محمد یوسف [※]

قاضی و رئیس یارمیش داملا بابا جان مخذوم [※]

Document 35

وزارت پناه یساولباشی اقامیز نینک خذمتلاریغه معلوم بولغایکم قربان نیاز دیکان ني ارابه[55] یولی سی غه قوش نیاز قربان نیاز و روز محمد و بابا و آتا نیاز و جمعه نظر و سیّد و صفا و اسکندر دیکان لار شریعت امریغه هم رضا بولمای زورلیق ایتب یورکانلاری اوچون ایکی طرف لاری نی قمتو سوزلا شتوروب عرضه کوی قربان نیاز مذکور نی مدّعاسیغه موافق اوّلغی تعاملی بویونچه ایل آت نی نایب اقسقال کدخدالاری نی اتیفاق[56] لاری بیله ارابه[57] یولی نی آلیب بریب رضا لاشتورلدی اوشبونی خذمتلاریغه معلوم قیلورمیز دیب ۸ نچی رمضان شریف دا خط بتلدی ۱۳۳۶

مهر: محمد یوسف بای ابن پهلوان محرم ۱۳۳۴

---

55 sic.

56 Textual variation of اتفاق.

57 sic.

Document 36

وزارت پناه یساول باشی آقانی معلوم لاری بولغایکم بیر مسجد قومینی ادم لاریدن عبدالرحمان
الله برکان محمد نیاز خواجه و ایش نیاز و قوشه خواجه و محمد یعقوب خواجه دیکان لاری
دربار عالی لاریغه عرض قیلغان ایرکان یموت طایفه لاری بیش آریق طرفیکا بارغانده
ایتکان خراجاتی درکلی چقون فلی سوراش دورلار دیب مذکور یموت جماعه لاری
مهمان توشکان یریدن سوراشسه لار دیب ایمدی مذکورلارنینک حقیده معلوم
قیلادورمیز اورسیه عسکرلاری چقون فلی غزنه[58] ده فل بولملغان سببلی بیش آریق
تابعی لارنی آقا نایب آقسقال کدخدالاری ایلات دین اندازسی مقداریده
هر برلاریغه سالاشیب ایتکان خرجی لارنی برسونلار دیب دربار عالی لاریدین
نشانه کیلکان سببلی و ینه یموت جماعه لاریدین اوشاق نینک بیکی بیله امان نیازبیک
دیکان لار بیش آریق ایچی غه دربار عالی لارنی فتک لاری بویونچه هر یرده

[verso]

بولوب توشکانده آقا نایب لاری اتفاق ایلان خراجات ایتکان سبب لی
و ینه بای لار بیله فقرالاریدین بیش آتار بویرلغان سببلی جمع خراجات نی
اتفاق ایتب اوز بلی اوزلاری هر بر واحدیغه سالاشیب مذکور
عرضه کویی لاریدین غیرلاری منوت پادشاهی بیله چقون فلی بریب دورلار داغی
مذکور عرضه کویی ایل اتفاق لاریغه ایتمای سرکش لیک ایتب
یورکان سببلی جمع آقا نایبلار اتفاق ایتب مهرلاریمیزنی باسدوق
مذکور عرضه کویی لارغه ینه جزا برماسه لار بزلار جماعه لارنینک تمام منوت چقون فلی
لاریمیز بتمای تاٴخیر تاپیب و ینه برکان فقرا هم قایتوب آلماقچی بولوب تورور دیب ماه جمادی الاولده

58 Textual variation of خزینه.

اوشبو عریضه اخلاص بیتلدی ۱۳۳۶

مهر: محمد یوسف بای ابن پهلوان محرم

حسن آقا ابن خدای برکان ۱۳۳۶

محمد یعقوب بای ابن اسماعیل جان بای

[※]

آ نیاز بای ابن محمد نیاز بای ۱۳۱۷

Document 37

وزارت پناه یساولباشی آقامیزنینک معلوم لاری بولغای کیم خواجه لیقلی قوشنظرنی بی وجه شرع[59] قربان نیاز و روز محمد و آتا مراد و تینکر بردی و الله بردی و مولام بردی و صابر دیکر قربان نیاز قوتلوقمراد و خواجه دوردی دیکانلار اوروب اعضالار ینی جراحت لاندروب و بر قولینی معیوب ایتوب یانیدن ایکی مینک مناتی نی الدیلار دیکان عرضه سیغه موافق عرضه کوی مذکور بیله دعواکرلاری نی الدروب ایل آتی نی نایب آقسقال کدخدالاری نی اتیفاق[60] لاری بیله جبرلاندیم ایکی مینک منات تنکام الیندی دیکان دعواسی نی خالیص اوتوب ایکی طرفی نی رضالاشتورولدی دیب ۸نچی ماه رمضان شریف ده خط بتلدی ۱۳۳٤نجی یلدا

مهر: محمد یوسف بای ابن پهلوان محرم

59 Textual variation of بی وجه شرعی.
60 sic.

Document 38

وزارت پناه یساولباشی آقامیزنی خدمت لاریغه معلوم بولغایکم
سارت آلاچه لی سیید آقسقالنی قومیده محمد رحیم دیکان نی جولی
سیغه اوغری توشوب تورت باتمن بوغدای تورت
کیملیک اشتوف تورت ایفاک چفانینی الیب چیقب
کیتکانینی حولی ایکه سی تویونوب ایزیدین قاوب
خواجه نیاز دیکان نی توتوب کیلتوردی یولداش لاری
قاچیب دور مذکور خواجه نیاز نی تیاقلاماقچی بولوب
سیاست ایتوب الغان وجه لاری بیله یولداش لاری سورا
لغانیدا یولداشی توره و منکلی دیکانلار مذکور بولغان
وجه لارنی الار آلیب کتدیلار کن قولغه توشدوم دیب

[verso]

اقرار بولدی سونکره مذکور ایکی یولداش لاری نی آلدوردق
الار هم اقرار بولدی مذکورلارنی اوغری لیغی ظاهر بولغانی
اوچون نایب اقسقال کدخدالار آلینغان وجه لار
اوچون تورت یوز طلا محمد رحیم مذکورغه الیب بردیلار
و مذکور اوغریلار نی اوشبو جینایتی توغریسیدا
خذمتلاریغه بباریلورمو یاکه موندا اوبکه سالیب
قویابیرامیزمو و یاکه کفیل غه بریلورمو اوشبو
توغریدا نه مهربانلیق لاری بولسه خط بیله معلوم
قیلسه لار دیب ۲۵ نچی

ذالقعده[61] دا جط بتلدی ١٣٣٤ نچی
مهر: محمد یوسف بای ابن پهلوان محرم ١٣٣۴

اوغریلارنی حاکم نی اوزی ساقلاب بولغاندا
چقارماقغه جواب یازیلدی

61 Textual variation of ذی القعده.

Document 39

وزارت پناه یساولباشی آقامیزنینک خذمت لاریغه معلوم اولغایکم سوسه لاقلی عوض محمد آقسقال نی قومیده خواجه مراد دیکان نی حولی سیدین بیر آطنی اوغورلانیب مذکور آطی نی ایزینی ایزچی بیله بارلاغانیده روز محمد چوچی دیکان نی اویغه آطنی ایزی باریب دور آطنی ایکه سی خواجه مراد بیله ایلاتی نی اقسقال کدخدالاری اوشبو حادثه نی بیزغه کیلب معلوم قیلدی بز آدم یباریب چوچی نی آلدروب اوغورلانغان اطنی ایزی سنینک اوینک غه باریب دور راستی نی ایتغن دیب یکرمه اوتوز قامچی اوروب سورادوق روز محمد چوچی ایتدی خوجه مراد نی اطی نی

[verso]

عبدالرحیم یوسف خواجه ابدال خواجه الاک تای نو دیکان لار بیله خواجه مراد نی دروازه سی نی بر یان طرفی نی تورومی تایدروب اطی نی الدوق دیب اقرار بولدی مذکور نی اقراریغه موافق مذکور یولداش لارینی آلدروب الارغه سیاست ایتوب سورالدی الارهم روز محمد چوچی نی ایتغانیغه موافق اقرار بولدیلار شولتوغریدا مذکور بش نفر اوغری نی اویکه سالیب اوغریلاردین سورالدی آطنی تاپنک لار فایده قویغان بولسانکزلار دیب اوغریلار آط یوق بولدی تاپلماق علاجی یوق دیدیلار سونکره خواجه مراد دین سور آلدی آطینک نه بهالیق ایردی دیب

[recto]

جوچه مراد ایتدی آطم نی بیر مینک ایکی یوز طلا غه سوراغانیده بیرمای یورور ایردوم دیکانی اوچون حسن اقا بابا ایلاتی نی

اقسقال کدخدالاری بش اوغریدین بر مینک اکی یوز طلا اطنی فلی اوچون اوچیوز طلا ایزچی فلی و غیر چقغون کدخدا فلی لاری اوچون آلیب دورلار جمعه بیر مینک بیشیوز طلا نی بیز موندا آلیب قویدوق ایمدی شونی خذمتنکیزغه معلوم قیلورمیز مذکور الینغان تنکه نی موندا اط ایکا سیغه تیکیشلی‌سی نی بریب و قالغانی نی ایزچیغه وکدخدا لاری بیله وغیر چیقغون لاریغه بریلورمو یا اوغریلارنی اویده ساقلانیب یاکه کفیل غه برورمیزمو و یاکه همه سی نی

[verso]

انجام بولغان تنکه سی بیله خذمتلاریغه بیاریلورمو اوشبو توغریده نه مهربانلیق لاری بولسه خط بیله معلوم قیلسه لار دیب ٢٥ نچی ذالقعده[62] دا خط بیتلدی ١٣٣٤ یلی

مهر: محمد یوسف بای ابن پهلوان محرم ۱۳۳۴

بر مینک ایکی یوز طلا نی آط ایکاسیغه بریلیب اوچ یوز طلا نی آلینغان لارغه بیریلماکا
بویروق بولوب اوغریلار نی کفیل غه تاپشورولماقغه جواب یازیلدی

62 sic.

Document 40

وزارت پناه یساولباشی آقاغه اعلام اولکیم اوشبو یلی ۳ نچی جمادی الثانیدا چواندور موضع دا بولغان حادثه خدای بیرکان بن اسماعیل نی کیچه نا معلوم

اولتوروبدورلار دیب خبر بیردی لار اندین سونکره شریعت شعار قاضی ایشان لاردین و اوزیمیزدین امین یباریب مذکور امین لار

موضع مذکور نی کدخدا آقسقال لاری ایل آدم لاری ایلان باریب کوروبدورلار مذکور نی یاز طرف داغی قفوسی نی سیندوروب و دهلیز داغی

قفوسی نی یقب کیریب مذکورنی اولتوروبدورلار مذکور مقتول نی کوروبدورلار کله سی نی اوستی و چپ قباقی جراحت دار بولغان

و مقتول نی اوغلی بردی شکور و خاتونی درجان بیکه و جمعه بیکه و قیزی راضیه بیکه لاردین سوز سورآلدی آلار جواب بردی لار اویمیزغه

اون بیش نفر نا معلوم آدم لارکریب شونداغ ایتی لار دیب مذکور بردی شکورنی ایکی چکه سی و منکلایی جراحت دار بولغان مذکور نی

خاتونی زلیخا بیکه نی کله سی جراحت دار بولغان و راضیه بیکه نی ساغ قولی جراحت دار بولغان آلاردین سورالدی مذکور آدم لاردین هیچ برین

تانیمادینکزلارمو دیب آلار تانیمادوق دیب جواب برورلار مذکور بردی شکور غه درک ۱۵ باتمان بوغدای و یکرمه طلالیق کاغذ مناة برغان

و راضیه بیکه نی بیر امیرکانی رویمال و بیر تیرما و آلتی قوشه رویمال و یتی قوشه عالچه رویمال اوچ یفکلی یلاک و ایکی کوینلاک و آتاسیغه

درک ۲ طلالیق تنکه ۴۵ طلالیق کاغذ منات ایکی کورفه لاریمیز نی آلیب کتیب دور لار و ینه مقتول نی اوغلی خدایشکر ایتادور تخمیناً ۳۵ باتمان

بوغدایم نی الغاندورلار دیب صورت واقعه شول تورور سونکره تورت لانچی ماه مذکوردا یعنی سه شنبه آقشامی موضع آتالقدا محمد جان قره

قربان خرات اوغلی دیکان نی اویکا خفتن دین اول راق بر بله باریب دور و یغلابدور من بیک آبادلی دورمن و یتیم دورمن منی هیچ کیشی

مهمان ایتمادی لار دیب شولوقت دا محمد یعقوب مؤذن دیکان آیتب دور بو بله آری یاقلی دور زیادا یمان اوغریدور من مونی

آری یاق دا بازارچی لیق ایتب یورکانیم سبب لی بیلورمن دیب دور سونکره مذکور بله نی ایل قراول لارینی یانیغه آلیب باریب دورلار

قراول لار ایل کدخدالاری نی یانیغه باریب باباجان شیخ دیکان نی مهمانخانه سیدا اولتورغان لاریدا ایچکری دین بر ناچاره چیقب خبر

بریب دور اوی اطراف لارینی آطلیغ آلدی و اوچاکگا ایکی آدم چقدی دیب سونکره کدخدالار دیشانغه چقسه لار ایکی آطلیغ

ایلان برنچه فیادا طیار ایرکان مذکور بله نی آلیب کیتماکگا هجوم اتیب دورلار سونکره آلار قورقوب دروازه نی بند ایتب احتیاط

ایلان اولتوروب چیقیب دورلار داغی ایرتنکی بیزنی یانیمیزغه آلیب کیلدی لار مذکور بله دین سورالدی آدینک کیم دور

جواب بیردی آدیم رجب قربان نیاز اوغلی عوض یخشی نی تیره شی دور من تورتکل بولوشی نینک ... (؟)

[verso]

مدة بر آی مقداری بولدی بو طرفغه اوتدیم بو طرف دا قویباق قزاق و بای نظرلار ایلان شرشالیغ جمعه نیاز و خواجه نیاز محمد صفا و سید مراد

و ینه چواندورلی صفا دیکان لار یولداشلاریمیز اوغری لیق ایتارمیز مذکور چواندورلی صفا نی ملتوقی و فیشنک لی اوقی باردور دیب جواب بردی

کیشی یباریب بارلاندی مذکور صفانی بر قره ملتوقی بر تفانچه سی ۲۳دانه بر دانکه اوقی بار ایرکان تافیب آلیب کیلدی لار

صفادین سوز سورالدی اوشبولارنی نه یردین آلدینک جواب بردی اوتکان ییلدا رسیه عسکرلاری نی ارابه[63] لی تاش سقاغه آلیب

بارغانیمدا بر مناتغه عسکردین ساتغون آلغان ایردیم مذکور ملتوق ایلان تفانچه نی مدة ایکی آیلقدا ایل آدم لاری ایلان کدخدالارینی

63 sic.

25 سوزی ایلان آری یاق دا آق قمیش منزلیدا قرینداشلاریم حاجی عبدالله و حاجی و نیاز محمد دیکانلاردین امانت آلیب کیلدیم

دیب جواب بردی مذکورلار نی اتاسی نی اسمی نی سورالغاندا بیلمادی اوشبولارنی هزاراسب کذریدین آلیب اوتدیم هیچ کیشی

بیلمادی دیب جواب بردی مذکورنی سوزی نی ایلات آدم لاری وکدخدالاریدین سورالدی آلار آیدیلار بیزلار ملتوق سقلا دیب

آیتغانیمیز یوق دور مونی یراغی بار ایرکانیدین خبریمیز یوق دور دیب جواب بردی لار سونکره شرشالی قچاقچی چواندور موضع دین

جمعه نیاز و خواجه نیاز و محمد صفا سید مراد و صفا ایسملی آدملارنی همه لاری نی جملاب مذکور بله غه کورساتیلدی مذکور چواندورلی صفادین

30 باشقه هیچ بری نی تانیمادی مذکوردین سوز سورالدی منکر بولدی مذکور بله رجب دیکان انکا آیتدی هر آقشام تانکدا منی آق میداندا غی

کول نی یانیغه آلیب باریب تاشلار ایردینک نماز شام دا مذکور کول نی یانیدین آتغه میندوروب آلیب کیتار ایردینک یوقاریداغی

بیان بولغان مقتول نی اویکا داغی بیزلار باردوق من آطلارنی توتوب توردیم اشیک نی یقدب لار مذکور بیان بولینغان یولداشلاریم

اویکا کیردی لار سونکره غوغا بولدی نه طریقه ایرکانین بیلمای دور من دیدی سونکره سورالدی نچند آدم بولور سیزلار دیکاندا

یکرمه چاقلی بولورمیز دیب جواب بردی مذکور محمد جان قره نی داغی آتی نی اوغیرلاماقچی بولوب مذکور قوبباق قزاق اوچ منات بیریب

35 منی یباردی مذکور صفا اوینی کورساتدی دیب جواب بردی و ینه معلوم لاری بولسون هزاراسب دین یقین وقت لاردا

اوغیرلانغان برنچه آط و برنچه اوی لار اوغیرلانغان ایردی آلارنی درک نی سورالساق آلارنی داغی بیزلار اوغیرلادوق دیب علامت

لارینی آیتب جواب بردی صورت واقعه اوشبو طریقه مذکور رجب دیکان بله نی آیتغان علامت تاپیلغان سبب لی مذکور صفا نی

میرشب غه تاپشوروب قویولدی مذکور رجب نی تاپیلغان ملتوق تفانچه نی ٢٣دانه اوق نی آطلی غه قوشوب خدمت لاریغه یبارولدی دیب اوشبو مکتوب بتیلدی ١٥نچی جمادی الثانیدا ١٣[64]لانچی یلدا [؟]

مهر: اسماعیل خواجه ابن ابراهیم خواجه

64 A damage in the text.

Document 41

معتمد الدولت مقرّب الحضرت یساول باشی آقامیز خدمت لاری غه معلوم اولغایکم آخری ماه جمادی الثانی دا پنجشنبه کونی آذانده جنکانلی مسجد ملاّ محمد رحیم دین جبار برکان آقسقال کیلیب معلوم قیلدیکم آقشام ایشجان دیکان نی اویی غه اوغری توشوب مذکور ایشجان نی قولینی سندوروب اینی‌سی قل محمد دیکان نی تیاق بیلان باشیغه اوروب باشینی یپجیب و یوغون سانی دین پچاق بیله بر آز کوشتی نی کسیب اویی نی تمام اشیالاری نی آلیب کیتب دورلار دیب درحال معلوم بولغاچ

قاضی ایشان لارنی بویوروب یباریلدی قاضی ایشان لار باریب صورت واقعه لاری نی خط ایتب کیلکاندین سونکره بر ایکی ساعت کین مذکور قل محمد دیکان

فوت بولغان ینه خبر برکانلاریدین سونکره قاضی ایشان لاردین کیشی بویوروب مذکور اولکان آدم نی مدفون ایتماکلاریغه بویرولدی سونکره ایزچی غه کیشی بویروب یبارکان دین سونکره پشین وقتیدا محمد یعقوب خواجه دیکان متولی بیله عبدالله دیکان همراه تیوه بیلان بیر آز نمرسه آلیب کیلدی لار خانقاه یاش کتّه لاری

حضوریدا مذکور نمرسه لارنی کوروب مذکور ایشجان دیکان لارنی کیشی بویوروب آلارنی آلدوروب مذکور نمرسه لارنی آلارغه کورساتیلکانده تمامی

نمرسه لاری آلارنینک مال لاری ایرکان اوشبو سبیلی مذکور مال لارنی خانقاه یاش کتّه لاری و هم ایلات کدخدالاری حضوریدا مذکورنی آقسقال جبّار برکان غه تاپشورولدی سونکره محمد یعقوب خواجه لاردین اوشبو مال لارنی نه یردین تاپدینکزلار دیب سورالغانده عبدالله خامباش دیکان جواب بردیکیم

منینک مورنی قبله سیداغی یریم نی اوستیدا بر دولام بار ایردی مذکور دولام غه باریب بعضی دهقانچلیق اسبابلاریم نی آلماقچی بولوب بارسام ایچینده

بر آز نمرسه تورغان کوروب محمد یعقوب خواجه میز نی یانیغه باریب آیتب خواجه میز بیلان همراه کیلیب کورکاندین سونکره خواجه میز اوشبو نمرسه

لارنی آرابه[65] غه یوکلاب بای آقانی حولی سیغه آلیب بارادورمیز دیدی من درحال
تیوه م نی آلیب کیلیب یوکلاب مونده آلیب کیلدوک دیب جواب بردی
ایزچی کیلکاندین سونکره ایزلارنی آلیب اوّل مذکور مال تاپلغان دوله غه آلیب باریب
آندین اوتوب قیاتلی قربان بای و همراه دیکان لارنی
اویی غه آلیب باریب دور آلارنینک اویی دین چیقاریب نوخاصلی محمد شریف دیکان
اوغری نی اویی غه آلیب باریب دور مذکور ایزچی یانیداغی قوشغان
خذمت کاریم غه اوشبو اوچ نفرلاری اوغری لارینکیز دیب توتوب بیرکان دین
سونکره آلارنی توتوب آلیب کیلدی لار مذکور اوچ نفر
لاریدین سورالغانده اوچ لاری هم انکار بولادورلار اوشبونی خذمت لاریغه معلوم
ایتادورمیزکیم مذکور محمد شریف دیکان اوغری اوّل
دین نیچه مرتبه خیوه غه باریب قوتولوب یورکان ایردی مذکورنی ایلات کدخدا
آقسقال لاری و هم قربان بای و همراه دیکان اوغری لارنی ایلاتی و هم
کدخدا آقسقال لاری کیلیب عرض ایتادورلارکیم اوشبو اوچ نفرلاری نی خذمت
همایونلاریغه آیتیب اولتورتوروب بیرماسه نکیز بیزلار
فقرا بولوب اویی میزدا فراغت اولتورا بیلمایدورمیز دیرلار اوشبو سببلی سیز حرمتلو
غه معلوم ایتادورمیزکیم اوشبولارنی هم
خذمت همایونلاریغه آیتوب اولتورماکغه تردود[66] قیلسه لار ایرکان اکر قوتولوب
خلاص بولوب کیلسه لار مذکورلارنی ایلاتی بیله و غیری
فقرالار فراغت بولمایدورغان کورونادور مذکور اوچ نفرلاری نی و هم قاضی ایشان
لارنی صورت واقعه یازغان خط لاری نی اوشبو
خط غه قوشسه خانقاه دا تورغان قراول قهقه بیک بیلان خذمت یباریلدی دیب
صورت واقعه اوشبو دورکیم
خذمت لاری غه تحریر ایتلدی ۵نچی ماه رجب ایی دا ۱۳۳۶نچی یلي

65 sic.
66 Textual variation of تردد.

بیکجانبای حاجی محمد یار قاضی اوغلی الله برکان کوادن اوغلی حاچی کریم قولی ترسوم بای اوغلی

بز نجم الدین الله برکان حاجی اوغلی یوسف بای حاجی اسکندر اوغلی

مهر: آقمهر حاجی محمد بای

Document 42

عزت نشان یساول باشی اقا زیدعمره نی خذمتلاریغه معلوم لاری بولغایلارکیم خواجه ایلی شیرین مسجد قومیدین مسماة حنیفه بیکه دیکان نینک ایریم صادق دیکان بی وجه شرعی اوروب بدنیم غه جراحت سالدی دیب حاکم غه عرض ایتب یساول یباریب مذکور ایری نی الدوریب آکی لاری نی بزلارنینک حضورلاریمزغه یباردی بعده مذکور ایریدین سوراغانیمزدا اورغانلقی غه مقیر[67] بولدی بعده مسماة مذکوره نی مؤمنه و متدینه بر خاتون نی امین ایتب کورساتیلدی اعضالاریده جراحتی بار ایرکاندیب امین مذکور بزلارغه خبر بردی مسماة مذکوره نی مسئله غه بویوریلدی مسئله مفتی بهاء فی الضمن نی مضمونیغه عمل ایتلیب شریعت پرمایشی[68] بیله تعزیر اورماقچی بولغانمزده توروب یوقدیب کتدی شول حادثه دین باشقه بزلارنینک حضوریمزدا فول تنکه حادثه بولغانی یوقتورور دیب صورة واقعه تحریر ایتلدی

مهر: قاضی [※]

قاضی خواجه ایلی [※]

قاضی خواجه ایلی داملا محمد صالیح خواجه [※]

قاضی خواجه ایلی داملا بابا جان خواجه [※]

67 Textual variation of مقر.

68 Textual variation of فرمایشی.

Document 43

وزارت پناه نجابت دستگاه یساول باشی اقامیزنینك خدمت لاریغه معلوم بولغای کیم کورلان لی

باباجان یوزباشی نینک قومی دین محمد یعقوب ایش محمد اوغلی دیکان طلب کارلیغ قیلب اورکنج غه

کلیب کسل بولوب دانش لیق[69] وجهی دین اورکنج لی خواجه فارسانی قومی داغی ویس بای دیکان نینک

اویغه بارغان ایرکان شولتوغریدا مذکور ویس بای دیکان بیزغه و قاضی ایشان لارغه معلوم قیلدیکیم

کورلانلی محمد یعقوب دیکان بیزنینک جایمیزدا کسل بولوب یاتیب دور دیب شونی برابریندا قاضی ایشان

لاریمیزدین و اوزیمیزدین بر آدم یباریب سوراولدی طلب قیلغان فلوینک بارمو و نمرسه قرالارینک

بارمو دیب آنی برابرینده مذکور قوم نی آقسقال کدخدالارینی حضوریده محمد یعقوب دیکان ایتغان سکیز منات

وبر اوراق بر ایشک باشقه نمرسه قرام یوقدیب ایشکین مینب اویغه کیتماقچی بولوب کیتب فشین[70]

وقتیدا یولده فوت بولغان ینه بیزغه خبر کلیب قاضی ایشان لاریمیزدین بر آدم نی و اوزیمیزدین بر آدم نی

امین قلیب یباریب یوغوچ لارنی الدوروب کورکفن ایتدوروب جنازه اوقوب قرا علم بابا

[verso]

علیه الرحمه غه امانت دفن ایتدوروب قویدوق و متوفا مذکور نی ایشکی نی و اوراقی بیله

69 Oghuz rendering of تنیشلیک.

70 Textual variation of پیشین.

سکیز منات تنکه سی نی اوچ کهنه چفان وبر کهنه چکمان وبر جوکرمه لارینی یوغوچی
خدای بیرکان
دیکان غه تاپشوردوق دیب اوشبو صورت واقعه نی خذمت لاریغه معلوم قلیب
داغی
ماه شعباندا خط بتلدی ۱۳۳۵نچی یلدا
مهر: الله برکان (؟) ابن عبد الرحیم بای
قاضی اورکنج داملا عطا الله ابن [※]
قاضی اورکنج داملا آتا جان ابن بابا صوفی مرحومی (؟) ۱۳۳

Document 44

وزارت پناه نجابت دستگاه امانکلدی بای یساولباشی اقامیزنینک معلوملاری
بولغایکم۱۶نچی ماه شعبان ده ایردیکم قره ماضولی جبار بیرکان آقسقال و تنکری بیرکان بای
و اوستا یعقوب لار مونده بیر ناچار بیله بیر یکیت نی توتوب کیلتوروب معلوم ایتدیلار
اوشبولار ایلاتمیزغه کیلیب مهمان بولوب ایردی لار یوروشلارینی ناقولای
کوروب توتدوق دیب شول سبب لی مذکور قاچقونچی لاردین سوراشیب
کورساک ناچار آلیب قاچقان یکیت تاشحوض لی و قیز مناق لی ایرکان مذکور
ناچار تاشحوض ده باباسی خدای بیرکان چوپچی دیکان نیکیغه کیلکانیده مذکور
تاشحوضلی اسکندر دیکان یکیت ناچارنی آلیب قاچیب چقیب تاشحوض ده اوزیم نی
جاییم ده ایکی آی ساقلاب آندین سونک چاتکوفروکلی آته مراد دیکان نینک
کیمه سیغه یتیب کیلیب قره ماضو توغریسیدین چقیب خانقاه تابع لارغه عبدالله دیکان
و ینه اشتمیرنیکیغه بارياتور ایردوک دیر نمرسه قره لاریمزنی هم عبدالله نیکی غه یباردوک
قیزدین سورادوق سن کیشی غه نکالی[71] یاکه فاتحه لی ایردینک مو دیب جواب

[verso]

بیردی من هیچکیم غه فاتحه لی یاکه نکالی[72] هم ایرماسمن دیب شول سببلی مذکور
قیزنی اتاسی نی مناق دین آلدوروب آلارنی و قیز آلیب قاچیب یورکان یکیت
اسکندر دیکان لارنی قوشیب خذمتلاری غه یباردوک ایمدی نه دیب

71 Textual variation of نکاحلی.
72 sic.

مهربان بولسه اوزلاری بیلورلار دیب ۱۸نجی ماه شعباندا بو خط بتلدی
۱۳۳۴نجی یلدا
مهر: عبد الرحیم بای ابن محمد یوسف بقال

Document 45

عزت نشان یساولباشی آقاغه معلوم بولسونکیم اوشبو یردا قربان محمد سردار آقانی جایی دا اولتورغانمیزدا غازی آباد فقرالاری سردار آقاغه عرض ایتدیلار اوستا محمد نیاز دیکان نی قیزی نی شوهری اوز رضالیقی بیله آیریب ایردی مذکور ناچارنی اوز ایلاتی و اوز قرینداش لاری ملا عثمان دیکان اوچون نفقه کسیب ایرکان لار مذکور ناچارنی نوخاصلی جمعه نیاز دیکان آلیب قاچیب کتیب دور ایمدی مذکور ناچارنی تافدوسدوروب حضرتمیزغه معلوم ایتوب آکاسیغه قوشوب یبارینک دیب ۲۴ نجی ماه جمادی الاولدا خط بتلدی ۱۳۳۶

مهر: عبد الکریم محرم ابن عبد الرحیم محرم ۱۳۳۱

Document 46

معتمد الدولت مقرب الحضرت يساول باشى آقاميز خدمت لارى غه معروض اولكيم ۳ نجى ماه جمادى الثانى آيى دا قولان قره باغلى مسجد حضرت پهلوان

دين ساتم بيله اتاجان ديكان لار معلوم قيلديلاركم آقشام محمد يعقوب آقسقال نينك اوبى غه اوغرى كيليب اوچاكى غه كيشى چقيب مذكور محمد يعقوب

آقسقال نى اوغلى اوزى اوچاكيدا قراول ليق ايتب ياتغان ايركان مذكورنى بوغوب اولتوروب دورلار داغى اوبى غه توشوب

اوى آسبابلارى نى آليب ينه بر جايى دا بر ناچار بيله محمد يعقوب آقسقال نى كچيك اوغلى ياتغان ايركان آلارنى اوستيغه كركانلاريدا مذكور

بله عبدالله دايم ديب تانيغان مذكور باله نى عبدالله ديكان اغزى نى توتوب سونكره مذكور اوى نى تمامى آسبابلارى نى آليب كيب دورلار

سونكره آزانى مونده كيليب معلوم قيلغاچ قاضى ايشان لاردين بر امين آلدوروب يانيغه بر خدمت كاريم نى قوشوب يباردوم آلار بارغاندين

سونكره مذكور اولكان آدم نى كوروب دفن ايتماكيغه بويوروب ايزچى آليب كليب مذكور ايزچى اوغرى لاردين بر پياده بيلان

بر تيوه نى ايزى نى آليب بويقزاقلى مذكور عبدالله ديكان نى اوبى غه آليب باريب دور سونكره مذكور محمد يعقوب آقسقال ديكان نى اوزى كيليب

اوشبو نى معلوم ايتديكيم مذكور عبدالله ديكان نينك كماندارييم هم اوشبو تورور ديب معلوم قيلدى سونكره مونداغى يموت نوكرلاردين

ايكى نفرى نى بيش آريق حاكمى نى آويغه فتك يازيب يباريلدى بيش آريق حاكمى الارنى يانيغه كيشى قوشوب همراه مذكور عبدالله ديكان نى اوبى غه

باريب مذكور عبدالله ديكان بيله جماش ديكان مونده آليب كيلديلار اوشبونى خدمت لارى غه معلوم ايتادورميزكيم مذكور عبدالله ديكان بيله

جماش ديكان اوغرى لارنى و هم مذكور محمد يعقوب آقسقال و ايشجان آقسقال و ساتم ديكان لارنى خالباى قاضى بيله قوشوب خدمت لارى غه يباريلدى

داغی معلوملاری بولغایکم دور غاویک لی محمد رحیم بای دیکان نی یاز ایامیدا بولادورغان جایی غه اوغری توشوب دهقانچلیق آسبابلاری بیله بر پشه خانه

بر چای نیک کاسه بر تونچه بر پازه بر آز سامانی نی آلیب دورلار آزانی ایزی نی آلیب بوای لی جمعه نیاز دیکان نی اویی غه آلیب بارغانلاریدا مذکور

جمعه نیاز دیکان اویی نی قراتمای دور کیلیب مونده معلوم قیلغاچ مونداغی یموت قراول لاردین ایکی نفر لاری نی بویوروب آلار باریب مذکورنی اویی نی

و ایکی طرف ایلات نی کدخدا آقسقال لاری بیله بارلاغانلاریدا مذکور نی اویی دین بر پازه بر تونچه بر پشه خانه بر چای نیک کاسه سین تانیب دور سونکره مذکور اوغری لارنی مونده آلیب کیلکاندین سونکره مذکور جمعه نیاز و باباجان دیکان لار دین سورالغانده اول انکار بولوب سونکره بویون بولدیلار

اوشبو نی هم خذمت لاری غه معلوم ایتادورمیزکیم مذکور تاپلغان نمرسه لاری نی محمد رحیم بای غه تابشوروب مذکور ایکی نفر لاری نی هم خالبای

قاضی بیله قوشوب خذمت لاری غه یباریلدی دیب صورت واقعه اوشبولاردورکم خذمت لاری غه تحریر ایتلدی ۷ نچی ماه جمادی الثانی دا ۱۳۳۶ نچی یلی

داغی معلوم لاری بولغایکم حانقاه یاش کته لاری التماس ایتادورلارکیم اوشبو طریقه نامدار اوغری لاردین اوچ تورت نفرلاری غه اولوم جزاسی

بریلسه ایرکان اکر جزا و تنبیه بریلماسه کون کوندین اوغری کوپراق بولادورغان کورونادور دیب تحریر ایتلدی

مهر: آقمهر حاجی محمد بای

Document 47

وزارت پناه نجابت دستگاه امانکلدی بای یساولباشی
آقامیزنینک معلوم لاری بولغایکم اویغورلی عبدالله
دیکان نی خاتونی نی عبادالله دیکان بی وجه اوروب
بیرکوزی نی جراحت دار ایتکانی سبب لی مذکور عبادالله نی
مونده آلدوروب سوراماقچی بولغانمیزده قاچیب کتیب
آندین سونک آقسقالی غه بویوردوق مذکور عبادالله نی
تابغین دیب شولوجه دین ایرتنکی کونی قوشاق دیکان
نکیدین تاپیب کلتوروب همه آقسقال کدخدالاری
اوزلاری تاشقاریده یراشتوروب جراحت
دارغه ملحم فلی دیب اون طلا و یساول حقی وکدخدا
فلی دیب جمی اوتوز آلتی اوتوز یتی طلای چقیب ایردی

[verso]

شوندین سیزنینک سی[73] قلونکیز دیب بیزغه
اون یتی طلا قویدیلار باشقه لاری نی کدخدالاری
و یساول لاری و ملحم فلی لاری غه کتیب دور
ایمدی مذکور عبادالله دیکان نی یساول آلیب
کلیب دور ملا قربان بای و یولداش آقسقال لار
اوروب یتمش بیش طلام نی آلدیریب آنینک
اول سوزی بیکاره دور صورة واقعه
اوشبو دور دیب ۱۷ نچی ماه ربیع الثانیدا
خط بتلدی
۱۳۳۵ نچی
یلدا
مهر: عبد الرحیم بای ابن محمد یوسف بقال

---

73 Textual variation of سعی.

Document 48

وزارت فناه[74] یساولباشی آغامیزنینک خدمت لاریغه معلوملاری بولسونکم تاشحوضلی قوتلوق مراد صوفی دیکان کیلب معلوم قیلدی مناق ده اولتوروملی قوربان بای دیکان موندین مقدّم التی ای لیق ده اویومده مهمان بولوب آطم نی اوغورلاب و ینه بر ککز فوستون لاریم نی آلیب کیتیب ایردی الحال مناق بازاریده تافدیم دیب مذکور قوربان بای دیکاندین سوراساق منکر بولدی مذکور قوربان بای دیکان نی یانیغه نوکر آطلی قوشوب آط ایکاسی قوتلوق مراد صوفی دیکان نی هم خدمت لاریغه یباریلدی اوشبو نی معلوم قیلورمیز دیب ۲۲نچی ماه ربیع الثانی دا ساغ سلامت لیک لارین تیلاب خط بتلدی ۱۳۳۵

مهر: محمد یعقوب بای ابن جبار قلی محرم ۱۳۳۴

74 sic.

Document 49

وزارت پناه حکومت دس کا[75] یاسول باشی[76]
اقامیزنینک جناب لاریغه مع روز[77] اولکیم قره داشلی
آغا دی کان ربیع الاول آی نی سکز لانچی کونی کیلب
عرض ایتدی فخر دیکان اکه سینک قیز[78] بیلان بر یکت نی
اولدروب دور بزلارکا بر امین بیرونک دیب
قازی[79] ایشان نیک یانلاریغه بر امین نی قوشوب
یوبردوک باروب برکا کورینک لار دیب باریب
میت لارین کورب میتنی میت ین ایکالاریغه
بیروب یوبردوک دیرلار جاراجتی[80] بارمو دیب
قازی[81] ایشان دین سورادوق بر یکی یریدین
فیچاق و تیاق جراحتی بار دیرلار اول کان کیشی
لارنی خوس تار لاریدین سورادق دوانکز[82] بارمو دیب
آلار آی دیلار ایکی سینی برکا اول درکان دین سونک

[verso]

دوامیز[83] یوق دی دیلار دیب ربیع الاول
آی نی ۲۲ سیده خط بیتلدی سنه ۱۳۳۵
مهر: محمد کریم یوزباشی ابن اسماعیل ۱۳۳۴

---

75 Textual variation of دستگاه.
76 Textual variation of یساولباشی.
77 sic.
78 sic.
79 Textual variation of قاضی.
80 Textual variation of جراحت.
81 sic.
82 Textual variation of دعوا.
83 sic.

Document 50

هو

عزت نشان یساولباشی اقانینک معلوم لاری بولغایلارکیم و یارمیش بویلی مسجد چعش میراب کاتلی دا رحیم بای و اتامرادلارنینک اویکا تورت آطلی و آلتی فیادا قوشولوب مذکور رحیم بای نینک بر جوفت اوکوز و بر سیغیری نی آلیب و اتامراد مذکورنینک خاتونین اطیب اولدوروب و بر دهقانین هم فیچاقلاب یارادار اتیب کیتب دور و ینه چلنک توابعدا حیتن دیکانینک هم اویکا بیش آلتی قویولوب و بیر سیغیری نی آلیب مذکور حیتن نینک اوزی نی آطیب اولدوروب کیتب دور ایمدی تاشحوض توابع نینک چار[84] اطراف لاریده بیر یکی اوچ کوندین بری شونینک و دیکار ایش لار قوزغالیب توروب دور و شول مذکور جای باسیب و مال آلیب و آدم اولدوروب یورکان اطلی و فیادا یموتلارنی سیدنیازنینک اطلی و فیاداسی دیب آیتوشورلار و ینه داغی تاشحوض فقرالاریغه بی تیکیش بی اورون و بیر قاره ایش لارنی

[verso]

ایتیب سن دا فلان نمرسه و فلان وجلاریم[85] بار دیب بی تیکش بی شریعت بی وجی شر[86] ایشلارنی ایتیب یروب دورلار تاشحوض توابع لاری کوب نادینچ[87] دور و ینه داغی فقرالارغه بیر نمرسه آد[88] و قوی نی مینک منات و یکی مینک منات لارین هم آلیب یوروب دورلار ایمدی اوشبولارنی خدمت لاریغه معلوم قیلامیز دیب خط بتلدی

۱۸ نچی ماه رجبدا ۱۳۳۶ نچی یلدا

مهر: جمعه نیاز محرم ابن محمود دیوان

84 Textual variation of چهار.
85 Textual variation of وجه‌لاریم.
86 Textual variation of بی وجه شرعی.
87 Oghuz rendering of ناتینچ.
88 Oghuz rendering of آت.

Document 51

عزت و سعادات نشانه یساوباشی[89] اقانینک معلوم لاری بولغای لارکیم ایش جان بای دیکان نی اویکا اوغری توشکان سبب لی خدای برکان قول دیکان نی قولیدین و بر تونک نی دانیب[90] بیزنی یانیمزغه آلیب کیلدی لار و بیز سوراش غانیمزدا آیتورمان ینه بر ادم بیله همرالوغدا[91] بوغدا[92] و قوی و تونک لارین الدیم دیب ایقرار[93] بولدی و شوندین سونکرا اقسقال وکدخدا لاری بیزلار ایلات غه باریب اوشبو سوزلارنی سوراشیب سونکرا یانیکیزا کیلتورورمیز دیب کفیل بولوب الیب کتیب ایردیلار و شول اقشامی خیوه غه کتیب ایش جان بای دیکان نینک اوستیکا اطلی یباریب دور ایمدی اوشبو خدای برکان قول

[verso]

دیکان کوب بیهوده یمان آدم دور ایمدی اوشبونی خذمت لاریغه قیلامیز دیب ماه جمادی الثانی دا خط بتلدی ۱۳۳۵

مهر: جمعه نیاز محرم ابن محمود دیوان

89 Clearly یساولباشی.
90 Oghuz rendering of تنیب.
91 Fonetic rendering of همراهلیقدا.
92 بوغدای.
93 Textual variation of اقرار.

Document 52

وزارت پناه و حکومت دستگاه یساولباشی آقامیزنینک خدمتلاریغه معروض اولکم قونکرات آچی قوبی لی باباجان اقسقال دیکان فوت بولدی دیب معلوم ایتکانی اوچون قاضی ایشان بیله اوز طرفدین بر آدم یباریب متوفای مذکورنی وارث لارینی بارلاب سوراشغانلاریدا بر سینکلسی بار ایرمیش قوچقار اقسقال دیکان من یقین قرینداشی من مونی مال اشیألاریغه وارث بولورمن دیر ایمش انی وارث لقیغه ایلی نی اقسقال و غیر کدخدالاریدن اعتبار ایتمایدور باشقه اوغلی و قیزی یوق ایرکان شول سببلی مذکورنی قرض لاری بیله یر ملک و غیر اسبابلاری نی اقسقال کدخدالارینی حضورلاریدا رویخط ایتوب مذکور رویخط نی خدمتلاری غه یباریلدی مذکور قوچقار اقسقالنی ایل اتی نی بعضی کدخدا

[verso]

لاری وارث لیق و قرینداش ایرکانلیک لاری راست دور دیر مذکور رویخط دا بیان بولغان مال اسباب یوق بولماس دین اوّل نه مهربانلق لاری بولسه خط بیله معلوم قیلسه لار دیب

۵نچی ماه شعباندا خط بتلدی ۱۳۳۶نچی

مهر: محمد یوسف بای ابن پهلوان محرم

Document 53

وزارت پناه یساولباشی اقامیزنینک خذمت لاریغه معلوم بولغایکم
قونکرات لی مسجد ایل امان یوزباشیدا الله بیرکان اقسقال نی
قومیدن جمعه نظر دیکان اوتکان یلي کوزاک فصلیدا حانقه
بازاریدا بر آطین اوغورلاتیب اوغری سی نی هنوزغچه
تاپمای یورکان ایرکان اوشبو یلي ۸ نچی ماه ذالقعده[94] دا
قوش نظر ولد دولت مراد دیکان نی اطیدا یوق بولغان
آطیداغی سالیب یورکان یونه سی نی تانیب مذکورنی توتوب
حضوریمزغه کیلتوردی بز سورادوق سن بو یونه نی قایدین
الدینک مونی اوغورلانغان اطی نی اوستیده کیتکان یونه
ایرمش دیب اول ایتدی من بو یونه نی حانقه نی
بازاریدن ساتغون الیب ایردوم دیب بیز ینه احتیاط

[verso]

بیله تفتیش ایتب سورادوق یوق بولوب اوغورلانغان
آط اوستیداغی یونه سندین چیقدی سن توغریسین ایتماسانک
سینکا جزا بیریلور دیب شولتوغریدا قوش نظر ایتدی
من مونی آطی نی حانقه بازاریدن اوتکان یلي کوزک وقتیدا
اوغورلاب الیب بیر قزاقغه اوتوز طلا غه ساتیب
تنکسینی الدوم دیب سونکره ایکی طرف نی کدخدا اقسقال لاری
مذکور قوش نظرنی آطی نی جمعه نطرنی اوغورلانغان آطی اوچون
الیب بریب رضالاشدوردیلار و اوغری قوش نظر
مذکورنی اقسقال کدخدالاری ایلتماس[95] ایتب کناهی نی

94 sic.
95 Textual variation of التماس.

تیلایدورلار شول سببلی مذکورنی ساقلاندی ایمدی مذکورنی
کدخدالارینی ایلتماس[96] لاری بویونچه مهربانلیغ لاری بولسه

[recto]

بوشاتیب یبارورمیز واکر موندا یبارسونلار دیکان
پرمایش لاری بولسه خذمتینکزغه
یبارورمیز دیب ۱۲ نچی ذالقعده[97] دا خط بتلدی ۱۳۳۶ نچی

مخفی قالماسونکیم مذکور قوش نظرنی اقسقال کدخدالاری نی ایلتماس[98]
لاری سببلی قهقه وکیل بیله قربان اقسقال نی کفیل ایتب
تاپشوردولار

مهر: محمد یوسف بای ابن پهلوان محرم

96 sic.
97 sic.
98 sic.

Document 54

عزت نشان یساولباشی آقانی معلوم لاری بولسون ۱۳ نچی جمادی الاول دا دوشنبه کیچی یعنی کیچه چواندور
موضع دا بولغانحادثه خدایبرکان اشنیاز دیکان نی ایشکی نی آلدیدا بر درخت دین آسیب
اولتوروبدورلار وآقعه نی خبر بردی لار شریعت شعار قاضی ایشان لاردین و اوزیمزدین امین
یباریب موضع مذکورنی آقسقال کدخدا مردم لاری ایلان مذکور امین لار کورکاندین سونکره دفن
ایتماکا جواب بریلدی مذکور کدخدآلارنی خضوریندا واقعه نی سورالدی مذکور کیچه دا مقتول نی اویوندا
آتاسی اشنیاز وآناسی جمعه بیکه وآفاسی شکر بیکه وانی ایری پهلوان وعمکی لاری حسین و عبدالله لار
یاتغان لار مذکور مقتول خاتونی رحمیه بیکه بیله بر اویدا یاتغان لیک دا اوشبو واقعه دین
هیچ برلاری خبر تاپمغان لار تانک دا عبدالله دیکان طحارت اوچون دیشان غه چقیب انی کوروب
نی کاره ایرکانین بیلمای مذکور حسین دیکان غه خبر بریب دور چقیب کوروبدورلار واقعه
شولطریقه ایرکان اندین سونکره مقتول نی خاتونی رحمیه بیکه دین سوز سورالدی ایتورکیم
کیچه ویسنیاز و عبد الرحمن و آدم بای تقلاق دیکان لار بیله ینه بر ادم کریب مذکور
نام لاری بیان بولغان اوچلاری ایریمنی آلیب کیتدی لار بری منی باسیب اولتوروب قالدی

[verso]

مناداغی بیخور[99] بولوبمن باشقه ایش نی بیلمای دورمن ققو اوستدین ایلیک ایرکان دیب چواب بردی

سنی باسیب اولتوروب قالغان کیمدور دیکاندا کورسام تانیدورمن دیب نشانه لارین

آیتدی کورساتیلدی قربان نیاز دیکان نی اوشبودور دیدی مذکور آدم لار نچون ایرینک نی

بو طریقه ایتدی لار دیکاندا ایریم نی مذکور ویسنیاز خاتونی بیله ایشی بار ایردی شولسبب لی

دیب جواب بردی سونکره مقتول نی حوستارلاری اشنیاز جمعه بیکه شکربیکه لاردین

سوز سورالدی آلار ایتورکیم بزلارنی قاندار یمز ویسنیاز بیلان عبدالرحمن

دیکاندور اوغولیمزنی خاتونی رحمیه بیکه درکلی اولتورماکچی ایردی لار اوشبونی

موندین مقدم یاش اولوغ لاریغه معلوم ایتب ایردیم دیب چواب بردی

مذکورنی سوزی نی قلندر آقسقال غایب نظر ارباب لاردین سورالدی معلوم ایتب ایردی

دیب جواب بردی لار سونکره ویسنیاز و عبد الرحمن ادم بای تقلاق قربان نیازلاردین

سوز سورالدی آلار منکیر[100] اندین سونکره مذکور تورت لاری نی میرشب غه تاپشوروب

مذکوره رحمیه بیکه نی کفیل کا بریب صورت واقعه نی خدمت تحریر قیلنب

مهربانچیلق لاریغه قرالدی دیب اوشبو ماه مذکورنی ۱۵ لانچیندا

مکتوب بتلدی ۱۳۳۵ لانچیسیدا

مهر: اسماعیل خواجه ابن ابراهیم خواجه

---

99 Textual variation of بیخبر.

100 Textual variation of منکر.

Document 55

هو

وزارت پناه نجابت دستگاه یساول باشی اقامیزنینک خذمتلاریغه معلوملاری بولغایکم اورکنجدا

غایبو موضعی دا آطلیغ یرده اولتوروملی سیّد حاجی بای اوغلی نینک درگاه عالی لاریغه عرض ایتب اوشبو

یکرمه آلتی لانجی ربیع الثانی دا دوشنبه کونی فوچته[101] خذمتی غه تورتکل غه کیتیب ایردیم عیالیم اوغول بیکه پهلوان قیزی

اویوم دا تنها قالیب ایردی یکرمه یتی لانجی ربیع الثانی دا فوچته نی تاشلاب اویوم غه قایتب کیلیب قراسام

دربازم ایلیک دور شولوجه دین قیچقوردیم هیچ بیر خبر اشیتمادیم آندین سونکره اوزوم نینک

بیر یقن قونکوشیم حاجی پهلوان اوغلی نینک اویدین خبر آلماقچی بولوب بارور ایردیم اویوم نینک یاریم طناب

اوزاقیده مذکور عیالیم نینک اولوکین کوردیم آنی قیچاق ایلان اوروب اولتورلوبدور اوشبونی اولتورکان

حاجی پهلوان اوغلی تورور و هم مذکور عیالیم نی قولیده بیر یوز ایلیک منات تنکه سی نی بارلغین بیلور ایردی شول سبب لی

آندین کورورمندیب امین آلیب باریب مذکور اولوک نی جایلاب قایتب کیلکان ایرکان مذکور اولوک نی و هم

حاجی پهلوان اوغلی نی توغری سیده آلارنینک عنایت نامه لی اقسقالی ایش محمد اقسقال بابانیاز اوغلی و جمعه نیاز اقسقال

ابراهم اوغلی و باباجان اقسقال عبدالله اوغلی و قربان بای اقسقال رحمانبیرکان اوغلی و حاجی نیاز بالطه نیاز

101 Phonetic rendering of the Russian word *pochta*.

اوغلی و سلطان بای شیریم اوغلی ویس نیاز عبدالله اوغلی و ایرنیاز توره اوغلی و باباجان بالطه نیاز اوغلی و ستارقلی

محمد سعید اوغلی دیکانلارنی آلدوروب اوشبو ایش حقّی دا تفتیش ایتب سوراشغانمیزدا آیتادورلارکیم مذکور

سید حاجی بای اوغلی دیکان ایلان حاجی پهلاوان اوغلی دیکان ایکی لاری یقن قونکوشی بولوب اولتورغان اوشبو ایکی

لاریدین غیری اوزلاری نینک یانلاریدا قونکوشی بولوب اولتورغان هیچ بیر کیشی یوقدور بیزلارنینک اولتورغان

یرلاریمز مذکور ایکی لاریغه چهار یک فرسق[102] دیک اوزاق ایردی مذکورنینک نه طریقه دا بولوب اولتورولکانی نی بیزلار

بیلمایدورمیز مذکور حاجی پهلوان اوغلی نینک موندین مقدّم وقت لار دا هم مونکا اوخشاش ایشلارغه مباشر بولوب یورکانی نی

بیزلار اشیتمادوک اوشبو واقعه هر نچاقلی تردّد ایتب کورکانیمزدا هم بیزلارنینک مونکا فهمیمز یتوشمایدور دیب

داغی مذکور سیّد حاجی بای اوغلی آیتادر مذکور عیالیم نی اولتورکان شول حاجی پهلوان اوغلی دیکاندور باشقه آدم ایرماسدور

دیب شول وجه لی مذکور پهلوان اوغلی دین سوراشغانمیزدا آیتادورکیم منینک اوشبو طریقه داغی ایشلاردین اصلا خبریم یوقدور

دیب ایمدی مذکور توغریده

اقسقال کذا و مدّعی و مدّعی علیه لارنینک

سوراشغانمیزداغی بیرکان اوشبو جوابلارین

خذمتلاریغه معلوم قلامیزکیم صورة

واقعه اوشبودور دیب

اوشبو مکتوب ٥نجی جمادی الاولدا

مرقوم بولدی ١٣٢٩نجی یلدا

102 Textual variation of فرسخ.

[verso]

سید بوچته چی اقرار قلدی حاتونوم اوغول بیکه بنت

پهلوان نی اولکانی درکدین حاجی بن پهلوان دین ایکی ایلک طلا صلح غه راضی

بولدوم دیب ماه جمادی الثانی ۶نجی سیدا کدخدالاری باباجان اقسقال و جمعه نیاز

اقسقال

و ایش محمد اقسقال و قربان بای اقسقال ۱۳۲۹

[no seal]

Document 56

وزرات پناه حکومت دستگاه یساولباشی آقامیزنینک خذمتلاریغه معروض اولکیم اون ایکی لانچی ماه صفر دا قم سنکرلی

اوغول کمفر[103] دیکان کیلب معلوم قیلدی کیم اویوم غه یتی آدم کریب بیر قره توری بایطال و بر تازه آرابه[104] و اوچ

باققی قوی بر آرجه شونی ایچنده اون آلتی باتمان تخته نی تنکه سی اون بیش قداق یفاک تورت یفاک میسک

تورت پادشاهی ایکی یکتای تورت یفاک تون تورت آی رویمال ایکی تورمه ایکی قتیغ شاهی و اوچیوز مناتلیق کاغذ

بر کموش بیلازک اوشبو نمرسه لاریم نی آلیب کیتدیلار دیب کماندارینک بارمو دیب سوراغانیمزده اویوم کا کیرکان

یتی آدم نینک بری سارقبای دیکان نی تانی دیم کمانیم شوندین تورور دیکاندین سونکره مذکور سارقبای نی آلدوریب

سوراشغانیمز دا منکر بولدی شول سبب لی آقسقال کدخدالاری بولوب سارقبای اوغری ایماس بیشاآلتی کون آختاریلسون

شاید باشقه براولاردین چقغای دیب سونکره آقسقالی ایشنیاز بیله بالته بای دیکانلار آریاقنی بارلاماق غه

بارغانلاریده صفر قزاق دیکان آیغاق بولوب یوز منات آلیب آیتوبدور سزلارنی اوغرینکز قم سنکرلی

تنکری بردی دوستان ایشجان قزاق اوغلی بیله کلیب آط آرابه[105] نی ساتدی دیب بال محمد دیکان نی اویونده اولتورغانیمزده

مذکور تنکری بردی کیلدی آریاقده مذکور تنکری بردی غه هیچ اوندامادوک بو طرفغه اوتکونچه سونکره مذکور تنکری بردی بیله

103 Fonetic rendering of کمپیر.
104 sic.
105 sic.

یولداشی قزاق دستان نی خطای بازاریده ابراهیم یوزباشی بیله مذکور ایشنیاز آقسقال لار توتوب دورلار ابراهیم یوزباشی

آدمی میز سوراغانده تنکری بردی آیتوب دورکیم مذکور بایطال بیله آرابه[106] نی آریاقده عنایت بولوش نی قول آستیده

ساتدوق اوچ قوی نی قم سنکرلی یوسف مخذوم نی اوغلی اوراض محمد آقسقال نیکی ده سویولدی یولداشلارینک

کیم دیب سوراغانده برکان جواب لاری قم سنکرلی دولت و قل محمد والّش آرانلی و اوراض محمد مخذوم و قزاق

خفر بای دیکان لار تورور دیب مذکور اوغری لارنی ابراهیم یوزباشی بیله آقسقال بزنی حضورمیزغه آلیب کیلدی لار

مذکور اوغری لاردین سورادوق تنکری بردی بیله قزاق دستان آیدی بایطال بیله آرابه[107] اوچ قوی نی آلدوق

باشقه نمرسه لارین آلغانیمز یوق دور دیب آیدی سونکره مذکور تنکری بردی بیله دستان دیکان لارنی یولداشیمز

دیب آیتغانلاری دولت و قل محمد والّش آرانلی دیکانلاردین سورادوق شونده برکان جواب لاری

بزلارغه تهمت تورور لیکن مال نی تولا دیسانکیز تولارمیز دیب آیدیلار و ینه یولداشم دیکان اوراض محمد مخذوم

بیله قزاق خفر بای قاچیب دور حاضر تافیلمادی شول سبب لی بویون بولغان تنکری بردی و قزاق دستان دیکان نی

[verso]

وهم مذکورلارنی یولداشیم دیکان دولت و قل محمد و الّش آرانلی دیکانلارنی ابراهیم یوزباشی بیله قوشوب

106 sic.

107 sic.

خذمت لاریغه یباردوک بعده معلوم لاری بولسون کیم مذکور اوغری لاردین تنکری بردی دیکان اوچتورت یلدین

بویان یمان اوغری بولوب هیچ تاپدورمای آریاقده قاچیب یورکان ایردی اتاسی هم مذکور تنکری بردی دین

بیزار تورور صاحب اختیار دورلار صورة واقعه شول تورور دیب اوشبو عریضه نامه

۲۵ لانجی ماه صفر دا مرقوم بولدی ۱۳۳۵ نجی یلدا

مهر: محمد نیاز بای ابن قاسم دیوان

Document 57

فضیلت نشان یساولباشی آقامز نی خذمتلاریغه معروض بوکه عوضمراد یکلیب معلوم قیلدی اوزوم منغت بازاریغه کتکانیم دا اویمکا اوغوری توشوب آلتی مناتی کم بر مینک طلالیق کاغذ مناتیم نی اوغورلاب دور دیب آقسقال کدخدالاری یکلیب جواب سورادی محلت برینک بر ایکی کون توفراق توکوروب کورای دیب سونکرا یکلدیلار توقوز یوز اوتوز منات نی توفراق بیله تاشلادیلار دیب سونکرا مذکور عوضمراد یکلدی منینک کماندا‌ریم ویس و خالمراد و ایرکین بایلار دیب مذکور اوچ آدمدین تفتیش ایتب سوراشغانیمز دا منکر بولدیلار عوضمراد من دولت آعلاغه بارورمن بایلو خطی برینک دیب بوکوندین بش کون سونک یعنی ایمدی یکلور سه شنبه کونی خذمت ینکزدا تاپیلماقچی بولدیلار مذکور اوچ آدم غه یوسف صفاش اوغلی کفیل تورور صاحب اختیار دیب ۲نچی جمادی الاولدا جمعه کونی خط بتلدی ۱۳۳۵نچی یلدا

مهر: [※] یوزباشی ابن رحمت الله یساولباشی

Document 58

وزارت پناه و حکومت دستگاه یساول باشی اقامیزنینک خذمتلاریغه معلوم بولسونکیم شه اباد موضعیداغی قم یافلی محمد مرادبای نینک قومیده تاجی نیاز دیکان نینک دوشنبه کچه سی یاریم اقشام وقتدیده اویکا بر نچه اوغریلار باریب مال اشیاءلاریدین بر جوفت[108] اوکوز و بر یابو و بر قوچقارلارنی و اوی اسبابلاریدین بر ینکی ایتوک و ینه بر کهنه ایتوک و ینه ایکی چفان و ایکی کیکز و آلتی قوشه رویمال و ناجار کویلاکی و بر آلاچه یلاک و بر قومچه و اوچ قوزی تریسی و بر چای نیک و ایکی کاسه و بر باتمن توقوم باش و بر باتمن تاریغ و ینه یوز منات لیق کغاز اقچه مذکور بولغان نمرسه لارنی الیب خواتونی[109] و بر اوغلی نی اویکا سالیب اوستیدین ایلب مذکور تاجی نیاز نی ایکی قولینی ارقه سیغه بغلاب یلکاسیدین چالیب کیتکان ایرکان لار دیب مذکور ایلات نی اقسقالی خبر برکان حالده قاضی ایشان لارنینک تلابی[110] بیله بر ادم یباریلدی ایمدی مذکور آدم نینک کیتکان مال اشیاءلاری بیله اوزی نینک بولغان واقعه لارینی خذمتلاریغه خط اتیب یباریلدی

[verso]

نی طریقه مهربان بولسه لار اوزلاری بیلور دیب ماه رجب نینک یکرمه یتی لانچی کونی یردی خط بتلدی ۱۳۳۹

مهر: محمد صفا آتالیق ابن عبدالله آتالیق ۱۳۳۵

108 Textual variation of جفت.
109 Textual variation of خاتون.
110 Textual variation of طلب.

Document 59

هو العزیز

وزارت پناه حکومت دستگاه یساول باشی آقامیزنی جنابلاریغه عرضمیز بوکیم دعاکوینکیز مسافر خانه ده استقامت قیلیب دعای خیرینکزنی تیلاب خوارزم شاه علیه الرحمه کا باریب دام دولته نینک حق لاریغه دعای خیر ایتب مریدلار بیرلان صدقه بیرماک اوچون باریب ایردوک صدقه نی بیریب خفتن دین سونک قایتیب کیلیب قوشومیز غه کیلساک یازیان درچه میز نی بیر آدم دیشانغه چیقسه زلف نی بوزوب دورغان ایرکان کیمسین دیکان دین قاچیب کیتکان ایکان تانیبسه نظام ایکان پچاقی قالیب ایرکان آقسقال باباغه باریب معلوم ایتب قوشومیزغه کیلیب اولتورساق بیر ایکی آقا اینی‌سی بیرلان آتاسی اورونک دیب بویوروب اوچ تورت آدمیزنی اوزیمیز نی اوروب کوب حقارت بیریب حریت دیب اوروب ینه بیر باله سی مانکلای نی زلف غه اوروب قانیتب بیزلار نی اوستومیزدین عرض غه باریب باراب دی مذکور بولغان حادثه شول تورور

مهر: عبدالله سالم

Document 60

عزتماب مالا اکتساب یساول باشی اقامیزنینک معلوم لاری بولغایکم طمه لی آدینه مراد دیکان جمعه نیاز و محمد یعقوب بای

دیکان لارغه بلتورغی یلي بر مینک ایکیوزکلته قامیش حقی بار دیب یکرمه توقوز طلا الیب دعواسنی اوتیب

خط بریب ایرکان و ینه برادرلاری خدای بردی و محمد شریف دیکانلارغه التی کولته بیده حقی بار

دیب اون بیش طلا الیب خط بریب ایرکان ایمدی بو یل ینه شول لارنینک ینه بر برادری

باباجان دیکان غه اون بر یاریم باتمن شالیم بار دیب دعوی قیلب قاضی ایشانلارنینک حضورلاریغه الیب باردی مذکور ایشانلارنینک حضورلاریده ۲ نچی آدینه مراد اوزی نینک

ایلاتی نینک نایب اقسقال کدخدالاری جمع بولوب آدینه مراد مذکور اوزی ناحق توتغوچی

دعوای قاق تورور دیب اقرار بولوب اخبار قلدیلار قلندر نایب و باباجان بای و دربیک

بابانیاز سید و باباجان بای و مدعًا علیه جمعه نیاز و باباجان لارنینک ایلاتی دعواسنی ناحق دیب

اخبار قیلغان لار بغت لی سید محمد اقا و رحمان بردی اقسقال وتازه بای و یعقوب بای دیکانلار

تورورلار آندین سونکره مذکور خط لارنی کوروب و هم مذکور ادم لار بر نجه دفعه قسم ایتدی

دیب خبر برکانلاری وجهدین ایشان لار مرافعه سنی سورامادیلار ایمدی اوزلاری بیلورلار

دیب عریضه نامه بتلدی ۱۳۳۵

مهر: شاه مراد بای ابن دولت مراد بای

Document 61

وزارت پناه و نجابت دستگاه عزت نشان یساول باشی آقاغه اعلام اوکم آریاقلی آغه جان ایشانمیز بزدین التیماس[111] قیلدیلار کم فتنک بیله درغان آتا علیه الرحمه اورتا لیق داغی آریاقلی آتالارنی دعوا جنجل لاری اوچون بر قاضی بولسه دیب شولوجه دین مذکور آریاقلی آتالاردین ملا نجم دیکان غه حضرتیمز بله قاضی کلان ایشانمیزنینک خذمتلاریغه معلوم ایتب یارلیق بیله مهر آلیب برسون لار ایشانمیزنینک التیماس[112] ایتکان سببلی دیب ٤١نچی ماه ذو القعده اینده یکشنبه کونی ١٣٣٧ خط بتلدی

مهر: محمد قربان سردار ابن حاجی بای ١٣٣٧

111 Textual variation of التماس.

112 sic.

Document 62

قیلیچ بایلی خالنیاز یوزباشی و صفر محمد نوکارلارنینک حمزه قزاق بیله دعوا لاری حقّیدا حضرتمز دام دولته نینک درکاه عالی لاریده صاف بولماقچی بولوب مدة اوچ کون وعده قیلب هر قایسی‌سی مذکور اوچ کونده درکاه عالم پناه لاریغه باریب تافیلماسه بارغان آدم معلوم قیلیب یساول آلسه قالغان آدم یساول حقین برسون دیب وعده قیلدی لار دیب ماه رمضان نینک ۸ نچی جمعه کونی اوشبو خط مذکور خالنیاز یوزباشی لارغه بریلدی

دیب ۱۳۳۲ بتلدی

مهر: محمد لطیف خواجه ابن عبد الکریم جواجه ۱۳۳۱

Document 63

چپان بای قزاق بیله قیلچ وکیل دیکان قراداشلی نینک بر تیوه اولکان دراکلی دعواسی حقّیدا [*][113] نینک درکاه عالی لاریده باریب صافلاشماقچی بولوب مدّة بیش کون وعده قیلیب مذکور بیش کونده درکاه عالم پناه دا تافیلماقچی بولدی لار هر قایسی سی مذکور مدّتلی کونده باریب درکاه عالم پناه لاریده تافیلماسه بارغان آدم یساول آلسه بارمای قالغان آدم یساول حقین برسون دیب حضوریمیزده وعده قیلدیلار دیب ماه ربیع الثانی نینک ۲۴ نچی دوشنبه کونی اوشبو بایلو خطی قیلچ وکیل غه بریلدی معلوم بولغایدیب ۱۳۳۲

مهر: محمد لطیف خواجه ابن عبد الکریم جواجه ۱۳۳۱

113 Invocation has been missed.

Document 64

هو العفو
حضرت امین السّلطنه و رکن الدّوله محب علما
و مشفق فقرا و غربانینک دربار فلک مدارلاریغه یوز مینک دعا
و آلقیشدین سونکره معلوم ضمیر آفتاب تنویرلاری بولغایکیم خدمت لاریغه
معروضه بولغان ماما جان بیکه نینک ایری نینک اولکانیغا آلتی آی بولدی دیب
ملا ایر نیاز و جکان صوفی و محمد نیاز میراب و رزاق بیردی مخذوم و عباداللّه محرم
و بابا جان چرچی و محمد نیاز بای و داغی مونداغ آدم لار اقرار بولدیلار
و بولارنینک آیتغانلارینی باور قیلماین نکاح قیلمادوق سید رضا خواجه ایشان
شول خاتون نینک عدّه سی اوتکانغه بیز هم شاهدمیز تیدیلار آندین
سونکره اوزومیز مباشر بولوب حملین و عده سین سوراشیب تحقیقلاب
آنت بیریب پهلوان نیازغه عقد قیلیب بیردوک تورت آی مونده
اولتوروب اورکانج غه بارغان ایرکان آنینک رئیسلاری هم اویلانیب سین
دیب زوردین قولیغه خط بیریب نکاحانه آلیب دورلار دعاکویلاری نکاح
قیلغاندا مذکور بولغان آدم لار هم حاضر بولوب آلارنینک سوز
لاری بیله نکاح قیلیب ایردوک بیارکان محرم لاریغه بیزنی هم چارلادی
لارمو دیکانیمیزده یوق تیدی شول وجهدین خدمت لاریغه
یوز اورماین بیان واقع نی قلم تیلی بیله بیان قیلیندی یوق
ایرسا دعاکویلاریغه مونداغ بی ادب
لیکغه قلم اورماقغه نی حد و نی پارا
بولغای السّلام علیکم
و داغی محمد رضانینک بیرکان
کاغذی صاف بولدی
دعاکویلاری صحرادین
کتابلاریغه مناسب
کاغذ تاپمادی

یکرمه دسته مقداری
کاغذ کرم قیلسالار
اوزلاری بیلورلار
و یا هر نچوک کاغذ
تاپسا یازه بیرسون
دیرلارمو اکر کاغذ
بیریلسا عبا{د} الله محرم
دعاکویلاریغه
قریب راق اولتوروب
دور تقصیر
تقصیر تقصیر

مهر: قاضی و رئیس محمود ابن داملا محمد کریم

Document 65

قُضّاة اسلام و حکام زوی الاحترام نینک معلوم لاری بولسونکیم تاجی نیاز دیکان بزّاز من بازار باشیده بر آدم نینک بیکار تورغان دوکانیغه مالیم نی توشوروب اولتوروب ایردیم خدای برکان دیکان برله شفیع بابا دیکان سین بو دوکاندین تور دیب منی بیوجه شرعی اوروب بر تشیم نی سیندوردیلار و ینه بر تشیم نی توشکودیک و ینه ایکی تیشیم نی بیجا قیلدیلار دیب بر تیشی قولیده و اوچ تیشی اغزیده تبرانیب تورغان کیلیب عرض قیلدی و خدای برکان برله شفیع بابا اورغان لاریغه انکار قیلدیلار و الارنینک اورغان لارین اوچ تورت آدم کیلیب اخبار قیلدیلار و دیکر خدای برکان مذکور برله شفیع بابای مذکور تیشلاری چیقغاندین سونکره بیش طلا بیرورمیز دعوانک نی قوی دیب صلح قیلماقچی‌هم بولوب تورور لار دیب صورت واقعه عرض قیلیندی ایمدی اوزلاری صاحب احتیار تورورلار دیب ۷ ماه شعبانده خط بتلدی ۱۲۶۷

مهر: قاضی و رئیس عبد الغفور [※]

Document 66

نیابت پناه حکومت دستگاه دقیقه شناس رمزرس فلاطون اساس توره میزنینک جناب کیمیاتأثیرلاریغه یوز منک دعا اداسیدین سونک عرض بوکیم مؤمن‌خواجه برله اغالاری نینک اوغول لاری استانه دا بزنینک اللیده مزده[114] کیلیب مرافعه غه اولتوردیلار هر قایسی لاری بر خط چیقاردیلار مؤمن‌خواجه غه اناسی مُلکیم دیب خط برکان ایرکان و بولارغه باباالاری مُلک منیک کی دیب خط برکان ایرکان و بولار آیتورلار یرلارنی بابامیز اوز ملکی ایتیب بزلارکا خط بریب ایردی دیرلار انینک اوچون بولارنی کواه غه سالیب ایردوک بولارکواه لارین الیب کیلسالار مؤمن‌خواجه شهرغه کیتیب تور دیب خبر تاپدیلار بیزنینک اللیده میزده[115] بولغان صورت واقعه شول تورور ینه اوزلار صاحب اختیار تورورلا[116] باقی السلام علیکم و علی من تبع الهدی التقصیر التقصیر و ینه کوب آدم لار ایتورلار یر امین خواجه نینک ملکی تورور

مهر: قاضی شرع شریف استادکریم عصر و حشیم از حد زیاد

---

114 Clearly: آلدیمیزکه.

115 sic.

116 تورورلار.

Document 67

بجناب عالی حضرت ارکان دولت رفیع منزلت ستوده خصلت فریشته طینت عمده الامدی

زبدة الکبری معین الفقرا ظهر الضعفا مروج دین احمدی حامی شریعت مصطفوی باعث الامن و الامان

توره بیک میزنینک خذمت لاریغه بو دعاکوی قدیم الخذمت لارنینک بصد هزار عجز

انکسار یوزیدین عرض اخلاص لاری بوکیم بورینجق دوردی دیکانکه نشانه

مهربان بولوب ایرکان سیز دوردی مذکور بیله محمد نفس و محمد قیلچ نینک دعوالارینی

ایکی طرف نینک کدخدالارینی جمع ایتیب اوز دستورلاری برله صاف لش تورسونلار

دیب بجان دل قبول قیلب دوردی مذکوردین محمد نفس و محمد قیلچ مذکورلارغه

خط یباردیک محمد نفس مذکور کلدی و محمد قیلچ مذکور کلمادی بلکه ایزا[117] و حقارت

بروب تور دیب ایشتدوک ایمدی سیز صاحب اختیار تورورسیز تقصیر

تقصیر تقصیر

مهر: قاضی جان محمد ابن ملا محمد دوردی

117 .ایذا

Document 68

خلیفه السلطان الاعظم و نایب الخانان المحترم مُحبّ العلمأ مشفق الفقراءغه
عرضیمیز بوکیم داملا رحمت الله جمعه کونی نماز جمعه دین اول کیلب آیتدی عبد الرحمن
دیکان وقف نینک غلّه سی اوچون بارغانده بیزنی اوردی و اینسی سوکدی اندین
سونک کیشی بیردوک اینسین آلیب کیلدی مرافعه قیلدیلار اینیسی منکر بولدی اندین
سونک بر بولاک جماعه شاهد بولدیلار سوکنی راست دیب اندین سونک تعزیر
قیلدوق
آلتی تعزیر اورغانده ملا مذکورنینک اوزی تیلاب آلدی اندین سونک خفتن وقتیده
عبد الرحمن مذکور حاضر بولدی ملا مذکور بیلان مرافعه قیلجق بولوب بز آیتدوق
ایرتنک
کیلونک دیب شنبه کونی ایرتنک نماز وقتیده عبد الرحمن مذکور کیلدی اقشام قایتب
بارياتورده ملا مذکور قرینداشلاریدین اوچ کیشی بزنی اولتورجک بولدیلار
بازارچیلار
قول لاریدین یازدوروب الیب یباردیلار توره حضرتیمیزغه عرضیمیز بار دیدی بز
ایتدوق
حقارت دعواسی صافلاشسون اندین سونک کیتارسز دیدوک ملا مذکور کیلکانچه
توقف
قیلسون ملا مذکور کیلمس دین بورون سزکا عرض
قیلمق اوچون کیب تورور دیب عریضه نامه بتلدی

مهر: قاضی [※]

Document 69

حضرتمیز دام دولته [*]
حضرت خلیفه الرحمان ظل السبحان اسکندرنشان قیصرپاسبان
باعث الامن و الامان [*] نینک استان عالی لاریغه یوز منک دعاء
و القیش اداسیدین سونک عرض بوکیم فتنک کدخدالاری
نی یکلتوروب سوراشدوق آلار ایتورلار سونک
ضعیفم بیله کوردوم دیکانی یلغان سوز تورور
اما اوزی محروم میراث ایرکان انی اولتوروب
ملکی کا ایکا بولماقچی ایرکان و ینه شول اولکان نینک
صغیرلاری نینک قولیدین خط لارین هم باسیب الیب
ایرمیش شول واقعه لارنی سوراشیب جنابلاریغه
یباریب ایردوک کدخدالاری هم اولکانین یخشی
راق کورارلار ینه اوزلاری صاحب اختیار تورور
لار باقی الهی ایام بکام دولت مستدام بولسون
مهر: [※]

Document 70

توره بیکیمزنیک جناب عالیلاریغه عرضلاریمز بوکم قره توفه‌لی فقرألارخذ متیکزغه عرض ایتکان ایرکانلار بزنیک اوستی میزکا عرب طایفه سی قوتلی مراد دیکان آدمنی یساول دیب کیلتوروب عبد الرحیم صوفی دیکان آدمنی کوب اوروب مجروح ایتدی شول ضرب سببلی صوفی مذکور اولدی و ینه سزمهربان بولغان ایرکان سز بودعاکوی لارغه بزنیک آدمیمز برلا و برنجه کدخدالار بیله اولکان آدمنی کورونکلار دیب بودعاکویلار شول موضع کدخدالاری برلا اولوکنی کوردی ارقه سیده کوک بار ایرکان بودعاکویلارغه معلوم بولغان شونجالی تورورایمدی اوزلاری صاحب اختیار توروروا ضح باد السلام السلام علیکم

مهر: قاضی و رئیس عمرخواجه [※]

مهر: قاضی رحمان بردی [※]

Document 71

دعای سلام بلا نهایه و بلا غایه زاده عمره و مسنده توره بیکیمزکه بعده مخفی قالماسون بویورغان

امرلارین مهماامکن (؟) قولیمیز دین کیلکانیچه قیلدوق شول میت نینک بری آق سقال لیق تورور وقل چماق تورورشول آق سقال نینک ایکی کونه[118] تونی هم بارتورور ینه هم قزاقی برچکمان هم بارتورور و ینه برکونه[119] فچاقی و برکونه[120] ایدوکی هم بارتورور و ینه بری بی سقال

یکیت توروراوچ تونی بار بری قیزیل و ینه بری آق بالقی و ینه برکهنه تونی بارتورور و ینه برآق بالقی تقیه سی بارتورورو ینه هم برکوک شفرمه سی هم بارتورورشول ایکی میت نینک یاتغان یرلاری خان حضرت میزنینک یرلاری تورور و ینه شول میت لارنینک یاتغان

یرلاری راه عامه توروراطراف لارینده قان هم یوق تورورو ینه میانه میت مذکور ومیانه اهل منکغیت تخمینایکرمه طناب یرتورورو ینه کارنده نینک کت خدالاری وقبچاق نینک کت خدالاری وارباچی نینک کت خدالاری ومنکغیت نینک کت خدالاری همه لاری کیلیب دفن قیلدوق و ینه قبچاق عمل دارلاری آکاه ایرماس ایرکان و ینه کارنده لار قاضی سیغه خبر برکان ایرکان و ینه منکغیت کت خدالاری هم ایشیت کان ایرماس ایرکان

مهر: [※]

118 Textual variation of کوهنه.

119 sic.

120 sic.

Document 72

حضرتیمیز دام دولته [*]
خلیغه الرحمن ظل السبحان [*] نینک استان فلک مدارلاریغه تومان منک
دعاء ارسالیدین سونک عرض بوکیم خاصه بوینده بر آدم اوز ضعیفه
سینی اورب اولتوروب حضرت شاه بابانینک
مزاراتی نینک بر طرفیغه کیلتوروب تاشلابدور کدخدا
لارنی جمع ایتیب سوراشدوق کدخدا آیدیلار اوز
کیاوی اولتوروب تاشلابدور اندین سونک شول
کیاو بولغوچی نی قینادوق اقرار ایتدی اوزیم اولتوروب
ایلتیب تاشلادیم دیدی حتی کدخدالاری هم ایتورلار
بول بدبخت زیاده یمان تورور اگر بول حادثه دین
قوتولوب چیقسه بزلار همه میزنی کوچورور دیرلار
ینه اوزلاری صاحب اختیار تورور دیب عرضه داشت ایتلدی
باقی ایام بکام دولت مستدام بولغای آمین و رب العالمین
و ینه عرض
بوکیم اولکان
ضعیفه نینک هیچ
خوسداری و
کیشی سی هم یوق
ایرکان اصلاً

مهر: [※]

Document 73

عریضه داشت اداسیدین سونکره حضرت توره بیکیمیزنینک
خذمت عالی لاریغه عرض لاریمیز بوکیم شهری بیکه نینک اوغلی عظیم بای نینک اولوکین کوروب
هر نه اعضاسیده جراحت و داغ و نشانه سی بولسه کوروب جنازه سین
اوقوب دفن قیلدوروب کورکاندیک یساول برله خط قیلیب یبارسونلار دیب
امر عالی لاری بولوب ایرکان بو امرنینک امتثالی اوچون اولوک نینک
اوستیکا یساول برله باریب اولوغ وکیچیک لارین جمع ایتیب اولوک نی
یلانغاچلات توروب کوردوک اغزی و بورنیدین قان کیتکان
وکوکراکیدین تاکیندیک نینک اشاقیغاچه کوک و قولتوقی نینک تکیده
هم کوکی بار ایرکان و سینغان و بوزیلغان و جراحت بولغان
یری یوق و بزلارکا نه وجهیدین کوک بولغانی معلوم ایرماس
و ینه عرض بوکیم بو حادثه دین برار آی بولدی شهری بیکه نینک دعوی
کرلار برکهنه تون و بر پیچاق توزوکنی الیب کیلدیلار اقشام اوچاکده
عظیم بای دیکان نی توتدوق بزلارنینک قولومیزدین
قاچیب کیتدی یماق و توزوکین الیب قالدوق دیب
کلیب ایردیلار صورت واقعه بو ایردی
عرض قیلندی ایمدی اوزلاری
صاحب اختیار تورورلار
التقصیر التقصیر التقصیر

مهر: [※]

Facsimiles

Section One

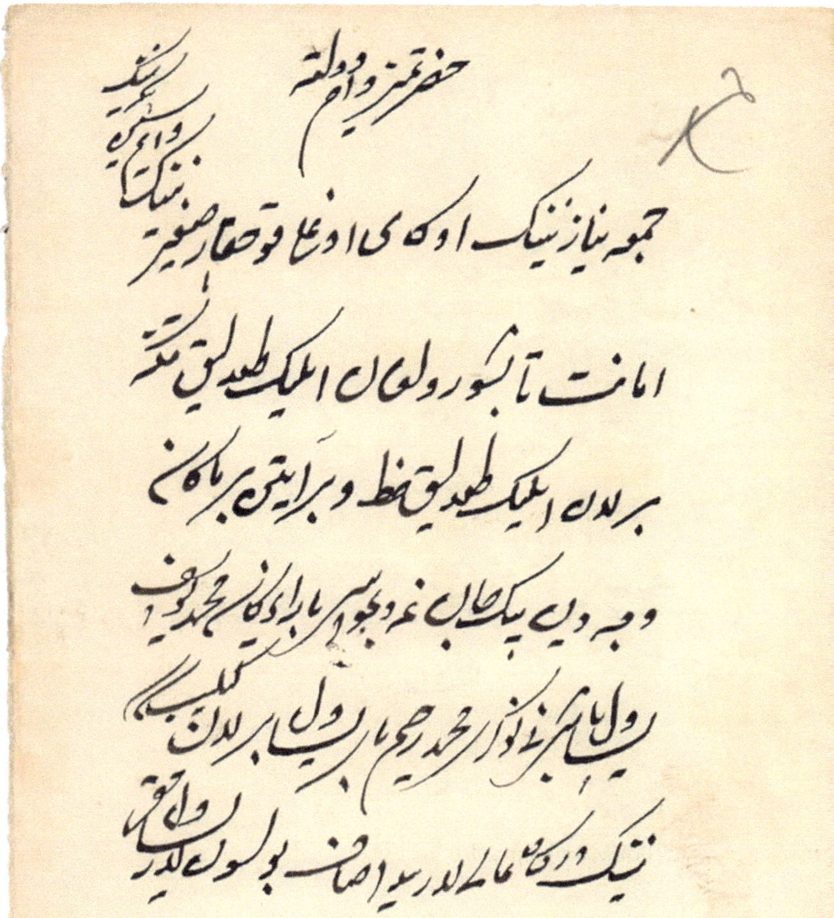

DOCUMENT 1A TsGARUz, I-125, op. 2, d. 633, l. 7

© KONINKLIJKE BRILL NV, LEIDEN, 2020 | DOI:10.1163/9789004427907_008

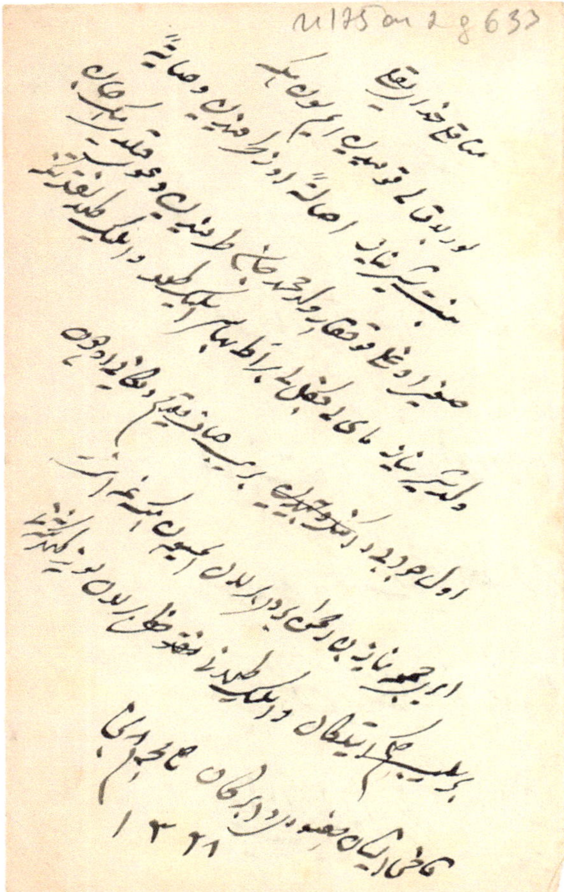

DOCUMENT 1B TsGARUz, I-125, op. 2, d. 633, l. 7 ob

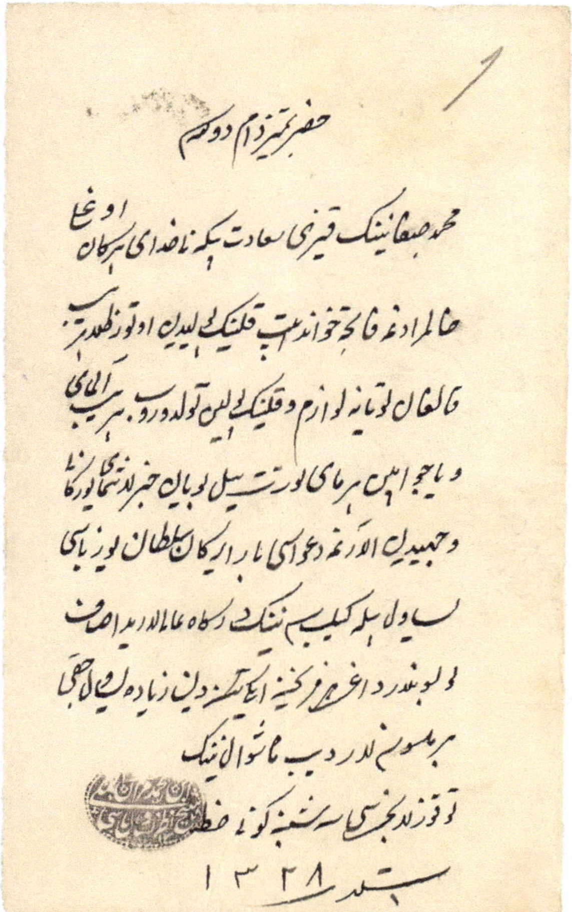

DOCUMENT 2A TsGARUz, I-125, op. 2, d. 633, l. 1

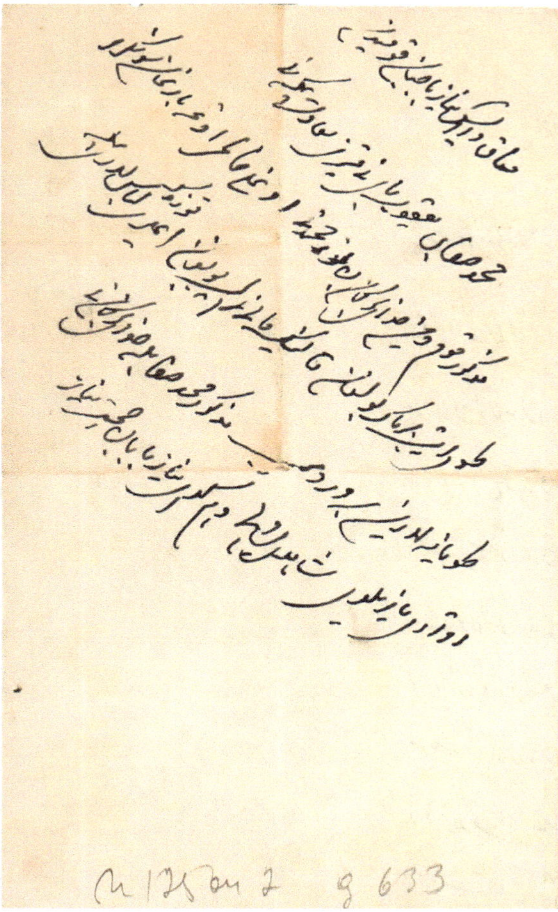

DOCUMENT 2B TsGARUz, I-125, op. 2, d. 633, l. 1 ob

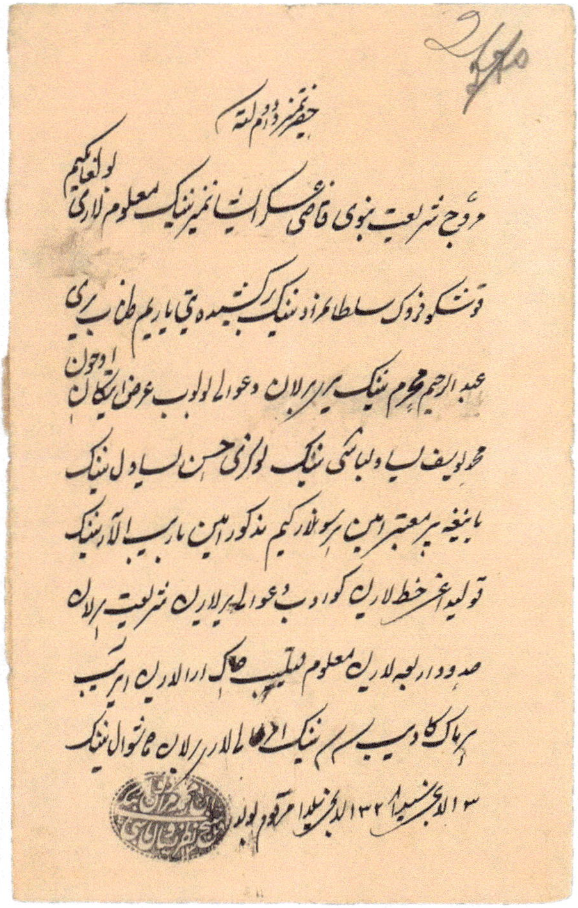

DOCUMENT 3A TsGARUz, I-125, op. 2, d. 633, l. 24

DOCUMENT 3B TsGARUz, I-125, op. 2, d. 633, l. 24 ob

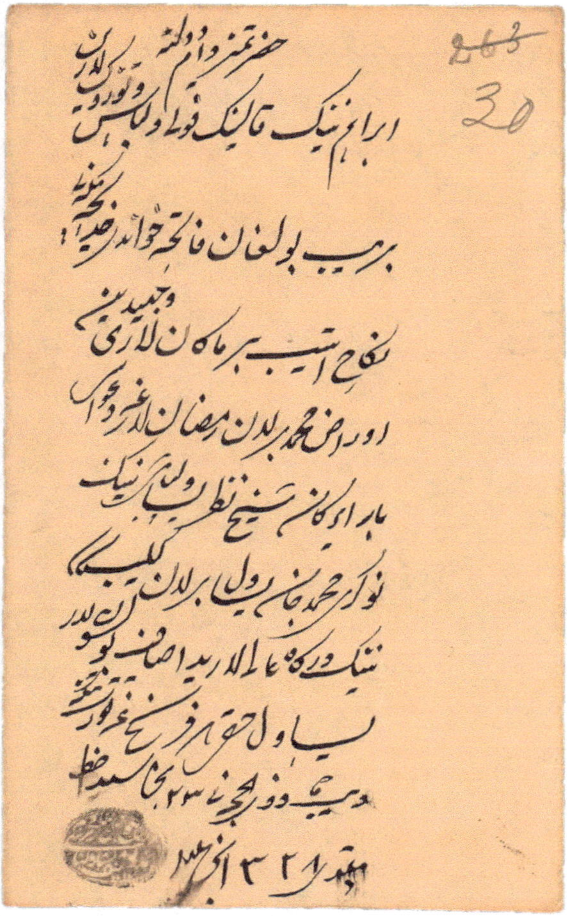

DOCUMENT 4A TsGARUz, I-125, op. 2, d. 633, l. 30

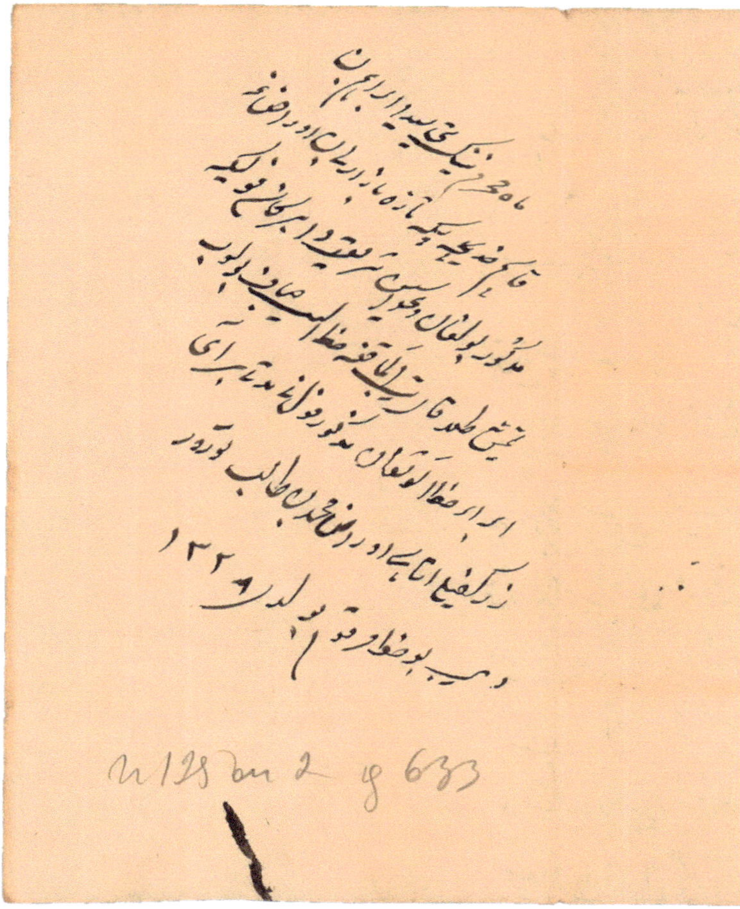

DOCUMENT 4B TsGARUz, I-125, op. 2, d. 633, l. 30 ob

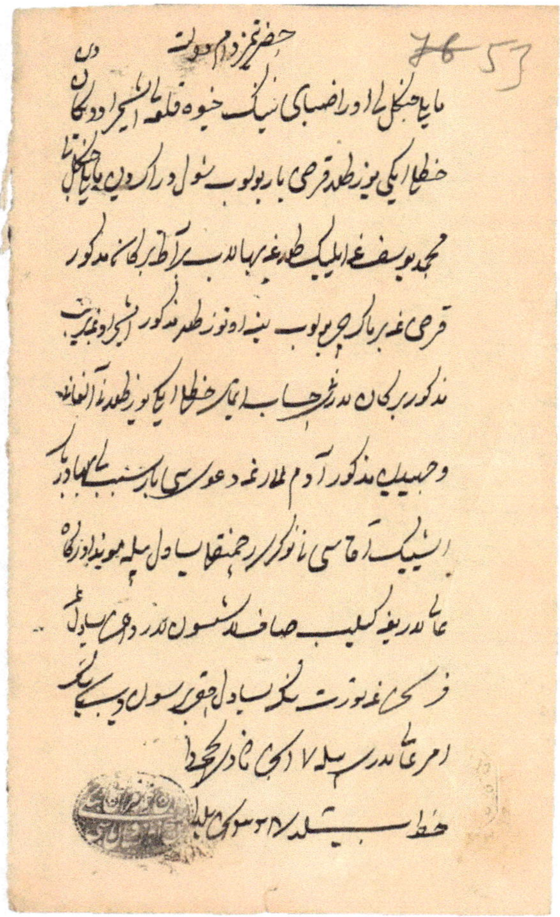

DOCUMENT 5A TsGARUz, I-125, op. 2, d. 633, l. 53

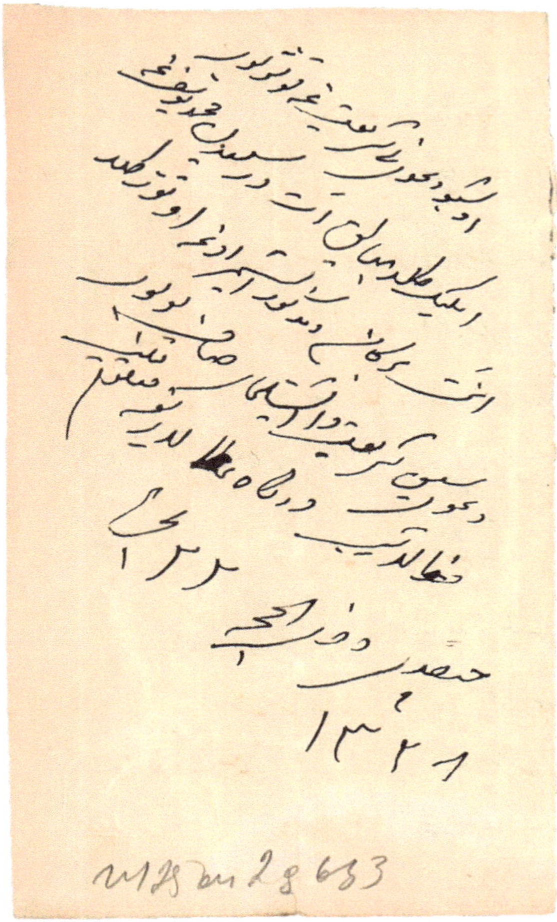

DOCUMENT 5B TsGARUz, I-125, op. 2, d. 633, l. 53 ob

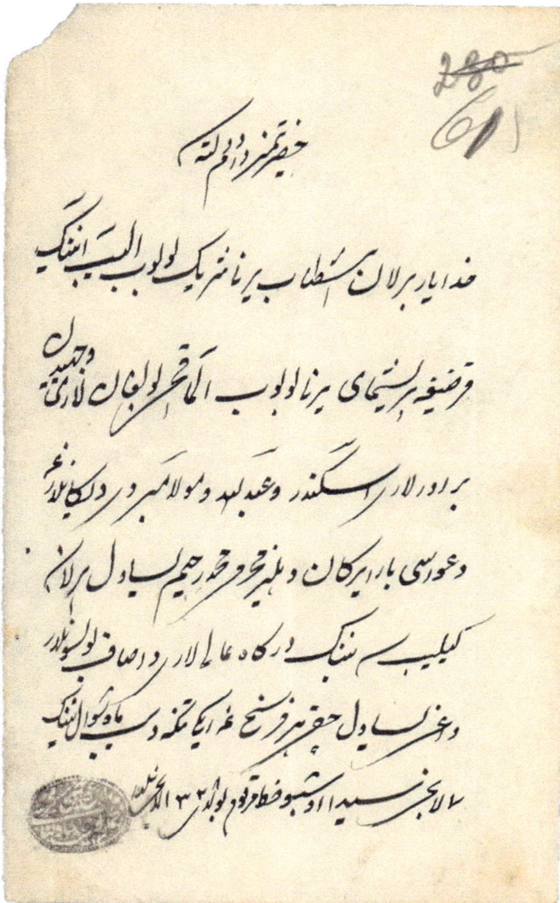

DOCUMENT 6A TsGARUz, I-125, op. 2, d. 633, l. 61

DOCUMENT 6B TsGARUz, I-125, op. 2, d. 633, l. 61 ob

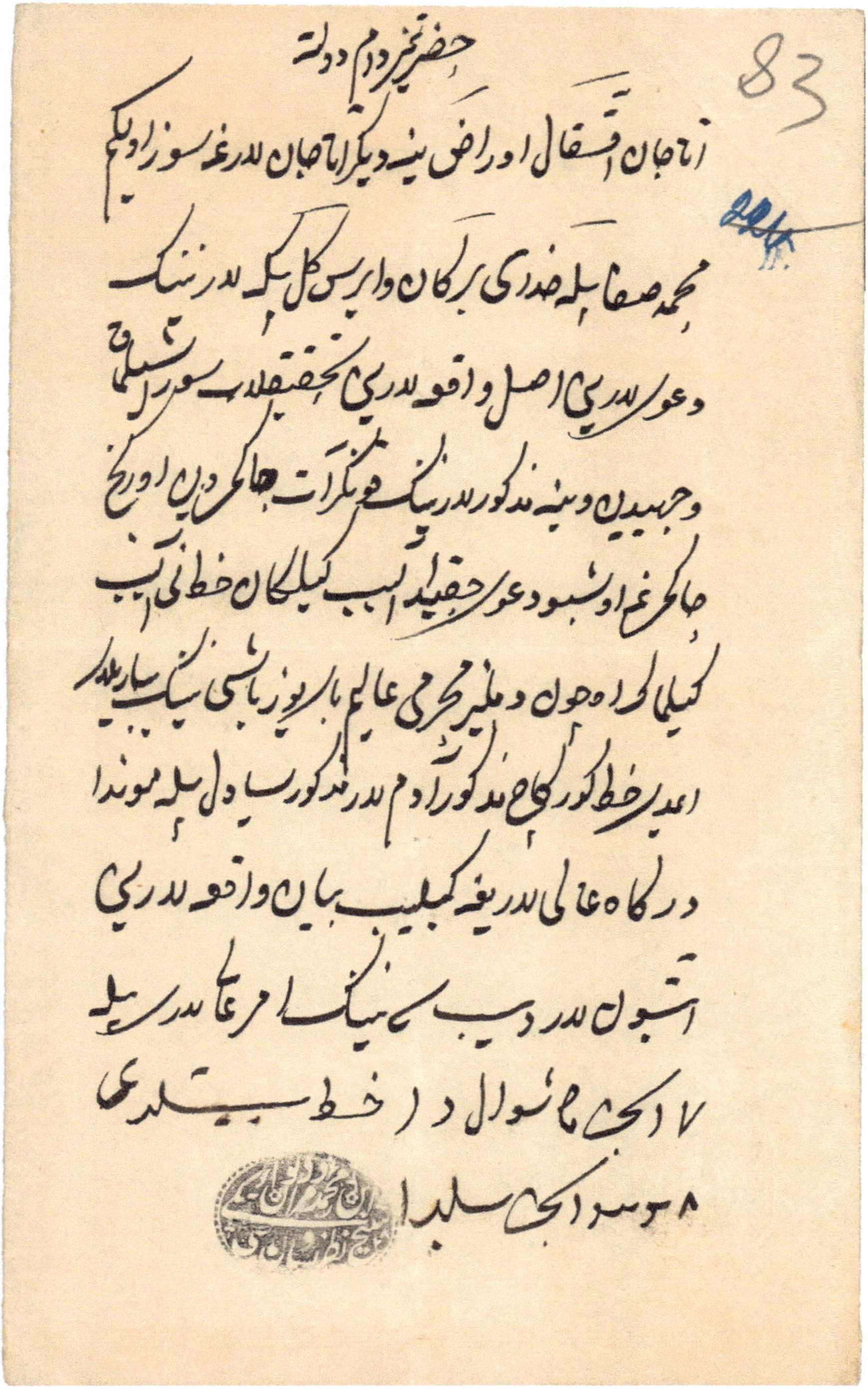

DOCUMENT 7A TsGARUz, I-125, op. 2, d. 633, l. 83

DOCUMENT 7B TsGARUz, I-125, op. 2, d. 633, l. 83 ob

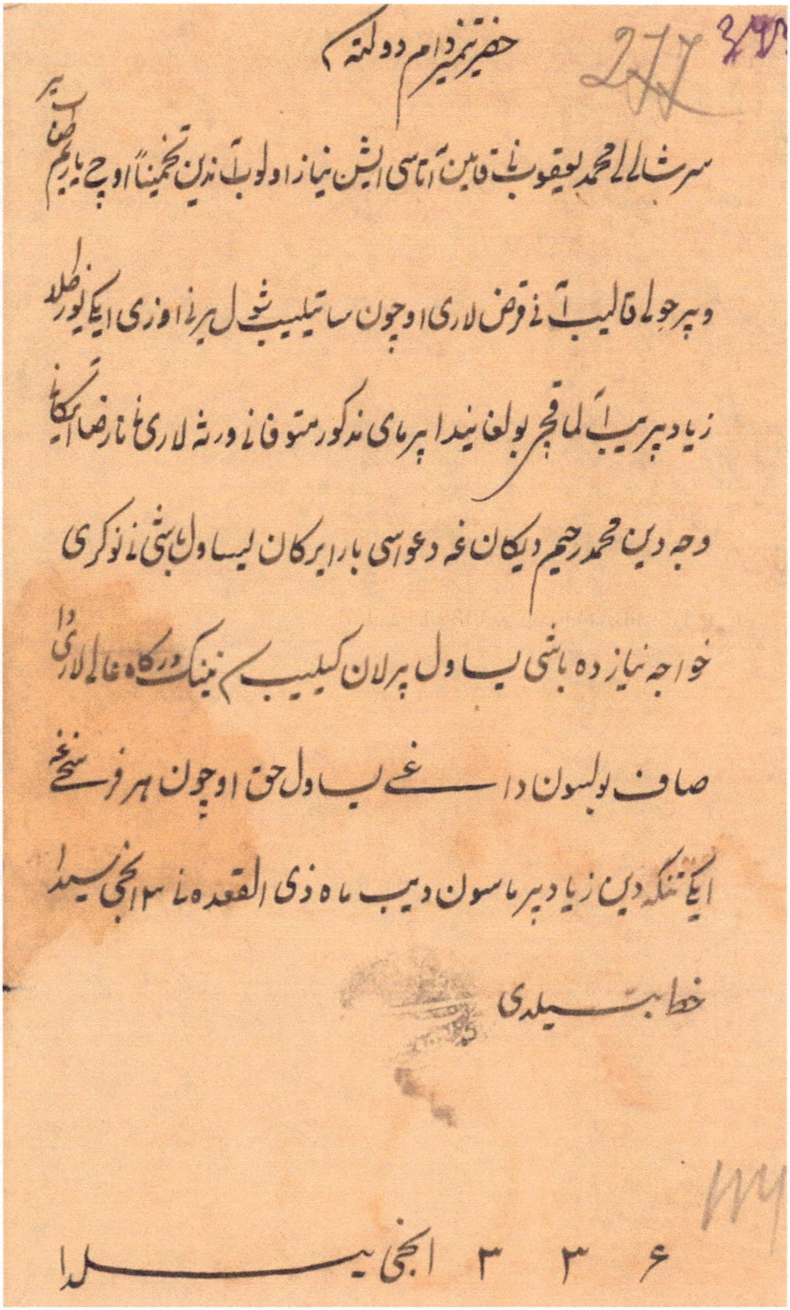
حضرت تقصیر دام دولته

سرشاه لار احمد یعقوب بای قاین آتاسی ایشن نیاز اولوب آندین تخمیناً اوچ یل

وبیر جوال قالیب آنه قرض لاری اوچون ساتیلیب شیخ ل بیرنه اوزی ایکی یوز طلا

زیاده بیر بیب آلماقچی بولغانیدا بیرمای مذکور متوفانه ورثه لاری نارضا ایکان

وجه دین محمد رحیم دیکان غه دعوی سی بار ایرکان لیسا ول بیتی نه نوکری

خواجه نیاز ده باشی بیب اول بیرلان کیلیب بیز نینگ درگاه عالی لاری دا

صاف بولسون داغی بیب اول حق اوچون هر فرسخی

ایکی تنگه دین زیاده بیرماسون دیب ماه ذی القعده نه ۱۳ انچی سیدا

خطابت سیلدی

۶ ۳ ۳ انچی ییلدا

DOCUMENT 8A TsGARUz, I-125, op. 2, d. 633, l. 114

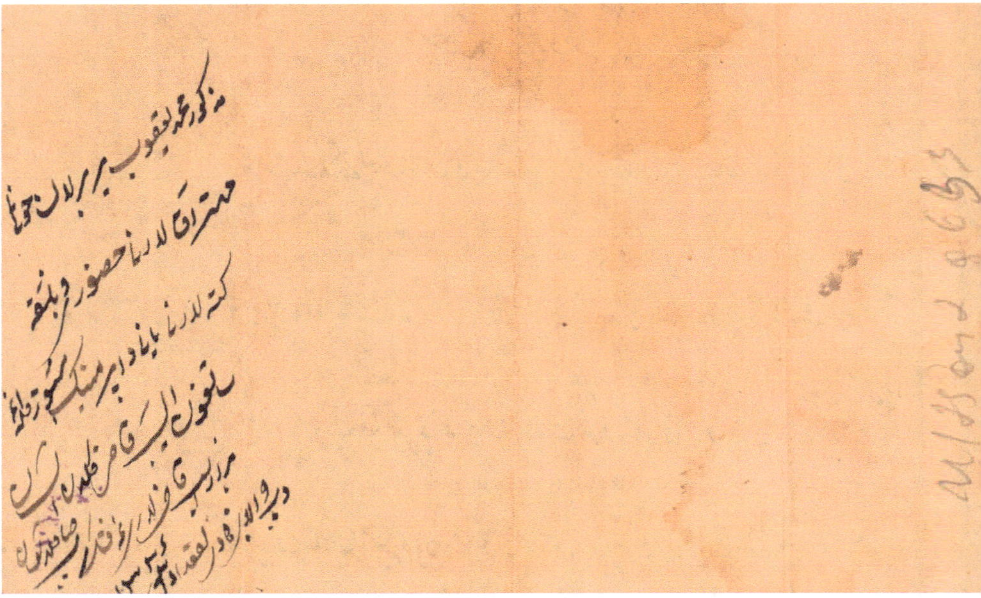

DOCUMENT 8B TsGARUz, I-125, op. 2, d. 633, l. 114 ob

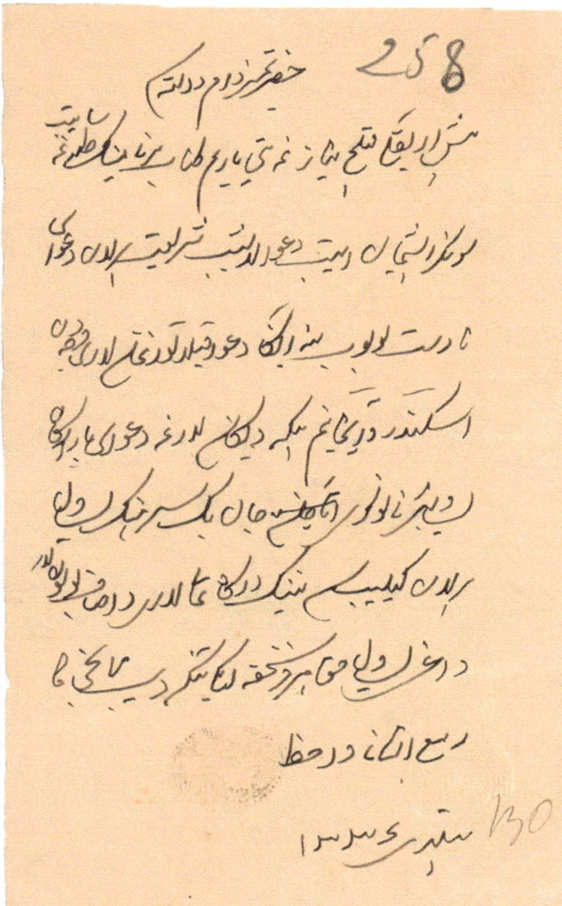

DOCUMENT 9A TsGARUz, I-125, op. 2, d. 633, l. 130

DOCUMENT 9B TsGARUz, I-125, op. 2, d. 633, l. 130 ob

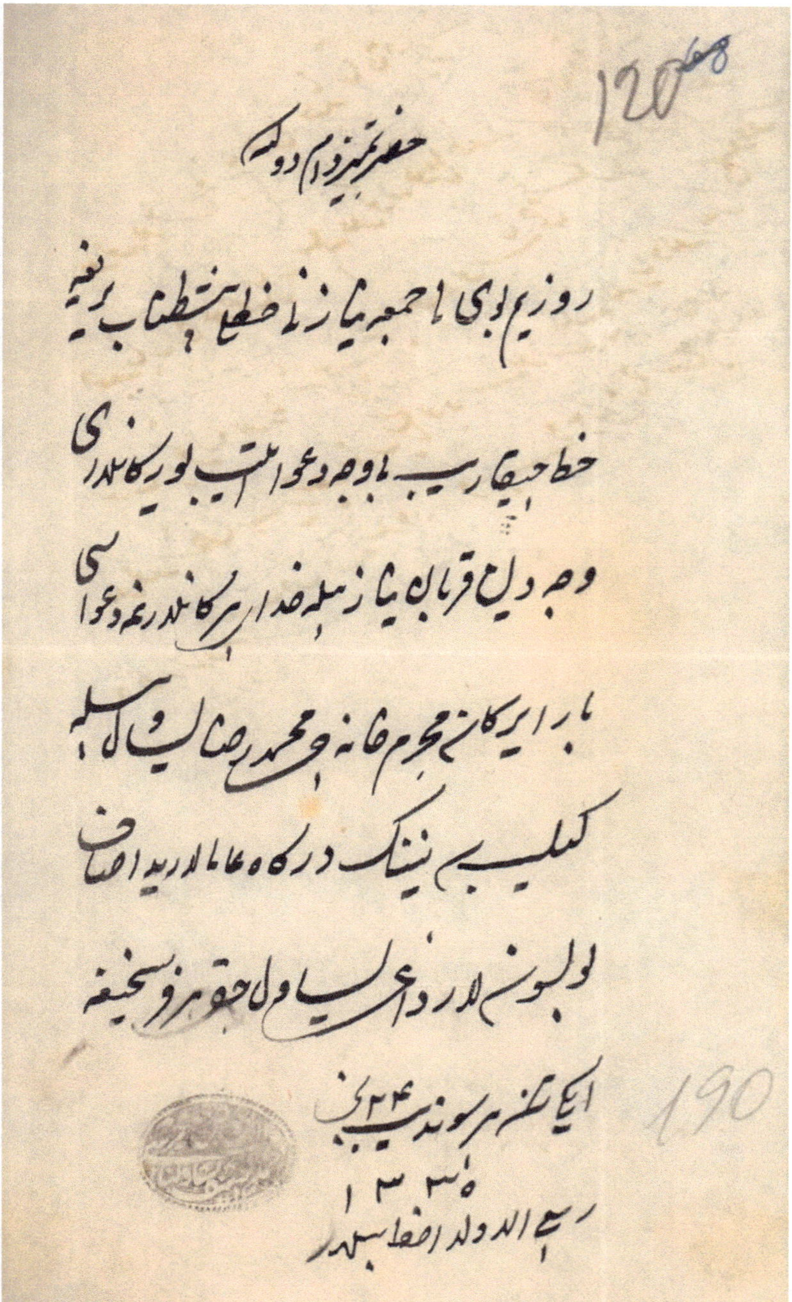
120
حضور تمیز دوام دولته

روزیم بوی ایا جمعه یازنه خطاب مستطاب رفیعه

خط حیدار ربیع ثانی وجه دعوا ایتیب بویرکاندری

وجه دیلیج قربان یازیلیه خدایرکاندر ریحیم دعواسی

بار ایرکان مجرم خانه محمد رضا ایکی سیلیه

کیلیب بینینک درگاه عالمه لاریدیه احیاج

بولبونلار داعی ایاول حقوق وسخنه

ایکی تخنه هرسوندنب ۲۴ ی
۱۳۳۵
ربیع الدوله افضل بهادر
190

DOCUMENT 10A TsGARUz, I-125, op. 2, d. 633, l. 190

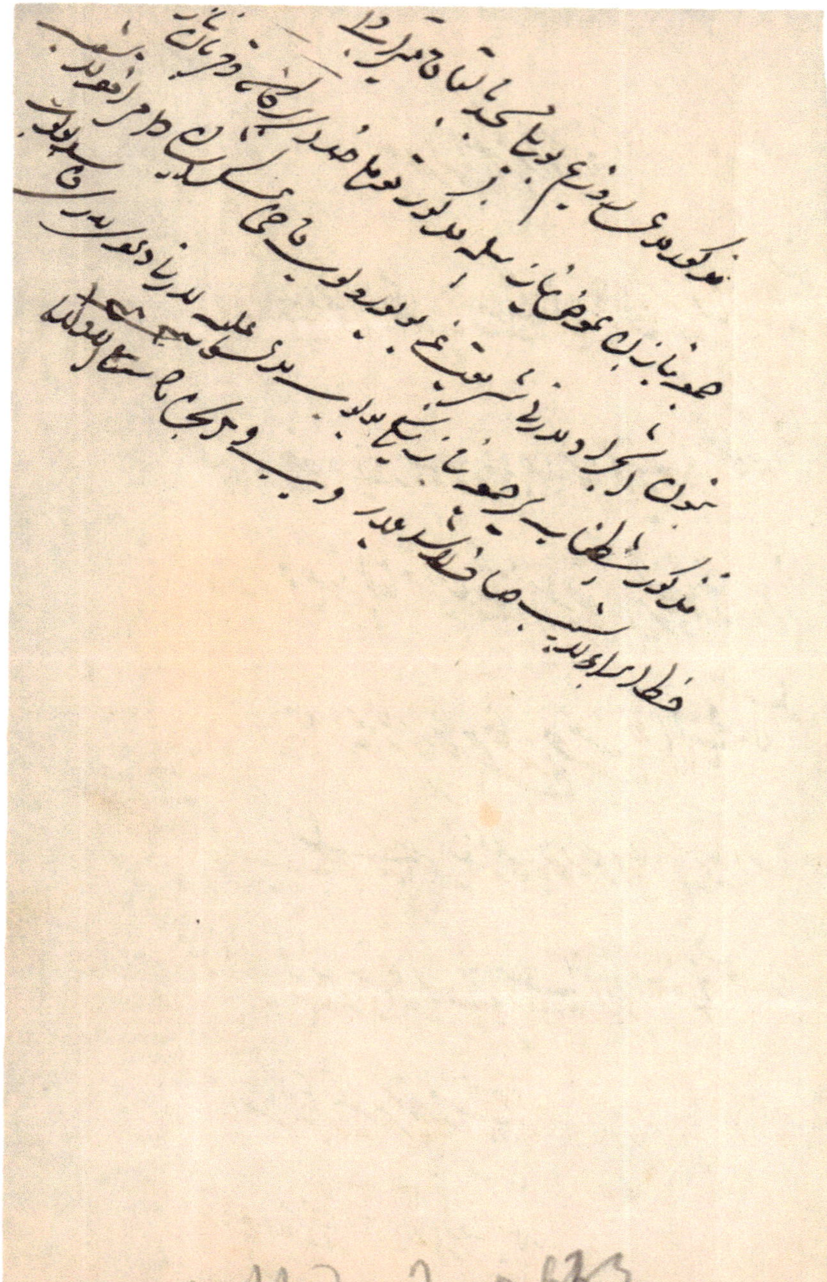

DOCUMENT 10B TsGARUz, I-125, op. 2, d. 633, l. 190 ob

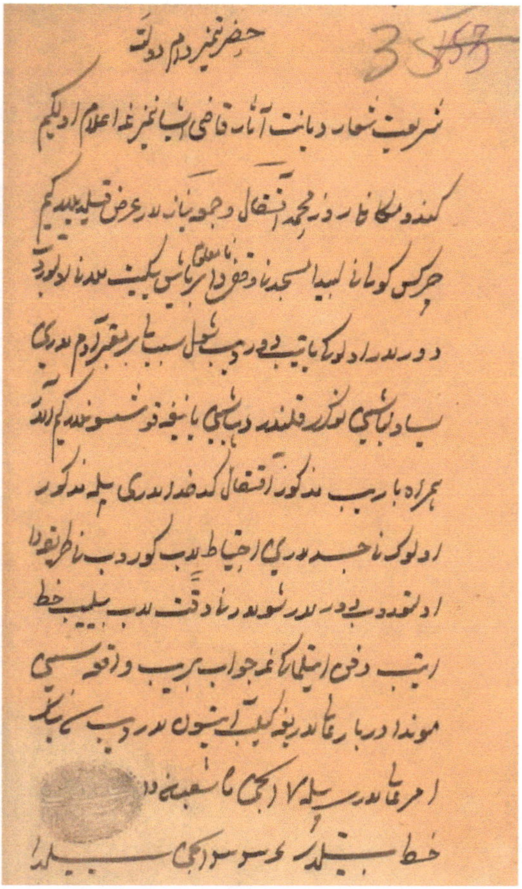

DOCUMENT 11A TsGARUz, I-125, op. 2, d. 656, l. 35

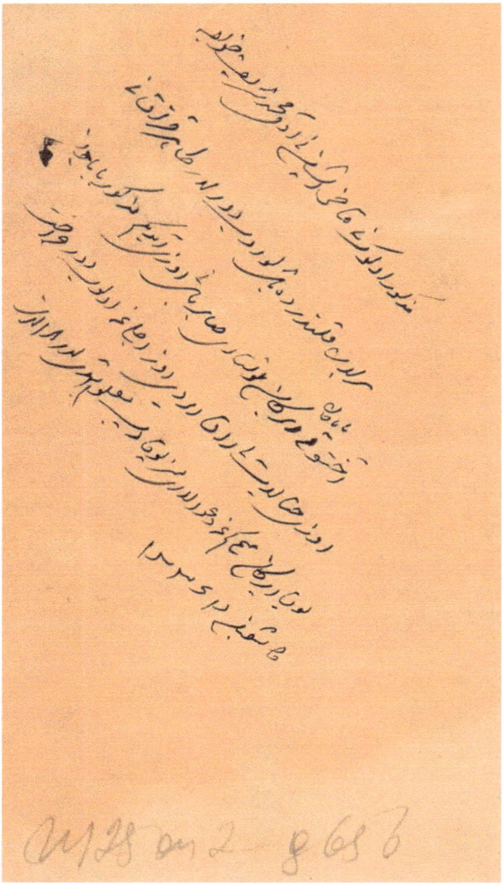

DOCUMENT 11B TsGARUz, I-125, op. 2, d. 656, l. 35 ob

Section Two

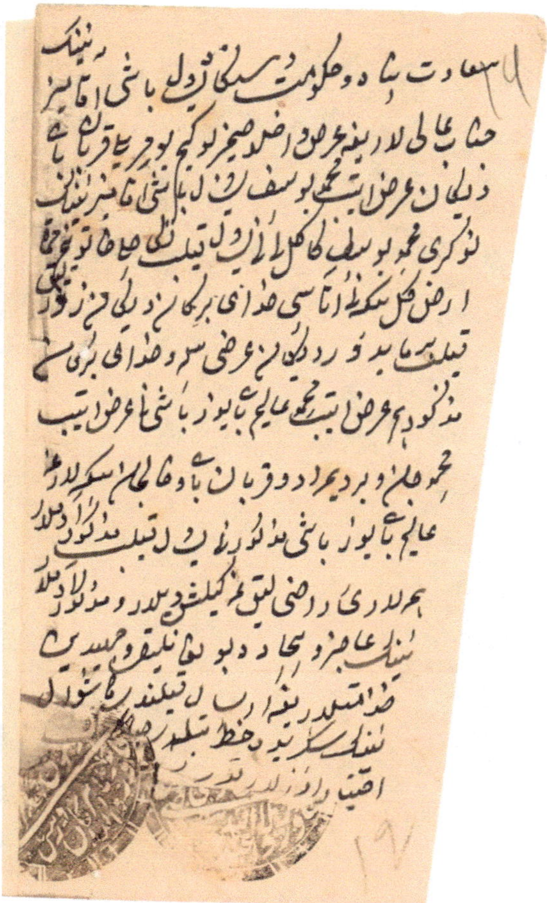

DOCUMENT 12A TsGARUz, f. I-125, op. 1, d. 498, l. 14

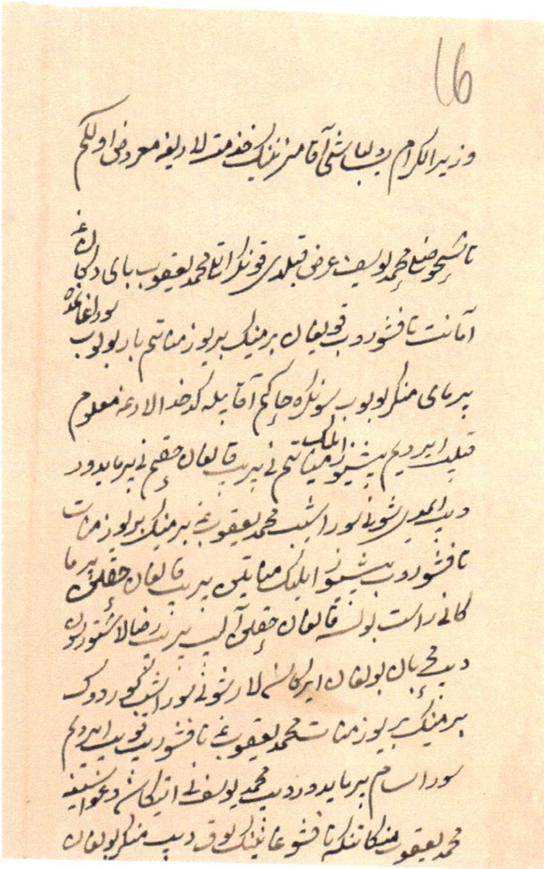

DOCUMENT 13A TsGARUz, f. I-125, op. 1, d. 498, l. 16

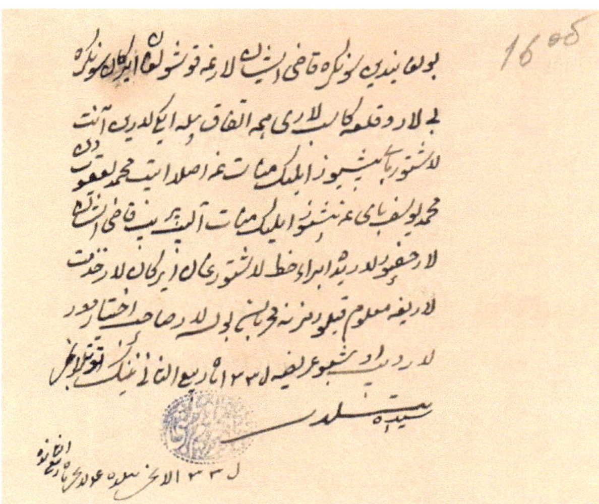

DOCUMENT 13B TsGARUz, f. I-125, op. 1, d. 498, l. 16 ob

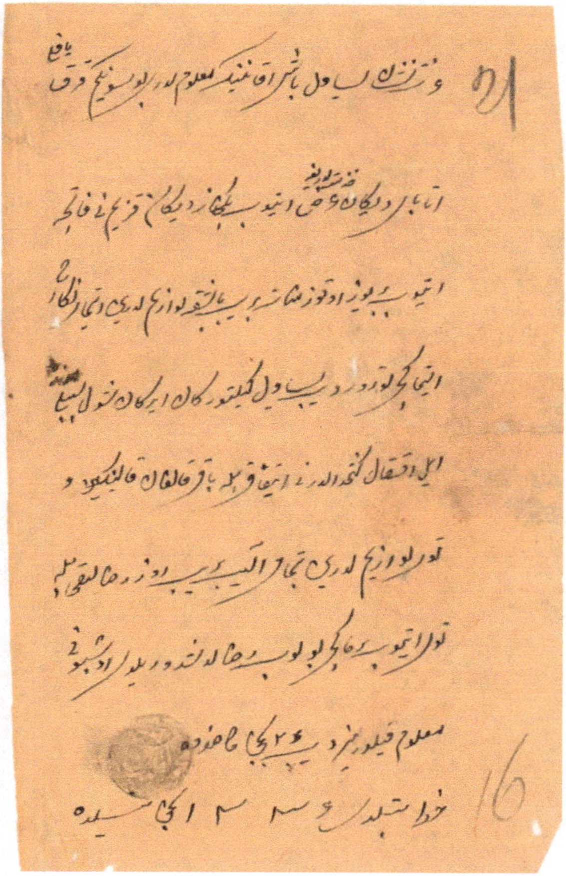

DOCUMENT 14A TsGARUz, f. I-125, op. 1, d. 498, l. 21

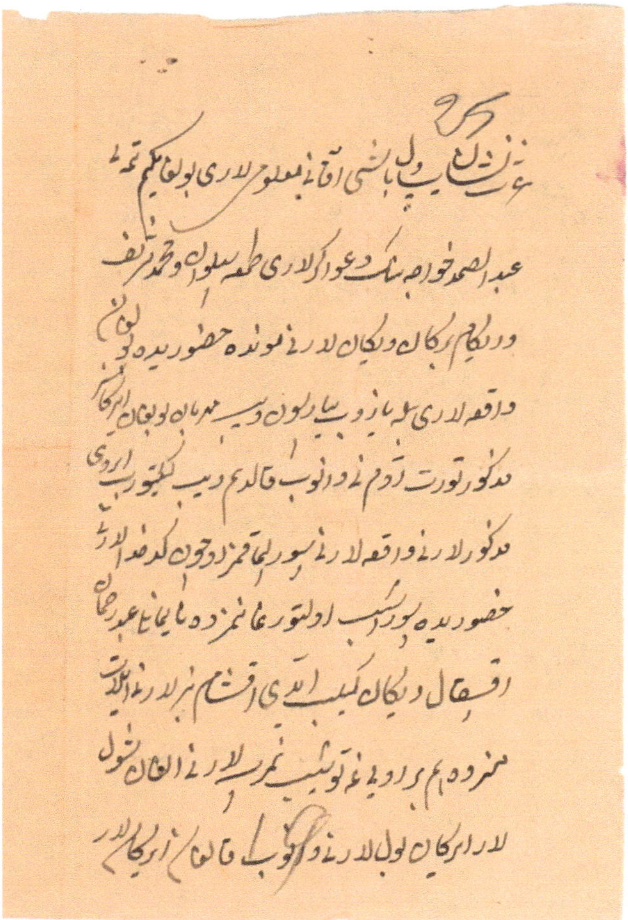

DOCUMENT 15A TsGARUz, f. I-125, op. 1, d. 498, l. 25

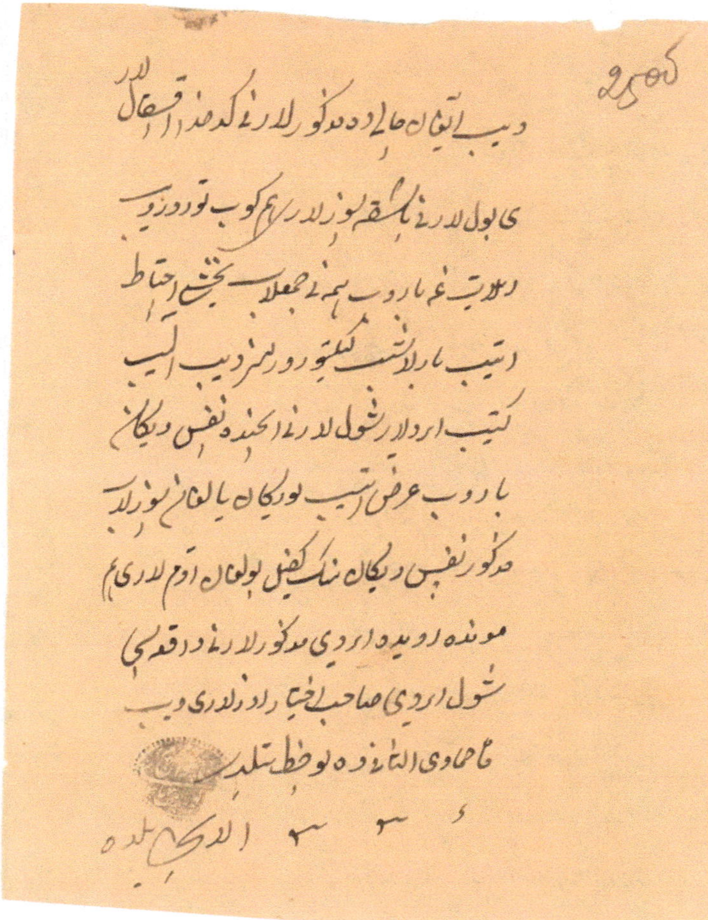

DOCUMENT 15B TsGARUz, f. I-125, op. 1, d. 498, l. 25 ob

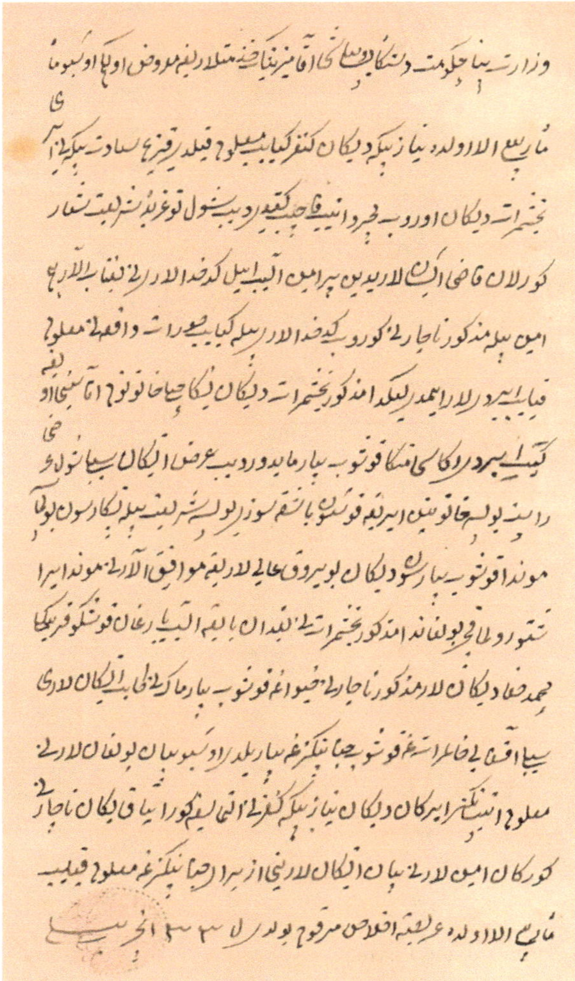

DOCUMENT 16A TsGARUz, f. I-125, op. 1, d. 498, l. 28

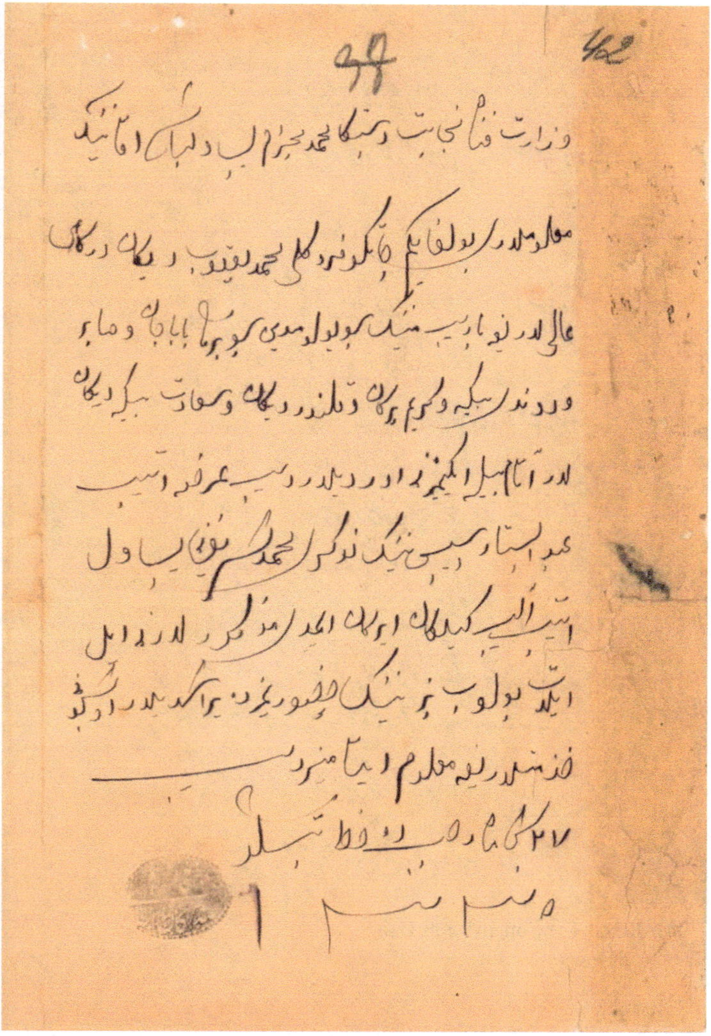

DOCUMENT 17A TsGARUz, f. I-125, op. 1, d. 498, l. 42

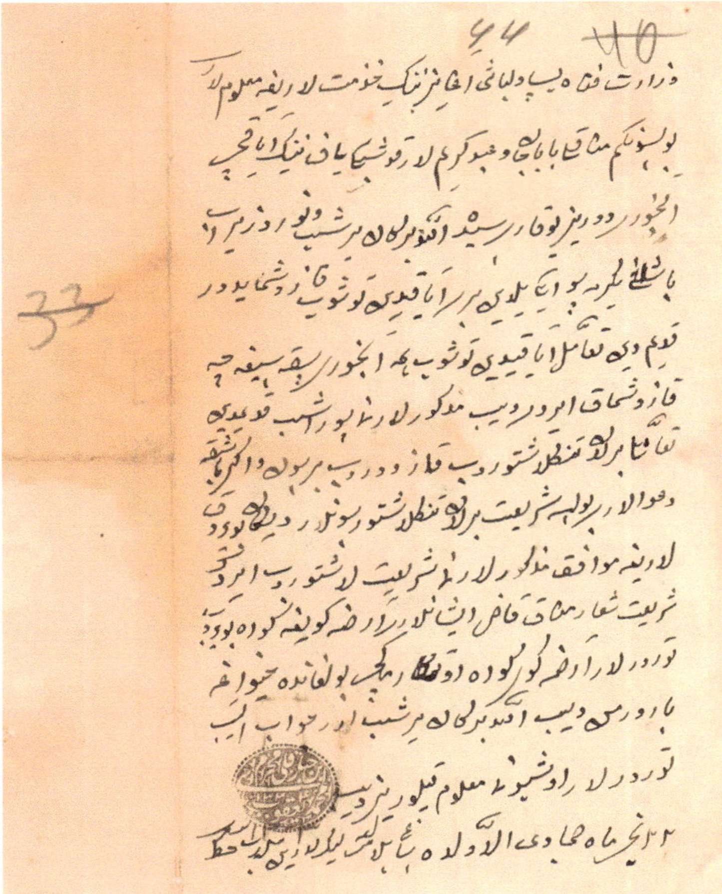

DOCUMENT 18A TsGARUz, f. I-125, op. 1, d. 498, l. 44

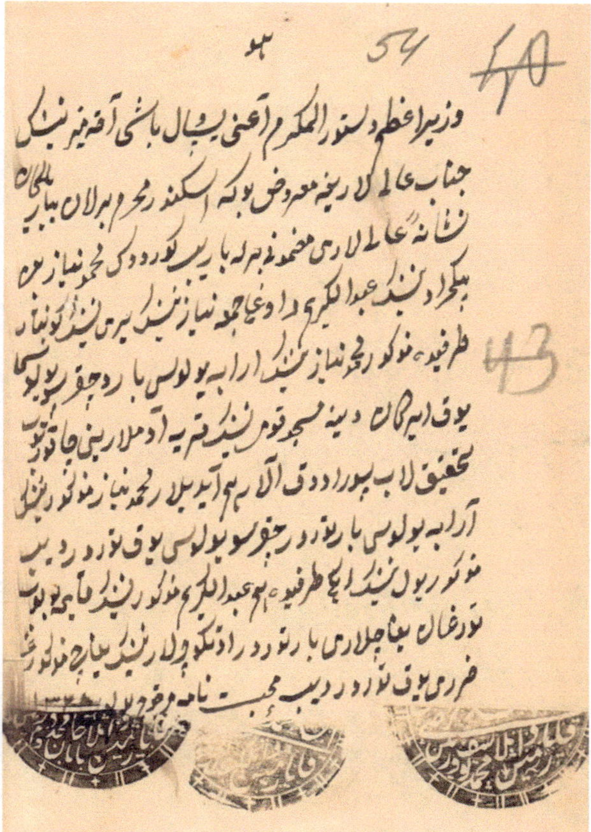

DOCUMENT 19A TsGARUz, f. I-125, op. 1, d. 498, l. 54

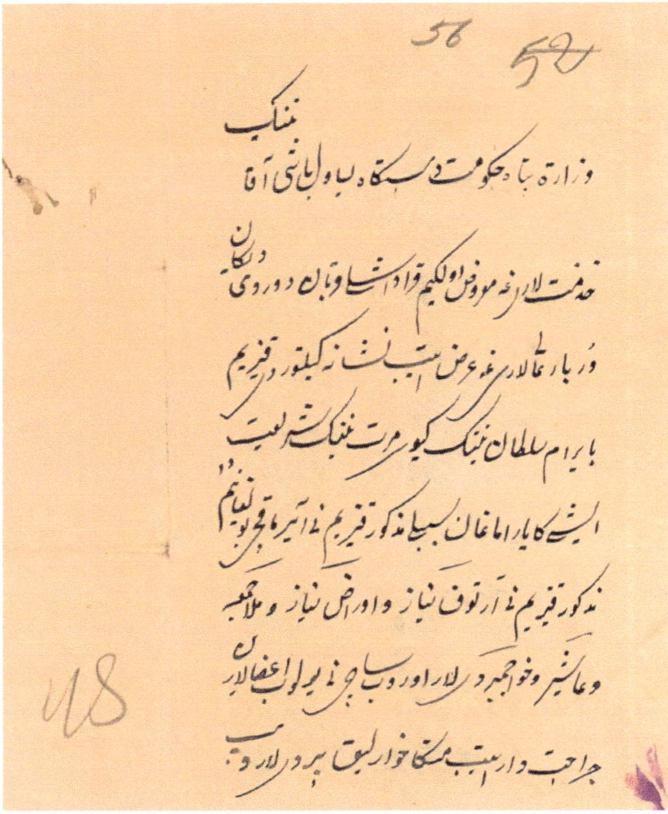

DOCUMENT 20A TsGARUz, f. I-125, op. 1, d. 498, l. 56

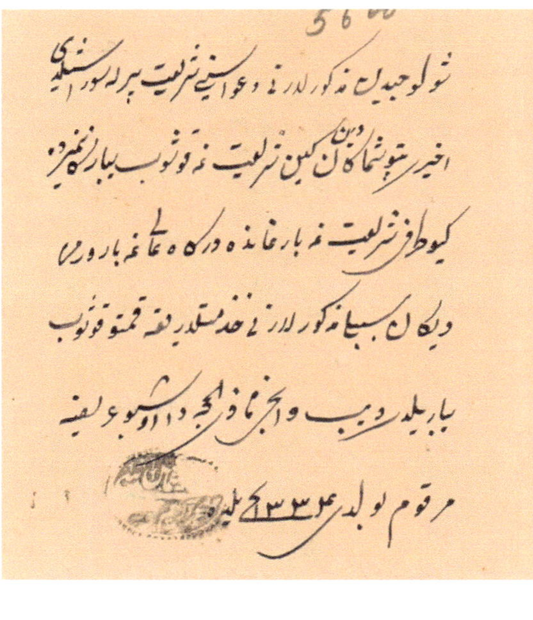

DOCUMENT 20B TsGARUz, f. I-125, op. 1, d. 498, l. 56 ob

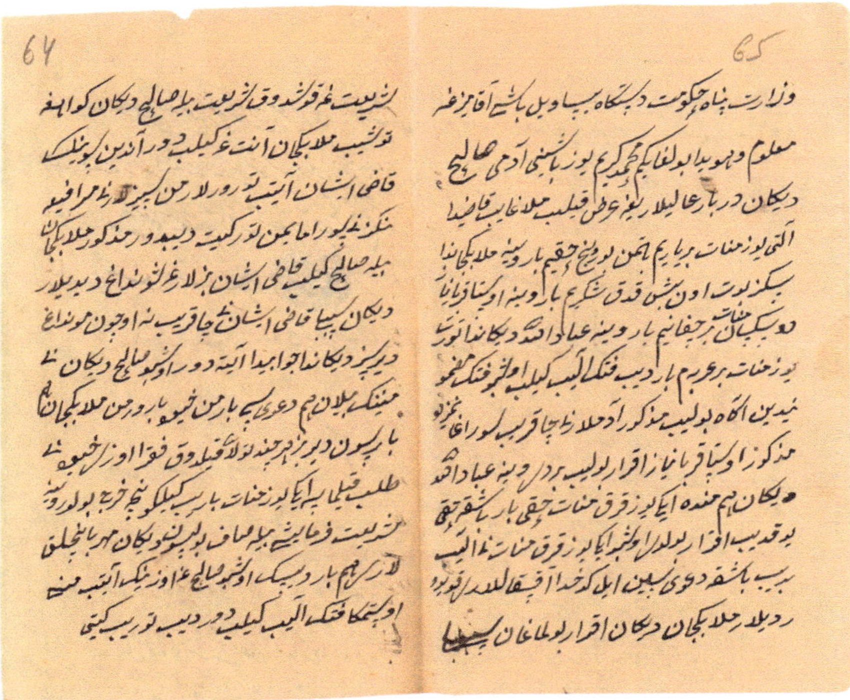

DOCUMENT 21A TsGARUz, f. I-125, op. 1, d. 498, ll. 65–64

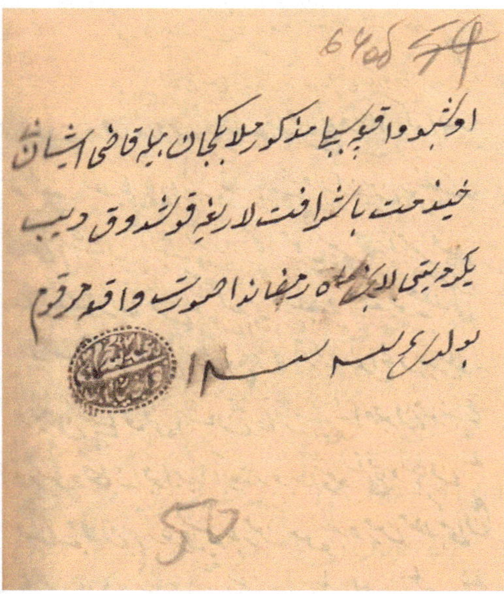

DOCUMENT 21B TsGARUz, f. I-125, op. 1, d. 498, l. 64 ob

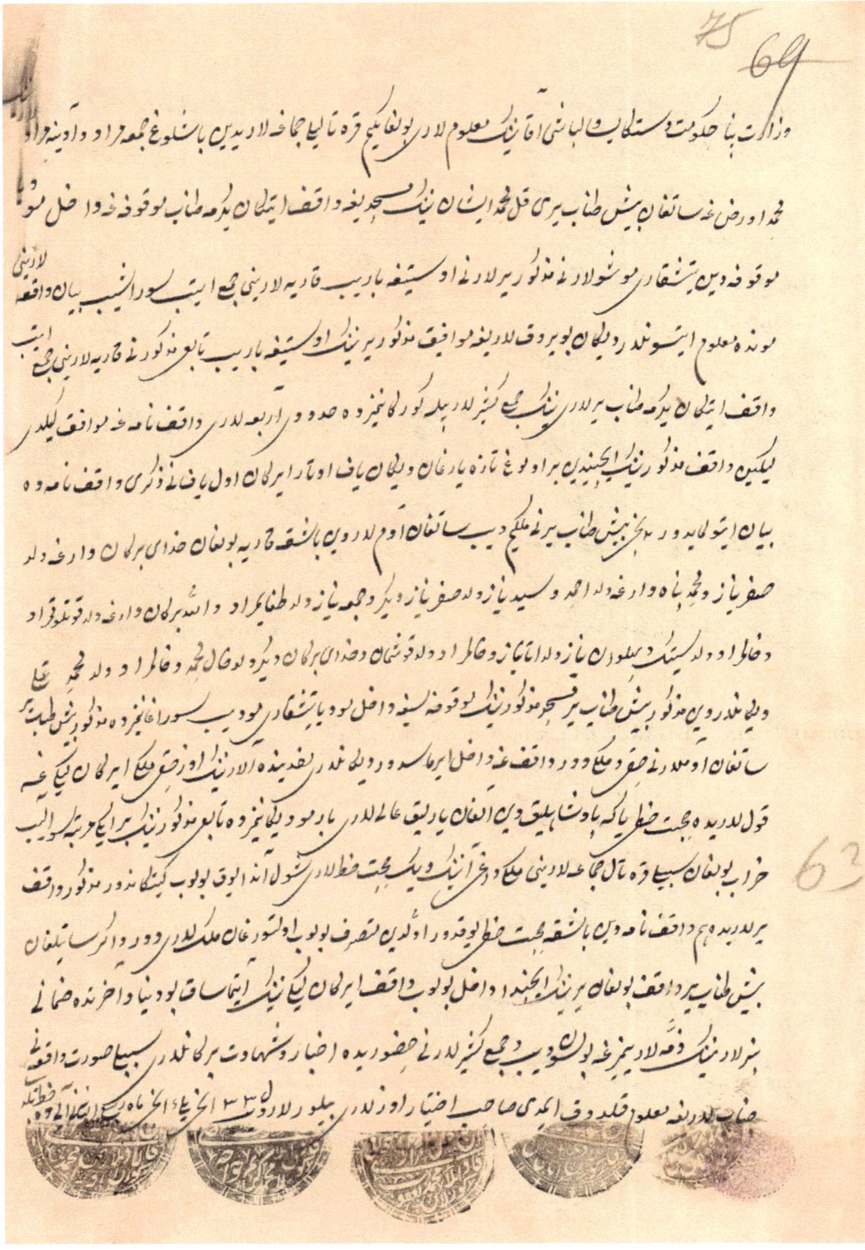

DOCUMENT 22A TsGARUz, f. I-125, op. 1, d. 498, l. 75

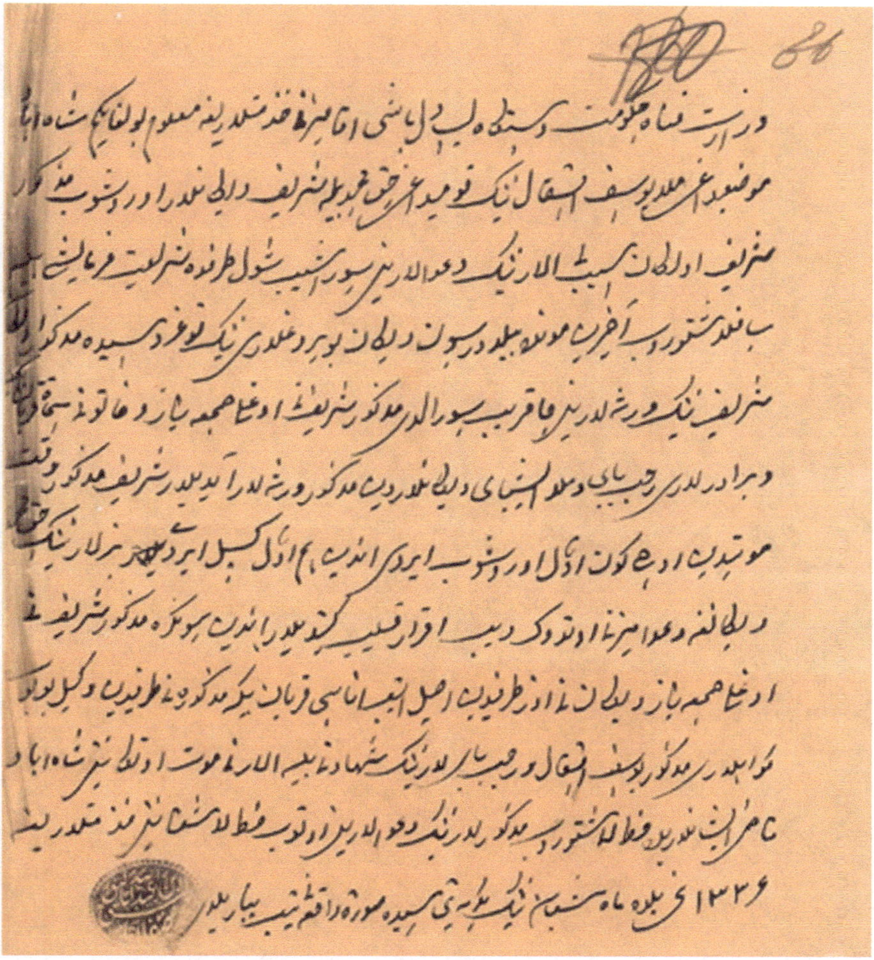

DOCUMENT 23A TsGARUz, f. I-125, op. 1, d. 498, l. 86

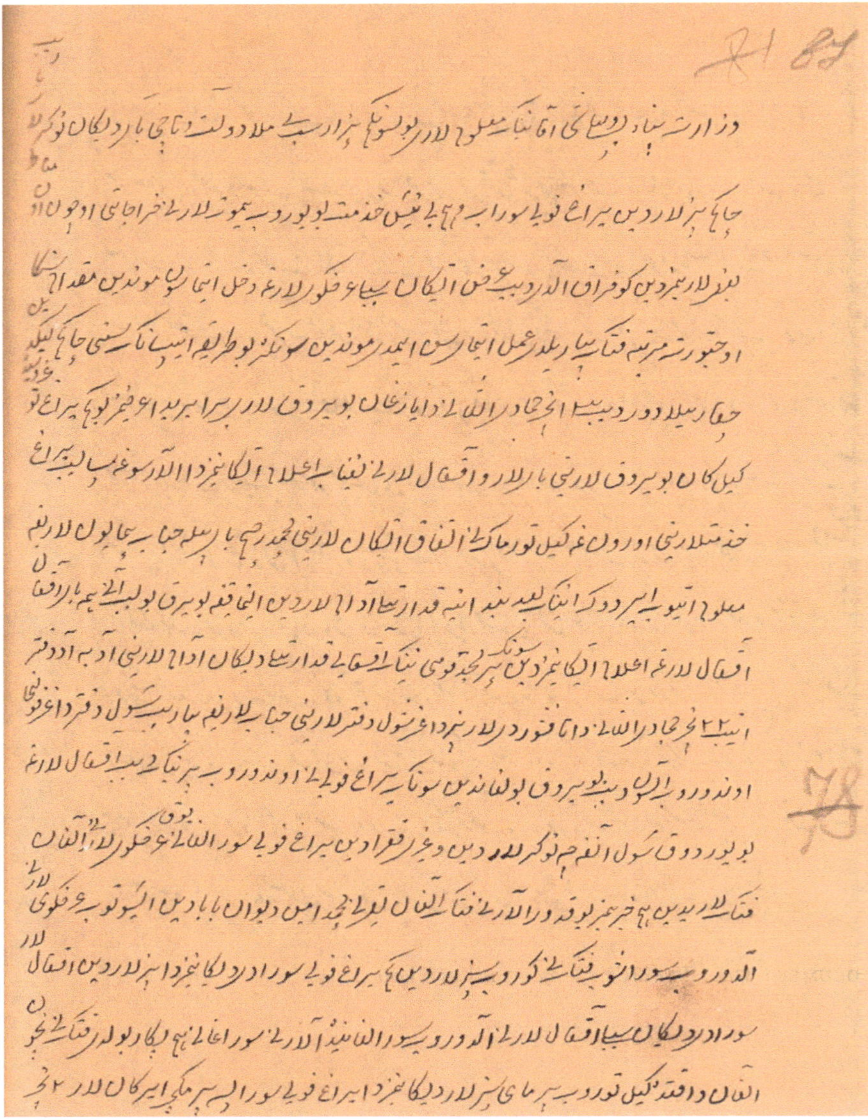

DOCUMENT 24A TsGARUz, f. I-125, op. 1, d. 498, l. 87

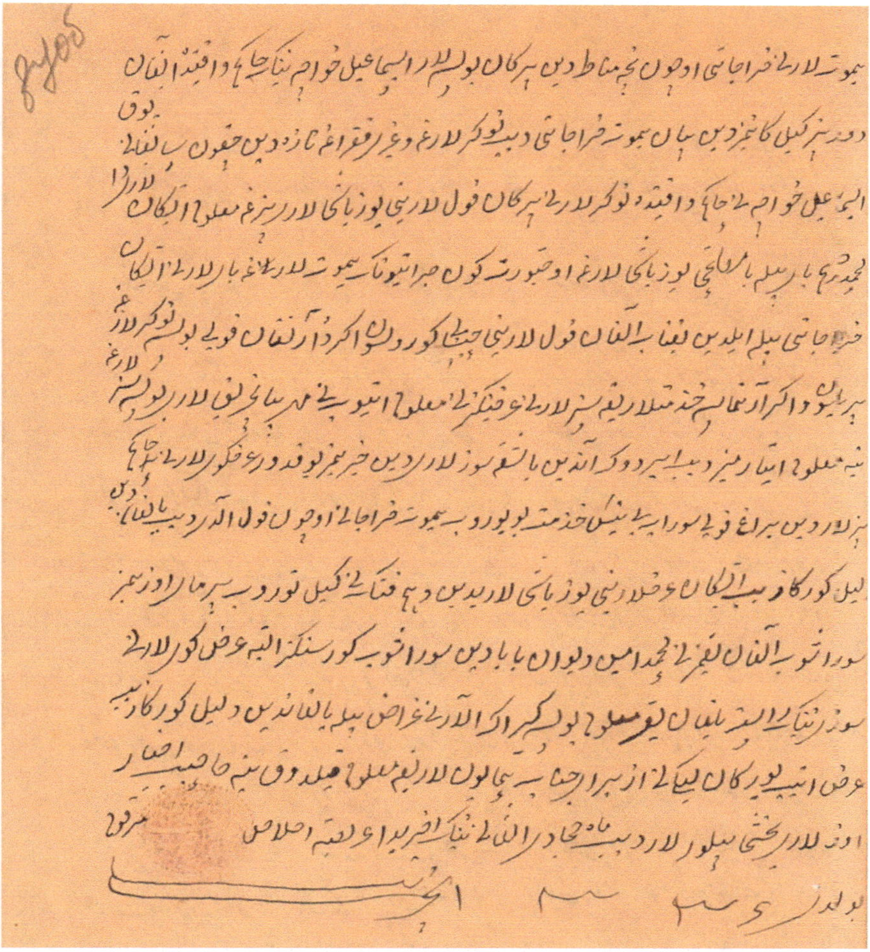

DOCUMENT 24B TsGARUz, f. I-125, op. 1, d. 498, l. 87 ob

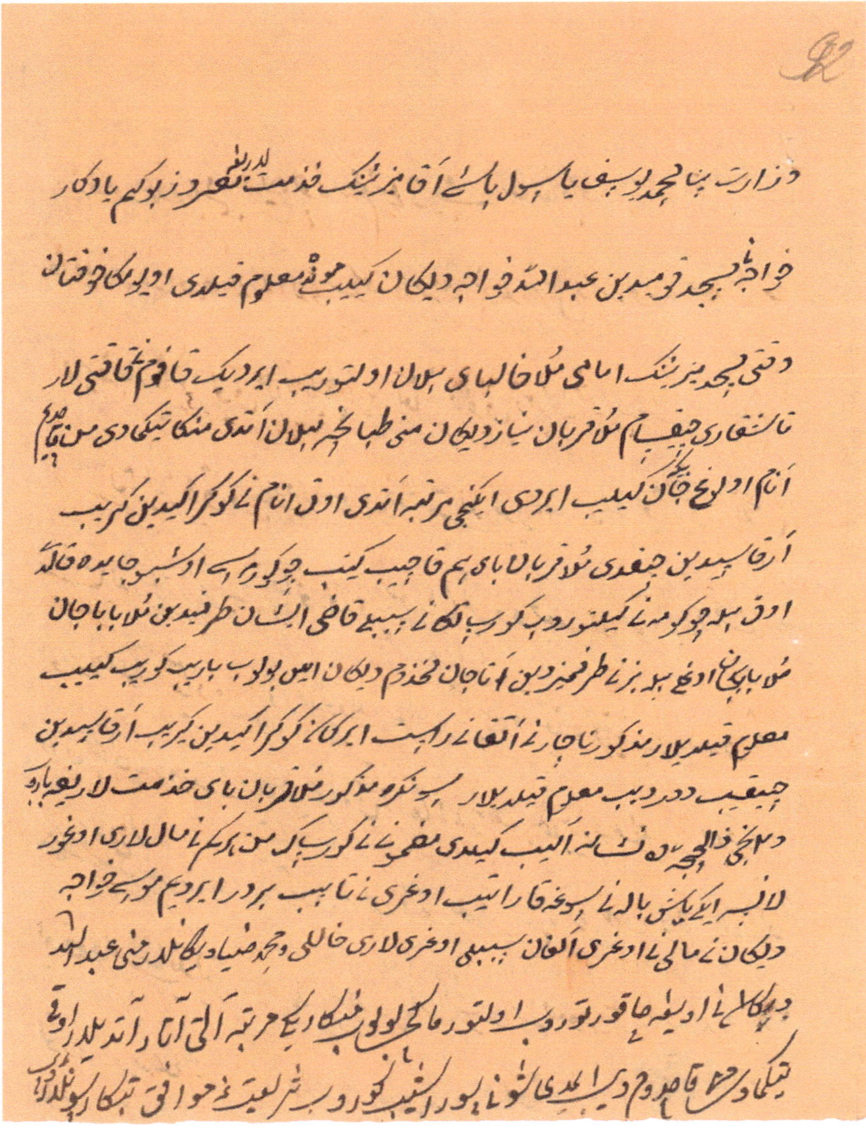

وزارت پناها محمد یوسف یساول باشی آقا میرزانینگ خدمت‌لریغه عرض دور بوکیم یادگار
خواجه نام محمد قاسم بن عبد الله خواجه دیگان کیشی موقوفه معلوم قیلدی اوزیلیک خوقندان
دفتی محمد میرزانینگ امامی ملا خالبای بیلان اولتوریب ایردیک قاقوم قاقیلار
تاشقاری چیقیب‌ام ملا قربان نیاز دیگان منی طپانچه بیلان آتدی منگا تیکیدی من قاچیم
آتام اورنیغ قاچقان کیشی ایردی ایکینچی مرتبه آتدی اوق آتامنی کوکراکیدین تیریب
آرقاسیدین چیقدی ملا قربان بای هم قاچیب کیتیب چوکور ارسی اوشبو جایده قالگه
اوق بیله چوکورمه‌نی کیلتوروب کوروب لیکن نی سببیدین قاضی الشان طرفیدین ملا باباجان
ملا بای ... اوغلی بیله برنی طرف محمد دین او تاجان مخدوم دیگان ایس بولوب باریب کوروب کیلیب
معلوم قیلدیلار مذکور تاجار نی اتقان راست ایرکانی کوکراکیدین تیریب آرقاسیدین
چیقیب دور دیب معلوم قیلدیلار سو تنکرو مذکور ملا قربان بای خدمت‌لاریغه باره
دور ... ذالحجه ... سنه الیب کیلدی ... ... من ... مال‌لاری اوغور
لاب ... بالانی ... قاراتیب اوغری ... بردر ایردیم موسی خواجه
دیگان نی مالی نی اوغری الغان سببی اوغری‌لاری خالی محمد ضیا دیگانلار حتی عبد الله
... ... اولتور ... مرتبه ... آتدیلار اوق
تیکمادی ... قاچدوم ... شریعت‌غه موافق ...

DOCUMENT 25A TsGARUz, f. I-125, op. 1, d. 498, l. 92

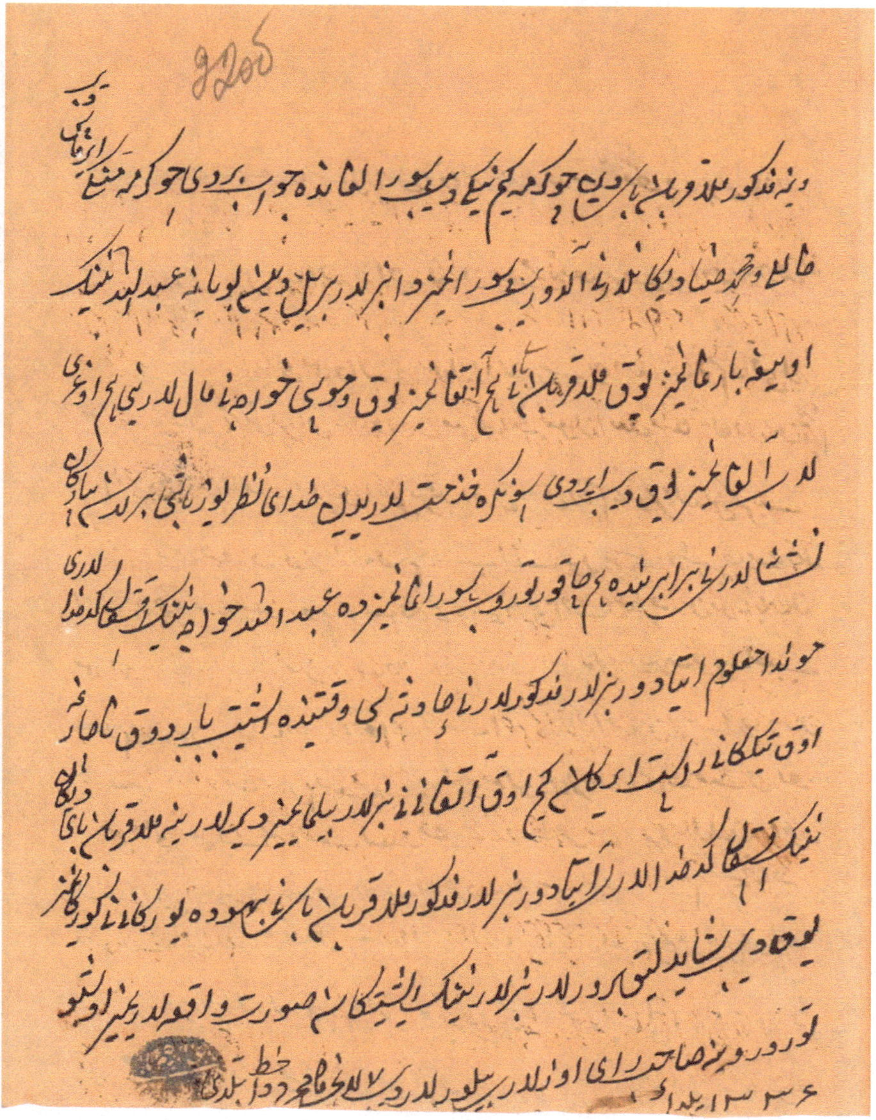

DOCUMENT 25B TsGARUz, f. I-125, op. 1, d. 498, l. 92 ob

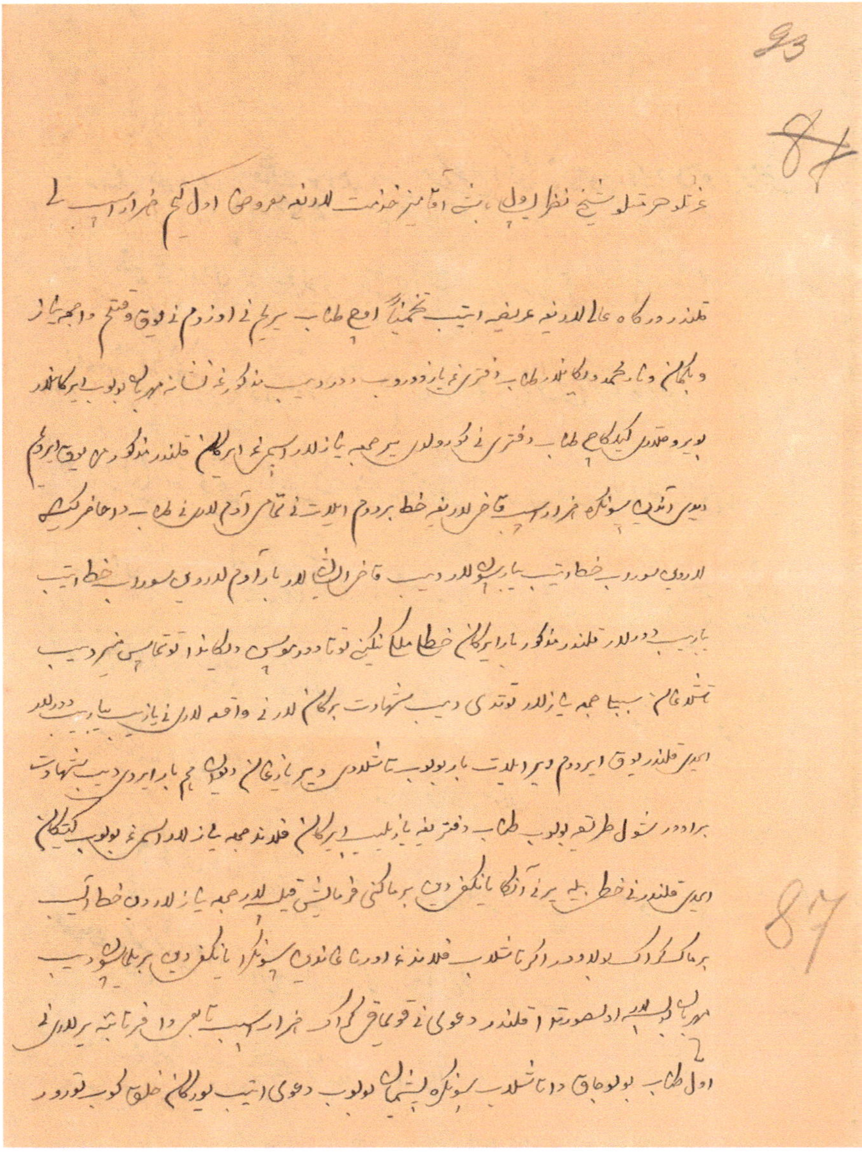

DOCUMENT 26A TsGARUz, f. I-125, op. 1, d. 498, l. 93

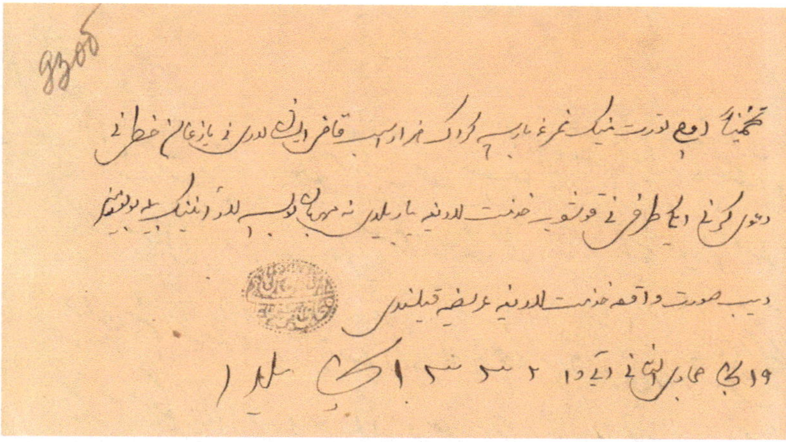

DOCUMENT 26B TsGARUz, f. I-125, op. 1, d. 498, l. 93 ob

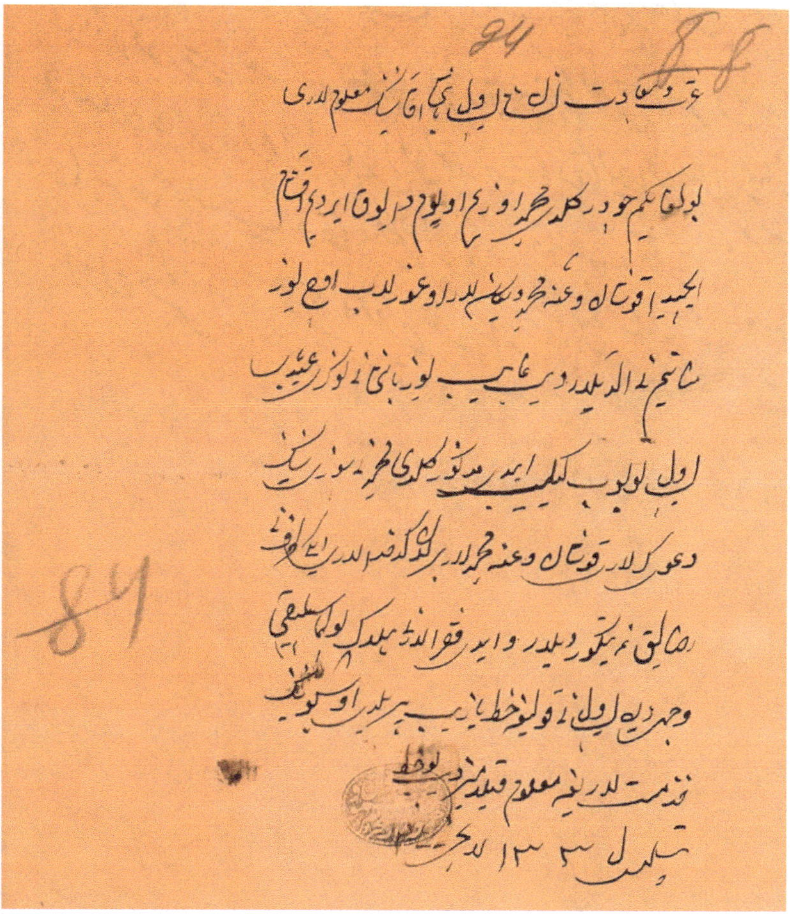

DOCUMENT 27A TsGARUz, f. I-125, op. 1, d. 498, l. 94

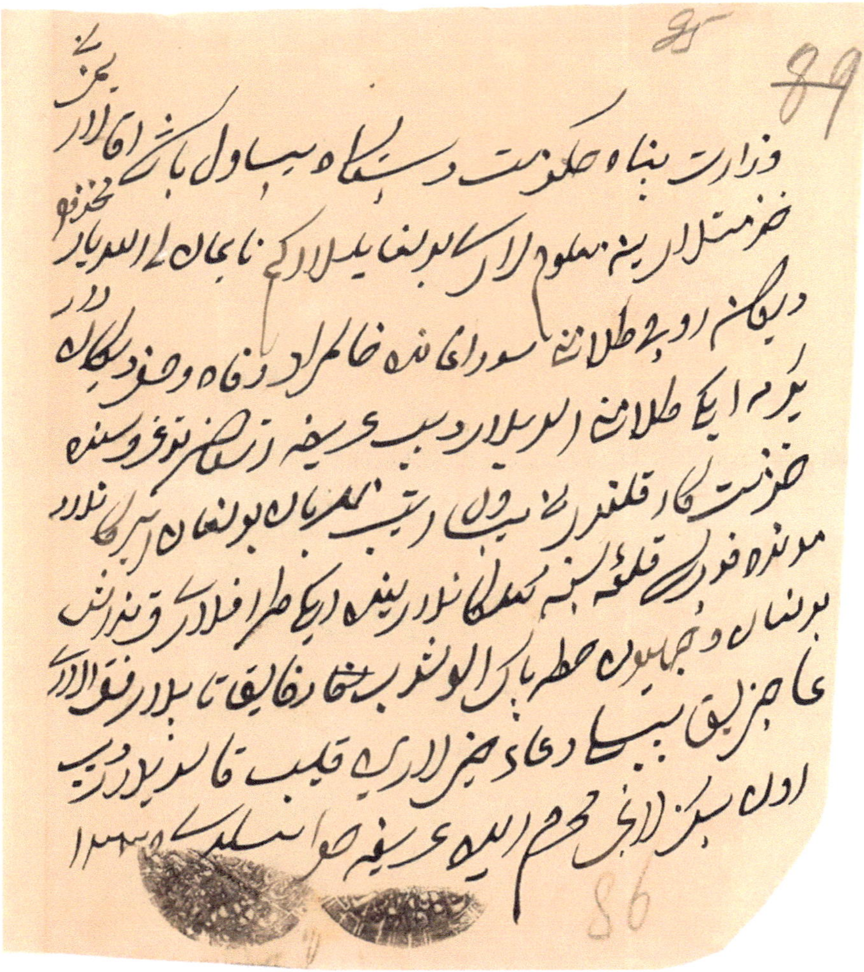

DOCUMENT 28A TsGARUz, f. I-125, op. 1, d. 498, l. 95

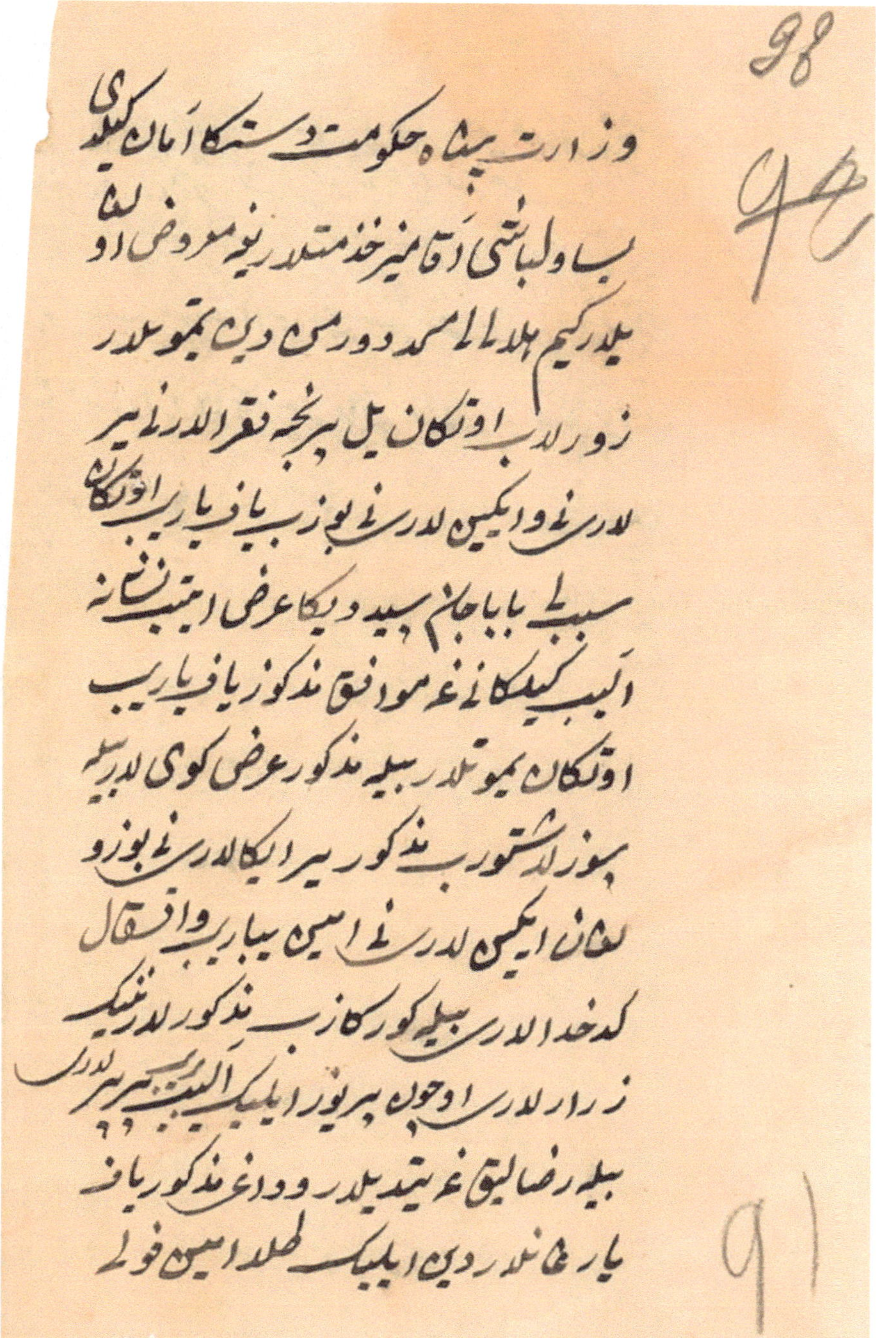
98
وزارت پناه حکومت دستگاه آمان کیلدی
ب ولباشی آقا میر خدمتلارینه معروض اولنغای
بیلدیرکیم هلالا لی سید دورمی دین تیمو بلدر
زورلادب اوتکان یل بیر نیچه فقرالارنی بیر
لارنی و ایکین لارنی بوزب یازیب اوتکان
سببی بابا جان سید دیکا عرض ایتیب نشانینی
آلیب کیلکانی غه موافق مذکور یازیب
اوتکان تیموتلادر بیله مذکور عرض کوی لادر سیم
سوزلادشتور ب مذکور یر ایکا لارنی بوزو
لکان ایکین لارنی امین ییباریب و اقسقال
کدخدالاری بیله کورکازب مذکور لارنینک
زرارلاری اوچون بیر یوز ایلیک آلیب بیر بیر لاری
بیله رضالیق غه یتیدیلدر و داغ مذکور یاف
یار ه نلدر دین ایلیک طلب امین قوله
91

DOCUMENT 29A TsGARUz, f. I-125, op. 1, d. 498, l. 98

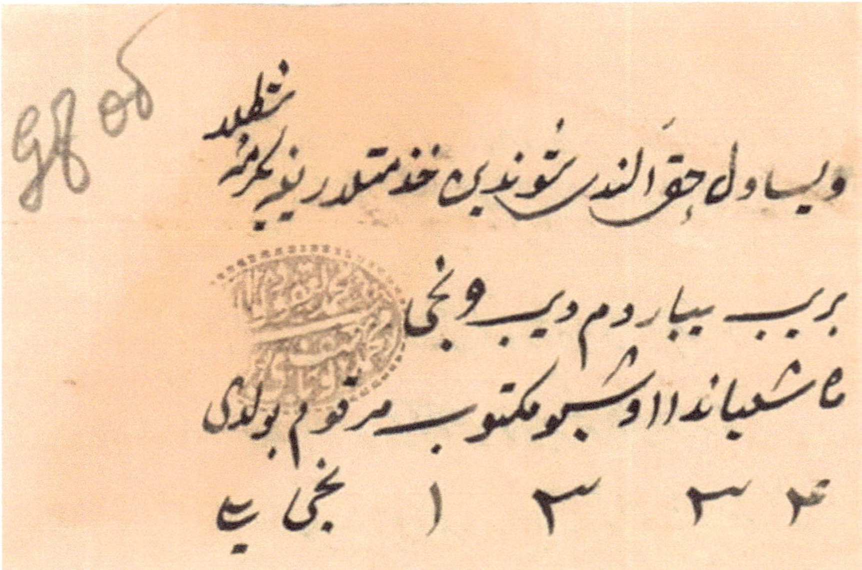

DOCUMENT 29B TsGARUz, f. I-125, op. 1, d. 498, l. 98 ob

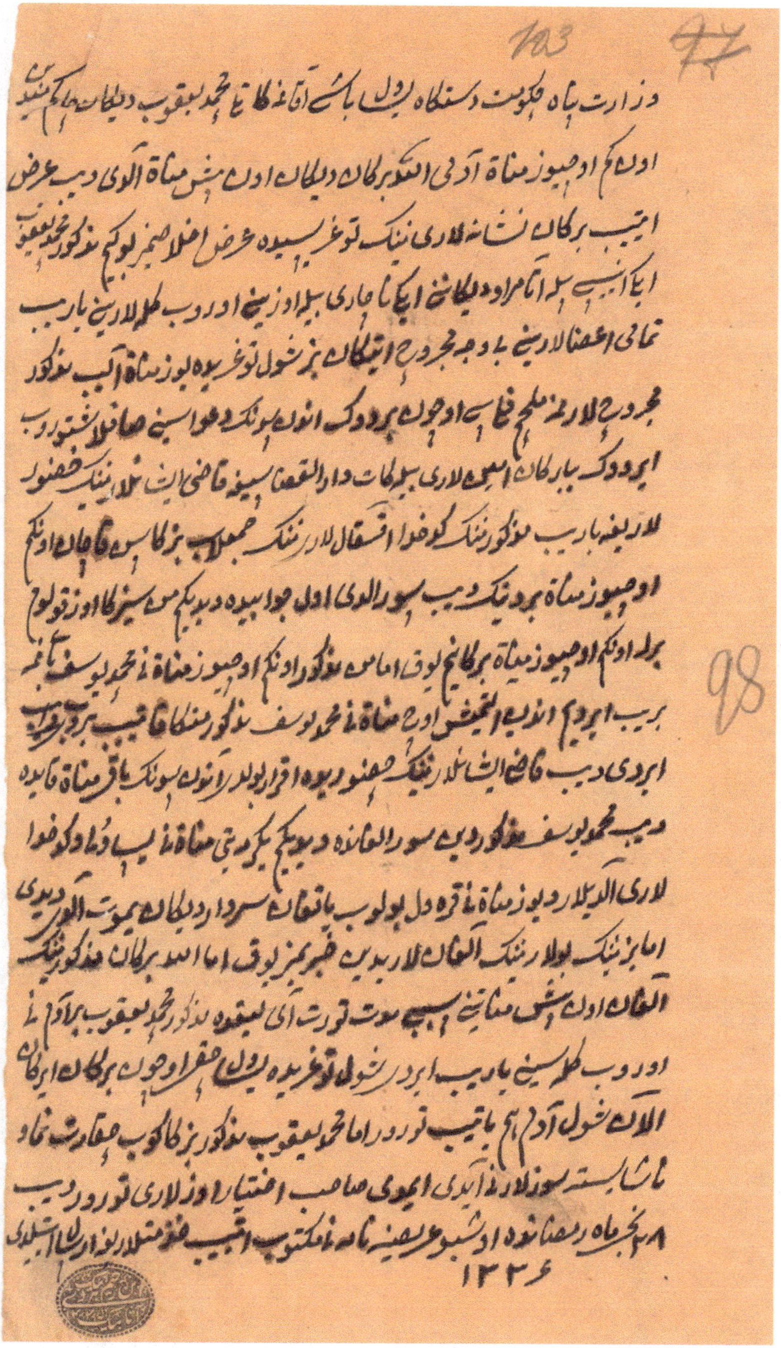

وزارت پناه حکومت دستگاه دولت پناه باش آقاغه کاتب محمد یعقوب دیلکان عالیجاهم منشید

اولکم اوچیوز منات آدی ایلکوبرکان دیلکان اون بیش منات آلوی دیب عرض

ایتیب برکان نشانه‌لاری نینک توغریسیده عرض اخلاصمز بولکیم مذکور محمد یعقوب

ایکی ایسپ بیله آتامراد دیلکانی ایکاتا جاری بیله اوزینی اوروب کلله‌لارینی یاریب

تمامی اعضالارینی باوجه مجروح ایتیکان بزشول توغریسیده یوز منات آلیب مذکور

مجروح‌لارمز ملحم خانه‌سی اوچون بیردوک اندان سونک دعواسینی صافلانغتوروب

ایردوک یبارکان اسمی‌لاری بیلکات دارالقضا سیده قاضی ایشانلار نینک حضور

لاریغه یاریب مذکور نینک گوفوا اقسقال‌لارینینک جملاب بزکا سوگ قاچان اولکم

اوچیوز منات بردی نینک دیب سورالوی اول جوابیده دیدیکم موسی کا اوز قولوم

بولاولکم اوچیوز منات برکانیم یوق اما مذکور اولکم اوچیوز منات محمد یوسف نامه

بریب ایردیم اندیب ایتکنی اوچ منات محمد یوسف مذکور مینکا قایتیب بردی دیب

ایردی دیب قاضی ایشانلار نینک حضوریده اقرار بولدیلار اندان سونک باقی منات قایده

دیب محمد یوسف مذکوردین سورالغانده دیدیکم بیر مدتی منات نی ایپادیکوفوا

لاری آلدیلار دیوزمنات نی قره دل بولوب یاتقان سردار دیلکان یموت آلوی دیدی

اما بزنینک بولار نینک آلغان‌لاریدین خبریمز یوق اما الله بیلکان مذکور نینک

آلغان اون بیش مناتینی سبب موت قورشاتی ایتیقوده مذکور محمد یعقوب برادم نی

اوروب کلله‌سینی یاریب ایردی شول توغریسیده دولت حقرا اوچون برکان ایرکان

الان شول آدم هم یاتیب تورور اما محمد یعقوب مذکور بزکا کوب حقارت تماو

ناشایسته سوزلار نی آیدی ایمدی صاحب اختیار اوزلاری قورور دیب

۸ نجی ماه رمضان نوده اوشبو عریضه نامه نی مکتوب ایتیب عرض ... ارسال ایتیلدی

۱۳۳۶

DOCUMENT 30A TsGARUz, f. I-125, op. 1, d. 498, l. 103

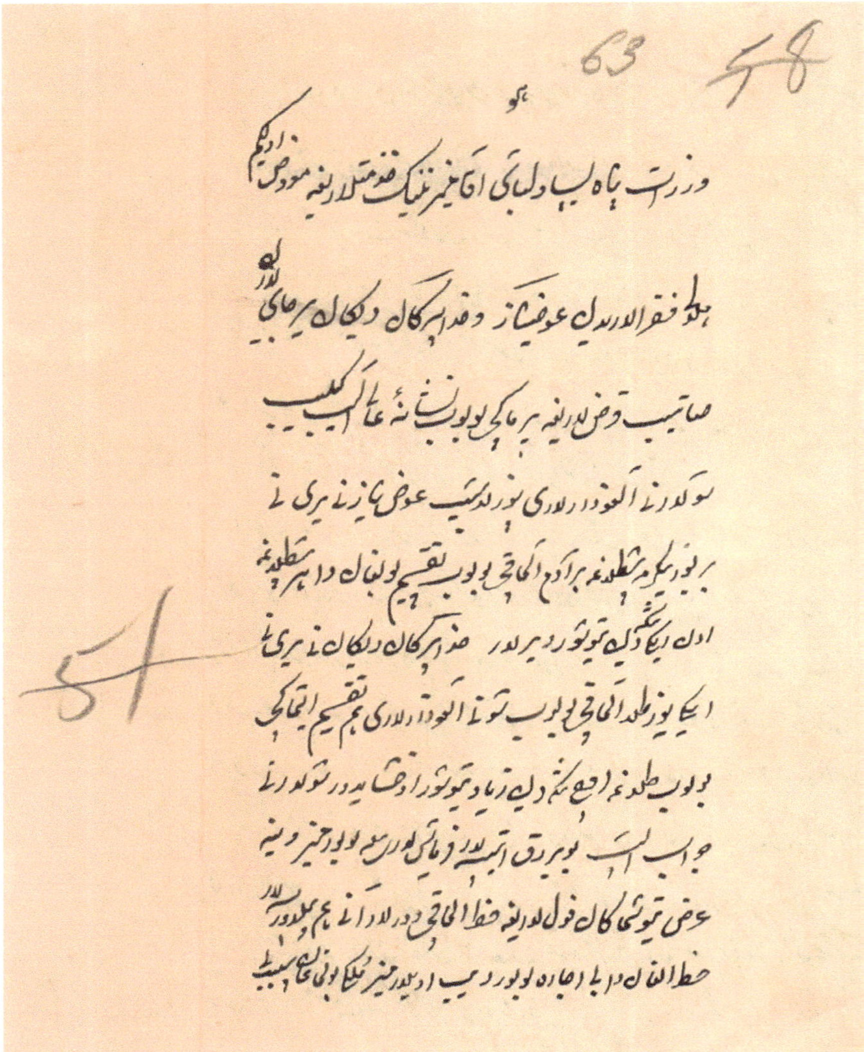

DOCUMENT 31A TsGARUz, f. I-125, op. 1, d. 498, l. 63

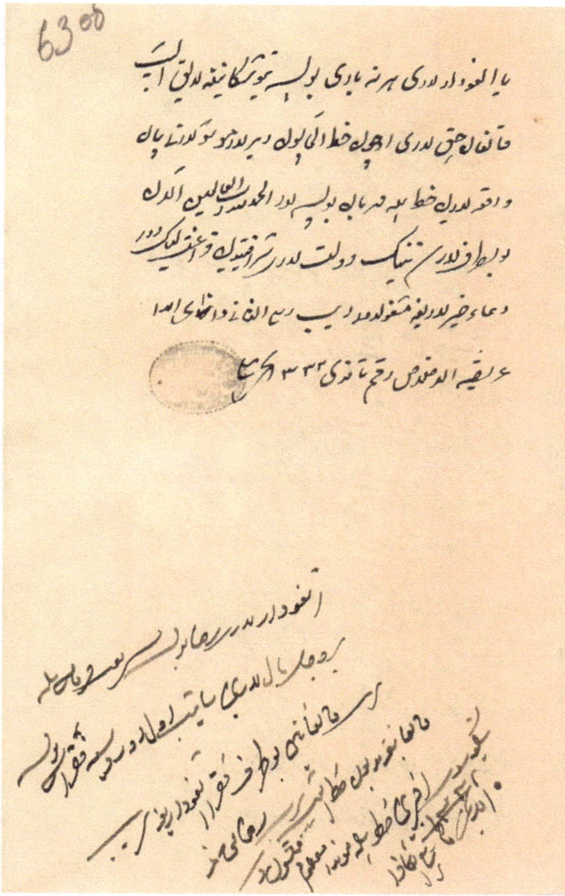

DOCUMENT 31B TsGARUz, f. I-125, op. 1, d. 498, l. 63 ob

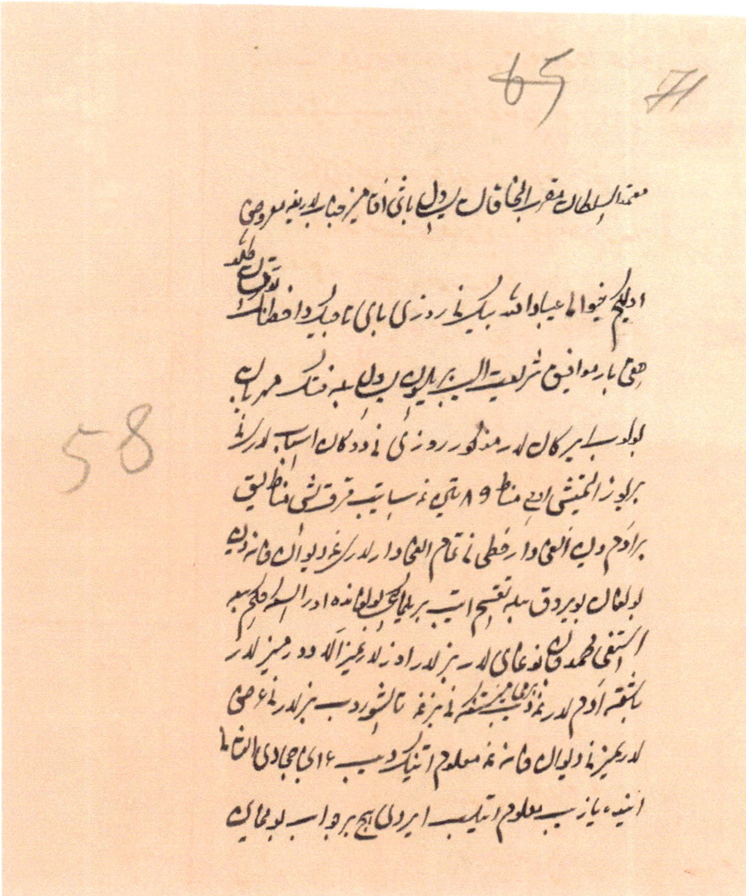

DOCUMENT 32A TsGARUz, f. I-125, op. 1, d. 498, l. 71

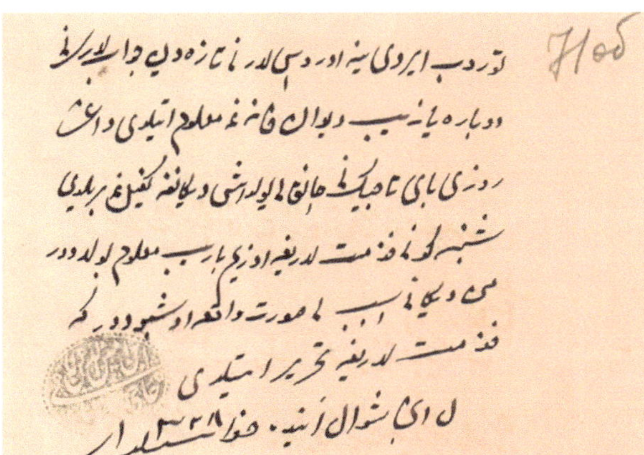

DOCUMENT 32B TsGARUz, f. I-125, op. 1, d. 498, l. 71 ob

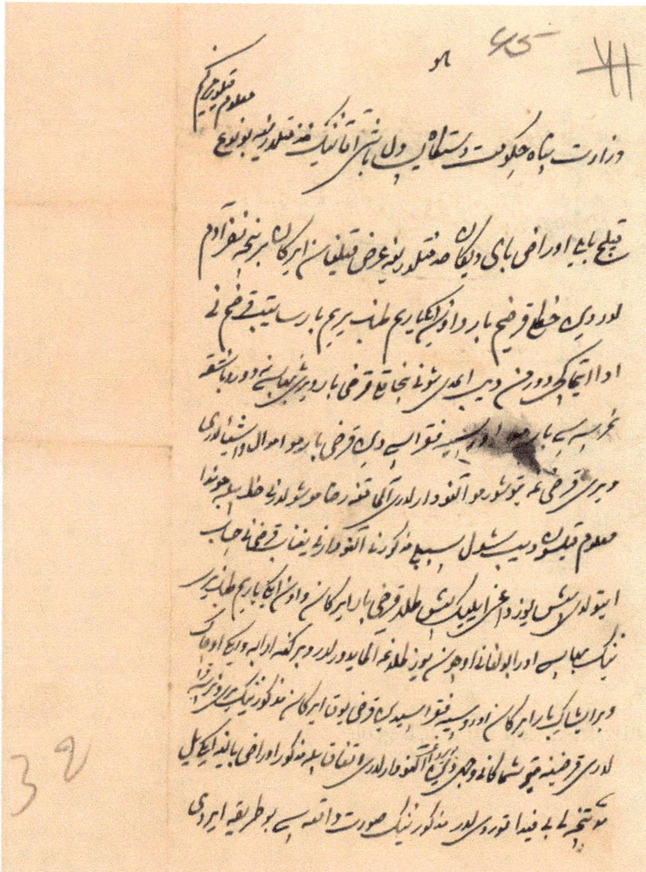

DOCUMENT 33A TsGARUz, f. I-125, op. 1, d. 498, l. 45

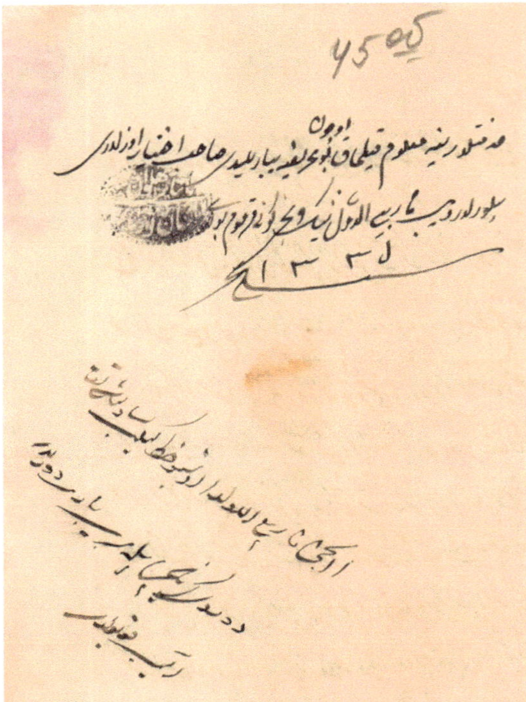

DOCUMENT 33B TsGARUz, f. I-125, op. 1, d. 498, l. 45 ob

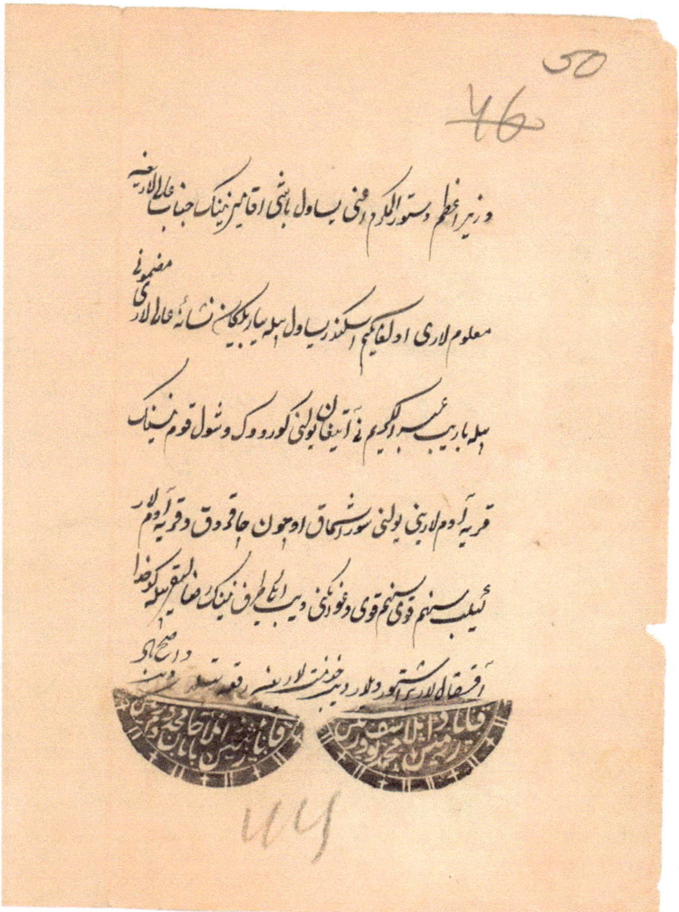

DOCUMENT 34A TsGARUz, f. I-125, op. 1, d. 498, l. 50

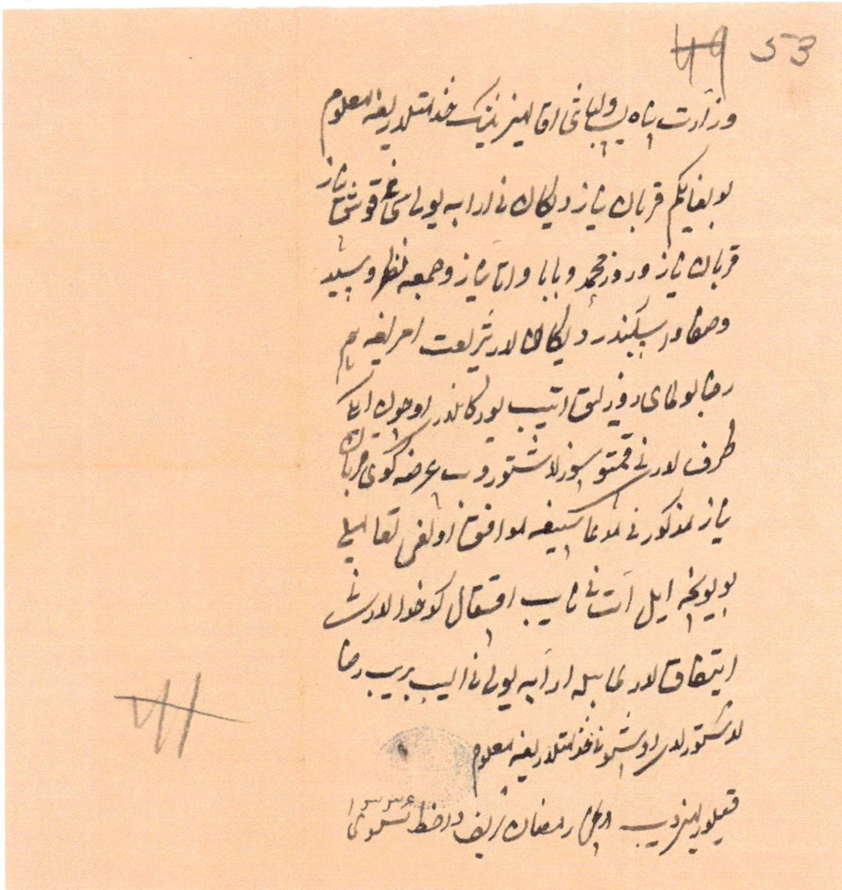

DOCUMENT 35A TsGARUz, f. I-125, op. 1, d. 498, l. 53

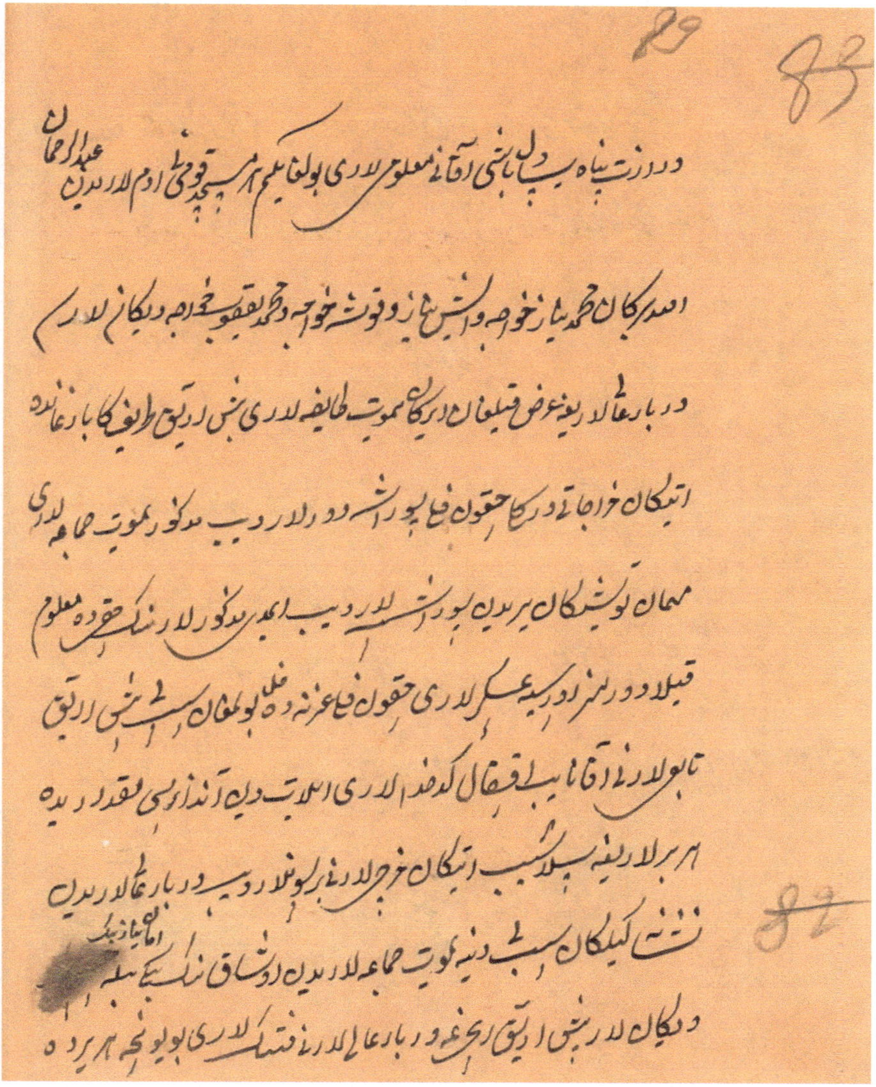

DOCUMENT 36A TsGARUz, f. I-125, op. 1, d. 498, l. 89

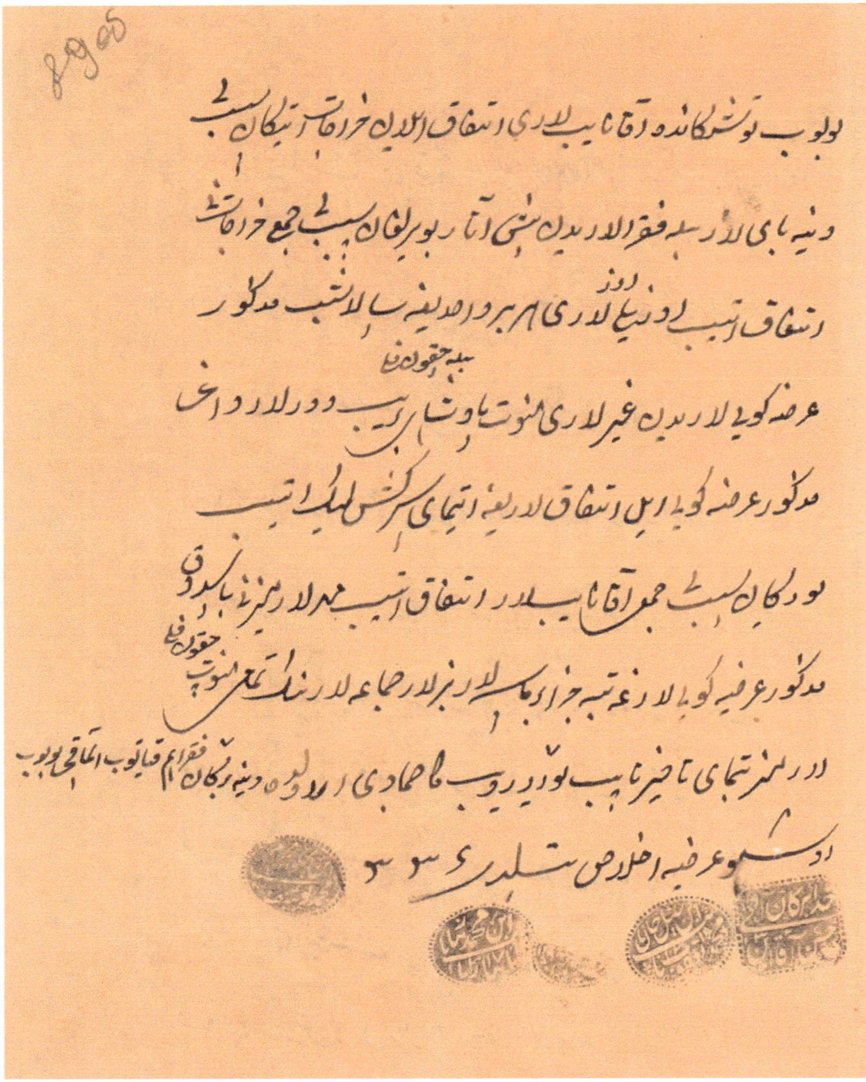

DOCUMENT 36B TsGARUz, f. I-125, op. 1, d. 498, l. 89 ob

Section Three

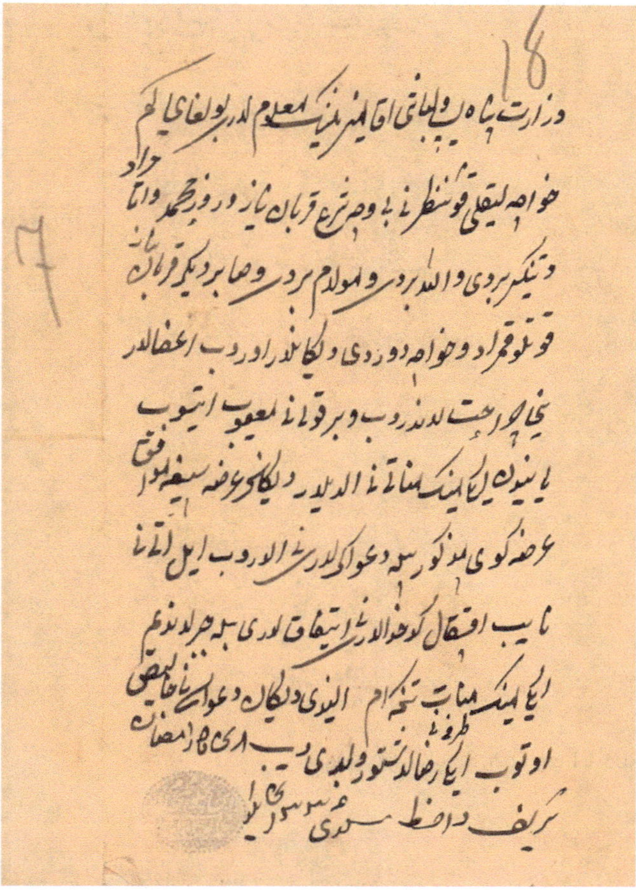

DOCUMENT 37A TsGARUz, f. I-125, op. 1, d. 498, l. 18

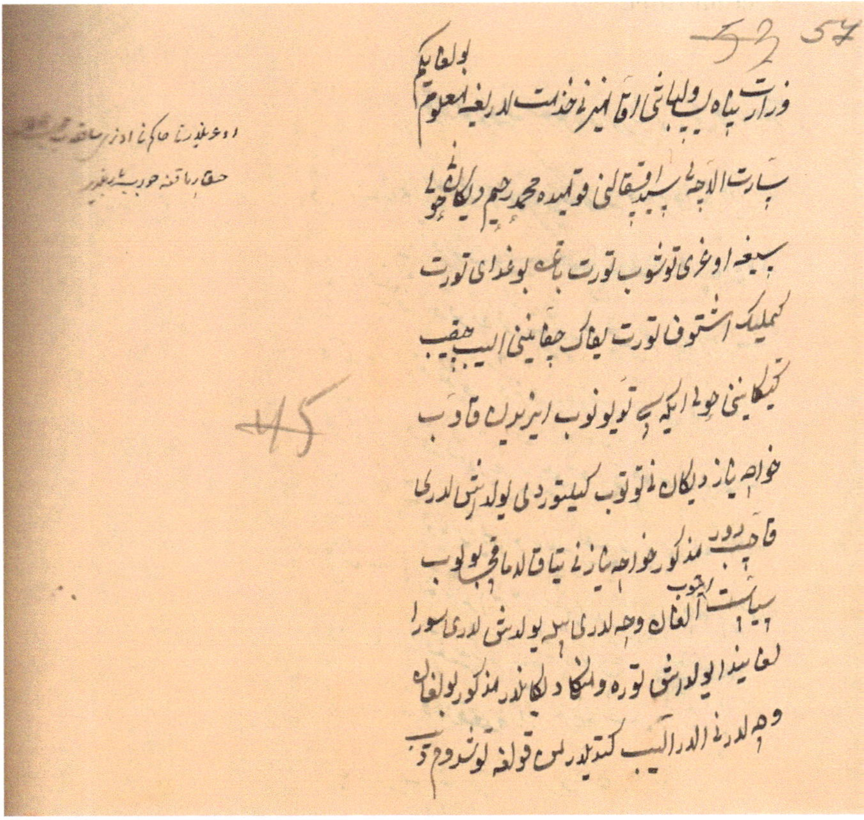

DOCUMENT 38A TsGARUz, f. I-125, op. 1, d. 498, l. 57

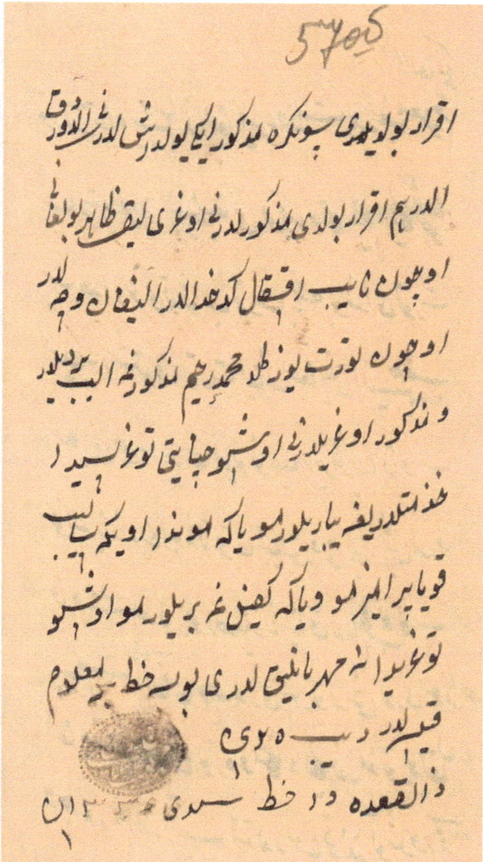

DOCUMENT 38B TsGARUz, f. I-125, op. 1, d. 498, l. 57 ob

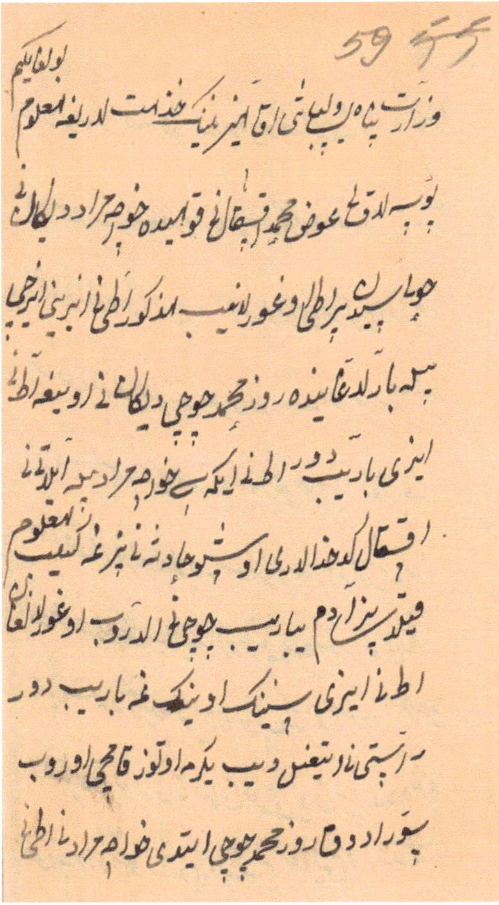

59

بولغایکیم

وزارت پناه ولی بای تی اراق ایمیر بلیک خدمت لریغه معلوم

بوبه الدق که عوض محمد قپچاق نی قوابیده خوجه مراد دیکان نی

چوپان پسیندی پیر اطی دغورلانیب مذکور اطی نی ابرینی اثرچی

بیله بار الدغ آیینده روز محمد چوچی دیکان نی اوریغه اطی نی

ایزی بار دیب دور الطنه ایکه سی خواجه مراد دیه ایلانی

اقسقال کدخدا الدی اوستوجادینه تاپر غه کیتیب معلوم

قیلدی پیر آدم بیا ریب چوچی الدروب ادغورلانغان

اطنا ایزی سیننگ ادینک ثم باریب دور

درستی نا راستیغنی دیب یکره ادلوز قاچی اوروب

سوراددق روز محمد چوچی ایتدی خواجه مراد نا اطی

DOCUMENT 39A TsGARUz, f. I-125, op. 1, d. 498, l. 59

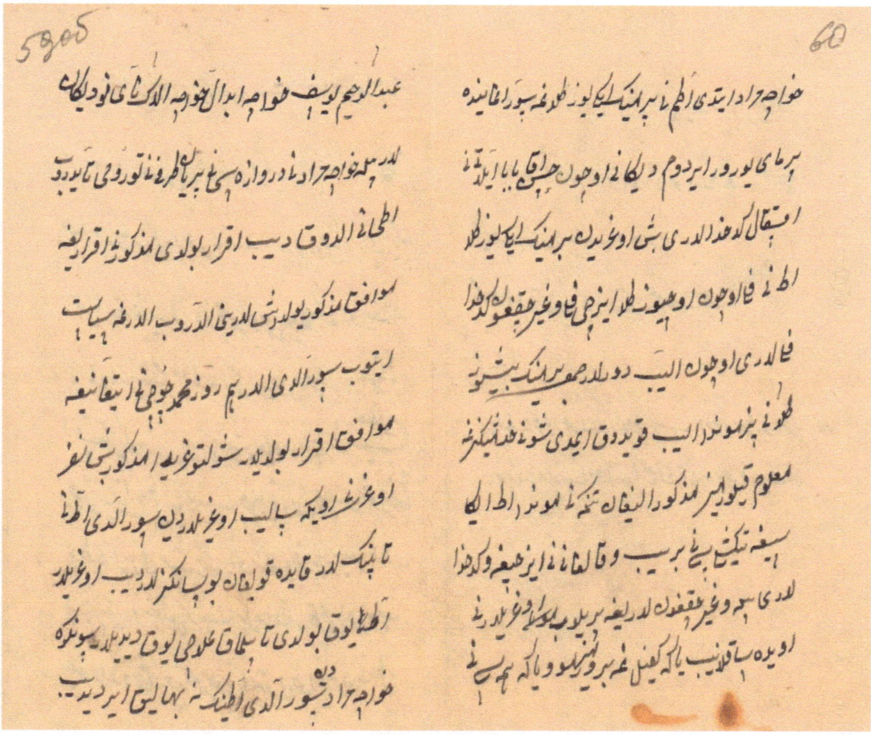

DOCUMENT 39B TsGARUz, f. I-125, op. 1, d. 498, ll. 59 ob.–60 ob

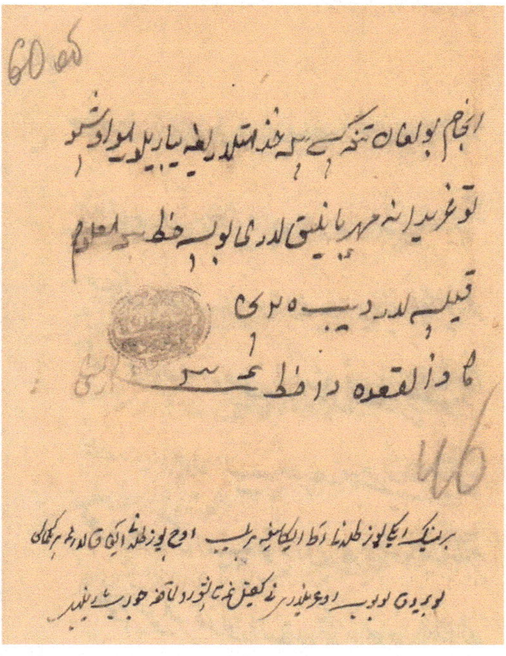

DOCUMENT 39C TsGARUz, f. I-125, op. 1, d. 498, l. 60 ob

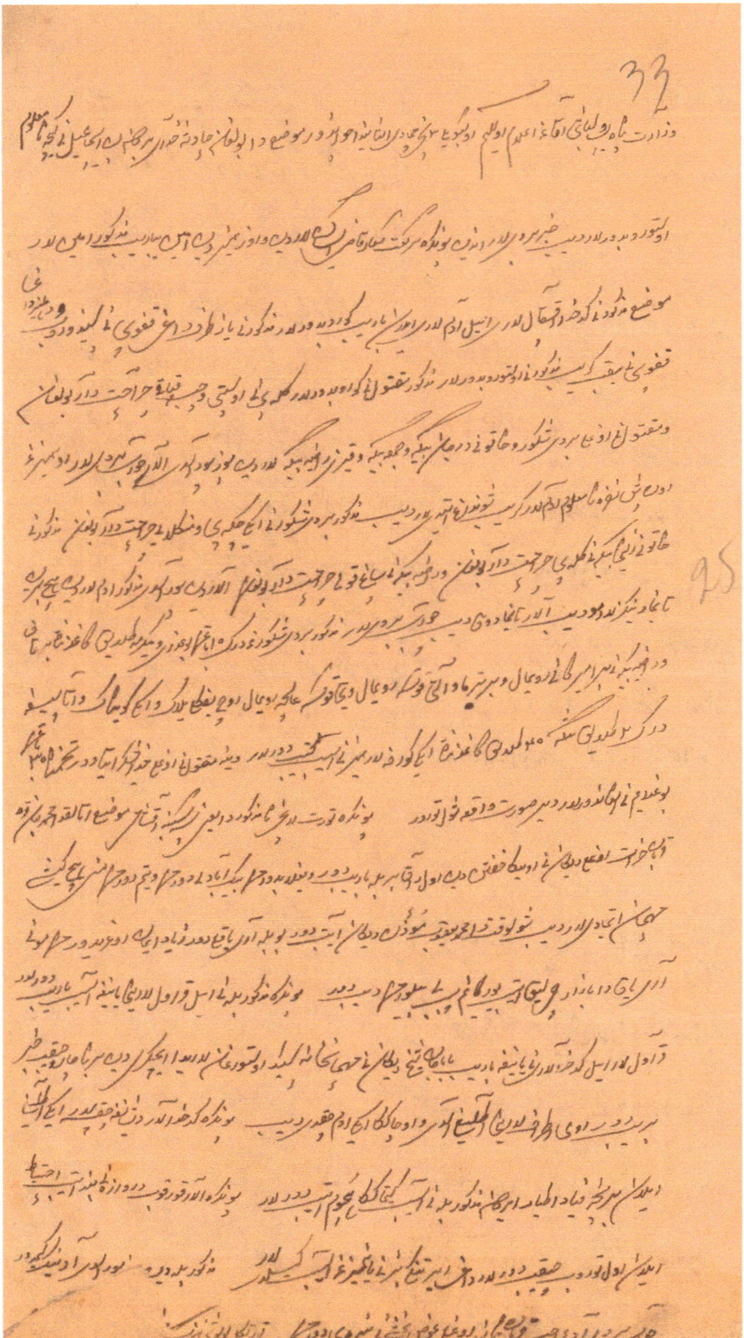

DOCUMENT 40A TsGARUz, f. I-125, op. 1, d. 498, l. 33

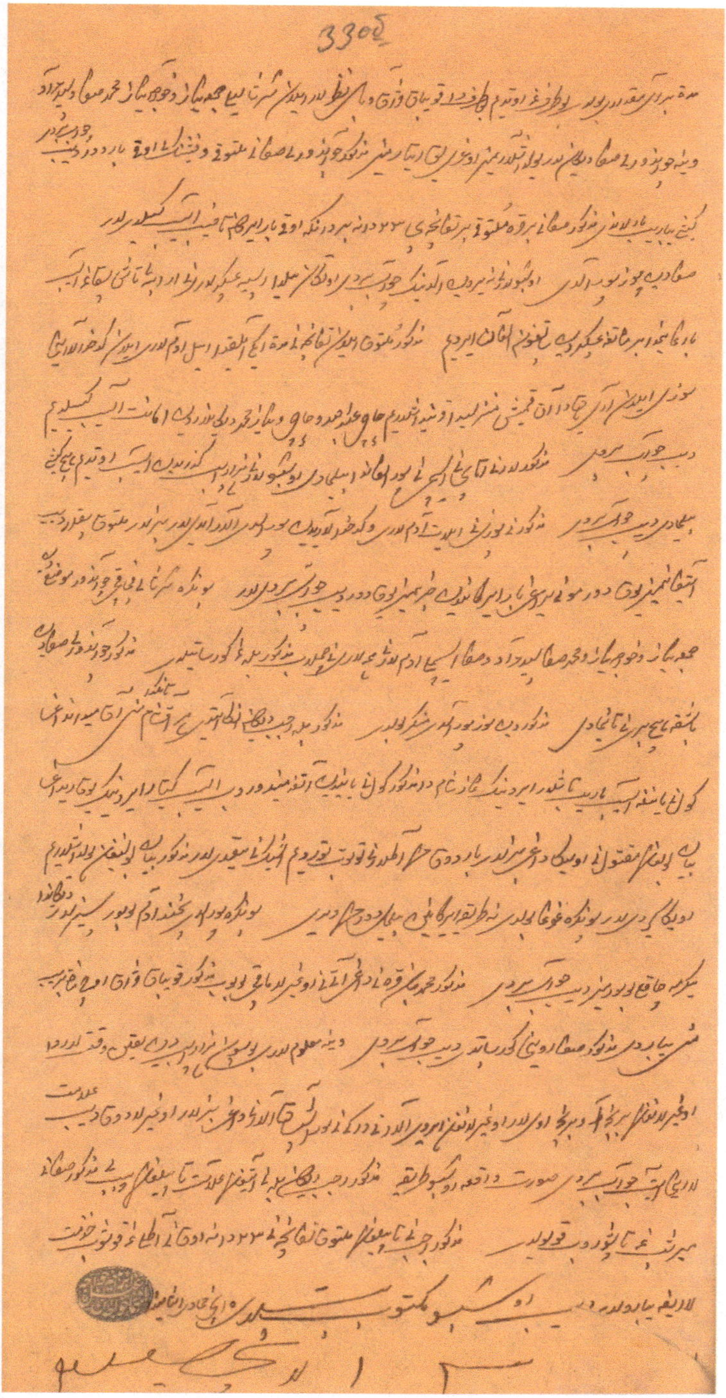

DOCUMENT 40B TsGARUz, f. I-125, op. 1, d. 498, l. 33 ob

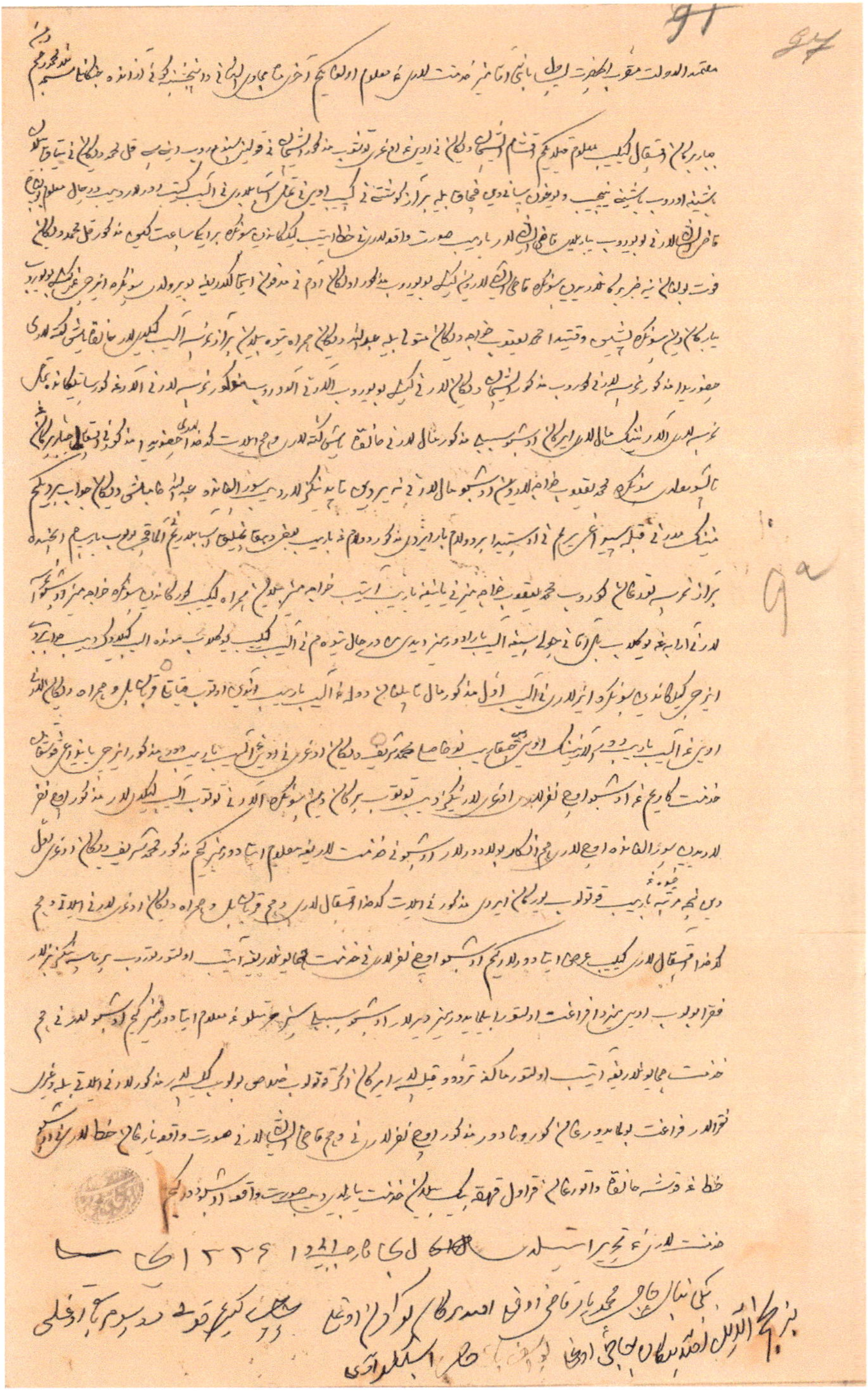

DOCUMENT 41A TsGARUz, f. I-125, op. 1, d. 498, l. 97

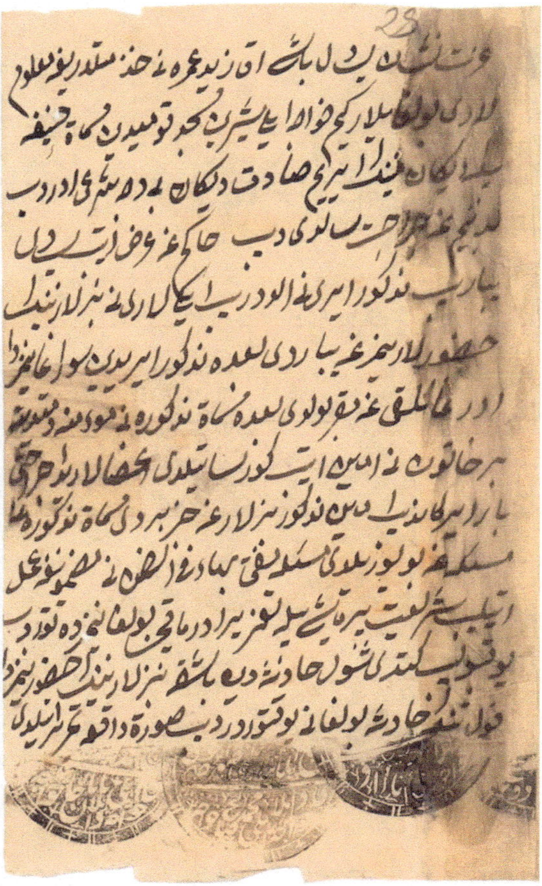

DOCUMENT 42A TsGARUz, f. I-125, op. 1, d. 498, l. 29

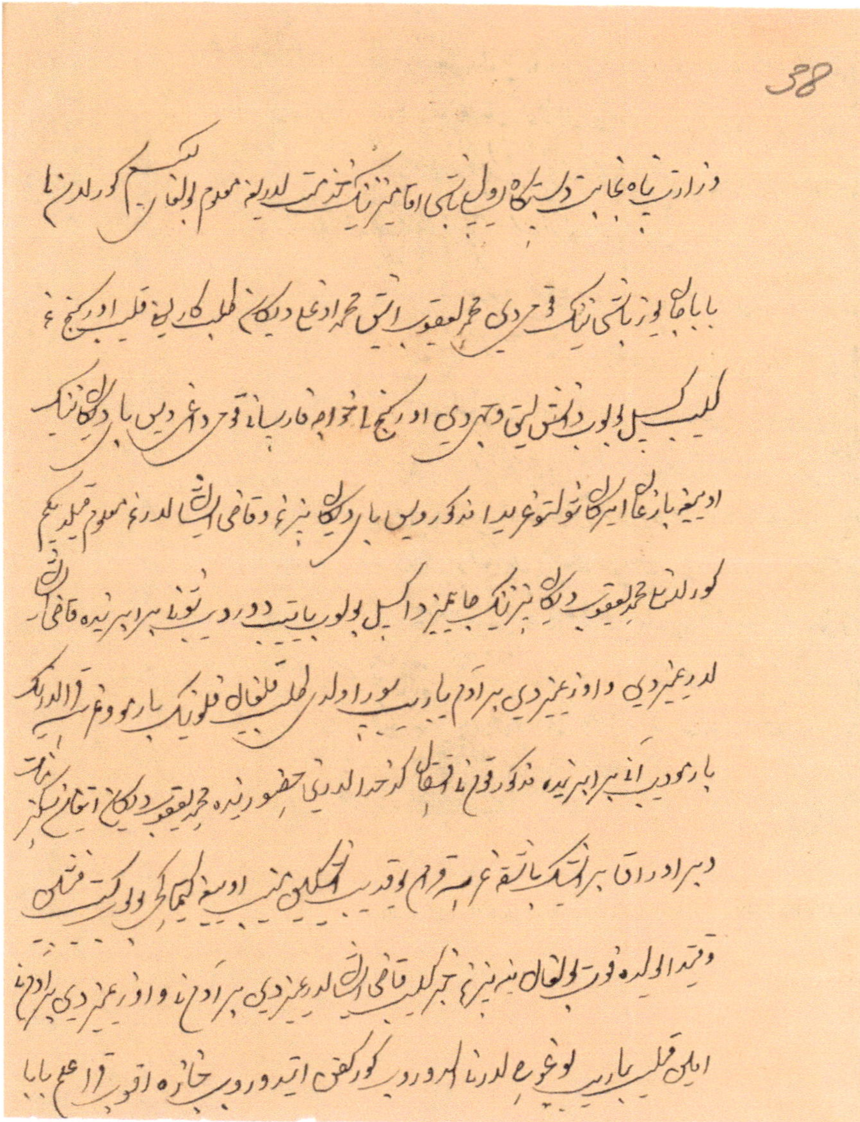

DOCUMENT 43A TsGARUz, f. I-125, op. 1, d. 498, l. 38

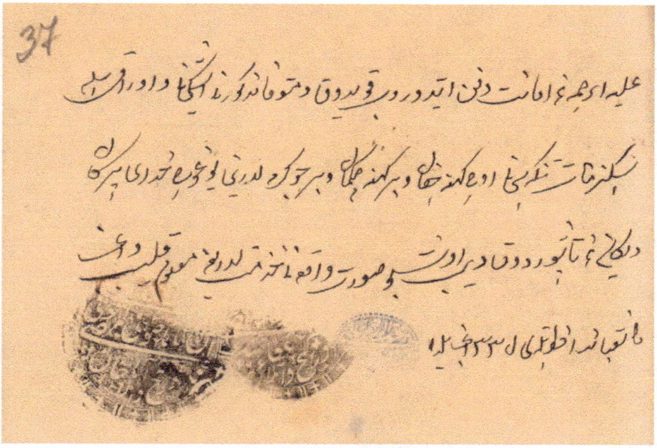

DOCUMENT 43B TsGARUz, f. I-125, op. 1, d. 498, l. 37

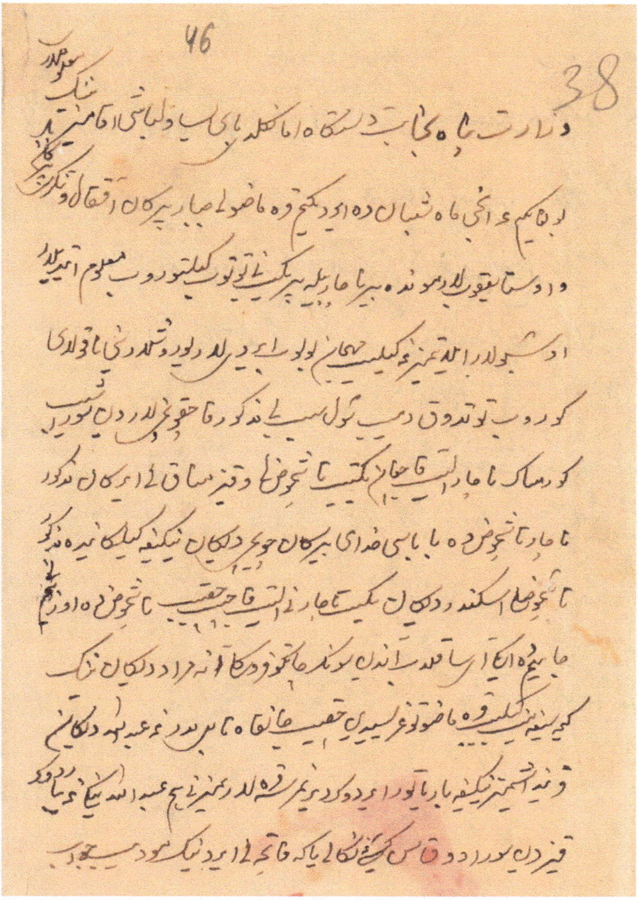

DOCUMENT 44A TsGARUz, f. I-125, op. 1, d. 498, l. 46

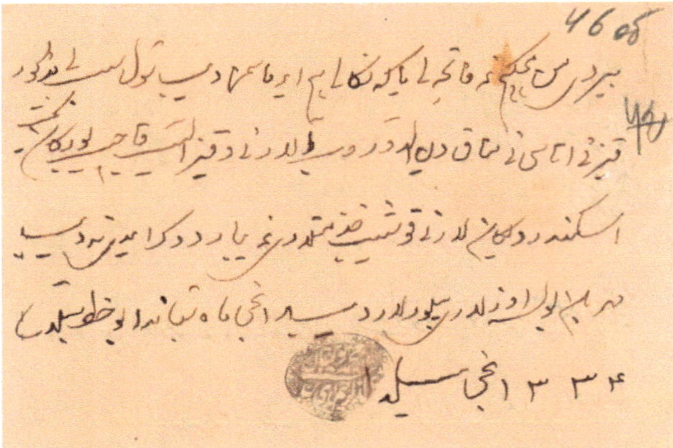

DOCUMENT 44B TsGARUz, f. I-125, op. 1, d. 498, l. 46 ob

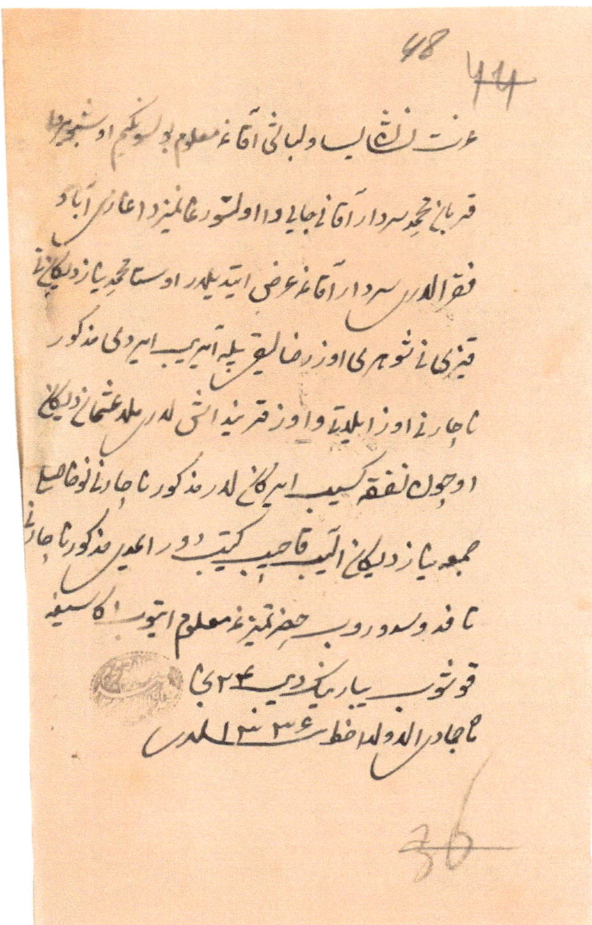

DOCUMENT 45A TsGARUz, f. I-125, op. 1, d. 498, l. 48

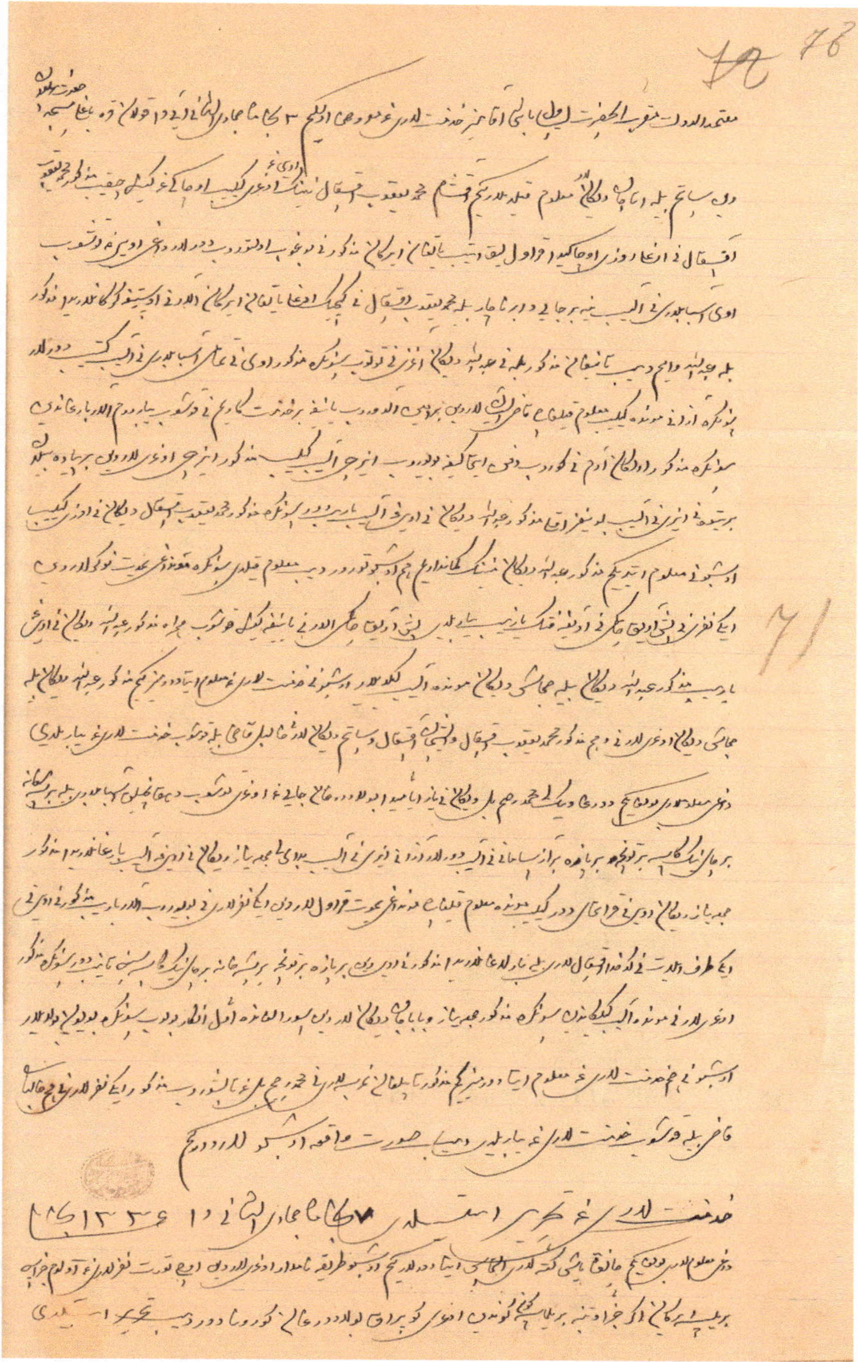

DOCUMENT 46A TsGARUz, f. I-125, op. 1, d. 498, l. 78

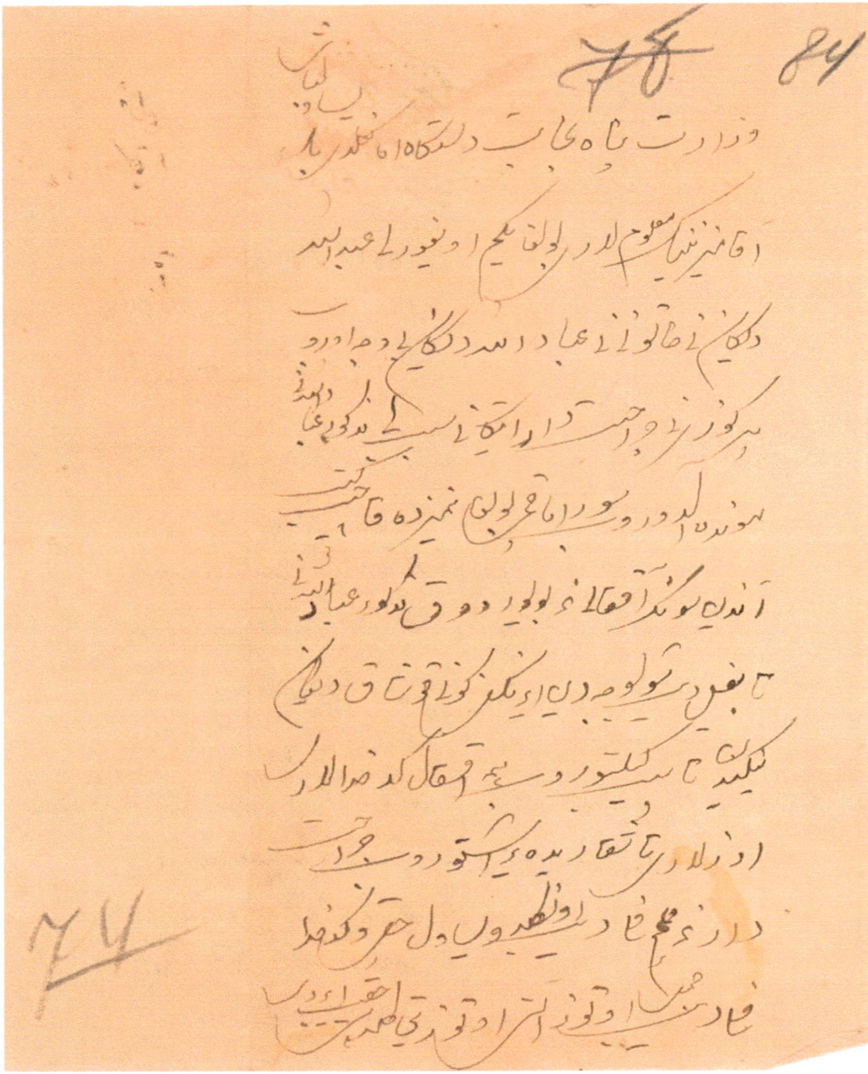

DOCUMENT 47A TsGARUz, f. I-125, op. 1, d. 498, l. 84

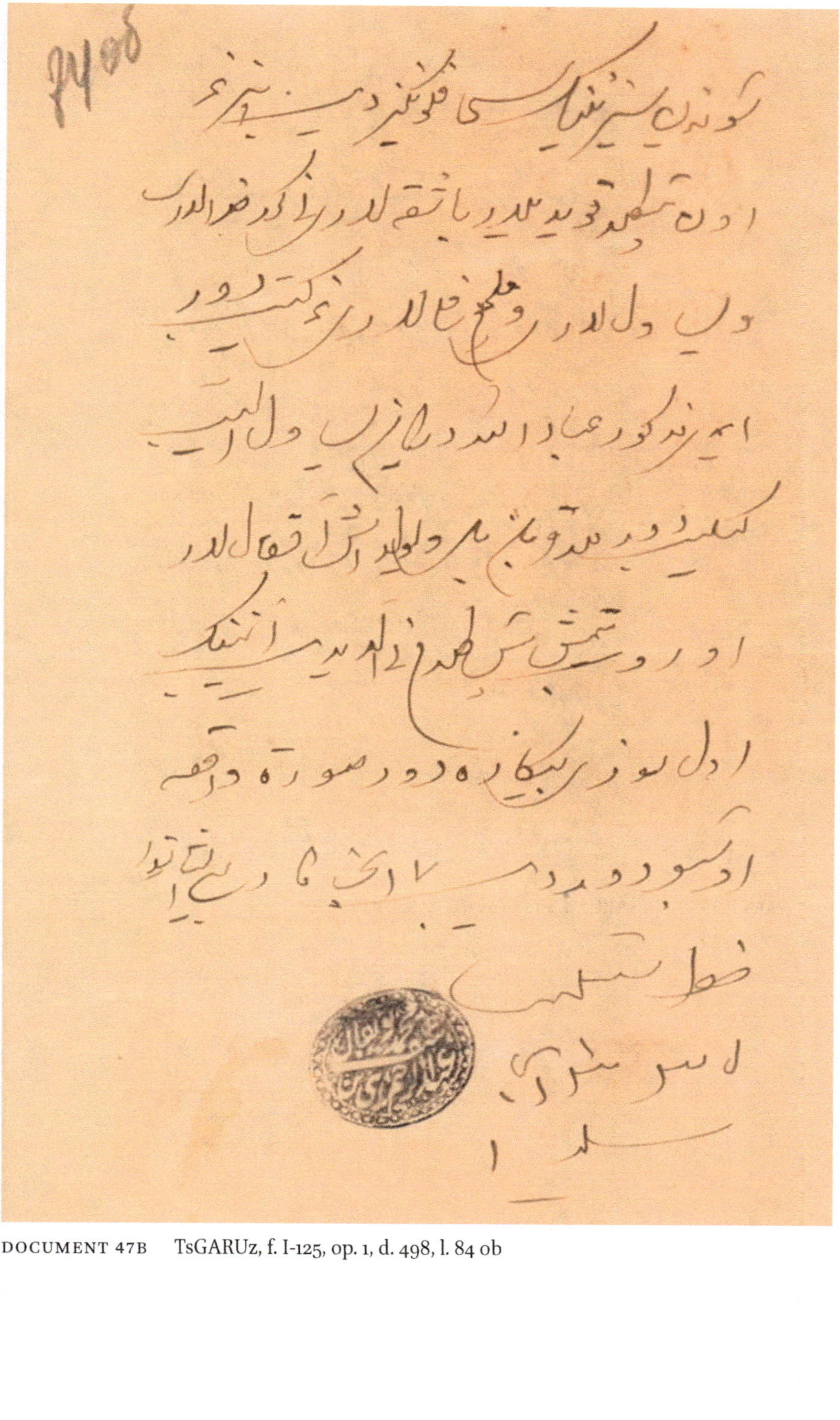

DOCUMENT 47B TsGARUz, f. I-125, op. 1, d. 498, l. 84 ob

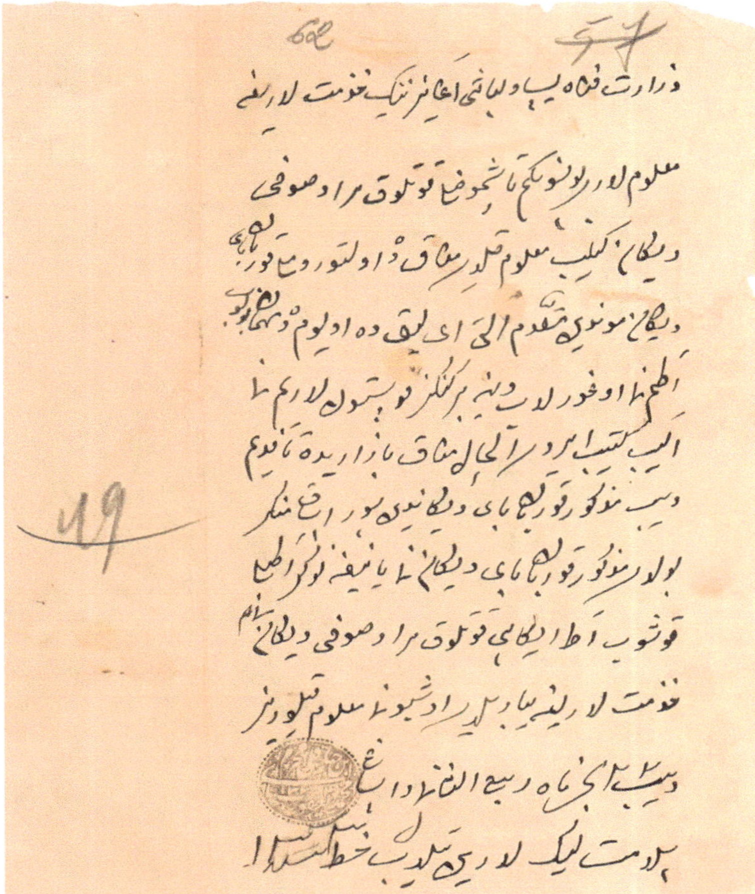

DOCUMENT 48A TsGARUz, f. I-125, op. 1, d. 498, l. 62

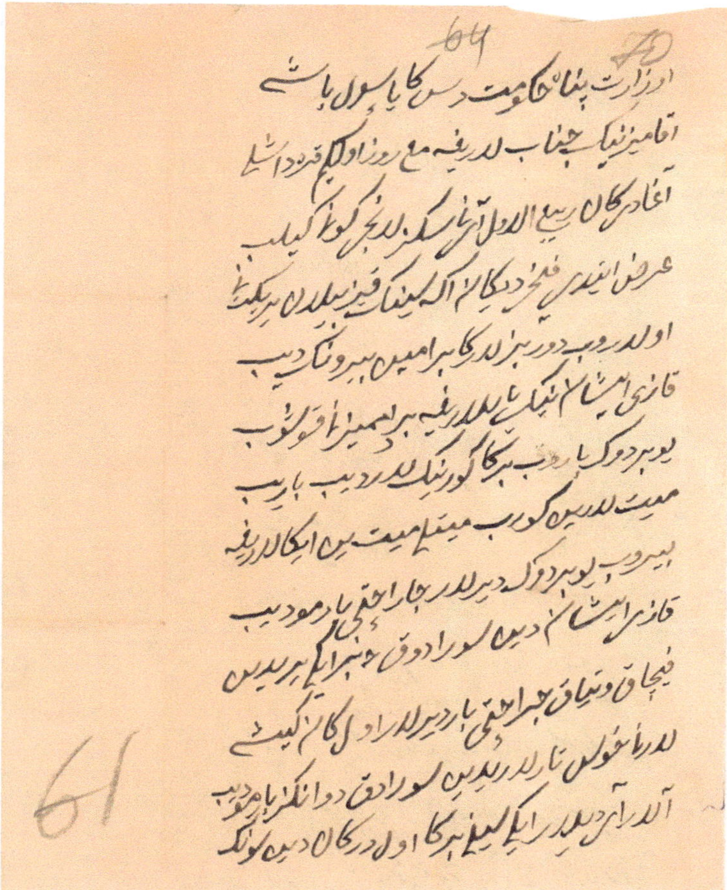

DOCUMENT 49A TsGARUz, f. I-125, op. 1, d. 498, l. 70

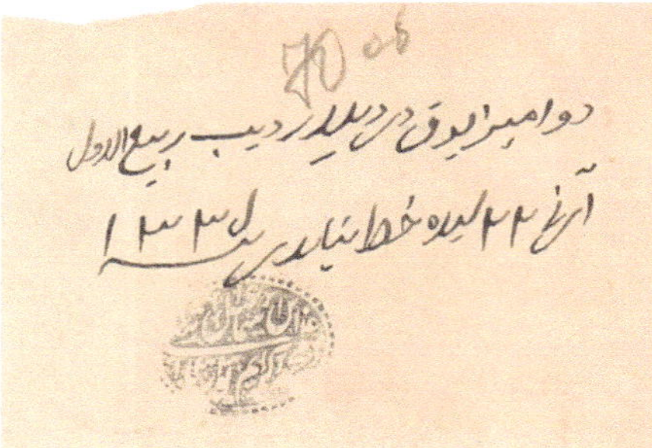

DOCUMENT 49B
TsGARUz, f. I-125, op. 1, d. 498, l. 70 ob

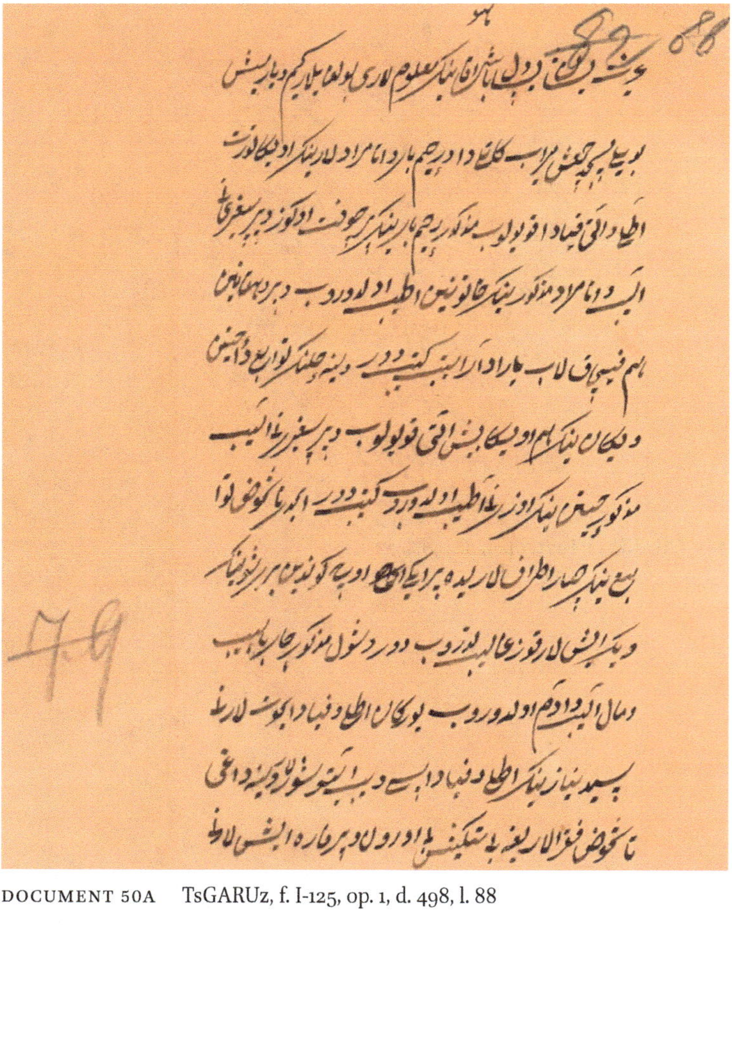

DOCUMENT 50A TsGARUz, f. I-125, op. 1, d. 498, l. 88

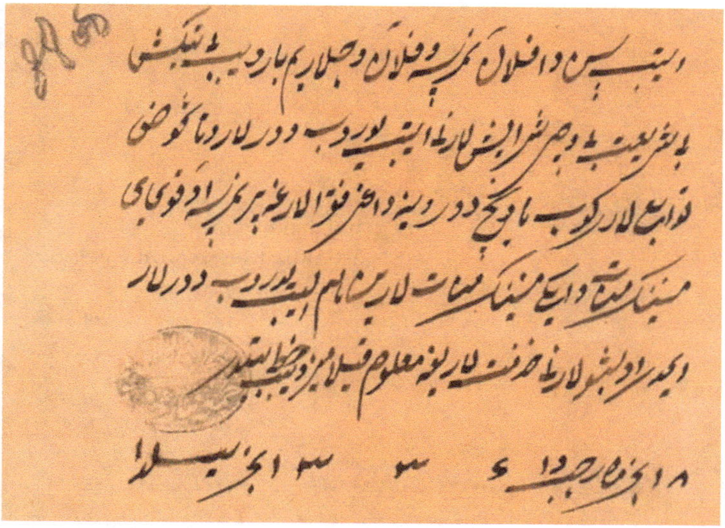

DOCUMENT 50B TsGARUz, f. I-125, op. 1, d. 498, l. 88 ob

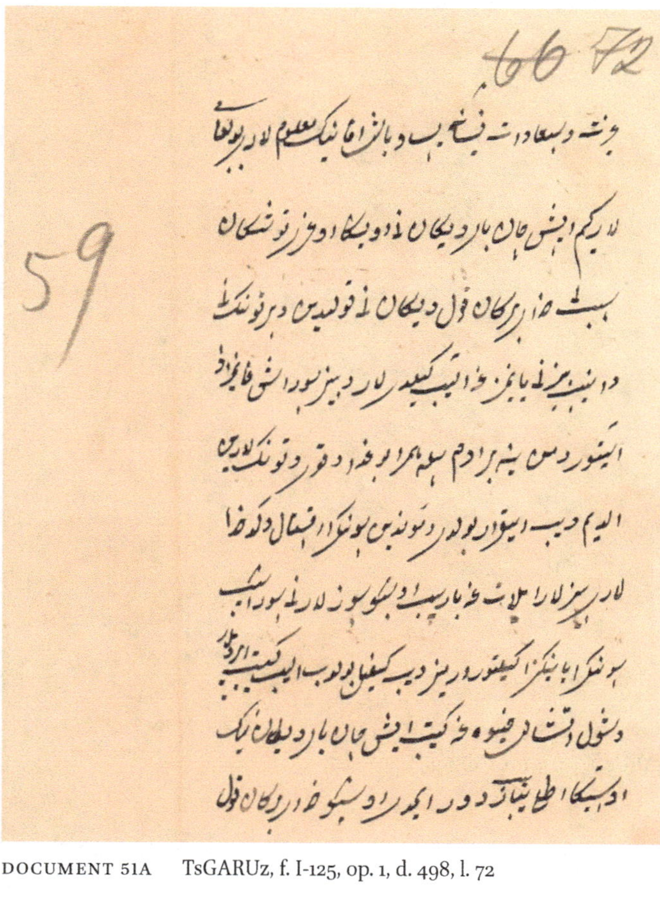

DOCUMENT 51A TsGARUz, f. I-125, op. 1, d. 498, l. 72

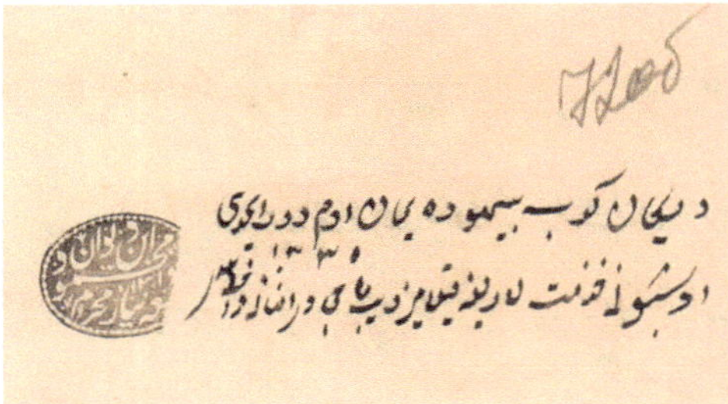

DOCUMENT 51B
TsGARUz, f. I-125, op. 1, d. 498, l. 72 ob

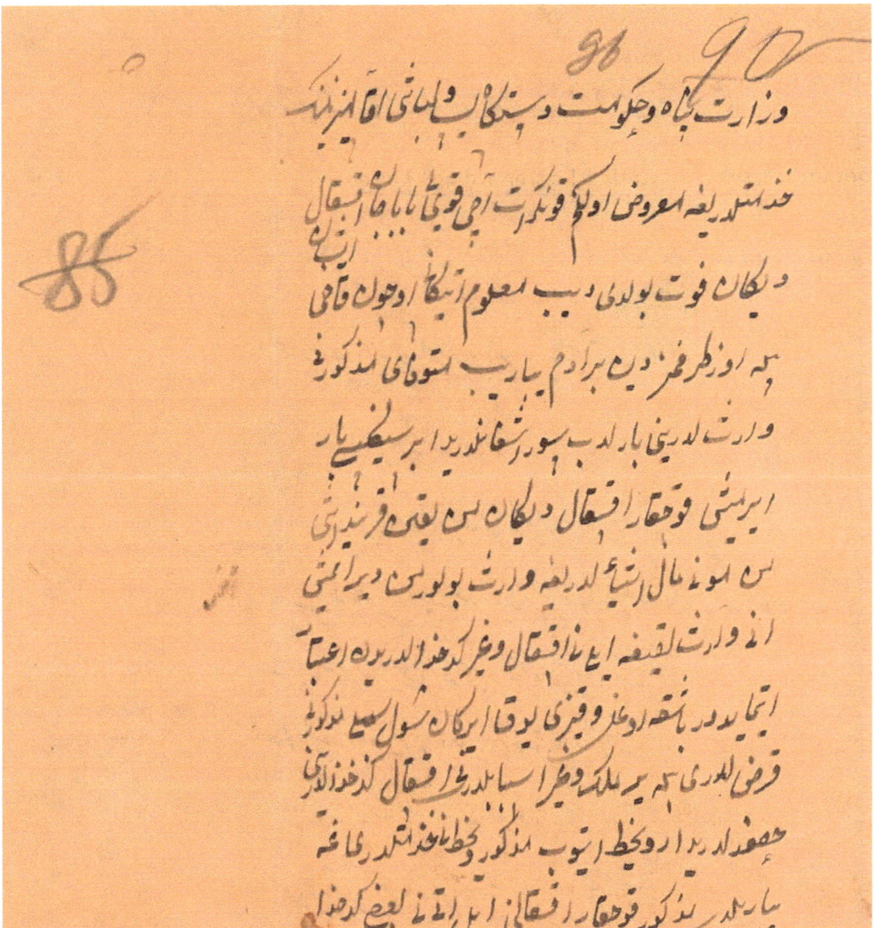

DOCUMENT 52A TsGARUz, f. I-125, op. 1, d. 498, l. 96

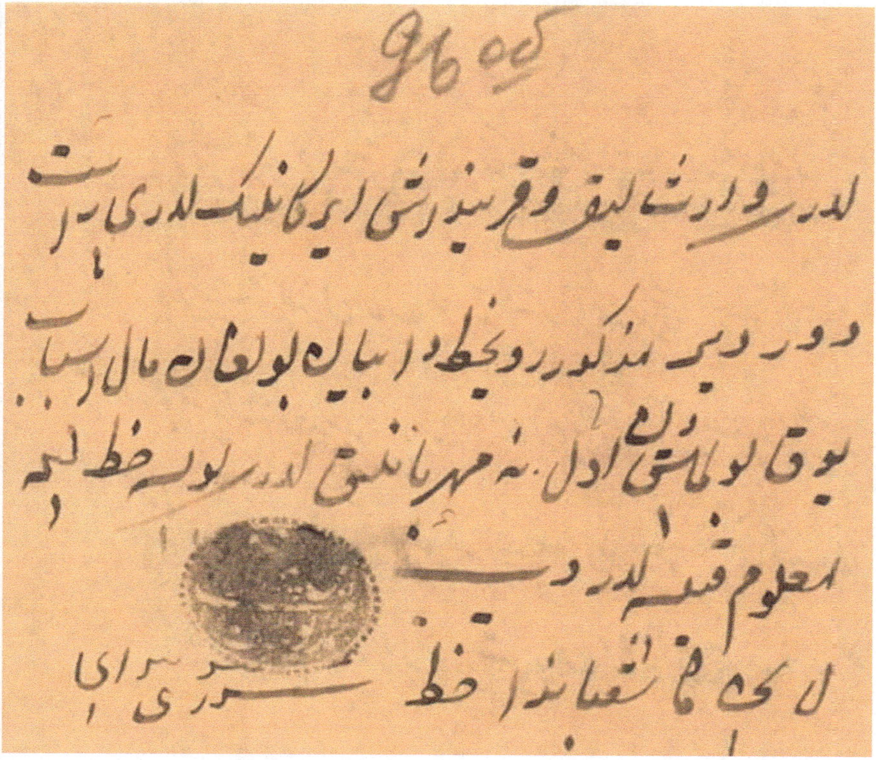

DOCUMENT 52B TsGARUz, f. I-125, op. 1, d. 498, l. 96 ob

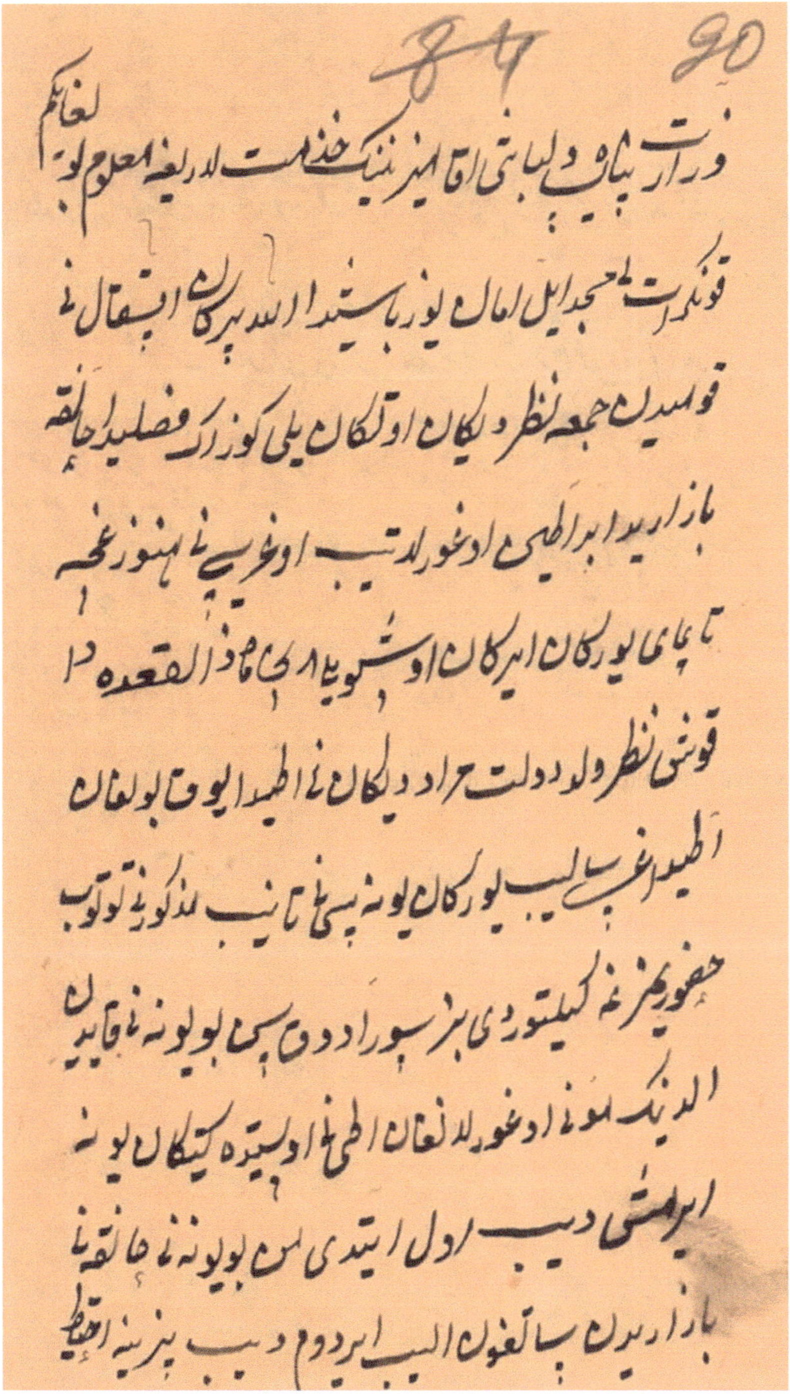

DOCUMENT 53A TsGARUz, f. I-125, op. 1, d. 498, l. 90

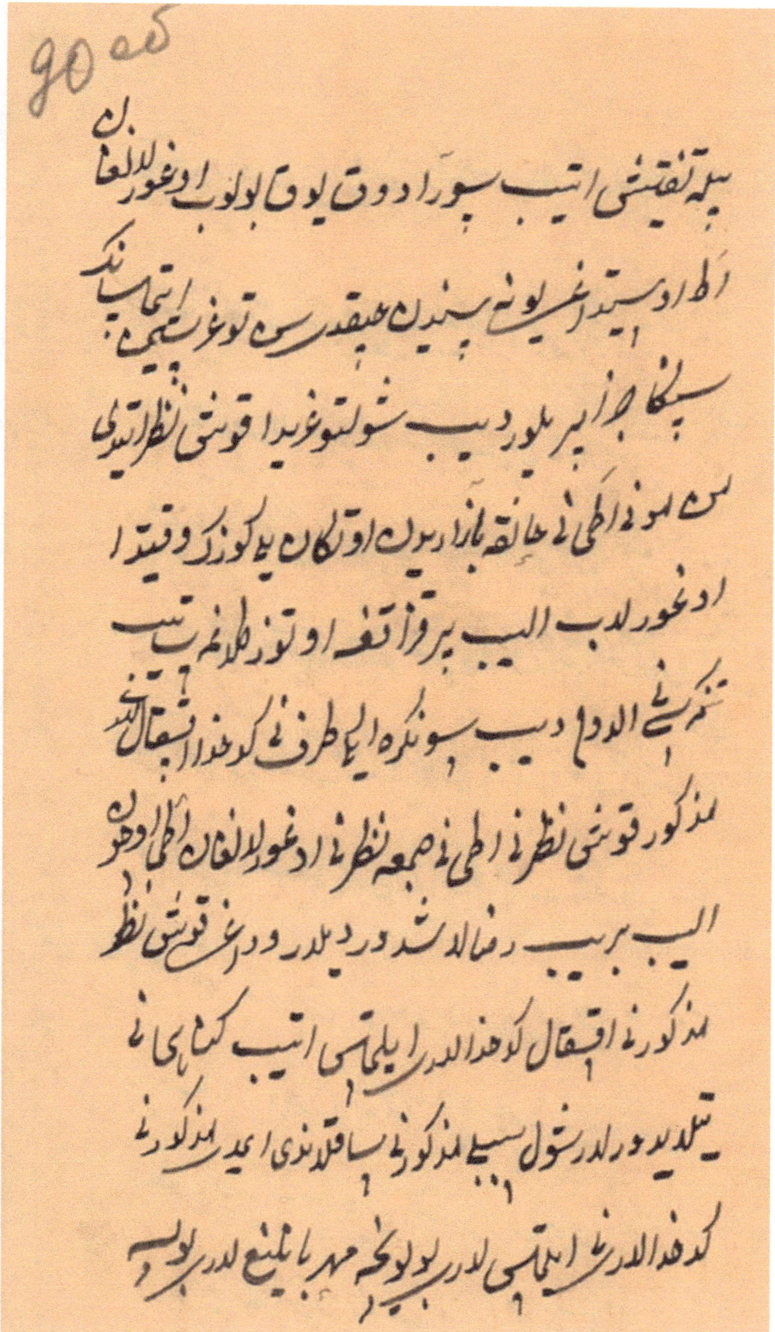

DOCUMENT 53B TsGARUz, f. I-125, op. 1, d. 498, l. 90 ob

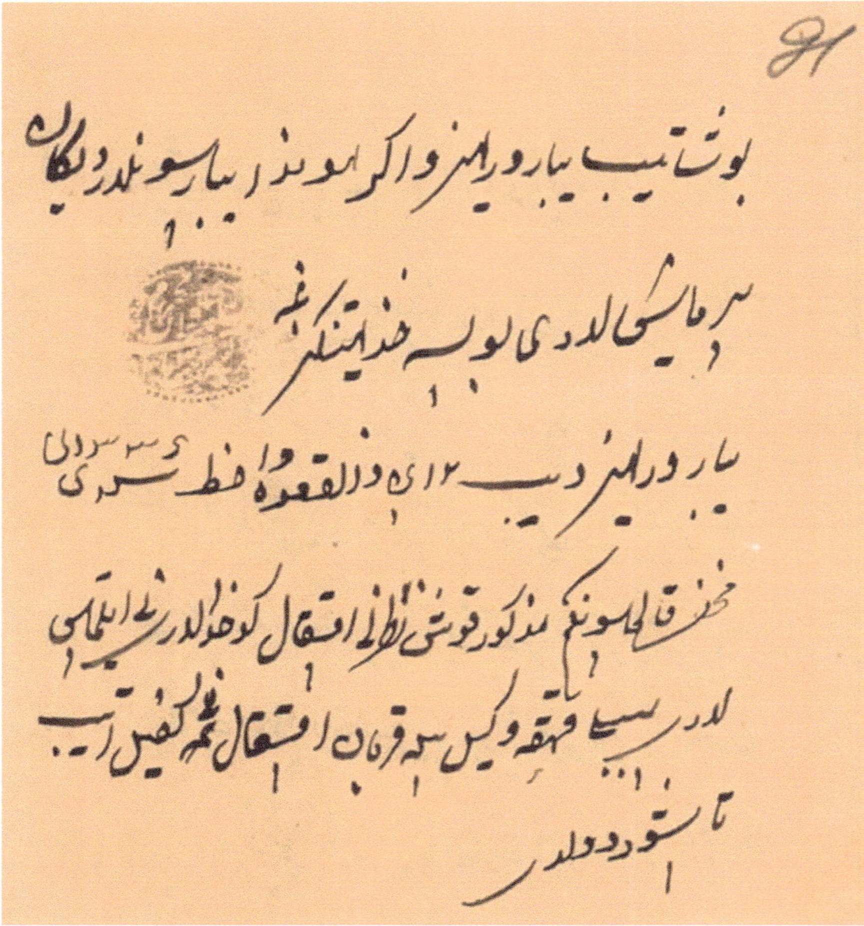

DOCUMENT 53C TsGARUz, f. I-125, op. 1, d. 498, l. 91

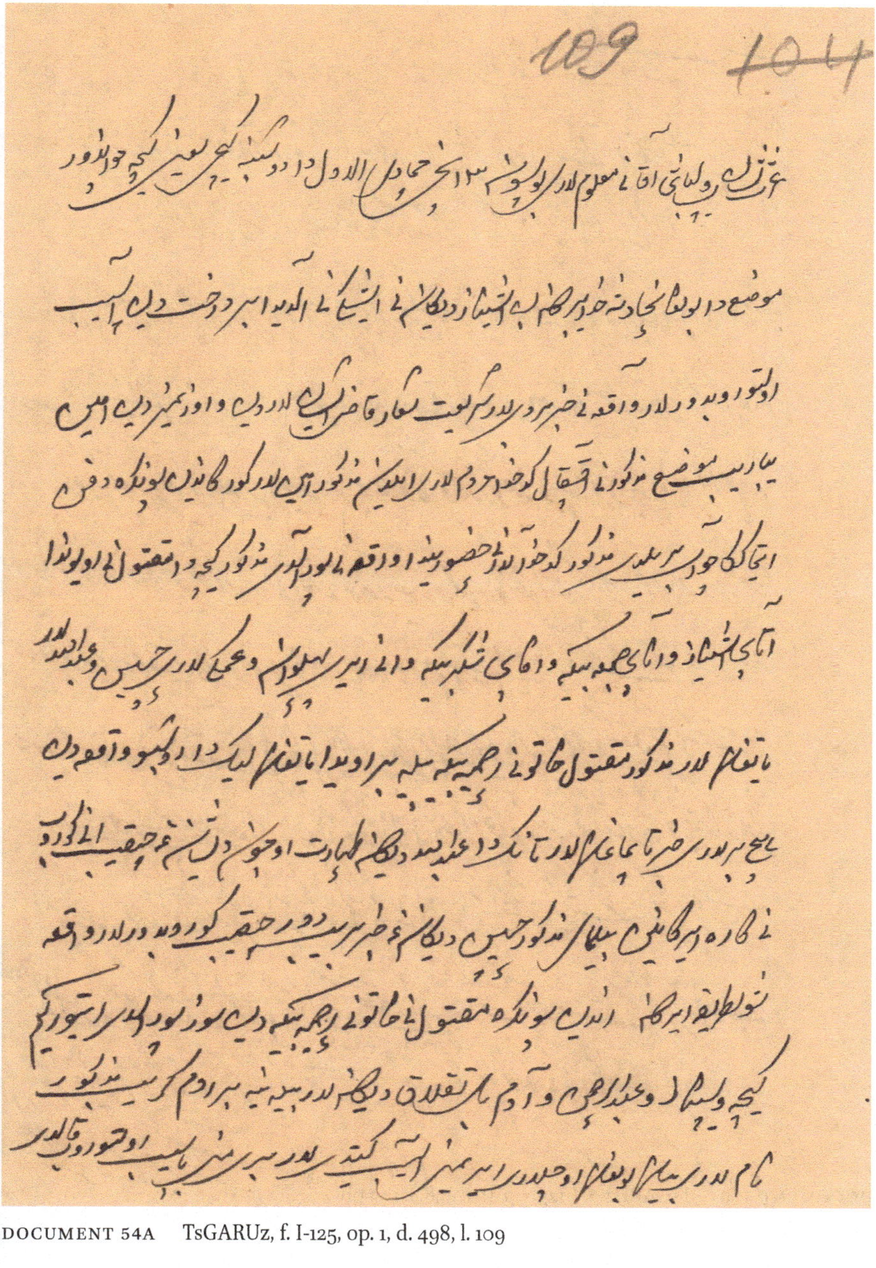

DOCUMENT 54A TsGARUz, f. I-125, op. 1, d. 498, l. 109

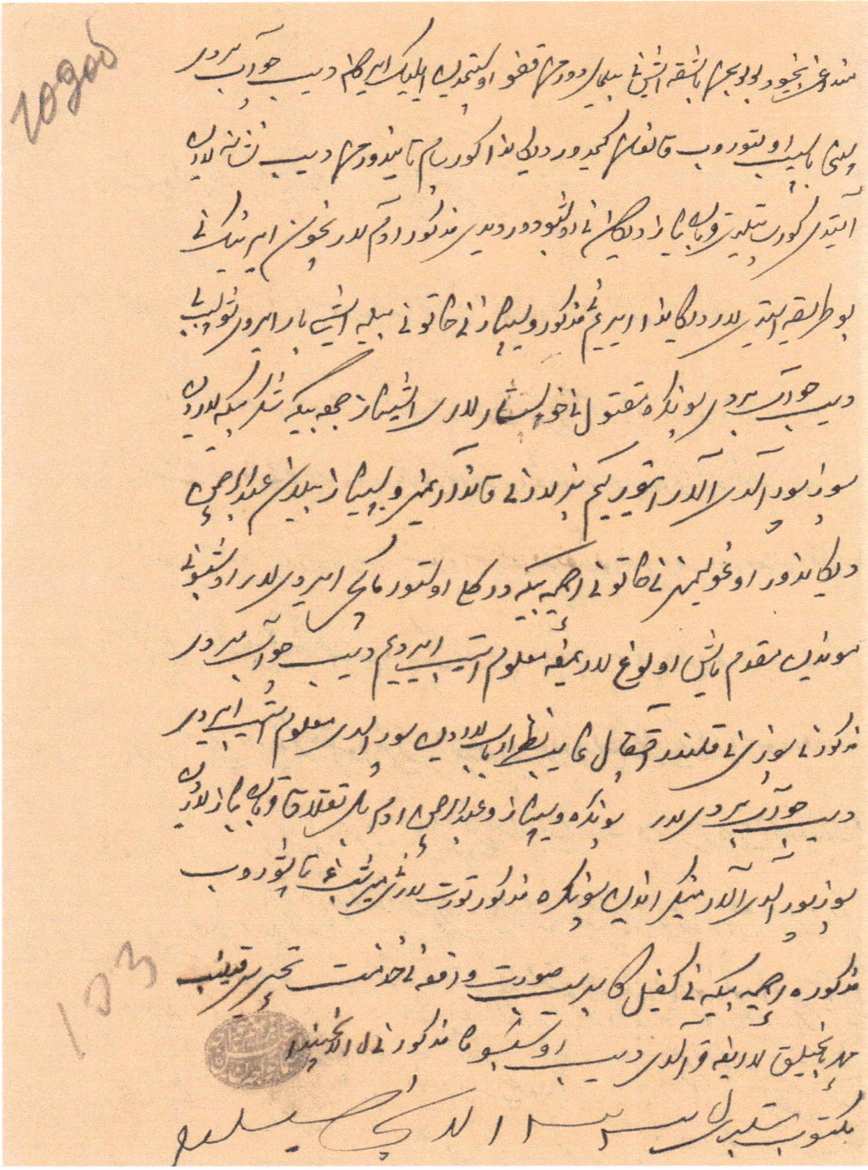

DOCUMENT 54B TsGARUz, f. I-125, op. 1, d. 498, l. 109 ob

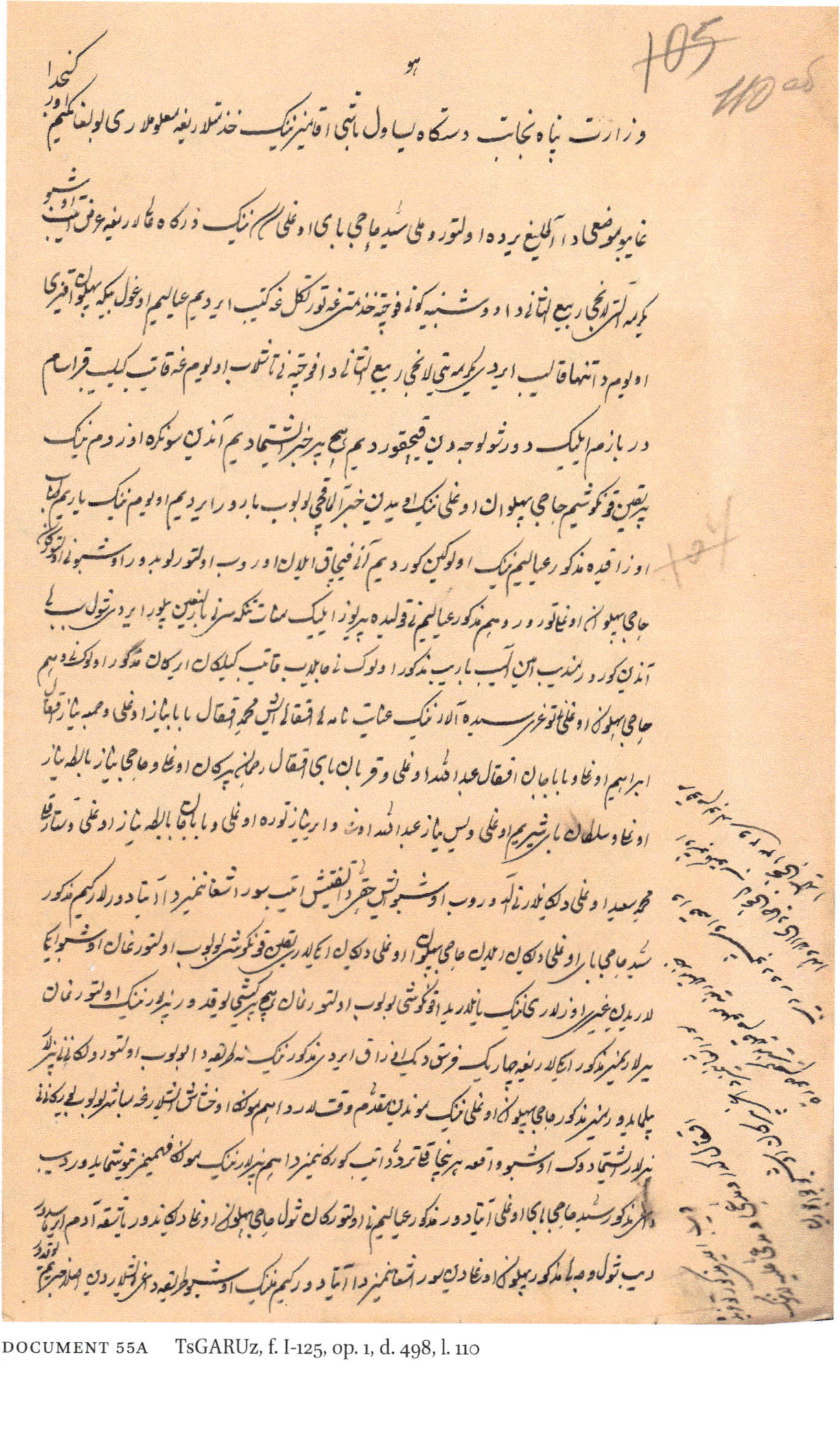

DOCUMENT 55A TsGARUz, f. I-125, op. 1, d. 498, l. 110

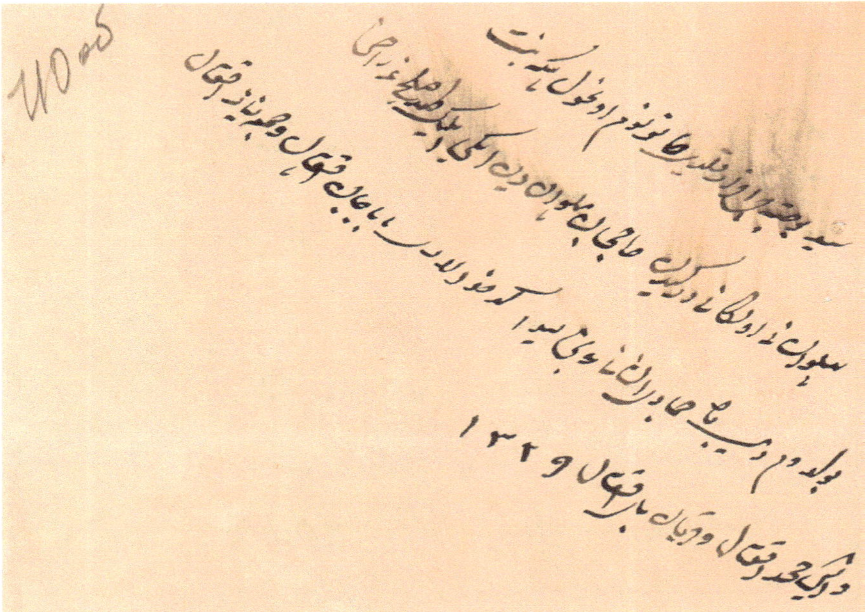

DOCUMENT 55B TsGARUz, f. I-125, op. 1, d. 498, l. 110 ob

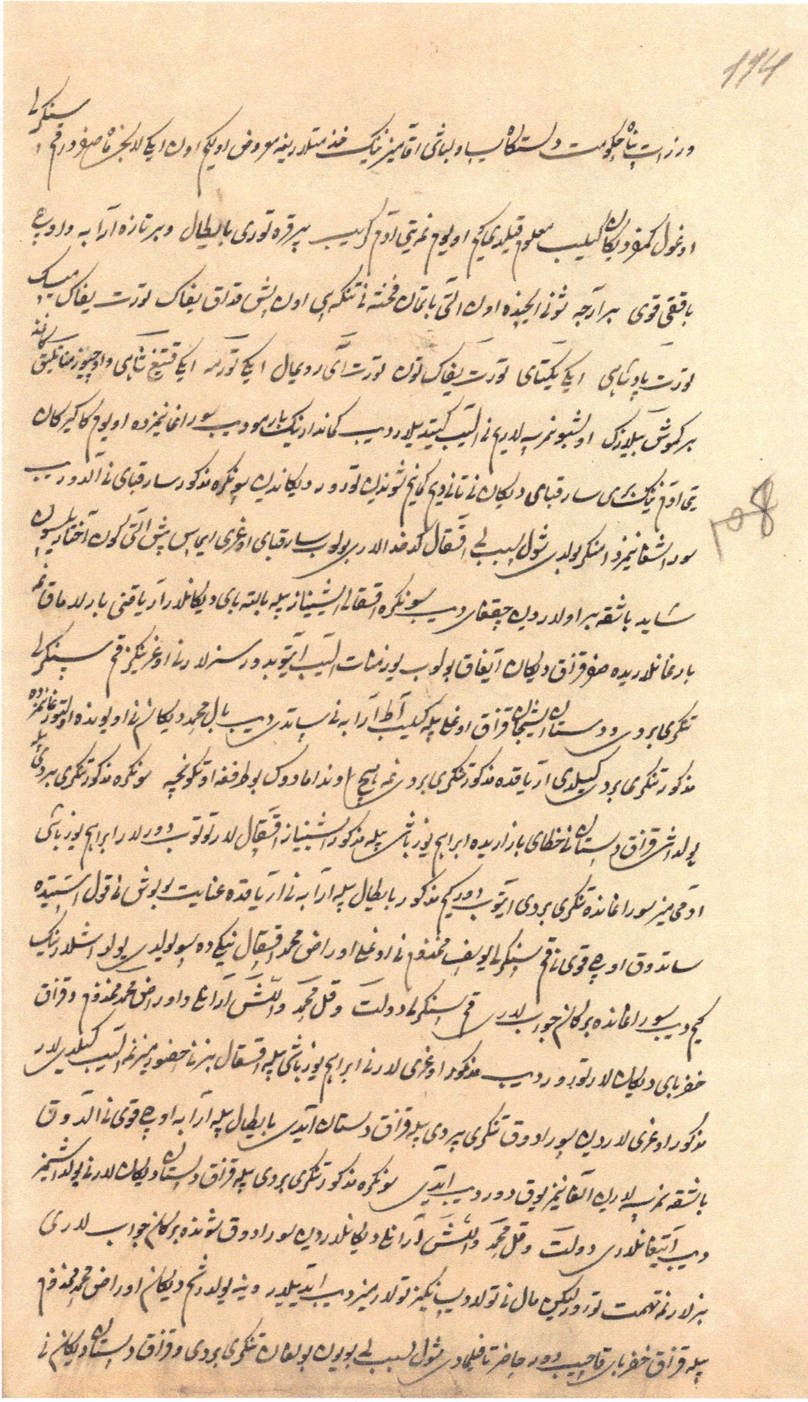

DOCUMENT 56A TsGARUz, f. I-125, op. 1, d. 498, l. 114

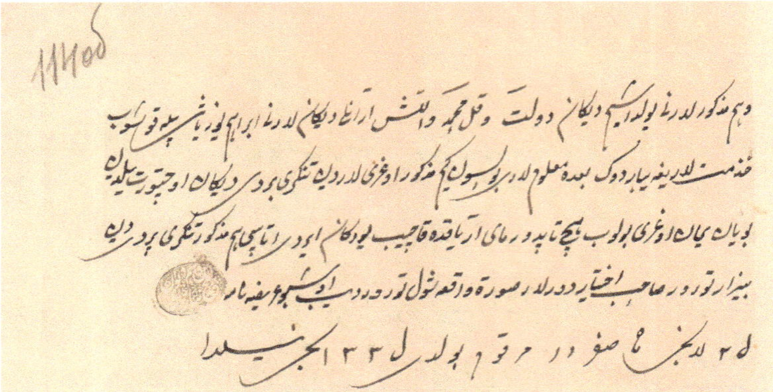

DOCUMENT 56B TsGARUz, f. I-125, op. 1, d. 498, l. 114 ob

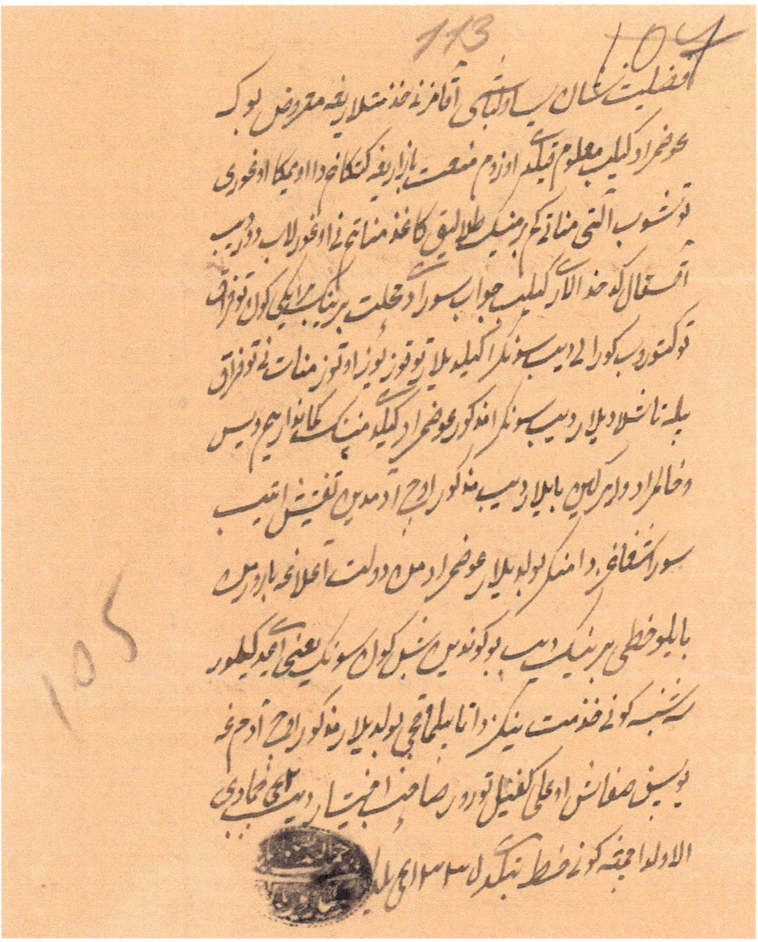

DOCUMENT 57A TsGARUz, f. I-125, op. 1, d. 498, l. 113

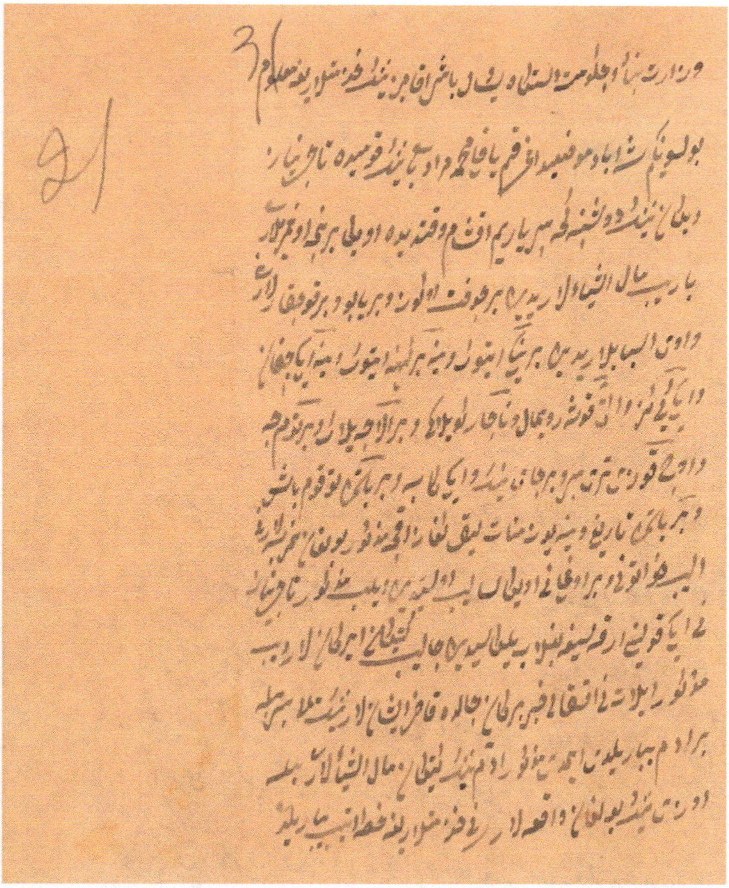

DOCUMENT 58A TsGARUz, f. I-125, op. 1, d. 498, l. 31

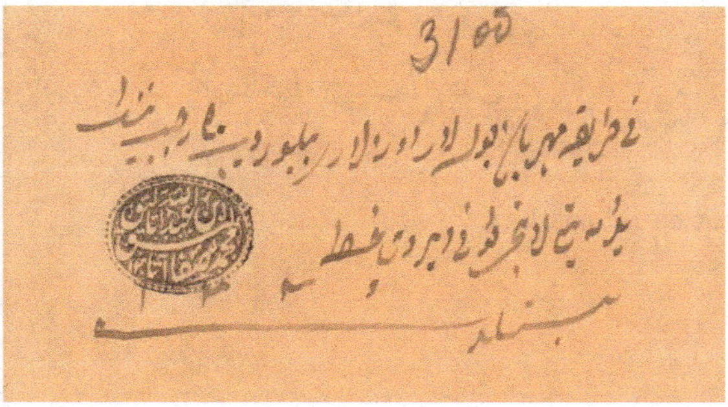

DOCUMENT 58B TsGARUz, f. I-125, op. 1, d. 498, l. 31 ob

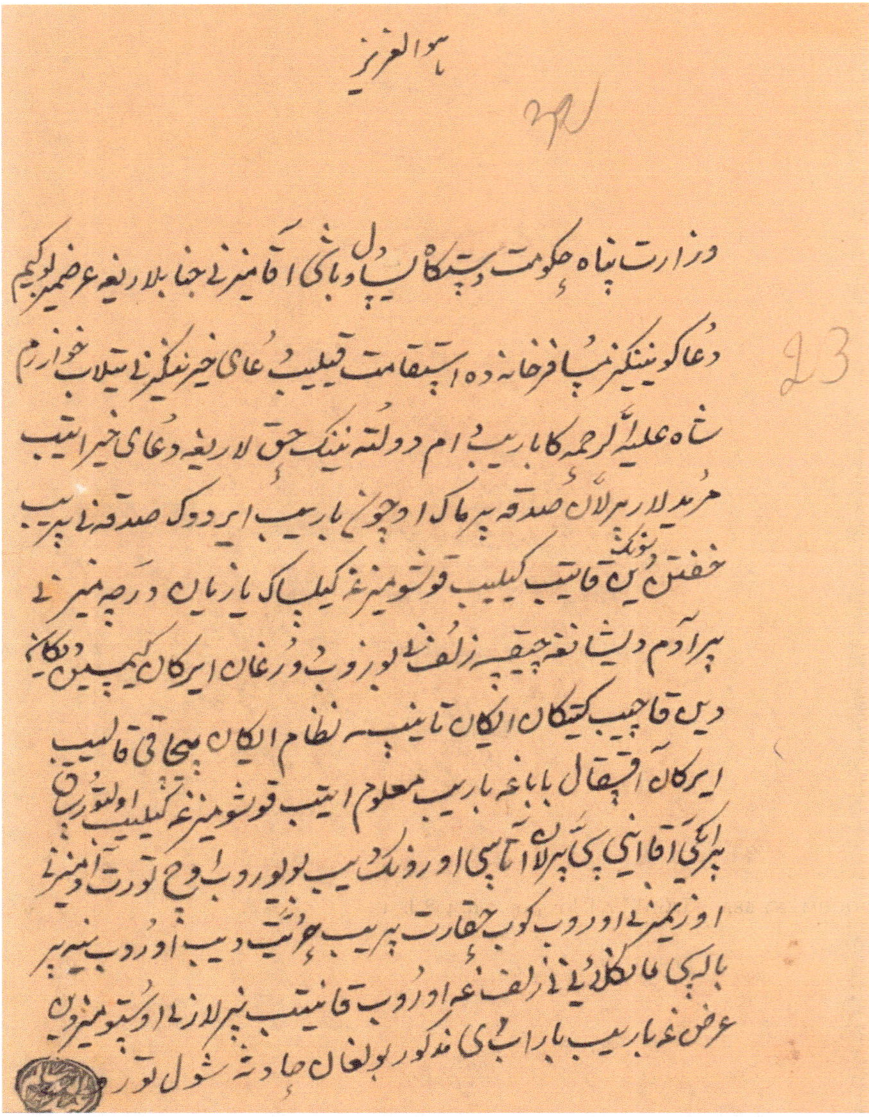
هو العزیز

وزارت پناه حکومت دستگاه دیوانبگی آقامیزنی جنابلاریغه عرضیم اولکیم
دعاگوینگیزنینگ پاخته‌خانه‌ده استقامت قیلیب دعای خیر تیلاب خوارزم
شاه علیه الرحمه کا باریب ام دولتخانه‌نینگ حق‌لاریغه دعای خیر ایتیب
مریدلاری بیرلان صدقه بیرماک اوچون باریب ایردوک صدقه‌نی بیریب
خفتن دین تونگ قایتیب کیلیب قوشونمیزغه کیلاک یازبان ورچه‌میزنی
بیر آدم دیش نعه چیقیب زلفینی اوروب اورغان ایرکان کیمپین دیکانه
دین قاچیب کیتکان ایکان تاپیب نظام ایکان بیچاق قالیب
ایرکان آقچال باباغه باریب معلوم ایتیب قوشونمیزغه کیلیب اولتور ریاق
بیر ایکی آقانی بی بیرلا آتاسی او روزنک دیب اوروب اوروب تورت آدمیزنی
اورمیزنی اوروب کوب حقارت بیریب حوث دیب اوروب بیزنی بیر
بالکی مانگلای زلفیغه اوروب قایتیب بیزلارنی اوشتومیزدین
عرض غه باریب بار ابدی مذکور بولغان حادثه شول تور

DOCUMENT 59A TsGARUz, f. I-125, op. 1, d. 498, l. 32

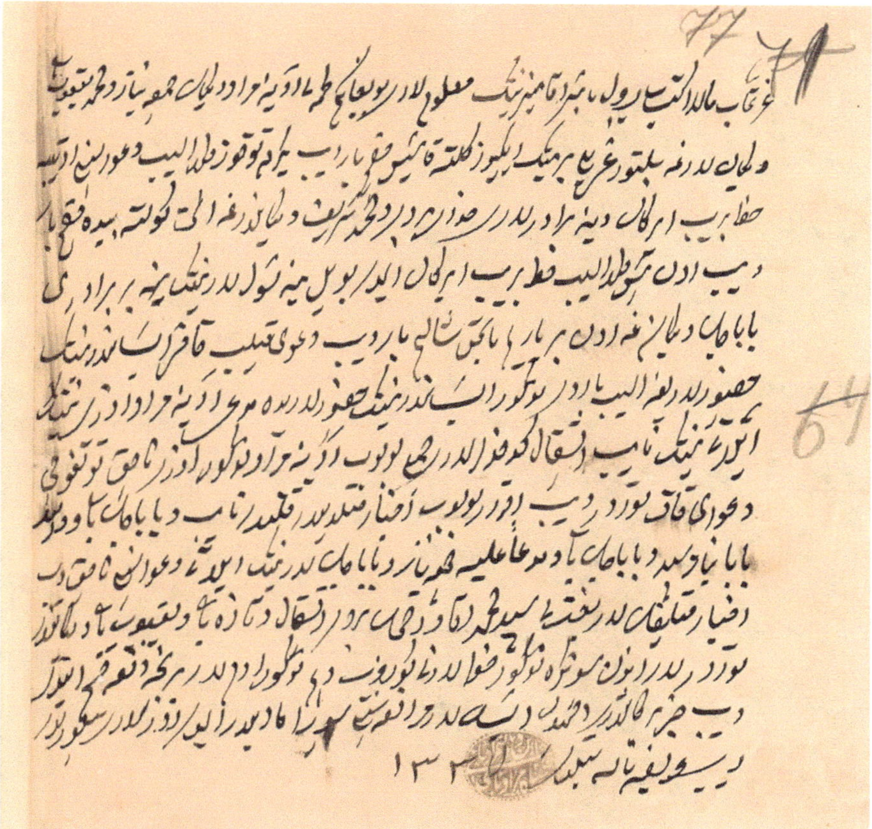

DOCUMENT 60A TsGARUz, f. I-125, op. 1, d. 498, l. 77

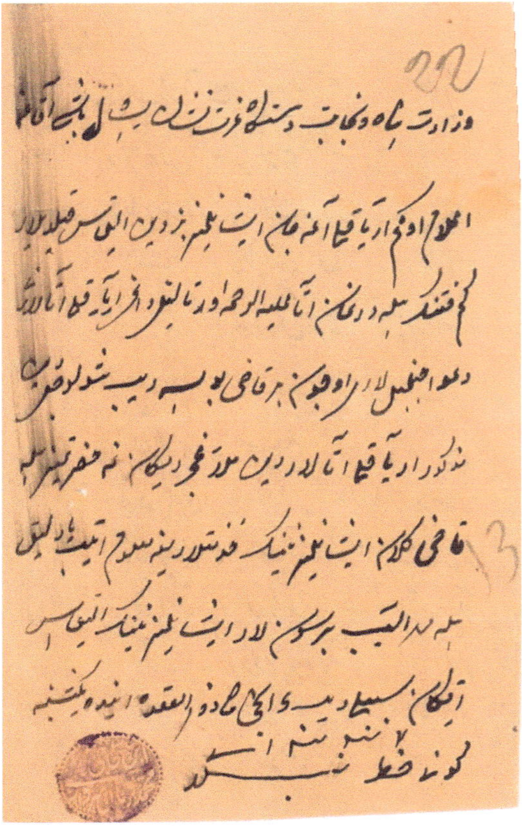

DOCUMENT 61A TsGARUz, f. I-125, op. 1, d. 498, l. 22

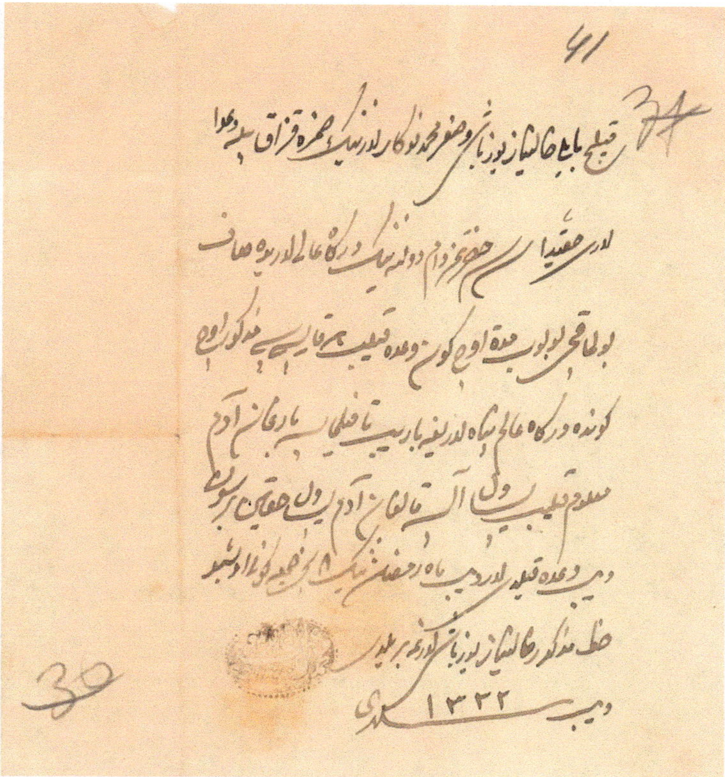

DOCUMENT 62A TsGARUz, f. I-125, op. 1, d. 498, l. 41

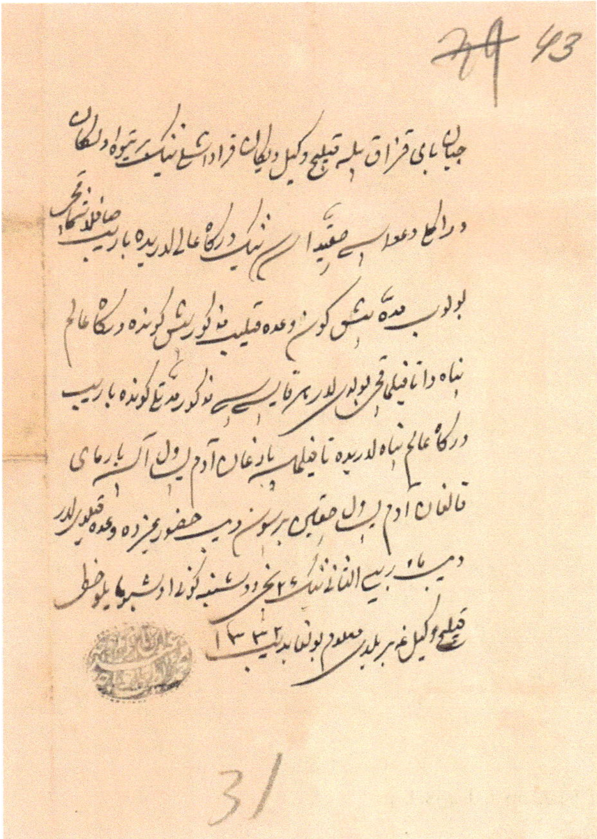

DOCUMENT 63A TsGARUz, f. I-125, op. 1, d. 498, l. 43

Section Four

DOCUMENT 64A TsGARUz, f. I-125, op. 2, d. 606, l. 1

DOCUMENT 64B TsGARUz, f. I-125, op. 2, d. 606, l. 1 ob

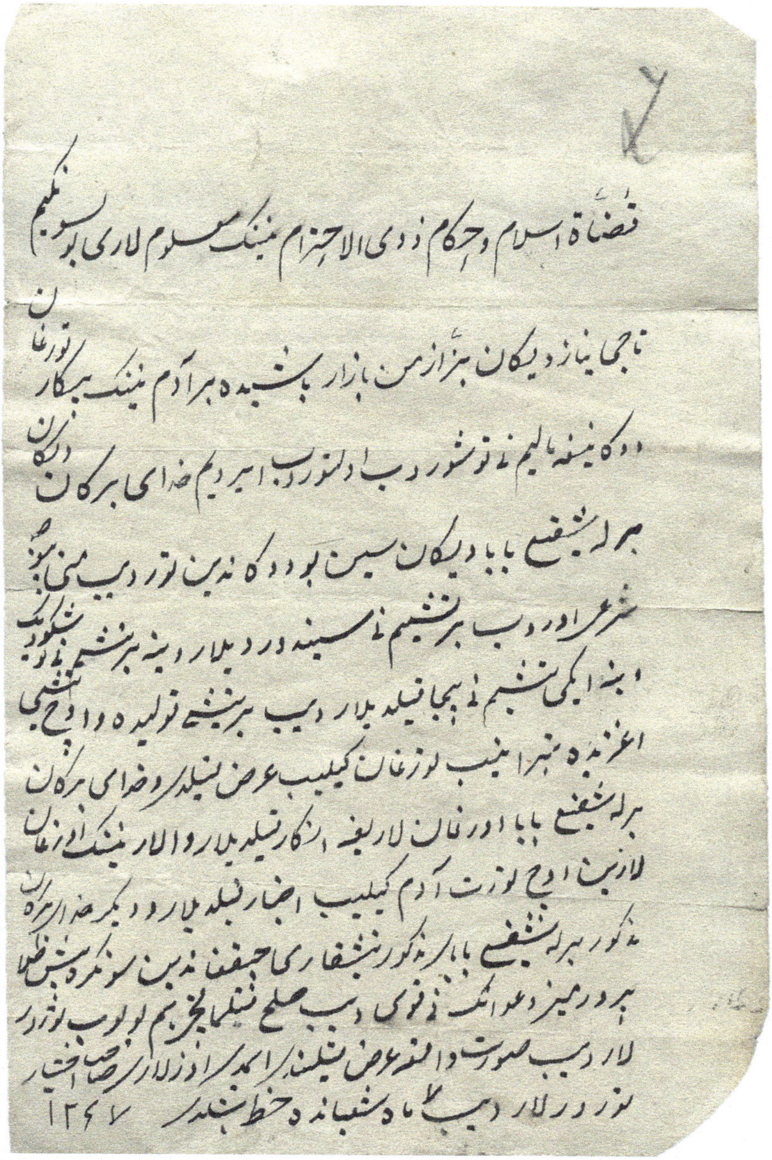

DOCUMENT 65A TsGARUz, f. I-125, op. 2, d. 606, l. 7

DOCUMENT 65B TsGARUz, f. I-125, op. 2, d. 606, l. 7 ob

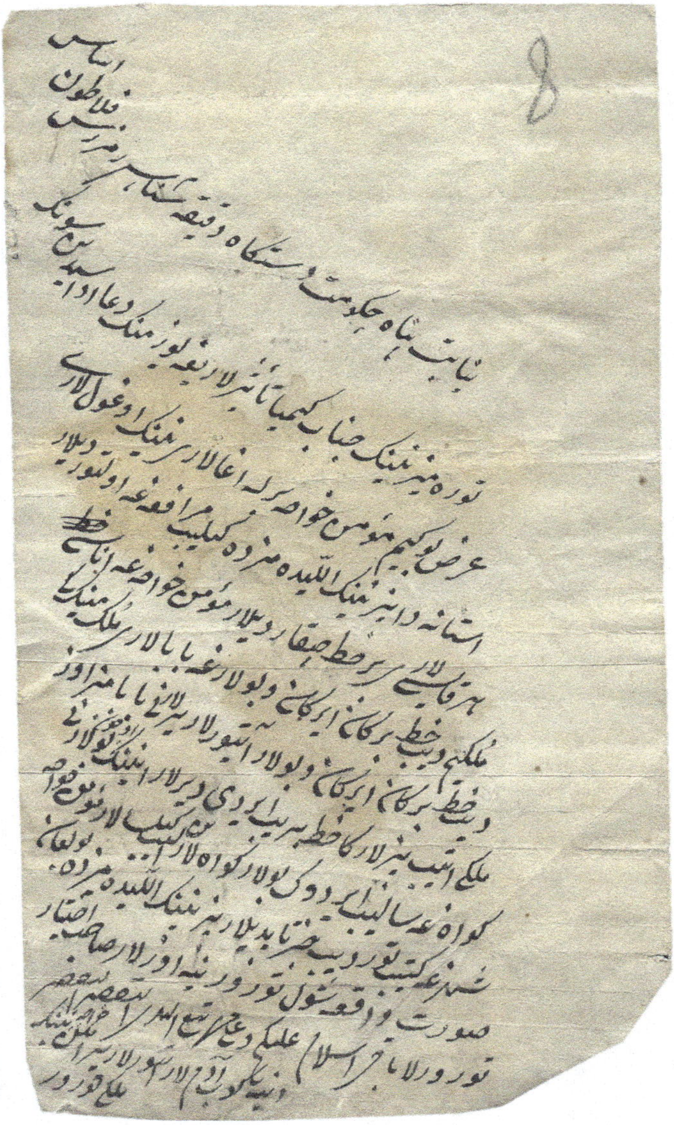

DOCUMENT 66A TsGARUz, f. I-125, op. 2, d. 606, l. 8

DOCUMENT 66B TsGARUz, f. I-125, op. 2, d. 606, l. 8 ob

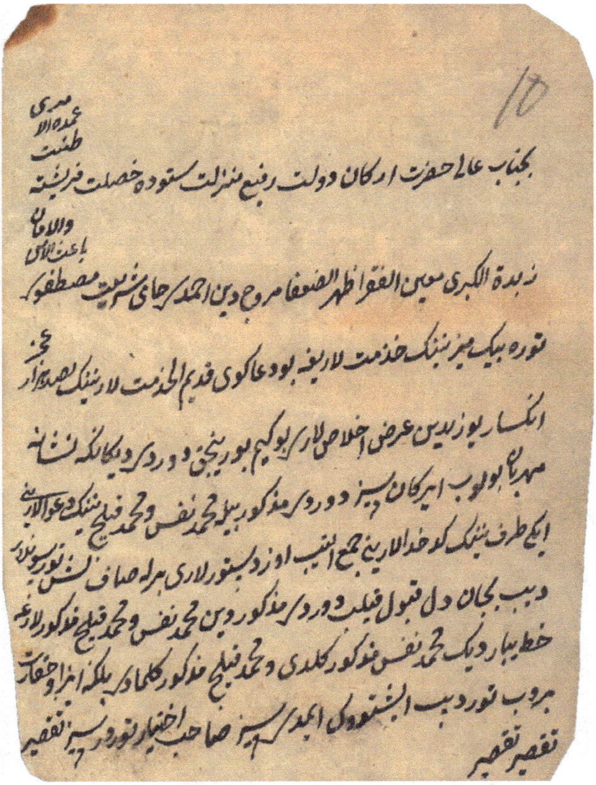

DOCUMENT 67A TsGARUz, f. I-125, op. 2, d. 606, l. 10

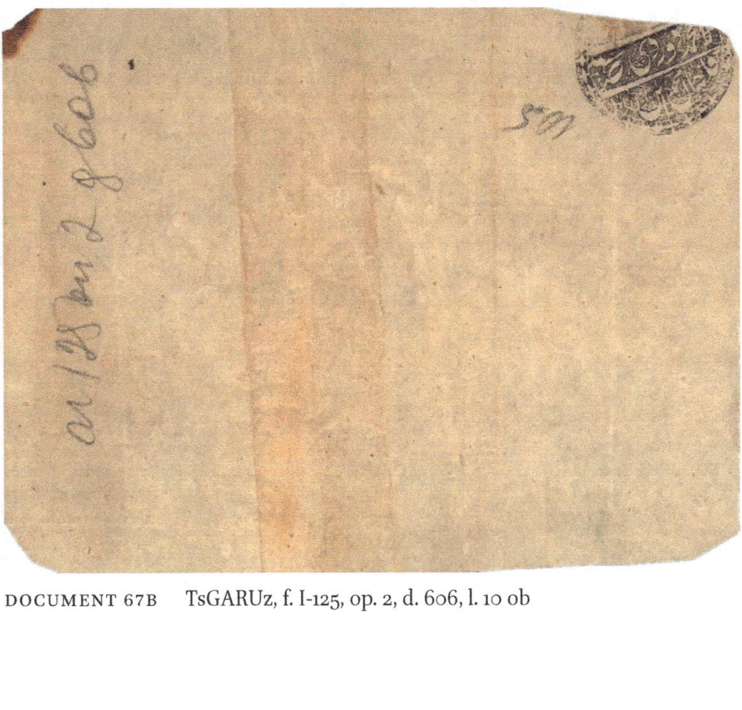

DOCUMENT 67B TsGARUz, f. I-125, op. 2, d. 606, l. 10 ob

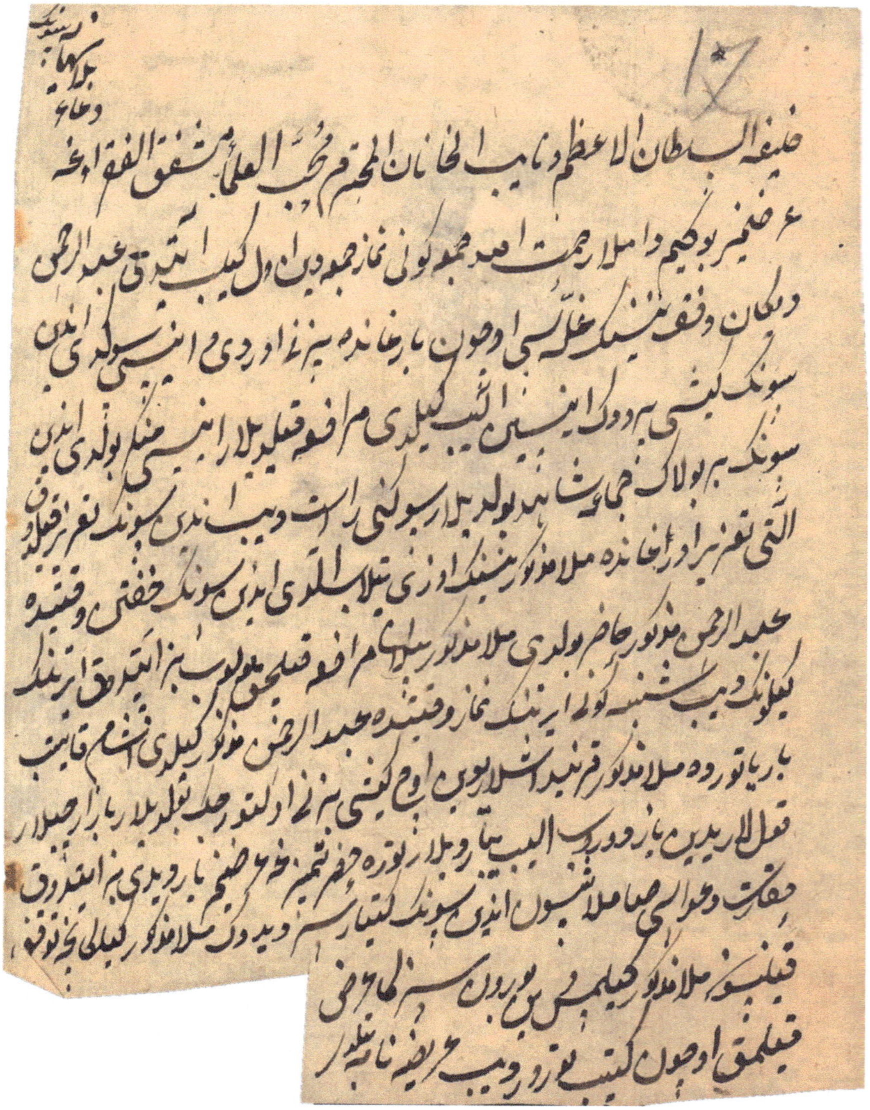

DOCUMENT 68A TsGARUz, f. I-125, op. 2, d. 606, l. 17

DOCUMENT 68B TsGARUz, f. I-125, op. 2, d. 606, l. 17

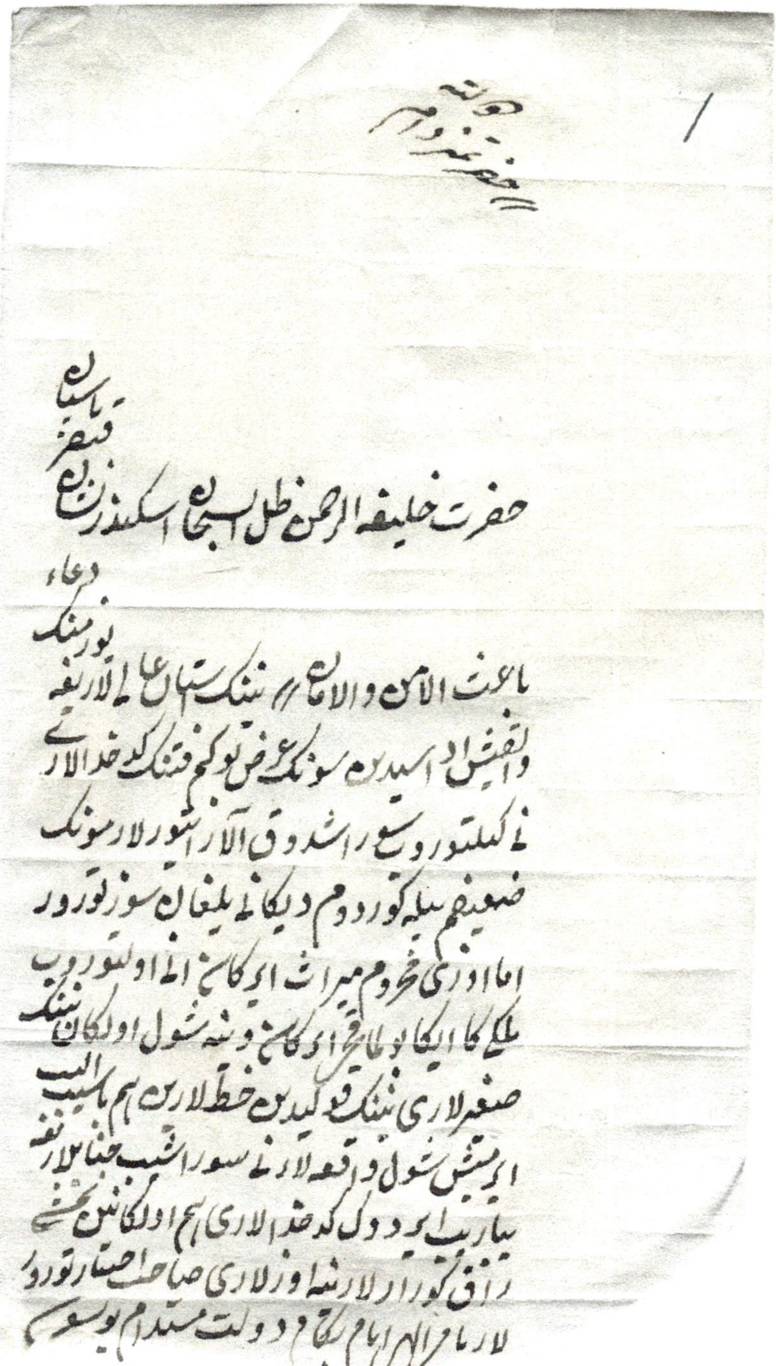

DOCUMENT 69A TsGARUz, f. I-125, op. 2, d. 37, l. 1

DOCUMENT 69B TsGARUz, f. I-125, op. 2, d. 37, l. 1 ob

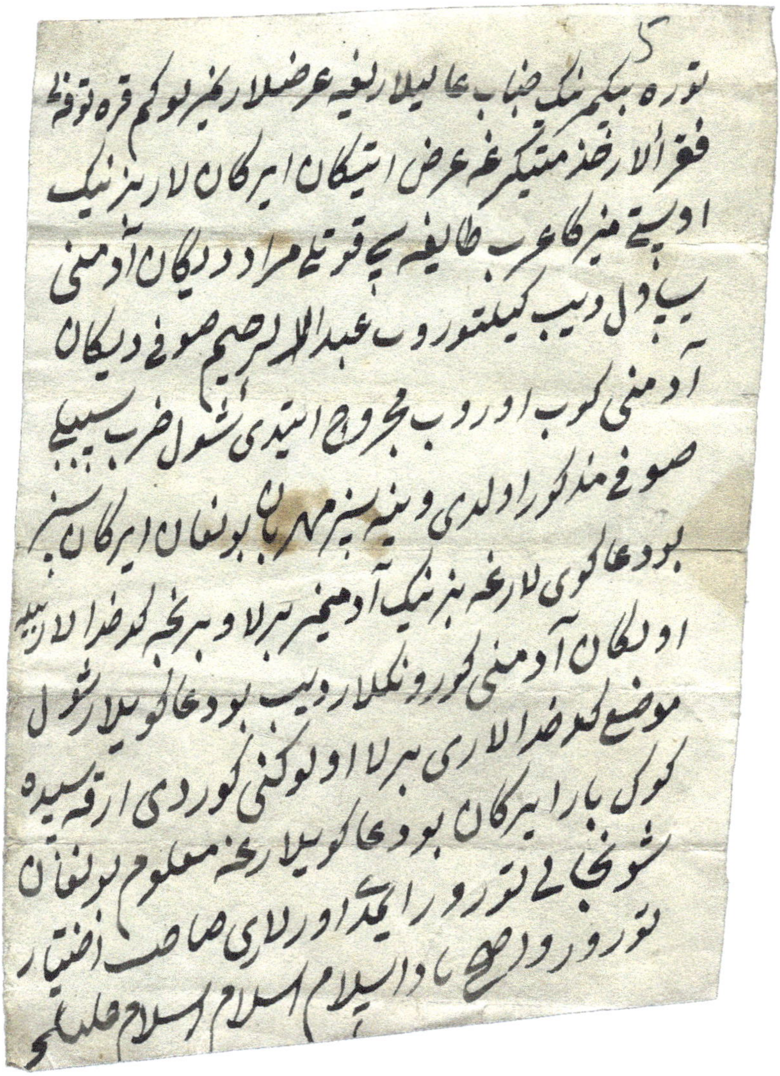

5

توره بیکیم نینک جناب عالیلاریغه عرضلار بیز بولکیم قره توقه‌لی
فقرالار خدمتینکیزغه عرض ایتیکان ایرکانلار بیزنینک
اوبسته میرزا عرب طایفه سیچ قبرتلی مراد دیکان آدمینی
یی‌دال دیب کیلتوروب عبد الرحیم صوفی دیکان
آدمینی کوروب اوروب مجروح ایتیدی شوال ضرب سیبیلی
صوفی مذکور اولدی و بینه بیز مهربان بولغان ایرکان سیز
بوداعاگویلارغه بیزنینک آدمیمیز بیرلا و بیرنچه کدخدالار بیله
اولکان آدمینی کوروننکلار دیب بوداعاگویلار شوال
موضع کدخدالاری بیرلا اولوکنی کوردی ارقه سیده
کوک بارا ایرکان بوداعاگویلاریغه معلوم بولغان
شونچانی توره ورایمگداورلاری صاحب اختیار
توره ورود صحیح ا دا السلام السلام السلام علیکم

DOCUMENT 70A TsGARUz, f. I-125, op. 2, d. 37, l. 5

DOCUMENT 70B TsGARUz, f. I-125, op. 2, d. 37, l. 5 ob

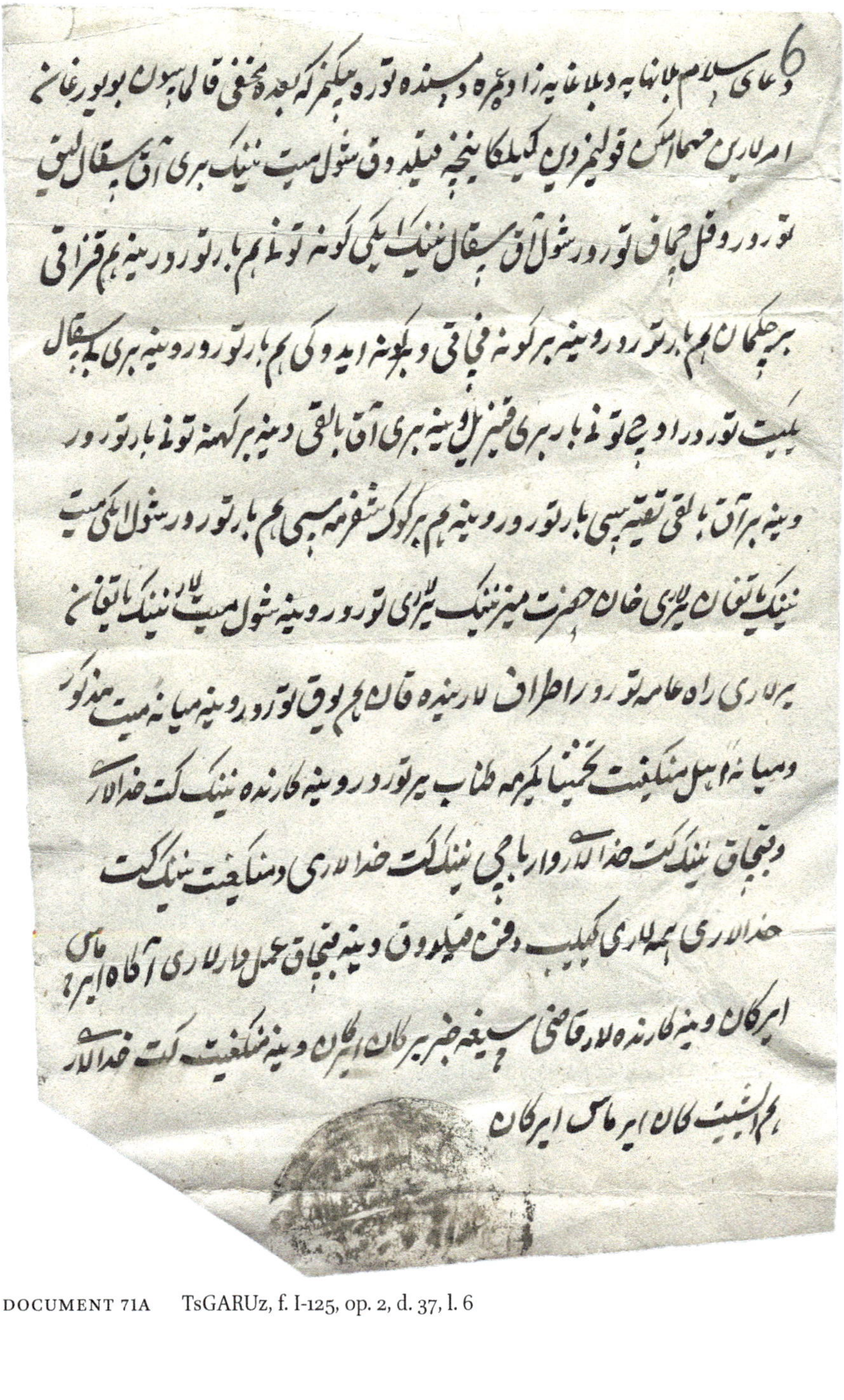
6
دعای سلام بالانها به دبلاغا یه زادعمره دسنده توره بیکم که بعده مخفی قالماسون بوبویرغان
امرلارین معمارلیک قولیم دین کیلکانینچه فیلیدوق شول میت نینک بری آق سقال لیق
توره وقفل جماف توره شول آق سقال نینک ایکی کونه توندیم بار توره وبنه هم قزاقی
بر چلکمان هم بار توره وبنه بر کونه فیاقی وبکونه ایدوکی هم بار توره وبنه بری کهنه سقال
بلیت توره در ادیچ تونذ بار بری قنبرلی وبنه بری آق بالقی وبنه بر کهنه تونذ بار توره
وبنه بر آق بالقی تعقیه سی بار توره وبنه هم بر کوک شقرمه سی هم بار توره شول ایکی میت
نینک بالیقلاری خان حضرت میرنینک یرلاری توره وبنه شول میت نینک بالیقلاری
برلاری راه عامه توره اطراف لارینده قان هیچ یوق توره وبنه میانه میت مذکور
ومیانه اهل منکیت تحمیناکم مه طناب بر توره وبنه کارنده نینک کت خدالاری
وقبچاق نینک کت خدالاری واریاچی نینک کت خدالاری ومنکیت نینک کت
خدالاری همه لاری کیلیب دفن قیلدوق وبنه قبچاق عمل دارلاری آگاه ایرماس
ایرکان وبنه کارنده لار قاضی سیغه خبر برکان ایکان وبنه منکیت کت خدالاری
هم ایشیتکان ایرماس ایرکان

DOCUMENT 71A TsGARUz, f. I-125, op. 2, d. 37, l. 6

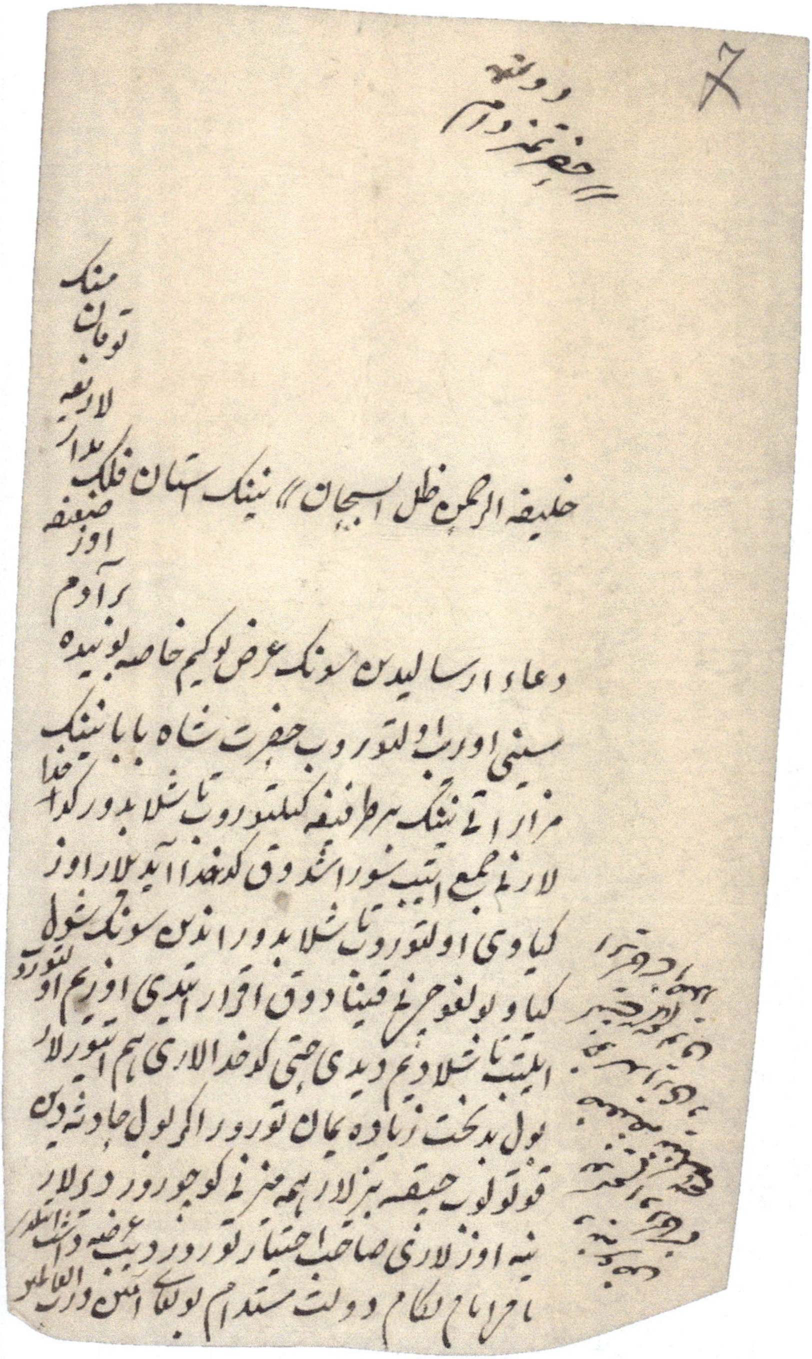
خلیفه الرحمن ظل السبحان // نینک آستان فلک
دعاء ارسالیدین سونک عرض لوکیم خاصه بونیده
سینی اوروب اولتوروب حضرت شاه بابا نینک
مزار اتا نینک بر طرفیغه کیلتوروب تاشلا بدورکه خدا
لارنی جمع ایتیب سورا ائتدوق که خدا آیدیلار اوز
کیاوی اولتوروب تاشلا بدور اندین سونک شول
کیاو بولغوجینی قیننادوق اقرار ایتدی اوزیم اولتوروب
الیتیب تاشلادیم دیدی حتی که خدالاری هم ایتورلار
بول بدبخت زیاده یمان توروردی اگر بول حادثه دین
قوتولوب حقیقه بیزلارنی هم مزنی لوجوروردیلار
نه اوزلاری صاحب اختیار توروردیب عرضه داشت ایتیلدی
باقی ایام بکام دولت مستدام بولغای آمین یا رب العالمین

DOCUMENT 72A TsGARUz, f. I-125, op. 2, d. 37, l. 7

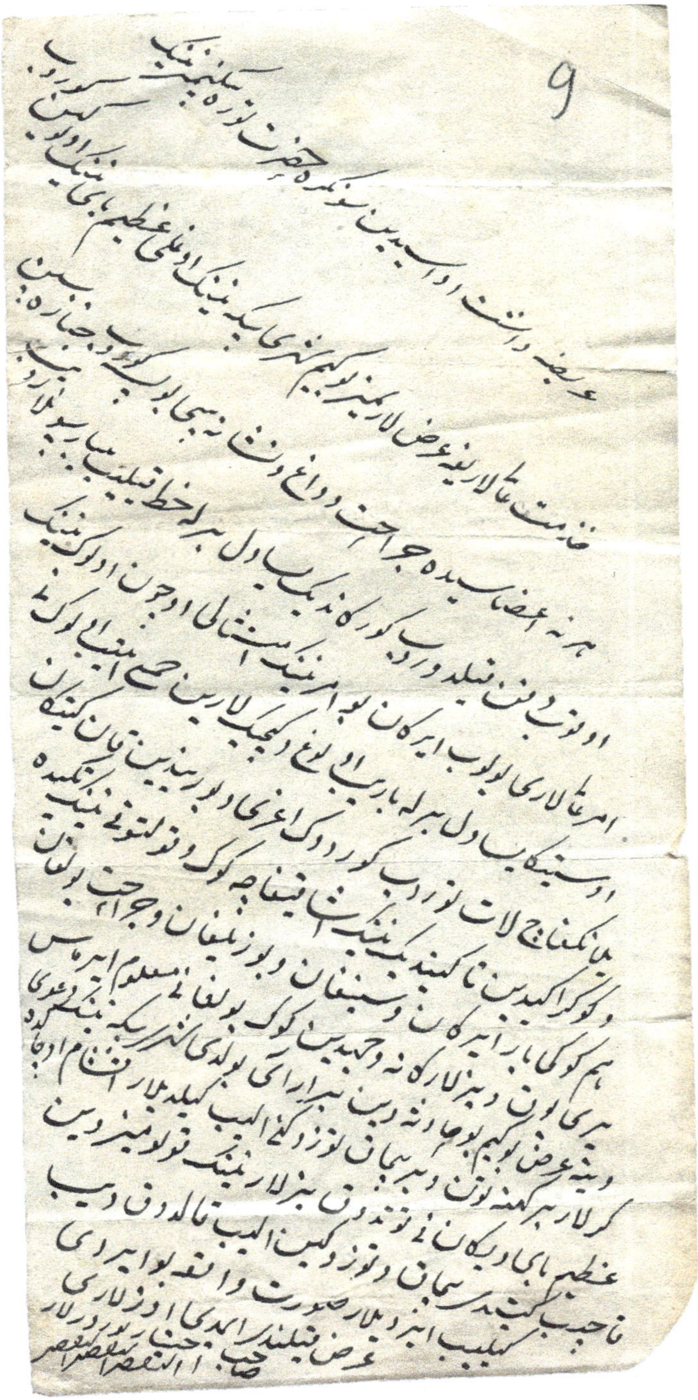

DOCUMENT 73A TsGARUz, f. I-125, op. 2, d. 37, l. 9

DOCUMENT 73B

Bibliography

Abbreviations

AIEARAN	Arkhiv Instituta etnologii i antropologii Rossiiskoi Akademii nauk, Moscow
GMIQ	Gosudarstvennyi muzei-zapovednik Ichan-Qal'a, Khiva
IVRRAN	Institut vostochnykh rukopisei Rossiiskoi Akademii nauk, St. Petersburg
IVANRUz	Institut vostokovedeniia imeni Abu Raikhana Beruni Akademii nauk Respubliki Uzbekistan, Tashkent
RGIA	Rossiiskii gosudarstvennyi istoricheskii arkhiv, St. Petersburg
RNB	Rossiiskaia natsional'naia biblioteka, St. Petersburg
TsGARUz	Tsentral'nyi gosudarstvennyi arkhiv Respubliki Uzbekistan, Tashkent

Primary Sources

'Abdullāh Bāltaev. *Khīva īsdalīklārī*. MS Tashkent, IVANRUz, inv. no. 11645.

'Abdullāh Bāltaev. *Khwārazm ta'rīkhīga matir'iallar, Khīva 1950*. MS Tashkent, IVANRUz, Tashkent, inv. no. 9320.

'Abdullāh Bāltaev. *Khīvada Tāsh ḥavlī bināsīning tāpāgrafiyasī, Khiva 1950*. MS Tashkent, IVANRUz, inv. no. 9321.

'Abdullāh Bāltaev. *Rivālūtsiyadīn avval qīshlāq khwājalīqīdā būlghān Khwārazm dīhqānlārīnī aḥvālī va kūrgan 'azāblārī*. MS Tashkent, IVANRUz, inv. no. 11978, fols. 13a–24a.

'Abdullāh Bāltaev. *Daftar (no. 22)*. MS Khiva, Private collection of Odilbek Abdullaev.

'Abdullāh Bāltaev. *Rivālūtsiyadīn avval qīshlāq khwājalīqīdā būlghān Khwārazm dīhqānlārīnī aḥvālī va kūrgan 'azāblārī*. MS Tashkent, IVANRUz, inv. no. 11978, fols. 13a–24a.

Bobojon Tarroh Azizov-Khodim. *Khorazm shoir va navozandalari. XIX asr okhiri–XX asr boshlarida Sayyid Muhammad Rahimkhoni soniy davrida iashagan shoirlar haqida esdaliklar*, ed. Rahim, Davlatior. (Tashkent: Ghafur Ghulom nomidagi Adabiiot va san'at nashriyoti, 1994).

Bobojon Tarroh Khodim. *Khorazm shoir va navozandalari*, ed. A. Otamurodova and O. Abdurahimov. (Tashkent: Tafakkur Qanoti, 2011).

Ḥasan-Murād Laffasī. *Gulshan-i sa'ādat*. MS Tashkent, IVANRUz, inv. no. 7797.

Ḥasan-Murād Laffasī. *Āzādnāma*. MS Tashkent, IVANRUz, inv. no. 12581.

[Ḥasan-Murād] Laffasī. *Tazkirai Shuaro*, ed. Polvonnazar Bobozhonov. (Urgench: Khorazm, 1992).

[Glushanovskii]. *Diplomaticheskomu Chinovniku pri Turkestanskom General-Gubernatore*, 20.02.1909. TsGARUz, I-2, op. 1, d. 253, ll. 7–7 ob.

Kun, Aleksandr L. [Alexander Kuhn]. *Ocherk istorii zaseleniia Khivinskogo khanstva s drevnykh vremen, sostav ego sovremennogo naseleniia, administratsiia i goroda khanstva, 1873*. MS St. Petersburg, IVRRAN, Arkhiv Vostokovedov, f. 33, d. 8.

Lykoshin, N.S. "O gadanii u sredneaziatskikh tuzemtsev." In *Spravochnaia knizhka Samarkandskoi oblasti 1907 g. Vypusk IX*, ed. M. Virskii (Samarkand: Tipo-Litografiia G.I. Demurova, 1907), pp. 163–197.

Lykoshin, N.S. *Zapiska Nachal'nika Amu-Dar'inskogo Otdela Polkovnika Lykoshina o sovremennom sostoianii Khivinskogo Khanstva, 1912 god*. TsGARUz, f. I-2, op. 1, d. 314, ll. 12–58.

Lykoshin, N.S. *Sovremennoe raspredelenie vlasti v Khanstve Khivinskom, 1912 god*. TsGARUz, f. I-2, op. 1, d. 314, ll. 63–69 ob.

Mirza Abdurakhman. *Zapiski Mirza Abdurakhmana*. MS St. Petersburg, IVRRAN, Arkhiv Vostokovedov, f. 33, op. 1, d. 134.

Mirza Abdurakhman. *Dnevnik Mirzy Abdurakhmana, vedennyi vo vremia khivinskogo pokhoda*. MS St. Petersburg, IVRRAN, Arkhiv Vostokovedov, f. 33, op. 1, d. 221.

Muḥammad Riżā Āgahī. *Riyāż al-dawla*. MS St Petersburg, IVRRAN, inv. no. D-123.

Muḥammad Riżā Āgahī. *Gulshan-i dawlat*. MS Tashkent, IVANRUz, inv. no. 7572.

Muḥammad Yūsuf Bayānī. *Shajara-yi Khwārazmshāhī*. MS Tashkent, IVANRUz, inv. no. 9596.

Pahlavān Niyāz Ḥājjī. [*Khāṭiralar*]. MS Khiva, Private Collection of Anvar Otaboev.

Safarov, Bābājān. *Khwārazm ta'rīkhī (1864–1934)*. MS Tashkent, IVANRUz, inv. no. 10231.

Safarov, Bābājān. *Khwārazmda būlūb ūtgān qūlchilīq aḥvāllarīnīng vāqi'alārī*. MS Tashkent, IVRRAN, inv. no. 11254/II.

Samoilovich, A.N. *Opisanie rukopisei knig, khraniashchikhsia v Khivinskikh pridvornykh knigokhranilishchakh i knigo-pechatniakh*. MS St. Petersburg, RNB, f. 671, op. 1, d. 145.

Sayyid Ḥāmid Tūra Kāmyāb. *Tawarīkh al-khawānīn*. MS Tashkent, IVANRUz, inv. no. 7717.

Şeyh Süleyman Efendi Buhârî, *Lugat-i Çağatay ve Türkî-i 'Osmânî* (Istanbul: Mihrân Matbaası, 1298/1880-1)

Shīr Muḥammad Mīrāb Mūnis, and Muḥammad Riżā Āgahī, *Firdaws al-iqbāl. History of Khorez*, ed. Yuri Bregel. (Leiden: Brill, 1988).

Shir Muhammad Mirab Munis, and Muhammad Riza Mirab Agahi, *Firdaws al-iqbāl: History of Khorezm*. Translated from Chaghatay and Annotated by Yuri Bregel. (Leiden and Boston: Brill, 1999).

Vaqf-nāma-yi khanaqāh-i Shaykh Sulaymān Ḥaddādī. MS Khiva, GMIQ, inv. no KP-1326.

Secondary Literature

Abashin, Sergei N. "Kalym i makhr v Srednei Azii: o "granitsakh" v sotsial'nykh otnosheniyakh." In *Chelovek i pravo. Kniga o letnei schkole po iuridicheskoi antropologii*, eds.

N.I. Novikova, and V.A. Tishkova (Moscow: Institut etnologii i antropologii RAN, 1999), pp. 155–161.

Abdullaev, K. *Naqshlarga bitilgan umr: Abdulla Boltaevning hayoti va ijodiy faoliyati* (Tashkent: G'afur G'ulom nomidagi Adabiyot va san'at nashriyoti, 1995).

Abdurasulov, A. *Khiva (Tarikhiy-etnografik ocherklar)*. Tashkent: Ŭzbekiston, 1996.

Abdurasulov, Ul'fat. "Tsentralizovannoe pravosudie i obshchestvennoe posrednichestvo v Khorezme: analiz dokumentov kantseliarii iasaulbashi." In *History of Central Asia in Modern Medieval Studies (in memoriam Prof. Roziia Mukminova)*, ed. D. Alimova (Tashkent: Yangi nashr, 2013), pp. 223–241.

Abdurasulov, Ul'fat. "Tainy khivinskogo dvora: politcheskaia bor'ba v Khive v period Rossiiskogo protektorata." *Vostok svyshe* 3 (2015), pp. 38–56.

Abdurasulov, Ul'fat, and Sartori, Paolo. "Neopredelennost' kak politika: razmyshliaia o prirode rossiiskogo protektorata v Srednei Azii." *Ab Imperio* (2016/3), pp. 118–164.

Abdurasulov, Ulfatbek. "The Aral Region and Geopolitical Agenda of the Early Qongrats." *Eurasian Studies* 14 (2016), pp. 3–36.

Abdurasulov, Ul'fatbek. "Konflikt kak resurs: anatomiia 'turkmenskikh besporiadkov' v Khorezme, 1914–1916." *Ab Imperio* 3 (2018), pp. 141–186.

Alam, Muzaffar, and Subrahmanyam, Sanjay. *Writing the Mughal World: Studies on Culture and Politics* (New York: Columbia University Press, 2012).

Andrianov, B.V. "Etnicheskaia territoriia karakalpakov v severnom Khorezme (XVIII–XIX vv.)." In *Materialy i issledovania po etnografii karkakalpakov. Trudy Khorezmskoi arkheologo-etnograficheskoi ekspeditsii*, III, ed. T.A. Zhdanko (Moscow: Izdatel'stvo Akademii nauk SSSR, 1958), pp. 7–132.

Anon. "Turkmeniia i Khiva." *Vsemirnyi puteshestvennik* 8 (1870), pp. 120–132.

Anon. "Razboinich'e gnezdo." *Illiustrirovannaia nedelia* 50 (St. Petersburg, 1873).

Ayoub, Sami. "'The Sulṭan Says': State Authority in Late Ḥanafī Tradition." *Islamic Law and Society* 23.3 (2016), pp. 239–278.

Babadzhanov, B.M., *Kokandskoe khanstvo: vlast', politika, religiia* (Tokyo-Tashkent: Yangi Nashr, 2010).

Balandier, G. "Kolonial'naia situatsiia: teoreticheskii podkhod (1951)." *Ab Imperio* (2013/2), pp. 29–64.

Baldauf, Ingeborg. "Kraevedenie and Uzbek National Consciousness." *Papers on Inner Asia*, no. 20 (Bloomington, 1992).

Baldwin, James. "Petitioning the Sultan in Ottoman Egypt." *Bulletin of the School of Oriental and African Studies* 75.3 (2012), pp. 499–524.

Basiner, Theodor-Fridrich. "Estestvenno-nauchnoe puteshestvie po Kirgizskoi stepi v Khivu." In *Istoriia Kazakhstana v zapadnykh istochnikakh XII–XX vv. Tom 5: Nemetskie issledovateli v Kazakhstane. Chast' 1*, ed. I.V. Erofeeva (Almaty: Sanat, 2006), pp. 283–360.

Batyrshin, Iskander. "Zapiska mladshego perevodchika Orenburgskoi pogranichnoi komissii Iskandera Batyrshina o Khivinskom khanstve i khane Prisyrdar'inskikh kazakhov Ermukhammede (Ilekee) Kasymove." In *Istoriia Kazakhstana v russkikh istochnikakh XVI–XX vekov. Tom VI: Putevye dnevniki i sluzhebnye poezdki po iuzhnym stepiam XVIII–XIX veka*, eds. I.V. Erofeeva, and B.T. Dzhanaev (Almaty: Daik-Press, 2007), pp. 300–318.

Becker, Seymour. *Russia's Protectorates in Central Asia: Bukhara and Khiva, 1865–1924*. Cambridge (Massachusetts: Harvard University Press, 1968).

Ben-Bassat, Yuval. *Petitioning the Sultan: Protests and Justice in Late Ottoman Palestine* (London: I.B. Tauris, 2013).

Binbaş, Evrim. "Condominial Sovereignty and Condominial Messianism in the Timurid Empire: Historiographical and Numismatic Evidence." *Journal of the Economic and Social History of the Orient* 61.1–2 (2018), pp. 172–202.

Bourdieu, Pierre. "The Force of Law: Toward a Sociology of the Juridical Field." *Hastings Law Journal* 38 (1986–7), pp. 805–53.

Bregel', Iu. E. *Khorezmskie turkmeny v XIX veke* (Moscow: Izdatel'stvo vostochnoi literatury, 1961).

Bregel', Iu. E., *Dokumenty arkhiva khivinskikh khanov po istorii i etnografii karakalpakov* (Moscow: Nauka, 1967).

Bregel, Yu. "The Sarts in the Khanate of Khiva." *Journal of Asian History* 12.2 (1978), pp. 120–151.

Bregel, Yu. *An Historical Atlas of Central Asia* (Leiden-Boston: Brill, 2003).

Danilevskii, G.I. "Opisanie Khivinskogo khanstva, sostavlennoe v 1842 g. podpolkovnikom G.I. Danilevskim." In *Zapiski Imperatorskogo geograficheskogo obshchestva*. Kn. 5 (St. Petersburg: Tipografiia Imperatorskoi Akademii nauk, 1851), pp. 62–139.

Davidovich, E.A. "Materialy po metrologii srednevekovoi Srednei Azii. Appended to Khintz, V. [Hinz, Walter]." *Musul'manskie mery i vesa s perevodom v metricheskuiu sistemy* (Moscow: Izdatel'stvo vostochnoi literatury, 1970), pp. 75–131.

Demidov, S.M. *Turkmenskie ovliady* (Ashkhabad: Ylym: 1976).

Dickson, Martin. "Uzbek Dynastic Theory in the Sixteenth Century." In *Trudy XXV Mezhdunarodnogo Kongressa Vostokovedov* (Moscow: Izdatel'stvo vostochnoi literatury, 1960), pp. 208–217.

Dresch, Paul, and Skoda, Hanna (eds.). *Legalism: Anthropology and History* (Oxford: Oxford University Press, 2012).

Dzhabbarov, I.M. "Iz istorii tekhniki i kul'tury zemledeliia v iuzhnom Khorezme." In *Istoriia material'noi kul'tury Srednei Azii*, 2 (Tashkent: Fan, 1961), pp. 272–295.

Erkinov, Aftandil. "How Muḥammad Raḥīm Khān II of Khiva (1864–1910) Cultivated his Court Library as a Means of Resistance Against the Russian Empire." *Journal of Islamic Manuscripts* 2 (2011), pp. 36–49.

Fragner, Bert. "Die 'Khanate': Eine zentralasiatische Kulturlandschaft vom 15. bis zum 19. Jahrhundert." *Zeitschrift für Kulturgeschichte* 9.1 (2008), pp. 33–75.

Gens, Georg von, and Helmersen, Gregor von. "Izvestiia o Khive, Bukhare, Kokande i severo-zapadnoi chasti Kitaiskogo gosudarstva." In *Istoriia Kazakhstana v zapadnykh istochnikakh XII–XX vv. Tom 5: Nemetskie issledovateli v Kazakhstane. Chast' 1*, ed. I.V. Erofeeva (Almaty: Sanat, 2006), pp. 12–84.

Girshfel'd, V.A., and Galkin, A.S. *Voenno-statisticheskoe opisanie Khivinskogo oazisa, pt. I–II, Sostavleno General'nogo Shtaba Kapitanom Girshfel'dom, pererabotano Nachal'nikom Amu-Dar'inskogo otdela General-Maiorom Galkinym* (Tashkent: Tipografiia Tashkentskogo voennogo okruga, 1902–1903).

Guliamov, Ya.G. *Istoriia orosheniia Khorezma s drevneishikh vremen do nashikh dnei* (Tashkent: Izdatel'stvo Akademii nauk Uzbekskoi SSR, 1957).

Iu.O.Ia. "Khivinskaia ten'ga v sviazi s nedavnim proshlym ten'govogo voprosa." *Turkestanskii sbornik*, Vol. 464 (Tashkent: 1908), pp. 122–128.

Ivanin, M.I. *Khiva i reka Amu-Daria* (St. Petersburg: Obshchestvennaia pol'za, 1873).

Ivanov, P.P. *Arkhiv khivinskikh khanov XIX v.: Issledovanie i opisanie dokumentov s istoricheskim vvedeniem* (Leningrad: Izdanie Gosudarstvennoi Publichnoi Biblioteki, 1940).

Kamalov, S. "Narodno-osvoboditel'naia bor'ba karakalpakov protiv khivinskikh khanov v XIX v." In *Trudy Khorezmskoi arkheologo-etnograficheskoi ekspeditsii, III. Materialy i issledovaniia po etnografii karakalpakov*, ed. T.A. Zhdanko (Moscow: Izdatel'stvo Akademii nauk SSSR, 1958), pp. 133–206.

Kaul'bars, A.V. "Nizov'ia Amu-Dar'i, opisannye po sobstvennym issledovaniiam v 1873 g." In *Zapiski Imperatorskogo Russkogo Geograficheskogo Obshchestva po Obshchei Geografii*, Vol. IX (St. Petersburg: Tipografiia Imperatorskoi Akademii nauk, 1881).

Kilevein, E.B. "Otryvok iz puteshestviia v Khivu i nekotorye podrobnosti o khanstve vo vremia pravleniia Seid-Mokhammed Khana, 1856–1860." In *Zapiski Imperatorskogo Russkogo Geograficheskogo Obshchestva*, Vypusk. 1 (St. Petersburg: Tipografiia Imperatorskoi Akademii nauk, 1861).

Kosbergenov, R. "Polozhenie karakalpalskogo naseleniia v Khivinskom khanstve v kontse XIX–nachale XX v." In *Trudy Khorezmskoi arkheologo-etnograficheskoi ekspeditsii. III. Materialy i issledovaniia po etnografii karakalpakov*, ed. T.A. Zhdanko (Moscow: Izdatel'stvo Akademii nauk SSSR, 1958), pp. 207–268.

Kostenko, L. "Khivinskoe khanstvo v sel'skokhoziaistvennom otnoshenii (s chertezhami)." *Voennyi sbornik*, 4 (St Petersburg: Tipografiia Deprtamenta udelov, 1874), pp. 373–388.

Kügelgen, Anke von. *Die Legitimierung der mittelasiatischen Mangitendynastie in den Werken ihrer Historiker, 18.–19. Jahrhundert.* (Würzburg: Ergon Verlag, 2002).

Layish, Aharon. Sharīʿa *and Custom in Libyan Tribal Society: An Annotated Translation of Decisions from the* Sharīʿa *Courts of Adjābiya and Kufra* (Leiden: Brill, 2005).

Levi, Scott. *Central Asian in the Global Age: The Rise and Fall of Khoqand, 1709–1876*. (Pittsburgh: Pittsburgh University Press, 2017).

Lobacheva, N.P. "K istorii slozheniia instituta svadebnoi obriadnosti (na primere kompleksov svadebnykh obychaev i obriadov narodov Srednei Azii i Kazakhstana)." In *Sem'ia i semeinye obriady u narodov Srednei Azii i Kazakhstana*, ed. G.P. Snesarev (Moscow: Nauka, 1978), pp. 144–175.

Lobasevych, Esaul. "Pokazaniia russkikh plennykh, byvshikh v Khive, dannoe 16-go iunia Orenburgskomu general-gubernatoru." In *Turkestanskii Sbornik*, Vol. 42 (St. Petersburg, 1871), pp. 86–89.

Logofet, D.N. *Bukharskoe khanstvo pod russkim protektoratom*, Vol. 1–2 (St. Petersburg V. Berezovskii, 1911).

Lomakin, A. *Obychnoe pravo u Turkmen* (*Adat*) (Ashkhabad: Parovaia Russkaia tipografiia K.M. Fedorova, 1897).

Mann, Kristin, and Richard, Roberts. "Slave Voices in African Colonial Courts: Sources and Methods." In *African Voices of Slavery and the Slave Trade, vol. 2: Essays on Sources and Methods*, eds. A. Bellagamba, S.E. Green, and M.A. Klein (Cambridge: Cambridge University Press, 2016), pp. 132–164.

Marglin, Jessica. "Written and Orality in Islamic Law: Documentary Evidence and non-Muslims in Moroccan *Sharīʿa* Courts." *Comparative Studies in Society and History* 59.4 (2017), pp. 884–911.

Meier, L. "Kirgizskaia step' Orenburgskogo vedomostva." In *Materialy dlia geografii i statistiki Rossii, sobrannye ofitserami General'nogo shtaba* (St. Petersburg: Tipografiia E. Veimara i F. Persona, 1865).

Melvin-Koushki, Matthew and James Pickett, "Mobilizing Magic: Occultism in Central Asia and the Continuity of High Persianate Culture under Russian Rule." *Studia Islamica* 111 (2016), pp. 231–284.

Mikhailov, N. "Rasskaz torgovtsa Ambrosimova o poezdke ego v Khivu." In *Materialy dlia statistiki Turkestanskogo kraia*, vol. 2 (St. Petersburg: Tipografiia K.V. Trubnikova, 1873), pp. 353–377.

Morrison, Alexander. "Sufism, Pan-Islamism and Information Panic: Nil Sergeevich Lykoshin and the Aftermath of the Andijan Uprising." *Past and Present* 214.1 (2012) pp. 255–314.

Morrison, Alexander. "Twin Imperial Disasters. The Invasions of Khiva and Afghanistan in the Russian and British Official Mind." *Modern Asian Studies* 48.1 (2014), pp. 253–300.

Morrison, Alexander. *The Russian Conquest of Central Asia 1814–1907. A Study in Imperial Expansion*. (Cambridge: Cambridge University Press, forthcoming).

Murav'ev, N.N. *Puteshestvie v Turkmeniiu i Khivu v 1819 i 1820 godakh gvardeiskogo general'nogo shtaba kapitana Nikolaia Murav'eva, poslannogo v sii strany dlia peregovorov, pt. 1–2* (Moscow: Tipografiia Avgusta Semena, 1822).

Müller, Christian. "*Maẓālim* Jurisdictions at the Umayyad Court of Córdoba (Eighth–Eleventh Centuries CE)." In *Court Cultures in the Muslim World: Seventh to Nineteenth Centuries*, eds. A. Fuess, and J.-P. Hartung (London and New York: Routledge, 2011), pp. 93–104.

Navruzov, S. "Puteshestvenniki i uchenye ob administrativnom ustroistve Khivinskogo khanstva XIX–nachala XX veka." *Obshchestvennye nauki v Uzbekistane* (1991/10), pp. 44–48.

Nielsen, Jürgen. *Secular Justice in an Islamic State: Maẓālim under the Baḥrī Mamlūks, 662/1264–789/1387* (Leiden: Brill, 1985).

Niiazmetov, M. *Poisk konsensusa. Rossiisko-khivinskie geopoliticheskie otnosheniia v XVI–nachale XX v.* (St. Petersburg: Peterburgskoe vostokovedenie, 2010).

Northrop, Douglas. *Veiled Empire: Gender and Power in Stalinist Central Asia* (Ithaca and London: Cornell University Press, 2004).

Paul, Jürgen. "Herrschaft und Gesellschaft. Einige Bemerkungen." In *Der islamische Orient. Grundzüge seiner Geschichte*, eds. Albrecht Noth, and Jürgen Paul (Würzburg: Ergon Verlag, 1998).

Péri, Benedek. "Notes on the Literary-Linguistic Term 'Čaġatay': Evaluating the Evidence Supplied by Native Sources." In *Altaica Budapestinensia MMII: Proceedings of the 45th Permanent International Altaisitic Conference (PIAC) Budapest, Hungary, June 23–28, 2002*, ed. A. Sárközi and A. Rákos (Budapest: Research Group for Altaic Studies, Hungarian Academy of Sciences – Department of Inner Asian Studies, Eötvös Loránd University, 2003), pp. 248–55.

Pianciola, Niccolò. "The Benefits of Marginality: The Great Famine around the Aral Sea, 1930–34." *Nationalities Papers* 48.2 (2019), pp. 1–17.

Pogorel'skii, I.V. *Ocherki ekonomicheskoi i politicheskoi istorii Khivinskogo khanstva kontsa XIX i nachala XX vv. (1873–1917 gg.).* (Leningrad: Izdatel'stvo Leningradskogo universiteta, 1968).

Pogorel'skii, I.V. *Istoriia Khivinskoi revoliutsii i Khorezmskoi narodnoi sovetskoi respubliki, 1917–1924 gg.* (Leningrad: Izdatel'stvo Leningradskogo universiteta, 1984).

Qo'shjonov, Otamurod, and Ne'matjon Polvonov. *Khorazmdagi ijtimoiy-siiosiy jarayonlar va harakatlar* (Tashkent: Abu Matbuot Konslat, 2007).

Rapoport, Yossef. "Royal Justice and Religious Law: *Siyāsah* and *Sharīʿah* under the Mamluks." *Mamluk Studies Review* 16 (2012), pp. 71–102.

Reichmuth, Philipp. "Lost in the Revolution': Bukharan *waqf* and Testimony Documents from the Early Soviet Period." *Die Welt des Islams* 50.3–4 (2010), pp. 362–396.

Sadykov, A.S. *Ekonomicheskie posledstviia ustanovleniia protektorata tsarskoi Rossii nad Khivinskim khanstvom*. PhD dissertation. (Moscow, 1954).

Sartori, Paolo. "Colonial Legislation Meets *Sharīʿa*: Muslims' Land Rights in Russia Turkestan." *Central Asian Survey* 29.1 (2010), pp. 43–60.

Sartori, Paolo. "Birth of a Custom: Nomads, Shari'a Courts and Established Practices in the Tashkent Province, ca. 1868–1919." *Islamic Law and Society* 18.3–4 (2011), pp. 293–326.

Sartori, Paolo. "The Evolution of Third-Party Mediation in *Sharīʿa* Courts in 19th- and Early 20th-Century Central Asia." *Journal of Social and Economic History of the Orient* 54.3 (2011), pp. 311–352.

Sartori, Paolo. "Murder in Manghishlaq: Notes on an Instance of Application of Qazaq Cutomary Law in Khiva (1895)." *Der Islam* 88.2 (2012). 217–257.

Sartori, Paolo. "Seeing Like a Khanate: On Archives, Cultures of Documentation, and 19th Century Khorezm." *Journal of Persianate Studies* 9.1 (2016), pp. 228–257.

Sartori, Paolo. "On Khorezmian Connectivity: Two or Three Things I Know about It" *Journal of Persianate Studies* 9.1 (2016), pp. 133–157.

Sartori, Paolo. *Visions of Justice:* Sharīʿa *and Cultural Change in Russian Central Asia.* (Leiden: Brill, 2016).

Sarybaev, K. *Agrarnii vopros v Karakalpakii (konets XIX–nachalo XX vekov)* (Nukus: Karakalpakstan, 1972).

Sazonova, M.V. "K etnografii uzbekov Iuzhnogo Khorezma (Polevye issledovania Iuzhnouzbekskogo arkheologo-etnograficheskogo otriada Khorezmskoi arkheologo-etnograficheskoi ekspeditsii v 1946–1948 gg." In *Trudy Khorezmskoi arkheologo-etnograficheskoi ekspeditsii,* I, eds. S.P. Tolstov and T.A. Zhdanko (Moscow: Izdatel'stvo Akademii nauk SSSR, 1952), pp. 247–318.

Schluessel, Eric. *An Introduction to Chaghatay: A Graded Textbook for Reading Central Asian Sources* (Mountain View, CA: Michingan Publishing, 2018).

Shioya, Akifumi. "Irrigation Policy of the Khanate of Khiva regarding the Lawzan Canal, 1830–1873." *Area Studies Tsukuba* 32 (2011), pp. 115–136.

Shioya, Akifumi. "Povorot and the Khanate of Khiva: A New Canal and the Birth of Ethnic Conflict in Khorazm Oasis, 1870s–1890s." *Central Asian Survey* 33.2 (2014), pp. 232–245.

Snesarev, G.P. "Materialy o pervobitno-obshchinnykh perezhitkakh v obichaiakh i obriadakh uzbekov Khorezma." In *Polevye issledovaniia Khorezmskoi ekspeditsii v 1957 godu.* Vyp. 4, eds. S.P. Tolstov and M.A. Itina (Moscow: Izdatel'stvo Akademii nauk SSSR, 1960), pp. 134–145.

Spies, O. 1991. Mahr. *The Encyclopaedia of Islam, second edition,* eds. P. Bearman et al. Leiden: Brill. Vol. VI, pp. 78–80.

Tashev, N. "Zanimal li Mukhammad Yusuf Baiani dolzhnost' Divan-begi?" *O'zbekiston tarixi* (2009/2), pp. 14–25.

Terent'ev, M.A. *Istoriia zavoevaniia Srednei Azii s kartami i planami,* 4 vols. (St. Petersburg: Tipo-litografiia V.V. Komarova, 1906).

Tukhtametov, T.G. *Rossiia i Khiva v kontse XIX–nachale XX v. Pobeda Khorezmskoi narodnoi revoliutsii* (Moscow: Nauka, 1969).

Tukhtametov, T.G. *Amudar'inskii otdel. Sotsial'no-ekonomicheskoe znachenie dlia Khorezmskogo oazisa* (Nukus: Karakalpakstan, 1977).

[Turpaev]. "Dnevnik perevodchika armianina Turpaeva, poslannogo v 1834 g. iz Novo-Aleksandrovskogo ukrepleniia v Khivu (perevod s armianskogo)." In Galkin, M.N. *Etnograficheskie materialy po Srednei Azii i Orenburgskomu kraiu M.N. Galkina* (St. Petersburg: Izdanie Ia.A. Isakova, 1868), pp. 264–285.

Urunbaev, A. et al. (eds.). *Katalog khivinskikh kaziiskikh dokumentov XIX–nachala XX vv.* (Tashkent – Kyoto: Izdatel'stvo Mezhdunarodnogo instituta po izucheniiu iazykov i mira Kiotskogo universiteta po izucheniiu zarubezhnykh stran, 2001).

Vamberi, Arminii. *Ocherki Srednei Azii (dopolnenie k "Puteshestviiu po Srednei Azii")* (Moscow: Tipografiia A.I. Mamontova, 1868).

Vamberi, Arminii. *Puteshchestvie po Srednei Azii.* (Moscow: Vostochnaia literatura, 2003).

Veselovskii, N.I. *Ocherki istoriko-geograficheskikh svedenii o Khivinskom khanstve s drevneishikh vremen do nastoiashchego* (St. Petersburg: Tipografiia brat. Panteleevykh, 1877).

Wilde, Andreas. *What is Beyond the River? Power, Authority and Social Order in Transoxiana (18th–19th Centuries)*, 3 vols. (Vienna: Austrian Academy of Sciences Press, 2016).

Winter, Stefan. "Le rôle du *kafīl* (garant) dans la governance locale selon les contrats d'affermage fiscal à Tripoli au XVIIe–XVIIIe siècle." *Islamic Law and Society* 23.4 (2016), pp. 392–409.

Wood, William. "The Sariq Turkmens of Merv and the Khanate of Khiva in the early Nineteenth Century" (Unpublished Ph.D. Dissertation. Indiana University, 1999).

Yastrebova, Olga, and Arezou Azad. "Reflections on an Orientalist: Alexander Kuhn (1840–88), the Man and His Legacy." *Iranian Studies* 48.5 (2015), pp. 675–694.

Yŭldoshev, Mukhamedzhan. *Khiva khonligida feodal yer egaligi va davlat tuzilishi.* (Tashkent: Ŭzbekiston SSR Davlat nashriyoti, 1959).

Zadykhina, K.L. "Uzbeki del'ty Amu-Dar'i." In *Trudy Khorezmskoi arkheologo-etnograficheskoi ekspeditsii, I. Arkheologicheskie i etnograficheskie raboty Khorezmskoi ekspeditsii. 1945–1948*, eds. S.P. Tolstov, and T.A. Zhdanko (Moscow: Izdatel'stvo Akademii nauk SSSR, 1952), pp. 319–426.

Zalesov, N.G. "Posol'stvo v Khivu i Bukharu Polkovnika Ignat'eva v 1858 godu." *Russkii vestnik* 2 (1871), pp. 421–449.

Zhdanko, T.A. "Karakalpaki Khorezmskogo oazisa (Materialy polevykh issledovanii Karakalpakskogo etnograficheskogo otriada Khorezmskoi ekspeditsii AN SSSR, 1945–1948 gg." In *Trudy Khorezmskoi arkheologo-etnograficheskoi ekspeditsii, I. Arkheologicheskie i etnograficheskie raboty Khorezmskoi ekspeditsii. 1945–1948*, eds. S.P. Tolstov and T.A. Zhdanko (Moscow: Izdatel'stvo Akademii nauk SSSR, 1952), pp. 461–566.

Zhdanko, T.A. *Ocherki istoricheskoi geografii* (Moscow – Leningrad: Izdatel'stvo Akademii nauk SSSR, 1957).

Zheliabuzhskii, E. *Ocherki i zavoevanie Khivy* (*s 9-kartinami*) (Moscow: Tipografiia A.I. Mamontova i K°, 1875).

Zhukovskii, S.V. *Snosheniia Rossii s Bukharoi and Khivoi za poslednee trekhsotletie* (Petrograd: Tipo-litografiia N.I. Evstigneeva, 1915).

Index of Places

Afghanistan 17
Akhal-Tekin oasis 16n45
Āmān Yūzbāshī, mosque community *190*
Ambar, see Manaq
Amu-Darya river 1, 3, 3n5, 6, 13, 13n31, 14, 20, 25, 45, 68, 69, 94, 111n71, 116, *147*, *164*, *165*, 165n207, 165n208, 170n219, 181n241, 197, *198*, *199*, 199n286, 207, 207n305, 208, *208*, 225n336
Amu-Darya Department (*Amudar'inskii otdel*) 3, 9, 14, 18, 28, 28n103, 45, 72, 115n78, 145, 165n205, 194, 195n277, *198*, 208, *208*, *209*
  right (Russian) bank of Amu Darya 3, 3n5, 20, 68, 69, *164*, *165*, 165n208, 181n241, *198*, *199*, 207, 207n305, 208, 225n336
Āq Maydān, locality *166*
Āq Qamīsh, locality *165*, 165n208, 207n305
Aral Province 170n219, 188n263
Aral Sea 6, 13, 13n31, 25, 62
Āryāq, see Russian bank of Amu Darya
Astana, town 216, *216*, 216n323
Ātāliq, locality *164*
ʿĀvaż Muḥammad Āqsaqāl, mosque community *162*

Bābā Jān Yūzbāshī, mosque community *172*
Baghat, town *206*, 206n301
Balkhan mountain 207n305
Bedrikent, locality 176
Bekabad (Begovat), town *164*, 164n202
Besh-Ariq (Bīsh-Ārīq), town and province 64, *98*, 98n47, 153, 154, *155*, 157, 159, 161, 178, *179*, 188n263, 205, 206n302
Bukhara, the Emirate 2, 10, 11, 33, 40, 41, 165n208, 183
Būmīrī, locality *105*
Būrlāq, locality *82*
Buvāy, locality *179*
Būyqazāq, locality 178, *179*

Caspian Sea 78
Central Asia XI, XII, XVII, XVIII, XX, XXn1, 1, 1n2, 2, 4, 6, 8, 8n19, 9, 10, 11, 14, 28n103, 33n126, 40, 47n179, 51n188, 67n214, 72n224, 74, 74n232, 83, 87n20, 100n52, 111, 125, 138, 164n201, 164n203, 190, 190n266
Chalang, locality *185*
Charjuy, city 18, 194n275
Charkas Lake 102, *102*
Chaʿsh [?] Mīrāb, mosque community *185*
Chātkūfrūk, locality *114*, *174*
Chavandur, locality 2, 3, *163*, *165*, *166*, *192*
Chimkent, city 31

Darghan Ata (Darghan), locality 207, 208, 208n310
Dūrghāvīk, locality *179*
Dūrman, mosque community *142*

Egypt XII

Gandumian (Gandūmqān), locality *102*, 102n54, 145
Ghāybū, locality *194*
Ghaziabad (Gazavat), canal 86, 86n17, 87n19, 176
Ghaziabad (Gazavat), town 48n180, 86n17, 176
Gurlen, city and province 39n156, *51*, 52, *52*, 52n190, 59, 82n5, 111, 111n71, *112*, 125, *127*, 140n143, 172, *172*, 197, 198n285

Ḥāfiq, locality *93*
Ḥasan Aqā Bābā, mosque community *162*
Hazarasp, city and province XXI, 2, 3, 70n219, 70n220, 93n30, 96, *97*, 98n47, 108n65, 130, *131*, *132*, 132n121, *136*, *137*, 153, 165n207, *166*, 166n210, 192, 193n273, 198n285, 226n339
Ḥażrat-i Pahlavān, mosque community *179*
Hilali (Yilanli) 48n180, 122n90, 141, *142*, 142n153, 145, *146*

Iran 17, 33, 51n188
Istanbul XXn1, 164n201

Jingān, locality *168*

Kaluga, town 24n88
Karabaili, Amu Darya's emissary 199n286
Karakalpak ASSR 13n31
Kat (New Kat), town 143, *143*, 143n156, *185*
Kazakh SSR (Kazakh ASSR) 13, 13n31
Kazakhstan 1
Khanqah, city and province 20, 62, 63, 109n67, 136, 137n136, 148, *149*, 149n170, 167, *168*, *169*, 169n213, 169n215, 174, *174*, 174n229, 178, *180*, 181n241, 190, *190*, *191*
Khāṣṣa, canal *226*, 226n338
Khidir-ili, canal 140n143
Khidir-ili Qal'a, fortress *140*, 140n143
Khitay (Khtay), town 68, 197, *198*, 198n285
Khiva, city and province XI, XII, XIII, XIV, XVI, XVIII, XIX, XXn1, XXI, 3, 5, 6, 8n18, 12, 14, 16, 17, 17n51, 17n54, 18, 19, 20, 24n88, 25, 26, 29, 30, 31n123, 33n126, 34n131, 35, 37n150, 38n154, 40, 41, 42, 44, 45, 46n176, 47n179, 47n180, 52, 53, 54, 55, 56n198, 57, 58, 59, 60, 61, 62, 64, 67, 68, 68n217, 70, 71, 72, 73, 74, 77, 78, 82n4, 84, 87n19, 90, *90*, 93n30, 94, 96, 98, 100, 102, 102n54, 104, *105*, 109n69, 111, 111n71, *112*, 114, *118*, 123, *124*, 128n115, 130, 131, 133, 138, 140, 140n142, 141, 142n153, 143, 143n156, 145, 146, 148, *148*, 150, 153, 154, 154n182, 157, 159, 165n205, 165n208, 167, *169*, 170, 172, 174, 176, 178, 181, 183, 184, 185, 187, *187*, 188, 188n263, 194n275, 199n286, 200, 201, 203, 206n301, 208, 210, 210n313, 212, 213, *214*, 215, 216, *216*, 216n323, 218, 219, *220*, 221, 222, 222n330, 222n331, 224, 226, 227
Khiva, the Khanate XI, XII, XV, XVI, XVII, XVIII, XXI, 1, 1n2, 2, 3, 3n2, 4, 4n8, 6, 8, 8n19, 9, 10, 12, 13, 14, 14n37, 14n40, 15, 16, 16n45, 17, 17n51, 18, 18n55, 18n56, 18n59, 20, 21, 21n67, 22, 22n76, 23, 24, 24n82, 24n85, 24n88, 25, 26, 27, 28, 28n103, 29, 31, 32, 33n126, 35, 36, 37n149, 38, 39, 39n156, 40n159, 41, 41n164, 41n166, 42, 44, 45, 46, 47n179, 47n180, 50, 50n184, 57, 62, 63, 64, 69, 70, 72, 73n227, 74n232, 75, 76, 77, 83, 86n18, 92n29, 93n30, 94n35, 95n36, 96, 97n42, 108n65, 111, 114n77, 124n97, 130, 134n128, 136, 137n135, 143n157, 145, 149n167, 154, 154n180, 161, 165n205, 172, 176, 178, 184, 194n275, 194n276, 197, *198*, 207, 207n305, 208
Khiva, post station 194n275
Khoja-eli, city and province XI, XXI, 6, 39n156, 40n159, 70, 170, *170*, 170n219, *171*
Khoqand, the Khanate 2, 10
Khorezm (*Khwārazm*) XI, XII, XIV, XV, XVI, XVII, XVIII, XX, XXn1, 1, 2, 3, 5, 6, 7, 8n15, 9, 10, 11, 12, 13, 17, 18, 19, 20, 20n66, 21, 22, 23, 31n115, 33, 37, 39, 40, 41n165, 47n179, 56n199, 63, 67, 69, 72, 83, 83n10, 83n11, 87n20, 94, 116, 117, 117n84, 122n90, 125n107, 129n116, 129n116, 138, 138n139, 140n144, 164n202, 165n204, 165n207, 183, 188n263, 194n276, 195n279, 207n305, 208, 208n309, 210, 210n313, 212n315, 213, 213n318, 215
Khorezmian Provincial Archive 4
Khorezm People's Soviet Republic 13, 19
Khwāja Fārsā, mosque community *172*
Khwājalīq, locality *157*
Kök-Tepe, locality 16n45
Krivoy Rog, town 19
Kunya-Urgench, city and province 70n220

Lavzan, canal 116

Mamluks XII
Manaq (Ambar-Manaq), town 61, *82*, 82n4 82n5, *84*, *117*, *118*, *174*, *175*, 183, *183*, 183n245, 198n285
Manghit, city and province XXI, 39, 39n156, 68, 129n116, 197, 198n285, 199n286, *200*
Manghit-Arna (Atalyk-Arna), canal 199n286
Manghit-Qal'a, fortress 199n286
Māylī Chungul (Māylī Jengel), locality *82*, 82n5, *90*
Muḥammad Amīn Khān, madrasa 87n18
Muḥammad Murād Bāy, mosque community *201*
Mullā Yūsuf Āqsaqāl, mosque community *128*

Nawkhast *169*, 169n215, *177*
Nayman, locality 109, *109*, 109n69, *140*, 140n142
New Urgench, post station 194n275

Ottoman Empire XII

Palvan-Yab, canal 165n207
Petro-Aleksandrovsk, town 3, 14, 17, 17n51, 17n54, 19, 30, 37n150, *165*, 165n205, 165n208, 194, 194n275, *195*, 195n277, 208
Pitnak (Fitnak), town 207, *208*, 208n309, 221, *221*

Qaraqalpaqstan XI
Qara-Bogaz, gulf 78
Qara-Mazi 174, *174*, 174n229
Qara-tupe 222, *222*, 222n330
Qibla Tāza-Bāgh Palace 37
Qlich Niyaz Bay (Qlich Bay), town *210*, 210n313
Qirq-Yaf (Qirq-Yab) *108*, 108n65
Qiyat, town 39n156, *168*, 168n213
Qonghrat, city and province 25, 56, 57, 94, *94*, 94n35, *106*, *190*
Qosh-Kupruk, locality 86, *87*, 87n19, *112*
Qum-Senger (Qum-Sangar), locality *197*, 197n283, *198*
Qūlān Qara Bāghlī, locality *179*
Qūshbigī Yāf, canal 116, 116n80, *117*

Rāfanīk, locality 37n147
RSFSR 13n31
Russian Empire (Russia) 3, 3n5, 6, 7, 13, 14, 14n40, 15, 16n45, 18, 20, 44, 94n35, 145, *147*, 148, *150*, 207
Russian protectorate over the Khanate of Khiva 4, 6, 9, 14, 15, 16n46, 19, 27, 148, 154n180, 194n275, 194n276
Rūzīm Būy, locality *100*, *101*

Sārt Ālācha, locality 159, *159*
Saint-Petersburg (Petrograd) 4n8, 7, 8n18, 14, 16, 17, 37n150, 38
Samarkand, city and province 18n56, 28n103
Sayyid Āqsaqāl, mosque community *159*
Shahabad, canal 56n198, 128n115, 142n153
Shavat (Shahabad), town XVI, *128*, 128n115, *129*, 129n116
Shīrīn, mosque community *170*,
Shumanay, town and province 71
Sirchali, canal 93n30
Sirchali (Sirshālī,) locality *93*, 93n30, *96*, *165*, *166*
Susalaq, locality 64, *162*

Syr Darya river 13
Syr Darya Province, Turkestan Governorship-General 38n154

Takhta, locality 176
Tama 109, *109*, 109n67, *205*
Tāsh Hawlī Palace 36
Tashhawz (Tashḥavuż), city and province 20, 38n154, 48n180, *56*, 56n198, 56n199, 57, 58, 70n221, 72, 106, *106*, 138, 139n140, 174, *174*, *183*, 185, *185*, 186n258
Tashkent, city XII, XVI, XVIII, XIX, 4, 16, 18, 19, 37n150, 46, 154n180
Tāsh-Saqā, locality *165*, 165n207, 165n206
Tāza Bāzār, locality *89*
Transcaspian Region (Oblast') 16n45, 66n211
Turkestan Governorship-General (Russian Turkestan) 9, 14, 28, 28n103, 31, 45, 75, 145, 165n205, 183
Turkmenistan 1
Turkmen SSR 13
Turtkul, see Petro-Aleksandrovsk
Tūyūklī, locality 165n207

Uil River 44
Ukraine 19
Ūlūgh Tāza Yārghān, canal *126*
Ural'sk 149n168
Ural, river 149n168
Urgench (New Urgench), city and provine XI, 4, 6, 70n219, 94, *95*, 95n36, 114, 115n78, 164n202, 172, *172*, 174n229, 194, *194*, 194n275, *214*
Ust Yurt plateau 44
Uzbek khanates XVII, 1, 6, 9, 10, 11
Uzbekistan XI, XVIII, 4
Uzbek SSR 13, 13n31
Uyghur (Yaman-Uyghur), locality 181, *181* 181n241, 225n336

Vazir (New Vazir), town *51*, 52, 52n190, 140n143

Yādgār Khwāja, mosque community *134*
Yangi-Ariq, canal 206n299
Yarmish, canal 119n87, 122n90, *185*
Yarmish, locality 119, 119n87, *120*, 152, 152n175

Index of Proper Names

'Abd al-Aḥad Sālim, shaykh 203, *204*
'Abd al-Karīm Maḥram b. 'Abd al-Raḥīm Maḥram, provincial governor *177*
'Abd al-Raḥīm Bāy b. Muḥammad Karīm Bāy, provincial governor *127*, *132*
'Abd al-Raḥīm Bay b. Muḥammad Yūsuf Baqqāl, provincial governor *175*, *182*
'Abd al-Raḥīm Maḥram *87*
'Abd al-Sattār Says *114*
Abdullaev, Odilbek XIII
'Abdullāh Īshīk-Āqāsī *93*
'Abdullāh Yasāvulbāshī b. Qurbān Niyāz Yasāvulbāshī 24
Abu'l-Ghāzī Khān (r. 1644–1663) 8n15, 22, 129n116
Achamayli, subdivision of Uzbek tribe Qonghrat *188*, 188n263
Āgahī, Muḥammad Riżā Mīrāb XXn1, 11
Agafonova, Zoia 4
Āgha Jān Īshān, Ata Turkmen 207, 208, *208*, *209*
Allāh Birgān Bāy b. 'Avaż Niyāz Maḥram, provincial governor 70n219, *115*, 115n78
'Ālim Bāy Yūzbāshī *94*
Alimova, Dilorom XIX
Allāh Birgān b. 'Abd al-Raḥīm Bāy, provincial governor *173*
Allāh Bīrgān Mīrshab *117*, *118*
Allāh Qulī Khān (r. 1826-1842) 11, 24, 35, 165n207
Āmān Kīldī Bāy Yasāvulbāshī b. Muḥammad Murād Dīvānbīgī 31n119, 33, 34, 34n132, 34n133, *142*, 142n152, *174*, *181*
Ambrosimov, Aleksey, merchant 41, 42, 43, 47n177
'Arabshahids, dynasty 10
Arabachi, Turkmen clan *225*, 225n336
'Aṣqar Maḥmūd Tūra b. Muḥammad Raḥīm Khān II (Fīrūz) 37n147
Ata, Turkmen clan 207, 207n305, 208, *208*
Ātā Bīk b. Raḥīm Birdī Bīk, provincial governor of Kat *144*
Atā Niyāz Bāy b. Muḥammad Niyāz Bāy *156*
'Avaż Khwāja, provincial governor
'Ayd Bāy Yasāvul *139*

Bābā Jān Yuzbāshī b. Pahlavān, governor 150, *151*
Bahādir Bāy Īshīk-Āqāsī *90*
Bahādir Maḥram Yūzbāshī, provincial governor 48n180, 106, *107*
Balghali, subdivision of Uzbek tribe Qonghrat 188n261
Bāltaev, 'Abdullāh (1890-1966) XI, XII, XIII, XIV, XV, XVI, XVII, XVIII, 22, 36, 45n173, 82n4, 87n18, 108n65
Bayānī, Muḥammad Yūsuf 25n91, 25n96, 36, 40
Basiner, Friedrich 26
Bayram-Shali, Turkmen clan 155n185
Becker, Seymour 22
Berdan, Hiram 165n204
Bolsheviks 7, 12, 17, 17n51, 17n54, 18, 18n56, 19, 35, 125n107, 154n180, 202n291, 208, 225n336
Bourdieu, Pierre 5
Bregel, Yuri 1n1, 11n26, 22, 24n82, 29, 34n131, 47n178, 47n179, 122n90, 155n183, 164n202, 165n204, 176n233, 181n241

Chawdur, Turkmen clan 24, 27, 125n107, *138*, 138n139
Chinggisids 10, 11, 12

Dāmullā Khudāy Birgān Ākhund 38n54
Dāmullā Muḥammad Karim Ākhūnd, mutavalli 53
Danilevskii, Gregor 26
Davlat Murād Maḥram b. Īsh Muḥammad 27n101, 34, 35, 38

Gandumian, peace treaty 14, 14n40, 15, 145
Galkin, A. S., Lieutenant General 17, 38n154, 141
Galkin, M.N. 78
Gens, Gregor 26
Ghāyib Yūzbāshi *139*
Guliamov, Yahya 86n17, 117n84

Ḥājjī Muḥammad Bāy b. Amīn al-Dīn Bāy, provincial governor *137*, 137n136, *149*, *169*, 169n217, *180*
Ḥasan Āqā b. Khudāy Birgān Āqā *156*
Ḥasan Murād Qūshbigī 116n80
Ḥasan Yasāvul *87*
Helmersen, Gregor von 26
Ḥusayn Muḥammad Bāy b. Muḥammad Murād Dīvānbīgī 31n119

ʿIbādullāh Maḥram *214*
ʿIbādullāh Tūra b. Muḥammad Raḥīm Khān II (Fīrūz) 37n147
Ibrāhīm Yūzbāshī *198*
Īgām Birdī Raḥim Birdī ughlī XVI
Īltūzār Khān (r. 1804-1806) 11
Imreli, Turkmen clan 125n107
Isfandiyār Khān (r. 1910–1918) XV, 12, 16, 17, 18, 18n55, 18n59, 28, 29, 30, 32, 34, 35n135, 37, 38n151, 38, 38n154, 39, 40, 45, 46, 48, 130, 146, 154, 176
Isḥāq Khwāja, provincial governor 70n220
Īsh Muḥammad Āqsaqāl Bābā Niyāz ūghlī *195*, *196*
Iskandar Maḥram *119*
Iskandar Yasāvul *152*
Ivanov, Pavel Petrovih 8n18

Jān Bik Sarhang Yasāvul *98*
Jumʿa Niyāz Maḥram b. Maḥmūd Dīvān, provincial governor 70n221, *139*, 139n140, *186*, 186n258, *187*
Junayd Khān (Qurban Muḥammad Sardar) 17, 17n53, 18, 18n59, 19, 33n130, 34, 35, 39, 40, 130, 154, 154n182, 176, *176*, 207, 208, *209*

Kalmykov, A.D. 14n40, 41
Kāmyāb, Sayyid Ḥāmid Tūra 11
Kaufman, Konstantin Petrovich von (1818-1882) 13
Khāl Murād Āqsaqāl *112*
Khāl Nīyāz Yūzbāshī *210*, *211*
Khān Īshān, Turkmen 39
Khorezmshah 11, *203*
Khudaybergenov, Komiljon XI, XIX, 34n131
Khudāy Birgān b. Ismāʿīl 3
Khudāy Naẓar Yūzbāshī *135*
Khwājam Khān, Turkmen 39
Khwāja Niyāz Bāy b. ʿAbdullāh Maḥram, provincial governor *124*
Khwāja Niyāz Dahabāshī Yasāvul *97*
Khwādjesh-maḥram 26, 26n97
Kilevein, E. 25
Kok-Uzak, subdivision of Uzbek tribe Qonghrat 188n261
Kosbergenov, Razambet 33n131, 62, 71
Kuhn, Alexander 22n76, 24n85, 26, 27, 58, 74, 74n230, 86n17, 95n36, 97n43, 129n116, 170n219, 207n305, 210n313, 222n331

Laffasī, Ḥasan-Murād (1880-1949) 18n59, 30, 31n118, 31n123, 33n127, 38, 56n199, 130, 141, 185n255
Lobacheva, N.P. 83n10
Lomakin A. 66n211
Lykoshin, Nil Sergeevich 28, 28n103, 28n106, 30, 32, 44, 45, 46, 48n180, 48, 49, 50, 53, 72, 74, 94n35, 129n116, 132n121, 137n136, 145, 146, 185n255, 194n275, 199n286

Maḥmūd Niyāz Yasāvulbāshī 24, 25, 25n91, 25n96
Mamat Yasāvulbāshī, see Muḥammad Maḥram Yasāvulbāshī b. Muḥammad Ḥusayn
Manghit, Uzbek clan 129n116, 224, *225*
Mann, Kristina 15
McChesney, Robert 12
Mirbadalov, Haydar Khwāja 18, 18n56
Mirzā ʿAbd al-Raḥmān 74, 74n230
Muḥammad ʿĀlīm Bāy Yūzbāshī *105*
Muḥammad Amiñ Dargha 39
Muḥammad Amīn Dīvān Bābā *131*, *132*
Muḥammad Amīn Īnāq (r. 1764-1792) 11
Muḥammad Amīn Khān (r. 1845–1855) 40, 41
Muḥammad Jān Yasāvul *88*
Muḥammad Karīm Yūzbāshī b. Ismāʿil, provincial governor *122*, *123*, *124*, *184*
Muḥammad Laṭīf Khwāja b. ʿAbd al-Karīm Khwāja, provincial governor *211*, *212*
Muḥammad Maḥram Yasāvulbāshī b. Muḥammad Ḥusayn 27n101, 32, 32n124, 33, 33n127, 33n130, 48n180, *114*, 114n75
Muḥammad Murād (Matmurād) Dīvānbīgī 24n88, 30, 31, 206n302

Muḥammad Niyāz Bāy b. Qāsim Dīvān, provincial governor, *199*, 199n286
Muḥammad Niyāz Yasāvulbāshī 23, 24
Muḥammad Raḥīm Bāy *131*, *132*
Muḥammad Raḥīm Bāy Yasāvul *81*
Muḥammad Raḥīm Khān I (r. 1806–1825) 23, 24, 24n82, 47n180, 49, 129n116
Muḥammad Raḥīm Khān II (Fīrūz) (r. 1864-1910) XI, XV, XVI, 14, 16, 25n91, 27n101, 30, 31n115, 32, 33, 35, 36, 37, 37n150, 37n151, 38
Muḥammad Raḥīm Yasāvul *92*
Muḥammad Riżā Yasāvul Maḥramkhānachī *100*, *101*
Muḥammad Ṣafā Ātālīq b. ʿAbdullāh Ātālīq, provincial governor *129*, 129n116, *202*
Muḥammad Sharīf Yasāvul *114*
Muḥammad Yaʿqūb Bāy b. Ismāʿil Jān Bāy *156*
Muḥammad Yaʿqūb b. Jabbār Qulī Maḥram, provincial governor *108*, 118, *183*, 183n245
Muḥammad Yaʿqūb Khwāja, mutavallī 62, 63, *168*
Muḥammad Yaʿqūb Yasāvulbāshī b. Muḥammad Yūsuf Yasāvulbāshī 34, 54n195, *97*, *98*, *99*, *102*, *103*
Muḥammad Yūsuf Bāy b. Muḥammad Yaʿqūb Divān, provincial governor *142*
Muḥammad Yūsuf Bāy b. Pahlavān Maḥram, provincial governor 109, *110*, *153*, *156*, *158*, 159, *160*, 161, *162*, *189*, *191*
Muḥammad Yūsuf Kākil Bī *105*
Muḥammad Yūsuf Yasāvulbāshī b. ʿAvaż Niyāz Maḥram (d. 1917) 28, 28n106, 30, 32, 34, 45, 70n219, 72, *81*, *82*, *87*, *89*, *93*, *101*, *105*, *134*, 134n124
Mullā Khāl Bāy, imam *134*
Munis, Shir Muḥammad Mīrāb XXn1, 1, 23, 47n180
Murav'ev, Nikolai 5, 50n184, 129n116

Nādir Shāh Afshār 10
Nāvāẕā Mīrāb *117*

Pahlen, Konstantin Konstantinovich 73
Provisional Government in Russia 17n54, 18

Qahqa Bīk Qarāvul *169*
Qalandar Dahabāshī *102*, *103*
Qalandar Yasāvul *140*
Qanjighali, subdivision of Uzbek tribe Qonghrat 188n263
Qaradashli, Turkmen clan *122*, 122n90, 184, *184*, 184n249, 212, 212n316
Qara-Tāylī, Turkmen clan *125*, 125n107, *126*
Qāżī Jān Muḥammad b. Mullā Muḥammad Dūrdī *218*
Qāżī Mullā Ghāyib *124*
Qāżī Raḥman Birdī *223*
Qāżī-yi sharʿ-i sharīf Muḥammad Murād *217*
Qāżī va rȧis ʿAbd al-Yaʿqūb *215*
Qāżi va rȧis Dāmullā ʿAbd al-Allāh *105*
Qāżi va rȧis Dāmullā Allāh Birgān *105*
Qāżī va rȧīs Maḥmūd b. Dāmullā Muḥammad Karīm *214*
Qāżī va rȧis Muḥammad Qurbān *127*
Qāżī va rȧīs ʿUmar Khwāja *223*
Qāżī-yi Gūrlān Dāmullā Bābājān Makhẕūm *127*, *152*
Qāżī-yi Gūrlān Dāmullā Muḥammad Yaʿqūb *127*
Qāżī-yi Gūrlān Dāmullā Ūrāż Muḥammad *127*
Qāżī-yi Gūrlān Muḥammad Karīm Khwāja *127*
Qāżī-yi Khwāja Īlī Dāmullā Muḥammad Ṣāliḥ Khwāja *171*
Qāżī-yi Khwāja Īlī Dāmullā Bābā Jān Khwāja *171*
Qāżī-yi Ūrganch Dāmullā Ātājān b. Bābā Ṣūfī-yi marḥūmī *173*
Qāżī-yi Ūrganch Dāmullā ʿAṭaullāh *173*
Qāżī va rȧis-i Yārmīsh Dāmullā ʿAbd al-Ghafūr *120*
Qāżī va rȧis-i Yārmīsh Dāmullā Bābājān Makhẕūm *120*
Qāżī va rȧis-i Yārmīsh Dāmullā Muḥammad Yūsuf *120*, *152*
Qīlich Vakīl Qarādāshlī *212*
Qipchaq, Uzbek clan 129n116, *225*
Qonghrat, dynasty XIV, XVIIn4, 1, 5, 6, 7, 8, 9, 10, 11, 12, 13, 19, 21, 22, 23, 24, 25, 26, 27, 27n101, 28, 34n131, 35, 36, 40, 41, 41n165, 44, 46, 47n178, 51, 72, 74, 75, 97n42, 97n43, 102n54, 117n84, 129n116, 146, 149n167, 167, 183, 184, 188n263, 194n276, 205, 207n305, 213, 215

Qonghrat, Uzbek tribe 188n263
Qurban Muḥammad Sardar, see Junayd Khān
Qurbān Niyāz Yasāvul 51
Qurbān Niyāz Yasāvulbāshī 23, 24

Rachinskii, doctor 38n151
Raḥman-Qulī Yasāvul *90*
Raḥmatullah Bāy Yasāvulbāshī b. Muḥammad Niyāz Yasāvulbāshī 24, 24n88, 25, 25n96
Rajab 2, 3
Roberts, Richard 15
Romanovs, dynasty 7, 17

Safarov, Bābājān 33, 33n130, 46, 46n176, 47, 47n179, 48, 50, 74, 77, 114n77
Ṣāḥib Naẓar Bāy b. Muḥammad Murād Dīvānbīgī 31n119
Samoilovich, Aleksandr 40
Sayyid ʿAbdullāh Khān (r. 1855) 24n88, 40
Sayyid ʿAbdullāh Khān (r. 1918–1920) XV, 12, 19, 32, 35, 40, 208
Sayyid Islām Khwāja b. Ibrāhim Khwāja, *vazīr-i akbār* (d. 1913) 28, 28n106, 31n117, 70n219, 70n220, 76, 132n121, 166n210
Sayyid Ismāʿīl Khwāja b. Ibrāhim Khwāja, governor of Hazarasp 70n219, 70n220, *132*, 132n121, 163, *166*, 166n210, *193*, 193n273
Sayyd Muḥammad Khān (r. 1856–1864) 207n305
Sayyid Niyāz, Turkmen 185, 185n255
Sayyid Riżā Khwāja Īshān *214*
Şeyh Süleyman Efendi Buhârî XXn1
Shāh Murād Bāy b. Dawlat Murād Bāy, provincial governor 206, 206n302
Shaykh Naẓar Bāy Yasāvulbāshī b. Muḥammad Murād Dīvānbīgī 30, 30n115, 31, 31n117, 31n118, 31n119, 31n123, 32, 34, 34n132, 34n133, 70, *84*, *87*, *88* *91*, *95*, *136*, 136n133
Shioya Akifumi 34n132
Shukur ʿAlī Īshīk Āqā 51
Stalin, Joseph 77
Sulṭān Yūzbāshī Yasāvul *84*

Tarrāh, Bābājān 30n115, 37, 37n149, 38, 50
Tukhtametov, T. 22n77

Ushak, Turkmen clan 154, *155*, 155n185
Uyghur, Uzbek clan 129n116

Wood, William 207n307

Yaqubov, Qahramon XIX
Yāsh khīvaliklār, see Young Khivans
Yomut, Turkmen clan 125n107, 130, *131*, *132*, 141, *142*, 144, 154, *155*, 155n185, 165n204, 176, *179*, 185, 185n255, 207n305
Young Khivans 18, 18n56, 19, 29, 38, 202n291
Yŭldoshev, Muhammadjon 22n77, 34n131, 46, 47n179, 114n77
Yusupov, Pahlavān Niyāz Ḥājī 18n59, 29, 30, 38, 39, 185n255
(?) Yūzbāshī b. Raḥmatullāh Yasāvulbāshī *200*

Zaitsev, I.M., Colonel 17n51, 17n54, 18n56, 154n180

Printed in the United States
By Bookmasters